Portland

This book was supported in part by generous gifts from

The City of Portland
Jean and Ray Auel
Doris Carlson
Maribeth Collins
Carolyn Kelly
Randall and Rachael Kester
The Kohnstamm Family Foundation
E. Kimbark MacColl
The Ruth Manary Fund of the Samuel S. Johnson Foundation
The *Oregonian*
Mary Fellows and John Russell
Caroline and Charles Swindells
Jane and Lawrence Viehl

Portland

People, Politics, and Power,
1851-2001

by
Jewel Lansing

Oregon State University Press
Corvallis

The paper in this book meets the guidelines for permanence and durability of the Committee on Production Guidelines for Book Longevity of the Council on Library Resources and the minimum requirements of the American National Standard for Permanence of Paper for Printed Library Materials Z39.48-1984.

Library of Congress Cataloging-in-Publication Data
Lansing, Jewel Beck.
Portland : people, politics, and power, 1851-2001 / by Jewel Lansing.
p. cm.
Includes bibliographical references (p.) and index.
ISBN 0-87071-559-3 (alk. paper)
1. Portland (Or.)—Politics and government. 2. Mayors—Oregon—Portland—History. 3. Portland (Or.)—Social conditions. 4. Portland (Or.)—Biography. I. Title.
F884.P857 L36 2003
979.5'49—dc21
2003007971

 First edition 2003, third printing 2004
Printed in the United States of America

OREGON STATE UNIVERSITY

Oregon State University Press
101 Waldo Hall
Corvallis OR 97331-6407
541-737-3166 • fax 541-737-3170
http://oregonstate.edu/dept/press

Preface

During my growing-up years, I began a life-long friendship with Portland, strengthened by many visits from my home in Western Montana. I remember riding along the now-historic Columbia River Highway, roller-skating on a concrete viaduct near my aunt's home in East Portland, discovering soft ice cream at a soda fountain near the Bagdad Theater, smelling roses along every sidewalk, riding a clanging trolley to and from a brief summer job at Montgomery Wards, carhopping at the famous Tik-Tok Drive-in on N.E. Twelfth and Sandy Boulevard, and viewing the unbelievable devastation of the 1948 Vanport Flood.

In 1961, my husband of five years and I bought a house in the Multnomah Village - Garden Home area three blocks inside the Multnomah - Washington County line. There we learned first-hand the importance of zoning laws and the need for citizens to monitor and challenge the actions of elected officials. In our case, it was the Washington County commissioners who, in the words of the Oregon Supreme Court, attempted an "egregious" case of spot zoning (*Smith v Washington County*, 1964).

I took the national certified public accountants' exam shortly after we moved to Portland, and soon started working for a CPA firm downtown. Later I established my own CPA firm specializing in audits of nonprofit organizations. I helped found an Oregon chapter of Accountants for the Public Interest, became active in the League of Women Voters, and joined the Oregon Women's Political Caucus.

Thirteen years after we settled in Portland, I was elected Multnomah County auditor. I served in that capacity for eight years, then began a four-year term as Portland city auditor. I first viewed city government from the inside, serving two years during Mayor Frank Ivancie's tenure, then two during Mayor Bud Clark's. My duties gave me insight into such city business as council agendas, budgets, ordinances, charter amendments, local improvement districts, annexations, union contracts, and the fire and police pension fund. The mayor's signature, and mine, were affixed to all city checks, mine attesting that the expenditures were properly authorized and paid from the correct fund—an oversight role for the auditor dating back to 1903.

These experiences with city government, together with the upcoming sesquicentennial of Portland's 1851 charter and the impending bicentennial observance of the 1805-1806 Lewis and Clark expedition, inspired me to undertake the research and writing of a comprehensive Portland history. Various aspects and time periods had previously been chronicled, but no book had focused primarily on Portland's political framework or encompassed its entire lifespan in a single volume.

This book is intended primarily as a reference, but for those ready for the journey, should also provide an enjoyable read. Copious notes have been included for readers who want to know additional details or seek sources for further research. The story unfolds chronologically, in segments corresponding to the regimes of the city's forty-four mayors and their forty-nine discrete tenures. Please note that old spellings have been retained in quoted texts, and that council proceedings are treated in far more detail in the first few chapters to give the reader a sense of early priorities and the trial and error tenor of pioneer city life. Also note that events occurring after mid-year 2001, such as the September 11, 2001, terrorist attacks on New York's World Trade Center, are beyond the 150th birthday time frame of this book.

In the forty-two years since my husband and I adopted Portland as our home, we have found it a wonderful place to raise children, to work, to participate in civic life, to enjoy a private back yard and an unparalleled out-of-doors. I am honored to have played a part in Portland's history—as a citizen, as its servant, and now as one telling its story.

Jewel Lansing
Portland, Oregon

Contents

Introduction

A small clearing along the Willamette River, surrounded by dense forest, had long been an overnight Indian campsite when a rudimentary town was hewn out of the woods. By 2001, that village had become the twenty-eighth-largest city in the United States—Portland, Oregon—a city cited as a model of urban livability and growth management.

Portland's story provides a fascinating microcosm of the American experience; a slice of Western Americana with its own unique tale. The story begins on April 14, 1851, and ends one hundred and fifty years later. In these pages, city leaders tackle issues of the day, struggle to find a workable government by trial and error, place the public good over private fortune and vice versa, and make growth their primary goal until the late twentieth century, when phrases such as "alternatives to growth" and "sustainable development" become a standard part of the lexicon. Always, it has been a struggle for power. Many issues have emerged again and again, adding new evidence that yesterday provides valuable lessons for today. More than any other single factor, transportation has been the city's lifeblood—first on the Willamette and Columbia rivers, next via a horse and wagon trail linking the Tualatin Plains to Portland's harbor, then progressing to railroads, interstate freeways, and an international airport.

Pondering the significance of what was leads inevitably to conjecture about what might have been. Future taxpayers could have saved millions of dollars spent reacquiring the waterfront if the second city council had exercised proper stewardship of the public's right to the levee. East Portland instead of westside downtown would be today's city center if Portland businessmen had not dug deep in their own pockets to meet the demands of greedy Ben Holladay so he would build his railroad terminal on the west side of the river. And Portland might have shaken its early spinster image had brewer Henry Weinhard pumped free beer through Skidmore Fountain on dedication day as he had offered to do.

Colorful characters emerge throughout this history. Picture Captain O. Travaillott, a dashing fellow who bedeviled and outwitted the citizenry after his brig *Duc D'Lorges* sank in Portland's harbor. Or pugnacious Oregonian editor T. J. Dryer, devious log-roller William King, irrepressible madam Nancy Boggs, idiosyncratic former governor "Silpester Annoyer," arrogant Judge Matthew Deady, "champion loud noise" George Baker, gravelly voiced Mildred Schwab, and tavern-owner Bud Clark. Mayor Stephen McCormick led irate citizens to the waterfront, where they tore down a warehouse built in defiance of council order.

Many blemishes mar city history. Blatant discrimination was practiced against African Americans, Chinese, and Japanese Americans. American Indians were both feared and shunned, and played no substantive role in Portland's recorded history. Hundreds of unfortunate sailors were shanghaied out of Portland harbor for distant sailings. The city was for many years a wide-open vice town, with police and city officials on the take. The 1912 "tin plate" law identified owners of buildings in which vice activities flourished, yet the ordinance had little effect in curbing such conduct. A woman mayor who was elected on a reform platform in 1948 and defeated after only one term nevertheless marked a turning point toward cleaner, more effective city government.

After its adoption in 1902, Portland voters used the initiative and referendum process to adopt many progressive laws, but also turned down sensible opportunities such as cheap public power and adequate funding for sewers. Urban renewal projects displaced hundreds of people from their homes and businesses, at the same time producing impressive long-term civic improvements. An era of outstanding Portland progress began with a far-sighted downtown plan conceived during the tenure of Mayor Terry Schrunk and brought to fruition with the aid of federal dollars and the forceful leadership of Mayor Neil Goldschmidt.

The first city council members—sixteen years younger, on average, than those of today—convened on the evening of April 14, 1851, to activate a frontier city government. That mud-inundated village had grown into the City of Roses one hundred fifty years later, a city widely recognized as an enviable place to live and work. Portland won kudos as a top recycling city, boasted the country's largest percentage of homes with internet access, and consistently ranked high in ratings for wise planning and growth. The one hundred fifty men who, in 1853, petitioned to disband Portland government and revoke its charter, would be astounded.

Acknowledgments

I am indebted to authors Harvey Scott, Leslie Scott, Joseph Gaston, Percy Maddux, Fred Lockley, Howard Corning, Ruby Lacy, Malcolm Clark, Jr., E. Kimbark MacColl (who loaned me his entire collection of notes from his three Portland histories), Carl Abbott, Fred Leeson, Eugene Snyder, William Hawkins, Paul Pitzer, Terence O'Donnell, and a host of others on whom I relied for basic information, as cited in the notes to this book. The *Oregonian* newspaper, throughout its one hundred fifty-year history, proved a valuable resource, as did the *Oregon Journal*, *Willamette Week*, and *Oregon Historical Quarterly*. Internet sites maintained by the City of Portland and a private web site maintained by Ernie Bonner provided solid background about contemporary issues.

In early fall 2000, I sent a questionnaire to several persons whom I knew to be knowledgeable about recent city history, and solicited their anecdotes and opinions about the city's most noteworthy accomplishments and failures of the last twenty-five to fifty years, along with important issues of the next ten to twenty. These responses helped guide preparation of the final chapters in this book. My heartfelt thanks to Carl Abbott, Gary Blackmer, Ernie Bonner, Ron Buel, Jane Cease, Ron Cease, Barbara Clark, Bud Clark, Don Clark, Elaine Cogan, Larry Hilderbrand, Jim Hill, Gretchen Kafoury, Vera Katz (by interview), Sue Keil, Bud Kramer, Fred Leeson, Kim MacColl (by phone), Chet Orloff, and John Terry for completing these questionnaires in full or part.

Among those who provided assistance concerning various topics were John Acker, Lloyd Anderson, Don Barney, Terry Baxter, Bill Blauvelt, Earl Blumenauer, Deborah Bogstad, James Brewster, Marino Bual, Linda Burglehaus, Laurel Butman, Doug Capps, Frank Dufay, Greg Everhart, Delma Farrell, Dick Feeney, Susan Francois, Frank Galida, Larry Grant, Jim Hagerman, Joan Hamilton, Marge Harding, Bill Hawkins, Neil Heesacker, Tim Hibbitts, Dorislee Riley Hoffpauer, Don Holm, Billy Hultz, Margie Humphreys, Shirley Johnson, George Joseph, Charles Jordan, Ted and Mason Kaye, Lloyd Keefe, Lee Kell, Judy Koonce, Jim Kuffner, Marianne Keddington-Lang, Ron Lansing, Adair Law, Paula Leach, Stephanie Leeper, Paul Leistner, Mike Lindberg, Elaine Lionberger, Karen Loper, Linc Mann, Joy Margheim, Suzanne Jo Miller, Dareth Murray, Nancy Niedernhofer, Ralph O'Hare, Rod O'Hiser, Britta Olson, Alan Percell, Denyse Peterson, Carolyn Philp, Carmen Piekarski,

Chris Powers, McKay Rich, Martha Richmond, Jeff Rogers, John Russell, Ken Rust, Ted Runstein, Mike Salisbury, Eugene Snyder, Phil Stanford, Erik Sten, Margaret Strachan, Jim Tompkins, Felicia Trader, Mark Turpel, Judy Tuttle, Joe Uris, Dan Vizzini, Ross Walker, Karen Whitman, Terri Williams, and Julie Williamson.

I am grateful to readers of all or part of various drafts of this manuscript: Carl Abbott, Sam Adams, Helen Barney, Gary Blackmer, Liisa Fagerlund, Carolyn Kelly, Cay Kershner, Ron Lansing, Fred Leeson, E. Kimbark MacColl, Ron Paul, and Dick Tracy. I take full responsibility, however, for errors and omissions.

Diana Banning and Brian Johnson of the Portland City Archives, Richard Engman and Shawna Gandy of the Oregon History Center manuscript room, Joe Stephens of the Oregon Supreme Court library, Dave Wendell of the Oregon State Archives, Cindy Gibbon of the Multnomah County library, Lynn Williams of the Lewis and Clark Law School Library, Susan Seyl, Mikki Tint, and Elizabeth Winroth of the Oregon History Center photo desk—all provided valuable research assistance. Amy Pratt assisted with the indexing, and Stephen Dow Beckham provided pragmatic indexing advice. The extensive Oregon history collection compiled by my husband, Ron Lansing, served as the basic research library for my six years of research and writing.

In addition to the major contributors listed in the front of this book who made publication possible, other financial assistance was provided by Nancy Bridgeford, Amy Bushaw, Barnes Ellis, Lynn Ferguson, Josie Henderson, Karen Hill, Renate Funk, Joe and Alyse Lansing Gass, Genevieve Goldy, Elizabeth Hadley, Annette Lansing, Mark and Jeanne Lansing, Judy Lawrence, Diana Kerman, Richard Meeker and Ellen Rosenbaum, Micki Naito, Owen Panner, Cheryl Perrin, Jim and Joan Redden, Betty Roberts, Steve Schell, and Norman Wiener.

The staff at the OSU Press— Jo Alexander, Tom Booth, Mary Braun, Jeffrey Grass, and Karen Orchard—brought this book to fruition.

My deepest thanks to all.

Chapter 1

A Clearing in the Woods

1845-1850

To this point I can bring any ship that can get into the mouth of the Great Columbia River.

—Captain John Couch, 1840[1]

I saw masts and booms of vessels that looked as if they had been left there. It took my eye. I had no idea of laying out a town there, but when I saw this I said: "Very well, sir, I will take it."

—Asa Lovejoy, November 1843[2]

The famous coin toss to christen Portland occurred in a village at the end of the Oregon Trail.[3] The Oregon Country was still a rough frontier then—a frontier claimed by both Great Britain and the United States.[4]

What the two coin-tossers had in common, besides a two-year friendship, was a claim on six hundred forty acres of dense forest twelve miles downstream with about an acre of open space along the riverbank. Lawyer Asa Lovejoy, Oregon City's mayor,[5] had gained his half-interest in the site by filing the claim and paying the filing fee on behalf of a wanderer named William Overton in early 1844. The same year, Overton traded his half-interest to merchant Francis Pettygrove[6] for fifty dollars' worth of supplies—equal to one thousand dollars' worth today—and moved on.[7]

Neither partner would concede the name choice for their townsite. Lovejoy wanted Boston, for his hometown, while Pettygrove had his heart set on Portland, as in Maine. (They apparently did not consider using a native Indian name.)[8] In 1845, they agreed to flip a penny and let chance decide. The copper[9] they tossed fell Portland side up two times out of three, and the name was set.[10] The flip of that coin became a legend re-enacted by Portland city commissioners and retold to generations of school children.[11]

Portland on the West Coast was destined to outgrow, several fold, its parent in the northeast corner of the United States. And, confusing as it has been for Portlanders over the years to explain that they were from Portland, Oregon, *not* Portland, Maine, at least Pettygrove didn't hold out for calling the site New Portland, as *Oregonian* Editor Harvey Scott later thankfully pointed out. In the year 2000, the population of Portland, Oregon, was eight times larger than that of her mother city, Portland, Maine—529,000 compared to 64,000.[12]

❧

When Portland was founded, there was no Seattle, no Tacoma, no Boise, no Spokane.

The states of Washington, Oregon, Idaho, and parts of Montana were all part of a vast expanse known as Oregon Country, with white settlement confined to the Columbia and Willamette rivers. Astoria, at the mouth of the Columbia River near the Pacific Ocean, had been established in 1811, but it was little more than a fur-trading post.The first white "civilization" centered around Fort Vancouver, on the north side of the Columbia River, built in 1825 by the British Hudson's Bay Company and administered by its factor, Dr. John McLoughlin—known as "White Headed Eagle" to the Indians because of his flowing mane of white hair and commanding presence. Fort Vancouver was a hundred miles inland near the mouth of the Willamette River. There Dr. McLoughlin "ruthlessly but openly crushed competition in the fur trade,"[13] preserved peace between the Indians and whites, planted thriving orchards and gardens, and extended a helping hand to mountain men, missionaries, and hundreds of Oregon Trail pioneers who began arriving in the early 1840s.[14]

Devastated by malaria and smallpox, the Indian population of the area had declined dramatically during the previous sixty years.[15] McLoughlin estimated that nine-tenths of the Lower Columbia River Indians had died off by 1835. Whole tribes, including the Multnomahs, were wiped out.[16]

"The revolt of the natives against the whites [in the Northwest] seems relatively brief and weak, in comparison with the resistance made by Indians in other parts of the American continent," said historian Leslie M. Scott. Without the diseases that ravaged the Northwest Indian population, Scott said, the influx of pioneers to the Oregon country would have been delayed ten or twenty years. Scott's article was titled, "Indian Diseases as Aids to Pacific Northwest Settlement."[17]

At the time of Portland's founding, ox-team pioneers were crossing the plains in ever-increasing numbers. Except for rules promulgated by Dr. John McLoughlin in the name of the Hudson's Bay Company, would-be settlers found no government in place when they got to the Oregon Country—unlike California, which had seventy years of Spanish habitation before the great western migration began.[18] Great Britain and the United States had signed a treaty of joint occupancy for the Oregon Country in 1818, but bitter jurisdictional disputes still broke out regularly, sometimes to the brink of war.[19] Along the Columbia River, McLoughlin's word held sway, but elsewhere joint occupancy meant continual conflicts between British and American law.

The United States claimed ownership of the Oregon Country primarily on three points: Captain Robert Gray's discovery of the "River of the West" (the Columbia) on May 11, 1792; the Meriwether Lewis and William Clark expedition of 1805-6, which wintered near the mouth of the Columbia River; and the fur-trading post at Astoria established in 1811.[20] Britain boasted not only busy Fort Vancouver, but a vast empire of fur traders employed by the Hudson's Bay and North West companies. British explorers such as Alexander Mackenzie and David Thompson traveled throughout the Northwest, and Thompson's trappers operated in the Willamette Valley.

Former president John Quincy Adams captured the American spirit and belief in Manifest Destiny in these words: "We claim that country—for what? To make the wilderness blossom as the rose, to establish laws, to increase, multiply, and subdue the earth, which we are commanded to do by the behest of God Almighty."[21]

In 1844, James Polk campaigned for president of the United States under the motto "54-40 or fight."[22] The United States sought all territory from the northern border of California to the southern tip of today's Alaska at 54°40' latitude. Covered wagons were seen on the Oregon Trail painted with "54-40—All or None" on their sides.[23] The British, for their part, insisted they were entitled to all land north of the Columbia River.[24]

A compromise treaty was finally signed in April 1846, designating the forty-ninth parallel of latitude, later the southernmost boundary of Canada, as the line between British and American sovereignty. Word of this treaty did not reach the nascent village of Portland for five months, and then the news came by way of the Sandwich Islands—now Hawaii—an early trade destination for vessels traveling the Columbia River.

The Oregon Country originally sought by the U.S. was roughly equivalent in size to the original thirteen colonies—357,000 square miles. After the treaty with Britain, the U.S. portion of the Oregon Country encompassed 286,541 square miles,[25] three times the size of present-day Oregon.[26]

Two years after the treaty was signed, Congress officially recognized the land it owned as the "Oregon Territory." After this official designation, United States law would fully apply. Land claims of pioneers could now be verified and land titles granted. Territorial officers would soon be appointed. The Pacific Northwest finally had a firm basis for governance.

But the early settlers had not waited. Five years before the 1848 treaty with the British, Americans in the Willamette Valley had established a provisional government. An early pioneer recounted how close was this famous vote for self-governance:

> The Americans held several meetings to see about organizing a government. Ewing Young had died in Chehalem valley [in 1841] and left his horses and cattle and other property. The settlers didn't know what to do about it. They called a meeting, at which they were going to discuss giving a bounty for killing wolves. At this meeting they discussed the question of having a government for the Oregon country. ... The French-Canadians who were there did not know what to do. Most of them had worked for Dr. John McLoughlin and knew and trusted him. ... Some wanted to have American government, some wanted to have Dr. McLoughlin for governor. ... Finally, Joe Meek said, "Those who are in favor of organization (under control of the United States) come to the right." ... When they counted those who were for American government, there were 52 of us, while there were only 50 in the group opposed to organization.[27]

This historic meeting took place in Champoeg, a landing on the Willamette River twenty-four river miles upriver from Fort Vancouver, on May 2, 1843.

John McLoughlin had claimed "The Falls" (Willamette Falls) and the nearby bank of the Willamette in the name of the Hudson's Bay Company in 1829. In 1842, still in the name of the Company, McLoughlin had Oregon City surveyed and laid out in town lots,[28] some of which he later claimed for himself. He directed the building of a log cabin, saw mill, grist mill, and store. He donated land to the Methodists for a mission. A sizeable community quickly grew up around the mission and mills, and it became the capital of the Oregon Country's provisional government in 1843. The first church west of the Rockies for white worshippers was built there the same year.[29] A jail was erected on a lot McLoughlin donated at the behest of the provincial legislature.[30] Soon thereafter, McLoughlin's relationship with the Hudson's Bay Company soured and he was forced to resign. He moved to Oregon City in early 1846, using up most of his life savings to do so. His claim was later stolen through an act of treachery by Oregon's first territorial delegate, Samuel R. Thurston, whom McLoughlin had not supported for election.[31] McLoughlin's contributions to Oregon were later recognized and honored, however. A statue of McLoughlin was placed in the Congressional Statuary Hall in Washington, D.C., in 1953 as one of Oregon's two honorees, along with missionary Jason Lee. The 1957 Oregon state legislature awarded John McLoughlin the title, "Father of Oregon."[32]

The Willamette Valley runs roughly one hundred fifty miles north to south and is forty miles wide. The Willamette River provided fast and inexpensive transportation for the early settlers, especially for northbound travelers, even though they had to portage around the falls at Oregon City. White swans, ducks, and geese frequented the river's environs; salmon and trout were plentiful; deer and elk provided venison to eat and hides to be tanned for buckskin clothing; wild berries and hazel nuts supplemented gardens planted by early pioneers. The Willamette Valley boasted a mild climate, rich soil, ample building materials, and abundant rainfall to reward human labors with satisfying harvests. The life of Oregon pioneers was hard, but productive, unhindered by the drought and grasshopper plagues of the plains. It was an Eden, though the green of its valleys came with downpours of rain that sometimes continued unabated for days.

Explorers Meriwether Lewis and William Clark originally bypassed the Willamette River, both on their 1805 canoe trip down the Columbia to the Pacific Ocean and on their upriver return the following spring. On April 2, 1806, the expedition camped near the Sandy River, which the men thought drained the Willamette Valley. Indians then told them of a larger river with a big falls that they had passed by. William Clark immediately took a party of seven men and an Indian guide back to investigate this great river that Indians called the Multnomah. In his journal, Clark drew a map showing their overnight campsite on the east side of the Willamette River, south of Sauvie Island. The next morning, Clark and his party continued upriver only a short distance before turning around to rejoin their companions at the Sandy River campsite. They probably did not reach the site that would become Portland forty years later.[33]

Portland was called "The Clearing" before the town had a name. Prior to 1845, The Clearing was nothing more than a meadow in the woods halfway between Fort Vancouver and Oregon City—twelve river miles in each direction. The Clearing had long been a camping ground and rest spot for travelers, both Indian and white, between the falls at Oregon City and the mouth of the Willamette River. In cutting brush and trees for campfires, Indians had gradually cleared about an acre of land.[34]

The first cabin near the future Portland townsite was built south of The Clearing in 1843 by a British sailor named William Johnson, who lived there with his Indian wife and two children, but left when other settlers started arriving.[35] William Overton and Asa Lovejoy stopped at The Clearing on a return canoe trip from Fort Vancouver to Oregon City in November 1843. The canoe was propelled by four Indians wielding sturdy paddles, according to Lovejoy. Overton had been eyeing this land for a claim, but he was broke—so he offered lawyer Lovejoy half-interest in the site if Lovejoy would prepare the papers, do the necessary surveying, and pay the twenty-five- to thirty-cent filing fee.[36]

Lovejoy filed this claim, as provided for by the provisional government, in early 1844.[37] By spring, the penniless Overton wanted to leave Oregon, so he traded his half-interest in the six hundred forty acres to store-proprietor Pettygrove, and eventually ended up in Texas, where, folks said, he was hanged.[38]

In winter 1844-45, Lovejoy and Pettygrove hired a man to build a small log cabin on the claim (although the fleas and mosquitoes were so bad he almost abandoned his work).[39] In summer 1845, they hired surveyor Thomas A. Brown to lay out the townsite, then started selling lots before agreeing on a name.[40] Pettygrove built a small log store at Washington and Front streets (today's Naito Parkway) near the river. Soon he commissioned the building of a wharf. He stocked the store with goods from his Oregon City store and hired a married couple to run it.[41]

Surveyor Brown was assisted by blacksmith James M. A. Terwilliger, who had filed for 640 acres south of the Portland claim.[42] Brown and Terwilliger laid out the Portland townsite in a sixteen-block grid, with eight lots, each fifty by one hundred feet, in each of the two-hundred-feet square blocks. An eighty-foot public right-of-way was marked off for north-south streets, sidewalks and curbs; and sixty feet was allowed for cross streets. No alleys were provided.[43] The grid built from Brown's survey was to frustrate future city planners, with its cramped eighty- and sixty-foot public right-of-ways—although in modern times the additional sun and light provided by short blocks has made downtown Portland attractive for pedestrians.[44] Portland's streets were probably laid out compactly to create more corner lots and to spare builders from having to fell so many trees and remove so many stumps.[45]

A woman pioneer later recalled a 1845 trip from the Tualatin Plains to Fort Vancouver when she was seven years old:

> There were no roads then and but few trails. We followed game trails, or the lay of the country. We climbed the hill north of Tuality Plains. This hill is now called Council Crest and is one of the show sights of Portland. There was a winding trail down to the river. We were on horseback and father said, "Hold your legs tight to your horse, Marie, the trail is narrow—you may get your knees hurt." I was a little thing, not yet eight years old and I was frightened at the steepness of the trail. It was very narrow and wound through heavy timber. … I remember there were two log houses where Portland now is. It was not called Portland then. We and others called it Middletown, because it was midway between Oregon City and Vancouver. There was a store near the bank of the Willamette. On the river bank at what is now the foot of Morrison and Washington streets were Indian tepees.[46]

Stumps were left standing in unbuilt lots, thus providing a derisive new nickname for the rudimentary village: Little Stump Town.[47] At first, many trees were burned instead of being chopped down and the townsite was "disfigured with the blackened shafts of immense trees denuded of their branches by fire."[48]

> "To give you an idea of the density and size of the timber, it is only necessary to say that Colonel Chapman, one of the prominent residents of the city [around 1853] had a stick of fir timber cut on W. S. Ladd's lot, and when it was trimmed up and a considerable part of the top cut off, it measured 130 feet in length [equal to a sixteen-story building].[49] He shipped it to San Francisco as a present to the people of the City by the Golden Gate, to be used as a flagstaff."[50]
>
> —George Collier Robbins

Lovejoy and Pettygrove were the first "proprietors" of Portland—meaning they held exclusive title to the six hundred forty-acre townsite insofar as ownership could be ascertained under provisional government law. Even so, historian Joseph Gaston makes a compelling case that credit for Portland's founding belongs solely to Asa Lovejoy.[51] Lovejoy's imposing gravestone at Lone Fir Cemetery also names him as the city's founder. The headstone says:

In memory of
ASA L. LOVEJOY
1808-1882
FOUNDER
OF
PORTLAND
He endured the adventures of the plains
and mountains and here–
beside the Willamette chose and wisely developed
the site of the greatest city of the Columbia Valley. Afterward
holding many offices of public trust,
and passing the esteem of all.
ERECTED BY HIS FRIENDS, 1943[52]

Perhaps these friends of Lovejoy's were influenced by Pettygrove's later unwillingness to concede that he and Lovejoy had intended Portland's waterfront to be publicly owned. In an 1853 court case, Pettygrove swore that he didn't remember any such intention, in spite of testimony by Lovejoy and ten other witnesses that the land fronting the river had always been designated for public use.[53]

On the other hand, a front-page *Oregonian* headline printed June 28, 1880, awarded the title of "Man Who Founded Portland" to Pettygrove. The *Oregonian* article based on an interview with Pettygrove says that he understood at the time he founded Portland that he was establishing a city for the future. Pettygrove had stopped by the *Oregonian* office on a visit while attending a reunion of the Oregon Pioneer Association when this interview took place. "Mr. Pettygrove told with great glee of the chance which resulted in naming the new town [after his own home town,]" the article says.

Neither Lovejoy nor Pettygrove retained his ownership in the Portland townsite for long.[54] Lovejoy retained his half for only a year, although he was to move his home to Portland twenty years later and spend the last nine years of his life in the city he had wanted to call Boston.[55] Pettygrove held his share for nearly four years, and left the area entirely in 1852 for the Puget Sound in Washington Territory, where he helped found Port Townsend.[56]

A good deal of credit for the early growth of Portland belongs to yet a third man—Captain John H. Couch—merchant, mariner, financier.[57] Captain Couch was highly regarded by other sea captains, and he spread the word among them that Portland was located at just the right spot to reach inland markets without grounding one's ship on sand or gravel bars. As early as 1842, Couch brought the sailing vessel *Chenamus* with a load of trading goods to Oregon City, twelve miles beyond The Clearing,[58] but he found the going difficult for the last few miles. Of The Clearing, Captain Couch declared: "To this point I can bring any ship that can get into the mouth of the Great Columbia River."[59]

Several rival towns emerged on the Willamette and Columbia rivers at about the same time, so Portland had to prove that it was the most direct and accessible route for farmers' produce to reach ocean-going ships. St. Helens, a town several miles downstream (west) from Portland, boasted a deep harbor on the Columbia. Other logical places for a major port city included Astoria and Fort Vancouver on the Columbia River, Linnton near the mouth of the Willamette, and the upstream Willamette settlements of Milwaukie and Oregon City.[60] But Portland had the advantage of both Willamette and Columbia river frontage as the city grew.[61]

Author Joseph Gaston, who knew Captain Couch well, describes the site Couch selected for his six hundred forty-acre claim, filed the same year the Portland townsite was surveyed. Couch's claim adjoined the Lovejoy and Pettygrove land on the north.

Portland's original city limits when the city was chartered in 1851 included a one hundred fifty-four-acre parcel of the Couch claim.[63] Couch and his brother-in-law George Flanders—the first city treasurer—donated ten city blocks of their land for a railroad depot and terminal grounds in the late 1860s.[64]

Shortly after Pettygrove built his store and Captain Couch filed his claim, thirty-eight-year-old Daniel Lownsdale filed on six hundred forty acres immediately west of the townsite in a heavily wooded area on a small stream. There he built a tannery. The stream became known as "Tanner's Creek." Almost immediately, Lownsdale's enterprise attracted

> "The first home of Capt. John H. Couch, where he lived all his life … stood on the west side of Couch lake, and Captain Couch could sit on his front porch and shoot a duck in the lake any day for dinner. Couch lake was a real lake covering about forty city blocks. … The present Union Railroad Depot stands [at the site of] the old lake … the whole of the lake having now been filled up to the established street grade by pumping sand out of the river opposite."[62]

a widespread following. The following ad for the tannery appeared in Oregon City's *Spectator* newspaper:"This establishment is situated in the midst of plenty of hemlock, the only good tanbark which can be procured in the Territory.—Daniel Lownsdale."[65]

"Trade came from far and wide to the tannery, for it was the only one in all the Oregon country," said author Percy Maddux, who rated the tannery as one of the three factors which contributed most to Portland's initial growth.[66] Harvey Scott's *History of Portland* is equally laudatory: "This was the first leather making establishment of any importance on the coast, and well nigh made Portland," Scott says.[67] An early pioneer later recalled that D. H. Lownsdale "had the honor of introducing a new circulating medium [in place of coins], which was Oregon tanned leather."[68]

Pioneers used leather for harnesses, saddles, hinges, partitions, saddlebags, boots, gloves, pants, jackets, and shirts. The raw materials—hides and tannins—were close at hand in the wild life and forests of the area. Animal skins were soaked in lime to loosen hair and flesh, scraped, then tanned in vats of tannins to soften the leather. Portland's PGE Park (formerly Multnomah Stadium) now stands where Lownsdale tanned his hides.[69]

About the same time that Couch and Lownsdale filed their claims, Lovejoy sold his interest in the Portland townsite to Benjamin Stark. Stark came to Portland in 1845 as a supervisor of cargo on the bark *Toulon* that carried goods for Pettygrove's new Portland warehouse. Lovejoy's wife was ill, so he sold Stark his half of the undivided six hundred forty-acre claim for three hundred ninety dollars in cash.[70] Stark bought his interest as an investment and continued to sail the seas with business interests in many ports, visiting Portland only occasionally.[71] Pettygrove, therefore, was the proprietor in charge of the town for three years, even though he retained business interests in Oregon City.[72]

A Portland post office opened November 8, 1849, across the street from Pettygrove's store and warehouse.

But in 1848, apparently for health reasons, Pettygrove sold his half of the claim to tanner Daniel Lownsdale for five thousand dollars' worth of leather.[73] This meant a tidy hundred-fold profit for Pettygrove, from his fifty dollar purchase price four years before.[74] Lownsdale thereupon sold his tannery to devote himself full-time to promoting Portland.

Already, with the townsite little more than a speculative dream, half of the original claim had changed hands twice and the other half had changed once. More swaps were soon to come.

By 1848, Portland consisted of "two white houses and one brick and three wood-colored frame houses and a few cabins." Visitors traveled through the thickest woods they had ever seen, woods infested with "wildcats, panthers, bears and wolves."[75]

Lownsdale's energy and drive, combined with an infusion of capital from the California gold fields, thrust Portland forward in a burst of new development. Lownsdale had traveled widely,[76] and in his initial concept of Portland, displayed laudable foresight in setting aside land for parks, public squares, market squares, and a cemetery. Over the years, however, he was to backpedal again and again, undermining his original plans so that some were never fully realized and others came only at great cost to the public.

Historian Malcolm Clark considered Lownsdale "a promoter by disposition, a man of overly flexible ethics."[77] Deals put together by Lownsdale ended up in costly litigation that cast a shadow over hundreds of early Portland land patents. Because the Oregon Country was not yet an American territory at the time the bargains were made, these earliest transactions dealt only with presumptive titles. After Congress gave the Oregon Territory official status in 1848, the federal government still had a long process to complete before official land patents could be issued.[78] Historian Joseph Gaston summarized the reason for this confusion: "[Portland] started and grew out of the most difficult and trying circumstances that ever attend the founding of any American city. There is not a single large city in the United States, except Portland, but what had for its foundations some sort of authority or law from a sovereign ruler or government."[79]

Lownsdale expanded the original townsite by a hundred additional blocks, reserving twenty narrow blocks for a park[80] and designating

Meanwhile, gold fever struck!

Gold was discovered at Sutter's Mill, California, in 1848. Men from the Oregon Country rushed to join the stampede. "The late Indian disturbances were forgotten. ... Even their beloved land-claims were deserted; if a man did not go to California it was because he could not leave his family or business. ... Far more went to the gold mines than had volunteered to fight the Cayuses. ... Tools were dropped and work left unfinished in the shops... abandoned to women and boys."[81]

In summer 1849, "Portland was almost depopulated, there being but three men left—D. H. Lownsdale, Colonel King, and Mr. Warren," says writer Fred Lockley.[82]

two blocks near the present County Courthouse and City Hall as public squares.[83] The fate of these twenty-two blocks, plus one designated for a public market place and another for a custom house, would eventually be decided by extensive court and public relations battles. The fate of four park blocks had still not been resolved to the public's benefit as the twenty-first century began.[84]

The 1850 townsite survey commissioned by Lownsdale and undertaken by Robert V. Short divided the bank along the Willamette River into individual lots. The original Thomas Brown map of 1845 had shown all land fronting the river—the "levee"—as undivided and therefore not to be sold. The word "levee" is modernly understood to mean an embankment used to prevent flooding, but that is not its meaning here. There was no dike along Portland's harbor. The levee was simply the west bank of the Willamette River, where wharves, docks, ferry landings and piers were being built. The east shoreline of the Willamette, by contrast, was swampy and flat, so was not spoken of as a "levee." John Brady drew a map reflecting the Robert Short survey. Soon the Short survey and Brady map would be the basis for high-stakes, acrimonious lawsuits over ownership of the levee that would drag on for many years.[85]

Daniel Lownsdale took on two partners that year: Stephen Coffin and William Chapman. The forty-two-year-old Coffin[86] of Maine had crossed the plains in 1847 and accumulated enough money from various Oregon City endeavors to buy a half-interest in Lownsdale's share of the townsite for six thousand dollars.[87] In December 1849, Lownsdale and Coffin each sold a third of their shares (totaling a one-sixth share of the townsite) for 26,666 dollars to lawyer W. W. Chapman, age forty-one. Chapman had served as U.S. attorney for the Wisconsin Territory and had represented the Iowa Territory in Congress.[88]

The Lownsdale-Coffin-Chapman trio formed the Portland Townsite Company, with Coffin as president and Chapman as secretary.[89] They offered lots at very low prices to those who agreed to build homes on the land.

An observer wrote a friend in November 1850: "You will perhaps be astonished when I tell you that Portland has become the principal town of Oregon. It now outnumbers Oregon City in houses, inhabitants, and as to business there is more done here now than there. There are now under way not less than one hundred and fifty new houses."[90]

That year, Lownsdale journeyed to San Francisco and met with co-owner Benjamin Stark to sort out exactly which land belonged to whom in the mile-square Portland townsite. The two finally agreed that all land south of what is now Stark Street would go to the Portland Townsite

Company, while Stark would retain ownership of the developed, but much smaller, parcel—a triangular-shaped segment bounded on the north by Burnside Street (John Couch's claim), on the south by Stark Street, and on the east by the Willamette River. In exchange, Lownsdale, Coffin, and Chapman agreed to pay Stark all money received for land they had already sold in his acreage. Stark's portion was approximately forty-eight acres, while the trio retained nearly six hundred acres (mostly undeveloped). Stark's share included almost all of Portland's booming "downtown."[91] See table below.

Even though he bore the distinguished title of former U.S. Senator from Oregon (appointed for the 1861-62 term), Benjamin Stark later refused to deed the two narrow blocks of his land needed to connect the twenty park blocks designated by Lownsdale's plat map[92] to the five additional blocks Captain Couch had dedicated for parks. Stark was in poor financial condition in spite of his travels, his investments, and his reputation as a wealthy man. He overextended his credit and never remained in Oregon long enough to properly tend to business affairs.[93]

Table 1: Ownership of the Original Portland Townsite

Year	*Transaction*	*Price paid*	*How much traded*		*Resulting ownership*
1844	Overton to Lovejoy	25-30 cent filing fee	1/2	320 acres	1/2 Overton, 1/2 Lovejoy
1844	Overton to Pettygrove	$50 worth of supplies	1/3	320 acres	1/2 Pettygrove, 1/2 Lovejoy
1845	Lovejoy to Stark	$390 in cash	1/2	320 acres	1/2 Pettygrove, 1/2 Stark
1848	Pettygrove to Lownsdale	$5,000 in leather	1/2	320 acres	1/2 Lownsdale, 1/2 Stark
1849	Lownsdale to Coffin	$6,000 in cash	1/4	160 acres	1/4 Lownsdale, 1/4 Coffin, 1/2 Stark
1849	Lownsdale and Coffin to Chapman	$26,666 in cash	1/6	106 acres	1/6 Lownsdale, 1/6 Coffin, 1/6 Chapman, 1/2 Stark
1850	Stark to Lownsdale, Coffin, and Chapman	Negotiated agreement	5/13	272 acres	12/13 Lownsdale, Coffin, and Chapman, 1/13 Stark

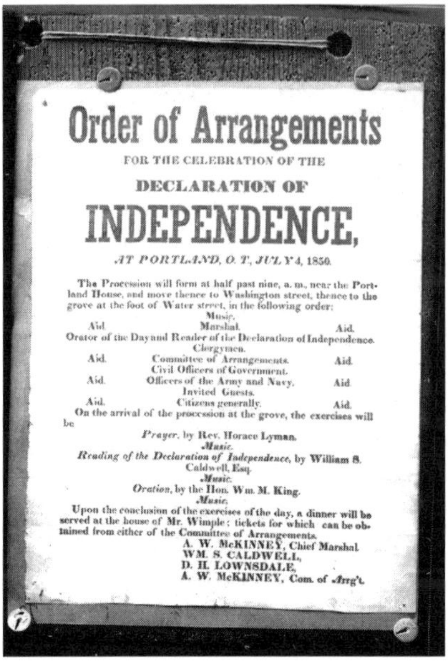

Controversial William King used oratorical skills to garner early political power. (Photo: OrHi #26614)

Some Portland lots changed hands several times before the federal government finished its long process of awarding titles. In 1850, Congress passed the Oregon Donation Land Claims Act that granted six hundred forty acres of free land to every married couple who had claimed acreage *before* December 1, 1850—one-half each to the husband and wife—provided that they cultivate the claim and live on it for four years. Between December 1850 and December 1855, married couples could claim three hundred twenty acres, single settlers, one hundred sixty acres.[94] After December 1855, these special Oregon Territory provisions ceased. Then it took years for government agents to survey the land, mark it off into townships and sections, and set up a procedure for receiving claims, taking sworn testimony, and awarding title. Lownsdale received his patent for title in 1860, Couch in 1865.[95] (The national Homestead Act that opened up free land for homesteading in other parts of the United States was passed in 1862.)[96]

By 1850, Portland, with eight hundred twenty-one people, already had more residents than any other Northwest white settlement. The closest rival was Oregon City, with six hundred ninety-seven inhabitants. Astoria had only two hundred fifty-two.[97]

Thomas J. Dryer, editor of the newly-founded *Oregonian* newspaper, described Portland in December 1850:

> The buildings are mostly new, of good style and taste, which with their white coats of paint, contrasted with the brown and dingy appearance of towns generally on the Pacific coast, gives it a most home like aspect. We have a steam saw mill already in operation and another about being erected, as well as a flouring mill, machine shop, planing mills, etc., which will add much to the importance of the place.... We have a Methodist Church just completed, which combines beauty and convenience with

> a substantial building of good size, also a Presbyterian church of modern style and large dimensions nearly completed.... A spacious School house has already been built.[98]

Exports from the Oregon Country to California during the gold rush years included lumber, beef, butter, bacon, and vegetables.[99] Fresh apples were in high demand.[100] A pioneer family named Luelling had brought two boxes of year-old grafted fruit-trees across the plains, faithfully watering and sheltering the tender plants throughout the six-month journey. They settled on a claim across the Willamette from Portland near the rival town of Milwaukie, and offered their first apples for sale in 1850. The fruit proved enormously popular. Luelling's apples sold for a dollar each in Portland, while the cost of a single apple to a California gold miner in the field—if indeed it ever reached him—was five dollars, the equivalent of one hundred dollars today.[101]

For almost the same price as two fresh apples, an early Portlander could buy a gallon of whiskey and still have enough money left over for a pound of tobacco.[102] Was it any wonder, with liquor so inexpensive and available, and with gold dust weighing down the pockets of returning miners, that the need for law and order helped create demand for a city government?

An early memoir by a woman pioneer describes prevailing attitudes of the time:

> [T]he old men talked over the possibilities of Oregon. One thought bridges would span the Willamette; others shook their heads, saying not while we live. Our children may live to see one. Others thought railroads would be built across the continent; all looked at the speaker and echoed "A railroad! Never, over those mountains. Why man, no one in God's world will live to see that day. Steamers and ships will come, but no railroad."[103]

In December 1850, five years after the city's founding, Portland citizens set forth a petition for self-governance to the territorial government.

Chapter 2

Treason and Spoils

December 1850 – January 1851

I well remember (in 1849) scrambling over logs, through brush and briar, and creeping under and through thickets of vine maple in the discharge of what proved to be a very laborious and disagreeable duty in locating and opening the (Canyon) road.

—Joseph Showalter Smith, in a letter to the *Oregonian*[1]

U. S. 26 serves almost every role a road can play. … It's an urban freeway, a mountain pass, a freight line, a scenic route, a tourist link and a gateway to recreation. It is a major highway for travelers, a commuter circuit for workers and a main street for rural residents.

—*Oregonian*, July 6, 1999[2]

Mud, stumps, rain, and more rain.

Throughout Portland's history, transportation has played a dominant role in the city's progress, never more prominently than in its earliest days. Even the chartering of the town became entangled with the need for a road to Portland from the farmlands to its west and south. The Portland–Tualatin Valley route targeted for a plank road had been hacked out of underbrush and dense forest, and was little more than a blazed path of roots and mud.[3] Planking would make it wider and more passable. Without such an access road, Portland was virtually an island, unreachable except by boat.

Two bills essential to Portland's future were introduced at the 1850-51 territorial legislature, both dealing with incorporation. The granting of charters to all kinds of enterprises was the way this early legislature did business. One Portland bill would create a city government. The other authorized a private company to raise funds for a plank road from Portland to the Tualatin Plains and beyond, so that log planks could be laid over a narrow trail then little more than a quagmire of muck.[4]

Politics became intricately involved in the approval of both these potential charters. Many projects demanded attention from territorial legislators: roads, schools, jails, libraries. Other towns were growing fast—Salem, Marysville, Milwaukie, Linnton, St. Helens—and there was talk of building a railroad from Portland down the Willamette Valley. Downstate legislators had other bills they were eager to pass. Uppermost on the legislative agenda was the question of where to build territorial institutions. Construction of such buildings would bring needed federal dollars to cash-strapped towns.

As for "Stumptown," its streets and roads were a territorial joke. Stumps were whitewashed to help revelers avoid bumping into them in the dark. Mud clung to ladies' skirts when they crossed Portland's streets, and the crude sidewalks offered little protection.[5] Territorial Governor Gaines was unable to visit much of Portland because of "vast quantities of mud and water" that lay in his course.[6]

A controversial character named Colonel William King now entered the picture.He had been elected as one of two members of the territorial house of representatives from Washington County, of which Portland was a part. There King served on the judiciary committee and chaired the incorporation committee. In these capacities, he was about to play a lead role in the 1850-51 legislature. William H. King was Portland's "first politician and statesman."[7]

King had held the rank of colonel in the New York militia, and the title stuck. Born in Connecticut in 1800, he moved first to New York, then Pennsylvania, then Missouri, before setting out for Oregon country in 1848.[8] The colonel's advanced age of fifty gave him considerable status in pioneer Oregon. He gave the "Oration" at the 1850 Fourth of July celebration in Portland.[9] Although a lawyer, he practiced little law. He set up a construction business, and built Portland's first sawmill in 1849 (which was destroyed by fire shortly after it was completed),[10] as well as Portland's first schoolhouse.[11]

A letter addressed to "Mr. King, Esquire, Member of the House of Representatives (Oregon City)" reads as follows:

> Portland, December 17, 1850
>
> Mr. King—Dear Sir—
>
> Accompanying this will be a petition for a charter for Portland. I understand that you are honored with the office of Chairman of the Committee on incorporations. Therefore I doubt not but due respect will be payed to the said petition. I took this petition from the stump, and every name that is on it has been put on in my presents and my opportunity to know the wishes of yon petitioners

> relative to the said charter is better perhaps than many others. Allow me then to state: that if your honorable body should think that Portland is to small or that it would be to expensive for her now to support a City organization, that a majority of the inhabitants of Portland would be as well pleased to receive only a town incorporation. Several have suggested the propriety of allowing the officers no remuneration in her infancy; this perhaps she can regulate after she has received her Charter.
>
> In haste, your obedient servant,
> L. B. Hastings.[12]

The petition sent by Loren Hastings read as follows: "We the undersigned residents of Portland humbly represent that it must be for the public good that the town of Portland should be incorporated as a city—We therefore pray your Honorable Body that you will grant a Charter giving all the rights and privileges usual in such cases."[13] The first signature was that of S. A. Clarke, who was later to be an *Oregonian* editor.[14] Other modernly recognizable names included Hugh D. O'Bryant, Thomas J. Dryer, W. W. Chapman, John H. Couch, Finice Caruthers, A. R. Skidmore, and James Terwilliger.[15]

"After Col. King came to Portland, if there was anything going on he was sure to have a hand in it, and perhaps to be very near the bottom of it," says Harvey Scott's *History of Portland.*[16] In an 1876 address before the Oregon Pioneer Association, Judge R. P. Boise said of King:

> In the Legislature of 1850, I first met Col. Wm. M. King. … Col. King was even then advanced to the prime of life. He was a veteran politician … and knew well the various evolutions of legislative tactics. He was a ready debater and could use with equal earnestness sound argument or sophistry, and could marshal the selfish desires, interests and prejudices of men with consummate skill, and like most men who aim at carrying a point, he was not over-scrupulous as to the means by which it was attained. He was a firm, and faithful friend, and a bitter enemy. He had faults which caused him much trouble and suffering – but who has not faults? He … possessed a keen and penetrating mind, and much intelligence, which would make him a marked man in any community.[17]

In short, Col. William King[18] was a nineteenth-century wheeler and dealer. His influence extended to such peripheral matters as the naming of Washington and Marion counties.[19] King made sure they were solid "American" names instead of the historic Indian names with multiple possible spellings previously considered by the legislature.[20]

Col. King, in his capacity as judiciary committee chair, received at least two more letters from prominent Portlanders during the 1850-51 legislative session, both from townsite proprietors. The two letters help explain the political climate surrounding the plank road and charter bills. The first was written two days after the Hastings petition had been dispatched to Col. King:

> Portland, December 19, 1850.
> Hon. Msrs. King, Deady and other
> Friends of the Portland and Valley improvement.
> Gentlemen.
>
> Since I saw you at the City and since hearing considerable said upon the subject, I am inclined to think it of the utmost importance that the [Road] Charter contain a Proviso for a Plank Road part of all the way. A Plank road may be made the first year, which in due season a Railroad will be completed.
>
> Yours, W.W. Chapman."[21]

Railroads were the coming thing, but building them required capital, materials, and know-how not yet available in the remote Oregon Country. But plank roads on which horses and buggies could travel were more within pioneer means. "At the start of the 1850s, Americans throughout the Midwest and South were seized by a mania for plank roads—highways with a surface of sawed planks spiked to wooden stringers. They were touted as 'the farmers' railroad,' easy for amateurs to build and almost as cheap as dirt in the states around the Great Lakes and in the Northwest where lumber was virtually free for the cutting."[22]

The second letter from a Portland townsite proprietor was to remind Col. King of the need for both a plank road and a city charter, while also touching on future plans for a railroad.

> Portland, January 13, 1851.
>
> Dear Col.—
>
> ... We have been looking for some action in regard to Legislative matters through the papers but nothing of note appears to come. ... We should like to have that R Road shoved ahead a little but the majority has come to the

> conclusion that a plank road will be the first advantage therefore if it could be fixed soon to give us a charter for a plank road with the privilege of increasing the stock and within five years to erect a railroad over the same space—from this to Yamhill falls—please write me at the first opportunity—please take your own way about business but shove on our corporation of—City of Portland—In a hurry your obtsvnt
>
> —D. H. Lownsdale.[23]

Lownsdale's plea to "shove on our corporation" reflects understandable anxiety about the lack, thus far, of legislative action on Portland's city charter. Nearly a month had transpired since Loren Hastings had sent King the petition with 145 signatures requesting incorporation for the city. The legislature was due to adjourn in little more than two weeks.

Three lawyers comprised the committee to whom this petition was referred: William King of Portland (committee chairman), pioneer William T. Matlock of Oregon City, and Matthew Deady of Yamhill County, later to be an eminent United States District Judge.[24]

On January 14, 1851, the Oregon territorial house of representatives passed Portland's charter. The territorial council (senate) approved the bill on January 23; and Governor John P. Gaines signed it on February 8. It was printed as a broadside by the *Oregonian* Press on March 16, three weeks before the date set for election of city officers (see Appendix A).

The city of Portland therefore received its charter eight years before Oregon became a state in 1859 and three years before the creation of Multnomah County in 1854. Only one town was incorporated before Portland: Oregon City, chartered in 1844, was the only city awarded official status by the *provisional* government. In 1849, Oregon City received a second charter[25] to become the first town recognized by the *territorial* government. Five days after passage of Portland's 1851 charter, the territorial assembly approved a third charter for Oregon City.

The two 1851 charters were not identical, however.[26] Portland men were required to donate two days of labor a year to build city streets plus one day for territorial roads, whereas Oregon City men had to work only one day a year on their own streets and none on territorial roads. All other able-bodied men in the territory over age twenty-one were required to donate two days of work on territorial roads. The end result was three days of annual labor for Portland men, one day for men of Oregon City, and two days for other men in the territory.[27] Log rolling—of which more will soon be said—was probably behind the differences.

Portland's charter gave the city council power to build streets, lanes, sidewalks, and public levees, and required property owners to repair and improve sidewalks, alleys, and gutters adjacent to their property. If the owner did not do so, council was authorized to make such repairs and improvements and assess the cost to the owner.[28] Except for the omission of these provisions, the two charters are virtually the same. Both cities were to be governed by a council consisting of a mayor, recorder, and five councilmen. Both had the word "town" scratched and the word "city" inserted instead. A "one-fourth of one per centum" property tax was authorized to cover the cost of each government.[29]

The contentious issue that overshadowed all other matters at this time was the territory-wide question of where to locate institutions such as the territorial capital, penitentiary, and college. The parts were rolled into one pork-barrel bill.

Until two days before adjournment, the issue was deadlocked. On January 28, 1851, a compromise bill was introduced with the exact locations of the government institutions left blank. The bill moved smoothly through first and second readings the same day. On January 30, the final day of the session, the blanks were filled with "Salem" for the capital, "Portland" for the penitentiary, and "Marysville" (now Corvallis) for the university. The House then approved the bill ten to eight.[30]

Also on the final day of the session, both houses of the legislature passed the plank road bill for Portland. The act provided that Thomas Carter, Daniel H. Lownsdale, and five others, "together with all other persons who shall become associated with them, by subscribing to the capital stock of said company," should constitute a new corporation to construct a plank road from Portland through the town of Lafayette in Yamhill County to some point on Mary's River (near present-day Corvallis, eighty miles south).[31]

The Oregon City *Spectator*, the foremost newspaper in the territory, published a stinging criticism of the 1850-51 legislature soon after it adjourned.

> It is said that "every dog has his day." Truly may this be said of some of the Legislative Solons—they have had their day; they have been tried and were found wanting. The

> people will *relieve* them of any further public trust. They are not satisfied with the tactics of the immortal nine. They do not believe in the system "you vote for my plank road and I'll vote for giving you the University—you vote for the Penitentiary for *me* and I'll vote for giving you the seat of Government." Here is the bargain and sale entered into by the immortal nine. "We must incorporate all these projects into one bill or they cannot be carried through. It will not do to risk them separately—we must rush them through as speedily as possible."[32]

That Col. King masterminded this vote trading is virtually certain. His prior legislative and leadership experience would have taught him to give a little here and take more there as the way to get things done. He knew how to count votes and out-maneuvered his opponents. Oregon City got left out of the bargain.

The newspaper article refers to a territorial law which specified that each bill was to address only one subject, a provision that continues to the present day. The current Oregon Constitution says: "Every Act shall embrace but one subject, and matters properly connected therewith ..." (Article IV, Section 20).

Another article in the same issue of the *Spectator* lambasted Col. King more directly:

> A Meeting, we are informed, was held at Portland, last week, to take in consideration the action of King and company, relative to gambling off the rights of the people who elected them to office, in peddling out the locations of the public buildings; distributing them far and wide, to catch the nincompoops who had not mind enough to stand, each, on his own platform; but who, like lambs to the slaughter, were led [by King]. ... One purpose of the meeting was to endorse the onslaught of Mr. King upon the Governor [Gaines].

The hero of this meeting, according to the *Spectator*, was Thomas Jefferson Dryer, editor of the two-month-old weekly *Oregonian*, the *Spectator*'s new rival.

> The meeting progressed and several speeches were made. Bro. Dryer gave Mr. King a sound drubbing for his disreputable course in the Legislature—for the bargain and sale he was engaged in, and for selling himself out,

> body and breeches to men less cunning than himself. King essayed a reply. His excuse for the bargain and sale was, that he thought it was necessary to sell-out that he might secure the passage of the Plank Road Bill, from the Willamette river to the Plains. Mr. Dryer, it is said, gave King a severe castigation—moved an adjournment of the meeting, and ruined King's prospects for the Mayoralty. Mr. Couch is to run for Mayor; there is no doubt of his election by the good people of Portland.[33]

Partisan political feeling ran deep throughout the Oregon Country, and Col. King was solidly in the Democratic camp. *Oregonian* editor Dryer was already a chief spokesman for the Whigs. The Whig Party had been formed in opposition to the Democratic Party and would soon be succeeded by the Republican Party. The newly appointed Whig governor of the territory, John Gaines, had recently arrived from the East Coast and had been coolly received by the Democrats. (Abraham Lincoln had been offered the job of territorial governor but had turned it down.)[34]

The territorial assembly was made up of a council (counterpart of today's senate) of nine members and a house of representatives of eighteen. Both Washington County representatives, Col. William King and Dr. Ralph Wilcox of Portland, served again in the 1851-52 legislature, which was even more contentious than its predecessor. The 1851-52 Democratic assembly met in Salem, while the Whig contingent, including the governor, remained in Oregon City.[35] A territorial audience that witnessed such divisive political shenanigans could fully appreciate the wit and innuendo of a biting satire called, "Breakspeare: Treason, Stratagems and Spoils," written anonymously by William L. Adams, a prominent Whig.[36]

This five-act parody of the 1850-51 legislature was to become a best-seller throughout the territory.[37] It was written to imitate Shakespeare, and was first published in five installments in the *Oregonian* in early 1852. The parody was an instant sensation.[38] The names used were fictional, but most were readily recognizable as those of leading Democrats of the territory. All lists which deduced the real-life counterparts of each of the characters identified Rex as Col. King.[39] A fictional Mormon conspiracy was added to the plot, but otherwise the story paralleled actual events of the 1850-51 legislative session."Crowds flocked to every post office to get a copy and read it, till half the people of Oregon had committed most of it to memory," one history says.[40]

Logroller William King (center) is satirized in this woodcut from the "melodrame" Treason, Stratagems and Spoils, *depicting a drunken scene at Grubs Grocery and pork-barrel politics of the 1850-51 territorial legislature. Text of melodrame by William L. Adams. See bibliography.*

Act II of "Treason, Stratagems and Spoils" begins with legislators arriving in Salem on December 1, the night before the first session starts. Five characters, including Rex (Col. King), meet at Grub's Grocery. In early Americana, the term "grocery" meant "dramshop, saloon, or tavern"and the characters at Grub's are imbibing liberally of alcoholic beverages.[41] (This definition of "grocery" was embodied in Oregon law.[42])

Rex boasts to his drinking buddies, obviously fellow-Democrats, of his log-rolling prowess. His title of log-roller—one who trades votes—referred directly to King's role in negotiating the compromise locations bill:

REX: *I tell you, Ned, if you will but consent*
To place yourself under my guardianship
And tutorage, in the dark, secret school
Of tactics political, if I fail
To tone up the liver of your conscience
To such a pitch, as certainly to prevent
The recurrence of those weak qualms again
Without the hope of a reward, I'll act
As your accoucheur, and deliver you

Of the last of these hateful "gnawing worms."
I, being an old hand at underground
Political machinery, why you see,
The people have conferred on me
The title of Rex, "King of log-rollers."[43]

The Oregon territorial supreme court ruled the 1851 location bill invalid; but Congress then validated it. The January 1855 territorial legislature moved the territorial capital to Corvallis; in December the next legislature moved it back to Salem. The controversy over the location of the capital was to smolder for nearly fifteen years before it was finally awarded to Salem by a decisive vote of the people in 1864.[44]

A penitentiary was indeed constructed in Portland (paid for by federal funds), with Col. King and his partner George Kittredge providing construction supplies.[45] (Kittredge was to serve on Portland's City Council in 1854 and 1855.) The *Oregonian* questioned King's land speculation in the penitentiary lots and the double salary he drew as commission chairman and for "simultaneously filling a commission vacancy."[46] In February 1854, the legislature removed King from the penitentiary commission. The penitentiary remained in Portland until 1866, when the legislature directed that convicts be moved to Salem, where most other statewide activities would ultimately be centered.[47]

And the Portland charter provision requiring two days of labor on city streets plus one day on territorial roads? A fitting postscript is contained in a May 28, 1869, order preserved at the Oregon History Center; it is the same kind of order sent to all able-bodied Portland men aged twenty-one and over:

> Mr. Wm King—
>
> You are hereby notified to appear on the road in District No. 18, at 1/2 miles west Canion Garden with Pick & shuvel to wok on Road on the 2nd day of June 1869.
>
> R. R. Riley, Supervisor.[48]

Chapter 3

A Four-Vote Victory

March – April, 1851

The town that [the first mayor] and his successors tried to govern was more like a giant fraternity house than a real community. Three quarters of the 805 residents recorded in the 1850 census were male. Nine-tenths of all Portlanders were in their twenties.

—Professor Carl Abbott, 1997.[1]

A four-vote margin. That's how close Joseph Showalter Smith came to being elected Portland's first mayor.

If he had known a public square would be named after the mayor one day, would Joseph Smith have tried harder? Would other possible candidates have sought the office? For it might well have been Couch Square, King Square, or Dryer Square in today's downtown Portland instead of O'Bryant Square. But only two names appeared on the first ballot for mayor: Hugh O'Bryant and Joseph Showalter Smith.

Portland's charter specified that the mayor would preside at council meetings, and cast an equal vote with other council members. He also functioned as the city's justice of the peace and received a portion of all the fines he collected. Otherwise, no salary was provided for either the mayor or council.

At a schoolhouse town meeting convened three weeks before the election, Thomas J. Dryer was nominated for mayor and W. S. Caldwell for recorder. Thomas Jefferson Dryer was the opinionated, feisty, civic-minded editor of the *Oregonian*, Portland's only newspaper, begun three months before. Dryer also was a hard-line Whig. He had worked on newspapers in the East, and ventured to San Francisco at the age of forty-two, taking along an old hand press and some battered type, looking for a promising spot to ply his trade. In San Francisco, he met two Portlanders who happened to be searching for someone to start a newspaper. Stephen Coffin and William Chapman convinced Dryer that their promising city would provide the opportunity and challenge he sought. The first issue of the *Oregonian* was published on December 4, 1850, less than two months before Portland's charter was approved.[2]

Four days later, at a second town meeting, Dryer declined the nomination in what the *Oregonian* termed "a short pertinent speech." The meeting ended with the following "excellent ticket" of city officers:

> *For Mayor*—J. S. Smith
> *Recorder*—W. S. Caldwell
> *Council*—S. Norris, R. Thompson, L. B. Hastings, T. G. Robinson, G. A. Barnes.[3]

The Oregon City *Spectator* had said that Captain John Couch planned to run for Portland mayor, and prophesied his election. Whether Couch ever seriously considered the race is not known. The same *Spectator* article recounted a meeting at which Dryer gave Colonel King such a "severe castigation" that it "ruined King's prospects for the Mayoralty."[4] That Col. King might have harbored such ambitions is certainly possible. On the other hand, Dryer could simply have been engaging in partisan hyperbole, with the Whig-leaning *Spectator*[5] adding its own spice.

Assuming the *Oregonian* and *Spectator* newspaper accounts were reasonably accurate, that made five potential candidates for Portland's first mayor: Thomas J. Dryer, Joseph S. Smith, Capt. John Couch, Col. William King, and a fifth contestant—previously unmentioned—Hugh D. O'Bryant.

Hugh O'Bryant had served as a first lieutenant during the Cayuse Indian War fought to avenge the brutal deaths of Dr. Marcus and Narcissa Whitman and twelve others on November 29, 1847, near present-day Walla Walla, Washington, two hundred miles east of Portland.[6] The Cayuse had attributed the many deaths from disease sweeping through their tribe to Whitman, a medical doctor who was also a Protestant missionary; the Indians thought Whitman was poisoning them.[7]

Hugh O'Bryant was born in Georgia and was thirty-six years old in 1851.[8] He grew up among the Cherokee Indians, the son of a Methodist missionary, and received little or no formal education. He "crossed the plains by ox team and prairie schooner," with his brother Humphrey, thirteen years younger than he.[9] They arrived at Oregon City in October 1843.[10] As a preacher's son who had apparently inherited his father's driving energy, booming voice, and missionary zeal for causes, Hugh O'Bryant was the sort of man who might offer the kind of leadership a new city needed to get things done.

O'Bryant was already a justice of the peace for the Portland townsite before the city charter was granted.[11] O'Bryant's membership in Portland's Masonic Lodge would also have earned him votes at the ballot box. Author E. Kimbark MacColl rates membership in the Masons as a strong status symbol in early Portland:

> Masonic membership thrived in Portland among white, non-Catholic males who preferred exclusively male company. Early Masonry was not unlike the private gentlemen's clubs of later years. On July 17, 1850, Willamette Lodge No. 2 held its initial meeting on the upper floor of Captain Couch's warehouse on North Front Street. Led by Benjamin Stark, the secret fraternal order dedicated itself to benevolence and charity. It drew many of Portland's early business and civic luminaries including Couch, Dryer, Flanders, Lewis, Lownsdale, T. J. Holmes, W. M. King, H. D. O'Bryant, G. L. Story, and John Logan. Within a year, 116 men belonged to Masonic lodges in Portland and in Oregon City.[12]

Hugh O'Bryant was Junior Warden of the Portland Masonic chapter, and William S. Caldwell, soon to be Portland's first recorder, was lodge secretary. Thomas G. Robinson and Robert Thompson, members of the city's first council, and Allison C. Bonnell, later to serve as Portland's second mayor, were also members of the newly established lodge.[13]

Although candidate Hugh O'Bryant is often credited with founding Portland's first public library in 1850 as a library reading room "paid for out of his own pocket,"[14] this claim is either grossly overstated or a mistake, because other records document that the twelve hundred dollars collected for library books purchased in New York City was contributed by sixty-five Portland businessmen who formed the Portland Library Association in that year.[15] Hugh O'Bryant was not a member of that group (see Appendix B).[16]

In 1847, Hugh O'Bryant claimed Swan Island—named for the white swans that stopped there on semi-annual migrations from Canada to Mexico and back[17]—in the Willamette River as a donation land claim.[18] Swan Island would one day boast Portland's first airport, and later a Henry Kaiser World War II shipyard.[19] At the time O'Bryant filed his claim, the main channel of the Willamette River ran between Swan Island and the east-bank mainland.[20] Whether O'Bryant ever built a cabin on Swan Island is unknown,[21] but we do know that he abandoned his original intent to own the island before he gained title.[22] Congress did not pass the Oregon Donation Land Claims Act until 1850, and it took ten years or more for actual titles to be awarded. Long before he gained title to the island, O'Bryant had left the Portland area.

Hugh O'Bryant's brother, Humphrey,[23] claimed six hundred forty acres at Tansy Point on the Columbia River across the mouth of Young's Bay from the city of Astoria,[24] but he also left the area without gaining title.

When O'Bryant was not off fighting Indians, or performing justice of the peace duties, or possibly prospecting for gold, he built cabins for other settlers. While most buildings of the time were constructed of round logs, O'Bryant erected one of split cedar boards.[25] His carpenter skills would have been in great demand with new immigrants continually arriving in Portland. (The 1850 census-taker found many people by listening for the sound of axes felling trees.)[26]

And O'Bryant's opponent—Joseph Smith? He started life as a poor farm boy whose family moved often. His middle name, Showalter, was the maiden name of his mother, who died when he was ten.[27] Joseph left home at age eighteen, after his father married again. He eventually saved enough money working in a grocery store to buy a horse, then started west in 1844. He arrived at Oregon City in 1845, where he found work and studied law. He was Oregon's first law student.[28]

The 1850 Oregon territorial census shows Joseph Smith "age 29, born Pennsylvania," living with wife Julia Carter Smith and their four-month-old daughter Anna at the spacious home of Julia's parents, Thomas and Minerva Carter.[29] By that time, Smith was practicing law; Gaston's *History of Oregon* identifies Smith as one of only four lawyers practicing in Portland prior to 1852.[30] He was also preaching at a local Methodist church[31] and was a Methodist circuit rider assigned to the Yamhill Circuit, of which Portland was a part.[32] He and Father Kelly conducted religious services in Portland by "coming down from their homes at stated times to hold worship in the cooper shop [a workshop where casks and barrels were made] which was the most commodious building for the purpose."[33]

Smith also helped hack out the first route for farmers to transport their produce through the steep forested hills west of Portland.[34] A committee consisting of Stephen Coffin, Smith, and a third person were appointed to "raise funds to meet the expenses and superintend the construction of the road," Smith said in a letter to the editor. "I paid fifty dollars out of a very slim purse toward the expense of the enterprise."[35]

Julia Carter Smith had conducted a private school for about thirty-five pupils in a log cabin at Second and Stark streets[36] the winter after she arrived in Oregon in 1848.[37] Her parents' land claim was to become fashionable Portland Heights, as well as part of Washington Park and old Canyon Road.[38]

Mayor Hugh O'Bryant. (Photo: OrHi #222)

In spite of Joseph Smith's worthy credentials, that first Portland election on April 7, 1851, pitted him against a better-known opponent. Hugh O'Bryant was six years older than Smith, who was then thirty years old, and had been in the Oregon Country two years longer. Both were active Democrats. Unlike Smith, O'Bryant was a single man, and may have frequented Portland saloons where much social life of the times occurred.[39] His rough-hewn manner may also have appealed to other 1851 frontiersmen.

On April 7, 1851, two hundred twenty-two male citizens cast their ballots for a mayor, recorder, and five council members.[40] Hugh O'Bryant received one hundred thirteen votes for mayor and Joseph Smith, one hundred nine—a harbinger for many close election results to come. The recorder and five council members nominated by the March 18 town meeting were elected without apparent opposition.

Joseph Smith left Portland two years after his mayoral defeat for the Puget Sound area. There, he was elected to the Washington territorial legislature, and served as U.S. District Attorney for the Washington Territory.[41] After five years, Smith moved to Salem, where he ran the state's oldest and largest woolen mill—the Willamette Woolen Manufacturing Company, founded in 1856—which prospered greatly, especially during the Civil War.[42] In 1868, Smith was elected as Oregon's representative to Congress (1869-71) and, while there, "with his own hand he penned the amendment to the [Northern Pacific Railroad] bill by which the company was required to build its main line down the Columbia River to Portland."[43] By 1879, he had moved back to Portland, and was one of the six richest men in Portland.[44] Smith was the Democratic party nominee for Oregon governor in 1882, but was defeated by a healthy margin.[45]

The same day that Portland elected its new city officials, Oregon City citizens elected the venerable Dr. John McLoughlin as their new mayor by a two-to-one margin.[46] Sixty-six votes were cast, of which McLoughlin won forty-four votes to twenty-two for incumbent mayor W. K. Kilborn.[47]

Hugh O'Bryant had wanderlust, ambition, and an amazing capacity to get himself elected to public office. O'Bryant left Portland almost immediately after completing his mayoral term, and moved south two hundred miles to the town of Roseburg, where he was elected to represent Douglas, Umpqua, and two other southwest counties on the nine-member Oregon territorial council . His fellow legislators elected him council president.[48] In 1860, he moved to the Walla Walla Valley in Washington Territory, about two hundred miles east of Portland.[49] There he served as a Walla Walla county commissioner, a Washington territorial assemblyman, a joint councilman for Walla Walla and Stevens counties,[50] chairman of the Coppei Precinct Democrats, and was active in county Democratic affairs.[51]

While living in Roseburg, O'Bryant had married and started a family. The 1870 federal census for Walla Walla County lists O'Bryant as a farmer with a wife, Matilda, ten years his junior, and seven children, ages two through sixteen, all born in Oregon or Washington territory.[52] O'Bryant was still residing in the Walla Walla Valley in 1874,[53] but after that his location is difficult to trace. Federal census records show that by 1880, when he was sixty-seven years old, Hugh O'Bryant was living with his family[54] in Merced County, California. However, no 1890 census record was found for any family member with the last name of O'Bryant in Oregon, Washington, or California.[55] Former Mayor O'Bryant had probably passed away by that time.

Was Hugh O'Bryant a good mayor? Thirty years after his term ended, the *1882 Portland City Directory* provided this evaluation:

> The first mayor of Portland was not a shining monument of scholastic veneering, neither did he represent much of the filagree and fresco of the *beau monde*; but his fibre was sound and his colors would wash. He was a man of tried probity and great force of character, and brought to the discharge of the duties of the work-day world an ample reserve of what Judge Kelsay would pithily term clean, hard sense.[56]

Certainly Mayor O'Bryant was a maverick, even in a part of the country that attracted independent spirits. His portrait hangs in row one, space one, in the Portland city hall mayors' gallery. In 1973, he was honored by the naming and dedication of O'Bryant Square, located between S. W. Washington and Stark streets on the northernmost of the Lownsdale park blocks.[57] O'Bryant Square is eight blocks due west of the town's first store and wharf.[58]

Chapter 4

The Supporting Cast

April 1851

[The] Mayor, Recorder and councilmen shall constitute a City Council, any five of whom shall constitute a quorum.[1]

In the mayor's absence, the recorder was to preside over meetings and perform all other mayoral duties. He was to serve on council committees, keep the official written record of council proceedings, and vote with his fellow council members. This role was quite different from today's hierarchy, in which the auditor—the modern counterpart to the recorder—is the only elected official with no vote or voice in city policy. Otherwise, however, this first configuration of the council was more like the city's 2001 commission form of government than those in any of the eight charters in between.

Accountant William S. Caldwell, age twenty-six, was this second-in-command. He lived with his twenty-one-year-old brother Richard, along with Councilman Robert Thompson and Captain George Flanders.[2] The Caldwell brothers had arrived by ship early the year before his election.[3] Although Caldwell served as secretary or treasurer for virtually every early organization in Portland, he was never to acquire the wealth or power that many of his contemporaries did.[4] His written journals constitute spare, but meticulous, records.[5] During Caldwell's one-year tenure as city recorder, he also served as Washington County Auditor.[6] In 1867, he returned to government as the city auditor, a position he held for eleven years.[7]

Little is recorded of the politics surrounding the election of the first five council members—George Barnes, Loren Hastings, Shubrick Norris, Thomas Robinson, and Robert Thompson. Whether they were eager volunteers or reluctant recruits is not recorded. None of their positions were apparently contested, and the election proceeded quietly with no local or political issues at stake.[8] All but one of them were bachelors[9] and probably frequented saloons, "groceries," and restaurants where they would have been known by many of their fellow townsmen.

Councilman George Barnes[10] arrived in Portland in August 1850, only eight months prior to his election, and opened a general merchandise store. Born in New York State in 1821, Barnes was thirty years old. But before his one-year council term was up, he left Portland for the tiny settlement of Olympia in soon-to-be Washington Territory, where he opened a store[11] and lived until his death at age ninety-one.[12]

Barnes says in his autobiography, written when he was eight-one years old, that he and his wife made a "long and tiresome" trip of five and a half months to Oregon by ox team and wagon in 1848. They wintered in Oregon, then went overland to the California gold mines, again by ox team, with six months' provisions. He purchased a "miners stock of goods" in Sacramento and took the supplies seventy-five miles up river, where he opened a store. The venture must have been successful, because by November he sold out and traveled back to Indiana by steamer via San Francisco, the Isthmus of Panama, and New Orleans, to outfit wagons with which to bring his father's family back across the plains. This time the wagon trip took only three months.

Loren Hastings hand-carried the petition to gain signatures for a Portland charter, so his election to the council was virtually assured. He was an ambitious man with strong leadership qualities and a willingness to assume responsibility. He had arrived in 1847 by wagon train with his wife and an infant son. When Hastings first saw Portland in December 1847, the settlement contained a dozen homes, one store, and a boarding house. Emigrant wagons, transported there by raft, lay on the riverbank in pieces. Portland "had a gloomy and strange appearance," Hastings wrote in his diary.[13] He bought a plot of land, erected a log house, and opened a general merchandise store in partnership with another man.[14] Then Hastings joined the California gold rush and came back with a nest egg of over ten thousand dollars.[15]

Hastings departed Portland before his council term was up to relocate two hundred miles north in the Puget Sound area. One source says he left because his wife's health was adversely affected by fever and malaria caused by floods prevalent along the Willamette River.[16] (However, a doctor writing from Portland in 1850 said there was *less* sickness in Oregon than he had ever seen in any other place.[17]) Another source says simply that Hastings was "not fully satisfied" with conditions around Portland.[18] In Port Townsend, the new town that Hastings and Francis

Pettygrove helped found, Hastings established a prosperous mercantile business, served in the Washington territorial legislature, and was elected as a justice of the peace, sheriff, probate judge, and county treasurer.[19] A 1900 Portland magazine says his wife, Lucinda, was the first white woman in Port Townsend.[20] The Hastings' first child, born in Illinois the year before they started their overland trek westward, was named Oregon Columbus Hastings.[21]

Shubrick Norris was the youngest councilman at age twenty-three. An articulate merchant (later an accountant),[22] Norris was ultimately to serve seven different terms in city and county office—four times on the city council, once as county auditor, once as county clerk, and at least one term on the Portland Board of Police Commissioners (1874-75).[23]

A fiftieth-anniversary *Oregonian* article entitled, "Names in the Paper, Advertisers and Other Persons Whose Names Are in the First Oregonian," contains the following paragraph concerning Norris:

> Shubrick Norris was long a man of affairs in Portland. The advertisement of Norris & Co. discloses the fact that he was then a grocer [ran a saloon or dramshop] and commission merchant, with Gabriel Winter and B. G. Lattimet as his partners. These latter were located in San Francisco, and were conducting a similar partnership business there. They became embarrassed and failed, involving Norris. This was about 1852. Norris was a young man, and he reapplied himself to business with much energy. In course of years he became prominently connected with the old Oregon Steam Navigation company. He acquired considerable property. In the early '80s he went to San Francisco and later to Los Angeles, where he died several years since.[24]

In 1854, Norris was elected to Portland's first public school district board.[25] That September, he was elected assistant engineer of the newly created city fire department.[26] He was a member of Trinity Episcopal Church, destined, according to historian E. Kimbark MacColl, "to become Portland's most socially prestigious church."[27]

An ardent Democrat, Norris corresponded frequently with Asahel Bush of Salem, the leading Democrat of the territory. Two Norris letters to Bush are reprinted below:

October 13, 1854

Dr. Bush—

Give Dryer h-l also the know nothings as they are getting quite numerous in this place and we are making a desperate effort to get all the foreigners which I think can be done by all the Democratic papers pitching in but it wants to be done right away as we are to have an election in a few weeks for a Councilman.

Yours, Shubrick Norris

April 11, 1857
Bush Esq.

Dr. Sir.

Our Democratic friend David Powell one of the Delegates to the Territorial Convention has some money for you. You will confer a favor upon the *Clique* of Multnomah by paying all the attention to him you can and treat him D— polite, get him to take the Statesman if you can.

Yours in haste, J. Shubrick Norris.

He Powell is the strongest man we have. Norris.

The G D fool has backed down and [undecipherable] Leland in his place, this is the D— outrage of a D— Leland could not of got five votes in the County Convention.[28]

The hot-blooded tenor of these letters helps illustrate how a bitter feud was subsequently to develop between Norris and another spirited Portland public servant, Thomas J. Holmes, of which more will be said later.[29]

❧

Council member Robert Thompson, age thirty-nine, was *not* wealthy transportation tycoon "R. R." Thompson, who served on the Portland city council in the 1860s and 1870s and became one of the city's most powerful figures. Perhaps the reason that the later council member Robert Thompson became known as "R. R." was precisely to avoid confusion between the two men, both of whom were active in early Oregon Country affairs. Both attended the first Oregon Masonic Grand

Lodge meeting in Oregon City in September 1851, and they served together on the credentials committee for that occasion. R. R. Thompson was living in Oregon City and was a member of its lodge, while council member Robert Thompson, who was eight years older, belonged to Willamette Lodge No. 2 in Portland.[30]

The Willamette Lodge one-hundred-year anniversary book calls Robert Thompson "a brusque hearty man, well liked by his associates and prompt in the discharge of his lodge duties."[31] Thompson was a "native of *Iowa*," the lodge book says, whereas historian Leslie Scott gives Robert Thompson's birth place as *Ireland*, and says he was at one time postal agent for Oregon.[32] The confusion may be due to illegible handwriting on census records and because census takers used various abbreviations for states and countries. [33] Thompson's Masonic membership would make Iowa the more logical place of birth.

Thompson was a wholesaler and retailer, dealing in "dry goods, groceries, hardware, provisions, furniture, etc.," a well-to-do man who also built houses and loaned money. He was a Democrat who served in the 1853 territorial legislature as a representative from Washington County, of which Portland was then a part, but was defeated when he sought reelection in June 1854.[34] According to a 1900 *Oregonian* article, "He was accidentally drowned in the Willamette River, one night in the Winter of 1855-56. He left no relatives, so far as known."[35]

Robert Thompson died without a will, so the court appointed an administrator for his estate.[36] An invoice from Brelsford & Ewry, "cabinet makers and undertakers," dated June 23, 1860, reads: "One silver mounted coffin—$145; one engraven silver plate, $15; another engraven silver plate, $10; tending funeral with hearse, $25; digging one grave, $5. Total $200." This would be roughly the equivalent of four thousand dollars today. His personal property and effects were sold to the highest bidder, and consisted of "one horse, two colts, two pistols, one gun, 'crops now growing,' books, and a variety of household furniture." Six years later, in 1866, a full block of Portland land (Block 260 at Taylor and Salmon between 11th and 12th) was divided and sold at various auctions on behalf of Thompson's two distant heirs, who had by then been located.[37]

The shortest tenure of any council member was that of Thomas G. Robinson, a forty-four-year-old bachelor and seven-year resident of the Oregon Country.[38] Robinson resigned in May 1851 for unstated reasons, after serving only six weeks on the council. Sixteen months later he married a young Irish woman named Bridget Teresa Clarke, who had come to Portland with her sister and brother-in-law Stephen McCormick, publisher of Portland's first city directory and Portland mayor in 1859-60. Robinson and Bridget Clarke received special dispensations from the Catholic church to be married because she was Catholic, but he was not. Witnesses at the wedding included the McCormicks and Portland township proprietor Benjamin Stark.[39]

Robinson owned the first quarters rented by the city council, and charged the city thirty dollars a month, twice the amount that the council paid to its next landlord.[40]

Robinson filed three land claims, but gave up both the first, near present-day West Linn, and the second, above the falls at Oregon City. After his service on the council, he filed a smaller claim on land in the Southwest Portland hills.[41] Robinson's Hill, the scenic twenty-eight-acre donation land claim filed by Thomas and Bridget Robinson in 1854, is their lasting legacy. The site is above today's S.W. Broadway Drive and commands a glorious view of Mt. Hood and Mt. St. Helens with the Willamette River and downtown Portland in the foreground.[42]

The least-known councilman was Harley McDonald, appointed to Robinson's council seat in June. McDonald attended all five council meetings held during his three-month tenure. He resigned in September, and departed for the East soon thereafter. He was a twenty-five-year-old carpenter, born in Massachusetts, and, at the time of the 1850 territorial census, was living with a young merchant from England and his wife.[43] A small bound log and journal kept by McDonald for two of his ocean voyages has been preserved at the Oregon Historical Center.[44] He returned to Portland for at least for a short while, because he voted for T. J. Dryer as mayor, as recorded in the November 1857 Portland poll book.[45]

The man appointed in September to fill the seat vacated by Robinson and McDonald was twenty-nine-year-old Seth Slater. He is listed as a painter in the 1850 territorial census,[46] but in 1859 ran a front-page *Oregonian* ad for a "Boot and Shoe Store" at the corner of First and Alder streets, offering men's, boys', youths', ladies', misses', and children's boots and shoes of "all styles and best quality."[47] Slater later served five months as city recorder, two years as city assessor, and another full year on the city council (1855-56).[48]

Slater had perfect attendance after his September appointment. Robert Thompson missed only one meeting the entire year. Councilman Norris and Recorder Caldwell each missed two. However, Hugh O'Bryant, George Barnes, and Loren Hastings were frequent absentees. They racked up seven, eight, and ten absences, respectively, out of thirty-one council meetings held that first year.

Before a new slate of officials was elected in April 1852, O'Bryant, Barnes, and Hastings had all left Portland for good. City government had ceased to be a high priority in their lives, and they retained city office in name only.

These six characters now join the mayor on center stage, as Act I of Portland city government begins.

Chapter 5

The Missing Fire Engine

1851 – 1852

Mayor

No. 1: April 1851 - April 1852

Hugh D. O'Bryant

> *Be it remembered that on this fourteenth day of April A. D. 1851, Hugh D. O'Bryant, who had been declared elected as Mayor, William S. Caldwell, who had been declared elected as Recorder, and Robert Thompson, Shubrick Norris, Thomas G. Robinson, George A. Barnes, and Loren B. Hastings, who had been declared elected as Councilmen at an election held on the seventh day of April A. D. 1851 in Portland in the County of Washington, Territory of Oregon, the said Mayor, Recorder and Councilmen having taken and subscribed to an oath, to support the Constitution of the United States. ... The aforesaid persons constituting the City Council of said City, held a meeting in said City on the day and year aforesaid.*
>
> — Proceedings of the Common Council, 1851, page 1

They came from seven eastern states; their ages ranged from twenty-three to forty-four: four merchants, one carpenter, one accountant, and the other (Robinson) probably a real estate investor.[1] Four of the men—O'Bryant, Barnes, Hastings, and probably Robinson—crossed the plains in covered wagons while the other three came west the short way, by ship, either around Cape Horn or with a portage across the Isthmus of Panama.

With their diversity of backgrounds, each man had different expectations of how a city ought to operate. Their meetings took place in the evenings, and they had little time to talk things through. Service on the council was a volunteer job. They were busy men—busy making a living, clearing land, planning new ventures, building homes. They

Table 2. Members of the first Portland City Council.

	Age	Occupation	Born
Thomas Robinson (councilman)	44	Real estate	Kentucky
Robert Thompson (councilman)	39	Merchant	Iowa
Hugh O'Bryant (mayor)	36	Carpenter	Georgia
Loren Hastings (councilman)	32	Merchant	Vermont
George Barnes (councilman)	30	Merchant	New York
William Caldwell (recorder)	26	Accountant	Massachusetts
Shubrick Norris (councilman)	23	Merchant	Maryland

were charged with creating a government from scratch, with no guidelines except those provided in the city charter, and no shared model to follow.

The jurisdiction of the new city covered a little more than two square miles, with a population of around nine hundred.[2] It was a rough frontier town, catering to sailors whose ships were laying over in the harbor, miners returning from California, farmers visiting for a day or two from the Willamette Valley, and new immigrants looking for a place to settle. The town's New England businessmen[3] found themselves "planted on the soil of two civilizations"—those of the Hudson's Bay Company and the church missions that had pioneered the Oregon territory. "This made it needless for Portland—like so many other frontier towns—to build law and order all anew," said journalist Dean Collins in 1925.[4]

Although comparatively little bloodshed occurred during Portland's beginnings, the city needed police and fire protection, and written rules of conduct. Two April 1851 *Oregonian* stories illustrated the need for a Portland police force. "Another Man Hung," said one headline. A second story said, "On Thursday a serious and brutal riot again disgraced our city. Several of the hands from the steamer *Goliah* became intoxicated and commenced a general fight on shore among themselves which resulted in the biting off of a piece of the nose of George Robbin, coal heaver, who in return stabbed with a dirk knife Henry Wood, fireman, in several places."[5]

In the first two months, the council met sixteen times, more than half the meetings held the entire year. Organizational matters moved along smoothly at first, but by summer, council business had begun to bog down.[6]

Meeting #1. April 14, 1851. As its first order of business, the council voted seven times before it chose "a competent and discreet person" to act as marshal. Then four council members switched positions to give five votes to Hiram Wilbur, leaving one lone holdout for William Higgins.

A committee of three was appointed to secure a suitable room and furniture for council meetings. Another three-person committee, composed of Councilmen Robinson and Barnes plus Recorder Caldwell, was to draft by-laws for governing the city. Then the council adjourned, perhaps to the Canton House to toast the beginning of Portland city government as the *Oregonian* article in the sidebar suggests. No record was found indicating where this first meeting was held.

Meeting #2. April 15. The following evening, the council met at 7:30 p.m., again at an unnamed location. Council members accepted a committee recommendation to lease a house owned by Councilman Robinson at thirty dollars a month for three months.[7] (This was a handsome price, and a transaction that would later be forbidden as a conflict of interest.)

A 1964 *Oregonian* article visualized the end of the first city council meeting this way: "On the warm, soggy evening of April 14, 1851, seven men recessed their deliberations and slogged up muddy Front Street to the Canton House. Three or four of them wore wrinkled waistcoats with high collars and elegant stovepipe hats. The others wore homespun coats and pantaloons and Mormon hats. … They had just come from their first council meeting."[8]

Meeting #3. April 16. The council met for the third night in a row. They adopted "Rules and Orders for Government of the City of Portland." The rules said the mayor could sit while he read or spoke, but had to rise to put a question. Members were to stand in their places to speak and address the mayor, and when done speaking, to sit down.

Six standing committees were designated:

1. Ways and Means: matters regarding revenue
2. Accounts: demands against the city
3. Streets: roads, streets and thoroughfares within the city limits
4. Landings: public levees, wharves, landings on the Willamette River
5. Current Expenses: printing and similar expenditures
6. Public Buildings: erection and repair of a jail, market house, and such other buildings as necessary.

The mayor was to nominate committee members, with the entire council to approve or reject his choices.

Council directed the recorder to determine the total taxable property within the city limits as listed on the books of the probate court clerk for Washington County.

Meeting #4. April 21. The council revisited its first two orders of business and voted again for a city marshal and treasurer. Two members were absent, so only three votes were necessary for a majority. Hiram Walker was again elected marshal, and George Flanders again elected treasurer.

The council approved a proposal from *Oregonian* editor Thomas J. Dryer that he print city by-laws and ordinances from time to time as the council should direct. (However, the *Oregonian* was soon to have competition from a Portland rival. J. Orvis Waterman and W. D. Carter floated their printing presses across the river from Milwaukie at night, to the dismay and indignation of Milwaukie citizens. On June 5, 1851, the first edition of the renamed *Oregon Weekly Times* was printed in Portland.[10])

> The April 19 issue of the weekly *Oregonian* carried the following news item:
>
> PORTLAND CITY COUNCIL.—The city council has been duly organized, but what progress has been made by way of creating ordinances, we are not informed. It is to be hoped, however, that something will be speedily done to protect the persons and property of our citizens from lawless violation, at the hands of desperadoes, who came here to gamble, cheat, rob, and steal, and murder if it suits their fancy, or subserves their interests.[9]

Meeting #5 April 29. The office of city attorney was established.

A new ordinance required removal of "all animal or vegetable substances, rubbish or filth of any kind whatever in any house, cellar, yard or other place which the city marshall shall deem necessary for the health of the city." No slaughterhouse was to be erected within the city limits or within half a mile of any residence. The law forbade selling any "unwholesome, stale or putrid meat, fish, fruit or any other articles of provisions." Fifty posters containing this ordinance were ordered printed.

Meeting #6. April 30. A property tax of one-fourth of one percent of assessed value was levied. The recorder and marshal were directed to send out bills and collect money due.

Meeting #7. May 1. The city's first business license was approved, covering auctioneers and commission merchants. (A commission merchant sold goods on behalf of someone else, typically for a percentage of the sales price. The "someone else" was usually an East Coast or California firm. Local owners did not have to pay this tax.) The recorder was to collect a fee of two dollars for each license issued and fifty cents for each monthly statement filed.[11]

Meeting #8. May 5. Erecting a building, or in any other way obstructing the public levee, was prohibited by Ordinance # 7. A fine of fifty to one hundred dollars was to be levied for violations, with the buildings or obstructions removed at the expense of the trespasser. This ordinance related to a court case filed a year before. Proprietor Daniel Lownsdale had constructed a building between the Willamette River and a lot owned by the Reverend Josiah Parrish. Parrish sought to force Lownsdale to tear down his building. This lawsuit was the first of many confrontations over ownership rights to the levee.[12]

Other ordinances adopted provided that no person could discharge a firearm within city limits; any person riding horses or driving horses with wagons at a furious pace would be fined five to ten dollars; and any person found drunk, rioting, or in any way disturbing the peace would be fined five dollars for the first offence and twenty-five dollars thereafter.

Meeting #9. May 6. An *ad valorem* tax (based on value) of one and a half percent was approved on goods and merchandise offered for sale from on board any vessel in the harbor. The marshal was empowered to board vessels to determine the value of goods offered for sale. This ordinance was passed in response to a petition signed by thirty-eight Portland businessmen, pleading that legitimate trade was being ruined by vessels selling goods without paying property taxes or buying licenses, thus damaging the "regular business of permanently established merchants."[13]

T. J. Dryer offered the services of volunteer Pioneer Fire Company No. 1 to the city, which were accepted unanimously.

Meeting #10. May 7. Councilman Hastings, who had been absent for three of the nine previous council meetings, appeared late and, on motion of Councilman Robinson, was fined five dollars for late attendance. After Hastings explained the reason for his tardiness [reason not recorded]; his fine was dropped.

Pioneer Fire Company No. 1 sent a petition asking for a first-class fire engine "capable of bringing water from the river to any portion of our town ... and an engine house, to preserve it in good order, and an upper room for the use of the company. ... (Also) hooks & ladders, fire buckets & axes" to use in case of an emergency before the engine arrived. An estimated thirty-five hundred dollars would cover all expense of purchase and transportation of the engine."[14] An election was set for Monday, May 26, 1851, at City Hall (Councilman Robinson's building)[15] for voters to accept or reject a special tax for buying the fire engine. Polls were to be open from 9 a.m. to 4 p.m.

Meeting #11. May 13. Simon B. Marye (future mayor) was elected city attorney on the third ballot. Others receiving votes were R. P. Boise, D. B. Brennan, W. W. Chapman (a townsite proprietor,) and William King, log-roller and legislator.

Meeting #12. May 15. After Mayor O'Bryant left the meeting, Recorder Caldwell took the chair and appointed a recorder *pro tem.* An ordinance passed dividing the city into two road districts. The first priority for work on a road would be Front Street, then First Street. Another ordinance requested all persons owning lots on Front, Taylor, First, Second, and Third streets to lay a "good and substantial sidewalk of brick, stone or plank, not less than six feet wide."

Meeting #13. May 22. Two road supervisors were elected and told to warn all persons liable to be called out to labor on the roads to be ready by the second Wednesday in June. Councilman Thomas Robinson resigned. City government had been in operation for five weeks.

Meeting #14. May 26. (Mayor absent.) Portland citizens gave resounding approval to a fire engine property tax: yes, thirty-one; no, two. The mayor's name was absent from the list of persons who voted, and no explanation was given.[16]

Meeting #15. June 4. Hiram Wilbur resigned as city marshal and was replaced by William L. Higgins,[17] a twenty-eight-year-old sailor born in Rhode Island[18] who had lost out on the job to Wilbur only two months before.

Meeting #16. June 10. A new committee would look into how stove pipes and chimneys could be improved for the prevention of fires. The marshal was instructed to take charge of an insane person reported to be in town, and to present his bill for this service to the city. The committee on buildings was to furnish an estimate of the cost of building a log jail.

Meeting #17. June 17. (Mayor absent.) A petition from Captain Couch and others concerning disturbances was read. Proposals for the erection of a jail would be taken until June 23.

Meeting #18. July 2. A committee was appointed to solicit private subscriptions to help cover the cost of building a jail.

Meeting #19. August 5. Councilman McDonald was to prepare a cost estimate for building a jail of timber, twenty-five by thirty feet, one story high. (However, McDonald left town before completing this job. The actual jail built was only about half this size—sixteen feet by twenty-five feet—see Meeting #28.)

Meeting #20. August 13. The recorder would be paid three dollars per meeting for keeping the minutes. The two street supervisors were to make monthly reports to council. The marshal was directed to attend all future meetings of council unless ill or absent from the city.

Meeting #21. September 11. (Mayor absent.) Harley McDonald's seat was declared vacant because he had departed for the East. Five ballots were required to elect Seth Slater as his replacement. The office of fire warden was created, to be filled annually by the council, "to examine the condition of stove pipes, chimneys and enforce such regulations as may be made for the prevention of fires."

Meeting #22. September 17. The committee on buildings was authorized to contract for the erection of a jail, and to procure a lot for such purpose. After three ballots, Thomas J. Dryer and Steve Coffin were chosen as the city's first two fire wardens.

Meeting #23. October 2. Recorder Caldwell reported that he had prepared the property tax bills. A gambling ordinance was adopted unanimously, prohibiting all gambling or playing at games of chance. Violators were subject to penalties of one to two hundred dollars, or imprisonment for thirty to ninety days.

Meeting #24. October 8. Two lots located at "approximately Alder Street between Front and First" were purchased for a city jail from J. P. Sheppard for one hundred and thirty dollars.[19] The committee on buildings was to procure a different room for council meetings, and to furnish the room with necessary furniture. The marshal was to take charge of furniture already on hand.

Meeting #25. October 17. (Mayor absent.) The marshal was to be fined five dollars for every council meeting he missed.

Meeting #26. October 22. Riding or driving a horse upon any sidewalk was prohibited by a new ordinance, with a fine of five dollars for the first offense, and ten dollars for each subsequent offense.

Meeting #27. November 15. (Mayor absent.) The marshal was directed to report all his official acts in writing to the next meeting of the council.

Meeting #28. November 21. A bill for rent of a new council meeting room at fifteen dollars per month was received from Stephen Coffin. This second city hall was probably in the schoolhouse and public building at First and Oak built by Coffin and William King.

An elaborate ceremony to mark the beginning of work on a plank road through the western forest and hills took place October 15, 1851. "A wagon load of planks were sawed out down at Reed and Abrams mill[20] and hauled out to the starting point, … and the whole town went out to celebrate the opening of the graded track and the commencement of the grand plank highway. The laying of the first plank along Jefferson was an occasion for high celebration—a gold coin buried beneath the plank, much oratory, and an ox roasted at the spot for the assembled guests."[21]

The occasion was a worthy one, for this great plank road bypassed the Tualatin River, the Willamette Falls portage, and Oregon City, effectively connecting Portland directly to the granary that was the Tualatin Valley.[22] However, actual construction of the road did not progress very far because the money raised soon ran out.[23] Daniel Lownsdale was the first president of the Portland and Valley Plank Road, and was succeeded by Col. William King, who became the paid project director.[24] "Management fell into the hands of the unprincipled, accounting procedures were lax and stockholders criminally abused," says historian Malcolm Clark.[25] The original plank road folded in the midst of scandal. It would be 1856 before another company was formed to finish the job.[26]

Portland's first public school opened December 15, 1851, with twenty pupils taught by John T. Outhouse. Classes were held in a public hall built by William King and Stephen Coffin on First Street, between Pine and Oak.[27]

The new jail, sixteen by twenty-five feet, was now complete except for a suitable lock. The treasurer was authorized to pay Ira Ward 1,175 dollars, the equivalent of twenty-four thousand of today's dollars, for constructing the jail. The council decided to meet the following Monday as a committee of the whole to consider the present city charter. (This meeting was either never held or no record was kept of the proceedings.)

Meeting #29. November 27. (Mayor absent.) Council heard a report from the city marshal and authorized payment of bills. A short meeting.

No council meetings were now held for four months.

Meeting #30. March 22, 1852. The council met to set a time and place for an election to choose new city officials to serve the following year.

The following resolution was offered by Councilman Slater and adopted: "Resolved that the mayor be requested to inform the council what disposition has been made of the ordinance levying a tax for the purpose of purchasing a fire engine and apparatus." The minutes then say:

> In compliance, the mayor submitted a communication which was received and ordered to be spread upon the record. The following is a true copy thereof:
>
> Gentlemen of the Council
>
> In answer to your Resolution inquiring to know of me disposition I have mad of the duplicates levying a tax to collect and raise a fund to purchase a Engine and hoes [sic] for the use of the City I will say for your Information that they are in my desk without my signature.
>
> March the 22nd, 1852
> H. D. OBryant, Mayor

Meeting #31. April 1, 1852 (Mayor absent.) The council accepted all bills reported for payment. A schedule of receipts and expenses was to be published in the *Oregonian* by the treasurer in accordance with the city charter.

The property tax statements drawn up by Recorder Caldwell to pay for a fire engine were never signed by the mayor. A committee appointed by the next council reported back that they were "unable to get the fire tax bills from the hands of the Ex-Mayor O'Bryant."

Thus ended the first year.

Chapter 6

By Trial and Error

1852 – 1853

Mayors

No. 2: April 1852 - September 1852

Allison C. Bonnell

No. 3: November 1852 - April 1853

Simon B. Marye

The undersigned citizens ... respectfully represent ... [that] the interest of Portland will be promoted by ... [repealing] the present City Charter ... [and] remonstrate against the passage of any and all acts incorporating the City of Portland.

—Petition signed by 150 citizens dated January 15, 1853[1]

[Each member of the smallpox committee shall] wear a Red Cockade in his hat and be compelled to sleep in Oregon City, Dine at Milwaukie, and walk on the waters of the Willamette. ... The mayor then appointed as committeemen His Excellency Gov. Gaines, Hon. E. Ely and F. W. Pettygrove.

—City Council minutes, March 12, 1853[2]

Despite growing disenchantment with the city's first charter, a new slate of elected officials stepped forward to volunteer their services for the city government's second year. Perhaps with new leadership, city affairs would fall into a more orderly pattern. Perhaps with a new mayor, the streets would be fixed. Perhaps with a new mayor, they would get a fire engine. The election took place April 5, 1852.

Once again, voters chose a safe elder as their chief over a younger challenger.

Mayor Allison Bonnell (Photo: OrHi 97631)

At fifty-one, Allison C. Bonnell, Portland's second mayor, was the oldest person thus far to serve on the city council. Born in New Jersey, Bonnell came overland to California in 1849 and to Portland by ship in 1850, where he "kept the books" for the Reed & Abrams sawmill.[3] After serving six months as mayor, Bonnell resigned when he left on a long business trip. The following year, after his return, he was elected city recorder, served three months, and moved to San Francisco permanently. His entire Portland residency spanned only three years. In San Francisco, he worked as the clerk and cashier for the *Evening Bulletin* newspaper.[4]

Bonnell won his mayoral election by fourteen votes out of two hundred sixteen cast: one hundred fifteen for Bonnell to one hundred one for Captain Zachariah C. Norton, the thirty-four-year-old former commander of the brig *Sequin.* Captain Norton and newly elected councilman Ani Dennison had been partners for a while, but ended their Portland-San Francisco trading business acrimoniously, with lawsuits filed on both sides.[5]

Zachariah Norton and his wife had anchored in Portland harbor during the winter of 1850-51, and Mrs. Norton found Portland's social life much to her liking. The Nortons later located permanently in Portland after several visits aboard the *Sequin.*[6] Mrs. Norton wrote: "We are remaining in this place sufficient time to load with flour and timber, during which time I enjoyed myself well, for the first time since I left

This first photograph of Front Street shows businessmen admiring a dray newly arrived from San Francisco in 1852. Left to right: Future city assessor Charles P. Bacon; drayman Adolph Miller (almost hidden); Oregonian *editor T. J. Dryer; future city treasurer and U.S. Senator Henry W. Corbett; future city treasurer W. H. Barnhart (behind, in doorway); future mayor John Breck; and merchant W. S. Ogden. Note ship in the harbor at far left. (Photo: OrHi #948)*

my home [New England] have found the society and customs correspond with those of our own happy land. In this little town the Sabbath is more regarded than in any country I have found while rounding the mighty continent."[7]

Captain Norton owned a wharf along Portland's waterfront, and later joined township proprietors Stephen Coffin and W. W. Chapman in vouching for the adequacy of Willamette River depth at the Swan Island bar in an 1885 letter to the *Oregonian*.[8] By 1910, Norton owned a small store on shore and "a ship at the river bank with a large stock of general merchandise."[9]

❧

Former councilman Seth Slater, who had forced an explanation from Mayor O'Bryant concerning the fire engine tax statements, won an easy victory as city recorder[10] Winner of the most votes for a council seat was Hiram Smith, who helped finance many immigrants with his own personal wealth.[11] However, Smith resigned after only one council meeting.

Another new councilman, sawmill owner William Abrams, resigned in June after ten meetings. (Abrams and a friend, U. N. Reamer, were the first white men to discover the Yosemite Valley while investigating possible lumber mill sites during the California gold rush.[12]) In 1850, Portland businessmen had entrusted Abrams with twelve hundred dollars collected to buy books for a public subscription library (see Appendix B). Abrams bought the books in New York while on a trip to buy parts for his steam sawmill and to bring his family back west.[13]

Newly elected councilman Abel Tripp missed thirteen council meetings before resigning. Ani Dennison was a natural-born politician and a colonel in the Oregon volunteer militia who would later be appointed Indian agent for the Warm Springs Indian Reservation.Thomas Pritchard was elected treasurer the following year, but resigned before taking that oath of office.

Council members were a little older this second year. Ani Dennison was the youngest at twenty-eight; Seth Slater was thirty; William Abrams, thirty-two; and Josiah Failing of New York, who took office at the council's third meeting of the year, forty-six.

Meeting #1. April 12, 1852. The mayor appointed a committee to make arrangements for a room for council use.

Meeting #2. April 15. Merchant Josiah Failing was unanimously chosen to replace Hiram Smith on the council. Widower Failing had arrived in Portland by ship only the previous year, bringing with him two sons—Henry, seventeen, and Edward, ten.

Meeting #3. April 22. A committee was appointed to consider abolishing the office of city attorney.

Meeting #4. April 29. Council adopted the plat map drawn by John Brady[14] in 1850 as the official city map. In doing so, the council took a big step backward from Ordinance #7, passed in May 1851 by the previous council, which specified that no building was to be constructed on the levee.

Brady's map was to play a major role in future lawsuits.[15] The original 1845 plat map drawn by Thomas Brown at the behest of Lovejoy and Pettygrove showed the levee as undivided public property. In deciding a case nine years later, Judge Deady said that Daniel Lownsdale had instructed surveyor R. V. Short and mapmaker John Brady to mark off the levee into lots for private ownership, which they did.[16] "By this stroke [adopting the Brady map], they [the council] signed away whatever right they had to the levee," said *Oregonian* editor Harvey Scott in 1890.[17] Nearly five years later, in January 1857, council was to repudiate the Brady map adopted by this council, but to little avail.[18]

At this same meeting, the council declared that "the public levee on Front Street granted in the compromise in 1850 by the proprietors of Portland" was city property, and the city would "act accordingly until otherwise instructed by the decision of a case now pending in court in relation thereto."[19] The mayor appointed a committee to call on the city proprietors to obtain a bond or deed for the streets and all land designated for schools, squares, and other public purposes.

Meeting #5. May 6. A committee was to ascertain the best possible offer of land suitable for burial purposes available from the city proprietors.

The *1882 City Directory* describes this colorful man: "He was a character, this Travaillot. … He had discharged cargo and was sitting in a saloon one night behind the best seven-up hand he had ever held when a sailor announced that the *Duc D'Lorges* had sunk. It was too true; she was anchored off the foot of D street, and getting weary of waiting for the captain, simply turned over and went to sleep on the bed of the river. … The captain was afraid to return to France and spent the greater part of the proceeds of his cargo in the city. He used to get mysteriously drunk, and then ascending the hurricane deck of a cayuse [pony], would careen down First street, a mounted simoom of alcoholic odor and broken English."[20]

Meeting #6. May 13. The office of city attorney was abolished. At the very time that the council was making costly and ill-informed decisions, council members cut corners by not hiring a city attorney—a decision that time would prove short sighted.

George Flanders, elected city treasurer for a second term, was to be paid a sum equal to 3 percent of all money he disbursed.

Meeting #7. May 20. The council decided to send Capt. O. Travaillot a letter requesting that he remove the sunken brig *Duc D'Lorges,* now in the channel of the Willamette River just below Capt. Couch's store, so the brig would not obstruct navigation. If the brig was not removed before June 15, the city would remove it at the owners' expense.

Meeting #8. June 3. A two-page letter from Capt. O. Travaillot explaining the circumstances of his brig's present location was accepted and filed.

Capt. Travaillot was to torment this council and succeeding councils for at least the next three years.[21] He had been fined twenty-five dollars by Mayor O'Bryant on May 30, 1851 for disregarding city law by riding "at a furious rate through the Streets of the City of Portland."[22] Travaillot appealed this fine to the Washington County District Court on the grounds that O'Bryant had no legal authority to receive such a fine. The court reversed the judgement against Travaillot in 1855, and the city council had to repay Travaillot his original fine plus an additional ten dollars.[23] Travaillot advertised himself this way in the Oregonian:

O. TRAVAILLOT
KEEPS CONSTANTLY ON HAND A GENERAL ASSORTMENT OF
Goods, Wares and Merchandise
LIQUOR, EVERY DESCRIPTION—HORSES FOR SALE
(ONE DOOR BELOW COUCH'S STORE.)[24]

Meeting #9. June 10. A request from O. W. Groom to exhibit a bull fight around the Fourth of July was rejected. The council agreed to rent the office of Mayor Bonnell (where they were probably already meeting) as council quarters for ten dollars per month.The council extended the deadline for removal of the brig *Duc D'Lorges* to July 1.

May 27. No quorum was present.

June 17. No quorum was present.

Meeting #10. June 24. A motion to publish a notice in the newspaper demanding that the owners of the Brig *Duc D'Lorges* remove the brig by July 3, 1852, or face forced removal, was tabled until the mayor could receive legal advice. The council wanted to sell its cargo, and even the brig itself, to pay the cost of removal.

Meeting #11 (special—unscheduled). June 29. Shubrick Norris received all five votes on the first ballot to fill William P. Abrams' vacant seat.

Meeting #12. July 1. The mayor appointed a fire department committee to consider whether or not to call another fire engine election.

Meeting #13. July 3, Saturday. It was time to work on the streets. Ordinance #20 provided that all males over twenty-one who had been Portland residents for thirty days had to contribute two days of labor on the public streets or pay the streets supervisor for laborers to perform the work in their stead. The street supervisor was to receive four dollars for each day that he supervised street improvements.

Meeting #14. July 15. An August date was set for another fire engine vote. The city printing contract was again awarded to T. J. Dryer (a good Whig), after a motion to contract with J. Orvis Waterman (a good Democrat and publisher of the *Oregon Weekly Times*) failed by three to two.

Meeting #15. July 22. A legal opinion regarding the brig *Duc D'Lorges* said the council could not sell Capt. Travaillot's cargo to pay the cost of removing the ship.

Meeting #16. August 5. The original date set for a fire tax vote came on a Sunday, and that time had passed. So the election was reset for a Wednesday.

Meeting #17. August 12. The committee on landings was asked to determine the most practicable and legal means for removing the brig *Duc D'Lorges* and other obstructions from the river.

Special election. August 18, 1852. Of seventy-one votes cast, thirty-eight approved adopting a special one-half of one percent fire engine property tax. The council would therefore levy this tax.

Meeting #18. September 16. Council granted permission to A. V. Cadwell to perform his circus on one or more nights for a fee of five dollars per night. City treasurer George Flanders was granted permission to construct a platform and hay scale on the street in front of his property.

Meeting #19, September 19. Seth Slater resigned as recorder because business matters would be taking him out of the city.

Meeting #20 (special). September 20. Charles B. Pillow, a thirty-year-old watchmaker and jeweler, took his seat as the new recorder.*25* The council adjourned to September 23.

September 23. No meeting was held.

September 27. The mayor resigned. Mayor Bonnell sent council the following letter:

> Monday evening Sept 27, 1852—
>
> Gentlemen, Expecting to be absent from your City during the ensuing three or four months, I herewith tender you

my resignation as Mayor of the City of Portland. With my best wishes for the prosperity of your city, and friendly greeting to each and all of you,

I remain, Gentlemen, Your Obedient Servant,
A. C. Bonnell.[26]

So, at virtually the same time, both the mayor and the recorder resigned to take care of out-of-town business. While the charter specified that the recorder was to act in the mayor's absence, Charles Pillow was unprepared to assume such a leadership role.

October and early November. No meetings were held.

Meeting #21 (special). November 13. Five men were present and entitled to vote: recorder Charles Pillow and councilmen Ani Dennison, Josiah Failing, Shubrick Norris, and Thomas Pritchard. Three votes would be needed to elect a new mayor.

Results of the balloting for mayor are shown in Table 3.

Table 3. Balloting for Mayor, November 1852

	First Ballot	*Second ballot*	*Third ballot*	*Fourth ballot*
Marquam, Philip	2	1		
Chapman, W. W.	1	1		
Davis, Anthony	1	1	1	
Lownsdale, Daniel		1		
Dennison, Ani		1		
Coffin, Steven			1	
Failing, Josiah			2	
Waterman, J. Orvis				1
Pritchard, Thomas				1
Marye, Simon				3
Blank	1		1	
Total votes	5	5	5	5

Young Simon Marye, former city attorney, was the compromise choice on the fourth ballot to fill the vacant seat.[27] Lawyer Philip Marquam and merchant Josiah Failing had each come within one vote of being elected mayor, and both times the tally included a blank ballot. The council agreed to meet at Josiah Failing's store the following Monday night.

Meeting #22. November 15. Simon B. Marye took the oath of office as Portland's third mayor.[28] Marye, at age twenty-seven, was Portland's second-youngest mayor to date[29] and younger than any of the council members with whom he would serve. His lack of worldly experience would be evident during his brief tenure.

Marye had arrived in the Oregon Territory in 1852 after graduating from William and Mary College in Virginia with B. A. and B. L. degrees.[30] In Portland, he married Sarah Chapman, the nineteen-year-old daughter of lawyer and city proprietor W. W. Chapman,[31] and they were living in Portland at the time of the 1853 census. Soon thereafter, they left for the South, where a daughter was born in Memphis in 1855.[32] During three months in late 1864, Marye ran " contraband cotton and other needed items for use behind the lines for the Confederacy."[33] He was practicing law in Vicksburg, Mississippi, at the time of his death in 1868 at age forty-two.

At the same meeting that Simon Marye was sworn in as mayor,[34] Philip Marquam was elected to replace Councilman Abel Tripp, who had resigned. (Marquam was later to become a prominent Portland judge, categorized in 1900 by author Joseph Gaston as "one of Portland's best citizens.")[35] Captain John Couch and two others sent remonstrances protesting the continued obstruction of river traffic by the brigs *Torquina* and *Duc D'Lorges*. The committee on buildings was asked to find a suitable room for council meetings. In the meantime, the council would continue to meet at 6:30 p.m. every Monday night at Failing's store.

Mayor Simon Marye. (Photo: OrHi #98075)

November 22—No meeting was held.

Meeting #23. November 29. Philip Marquam took the oath of office as councilman. Mayor Marye, presiding at his second meeting, appointed Marquam to fill Councilman Tripp's vacant positions on various committees. When someone moved to refer the street supervisor's report to the accounts committee for payment, Councilman Norris objected. (The street supervisor was Thomas J. Holmes, with whom Norris had an ongoing rivalry.) A vote was taken and the mayor ruled that the motion had carried. Norris appealed this decision to his fellow council members and overturned the mayor's ruling, with only Dennison supporting the mayor. Marye then entered the following protest: "Simon B. Marye, of the Common Council of the City of Portland protests against the vote of P. A. Marquam upon any matter before the said Common Council, he not being a member thereof, not having fulfilled the provisions of the charter requiring a member elected or appointed to qualify himself within ten days after such election or appointment." Although Marye had already assigned Marquam to serve on committees, the novice mayor now sought to disqualify him on a technicality. The contested council vote on the street supervisor's report was resolved by referring parts of the report to three different council committees. The list of able-bodied men who had not put in their required days of free labor was sent to a separate committee.

> T. J. Dryer's *Oregonian* carried the following story on November 27, 1852:
>
> GAMBLING—We are creditably informed that our city is at this time infested with several professed blacklegs, who are in the habit of inveigling into their den and swindling persons who can be induced to risk money upon the turn of a card. ... We have now an efficient mayor and a full board of aldermen, and ought to have a city marshal who would ferret out those sporting gentlemen. A few days in the *block house* on bread and water would have a tendency to purge our city from these bejeweled worthless.[36]

December. No meetings were held.

Meeting #24. January 10, 1853. Simon Marye's law office now became the fourth city hall. The following resignation letter from Marquam was read:

> Gentlemen—As there exists a difference in regard to the legality of my qualifications as a member of your body, I hereby resign the office to which I had the honor of being elected as the most expeditious and least objectionable mode of settling the difficulty referred to. Believe me gentlemen with great respect.
>
> Portland, December third, AD 1852.
> Yours most truly, P Marquam.

The council then voted, three to one, to reelect Marquam as councilman. Recorder Pillow was instructed to notify Marquam of his (re)-election.

Meeting #25. January 12. Marquam sent another resignation letter. A bill from Mr. Fountain for burying the dead was referred to committee.

Council minutes do not mention a document dated January 15, 1853, which forwarded a proposed new city charter to the territorial legislature. The letter is preserved in the Oregon State Archives. It states that a meeting of Portland citizens was held on that date at the school house "for the purpose of taking into consideration the Expediency of applying to the Legislature of the Territory of Oregon for a new city charter." A proposed charter was attached, which the letter said had been read aloud, discussed, amended, and "*unanimously* adopted by the meeting as containing substantially the advice of the Citizens of Portland with regard to a City Charter which they hoped and prayed the Legislature would pass into a law." The letter was signed by Simon B. Marye as chairman, and Henry Failing as secretary.[37]

A contrary petition, dated six days later, and signed by one hundred and fifty men, asked the legislative assembly to disband Portland's city government and revoke its charter. The signers said that in their opinion the interest of Portland would be promoted by "the passage of an act repealing the present City Charter, And, Also remonstrate against the passage of any and all acts incorporating the City of Portland."[38] Signers included well-known names such as Thomas Carter, Daniel Lownsdale, George Flanders, John Couch, Abel Tripp, Absalom Hallock, and future mayors Stephen McCormick, Thomas Holmes, and William Ladd.

Clearly nobody in Portland was satisfied with the first two years of city government. It had accomplished little. The question was, would the town be better off with a new charter or none at all? Governance in the Oregon Territory was still a hit-and-miss proposition.

❧

Meeting #26. February 7. The council asked the mayor to obtain a certified copy of an act passed by the territorial legislature on January 28 referring a new charter to the citizens of Portland for adoption or rejection. An election date would be set as soon as practicable.

Meeting #27 (special). Saturday evening, February 19. The marshal was asked to explain what had happened to bills presented to Daniel H. Lownsdale and others for labor on the streets.

Meeting #28 (special). Saturday morning, March 12. Doctors J. A. Davenport, Broy, and Wilson told the council, by letter, that smallpox was prevalent in the city. The council defeated, by one vote, a motion to procure a large "Pest House" where all persons afflicted with smallpox would be confined. Councilman Dennison then proposed that every house in which someone with the disease lived should be posted with a sign and the family cautioned against "having any communication with any persons except through the physician attending them."

Councilman Norris moved to add the words, "a flag 21 feet square (shall) float over each house in which the small pox exists." Mayor Marye then offered the following amendment: "That each [member of the committee to ascertain where smallpox exists shall] ... wear a Red Cockade in his hat and be compelled to sleep in Oregon City, Dine at Milwaukie, and walk on the waters of the Willamette."

The mayor then accepted an amendment (which was voted down) that the expenses of said committeemen were to be paid by the Portland mayor. The mayor then offered the following substitute: "(T)he Council believes in the transmigration of souls and that A. P. Dennison be a committee to seek out forthwith and conduct into the Council Room the largest black Cur that can be found for the moment, in which is supposed to rest the spirit of Aesculapius (Greek and Roman god of healing), as to the best mode of preventing the spread of the small pox in Portland—The city council being incompetent and unable to determine the matter themselves." The motion was voted down.

Dennison's first resolution was then taken up and passed by a four to two vote. The mayor appointed as committeemen "His Excellency Gov. Gaines," "Hon. E. Ely,"[39] and F. W. Pettygrove (who had moved to Port Townsend the previous year). McLaren then moved to reconsider the vote, which motion carried. "The mayor thereupon arose and stated that he declined sitting any longer at this time in consequence of the actions [taken] at this meeting of the council, deeming it trifling away the time of the council. The council thereupon dispersed.—Attest: Chas B Pillow, Recorder."

Meeting #29. March 14. The minutes of the last meeting were read. Councilman Failing objected to the inclusion of several amendments and moved that they should not be preserved in council records. His motion failed.

Marshal Higgins was directed to explain in writing why he had not enforced the collection of taxes for the years 1851-52 as prescribed by the city charter. The council ordered the marshal to produce a separate listing of bills owed by Daniel Lownsdale and others for road taxes, including how much of each debt he had collected.

While lots donated by the city proprietors for burial purposes were too low and marshy to be suitable, Norris and Dennison reported, two of the proprietors—Stephen Coffin and W. W. Chapman (the mayor's father-in-law)—were willing to give deeds or bonds for city streets and several other public blocks of land, to be placed in the hands of the city council for safe keeping, if Daniel Lownsdale was willing. (The townsite proprietors had become adversaries amongst themselves after the surveyor general's office ordered them earlier that year to partition the townsite by designating which parcels each of them owned to protect the rights of buyers.[40]) Lownsdale, however, said he could not do anything about deeding lots to the city until the legal questions were settled as to who was the owner of which part of the townsite claim.

The council did not push further. By its failure to get signed deeds for all property designated on plat maps for public use, this council again failed future generations. Had council obtained signed deeds for the park blocks, public squares, and market place blocks as originally platted by Lownsdale, several lawsuits and the expenditure of millions of dollars could have been avoided. The tenure of Mayor Marye was thus one of missed opportunities as well as youthful nonsense.

Meeting #30. March 16. Reports of the city marshal and treasurer were read and referred to committees.

March 19, 1853. Election day. By the slender margin of eight votes, a new city charter was passed. Of three hundred seventy-five votes cast, two hundred fifty-seven were for the new version. Two-thirds of Portland citizens, or two hundred forty-nine votes, were required before the charter became law.[41] The one hundred fifteen "no" votes were probably against any charter at all.

Perhaps the new charter, with a separate nine-member council, would work better than the inexperienced and disorganized city council that had muddled through the city government's second year.

Chapter 7

Falling Apart and Getting It Back Together (More or Less)

1853-1856

Mayors

No. 4: April 1853 - March 1854

Josiah Failing

No. 5: March 1854 - April 1855

William S. Ladd

No. 6: April 1855 - April 1856

George W. Vaughn

Hopes and expectations were high for Portland's second charter, and for the solid citizens who were volunteering their services to the city.

At least three signers of the petition to revoke the city's charter—John Couch, William Ladd, and Richard Field—were elected to the new nine-member council. The treasurer, assessor, and marshal positions were also now elective, doubling the number of elected officials from seven to fourteen.

This new city government was divided into three branches—executive, legislative, and judicial—like the federal and, later, the state governments. But the city charter came into being much differently than did the state and federal models. The United States Constitution was adopted after vigorous, open, public debate, and ratified by the states after more vigorous, open, public debate. Records were kept of deliberations. On the state level, elected delegates would be convened in 1857 to draft a state constitution for Oregon. Detailed records would be retained of the convention proceedings and debates.[1] By contrast, Portland's second charter was drafted hastily, with little public input. No records exist regarding arguments for or against various provisions. More signatures,—one hundred fifty—had been gathered to do away with city government entirely than the one hundred forty-five signers who had sought the city's first charter two years before. By trial and error, the city was about to find out whether a different configuration would work any better than had the first.

Portland's new executive branch consisted of a mayor (who was no longer part of the council), a treasurer, an assessor, and a marshal. The recorder constituted the judicial branch as justice of the peace. The nine council members, all elected at-large, became a legislative body that would appoint its own record-keeper. This second charter was the only one Portland citizens got to vote on for the rest of the nineteenth century, except for the consolidation charter of 1891.[2] All other charter changes would be made unilaterally by the legislature.

The council president, who would be elected by council members from among themselves, was to preside over council meetings and serve as acting mayor when the mayor was absent. The mayor would send an annual message to council, and otherwise communicate whenever he "deemed expedient." The mayor could veto council ordinances, with a two-thirds council vote required for override.[3]

The city was authorized to erect a waterworks, buy and hold real property beyond the city limits for burial purposes, and establish a hospital, workhouse, and house of correction. The council was given authority to prevent obstructions in the Willamette River and to compel their removal. Elections could not be held where intoxicating liquors were sold.

The two days of annual road labor for males was eliminated, offset by a doubling of the property tax allowed from one-quarter percent of assessed value to one-half percent. The city was to collect public school taxes for a school fund to be controlled by the council.

Josiah Failing—a businessman with a solid reputation for integrity and common sense—was elected mayor. Failing was known as the "Dean of Front Street" because of his advanced age (forty-seven) and responsible demeanor. He was a driving force in the founding of Portland's public schools.[4] His sons, Henry and Edward, were now old enough, at ages nineteen and twelve respectively,[5] to take active roles in running the family's general merchandise store.

The council first met at the law office of Philip Marquam, and elected William Abrams as council president. Finding suitable council quarters was again an initial order of business. By its fourth meeting, the council had rented a room on the second floor of Coffin's Building for fifteen dollars a month.[6] The council met sixteen times between April and October; the following items were discussed at these meetings.

Mayor Josiah Failing. (Photo: OrHi #99140)

Mayor Failing reported that the city treasury had a *deficit* of five hundred thirteen dollars, with bills totaling six hundred fifty-three dollars, but only one hundred forty dollars on hand. In a detailed six-page memo, the mayor urged the council to take immediate action to prevent fires, settle the marshal's uncollected accounts (both for property taxes and unserved road labor days), license various classes of businesses, procure a public burial ground, prevent contagious diseases, improve streets by assessing the adjacent property owners, compel owners to construct sidewalks at least nine feet wide, assess taxes on persons engaged in the sale of goods, and remove obstructions in the Willamette River.[7]

The council refused to accept bills for expenses incurred on behalf of a pauper, because it was not a city responsibility. The creditors were told to take their bills to Washington County.[8]

Mayor Failing vetoed an ordinance that would have imposed licenses upon wagons and drays because, he said, it could be unjustly interpreted to apply to wagons used for transporting goods belonging to the owner.[9]

Councilman Ladd was appointed as a committee of one to find a site for a public burial grounds and to raise subscriptions to pay for it. Daniel Lownsdale's petition to build a wharf was tabled.

William Abrams resigned as president of council in August, but withdrew his resignation later at the same meeting.[10]

At the council's final meeting, on the evening of October 12, 1853, business consisted mainly of trying to fill vacant council positions. Several blank pages follow in the council ledger, with no further meetings recorded.

This was the third winter in a row that the council had virtually stopped functioning before the end of its term. It would be six months before new officials could be elected. The council filled its own vacancies, so all that was needed was for a majority of councilmen present to vote for the same person as a replacement. The problem was finding acceptable candidates willing to serve. These were volunteer jobs, and profit-making opportunities abounded, most of which required a good deal of travel. Furthermore, separating the mayor from the council was not working well. The *Oregonian* was charging city government with malfeasance for failing "to improve the streets and sidewalks."[11] Starting a government from scratch was a very different proposition from stepping into a structure already functioning well.

The city's top two elected officials were also beset by misfortune. Mayor Josiah Failing lost a cargo of goods on the Columbia River bar.[12] In December, two Reed & Abrams steam sawmills co-owned by Council President William Abrams burned to the ground, and most of the lumber stored in the yard was destroyed.[13] These business reversals undoubtedly contributed to the breakdown of city government.

No fire engine had yet been purchased.

The judicial branch of Portland's 1853-54 city government continued to function, but the legislative branch—the council—had totally fallen apart.

March 1854 - April 1855

By March 1854, with little preamble, Portland had a third new charter[14] and a new set of city officials. The territorial legislature had adopted a new city charter in January, after less than a year under the second one. This third charter, which many historians erroneously took for the city's first, was to last ten years with no amendments until 1858. Note that the territorial legislature approved this new act with no vote of the people. Today, Portland citizens take for granted their authority to amend the city charter, but nineteenth-century Portlanders had no such right. It was not until 1906 that voters approved a state constitutional amendment that gave cities the right and responsibility to make their own charter amendments.[15]

Portland's next mayor, William Sargent Ladd, age twenty-seven, was the youngest person ever to hold that office in Portland's first one hundred fifty years. He was one of the best.

Ladd won the mayoral contest over sawmill owner William Abrams. Ladd, a Democrat,[16] won with 57 percent of the vote over Abrams, a Whig.[17]

A former New Hampshire schoolteacher, Ladd had arrived in Portland by sea shortly after the first city government convened in 1851, and started out in business by selling small consignments of merchandise on a commission basis. A year later, he opened a store in partnership with his former schoolmate Charles Tilton. In 1853, Ladd built the town's first brick building, got himself elected to the city council, and solidified his reputation for hard work and frugality. While serving as mayor in 1854, he was elected to Portland's first school board[18] and journeyed to San Francisco to meet and marry his fiancée, Caroline Elliot of New Hampshire, Tilton's cousin.[19] Together, Ladd and Tilton were to found the first banking house north of San Francisco, Ladd and Tilton Bank, in 1859. Ten years later, Ladd cofounded the Ladd and Bush Bank in Salem with Oregon's political kingpin, Democrat Asahel Bush.

William Ladd knew how to get things done, how to work with people, and how to set priorities. He had demonstrated his propensity for hard work by pulling stumps out of the ground to work off his road tax instead of paying someone else to do it.[20]

> He was … often … at hand as early as four o'clock in the summer mornings, to help off his customers with their wagon loads in the cool of the day. He economized his strength, avoided

Mayor William S. Ladd. (Photo: OrHi #60495)

> saloons, spent his nights in sleep, not in carousals. … He was a shrewd trader. … Not easily excited, he could view business affairs with coolness, and make the most advantageous moves in the hours of opportunity.[21]

William Ladd remained involved in civic and business affairs throughout his lifetime, continually giving back to the community of the wealth he accumulated. He would later serve another partial term as mayor (1857-58). For twenty-four years beginning in 1869, he donated space for a public library in his handsome bank building.[22]

❧

The third city charter retained a nine-member legislative council that operated at arm's length from the mayor and recorder. However, the recorder regained power as the mayor's substitute, a responsibility that had been given to the council president the year before. The new charter also gave council authority to levy an additional one-half percent property tax for specified projects (in addition to the previously authorized one-half percent tax for general government purposes). The start of the city's fiscal year was changed to July 1.

Planned street improvements would be halted if a third of adjacent property owners objected. In the absence of such protest, owners of adjacent property would bear at least two-thirds of the cost of improving city streets.[23]

In addition to the fourteen elected officials specified in the charter—mayor, recorder (justice-of-the-peace), treasurer, marshal, assessor, and nine council members—the charter required the council to appoint a city attorney, street commissioner, city surveyor, city collector, and council clerk. Neither the mayor nor council members were to receive any pay, but all other officials were to receive some kind of compensation, usually on a fee-for-service basis.

❧

The council convened for its first meeting at the office of Ani Dennison on March 24, 1854. James Field was elected council president. Once again, a committee was appointed to procure a suitable room and fixtures for the use of council. Another committee was to collect all records and papers of preceding city councils.

A room offered by Anthony L. Davis, at twenty-five dollars per quarter, was chosen as the most economical and suitable for council's needs. Friday evening at 7:30 p.m. was selected as the best time for the council to meet.

Councilman Shubrick Norris, with two years of previous council experience, reported back that he had obtained a record book and two packages of papers from the last council clerk. A motion was made that "certain books purporting to be the record books of some former City Council be returned to the person or persons of whom they were obtained by the clerk of the city council." The motion failed on a three-three tie vote (Norris voting against), with three council members absent. Exactly what these "certain books" were was not recorded. A committee was appointed to procure chairs, stationery, and candlesticks for the council room.

Over the next three months, the council imposed licenses on "bar rooms, drinking shops, taverns, theatricals, shows, and other public exhibitions, billiard tables, and bowling allies; hawkers, peddlers, brokers and pawn brokers; wagons, drays, carts and carriages"; authorized purchase of a half-acre of John Couch's land for a cemetery at a cost of two hundred dollars, with another two hundred dollars authorized to enclose the cemetery with a fence and one hundred dollars for clearing stumps from part of the land; and designated penalties for disorderly conduct or indecent and immoral practices.[24]

A fire department was created, and the process of purchasing one or more fire engines was begun. Another ordinance specified that anyone who refused to assist in extinguishing a fire or in removing goods endangered by fire could be arrested and fined.[25] The December fire that had destroyed two sawmills had provoked the following newspaper reprimand: "It is *disgraceful* to see men standing with their hands in their pockets, when their neighbors' property is being devoured, and the city endangered, without manifesting the least disposition to render aid, although entreated and implored to do so."[26]

At a special meeting in June, the council considered a petition from James Terwilliger and others urging the council to seek legal advice in the "levee case" coming before the U.S. Supreme Court at its next session. The mayor was directed to employ an attorney to prosecute the case now pending with J. B. Parrish as plaintiff.

No early Portland issue would have a more costly long-term effect, take longer to resolve, or was more contentious than that of control of the levee. It was a clear-cut matter of public versus private ownership of the land between Front Street and the Willamette River. The Portland townsite had changed hands several times, and different owners had commissioned plat maps that treated the riverfront differently. Frontage lots had been sold. Private entrepreneurs had built profitable enterprises there. The Parrish lawsuit, by its challenge to a building on the levee, was a critical test case for public ownership.

Council President James Field resigned his seat on the council after only three months. Councilman William McMillen was elected as his replacement.[27]

The council turned down a petition for sidewalks because of the present "embarrassed situation of the finances of the city." Samuel Farnham and others sent a petition requesting that owners of swine be required to keep them confined. No action was taken.

By late June, the council clerk had still not purchased a new set of books, so the council told him to continue using the old ledger and journal in which proceedings for 1851, 1852, and 1853 had already been recorded.[28] This thrift on the part of the council[29] was fortunate from the standpoint of historical preservation, for all council meeting minutes from 1851 through November 1858 are preserved in one ledger. The leather-bound volume weighs ten pounds, is nearly three inches thick, and is half again the size of today's standard office paper size.[30]

However, the council also made a confusing decision to start numbering ordinances with number one, thereby ignoring the twenty-three ordinances approved by the three preceding councils. This was to cause long-lasting misunderstandings by future researchers.By year 2001, over one hundred seventy-five thousand ordinances had appeared on council's calendar over its one hundred fifty years of existence,[31] all numbered consecutively except for the twenty-three laws passed from 1851 to 1854, and another eight ordinances inadvertently given duplicate numbers in 1855.[32] This renumbering of ordinances was probably the reason Portland's first two charters have been overlooked by many historians.

A typical council meeting took place on July 7, 1854, at the council's nineteenth meeting. An ordinance responding to an earlier citizen petition was introduced to prevent hogs from running at large, but was not voted on. A bill from Stephen Coffin for rent owed from the 1851, 1852, and 1853 councils was referred to the committee on ways and means because city treasurer George Vaughn refused to pay it. A committee of three was appointed "to ascertain the amount of outstanding demands against the city" for old debts.

During summer and early fall, the council passed ordinances authorizing and requiring the planking of part of Front Street, setting the grade and requiring planking for other streets, and requiring removal of obstructions from city streets and sidewalks. Willamette Fire Engine Company No. 1 and Vigilance Hook & Ladder Company No. 1, all

Glacier-capped Mt. Hood was climbed by a party of pioneers on August 8, 1854, although they may not have reached its highest point. Included in this ambitious party were high-spirited *Oregonian* editor Thomas J. Dryer and the council's nemesis, Captain O. Travaillot.[34]

volunteers, were admitted into the fire department. Council accepted a gift of five acres each from Finice Caruthers and James Terwilliger for a cemetery, and authorized funds to build a fence and mark off burial lots for sale to the public. Two ferry landings were established, one at the end of Taylor Street and the other at Stark Street.[33]

The council refused to pay claims by Marshal R. L. Perkins and Mayor Ladd for the arrest and keep of one Henry Marshall, "a lunatic," even though Perkins had taken this prisoner by order of city recorder Ani Dennison as justice of the peace. Perkins and Ladd were told to present their bills to Washington County because territorial law charged counties with providing for the care of insane persons.

The first fire department election was held, with H. W. Davis elected as chief engineer and Shubrick Norris as his assistant.

The council was still devoting a good deal of time to finding willing successors to fill city vacancies. They tabled the resignation of Charles P. Bacon as assessor and collector, then learned that Bacon had failed to deposit all money he received with the treasurer every month. His resignation was therefore accepted, and the city attorney was directed to file a law suit against Bacon and his sureties for 2,343.80 dollars, with damages, for not faithfully performing the duties of city collector as required by law.[35] Lewis M. Starr, brother of future mayor Addison Starr, was elected as new city collector.[36]

The street commissioner's salary was increased from five to ten dollars a day, and the city surveyor's from eight to ten dollars per day. Absalom Hallock, who had previously submitted his resignation from both positions, agreed to continue in these capacities.

The street commissioner was directed to drain Front Street between Washington and Morrison streets where the plank roadway sank beneath the ground.[37] The council's regular meeting time was moved to Saturday evenings. In November, Addison Starr was paid one thousand dollars of his 1,483-dollar contract for laying sewers in the city.[38]

No quorum was present for November 18 meeting.

No quorum was present for November 25 meeting.

On December 2, new marshal Thomas J. Holmes was instructed to "procure the stove belonging to the city, now in the hands of William Grooms, late city marshal, and to have the same put up in the Council Room."

Multnomah County was created from parts of Washington and Clackamas counties on December 22, 1854, with Portland as the new county seat. This was welcome news to Portlanders, because the horse and buggy ride to Hillsboro (county seat of Washington County), fifteen miles west, was a burdensome one.[40] Until elections could be held, city councilman Shubrick Norris was designated as interim Multnomah County auditor, city treasurer George Vaughn as a county commissioner, council president William McMillen as sheriff, and former council clerk Anthony L. Davis, whose room the council was renting for its meetings, as judge of probate.[41]

Mayor Ladd sent the council a letter noting that the brig *Duc D'Lorges* was still obstructing Willamette River traffic. A sand bar had built up around where the brig had sunk in the river.[39]

No quorum was present for the December 9 meeting.

On December 20, the council considered the ordinance prohibiting hogs from running at large, but after much discussion, the ordinance was postponed indefinitely.

At its fiftieth meeting, the council authorized the mayor to petition the legislature to pay the city twelve hundred dollars for the jail destroyed by fire while it was housing territorial convicts under management of the penitentiary commissioners.[42]

Two council replacements chosen in January subsequently declined to serve.

No quorum was present for February 3, 1855, meeting.

No quorum was present for February 10 meeting.

On February 13, a feeble attempt was made to fill the vacant council seat of J. Orvis Waterman, with Thomas Carter receiving one vote; T. J. Dryer, one vote; and the other four ballots left blank.

Simeon G. Reed and Francis Pfaff, proprietors of the Eureka Saloon, petitioned for a reduction of fees, arguing that while the rate of taxation on billiard tables and bowling alleys had not been excessive when the original law was passed "owing to the prosperous state of affairs then existing," the present depression throughout the territory was depriving them of any profit.[43] Their petition was favorably reported on, accepted, and placed on file. However, no ordinance amendment was proposed.

No quorum was present for February 17 meeting.

No quorum was present for February 24 meeting.

Other ordinances passed by this council during the last six months of their tenure included requiring the removal of slaughter houses;

authorizing the planking of another portion of Front Street; regulating the storage of gunpowder; and authorizing entry of three hundred twenty acres of the Portland townsite at the proper federal land office.

Council members completed their terms in March by directing the Ways and Means committee to employ "a competent person" to write up council minutes for the current year. Pro-tem clerks had been writing their minutes on scratch paper; now their notes were transferred to the permanent journal by a scribe. Ordinance numbers got mixed up during this time, with numbers thirty-five through forty-two used twice. Perhaps no permanent person was willing to take on the job of council clerk because the council had reduced the clerk's pay from five dollars per meeting to three (the approximate contemporary equivalent to reducing the pay from one hundred dollars to sixty), and previous council clerks had still not been paid.

A final billing from city attorney William Farrar summarized city business he had conducted during the year (the levee case was apparently handled by someone else):

> Consultation with Councilmen Norris and Fitch as to right of City Recorder and other officers to charge the city for (their) office rent, stationery, &c. —$10
>
> Viewing contract of city with A. M. Starr for building and constructing certain drains, sewers, &c in Front Street & to Willamette River —15
>
> Drawing duplicate contracts for city with Frush and Masters for the furnishing of material & planking of certain parts of Front Street & certain cross streets and constructing sidewalks —15
>
> Duplicate contracts for city with James Terwilliger & Finice Caruthers for deeds of land for cemetery—15
>
> Counsel & advice with Mayor Ladd with reference to said contract —10
>
> Examination of the law, and consultation and advice with members of Common Council as to right of city to plank streets where parties abutting protest against planking —5
>
> Consultation & advice with Mayor Ladd as to course proper to be pursuedfor removal of a sunken vessel in Willamette River within city limits, and preparing notice to Capt. O. Travaillot to remove said vessel, and notice toother persons upon the same subject —15

Drawing warranty deed to 10 acres of land, with special reservations, from Mrs. Thomas, Finice Caruthers & James Terwilliger to City of Portland for city cemetery—10

Attorney fee before Recorder Dennison in case of City vs. Johnson & Perkins for maintaining a slaughter house within certain forbidden limits in city —5

Counsel & advice given to City Recorder as to construction of sundry old city ordinances, and counsel given to other city officers—

Total billing $100

The 1854-55 council, which started out so briskly in the spring and summer, barely held itself together by the end of the term. Perhaps the general business slow-down distracted councilmen from their duties. Even so, the records of this council and mayor were a marked improvement over any of the previous three years. City government was operating, and, for the first time, the governance year ended with no petition circulating for a new charter or to abolish city government.

April 1855—April 1856

In early April elections, Republican George W. Vaughn defeated Democrat (and future mayor) Addison Starr to become mayor.[44] Vaughn was a wealthy hardware store owner and real estate investor who had come to Portland from New Jersey in 1850. He was one of twenty-six organizers of the Pacific Telegraph Company in 1855,[45] and later built a large brick flour mill on Main Street. (The mill burned completely in 1873, and Vaughn suffered an estimated two hundred thousand dollar loss, or almost four million in today's dollars.) A major street in Northwest Portland is named for him.[46]

The new mayor was a man of firm opinions with no reluctance to speak out. An advertisement he placed in the *Oregonian* in 1865[48] castigated one Jacob Mayer, to whom Vaughn had leased his "handsome brick store." Vaughn had accepted depreciated currency from Mayer as rent payments under protest, his ad said, and he wanted everyone to know that even if Mayer were to comply with his contract and pay in coin, "he would be getting the best bargain in the city." Vaughn concluded: "I make this statement to show the public what kind of man he must be."[48]

> In 1855, Portland retained its position as the most populous and richest per capita city on the West Coast north of the California border.[49]

In late April 1855, Mayor Vaughn notified the council that the city had received and expended over six thousand dollars during his term as city treasurer, leaving a balance of three hundred ninety-four dollars on hand. He urged council to collect the six hundred dollars allocated by the territorial legislature for loss of the city jail destroyed by fire; to secure a fire engine and appropriate apparatus for the prevention of fires; to build water reservoirs connected to each other for extinguishing fires; to provide for safe storage of gun powder; and to complete a city cemetery.

Three council members were assigned to investigate transactions made by the last city council and to obtain possession of their final council meeting minutes, if possible. Another committee was to investigate the expediency of putting down cisterns for use by the volunteer firemen. Cemetery lots were to be advertised for sale immediately.

No quorum was present for May 26 meeting.

No quorum was present for June 2 meeting.

No quorum was present for June 5 meeting.

No quorum was present for June 9 meeting.

On June 11, the council passed its first ordinance, "To encourage and regulate the growing of shade and ornamental trees within the city." Shade and ornamental trees were to be planted eight feet from the street, and trimmed as the street commissioner saw fit. He was authorized to trim such trees each April if he deemed necessary, with the expense to be borne by the adjacent property owner. Front Street was exempted from the ordinance.

The marshal was to procure a broom, pail, pitcher, and tumblers for use by council. A second committee was appointed to try to locate all missing papers of the last city council.

Several council members resigned during the summer, including council president George Kittridge. Ransom Clark was selected to replace him, but he also resigned a month later.[50] One councilman who remained on the job was Matthew Patton, for whom today's Patton Home for low-income residents was named.[51]

The affairs of Capt. Travaillot once again appeared on the council's agenda. The captain had won his lawsuit against the city on the grounds that Mayor O'Bryant had lacked jurisdiction to fine him twenty-five dollars for riding "at a furious rate through the Streets of the City of Portland" in 1851. The council authorized payment of thirty-five dollars as ordered by the court.

Mayor George Vaughn. (Photo: OrHi #92369)

The council levied an additional tax of three-eighths of one percent against all taxable property for purchasing a fire engine, hose and other apparatus at ten thousand five hundred dollars or less.[52] Chief fire engineer H. W. Davis told the council that he "entertained serious fears" that the all-volunteer fire department would disband if the council neglected to provide better equipment and facilities. The council received the report and placed it on file.[53]

No quorum was present for August 4 meeting

No quorum was present for August 11 meeting.

An ordinance to prevent dogs from running at large was adopted in mid-August. All dogs were to have collars of metal or leather secured around their necks with a number or name stamped thereon. Dog owners were to pay the city collector two dollars per quarter for these licenses. A one-hundred-dollar fine was specified for vicious damage done by a dog. If an owner failed to confine a vicious dog, the city collector was to kill the animal and receive two dollars for each such extermination.[54]

No quorum was present for September 1 meeting.

No quorum was present for September 4 meeting.

The ordinance against loose pigs was finally passed in September. After September 29, all persons who owned swine were to keep them confined in suitable enclosures that were clean and free from stench. All swine found running at large after October 10 would be put into a pound or enclosure with all legal charges to be paid by the owner. If the swine was not claimed and removed in five days, the marshal was to sell the animal at auction, with net proceeds to go into the city treasury.

On November 16, 1855, the first telegraph line opened from Portland to Oregon City. The first message, sent to T. J. Dryer, said: "Compliments of the Pacific Telegraph Company to the editor of the *Oregonian*."[55]

The threat of Indian attack was discussed at a meeting in mid October. Councilman Love suggested that guards be placed about the city—"there being danger of the Indians firing the town or committing depredations of some kind." Mayor Vaughn, who attended the meeting, recommended that a guard be posted at the city's expense. An ordinance was to be drafted regarding Indians and city safety because Portland was serving as the military supply point for hostilities occurring not far from the city; the militia was headquartered on the east side of the Willamette River, although most of the fighting was occurring east of the Cascades. Troops were being sent east on steamboats up the Columbia River. Travel was "dangerous if not impossible" both in the Oregon and the Washington territories.[56]

No quorum was present for October 15 meeting.

No quorum was present for October 20 meeting.

In November, owners of First Street property were ordered to grade and lay nine-foot-wide sidewalks of "good sound lumber or plank" at least two inches thick with square edges, at their own expense. A "good substantial brick sidewalk" was also allowed.[57] The minutes are silent regarding precautions needed for possible Indian troubles.

News came in November that the city's first fire engine could be expected to arrive in five months from New York City, purchased on behalf of the city by former governor George Abernethy.[58]

No quorum was present for November 24 meeting.

At a special meeting about sidewalks called by Mayor Vaughn on November 27, the council ordered sidewalks to be laid, at the owners' expense, on both sides of nine streets—from Pine to Salmon between Front to First Street—on or before February 1, 1856.

No quorum was present for December 8 meeting.

No quorum was present for December 22 meeting.

No quorum was present for December 29 meeting.

On January 12, 1856, at its thirty-sixth meeting, the council agreed to build a series of wood cisterns, fifteen feet square and nine feet deep, caulked and pitched, for use of the fire department.

No quorum was present for January 19 meeting.

No quorum was present for January 26 meeting.

In February, former mayor Josiah Failing requested that the sidewalk in front of his store be allowed to remain as already laid down. The street committee recommended that it stay as it was until the street was planked, but that the planned street grade should proceed. The resolution was taken up, and "after a grave silence of some length … action [was] indefinitely postponed."

Both fire wardens resigned. Council "justified itself" concerning these resignations and said that the council had done its duty. The minutes gave no further details.

No quorum was present for February 20 meeting.

No quorum was present for March 1 meeting.

No quorum was present for March 5 meeting.

No quorum was present for March 8 meeting.

On March 15, with seven members present, the meeting was adjourned for lack of business.

By March 27, 1856, numerous citizens had sent petitions urging a night watch "to protect our lives and property from the depredations" of their "common enemy"—the Indians. Council directed the marshal and mayor to procure the services of "eight reliable sober and trustworthy men to stand watch within the city limits at such places as they shall deem most proper and necessary" to protect the city. Each man was to receive five dollars per night for his services.

No quorum was present for March 29 meeting.

No hostile Indians appeared. The closest they came was forty miles from the city.[59] The marshal was ordered, at the next council meeting, to pay the several watchmen five dollars each for one night's duty. In other April business, the council rescinded a former resolution placing the elevation of Second Street not more than six inches above that of First Street. Thomas Ager was hired to construct four fire cisterns, a contract that the council said would be binding upon succeeding councils.

Communications received from George Abernethy in New York[60] concerning a fire engine were "commented on with remarks highly complimentary to Mr. Abernethy for the interest he has taken in his Agency for the purchase of a Fire Engine for the City of Portland in which it was supposed he could feel but little interest."[61]

The fiftieth and final meeting of this council was a perfunctory one. Seven members heard bills presented, approved their payment, and adjourned.[62]

Meanwhile, Canyon Road west of Portland was a morass of mud; it was virtually impassable. The road was outside the city limits, and therefore not under the council's jurisdiction. The portion of the road closest to Portland had been planked five years before by the now-defunct Portland and Valley Plank Road Company. On January 25, 1856, the territorial legislature chartered a new corporation, the Portland and Tualatin Plains Road Company. Businessmen such as former mayors William Ladd and Josiah Failing, former recorder William Caldwell, and future mayor Addison Starr, were among those who paid private subscriptions. Although this company finished its planking within a year, the road was still primitive.[63]

> "[T]he pioneers were confronted with a gigantic task. ... The immense stumps were solidly rooted, and, when removed by laborious effort, the roots and rocks in the roadbed had to be cleared away. The work was costly and the cost was always greater than estimated. ... The mud during the greater part of the year made wagon travel almost, if not quite, impossible. ... A wagon journey, with a load, made progress at the rate of eight or ten miles a day."[64]

Produce from the fertile Tualatin Valley reached Portland's harbor over a great plank road. The fifteen-mile journey from Portland to Hillsboro was nearly a full day's ride in the late 1800s when this picture was taken. (Photo: OrHi #20702-a)

Table 4. Ordinances passed, 1851-56

Year 1: 1851-52	18 ordinances passed	Mayor Hugh O'Bryant
Year 2: 1852-53	3 ordinances passed	Mayor Allison Bonnell (six months)
Year 2: 1852-53	0 ordinances passed	Mayor Simon Marye (six months)
Year 3: 1853-54	2 ordinances passed	Mayor Josiah Failing
Year 4: 1854-55	42 ordinances passed	Mayor William Ladd
Year 5: 1855-56	15 ordinances passed	Mayor George Vaughn[65]

Although council turnover remained high, and many meetings were cancelled for lack of a quorum, the mayor and council continued to work on improving the city's streets and sidewalks, and took steps toward the prevention and control of fires. The city was spared the ravages of Indian wars occurring in other parts of the territory.

The first five years of city government had been a time of trial and error, but of relative calm. At the urging of Mayor Ladd, the 1854-55 council had set many new ground rules under which the city could grow and prosper. A comparison of council productivity is revealing; see Table 4.

The city had had no natural disasters, no murders, no big scandals.

Free-flowing alcohol, endless mud, and the unresolved levee question remained; the battle over ownership of the west bank of the Willamette River between public and private interests still had many years to go.

Chapter 8

A Mayor Ousted, a Councilman Expelled, Portland's First Hanging, and a Near-Riot on the Levee

1856-1860

Mayors

No. 7: April 1856 – April 1857
James O'Neill
April 1857 – Nov 1857
James O'Neill (half-term)
No. 8: November 1857 – April 1858
William S. Ladd (again, for half-term)
No. 9: April 1858 – April 1859
Addison M. Starr
No. 10: April 1859 – April 1860
Stephen J. McCormick

A thoughtful description of the times was penned by future *Oregonian* editor Harvey Scott, then an eighteen-year-old passing through Portland from Washington Territory on his way to attend school west of Portland.

> Portland, in (October) 1856, contained about 1800 inhabitants. All business was in Front Street. … (W)est of First Street, only paths, trails and zigzag roads made by woodmen led the way through stumps and logs and over uneven places, out into that forest. The Canyon Road had been opened, but was yet almost inaccessible from the nascent city, and most difficult of passage or travel when reached. … In many places (this road was) so narrow that teams could not pass each other, and most of the logs had been cut out at lengths, or widths, that gave room for only

> a single vehicle. In the winter there was bottomless mud—though the Canyon Road was crosslaid with timber a portion of the way. No one who passes over these roads now can have any idea of the size of the trees or the density of the forest then; the logs, undergrowth, ridges and gullies, hills, steeps and sharp turns in the ravines rendering road-making a thing difficult now to comprehend or believe. …
>
> Western Oregon was so fully settled that the most desirable lands were all taken. The great donation claims of 640 acres, to man and wife, covered all, or nearly all, the open valley lands. Then country was everything, the towns comparatively nothing; and Salem as the center of agricultural Willamette, was in many ways a more important town than Portland.[1]

Another vignette was penned by Edwin Markham, an internationally known poet born in Oregon City in 1852, who left Oregon as a young boy:[2]

> I was not yet six years old when in 1857 mother sold her property in Oregon City and we packed our things and went by boat to Portland. … As we drove through the deep mud of one of Portland's business streets, I saw a group of convicts working on the road. They wore striped uniforms

Portland's nickname "Stumptown" was well deserved, as can be seen in this 1857 photo. The building at center was located between Fourth and Fifth at Hall. (Photo: OrHi #5487)

> and each of them had attached to his leg a ball and chain. One of the convicts was cursing horribly as we passed. I had not known until then that the men ever wore striped clothes and had balls and chains fastened to them. I did not know that men were ever chained like wild animals. It was years before this shocking sight grew dim. I would wake up at night and see them and wonder about them.[3]

The city's first two-term mayor, James O'Neill,[4] enjoyed great popularity. However, his tenure was to end ignominiously, mid-way in his second term, because he was absent from the city without permission from the council. Despite his forced exit, Mayor O'Neill was arguably the best-liked Portland mayor of the nineteenth century.[5] He won his first election handily over former councilman and recorder Ani P. Dennison.[6]

"Always pleasant and obliging, never a cross word for anyone," was how James O'Neill and his brother Dan were described.[7] James arrived from New York State in 1853, and was employed as Wells Fargo agent for the Oregon Territory when he was elected Portland mayor at age thirty-two.[8] Daniel, two years the junior, had preceded James to the territory by four years, and was a steamboat captain on the Willamette and Columbia rivers who took the 1850 territorial census as a deputy to U.S. Marshal Joe Meek.[9]

In June 1856, the council again warned offenders to remove obstructions to the levee, specifically cordwood and timber stacked there, and directed the street commissioner to remove these obstructions himself if the owners neglected to do so.[10] Brisk trading and shipping continued through Portland's harbor.

On July 26, 1856, the major event of the year occurred: *Portland's first fire engine arrived!* After its long journey by boat around Cape Horn from New York City, this "pride of the Northwest" evoked "awe and amazement" in the eyes of all who beheld the steam engine for the first time.[11] It had taken over five years, from that first May 1851 vote (which Mayor O'Bryant refused to implement), but Portland finally had a fire engine, and a modern one at that.

During Mayor O'Neill's first term, the council also granted a right-of-way to conduct water through city streets, provided that no pipes were laid that would interfere with the laying of sewers.[12] The council also required owners of adjacent properties to clean their streets; prohibited fast riding and driving; prohibited riding and driving on sidewalks; directed more surveying, grading, and planking of streets;

Mayor James O'Neill. (Photo: OrHi #104369)

and licensed bar-rooms, drinking shops, billiard rooms, bowling alleys, theatrical shows, and other public exhibitions.[13]

City Collector T. J. Holmes routinely posted public notices regarding pending property foreclosures. A notice dated April 13, 1856, said the city had purchased Lot 6 of Block 111 (between Clay and Market, Front and Water streets) by paying unpaid city taxes of two dollars and thirty cents at public auction, "being the amount of the taxes, charges and interest due on said tract." (This was next to a marshy area south of downtown; possibly it was unsuitable for building except on stilts.) The owner was given four years to redeem his land by paying all back taxes; after that, a deed to the property would be issued to the city.[14]

In January 1857, the council repudiated the Brady map adopted by the 1852-53 council,[15] fearing that the levee case before the U. S. Supreme Court might otherwise be compromised. The council said the Brown map commissioned by Lovejoy and Pettygrove when the town was first laid out in 1845, showing the levee as open space, was the correct basic map of the city.[16] Wise as this council action was, it came too late.

April 1857 - November 1857

Mayor O'Neill won a second term in April 1857, defeating merchant and future U. S. Senator Henry W. Corbett.[17] Soon thereafter, the council rented a new meeting room for twenty-five dollars a month in a building owned by Jacob Kamm adjoining J. L. Atwood's Saloon.[18]

The territorial supreme court had issued an injunction forbidding construction on the waterfront while the *Parrish vs. Stephens* levee lawsuit was on appeal to the U. S. Supreme Court. Nevertheless, on May 22, a large wooden building, an addition to the Metropolis Hotel, was moved onto the levee. Mayor O'Neill immediately called a special council meeting, at which the council authorized him to institute legal proceedings in federal district court to have the building removed, and to have those responsible arrested. Only one council member—N. S. Coon—voted nay.

The council soon received a petition signed by ninety-five citizens, including Thomas J. Dryer, Capt. O. Travaillot, and George Vaughn (note Vaughn's signature for what was to happen three years later), urging the city to remove the building without waiting for court action. On June 10, the council authorized the marshal to move the structure if owner Benjamin Smith did not do so within ten days.[19] The marshal, Samuel R. Holcomb, reported back on July 7: "I removed said building June 24th, 1857 and sold said building July 6, 1857 according to the provisions of said ordinance, for the sum of $475, and … after deducting expense to the amount of $161 … paid the balance of $314 into the city treasury."

The council was uncertain what to do with this three hundred fourteen dollars profit. On July 27, they voted to retain the money in the city treasury until they should direct otherwise.

By the council's August 11 meeting, councilmen Simeon Reed and Benjamin Goodwin had both resigned. Townsite proprietor Stephen Coffin was elected to fill Reed's seat and former councilman Shubrick Norris was chosen as Goodwin's replacement. However, Councilman Holmes opposed the seating of Norris. Historian E. Kimbark MacColl describes the rancor between fellow Democrats Norris and Holmes this way: "The Holmes-Norris feud was the most extreme example of political infighting during the decade. It began while grocer Norris served on the first city council in 1851. Over the next six years, the English-born Holmes, a politically ambitious and increasingly successful shoe merchant, grabbed appointive and elective offices. Some he held concurrently … [I]n 1854, Norris attacked Holmes's moonlighting and forced him to resign all other positions to retain the lucrative elected marshal's job. In the process, Norris created a bitter enemy."[20]

The council minutes of August 11, 1857, describe what occurred immediately following Norris' selection to fill the present council vacancy: "Mr. Couch tendered his resignation, which was read. … Mr.

Meanwhile, voters throughout the Oregon Territory overwhelmingly supported the convening of a state constitutional convention, a proposition that had been narrowly defeated three times in the previous three years.

This marathon constitutional convention was held in Salem in late summer 1857. Four future Portland mayors participated: Stephen McCormick (1859 mayor), William Farrar (1862 mayor), David Logan (1863 mayor), and George Williams (1902 mayor).[21] *Oregonian* editor Thomas Dryer was a delegate-at-large representing Washington and Multnomah counties.[22]

The convention met for only one month—from August 17 through September 18—and drew up today's Oregon constitution. Voters approved the document by more than two-to-one in November 1857. It would be more than a year, however, before Congress granted statehood. President James Buchanan signed the bill admitting Oregon as the thirty-third state of the Union on February 14, 1859, eight years after Portland received its charter from the territorial government.[23]

Holmes offered his resignation also. The chair ruled Mr. Holmes out of order. A quorum not being present by reason of the withdrawal of Messrs. Couch, Holmes, and Hardenburg, the chair directed the marshal to summon absent councilmen to attend. The marshal reported no absentees to be found. Council therefore stood adjourned."

By the next council meeting, Holmes had devised a new strategy to block Norris from council; he moved to direct a new three-member committee to review Norris's oath and qualifications, and got himself appointed to the committee. Two weeks later the committee reported back that Norris had indeed been duly elected and taken the oath within the required ten days, and was therefore "duly entitled to take his seat and officiate as a member of this Common Council." However, Norris was absent from that meeting as well as the next two, possibly on an out-of-town trip. At the third meeting, the minutes say, "On motion of Mr. Holmes, the seat of Mr. Norris was declared vacant."

By October 13, 1857, nearly half the council seats—four out of nine—were vacant. Citizens chosen to fill these vacancies included log-roller William King, Dr. R. B. Wilson (well-to-do son-in-law of Captain John Couch), and William McEwan (who had been city attorney the previous year.)

In the midst of this council upheaval, Councilman Holmes demanded an immediate citywide election to replace the mayor. Holmes argued that O'Neill had been absent from the city for more than thirty days without obtaining the council's permission, in clear violation of the city charter:[24] the 1854 charter stipulated that any absence without council approval created a vacancy in the office.[25]

O'Neill was probably on a business trip, although the minutes do not say where he was. Previous councilmen and mayors had been absent for four to six weeks and longer on business trips without the formality of obtaining council permission. A boat trip to San Francisco took about a week each way, while a round trip to New York with a land portage across Panama required at least four months. Such travels contributed heavily to high turnover and absenteeism in the ranks of city officials.

Holmes carried a grudge toward O'Neill, stemming from a lawsuit Holmes had filed as city marshal. O'Neill was fined one hundred dollars by the city recorder for engaging in money brokerage without a license. O'Neill refused to pay. Instead, he appealed to the territorial supreme court, which ruled in June 1856 that as a salaried agent of Wells, Fargo & Company, O'Neill was not a broker because he was not acting for a fee, or rate percentage, for others. The suit brought by Holmes was therefore dismissed.[26]

But O'Neill had indeed left town without seeking permission from the council and had not yet returned. On November 4, 1857, a special citywide election was held to replace him.[27]

November 1857 - April 1858

By a margin of only two votes, former mayor W. S. Ladd defeated *Oregonian* editor T. J. Dryer, one hundred forty-four votes to one hundred forty-two, as the next, but half-term mayor. Three votes were cast for former mayor George Vaughn. Because voting was done orally (*viva voce*) in 1857, we know exactly who voted, and for whom.[28]

The Democratic *Oregon Weekly Times* crowed over this defeat of Thomas Dryer:

> On Wednesday last huge posters were plastered about the street corners, announcing in blazing capitals that Thomas J. Dryer was an "Independent" candidate for Mayor. ... For an hour or two the public mind seemed staggered and appalled at the idea of Dryer's demanding an endorsement of his action[s] at the convention .... [I]n spite of Mr. Ladd's unequivocal declination and refusal to sanction the use of his name, Dryer was repudiated, condemned and beaten! ... Mr. Ladd does not seem to regard the result as

at all complimentary to himself in view of the fact that Dryer was his competitor.[29]

Mayor William S. Ladd (Photo: OrHi #60495)

At the same November 4 election, city voters turned down a special property tax levy of one and a half mills (fifteen cents on each one hundred dollars of property value) to procure legal counsel "to prosecute and defend the suit in the Supreme Court of the United Sates, to wit—Josiah L. Parrish vs. Thomas Stephens and others, being the same suit that is commonly known as the Levee suit."[30] The measure failed by nearly two to one (seventy-eight votes for, one hundred forty-three against).[31] Both Ladd and Dryer voted no. Councilman Holmes later raised private funds with which to pay the legal costs for Parrish.[32]

After the stormy council sessions of summer and fall, tempers cooled as winter set in. The marshal was directed to provide means for warming the council's meeting room. Deputy marshal J. F. McCoy soon thereafter presented two bills to the treasurer; one for three dollars and seventy-five cents to Henry Neeves for sawing and splitting one cord of wood for council chambers, and the other for the same amount to buy a pipe joint, elbow, and zinc for putting up a stove.[33]

The task of removing thirty-eight dead bodies from the "old grave yard" to the new city cemetery at a cost of eight dollars each was completed in late November. The council authorized three hundred and four dollars to pay this bill.[34]

Antagonisms again flared on December 28, 1857. During a debate about paying a federal court fee to enter the Portland land site in the city's name on U.S. land title rolls,[35] an argument ensued. Councilman

In April, the council approved payments to its members for attendance from January through April 15, 1858, as follows:

Absalom Hallock, council president	11 meetings	$33
Charles Hutchins	12 meetings	$36
Edward Hamilton	10 meetings	$30
Thomas J. Holmes	10 meetings	$30
Shubrick Norris	8 meetings	$24
William King	8 meetings	$24
R. B. Wilson	7 meetings	$21
Steven Coffin	7 meetings	$21
William L. McEwan	6 meetings	$18
Total		$237

Peter Hardenburg used "improper language and expressions," according to the minutes, and accused the courts of chicanery. Former city attorney William McEwan moved that Hardenburg be expelled. Council President Absalom Hallock ruled that Hardenburg might speak once, then must absent himself during the council's discussion. With Hardenburg gone, the remaining council members voted to suspend him until the next meeting, when further action concerning his case would be considered. Hardenburg returned to the meeting after this vote, and insisted on retaining his seat and on his right to address council, which the council clerk noted was "contrary to the rules of order and the orders of the President." The council then reconsidered its previous vote, and voted to expel him from the council immediately. Only R. B. Wilson voted nay. The minutes say, "Mr. Hardenburg was thereupon declared to be no longer a member of this council."[36]

Shubrick Norris was selected as Hardenburg's replacement, finally slipping back onto the council by a one-vote margin. (Undoubtedly, one of the votes against him was that of Councilman Holmes.) Charles Hutchins, who had resigned less than a month before, apparently changed his mind, for he returned to fill his own vacancy.[37]

Only three ordinances were passed during Mayor Ladd's short five-month tenure, and all three were signed by City Recorder Anthony Davis as acting mayor. These ordinances reorganized the fire department, specified measures to prevent fires, and codified legislative charter changes dividing the city into three wards and granting council members three dollars for each meeting attended. For the next fifty-five years, city council members would be chosen by wards.[38]

Portland's harbor was the subject of two additional charter amendments adopted by the state legislature in January and February 1858. One authorized the city to assess and collect port dues from all arriving and departing vessels. The other created an elected position of port warden to assess and collect these dues.[39]

April 1858 - April 1859

Portland's next mayor, Addison M. Starr, won election over former mayor George Vaughn by a resounding two-to-one edge (two hundred eighty-nine votes for Starr; one hundred thirty-eight for Vaughn),[40] a rematch and reversal of their 1855 race.

Addison Starr served as Multnomah County sheriff at the same time he was mayor—the first and only person to act in both these capacities simultaneously.[41] The mayor's job was a volunteer civic duty, while the sheriff was compensated on a fee basis, and was called upon only when needed. Starr served a four-year term as sheriff, whereas his mayoral term was for only one year.[42]

Addison "Ad" Starr, born in New York, was thirty-eight years old when elected mayor and sheriff, and had lived in the Oregon Territory for eight years.[43] The 1850 territorial census lists Addison Starr as a "clerk," and his brothers Lewis M. and L. V. Starr as "tinners." This probably means that Addison Starr managed the family tinsmith and stove business. Two young miners also lived in the Starr household at time of the census, which might indicate that the Starr brothers had recently arrived from the California gold fields.[44] Be that as it may, Addison Starr's penmanship, grammar, and diction (as evidenced by council documents preserved in the city archives) bespoke an educated man. He was the eldest brother—four years older than Lewis, and six years older than L. V.—and the first to take a lead in Portland's community affairs. A fourth brother, E. A., joined them in Portland later, and all four were active participants in city life.[45]

Mayor Addison Starr. (Photo: OrHi #227)

The Starrs opened Portland's first distillery and became wholesale liquor distributors. "Ad Starr's whiskey" distillery was located on the Willamette River north of downtown.[46] An advertisement in a local newspaper said: "Keep the money in the state. If people must and will have whiskey, let them buy Starr pure unadulterated white whiskey."[47]

In July 1865, Addison and Lewis Starr, along with three other men, incorporated the First National Bank of Portland, the oldest national bank on the Pacific Coast.[48]

> Mayor Starr's name is best known for the landmark court case of *Starr v. Stark*, in which the Oregon Supreme Court held for Addison Starr and his brother Lewis.[49] At issue was title to an entire city block that the Starr brothers had purchased in good faith from town proprietor W.W. Chapman in 1850.[50] The Starr block was part of the forty-eight acres Benjamin Stark received in an 1850 settlement over property rights with townsite proprietors Lownsdale, Coffin, and Chapman. Much of Stark's land had been sold by then, and the trio had agreed to pay Stark all proceeds from those sales.[51] Stark, however, refused to give the Starrs a deed to the property. The unanimous state supreme court opinion said: "Upon every principle of law and morals [Stark] should be fore ever enjoined from the commission of such injustice, and be compelled to quiet the [Starrs'] title by a release of all claim to the premises."[52]

The council chose backroom politician Col. William King as president during the first four months of Starr's tenure, after which time King resigned as president for unstated reasons.[53] Attendance at council meetings was dramatically improved now that council members were paid to attend, and council turnover experienced a sharp drop. Five 1858-59 councilmen remained on the council for at least another year, an unprecedented circumstance.

In late April 1858, the council reaffirmed its stand against obstructions on the levee.[54] However, later the same year, the U.S. Supreme Court dismissed a crucial case regarding the levee on the grounds that it "raised no federal or constitutional issues."[55] This did not settle the ownership dispute over the levee, however, for in effect the Court said only that no federal law applied in Oregon when Lovejoy and Pettygrove platted the Portland townsite.[56] (The claim had been filed with the provisional government while Great Britain and the U.S. still occupied the Oregon Country jointly.)

In another issue of public versus private ownership, Mayor Starr moved to regain two blocks set aside as public squares by the townsite proprietors. Contrary to his stated intent, Daniel Lownsdale had sold

This 1858 parade featured volunteer firemen and a spirited brass band. (Photo: OrHi #5488)

the two blocks designated as public squares to his lawyer, Lansing Stout. Stout, a future Oregon congressman (1859-61), paid Lownsdale thirty-eight hundred dollars for five blocks that included the two public squares, then sold a half-interest in those five blocks to City Recorder Alonzo Leland. Starr called a special council meeting, and urged immediate council action to establish the city's right to these blocks, noting that two of the blocks were being fenced in.[57] The city then filed suit against Leland and Stout. The case was to wend its way through the courts for several years before being decided in the city's favor.[58]

That fall, two one hundred-by-one hundred-foot lots were sold from the estate of one John Billings, who had died without a will. The two lots, at the southwest corner of S.W. First Avenue and Harrison Street, brought three hundred eighty dollars at auction, which would be roughly seven thousand dollars today. In fall 2000, the two lots were the site of a parking garage for Portland Center Apartments with modern office space on the top floor. The assessed value of the two lots was seven hundred eighty-five thousand dollars.[59]

In October, the council authorized construction of a new city jail. At the same meeting, they ordered that the "person or persons erecting a new house on the levee be notified to stop further improvement" and to remove the obstructions placed there in violation of a court order.[60]

In spite of this council order, ex-mayor George Vaughn began building a wharf on the waterfront. On January 7, 1859, the council

> Near the end of his tenure as sheriff, during the Civil War, Addison Starr was to face down a mob bent on vigilante justice. The incident started with men discussing the war in a saloon when one proposed a toast to the Union. A southern sympathizer named Patterson yelled, "To hell with the Union." A Captain Staples came after Patterson with a rope, and Patterson shot him. Deputy Sheriff Lewis Starr (Addison's brother) was summoned, and arrested Patterson. While Lewis was leading the prisoner to jail, a huge crowd, hundreds of men, gathered. A lynching party moved in. Sheriff Starr arrived and, with pistol drawn, threatened to kill the first man who touched Patterson. The crowd reluctantly parted for the Starr brothers and their prisoner to make their way to the city jail.[61]

notified Vaughn and others to stop making improvements on the public levee. One of the committee members who recommended this action was councilman Henry Corbett, future U.S. senator from Oregon (1867-73).[62] Council warnings apparently did not impress Vaughn, however. Convinced of his rights as a property owner, he continued to complete his wharf.

Meanwhile, Congress granted Oregon statehood on February 14, 1859.

The *Oregonian* obituary for Addison Starr, who left Portland in 1865 for San Francisco and died there a wealthy man at age seventy-one,[63] said Starr came to Portland as a Democrat, but acted with the Republicans after they organized as an Oregon political party in 1859.[64] Soon after Addison left Portland, Lewis Starr moved north to the Puget Sound area,[65] where he had been a silent partner in the founding of Tacoma City in Washington Territory.[66] In 1881, Lewis and Addison Starr sold their Puget Sound Navigation Company to the Oregon Railway & Navigation Company for six hundred thousand dollars and Lewis also retired to California as a wealthy man.[67]

April 1859 - April 1860

In 1859, the Democrats backed an Irishman named Stephen J. McCormick as mayor, and easily defeated a "Citizens Ticket" headed by Republican mayoral candidate Captain Alexander Ankeny[68] and also including townsite proprietor Stephen Coffin and future mayor Henry Failing. The lone Republican elected was Erasmus Shattuck, who had served as city attorney the previous year. The ward system of electing councilmen enacted by the legislature the previous year thus brought increased diversity of occupations, but not of party, to the council.[69]

Thirty-year-old Stephen McCormick was the city's tenth mayor, and the first of Portland's six foreign-born mayors.[70] McCormick arrived in Portland in 1851 at age twenty-two from Dublin, Ireland, accompanied by his wife and sister-in-law. He had been educated as a Catholic priest, but went into business as soon as he arrived, setting up a small job printing office in a seven-by-nine-foot room on Front Street. The following year, his sister-in-law Bridget Clarke married Thomas Robinson, a member of Portland's first city council,[71] and the newlyweds chose a donation land claim with a commanding view on a hill above present-day Broadway Drive.[72]

Mayor Stephen McCormick (Photo: OrHi #76680)

McCormick had published a small dictionary of Chinook jargon, the common language between the Indians and settlers. McCormick's dictionary became a "household book" for many families throughout the territory.[73] McCormick was also known to Portlanders as the publisher of *McCormick's Almanac*, "a breezy little pamphlet … of much value throughout the state."[74] He took part in the state constitutional convention, and was later elected to a two-year term on the Multnomah County Commission.

In 1863, McCormick began publishing an annual *Portland City Directory* which contained lists of businesses, services, and residents, complete with addresses, along with officers of governmental organizations, churches, lodges, banks, etc., and a full array of commercial advertisements. Most editions of the directory contained a copy of the city charter, rules of the common council, ordinances, the names of all volunteer firemen, and basic information such as the locations of cisterns for fighting fires. In 1867, a detailed city map was added.[75]

The council again elected architect Absalom B. Hallock as council president. Hallock was to serve a total of eleven years on the council, a phenomenal record for the times. A civil engineer, Hallock had been appointed as both the city and county surveyors in 1855, when he was twenty-eight years old.[76] Now, in 1859, and for the next three years, he served as city surveyor as well as on the city council. A December 1900 *Oregonian* article calls Hallock a political boss who "came near running the city,"[77] and who served several years as chief of the fire department.[78] Wearing his architect's hat, Hallock designed at least eighteen of Portland's fine brick buildings.[79] He was also appointed to the powerful Board of Police Commissioners in 1870, and served as its first president.[80]

As city marshal, the voters elected James Lappeus, co-owner of the popular Oro Fino Saloon and Theater. Lappeus would be an influential force in Portland's police community for the next twenty-four years, serving various terms as city marshal and later as police chief, until his removal from office in 1883.[81] Marshal Lappeus's eventual undoing stemmed from a charge of bribery dating back to his first year as marshal.[82] The accusation concerned a Portland murder committed in full daylight in front of numerous witnesses.

Anna Balch—the fifteen-year-old daughter of farmer Danford Balch—eloped with a young man named Mortimer Stump who had worked for Balch until ordered off the farm. After their elopement, the newlyweds stayed with Mortimer's family northeast of Portland for about a week. On Thursday, November 18, 1858, the entire Stump family, including Mortimer, Anna, and Mortimer's parents, journeyed to town to buy necessities with which the young couple would set up housekeeping. That afternoon, the two fathers encountered each other at Starrs' store and exchanged heated words. The words were so heated, in fact, that Balch rushed home for his double-barreled shotgun. As Anna and her new family boarded the Stark Street ferry for their return trip home, Danford Balch shot and killed Mortimer Stump.[83]

Balch later claimed that his gun had gone off accidentally; that he had merely intended to bring his daughter back home. Nevertheless, he spent the winter awaiting trial in a flimsy rented building being used as a city jail until the new jail was completed in March 1859.[84] Balch broke out of jail in early 1859 and hid out near his farm in today's Forest Park for several months, fed by family and friends.[85] He was still hiding when Lappeus was elected marshal. Lappeus discovered Balch's hideaway and arrested him in July 1859. Balch was tried and found guilty in late August[86] and hanged on October 18.[87]

Salem's *Oregon Statesman* newspaper carried the following account of the hanging: "Danford Balch was executed near the jail in Portland. The awful spectacle was witnessed by an immense concourse of people, among whom I was pained and surprised to observe a large number of women and children. … Some individual, a speculator, had erected some seats near the gallows, intending to turn an honest penny by leasing them to spectators of Balch's dying agonies. But during the night preceding, some persons threw the seats into the river, thereby spoiling a very mean speculation."[88]

In a final statement written on his behalf by a Methodist minister, Balch confessed that he had had two drinks on the day of the shooting, and had been imbibing alcohol frequently for several years. An *Oregonian* article spoke of Balch as an "unfortunate man, who, under the excitement of intoxicating drink, ignorance of the law, and evil advice, slew his fellow man."[89] Today a large commemorative stone marks the Danford Balch homesite at N.W. Thirtieth and Upshur in Lower Macleay Park, near the site of the famous 1905 world's fair Forestry Building. Balch Creek in Macleay Park bears the name of the hanged man.[90]

The following March, during Lappeus's 1860 reelection campaign, a man named Richard Loney printed a poster charging that Marshal Lappeus had offered to free Balch from the city jail for one thousand dollars. Nothing came of this accusation until twenty-three years later, when the *Portland Weekly News* reprinted the poster affidavits in a bold attack on Lappeus, then serving as chief of police. An extensive investigation followed. While Lappeus was exonerated, the 1883 mayor nevertheless removed him from office, and Lappeus did not return to public service. According to the affidavits published, Mrs. Balch had tried, but failed, to raise the bribe money.[91]

Two other troublesome incidents occurred while Balch awaited execution. The first concerned a petition that the council received on September 6, 1859, signed by forty-one people (including Marshal Lappeus and past and future mayors William Ladd, Thomas J. Holmes, and G. Collier Robbins), claiming that the recent election of a new chief fire engineer and assistant engineers had been illegally conducted. The petition said: "The ordinance reorganizing the Fire Department … [provides that] the voting shall be by ballot, and immediately on the closing of the polls the votes shall be publicly counted. … [However] the doors of the place of voting were closed and locked, and the counting of the ballots cast was done in secret. … We claim that by this illegality, the election to be a nullity, and that the Department is not bound to recognize the persons elected as their officers, and respectfully pray that you will ordain a new election."[92]

A committee of council members was appointed to look into these allegations. At the next meeting, committee chair William Blanchard asked for and was granted further time to report. No further mention of this investigating committee appears in subsequent council minutes, and Councilman Blanchard resigned in January 1860. By that time, the new chief and his assistants had long since been established in office.

The second incident involved a petition by Chinese residents asking the council to restrain some Chinese ladies of bad repute who they feared might cause disturbance of the peace. The *Oregonian* said a few "reputable" Chinese residents were "seeking the removal of a Chinese brothel by official action."[93] The council committee that investigated and reported back on September 7 said the problem was "not important enough to warrant further action."[94]

Near the end of his term, events coincided to thrust Mayor Stephen J. McCormick into one of the most memorable and action-packed moments in city government history.

Former mayor George Vaughn had defied a court order in January 1859 to cease building a wharf between Alder and Morrison. Now, in March 1860, Vaughn began constructing a building to enclose his wharf. This time the council ordered him to remove this levee obstruction within twenty-four hours. Instead of obeying this order, Vaughn hastily engaged a sizeable crew and completed the construction overnight. The *Oregonian* of March 24, 1860, reported it this way:

> Our city came very near being disgraced by a riot on Thursday last, in consequence of the refusal of Mr. G. W. Vaughn to recognize the authority of the city government over the public levee.
>
> The facts are briefly these: Mr. Vaughn claims to own the grounds in front of his store on Front street, by conveyance to him from Daniel H. Lownsdale and others. The city council claims the land as belonging to the city by right of donation from the original proprietors and under the decision of our courts. Mr. Vaughn built, during the past fall and winter, an extensive wharf upon the disputed ground, and was preparing to erect a building upon the wharf for commercial purposes.

> The city council, by an ordinance passed Tuesday night, instructed the city marshal to remove all obstructions from the wharf, after giving the parties interested twenty-four-hours notice. On Wednesday, Mr. Vaughn put a large gang of men at work, and before night had put up a building covering some fifty by twenty feet. The marshal … served upon him a copy of the ordinance, at the same time notifying the persons at work upon the building that they were trespassing upon the rights of the city. Neither Vaughn nor the persons employed paid the slightest attention to the city authorities, but *defiantly* trampled the ordinance underfoot.

The next morning, Mayor McCormick and Marshal Lappeus were preparing to remove the structure when they were arrested by Sheriff Addison Starr on a warrant to prevent destruction of private property. However, the charges against the two men were dismissed after a brief hearing. The mayor and marshal then led an indignant crowd of citizens to the waterfront, where they tore down the building in a few minutes. "Although there was intense excitement," the *Oregonian* concluded, "we are glad to chronicle the fact that there was no violence committed upon [any] person. …Some persons object to the manner of removing the building. If Mr. Vaughn had not, in a defiant manner, manifested a determination to erect the building, in an unusual way, and in such hot haste, with a full knowledge that the city authorities and a large portion of the people were opposed to it, and if he had not treated their authority with contempt by trampling their protest under his feet, the building would probably have been rolled off in place of demolished."[95]

Attorney William H. Farrar (former city attorney and future mayor) and Alonzo Leland (former councilman, recorder, and surveyor,[96] and now a newspaperman being sued by the city over public squares) printed a pamphlet that accused McCormick of fanning up "a flame of vengeance," arousing "passion and the mobocratic spirit of our community."[97]

Stephen McCormick could hardly have ended his mayoral career more dramatically. Few public officials in Portland's history can match the sheer audacity of Mayor McCormick's march toward the river to demolish a building, or George Vaughn's unbending defiance. For a time, former mayor Vaughn took up residence across the Columbia River in Vancouver in pique over being ejected from his holding on the levee.[98]

Chapter 9

Gold, the Levee, and Two Eccentric Mayors

1860 – 1864

Mayors

No. 11: April 1860 - April 1861

George Collier Robbins

No. 12: April 1861 – April 1862

John M. Breck

No. 13: April 1862 – April 1863

William Farrar

No. 14: April 1863 – April 1864

David Logan

Gold flowed into Portland from all over the Pacific Northwest following several discoveries of gold during the 1850s. Southern Oregon, British Columbia, Eastern Oregon, Idaho, Montana—throughout the Northwest, gold fever turned Willamette Valley farmers into miners as gold-seekers from all over the world passed through Portland on their way to and from the mines.[1]

No mayor personified this phenomenon better than George Collier Robbins, Portland's eleventh mayor. Although a watchmaker and jeweler in Portland, Robbins spent most of his life as a miner or a speculator in mining ventures. Robbins, a Republican who advertised himself as "independent," defeated Democratic candidate R. R. Thompson, who later amassed a fortune from Columbia River transportation.[2]

A month before the April 1860 election (and before Mayor McCormick's crew tore down George Vaughn's building on the levee), the *Oregonian* once again denounced city government:

> We have always had ... the most inefficient administration of our municipal affairs ... that ever cursed any corporate city. The reason and explanation of this is, that a few *old party hacks* have been elected and reelected to the city

> council without reference to qualification, honesty, or faithfulness to the public good. … Heretofore officers have been selected year after year with reference to availability, or in consideration of their devotion to party. The people have "paid dear for the whistle."[3]

The *Oregonian* left no doubt where it stood in the mayor's race the week before the election: "There is not a voter in the city who does not know the standing and character of G. C. Robbins, the independent candidate for mayor. His interests are all in the city; his honesty, ability and devotion to the welfare of a community, of which he has long been a member, cannot be questioned. He is the candidate of no political party."[4]

Robbins was also backed by future mayor Henry Failing, who later withdrew that support.[5] Robbins won by a 7 percent margin.[6]

Incumbent marshal James Lappeus was reelected in a three-way race in spite of the affidavits posted around town alleging that he had offered a one-thousand-dollar bribe to free convict Danford Balch the year before.[7] But he won by only thirteen votes.[8]

The new mayor told the council that the city's accounts were kept too loosely and unsystematically, noting that it was impossible to ascertain how much money had been spent for various activities. The city jail was unhealthy, he said, and urged the hiring of a night police force.[9] The council reelected Absalom Hallock as its president.[10]

Mayor George Collier Robbins. (Photo: OrHi #97639)

Townsite proprietor Daniel Lownsdale sent the council a letter offering to cease any new levee improvements except for a wharf already under construction, but made it clear he was not releasing any property rights. Rather, Lownsdale said, he was making the offer to stop further litigation and "for the sake of peace."[11] But court cases about the waterfront were already in progress, and Lownsdale's letter was laid aside. On October 17, 1860, the federal government granted certificates of levee ownership to Steven Coffin and Daniel Lownsdale under the Donation Land Claim Act.[12] This formality had been expected and did not settle any lawsuits in progress.

In Salem, state legislators struck out the Portland charter provision to pay council members three dollars per meeting, even though this compensation had substantially improved council attendance.[13] The legislature also said that any Portland city fireman who served for seven consecutive years was excused forever from state jury or militia service. Each Portland fire department company was to choose three delegates, and this board of delegates would elect its own officers and promulgate fire department rules. All firemen (they were still volunteers) would vote for a chief engineer and two assistants each December.[14]

That fall, presidential elector Thomas J. Dryer carried the news to Washington, D.C., that Oregon was casting its votes for Abraham Lincoln as president, albeit by a slim plurality. While in D.C., Dryer was appointed commissioner to the Sandwich Islands (now Hawaii). Portland thus lost a colorful character who had played a major role in public affairs since city government began.[15] As editor of the *Oregonian*, Dryer had informed, cajoled, rallied, and bombarded his readers with hyperbole, saving his strongest vitriol for the Democrats. In 1851, he had considered running for mayor; in 1857, he did run and was nearly elected. His rough-and-tumble character fit the era. By 1860, Dryer owed so much salary to his printer, Henry Pittock, that he handed over ownership of the *Oregonian* to pay this debt.[16] Pittock was to publish the *Oregonian* for half a century.[17] Pittock's name is preserved through the mansion he built overlooking downtown Portland, a commanding edifice now a city-owned historical landmark open for public viewing and private rentals.[18]

As if to prove that the newspaper had not lost its combative edge with Dryer gone, the *Oregonian* of December 29, 1860, lambasted city government on the front page:

> Was there ever a city government managed in such a worthless and imbecile manner as this our city of Portland? ... We have not a continuous street that is

> passable with a well loaded vehicle. Little botches of street improvements are made at private expense of a compact of mud and gravel joining on a patch of rotten plank, which is again connected with splashy logs, and all this again covered with reeking filth and puddled water in the winter and miasma and decay and noisome dust in summer. … [F]or the past few years the city has lost every [law]suit in which she was a party! … Either the common council have acted indiscreetly in engaging in the suits, or their legal advisor has failed in skill or attention in bringing or conducting them. . . .
>
> [C]urrent revenue of the city [is] sixteen thousand dollars. What becomes of this money? This year the city has bought no lands, erected no public buildings, dug no fire cisterns, bought no fire engines, paid no salaries, improved no streets, constructed no wharves, paid no back debts. … If the great bulk of the city's revenue is given for receiving and disbursing it … we think [the taxpayers] pay too dearly for the whistle, and would recommend the throwing up of the charter if a different order of things cannot be instituted.

City Attorney David W. Douthitt, who had held that appointive office for nearly two years, resigned shortly thereafter and moved away. In February, the council paid lawyer George H. Cartter one thousand dollars to represent the city in four ongoing lawsuits. Two of the suits had been initiated by the city and two were filed against the city; all four were critical land-title cases.[19]

In reminiscences about his pioneer days, G. Collier Robbins said that a watchmaker was needed when he arrived in Portland in fall 1852, so he opened a shop to fill that void. Usually clocks and watches simply needed cleaning, he found, and before long he learned enough about the trade to pick up "plenty of work." As his business prospered, he added more employees, and soon built one of the finest residences in the city. "With the discovery of gold on Frazer River … I added an assaying department and bought gold dust, as well as melting it down for others and establishing its value. As coin was exceedingly scarce, I added a mint … and issued fifty-dollar gold ingots … [which] were accepted as currency throughout the whole Northwest country. As the city grew, I … added a large stock of watches and jewels, guns and ammunition, as well as fishing tackle. Later I put in Indian trade goods and added a bank department. In the meantime I invested my surplus money in real estate and was soon one of the substantial citizens of the town."[20]

Yet when merchant Henry Failing was asked by a New York business associate for a credit reference for Robbins in 1865, he responded that Robbins had failed in Portland a few years before, though generally reputed to be rich.[21]

Robbins's autobiography describes his mining years in detail, but says nothing of debts or how he disposed of his flourishing Portland business or beautiful home.[22] His printed autobiography (which may have been abbreviated by his son) speaks no further of returning to Portland, although the *1870 Portland Directory* lists Robbins as a miner with a residence on North First Street between C and D streets.[23]

So the record on Mayor Robbins ends in ambiguity. Was he, as Henry Failing claimed, a business failure, a violent-tempered man who could not control his tongue, who left Portland owing a lot of money? Or was he an outdoor man who turned to mining because he found there "pleasure as well as profit" that gratified his "keen liking for the outdoors and the stirring life of the camps"? Robbins said the Wells-Fargo Company had furnished him a ten-thousand-dollar letter of credit, along with an open letter addressed to its agents requesting that they furnish Robbins all the facilities in their power.[24]

Robbins was nominated for a second term as Portland's mayor, but declined the nomination.[25] By the time a new mayor took the oath of office, Robbins was already camped out with hundreds of other miners on the banks of the Payette River in Idaho, waiting for deep mountain snow to melt so he could begin prospecting for gold.[26]

April 1861- April 1862

The *Oregonian*'s litmus test for candidates in the April 1861 city elections was simple: Were they sound on the levee question?

Col. William King nominated John Breck for mayor at a town meeting to nominate candidates for city offices. But before this nomination was voted upon, a committee of four from each of the three city wards was named to produce a slate of candidates for all city offices. After this group brought back their nominees (the list included Breck for mayor), not everyone was satisfied. So a rump group convened in council chambers to draw up its own slate. Incumbent George Collier Robbins was nominated at the council chambers meeting, but since Robbins declined to run, John Breck ended up as the sole mayoral nominee.

Both sets of names were printed in the next issue of the weekly *Oregonian*. Candidates judged to be sound on the levee question got a star in front of their names. Neither Col. William King nor his Ward 3 running mate, W. C. Hull, were honored with stars.[27] Both their opponents—former mayor William Ladd and incumbent councilman Erasmus Shattuck—were. Unfortunately for the cause of public levee ownership, King and Hull won out.[28]

Marshal Lappeus did not seek reelection. William Grooms, who had served as marshal seven years before, was returned to that post.[29]

❧

The city's twelfth mayor, John Breck, had already served as city assessor, county assessor, and city council clerk. Not only did he put in four years as a council member after his mayoral term ended, but he served as Multnomah County clerk and city assessor as well, a reversal of the usual sequence and an unusually long record of public service for the times.[30] Breck, from Pennsylvania and Wisconsin, worked as purser on various steamships when he first came to Oregon in 1850, and also engaged in merchandising. In 1860, his ship struck a reef and thirty-eight passengers and crew members were drowned. He was later hired as the steamship company's shipping agent in Portland. In 1855, he bought a lot across from the post office for two hundred dollars, which his wife sold for eighty thousand dollars in 1890.[31] (The equivalents

Mayor John Breck. (Photo: OrHi #223)

today would be a thirty-eight hundred dollar cost and a sales price of one and a half million dollars.)

Mayor Breck vetoed only two ordinances during his term, but both vetoes were overridden by the council. The first ordinance he vetoed fixed the salary of John. H. Mitchell, the new city attorney, at one thousand dollars per year. Previous city attorneys had simply billed the council for work performed. The next council would repeal this 1861 ordinance, and fix the city attorney salary at five hundred dollars per year.[32] Mitchell, a newcomer to Portland, would soon be well known as a commanding presence in Oregon Republican politics. He was to serve twenty years as Oregon's U.S. senator, and would be convicted in 1905 of receiving illegal timberland fees in one of the biggest scandals in Pacific Northwest history.[33]

The second Breck veto that the council overrode repealed an 1860 ordinance asserting that the strip of land east of Front Street was a public levee, and providing for "removing all obstructions therefrom."[34] Col. William King masterminded the veto override. This ordinance would be cited by Judge Deady in his ruling regarding the levee case, as would another ordinance passed by this council that "asserted said strip of land to be private property" and permitted private owners to build on their waterfront holdings.[35]

Federal Judge Matthew Deady issued his ruling against the city in its levee case against the Lownsdale family in early December 1861.[36] Deady said that Lownsdale "had not intended to have that piece of ground built upon, but intended it for wharves ... plainly implying a private ownership. " The judge also noted that the city could have joined the Parrish lawsuit after the city was incorporated in 1851, but failed to do so. The wharf being constructed on the levee by Daniel's son, James P. O. Lownsdale, would stay.[37]

The Brady map adopted by the city's second council in April 1852 had played a major role in the city's loss.[38] And although an 1853 lower court had ruled in favor of public ownership of the levee ("Public levies are almost as necessary ... as public streets," that opinion said[39]), the U. S. Supreme Court found that no federal law was applicable because the Oregon Donation Land Claims Act was not passed until 1850, and intentions of owners prior to that time did not pertain. In addition, Deady's 1861 opinion noted that the city had assessed waterfront lots as private property in 1854 and collected property taxes on them in both 1855 and 1858.[40]

Fifty years later city voters would approve the sale of municipal bonds to buy back parts of the levee for public docks.[41] Levee owner Stephen Coffin later dedicated a two-block portion of his riverbank to the city, reserving to himself only the right to operate a ferry thereon. The Coffin property was just south of today's Hawthorne bridge, between Jefferson and Clay.[42]

April 1862 - April 1863

The most mysterious mayor in the city's history now came to power. Consider:

- He was absent for at least half of his term as mayor, perhaps as much as two-thirds.
- People said there was a "non-understandable" element to his character.[43]
- He was said to be a brilliant man whose life seemed to have "no fruitage"; that he lived a "wasted life."[44]
- Only two mayors out of the forty-four in city history have no portrait or photograph hanging in the city hall mayors' gallery. One of the missing is Mayor William Farrar.[45]

A candid appraisal of Portland's enigmatic thirteenth mayor, William Farrar, is provided by John R. McBride, fellow-delegate with Farrar to the 1857 state constitutional convention. McBride says that he showed proposed language to forbid slavery in the state to William Farrar and David Logan for their approval before he took it to the convention as a whole. Both Farrar and Logan told him, "All right; go ahead."

> To my astonishment both voted against the proposition. Logan was an Old Line Whig and Farrar a professed free State Democrat. To say that I was amazed expressed my feelings lightly. "Too radical," was the only answer I received to my remonstrances ... (Another delegate) said, "It does not surprise me. ... Farrar has no convictions on any subject. He is as slippery as an eel, and can (not) be depended upon. ... He was elected on an independent ticket denouncing the Democratic party for trying to dodge the slavery issue, and then votes to dodge it himself."

McBride goes on in his remarks to ponder the character of William Farrar. He complimented Farrar's talents, but was puzzled by his actions.

> [Farrar], a native of New Hampshire, was a man of fine education and acquirements, a brilliant lawyer and powerful advocate. What his defect of character was I have always been at a loss to know. He was a man of fair

> complexion with light blonde hair. His bearing was elegant and his address winning, but there were always inconsistencies in his conduct that his friends could not explain, and he never attempted to explain anything himself—did not seem to realize that it was necessary. A noted instance of this occurred some years after the time of which I speak. He was invited to deliver the annual address at an anniversary of the state of New Hampshire in 1864. He was then living in Washington City. He accepted the invitation and was abundantly capable of performing its requirements with credit, for he was an elegant platform orator. Some weeks before the date of the services he disappeared from the city, and when the time for the journey came no one knew of his whereabouts, and when asked on his return about the anniversary proceedings, he quietly said he did not go and knew nothing of them.[46]

Mayor William Farrar, born in New Hampshire, is listed on the 1860 census at age thirty-four, living in Portland with his wife, Maria Farrar, age twenty-six. He had served a term as city attorney in 1854-55. He was a law partner of Lansing Stout, Oregon's congressman the previous term, against whom the city had a lawsuit pending regarding ownership of public squares.[47]

Portland was experiencing prosperous times when Farrar took office, while eastern states were suffering the ravages of the Civil War. An April *Oregonian* article describes Portland's situation: "Eighteen months ago any number of houses could be obtained for use, but to-day scarcely a shell can be found to shelter a family. Rents are up to an exorbitant figure, many houses contain two or more families, and the hotels and boarding-houses are crowded almost to overflowing. The town is full of people and more people are coming in. Buildings are going up in all parts of Portland, streets graded and planked, wharves stretching their proportions along the levees, and a general thrift and busy hum greet the ear, or attract the attention of a stranger upon every street and corner."[48]

> City government's record-keeping was indeed chaotic. The city had no city hall, no permanent staff, no central place to house its records. The mayor and councilmen were all volunteers.

As new mayor, William Farrar warned that he would reject all requests for city payment that were not fully documented. Farrar had queried the council clerk, recorder, and other city

On May 4, 1862, townsite proprietor Daniel Lownsdale died. His wife, Nancy, had predeceased him by eight years. Complicated land-ownership questions now became even more complicated because both Lownsdales had been married before, both had children by a previous marriage, and neither had prepared a written will. Daniel Lownsdale's 1860 federal land patent specified that he owned the east half of his claim and Nancy the west half; therefore, the park blocks designated on Lownsdale's 1850 townsite map were in Nancy's half.[49] It would be three more years before the courts ruled regarding conflicting land title claims filed on behalf of the Daniel and Nancy Lownsdale heirs.[50] Daniel's son by his first marriage, J. P. O. Lownsdale, was en route to Oregon from Indiana at the time of his father's death, and would stay in Portland to look after his estate.[51]

officials regarding a warrant for thirty-seven dollars and fifty cents he had been asked to countersign, though he could find no evidence that the claimant had ever served as a fire warden. In fact, he said, he could find no record of council proceedings whatsoever prior to 1858.[52]

An early ordinance approved by Mayor Farrar granted William S. Ladd and others a right-of-way to lay water pipes through the city streets. However, the ordinance was soon voided by the state supreme court because it granted unallowable "exclusive privileges" regarding a public thoroughfare.[53]

The *Oregonian* had previously castigated the council for its lack of attention to unhealthy conditions in the city:

> [Holes in the streets] or gutters, while in drying up exhibit a green surface, emit a poisonous and unhealthy air for breathing purposes.
>
> … [I]n many cases the offal of the kitchen, vegetables, dish water, suds, and other articles, which speedily corrupt and putrefy, are thrown about in the yards or in holes, where they rot and send out a stench and offensive air—causing contagion and death.
>
> In other cities there are Health committees, which, at certain seasons of the year, are required to examine the lots, the yards, the outhouses and the cellars in the city, to see that there are no causes to produce sickness, and if there are, to order their prompt removal, or subject those concerned to severe fines.[54]

A situation was soon to occur which demonstrated the wisdom of the *Oregonian*'s warning. In June 1862, the Willamette River flooded its banks and inundated Front Street.[55] A wave of smallpox threatened the city soon thereafter. In mid-June, the council required a red flag to be conspicuously placed on any building that housed a person with smallpox or another dangerous and contagious disease. Fines of fifty to one hundred dollars were mandated for failure to notify the city of such contagious diseases within twelve hours. Fines also applied to anyone who failed to put up a red flag, or who tore one down.[56]

In early July, council leased new chambers: a large second-story room in the Wasserman Building. This brick edifice, only two years old, was located mid-block on the west side of Front Street, between Alder and Washington.*57*

On July 30, Mayor Farrar notified the council that he planned to be absent from the city for three months to pursue a business engagement that had existed before the election. The council approved this absence for August, September, and October. Now began the longest acting-mayor term in the city's history. For over eight months, from August 1862 to April 1863, recorder J. F. McCoy signed every law passed by the council, a total of seventeen separate ordinances evenly spaced over the rest of the year. McCoy sent several messages to the council in his capacity as acting mayor. This author found no evidence that Mayor Farrar returned at any time during the last two-thirds of his term, or requested an extension of his leave. By 1864, Farrar was living in the nation's capital, as previously noted in the McBride quote. Perhaps he went east and simply decided to stay.[58]

J. F. McCoy deserves due credit for his long service as interim mayor. Even though he never bore the mayor's title, he performed mayoral duties longer than either Mayor Allison Bonnell or Mayor Simon Marye in the city's second year, or William Ladd in his second tenure as mayor. In May 1858, while serving as a Multnomah County deputy sheriff, McCoy had been shot and severely crippled.[59] He was elected to city office five times—twice as assessor and three times as recorder.[60]

One of the laws McCoy approved during this period authorized C. S. Mills to place numbers on all houses in the city limits and to collect thirty-seven and a half cents per house from each owner or occupant for doing so. Council added the word "North" to all street names in Couch's Addition.[61]

Hawkers who met incoming vessels and called out verbal advertisements for taverns, hotels, restaurants, and other public houses would henceforth have to pay a license fee of ten dollars per quarter.[62] To raise additional revenue, the city sought and received approval from the state legislature to tax wharfingers (those who operated wharves) and to levy property taxes on land not yet laid out in lots or blocks. This charter amendment was approved by the legislature in October 1862.[63]

Other ordinances adopted by the council and approved by Acting Mayor McCoy concerned licensing of auctioneers; prevented butchering within city limits; authorized purchase of a lot for Columbian Fire Company No. 3; recognized Protection Fire Company No. 4; licensed taverns and porters; levied a tax of three mills, and provided for the grading of public squares.[64]

April 1863 - April 1864

The city's next mayor was another brilliant lawyer who never achieved his full potential: David Logan.

Both William Farrar and David Logan had previously served as city attorney for one-year terms. Both were delegates to the 1857 state constitutional convention, where Logan, "with his sarcastic tongue, made many an opponent subside in silence."[65] Both men failed to support their colleague's proposal for constitutional language to prohibit slavery. Both were eloquent orators who ascended to the mayor's office in their late thirties. There the similarities end.

Mayor David Logan. (Photo: OrHi #38326)

David Logan, son of Abe Lincoln's law partner in Springfield, Illinois, was an avid Republican. He was a leading Whig of his era, and sought four times to represent Oregon in the nation's capital, always unsuccessfully, partly because his reputation as a superb lawyer was marred by his proclivity to drink.[66] An overview of mileposts in Logan's life reveals how often his aspirations were frustrated:

Oct 1849: Arrived in Oregon, at age twenty-five; first operated ferry, then practiced law;

June 1854: Elected to state legislature;

Aug 1854: Accused of public drunkenness and rape of an Indian woman;[67]

April 1857: Appointed Portland city attorney for a one-year term;

Aug 1857: Elected as a delegate to the Oregon constitutional convention;

June 1858: Candidate for U. S. Senate, unsuccessful;

June 1859: Candidate for Congress; lost by sixteen votes to Lansing Stout;

June 1860: Candidate for Congress; lost by seventy-six votes to George Shiel;

Sept 1861: Requested a federal judicial appointment; turned down by Lincoln;

April 1863: Elected mayor of Portland;

June 1868: Candidate for Congress, lost to Joseph S. Smith by 1,199 votes;

1871: Retired from practice of law to a farm in Yamhill County;

March 1874[69]: Died at age forty-nine, lauded as "the state's best trial lawyer."[70]

> In February 1864, a group of citizens established the Library Association of Portland, forerunner of the free public library that would come thirty-eight years later. Initially, the library was open only to those who paid a yearly subscription.[68] (See Appendix B for a history of Portland's previous public library founded in 1850.)

In his 1863 mayoral message, Mayor Logan gave an upbeat assessment of the city's state of affairs: "From a small and obscure village … the progress of twelve years finds us a large, flourishing and rapidly improving commercial city, bidding defiance to all competitors."[71]

Two noteworthy technological advances came during David Logan's tenure: a macadamized road and a telegraph wire connecting Portland to San Francisco.

A Scotsman named J. L. McAdam had invented an elevated road surface composed of bottom rocks for drainage and topped by compacted small broken rocks mixed with tar.[72] Macadamized roads were proving to be a significant improvement in rainy Oregon. In mid-July, the council gave the Portland and Milwaukie Macadamized Road Company (PMMRC) permission to operate a tollbooth within city limits.[73] The PMMRC then built a six-mile macadamized road south along the Willamette River to connect with a ferry to Milwaukie directly across the river. Present-day Macadam Avenue follows this early route.[74]

> A glorious celebration occurred March 8, 1864, commemorating an exchange of telegraph messages between Mayor Logan and the mayor of Portland, Maine. The first dispatch from San Francisco had arrived three days earlier, in time for the *Oregonian* to issue a special edition with news from New York only twenty hours old. The thirteen-year-old city of Portland now had a direct connection to the outside world.[75]

A popular racetrack, roadhouse, and hotel called the White House were built near road's end. By the 1870s and until the turn of the century, the White House was a fashionable destination for Portland's social set, many of whom raced their horses both on the race track and on the macadamized road.[76]

A fond epitaph for Mayor Logan was penned by author and railroad pioneer Joseph Gaston in 1911: "[O]f all the lawyers of Oregon of that time, or since, no man was the equal of David Logan in trying a cause, in everyday work in the court room, in readiness for every emergency, and for matchless ability in an appeal to the jury of twelve men. ... Logan was sincere and honest to the core. He could not tolerate deceit. He could not beg favors or solicit votes—and for that he did not succeed in Oregon politics."[77]

Note that Gaston did not equate serving as mayor of Portland with success in Oregon politics. It would be one hundred and five years before another lawyer, Neil Goldschmidt, would parlay his accomplishments as Portland mayor to election as governor of Oregon.

Chapter 10

Sacred Money, Apoplexy, and Spirituous Liquor

1864 – 1869

Mayors

No. 15: April 1864 - June 1865

Henry Failing (one year, three months, elected)

June 1865 – Nov. 1866

Henry Failing (one year, three months, elected)

No. 16: Nov. 1866 - June 1867

Thomas J. Holmes (eight months, appointed and elected)

No. 17: July 1867 - June 1868

James A. Chapman (one year, appointed)

No. 18: July 1868 - June 1869

Hamilton Boyd (one year, elected)

Mayor Henry Failing left an outstanding record of accomplishment as the city's fifteenth mayor. However, his second tenure as the city's twenty-first mayor nearly ten years later was to be beset by problems, though mostly through no fault of his own.[1]

Like former mayor William Ladd, Henry Failing acquired great wealth and gave much back to the community. He devoted time and money to the Portland Public Schools, Library Association of Portland, Port of Portland Commission, Portland & Tualatin Plains Road Company, Portland & Milwaukie Macadamized Road Company, River View Cemetery, and many other organizations and causes. Twenty years after he first served as mayor, in 1885, he was chosen unanimously as president of the Portland Water Committee that was to acquire the city's Bull Run water supply, one of the most successful and important long-term endeavors in the city's history. Failing was to serve as president of that board for fourteen years.

Henry Failing and his father, Josiah Failing, not only served as Portland's only father and son mayors, but were the only two mayors

Mayor Henry Failing. (Photo: OrHi #53226)

related to each other in any way. Josiah Failing, the "Dean of Front Street," completed his term as mayor ten years before Henry assumed the same office. The same year Henry was first elected mayor, the elder Failing, then fifty-eight, turned over management of the family store to his thirty-year-old son.[2]

At age seventeen, when he arrived by boat with his father and ten-year-old brother Edward, Henry was already experienced in the business world. He had left school at age twelve to work for New York City merchandising firms, and there had become an expert accountant. In Portland, he worked in his father's general merchandise store. At age twenty-four, he married Emily Corbett, sister of his friend Henry W. Corbett. The two Henrys later became business partners, first as owners of Corbett, Failing & Co., merchants, and later as bankers. In 1869, they bought controlling interest (along with Josiah Failing) in the First National Bank from Addison and Lewis Starr. Henry Failing served as that bank's president for the next thirty years.[3]

Henry Failing introduced dramatic changes to the internal workings of Portland's city government. Processes he instituted—forecasting and budgeting of revenues, spreading costs of street and sewer improvements, appropriating money in advance for designated purposes, and tracking of approved expenditures through ordinances—are practices still reflected in city governance today. Most of them were standard municipal procedures that Portland had not yet adopted. Failing's "marvelous judgment and powers of exact estimation" were

Mayor Henry Failing lived in this mansion, located kitty-corner (southeast) from today's Pioneer Courthouse Square. (Photo: OrHi #28186)

renowned; he could project the estimated receipts and expenditures for an organization with incredible accuracy.[4]

The new mayor's first priority was the condition of city streets. Portland's streets were "a reproach to the city and its inhabitants," Mayor Failing told the council in his inaugural message. "So pressing is the necessity for some action that all other improvements seem of little consequence in comparison."[5]

Failing proposed a charter amendment to require owners of real estate "permanently benefited and enhanced in value" to cover the entire cost of grading and paving adjoining streets. He asked that money be set aside in a special account whenever an expenditure was authorized, and "held sacred for that purpose only." Contract terms would be more advantageous to the city, he said, if contractors were assured that city funds would be available to pay bills when due.[6] In the past, vendors had sometimes been left dangling for months, having to hound the city to pay its bills.

By the time Failing resigned as mayor in November 1866, the council had passed two hundred thirty ordinances during his tenure. Compare this number with his predecessors; see Table 5.

Other officials who served with Henry Failing undoubtedly deserve credit for this speed-up of city business—council president John Sutton, council member and former- mayor Addison Starr, city attorney Joseph Dolph,[7] recorder J. F. McCoy (who had served as acting mayor during a considerable portion of William Farrar's term), and other city officials.[8]

The council named Marshal Henry L. Hoyt as the city collector because the two offices seemed to fit well together. Combined, the two positions paid Hoyt a good income, but also gave him a dangerous degree of control over establishments that sold alcohol—an invitation to graft and corruption.[9]

Crime was a growing problem for Portland. Criminal elements from the southern states had emigrated west to avoid the Civil War draft. Escapees from the Oregon state penitentiary south of downtown Portland often gravitated toward the central city, which was a convenient target for ready cash. (The penitentiary would be moved to Salem in 1866.) As population increased, the number of arrests rose and the recorder's court docket was crowded, even without a regular city police force.[10]

That fall, after Marshal Hoyt warned that thieves and roughs would be wintering in Portland, Failing hired two police officers at a salary of one hundred dollars each per month. This was the first time any full-time, salaried police officer had served the city, although the state legislature had adopted a new criminal code the month before which encouraged, but did not require, police attendance at "exposed places" to *prevent* crime—as opposed to arresting criminals after the fact—an emerging national concept.[11]

City ordinances passed in Mayor Failing's first year included a special tax levy to pay off prior city debts totaling fifteen thousand dollars; a second special levy of fifteen thousand dollars for a machine to dredge Portland's harbor; a five hundred dollar appropriation to remove snags from the Willamette River; codification of city ordinances; setting the width of city sidewalks at fifteen feet for eighty-foot-wide streets and at twelve feet for sixty-foot-wide streets; imposing and regulating various license fees; providing for gas street lamps; appropriating funds to defray

Table 5. Ordinances passed, 1861-66

John Breck	1861-62	6 ordinances during this one-year term
Farrar (and McCoy)	1862-63	28 ordinances during this one-year term
David Logan	1863-64	14 ordinances during this one-year term
Henry Failing	1864-66	92 ordinances per year (average)

the cost of "obsequies" after the death of President Lincoln; authorizing construction of a hose and bell tower for Fire Engine Company No. 4; preventing horses and cattle from running at large; and appropriating money for a Fourth of July celebration.[12]

To defray the expense of improving twelve blocks of Front Street from Morrison to Harrison, property owners were assessed twenty-eight thousand dollars.[13] The handwritten lien docket listing these owners, property descriptions, and amounts owed was amazingly similar in methodology, assumptions, and process to the city's Local Improvement District lien dockets of the year 2001, except, of course, that the lists were prepared with computers and laser printers in 2001.[14]

The council also authorized payment of two hundred dollars to Judge Matthew Deady for drafting a major overhaul of the city charter, a document approved by the state legislature with little debate.[15] The new charter, the city's fourth, specified two-year terms for the mayor, recorder, treasurer, and assessor, and staggered three-year terms for the nine council members. Councilmen from each of the three wards drew lots to see how long each would serve; thereafter, only one council position from each ward would expire every year. City elections would henceforth take place in mid-June, rather than April, with terms beginning ten days after election day. The terms of all incumbent officials were extended two and a half months to conform to the new election cycle.

The charter comprised twenty-six pages of text compared to only nine pages in the charter it replaced. It was a substantive improvement over previous charters in organization and detail, with subject matter grouped under titles and subtitles in each of its ten chapters.

The new charter stipulated that street improvements could be charged against properties that benefited directly, by placing a lien—a legal claim against the property that allowed the city to foreclose if the debt remained unpaid—against benefited properties. Two-thirds of adjacent property owners had to remonstrate before an improvement project would be abandoned—twice the percentage previously required.

The mayor was named *ex officio* council president to preside over council meetings, bringing the mayor back into regular contact with council after eleven years of isolation as a completely separate executive branch. The mayor could still veto ordinances, but had no council vote. A city debt limit of fifty thousand dollars was established.

Not only was the allowable property tax levy doubled to 1 percent of value, but an additional two-year levy was authorized to pay for the cost of dredging the Willamette River and otherwise improving navigation.[16] The council was authorized to fill vacancies in the mayor's office, and also to appoint the marshal.[17] Many unforeseen problems were soon to arise because of these appointment powers.

In December of the following year, the legislature authorized the council to appropriate private property if it was necessary to do so in order to establish and widen streets and alleys.[18]

June 1865 - November 1866

The public was so satisfied with Mayor Henry Failing's efficient administration that he was reelected for another term in June 1865 with only five dissenting votes—seven hundred eighty-five votes for Failing; five for others—the most unanimity ever recorded in Portland's mayoral history. Failing was a Republican, but believed municipal elections and activities ought to be nonpartisan, a principle which guided his actions and pleased the public.[19]

Council business included approving a contract for sewers;[20] more street projects;[21] erection of cisterns for use by the fire department; erection of lamp posts for gas lights; rental of space for a city dog pound; and specifying where shade and ornamental trees bordering streets could be located.[22]

Mayor Failing warned the council that police services and justice-of-the-peace court were costing five hundred dollars a month more than fines collected—an alarming situation, since these two functions were expected to pay for themselves. The council therefore increased liquor licenses to five hundred dollars a year; the same ordinance prohibited the hiring of females in saloons.[23] Both provisions of this ordinance proved unpopular, and many Portlanders lobbied the council heavily for its repeal, albeit unsuccessfully, during Failing's tenure.

Eastside farmer Colburn Barrell offered to sell the city Lone Fir Cemetery for four thousand dollars, but the council turned down the offer.[24] Lone Fir was located on a thirty-acre site with a partial meadow and good drainage on the east side of the river. The council said the distance from the city was too great, even though agitation for a Willamette River bridge was mounting and many Portlanders were ferrying back and forth to use the cemetery.[25]

For the first time, the mayor's position was not on the 1866 ballot because mayoral terms had been extended to two years. However, Marshal Henry Hoyt, formerly elected, now had to win a council appointment to retain his badge. On the thirteenth council ballot, Hoyt kept his job.[26]

In October the legislature authorized a method for financing sewer projects in the city: property owners could now be assessed for sewers and drains, with costs to be spread to owners of benefited properties in the same way street improvements were handled.

November 1866 - June 1867

After serving two and a half years, Mayor Henry Failing resigned in November 1866. Perhaps the mayor's job was taking too much time away from other business interests; council records do not give his reason. As specified by the 1864 charter, council members were charged with filling eight months of Failing's unexpired term until the next general election.[27]

The council chose vocal and excitable Thomas J. Holmes in a five to four council vote over well-to-do R. R. Thompson, who had lost his 1860 bid for mayor against George Collier Robbins.[28] Holmes had served as city marshal, assessor, street commissioner, collector, council clerk *pro tem*, and council member. This nemesis of Shubrick Norris[29] was the city's second foreign-born mayor.

Holmes was born in the county of Norfolk, England. He emigrated to New York City with his parents at age eleven, apprenticed as a shoemaker, started his own shop in Jersey City, married, and had six children. When his wife died, Holmes went to sea and ended up in Portland soon after the California gold rush. He started out as a shoemaker in Portland, but soon branched into real estate.[30] He was forty-seven years old and a wealthy man by the time he was appointed

Mayor Thomas J. Holmes. (Photo: OrHi #97630)

mayor. He had recently completed three years as an elected school board member.[31]

Mayor Failing was barely out the door before liquor license fees were reduced with the new mayor's approval, and women were again permitted to work in places where alcohol was sold.[32]

In his January 1867 message to the council, Mayor Holmes said an economic slowdown was affecting all areas of Portland business, and urged the use of convicts for city labor. Chinese "bawdy houses" should either be removed or heavily taxed, he said, and the police force should be reduced by one person. The boarding of prisoners ought to be contracted out to the lowest-bidding hotel, and the marshal and recorder placed on salary instead of a fee-for-service basis, so that a limit could be placed on the flow of money going to these officials instead of the city treasury.[33]

Holmes soon vetoed a council ordinance that would have *increased* the police force, and the council lacked the votes to override his veto. However, the council did override his veto of two other ordinances—one setting the marshal's compensation and another establishing a day and night police force.[34]

In early 1867, Congress appropriated sixty-six thousand dollars to improve the Willamette River below Portland by dredging.[35] That spring, Multnomah County's first courthouse was completed at S.W. Fourth and Main, where the present courthouse still stands.[36]

In order to continue as mayor, Holmes had to stand for election in June. He drew a Republican opponent with a well-known Portland name: James P. O. Lownsdale, the thirty-seven-year-old son of townsite proprietor Daniel Lownsdale.[37] Lownsdale had lived in Portland for five years, administering his father's estate. He had been appointed to vacancies on both the city council and the Multnomah County Commission, and had subsequently been elected to complete both those terms.[38] The *Oregonian* championed his candidacy against Democratic Mayor Holmes: "The Democrats of this city have been attempting for the past six months to ingratiate themselves with the people, by keeping up a furious out-cry against the extravagance of the [former] party in power, and clamoring for retrenchment. Ever since the present Mayor entered upon the duties of his office, the citizens of Portland have been harangued almost weekly about high taxation, exorbitant pay to city officials, and corrupt and wanton squandering of the people's money." "High sounding talk" by the Democrats was "utterly false and empty," the newspaper said. The truth could be found in the city archives that would reveal these Democratic leaders as "unscrupulous demagogues." The truth would show that prior to Mayor Failing's tenure:"... every department of the city government was managed and controlled by the Democratic party—and that party by Hallock, Holmes & Co. ... Let not the citizens of Portland be deceived by [their] specious falsehood[s]. The first message of Mayor Failing, in April 1864, disclosed the somewhat alarming truth, that it was impossible to arrive at any satisfactory understanding of the condition of the city finances, because there was *no record of the indebtedness of the city.*"[39]

The following day, the *Oregonian* attacked Mayor Holmes personally: "For several years he refused to pay his taxes, so strongly did he favor 'economical reform.' He always opposed street improvements, doubtless also through consideration of 'economy.' Every measure looking to permanent improvements in the city has encountered his opposition. His ideas of 'economy' are to pay no taxes as long as he can help it; to let the streets remain in a filthy and almost impassable condition (as they were two or three years ago,) and to rent his tumble-down shanties throughout the city, whereof he has a great number, to Chinese .... This is his record in favor of 'reform.'"[40]

On June 17, 1867, Thomas J. Holmes won his election for mayor over Lownsdale by a slim margin.

Now occurred one of the most bizarre twists in the history of city government. After addressing supporters with his "customary vigor" on election night, and after receiving congratulations from friends as he went about his business all the next day, Mayor Holmes was stricken with apoplexy (a stroke) and died within a few hours.[41] He was forty-eight years old.

The shocked community reacted with bipartisan goodwill in memory of this indomitable Englishman who had played such an active role in the life of his adopted city.

July 1867 - June 1868

The immediate challenge facing the council was to fill the mayor's office until the next election—one full year. The process that now took place created a mix-up in some historical records. At least three references,[42] including the thick volume that constitutes the *1923 Mayor's Report to the City*, credit Aaron E. Wait as being the next mayor, albeit only for a week (July 24-31, 1867). But Wait was never mayor of Portland.

Wait enjoyed a solid reputation as a lawyer and judge. He had edited the *Spectator* newspaper for a year while practicing law when he first came to Oregon in 1848. He had drawn up the deed by which Daniel Lownsdale purchased half-interest in the Portland townsite from Francis Pettygrove for five thousand dollars' worth of leather in 1848.[43] At the

The letter that Wait sent to the council says:

I was duly notified that at your last regular meeting you elected me to the office of Mayor of this city to fill the vacancy caused by the death of the Hon. T. J. Holmes.

Accept my heartfelt thanks for the unsought and unexpected honor thus conferred upon me.

My failure to qualify within the time prescribed by law leaves the office still vacant; and it is due that I assure you that I would have accepted the office had I felt that the condition of my health would have permitted it.

I cordially concur in the ardent desire of our excellent, and deeply lamented, late Mayor, to see the city expenditures regulated by strict economy, and except for the reason before stated, I should have cheerfully accepted the office, and have given to its duties my best abilities.

I am, very respectfully yours,
Portland, July 30th 1867
Aaron E. Wait[45]

first election after Oregon became a state, he had been elected to the Supreme Court of the State of Oregon and served three years as its first chief justice (1859-62).

Wait was the council's first choice, but he declined to serve.[44]

When Wait turned down its nomination, the council had to search elsewhere for a new mayor. With all nine council members present at its July 31 meeting, five votes would constitute a majority. Attorney John Mitchell received four votes on the first ballot, Dr. James Chapman three votes, and former mayor Stephen McCormick two votes. On the next five ballots, Mitchell and Chapman tied, four votes to four, while one council member stuck with McCormick. On the seventh ballot, one councilman switched to Chapman, one ballot was blank, and the five-to-three decision was made.[46]

❧

Dr. James A. Chapman, born and educated in New York State, had enlisted in the union army in 1861. He came to Oregon the following year as an army surgeon, then practiced medicine in partnership with Dr. William H. Watkins for many years, and was listed as one of seven druggists in Portland by 1870. During Governor LaFayette Grover's tenure (1870-77), Chapman would be appointed surgeon-general of the Oregon militia.[47]

Mayor James Chapman. (Photo: OrHi#38385)

Chapman was to serve three interspersed terms—as Portland's seventeenth, twenty-second, and twenty-fifth mayors, the only mayor in Portland's history to do so. The first time, he filled half the unexpired two-year term of T. J. Holmes. The second time, he was elected for a two-year term (1875-77), and the third time for a three-year term (1882-85).

"One of the worst mayors in Portland's history" was Portland historian E. Kimbark MacColl's conclusion about Dr. Chapman. The reason for this negative assessment will be evident to the reader during Chapman's last term. But as bad as Mayor Chapman would prove to be, he most likely did less damage than would have political kingpin John H. Mitchell, because Chapman was neither as sophisticated nor as powerful. Of Mitchell, MacColl says, "No one in Oregon's history has ever aroused more popular enthusiasm or more intense animosity."[48]

Another council brouhaha developed before Chapman began his term. This time it concerned the appointment of a marshal. Ironically, Mayor Holmes's criticism of excessive fees collected by the marshal motivated several people to seek that appointment.

At the council's initial July 24 meeting, members[49] voted *forty-three* times for marshal before adjourning without reaching a majority.[50] Here came the sticky part: Councilman A. Rosenheim was one of the nominees for the position, and had received four votes (probably including his own)—only one vote short of a majority—in thirty-one of the forty-three votes. At its next meeting, on the very first ballot, the council awarded Rosenheim the needed five votes to appoint him marshal.[51] But Marshal Henry Hoyt refused to surrender his office. Rosenheim had been illegally elected, he said.

Recorder J. J. Hoffman was thrust in the middle of this stand-off between Hoyt and Rosenheim. As justice of the peace, Hoffman issued fines and warrants that were orders a marshal or constable had to carry out. Hoffman attempted to sidestep the issue by dealing only with the Multnomah County constable at first, but by August 10, he returned to working with Hoyt as the *de facto* city marshal.[52] The council then filed suit against Henry Hoyt to vacate his office, and passed an ordinance to prevent anyone from "improperly retaining books, paper, etc., belonging to the city."[53]

The *Oregonian* sided with Hoyt, categorizing Rosenheim's election as illegal. His selection had been arranged by "corrupt leaders of a corrupt party," the newspaper said—even though Rosenheim had been elected as a Union [Republican] party member two years before. Rosenheim had apparently started voting with the Democrats shortly after joining the council.[54]

In the midst of this quarrel, a Portland police officer was killed in the line of duty for the first time. Officer Thomas G. O'Connor was shot after a running gunfight with Frank Miguel in front of the Oro Fino Saloon, an establishment owned by former (and future) marshal James Lappeus. Miguel, who had shot at police officers before, died on August 23, 1867, and Officer O'Connor died a week later. The council voted three months' salary paid to O'Connor's widow and family.[55]

The Hoyt - Rosenheim controversy was heard by the Multnomah County Circuit Court twice, and appealed to the Oregon Supreme Court. The supreme court ruled that Rosenheim's appointment was illegal. "The court found that the offices of marshal and councilman were incompatible and could not be held by one person, and that it was contrary to the policy of law for an officer to use his official appointing power to place himself in office," an *Oregon Historical Quarterly* article says.[56] Hoyt, therefore, remained as city marshal until a successor could be named and qualified.

Marshal Hoyt resigned in late September. In early October, the council selected David Jacobi, a thirty-seven-year-old Bavarian bookkeeper,[57] as his replacement.

Mayor Chapman's mayoral message stressed the need for street improvements and enthusiastically advocated adopting the Nicholson paving process for all principal city streets.[58] The city had been experimenting with this method, invented by Samuel Nicholson of Boston, which was purported to provide a lasting road surface. Parallel-sided wood blocks were laid in a checkerboard pattern, some lower and some higher. The lower blocks and narrow grooves were filled with small broken stones, then covered with melted tar or pitch. The *1866 City Directory* summarized the argument for the Nicholson process: "No improvement which had hitherto been attempted in this city seemed to meet with such combined opposition, when first contemplated, as the Nicholson pavement, and yet … no improvement yet made gives more general satisfaction … adding so materially to the appearance of the streets whereon it has been introduced—presenting at once a clean and healthy appearance to the city."[59]

Chapman also noted that the recently published auditor's report showed city financial affairs in "very satisfactory condition" with a treasury balance of over eight thousand dollars and outstanding license renewals and other revenues still to be collected.[60] Mayor Failing's

A private organization founded in December 1867 was to play an influential role in Portland history. The Arlington Club had no official connection to city government, but the thirty-five founding members of this exclusive all-male social club included Mayor James Chapman, former mayors Henry Failing and William Ladd, and past or future council members Simeon Reed, Lewis Starr, John McCraken, Alexander Ankeny, R. R. Thompson, Al Zieber, and Thomas Carter. The Arlington Club's one-hundred-year history notes: "No history of Portland is complete without reference to many of those members."[61]

The club founders agreed to pay one hundred dollars each to furnish "suitable rooms" for the organization. Ironically, the site on which the Arlington Club built its permanent home in 1892 (West Park at Alder) was part of the originally platted public park blocks awarded to the heirs of Nancy Lownsdale in an 1865 federal ruling. The attorney who had won that Lownsdale court case against the city, William W. Page, was an Arlington Club founder. With no apparent regret for the public's loss of those blocks, the club's history proudly notes, "The Arlington Club probably would not be where it is but for the case he [Page] won."[62]

businesslike approach had placed the city on the soundest financial basis in its history.

Of the ninety-three ordinances passed during Mayor Chapman's first term, most concerned street improvements, street grades, street repairs, and reports by the surveyor about new streets. The city was expanding westward. Plans were begun to start building Eighth, Ninth, and Tenth streets. Construction of four more fire cisterns was authorized.[63] By council decree, awnings and awning posts could no longer extend out beyond sidewalks.[64]

The street commissioner reported that gates around the public square fences had failed to "keep out the cows and other animals running at large in the city," so he had nailed up the gates. He recommended that these gates be replaced with turnstiles, and that two inches of coarse sand be laid on top of the gravel walks.[65]

The council authorized spending five hundred dollars to purchase a sturdy safe for the city auditor, four hundred dollars for the safe and one hundred dollars for putting it in place.[66]

One of the biggest Oregon battles of the century now began, a fight over the location of a railroad track to run from Portland to northern California. The controversial issue was whether the line should run down the west or east side of the Willamette River.

Planning for Oregon railroads had started as early as 1850, but no construction had yet taken place. The 1864 Oregon legislature had offered two hundred fifty thousand dollars to any company that would build a line from Portland to Eugene, but the carrot had not been large enough to draw any takers. In 1866, Congress authorized land grants of seven million acres ("worth about five million dollars at the time";[67] nearly seventy million adjusted for inflation today) to two companies, one of which would build north from Marysville, California, near Sacramento, while the other would build south from Portland, to meet somewhere in the middle.

"Opposition to the giving of the public domain to corporations had not yet developed," notes Scott's 1890 *History of Portland*. Proponents for congressional passage of this railroad bill stressed the vulnerability of the Pacific coastline, arguing that a rail line parallel to the coast would allow "speedy dispatch of troops to any point threatened."

A California corporation had already formed to build north from Marysville, California.[68] A group of Oregon businessmen now organized the Oregon Central Railroad (OCR) to construct the northern part of the line. Incorporators included former and future councilmen Henry Corbett, R. R. Thompson, Simeon Reed, John McCraken, and Erasmus Shattuck; former mayoral candidate Joseph Showalter Smith; and former city attorney John Mitchell (who was later to defect to the opposition company as a lead advisor and lawyer).[69]

The Portland city council supported the OCR project by agreeing to pay interest on two hundred fifty thousand dollars' worth of bonds over a period of twenty years.[70] Captain John Couch and his brother-in-law, former city treasurer George Flanders, donated ten city blocks of their north Portland claim for a railroad depot and terminal.[71] The railroad route would run south along the west side of the Willamette River, then west and south through Washington, Yamhill, Polk, and Benton counties to Eugene.

The conflict began when a second company formed to claim the same land grant under the same name and proposed to run its line down the east side of the Willamette. The eastside group filed a lawsuit alleging a secret fraudulent agreement and other irregularities by the westside company.

While that lawsuit worked its way through the courts, the federal district court ruled that Portland government could not pay interest on OCR's bonded indebtedness because that would violate its charter debt limit of fifty thousand dollars. Interest on the bonds for twenty years, the court found, would constitute a debt of more than three hundred thousand dollars. City Ordinance #468 authorizing payment of interest was therefore declared void—a major blow to the westsiders.

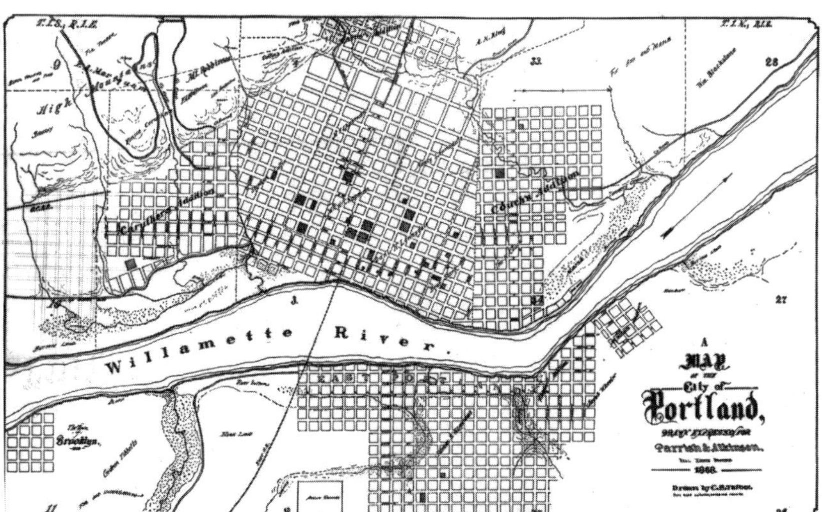

Portland in 1868—a rare old town map. (Photo: OrHi #25717)

On April 15, 1868, the westsiders broke ground for construction of their railroad. A large crowd was on hand for the ceremony. The route started at the head of Fourth Street in the Caruthers Addition and skirted the west Portland hills by running south along the river to Lake Oswego, where it turned west to Forest Grove in Washington County.

The next day, an even grander ceremony took place on the east side of the river, about three-quarters of a mile south of Portland's downtown, five hundred yards inland from the water.[72] There, promoters turned the first shovel of dirt for an eastside railroad line.

Mayor Chapman's first term thus ended quietly, completely overshadowed by the race to build a railroad.

July 1868 - June 1869

Voters chose Hamilton Boyd to complete the second half of Holmes's two-year term. Boyd was Portland's eighteenth mayor and the last to be popularly elected to a one-year term.

Hamilton Boyd served simultaneously as Portland mayor and as a Multnomah County commissioner,[73] the only mayor to do so in city history.[74] It is therefore particularly surprising that, even after this double exposure, no portrait or photograph of Mayor Boyd had been found as of April 2001.[75] Mayor Boyd not only served one year as Portland's mayor and two years as a Multnomah County commissioner, but he spent the remaining fourteen years of his life in Portland, where he was living at the home of his son when he died in 1883.[76]

The 1870 census shows Hamilton Boyd, age thirty-nine, living in Portland with his wife, Carolyn, age thirty-six, and son Henry, age fifteen, all born in New York State. Boyd was listed as a bank clerk with assets of forty-two hundred dollars. Neither his mother nor father was of foreign birth.[77] Boyd had come to Oregon around 1860, and was later the lead accountant for Ladd & Tilton bank for several years.[78] As a former assistant Multnomah County clerk and city council clerk, Boyd would have understood how government operated—useful experience for tackling the issues of crime, police protection, and the high cost of city services that would face him as mayor.

The new mayor had been in office for "forty days and forty nights" when the *Oregonian* challenged, through sarcastic innuendo, his methods and actions as county commissioner. A "great many people who could never see it before, are beginning to think as Mr. Boyd does, that he is a wonderful man. Mr. Boyd is *the* County Commissioner … there is little danger of the people's money being squandered in any way not consistent with Mr. Boyd's ideas of 'reform.'" Boyd had defied state law by passing county laws that conflicted with state provisions, the editorial said, attempting to override greater and higher wisdom. "Whether Mr. Boyd has fulfilled the pledges made for him in relation to reform and retrenchment, is a matter about which even as great men as he may differ. We feel quite too modest to express an opinion."[79]

Boyd had been elected as mayor on a platform promising reform—and the reform promised was to reduce the cost of government. About this same time, a petition circulated calling for the state legislature to consolidate the city and county to cut down on "ruinous taxes." The September 1868 petition said: "Your petitioners ... being opposed to the heavy and ruinous taxation carried on by the support of a separate government of the city of Portland, and believing that a consolidation of the government of the city of Portland with that of the County of Multnomah, on an economical and judicious basis, would greatly reduce taxation, retrench expenses, and promote the general good of the community. We therefor pray your Honorable Body to pass such law."[80]

Firm support for this petition came from the *Oregonian*, which presented San Francisco as the model to follow. Before consolidation in 1856, the city and county governments of San Francisco had together cost more than eight and a half million dollars for the preceding six years. For the six years after consolidation, the joint city-county government spent less than half as much, only slightly more than three and a half million dollars. The *Oregonian* used these figures to make a compelling case."Now if consolidation proved such a blessing to the tax-payers of San Francisco, may we not hope for a like result for Portland? There is one idea that seems to pervade every mind, and that is that 'our charter! our government! our financial affairs!' are in horrible and disastrous condition. ... [A]ll are satisfied that it would be next to impossible to make the matter any worse. Hence nearly every man is signing the petition."[81]

The commonsense argument for consolidation, which has changed little in well over a hundred years, was the same as that made for marriage: two should be able to live as cheaply as one: "It would certainly be cheaper to carry on one government than it is two. We would then have no use of paying but one assessor; we now pay two. One Treasurer would safely keep all the money that would at any one time be in the Treasury. ... We have a court house ample and sufficient for a council chamber, city hall, etc., without ever interfering with the workings of the Circuit Court. Our city jail is now in a wretched condition. We have an ample and commodious county jail, which would save the expense of building a new one for the city."[82]

The article failed to point out, however, the far-reaching changes such consolidation would require. Counties had been created as an arm of state government, as specified by the Oregon constitution.[83] Only insiders would have realized that the state constitution limited counties to five thousand dollars of debt other than to "suppress insurrection or repel invasion,"[84] while Portland's charter allowed ten times that much, and the limit could be increased by the state legislature simply by amending the city charter. Also, at that time Multnomah County was basically rural, except for Portland. Why would farmers want to share Portland's mud, crime, and harbor problems? The state constitution would have to be amended in order for the city and county governments to consolidate, and that could happen only through a statewide vote of the people.[85] Did reformers have the necessary zeal to push their proposal through all the hurdles it would need to pass?

At any rate, the petition did not go far. Only a few signatures out of two hundred sixty-two appended to the document were familiar names: James Terwilliger, Stephen Coffin, Erasmus Shattuck, Aaron Wait, George Vaughn, Stephen McCormick, and Van B. DeLashmutt. The five-foot-long petition of individual sheets glued together was referred to Multnomah County members of the House, but the petition died without even the assignment of a bill or resolution number.[86]

However, the legislature did amend the city charter to remove the council's power to appoint the mayor and other elective officials in case of vacancy. The council's appointments—Mayor Holmes, Mayor Chapman, and Marshal Rosenheim—had not been well received by state legislators. The authority to fill vacancies, except for council positions, was returned to the voters. In addition, four more elective positions were added, bringing the total number of elected officials to eighteen: mayor, recorder, auditor, assessor, treasurer, marshal, city attorney, street commissioner, surveyor, and nine councilmen.

Another charter change limited the percentage of fees the marshal and recorder could retain, with one-third of fees collected to go into the city treasury. However, when the marshal and recorder prosecuted violations of state law, they earned the full amount stipulated by state law. This created an incentive for the two officials to enforce state laws more vigorously than local ones.[87]

In August, a controversial entrepreneur named Ben Holladay had arrived in Oregon with the avowed purpose of creating a railroad empire.[88] Oregon was prime railroad country waiting to be plundered.

Immediately after Holladay arrived in town, "[H]e bought a large plot of land east of the river and declared that the city of the future would be on that side, that the grass would soon be growing on Front Street, and that he would make a rat-hole out of west-side Portland. He thus antagonized in a single breath the rich men of the city, all of whom owned west-side property, and their antagonism never abated."[89] Holladay was "a genuine specimen of the successful Western pioneer of former days, illiterate, coarse, pretentious, boastful, false, and cunning," according to his later rival, Henry Villard.[90]

By September, Holladay had bought out controlling interest in the eastside railroad company (a court order had forced the company to change its name; it was now known as the Oregon and California—the O&C—Railroad) and infused the project with capital from his own fortune earned from overland stage companies.[91] He now hired crews of Chinese immigrants to hack out underbrush, fell trees, construct bridges over rivers, streams and marshes, and build up a strip of land drained by ditches along either side of the elevated roadway.[92]

No track had yet been laid on either side of the Willamette.The westsiders were making slow progress. They lacked the East Coast financial resources of brash Ben Holladay. Author Glenn Chesney Quiett put it this way: "[Holladay] drove his Oregon railway project with all the breakneck speed, dust, and thunder of a runaway stage-coach, while staid Portland clasped her mittened hands and looked on in horrified fascination."[93]

Street improvements continued to dominate the council agenda, for few matters engaged the citizenry's attention more than potholes in the street—a phenomenon that continues to the present day. Other issues that dominated city politics, though they were seldom discussed by the council, were liquor issues, according to Joseph Gaston's Portland history, which states that around 1868-70 "Portland had for two years a city council of nine members, six of whom were saloonkeepers; and the mayor himself, Hamilton Boyd, was a patron of saloons; and the marshal (later chief of police), James H. Lappeus, was also the proprietor of a saloon. There were at that time about thirty saloons in the town; and it was a straight whiskey proposition. The marshal enforced the ordinances strictly, and the council gave the city a clean honest government without grafting contractors of any kind. The saloon was not then used as an aid to gambling, robbery, or the debauchery of women."[94]

On the downtown streets of Portland, tailors were doing a booming business. When they pressed suits, they used a heavy, oversized iron called a "tailor's goose," a long iron with a curved handle. A Portland tailor named George Neimeyer often sought guidance from other merchants in conducting his daily affairs. One day around 1869, Neimeyer came to his friend Jeff Hays for assistance: "'I have a telegram I want to send to San Francisco,' Neimeyer began. 'I wanted to order a tailor's goose, but coming down the street I met Mr. Borquest and he told me to order one for him also. Now I don't know what to say. I cannot tell the San Francisco firm to send me two gooses, or a pair of geese, and what will I say so that it may be understood?'"

This was a really hard nut to crack for anyone with even a more copious vocabulary than Mr. Neimeyer possessed. After a few minutes of thought and consideration the following message was indited: "Please send me one tailor's goose, and while you are at it, please send me another. [Signed] G. Neimeyer."[95]

That a general attitude of leniency toward saloons existed during this time is undoubtedly true, but Hamilton Boyd was mayor for only one year, not two, and the assertion that six of nine councilmen were saloonkeepers is questionable.[96]

As for the claim of "clean honest government," the autobiography of Edward Chambreau gives a different picture. Chambreau says one of the first things he did when he opened his Portland saloon was to "fix the Policeman" on his beat. Chambreau's diary describes the marshal's handling of gambling victims as a scam in which the policeman would publicly offer a one hundred dollar reward to anyone who told him where the guilty gambler had gone, then would convince the victim to go home. Chambreau would pay off the police officer and, Chambreau implies, the officer would take the money back to split with the marshal.[97]

❧

In January 1869, the council authorized the Oregon Central Railroad to lay track down the center of Fourth Street.[98] The County Courthouse had been erected on Fourth Street two years before. It was an unimproved street running parallel to the river four blocks west of Front. The council reserved the right to regulate the speed of trains within city limits, and to restrict the hours during which trains might run.[99]

On May 10, 1869, the last spike was driven into the ground at Promontory Point, Utah, to complete the nation's first transcontinental railroad. Within five days, passengers were traveling from the East Coast to California in eight to ten days.[100] However, not a single line of track had yet been laid in Oregon, although much preparatory work was in process. In the meantime, Ben Holladay's money was working its charm in Salem and Washington, D. C., greasing the way for future deals.

Now, seventeen years after the second city council had accepted the notorious Brady map, the 1868-69 council adopted the map drawn by C. W. Burrage, city surveyor, as the city's official plan of streets, blocks, and public property.[101]

Chapter 11

Police, Parks, and Unscrupulous Ben Holladay

1869 – 1873

Mayors

No. 19: July 1869 - June 1871

Bernard Goldsmith

No. 20: July 1871 – June 1873

Philip Wasserman

The city was growing fast. Drays lined up in the Portland harbor waiting to load and unload from ships. The warehouses and other wooden structures that lined the waterfront were built out over the river on stilts. Crowds of people thronged to buy goods along Front and First streets, in spite of smelly, unsanitary streets littered with horse dung. The salmon business and foreign commerce drew a rabble of foreign sailors with money in their pockets to spend.[1] Waves of foreign immigrants were arriving regularly, lured as cheap labor to build railroads.

Police protection was costly and spread too thin; citizens clamored for reform because taxes were too high. Volunteer firemen were ill equipped and without enough cisterns for adequate fire protection.[2] Two rival railroads were vying to complete their first twenty miles of track. Long-term city problems continued building, with the council focused on the here and now.[3]

Two civic-minded businessmen stepped forward to take a turn at the helm of Portland government: Bernard Goldsmith and Philip Wasserman. Their four years of combined mayoral tenure would prove to be a period of comparative calm before a gathering storm of anti-Chinese sentiment and temperance rumblings. E. Kimbark MacColl calls Goldsmith's term "one of the more successful in Portland history."[4]

Both Goldsmith and Wasserman, Portland's nineteenth and twentieth mayors, were German-born Jews of unquestioned integrity. They were close personal friends and leaders in the community; they were the city's third and fourth foreign-born mayors. Goldsmith served as the first of

Mayor Bernard Goldsmith. (Photo: OrHi #25945)

five Jewish mayors, Wasserman the second.[5] Bernard Goldsmith became the most prosperous Jew in Oregon,[6] and was the eighth-wealthiest Portland resident at the time he served as mayor.[7] This thirty-seven-year-old native of Bavaria measured barely five feet tall. At age fifteen he had emigrated to New York City, where he apprenticed as a watchmaker. Later, he worked as a stevedore in California and then owned a jewelry store. He began accumulating capital in earnest after he opened three stores in northern California and southern Oregon.

The young entrepreneur settled in Portland in 1861, when he was twenty-nine years old. He founded a Portland dry-goods store with "several of his seven brothers," played the gold currency market, and invested in northern Idaho mines, Willamette Valley wheat, and eastern Oregon cattle. He was one of twelve founding members of the elite Portland Stock and Exchange Board in 1865. His entry into the wheat market triggered awareness by others that the Columbia River valley could produce another kind of gold—wheat—which would dominate Portland's shipping industry in years to come.[8] Between 1850 and 1870, Willamette Valley wheat output was to increase tenfold, from two hundred thousand bushels to over two million.[9]

Goldsmith and Wasserman were both Democrats before the Civil War, as were most Jews nationally, and both followed the national pattern of shifting to the new Republican party in opposition to slavery and support of Abraham Lincoln. Goldsmith therefore ran as a candidate for Portland mayor on the Union (Republican) ticket, but in 1875 switched back to the Democratic Party.[10]

Goldsmith had been mayor only a short time when smallpox was suspected on board a newly arrived ship from China. The mayor ordered the marshal to quarantine the immigrants for ten days, and to hire four temporary policemen to keep twenty-four-hour watch.[11] He arranged for the immigrants to stay in a tent on the outskirts of town, and for Chinese firms to feed them during their isolation.[12]

In September 1869, the Oregon Supreme Court overturned a two thousand dollar verdict against the city on behalf of a woman who had fallen through a sidewalk. Catharine O'Harra and her husband had alleged in their complaint that Mrs. O'Harra, "while traveling over the sidewalk of said Fifth street, was, on account of a defect therein, precipitated through said sidewalk, whereby she was injured." The city denied defects and liability, and the court decided only the liability question.[13] The court held that Portland's charter exempted the city from such liability.[14]

The eastside O&C Railroad laid its first rail on October 28, 1869.[15] It had taken a year and a half to clear a path and build a roadbed that would support the wooden ties and iron rails on which the powerful iron horses would ride. The route would run south from East Portland to Oregon City and continue southward along the Willamette River. Ben Holladay was playing politics the way he liked best—by entertaining guests in ostentatious style with the expectation of future reward. He maintained "a lavish home at Third and Alder tended by a chef from New York and a retinue of servants";[16] an "elaborate cottage" on the Oregon coast in Seaside, and two beautiful mansions, one in Washington, D. C., and the other on the Hudson River in New York.[17] The Oregon legislature, heavily lobbied and feted by Holladay and his associates, had reversed its original recognition of the westside company as the certain recipient of federal largesse, on grounds of faulty procedures, and decreed that the first company to complete twenty miles of railroad would receive the promised seven-million-acre federal land grant.[18]

By November, ten miles of Ben Holladay's railroad were finished. On the day before Christmas, his workers completed the crucial first twenty miles.[19] The eastside route, in the person of Ben Holladay, had won.

The westsiders were stymied for the present, while Holladay continued to extend his empire. In addition to the steamship line he operated between Portland and San Francisco, he platted the Holladay subdivision in East Portland, and built a bridge across Sullivan's Gulch, a ravine that would one day serve as right-of-way for Interstate Highway 84 and a MAX light rail line.[20]

On May 4, 1870, Congress approved a second land grant specifically for Portland's westside railroad, again contingent upon completion of twenty miles of track. But the westsiders were out of money, and within two months sold out their railroad interests to Ben Holladay.[21]

During the next six months, business boomed on the east side, while little railroad activity occurred on the west. The O&C line reached the state capital in Salem on September 25. A month later, residents on the east side of the Willamette received a charter from the state legislature for a new city named East Portland.[22] The railroad fare from East Portland to Salem was five cents a mile, or five dollars for a round trip[23] at a time when a good quality all-wool suit cost around eight dollars.[24] This 1870 fare cost the equivalent of sixty-two dollars in year 2000 dollars, when a round-trip Amtrack ticket from downtown Portland to Salem cost fourteen dollars.[25]

> In 1870, Congress authorized Portland to erect a bridge over the Willamette River, and the council had plans drawn up for a bridge big enough to "obviate the necessity of building more than one bridge" across the river.[26] It would be another seventeen years, however, before a bridge would actually be built.

Politics was the driving force behind a bold power move in Salem. The Democratic clique, fearing that Ben Holladay and his followers were planning to buy a takeover of city government, bulldozed a charter amendment through the 1870 legislature that created a board of police commissioners with authority over all Portland police matters, a board that existed on and off until permanently abolished in 1903. The board's responsibilities included appointment of a chief of police (the former marshal's position), specifying police rules and regulations, deciding how many police to hire, and authorizing police expenditures. The council was to raise the money to pay these expenses. The three police commissioners would receive three dollars a day for their services,[27] although neither the mayor nor council members received any such compensation. The Board of Police Commissioners would prove to be one of the most controversial citizen bodies in the city's history. It not only shifted power from local to state government because the governor chose the commissioners, but also shifted power from elected city officials to an appointed citizen body independent of the council—the first of several such bodies that would play a significant role in Portland's future. Senate Bill 34 that created the police board was introduced by Democratic Senator Lansing Stout and passed the House on a party-line vote of twenty-nine to fourteen in spite of a petition signed by six hundred twenty-seven Portland citizens remonstrating against the bill.[28]

Ironically, the city's first day-and-night police department had been formally created by the council a month before. The council had also agreed, at the urging of Marshal Joseph Saunders, to replace the present city jail with a two-story building that would house the police judge court, police department, and an improved new jail.[29]

Governor Grover appointed three Democrats to the prestigious new police board: Absalom Hallock, architect and experienced councilman; William P. Burke, a forty-four-year-old carpenter who made sure his son-in-law got appointed police captain; and John H. Hayden, probably in the lumber business, who was frequently absent from commission meetings.[30] As president, Hallock became the dominant voice of the board for the next four years. Professor Emeritus Charles A. Tracy of Portland State University says Hallock was "almost dogmatic" as a police commissioner, but that he initiated administrative and operational procedures that were "consistent with the practices of twentieth-century police organizations."[31]

The commissioners chose former marshal James Lappeus, co-owner of the Oro Fino saloon, as the city's first chief of police.[32] The board adopted rules and regulations that Marshal Saunders had promulgated only two months before. Rotating police beats were instigated and records kept of citizen complaints. One police captain, six regular policemen, and three special policemen (who would serve as private watchmen) were hired from thirty-two applicants. The charter specified a salary of one hundred twenty-five dollars a month for the chief, one hundred dollars for the captain, and ninety dollars for regular policemen.

In its first few years, the Board of Police Commissioners worked comparatively well, partly because the three paid commissioners devoted more time and attention to the job than had the three council members on the health and police committee, who were "unpaid and often unconcerned."[33]

The city recorder position—which had been designated as deputy mayor for much of Portland's history—was eliminated in the same charter amendment that created the police board, and replaced with a position called police judge. The council president would henceforth act as mayor in the mayor's absence. The auditor, city attorney, street commissioner, and surveyor were once again made appointive. The city's general debt limit was doubled to one hundred thousand dollars. In addition, the charter authorized issuance of four hundred thousand dollars in bonds to erect a city water or gas works if votes approved.[34] (Note how dramatically this allowable debt differed from the five thousand dollars maximum specified for counties in the Oregon constitution.)

For seventy-five dollars a month, the council moved to new quarters—four rooms on the second floor of Henry Corbett's building located between Washington and Alder, probably on First Street.[35]

In late 1870, Ben Holladay issued a bold challenge to westsiders: For one hundred thousand dollars in cash, he would finish building the westside railroad and make downtown Portland the terminus for both his lines.

Mayor Goldsmith presided over a December 16 mass citizens' meeting to discuss Holladay's proposal. A committee of five was appointed to solicit contributions to meet Holladay's demand, with another five solicitors subsequently added. Three more citizen meetings in late December and early January aired concerns and reported progress.[36]

For westsiders, a downtown railroad terminus was crucial. A northern transcontinental line was building westward through the Dakotas and Montana, headed for Washington State instead of Oregon.[37] If westsiders did not act, Holladay threatened to keep his terminus on the east side of the Willamette or move it downstream on the Columbia to St. Helens. Although Portland was the most populous city and the obvious choice, Holladay could easily change all that.[38] The solicitation committee warned fellow westsiders: "[I]f this proposition fails real estate will decline in this city. … serious losses will ensue. … You must face the music and take the broth as it is cooked. … A city has been started here, and has prospered simply because the wagons from the valley in early times could not go any further down the river and the ocean steamers could squeeze along up. But to a man who is able to own lines of steamships and build lines of railroads, the 'natural advantages' will be at the point where he can make the most money by a connection between the two lines of transportation."[39]

By February 11, 1871, Portland had met its one hundred thousand dollar goal with contributions from three hundred thirty-five people. The largest donation of five thousand dollars came from George

Flanders, Portland's first city treasurer and brother-in law of John Couch, who had died the previous January.[40] Contributions from past and future Portland mayors included William Ladd (thirty-five hundred dollars), Henry Failing (fifteen hundred dollars), George Vaughn(one thousand dollars), David Logan (five hunded dollars), George H. Williams (five hundred dollars), Sylvestor Pennoyer (one hundred fifty dollars), John Breck (one hundred dollars), and Stephen McCormick (one hundred dollars).[41] A Goldsmith company contributed one thousand dollars and a Wasserman company, five hundred dollars.[42]

Yet only sixteen years later, the *Oregonian* was to downplay not only the importance of this impressive fund-raising fete, but to overlook the importance of Congressman Joseph Smith's amendment to a congressional bill that required the Northern Pacific Railroad to build its main line down the Columbia River to Portland. The *Oregonian* boasted that Portland's role as the "Railroad Cross-Roads of the Pacific Northwest" came as a natural consequence, simply because of its superior location. The great transportation lines came to Portland, the newspaper said, by force of the law of commerce as well as "the physical law which makes water run down hill." Furthermore, it insisted, "The situation of the city at the junction of the Willamette and Columbia valleys is invincible."[43] Yet East Portland might well have developed into the downtown core of Portland had westsiders not responded with their dollars in 1871.

❧

Bernard Goldsmith loved parks and knew from his years growing up in Europe what a precious heritage parks could be.[44] He pushed negotiations to regain the two blocks originally targeted for public squares that had never been deeded to the city. Both were now owned by former township proprietor W. W. Chapman. At Goldsmith's urging, the city struck a deal with Chapman to pay him six thousand two hundred and fifty dollars for nine blocks—the two plaza blocks[45] plus seven blocks west of downtown originally designated as park blocks on Lownsdale's first map. A similar, though less costly, purchase was negotiated with Stephen and Mrs. Coffin, whose seven park blocks and title to four hundred feet of public levee were deeded to the city for twenty-five hundred dollars in July 1871.[46]

An equally important purchase made during Goldsmith's tenure was that of forty wooded acres in the hills above downtown Portland, the nucleus of present-day Washington Park. The cost in early 1871 was thirty-two thousand dollars, a price that drew considerable criticism.[47]

Portland was surrounded by nature's parkland—why was the city paying good money for it?[48]

Another marvelous opportunity was lost, however, when the council failed to obtain an additional six park blocks still in private hands.[49] The heirs of Nancy Lownsdale offered to sell these blocks to the city for thirty-six thousand dollars; a council committee counteroffered only half that amount and the offer was rejected. By the following year, real-estate prices had inflated so astronomically that the next council agreed to call a special election on December 20, 1871, for voters to approve a ninety-two thousand dollar levy to buy the six blocks. Public sentiment was so negative, however, that the council cancelled the planned election.[50]

Meanwhile, responding to citizen demands to curb prostitution, the council adopted an ordinance to suppress brothels.[51] The chief of police was to crack down on violators and collect five dollars from every prostitute convicted. Chief Lappeus ignored this law for the most part, however, and prostitution continued unabated. During his first six and a half years as police chief, Lappeus and his force made only sixteen such arrests, an average of one arrest every five months.[52]

The council decided to make use of convicts as unpaid labor. A council ordinance approved by Mayor Goldsmith said that city prisoners, "after conviction, shall be liable to work upon the public square, lots, blocks, engine houses, streets, cisterns, sewers and … in cleaning all crossings of streets in the city. … No prisoner shall be allowed to labor more than 10 hours in one day. … This ordinance shall not be construed to require any female to perform labor, nor to require any prisoner to labor on Sunday."[53]

Mayor Bernard Goldsmith's greatest achievement, in his own estimation, affected Portland indirectly. He was the driving force behind the building of locks to navigate around the Willamette River falls across from Oregon City. Goldsmith and his associates obtained a state legislative grant of two hundred thousand dollars for the project, and when estimated costs more than doubled, Goldsmith paid an additional two hundred thousand dollars himself. When the locks were finished in 1872, boats could travel all the way from the Pacific Ocean to Eugene, 160 river miles south of Portland. The cost of shipping Willamette Valley goods to Portland was cut by half, thereby forestalling the kind of railroad freight monopoly that developed in other parts of the country.[54]

July 1871- June 1873

In June 1871, three-term state legislator Philip Wasserman[55] won 60 percent of the vote for mayor over former mayor Dr. James Chapman.[56] Wasserman, at forty-three, was four years older than his friend Bernard Goldsmith and had also been born in Bavaria. The new mayor had left Germany in 1850 at age twenty-two and arrived in Portland in 1858.[57] He was later to serve four years on the Portland school board[58] and was a founder of Portland Business College.[59]

Though not as adventuresome as Goldsmith in business dealings, Wasserman was nevertheless a respected merchant who, with his partner, T. Dittenhoeffer, ran a cigar store. Their ad in the *1870 Portland Directory* says:

PIONEER CIGAR STORE
WASSERMAN & CO.,
Importers and Dealers in
FINE HAVANA AND AMERICAN CIGARS
Tobacco, Snuff, Marches, Playing Cards, Cutlery
Combs, Brushes, Toys, Yankee Notions, Etc.
77 FRONT STREET, PORTLAND, OREGON.

The German word for "water" is "wasser." It was fitting, therefore, that Mayor Wasserman worked to improve Portland's water. A June petition signed by two hundred seventy-six citizens urged the council to find a cheaper water supply. It was up to the new mayor and council to respond.[60]

Until 1856, when Stephen Coffin and Finice Caruthers diverted water from Caruthers Creek to establish a water system, Portlanders drew their water from wells. By 1871, H. C. Leonard and John Green[61] owned both the city's gas works and the Portland Water Company, which had added water from Balch Creek in today's Forest Park to the Caruthers Creek supply. The Portland Water Company replaced hollowed-out logs with iron pipes, and erected reservoirs and pumping stations, but the supply was still inadequate for fire protection and many other needs of a growing city. Their water was also expensive.[62]

At Mayor Wasserman's urging, the council authorized a study of water supply alternatives.[63] The committee reported back the following year, recommending erection of a municipal waterworks using either Willamette River water or Stephens' Springs near Mount Tabor on the east side. The council forwarded the report to the 1872 state legislature, but legislators balked at the one-million-dollar price tag. The 1870

Mayor Philip Wasserman. (Photo: OrHi #365)

legislature had authorized four hundred thousand dollars for this purpose, and that was as far as legislators were willing to go.[64]

So Leonard and Green added a bigger pump and a bigger pump station, and city residents made do with water from this private waterworks. A proposal on the city's June 1873 ballot to buy out the private company failed by an overwhelming majority because the asking price was so high. The *Oregonian* said, "We regard the proposition to purchase the works at the price named one that ought not be entertained for a moment."[65]

Portland's first street railway started operation in 1872. The council granted a twenty-five-year franchise to sawmill owner Levi Estes to "lay down and maintain an iron railroad track or tracks."[66] The line utilized old rails from Ben Holladay's O&C Railroad. The franchise grant generated considerable opposition because people thought Holladay backed it, which he did.[67] A round trip on the mule-drawn streetcar up and down First Street took at least an hour. The car was a discarded San Francisco trolley that held twelve passengers.[68]

Proposals for improvements to streets, sidewalks, and sewers, along with remonstrances against them, consumed a great deal of council time. The city sloped upward from the river, so the degree of street incline, or grade, was an important component of every project considered, and good drainage was always a major problem. Portland had not yet won its battle with mud. The council also spent considerable time reviewing and adjusting assessed property values.[69]

For the thirteenth time since the council had begun deliberations twenty years before, it again moved its meeting room, this time to 93 First Street.[70]

The elections of June and October 1872[71] were rife with scandal; charges of illegal voting, bribery, and criminal conspiracy filled the newspapers and spread by word of mouth. Wasserman was only halfway through his term, so there was no mayor's race on the ballot, but there were three council slots to fill. Ben Holladay and former city attorney John Mitchell were trying to wrest control of the Republican Party from Henry Corbett and Henry Failing. Corbett and Mitchell were the two leading candidates for the U. S. Senate. E. Kimbark MacColl reports a 1872 meeting between Holladay and a man named Wicks as follows:

> "When I went to his office," Wicks said, "he had his feet on the table and was tipped back in a big office chair smoking a cigar." Holladay told Wicks that he was prepared to spend what it took to make a traditionally Democratic ward "go Republican." Holladay "furnished me with a sack of $2.50 gold pieces. I kept busy till election day," Wicks said, "moving from one hotel and lodging house to another. On election day I served as paymaster .... We carried the old Modoc ward—the Democratic stronghold—and for the first time in its history it went Republican."[72]

Judge Matthew Deady, in his diaries, quotes a letter from Holladay stating that said he had "spent $250,000 in coin to make Oregon a Republican State."[73] This included buying votes to elect three candidates to the city council and Mitchell to the U. S. Senate.

Henry Corbett, however, was not without means to fight back. He soon found an effective way to retaliate: in October, he bought controlling interest in the *Oregonian*, now a daily, and installed his own editor, a lawyer-journalist and city councilman named W. Lair Hill. Corbett ousted the existing *Oregonian* editor Harvey Scott, who went to work for the *Bulletin*, a new Ben Holladay venture.[74]

The October federal elections were as scandalous as any in the city's history. "Vote buying and repeating was conducted on such a flagitious scale that the *Oregonian* afterward estimated one-fourth of the votes cast in the city were illegal," notes Malcolm Clark.[75] Two federal grand juries were later impaneled to investigate bribery charges, but the first panel was discharged because it was fixed, and the second was rendered impotent because the U. S. Attorney, former Oregon governor Addison Gibbs, was fired by the U. S. Attorney General (and future Portland mayor) George Williams at the insistence of U. S. Senator John Mitchell. "Williams was not a particularly venal man," Clark says, "but he was a weak one."[76]

A stately new city jail and police headquarters opened for business July 27, 1872, as the city's first municipal building. The edifice resembled a New Orleans mansion complete with arched windows, decorative cast-iron entry porch, and ornate gable.[77] Policemen were issued silver stars to wear on their uniforms, and all officers were ordered to obtain standard dress by the end of the year. This first uniform was to consist of: "a dark blue coat, vest, and pantaloons and black hat of uniform style with cord and tassel. The coat to be Frock, single-breasted, velvet collar and the vest single breasted, both trimmed with brass buttons."[78]

The 1872 legislature revisited Portland's charter and voted to have the mayor appoint the members of the Board of Police Commissioners instead of the governor. However, Governor Grover vetoed the bill and the senate was unable to override his veto.[79]

About this time, Ben Holladay's empire began to fail. He had completed the westside line twenty miles south to the Yamhill River at a point called St. Joe just north of present-day McMinnville, where it stopped abruptly.[81] Through reckless spending, Holladay had accumulated nearly ten million dollars of indebtedness to his German backers, of which

In the early morning on December 22, 1872, fire broke out in the rear of a Chinese laundry between Morrison and Alder, where pitch was being boiled. Firemen from near and far battled the blaze all day before rain finally put out the fire. Two and a half blocks of buildings were destroyed, causing an estimated five hundred thousand dollars of damage, or seven million in today's dollars. The city's cisterns gave out after only two hours, and structures built out over the river on wooden stilts burned quickly.[80]

only five million was used building his railroads.[82] He now defaulted on the interest for these loans. The railroads were operating at a deficit. An unnamed Salem wag had predicted that the railroad would carry all the available passengers on its first trip, all the freight in the Willamette Valley on its second, and have to pull up the tracks behind it on the third.[83]

During Mayor Wasserman's last month in office, the council passed an ordinance prohibiting the hiring of Chinese workers on city contracts. Mayor Wasserman vetoed the measure, and his veto held.[84]

Twelve years before, in 1861, only 1 percent of Portland's population was Chinese—twenty-seven persons out of nearly three thousand. Four of the Chinese were women, probably prostitutes. The men had left their wives at home because they had come to America not to stay, but to make money they could take back to China.[85] By 1872, the Portland Chinese population had increased to over one thousand.[86] Jobs for Chinese were plentiful in summer, but disappeared in winter. Competition for off-season jobs was fierce, and many Chinese had to live on their summer earnings during their off-season months of unemployment, which meant they were unable to return to China laden with riches as they had planned. Unemployed Chinese from other parts of the Northwest also drifted to Portland in the winter months.[87]

The council passed a second anti-Chinese ordinance in 1873 for the "preservation of health and prevention of disease," commonly known as the infamous "Cubic Air Ordinance," which Wasserman signed. This law said anyone living in a building with less than 550 cubic feet of air per person should be arrested.[90] Police conducted sweeps of Chinatown on June 26 and 27, immediately after Wasserman left office, and arrested fifty violators each night,

In southern Oregon, conflicts between white settlers and the Modoc Indians turned into open warfare in spring 1873. The federal government had assigned the Modocs to a reservation and many refused to go. There was treachery on both sides. General Edward Canby and a companion, unarmed, were ambushed and murdered April 11, 1873, on their way to meet with the Modoc chief, hoping to arrange a "permanent and peaceful treaty."[88] Portland's city council issued a resolution of sorrow and homage to General Canby, and appointed a committee to confer with military authorities about a Portland reception for General Canby's remains.[89]

perhaps to deliver on campaign promises by newly elected officials. Most of these Chinese paid the five dollar fine and returned home to the same crowded conditions they had left. Enforcement dwindled. But anti-Chinese sentiment did not.[91] A "Committee of 27 Citizens of Portland" stated it this way:

> As honorable men, we disdain to demagogue on the Chinese question. We … feel that the influx of Chinese works a great hardship on the laboring classes of the Pacific States, and greatly retards their progress. … But [the Chinese] are here by virtue of existing laws and treaties. … We would therefore advise as the only remedy for the existing evil, petitions to our representatives in Congress … for such modifications of our treaties with China as will remove the evil which has fallen so heavily upon us. As long as such treaties exist, local laws discriminating against Chinese will not stand the test of adjudication.[92]

American ways were strange to these Chinese immigrants. A letter home from Portland merchant Ah-ning said:

> The American men don't work, they don't know how. They grow food, but not like China. They don't feed the land with land food; they waste land food and there are weeds all over. …The streets are wide, but are full of bad stumps and holes. … The women here are curious. … Their dresses spread around like a balloon. They can't go through a door without crowding both sides. The dress covers them all over down to their feet. … It doesn't cost much to live here, and when we go home to China, we can bring much money. … Don't come here; there are too many Chinese already.[93]

Chapter 12

The Big Fire, a Ladies' War, and a Grand Celebration

1873 – 1879

Mayors

No. 21: July 1873 – June 1875

Henry Failing (second term)

No. 22: July 1875 – June 1877

James A. Chapman (second term)

No. 23: July 1877 – June 1879

William Spencer Newbury

Henry Failing had a fight on his hands to get a return engagement as mayor seven years after his first tenure. In 1873, he headed the Citizens' Ticket against Democrat Eugene Semple and Republican John McCraken, former council president.[1]

The *Oregonian*, now owned by Henry Corbett, went gunning for McCraken, who, the newspaper said, had been hand-picked by Ben Holladay to draw votes from Failing. "If there is one man in Portland pre-eminent for neglecting every duty of a public nature which he undertakes to perform, that man is John McCraken," the paper said.[2] The *Oregonian* also charged Holladay with instigating voting irregularities:

> A carpenter in this city, who has always voted the Republican ticket, was engaged to work on the new Custom House. Last Saturday he received notice that if he voted for the (Citizens') ticket, he would be deprived of the job. ... To satisfy himself ... he went directly to Mr. W. L. Higgins, the Superintendent, to inquire about it. Imagine his surprise on being told by Higgins that he must lose his situation, or vote the ring [Holladay] ticket. ... Higgins [said] he had to do it, as he himself would lose his place if he did not exact this.[3]

Failing won the 1873 election by forty votes out of 2,036 cast.[4] The *Oregonian* predicted that five council members would vote for the Citizens' agenda and four votes would be "favorable to the schemes of Mr. Holladay."[5]

Mayor Henry Failing. (Photo: OrHi #53226)

A month after Mayor Failing took office, catastrophe struck the city.

At 4 a.m. on the dry summer morning of August 2, 1873, flames shot upward from the back of a furniture store near the river where oils and varnishes were stored. A policeman sounded the alarm and shouts of "Fire! Fire!" soon ripped the air. The most disastrous fire in Portland history licked at the wooden structures like a fire-breathing dragon.

Firewood stacked on the sidewalks, left over from a mild winter, provided instant kindling. Wooden sidewalks exploded in flames. Windows melted and smashed from the heat. The fire created "a concentration of heat so intense that it penetrated brick buildings and caused the contents to burst into flame."[6] The fire raced across narrow streets and wooden crosswalks. Flames jumped from awning to awning, rooftop to rooftop, street to street.

The volunteer fire department fought valiantly. Fire companies from neighboring towns joined in. But the firemen lacked control and direction, and were no match for such a conflagration. The city's fire-fighting capacity had not improved since the two-and-a-half-block fire only eight months before.[7]

The fire burned all day before it was finally contained. By then the devastation covered twenty-two blocks and had caused one and a quarter million dollars of damage. Less than a fourth of the loss was covered by insurance.[8]

The cause of the fire was never officially determined, but it was commonly understood that arson was involved—a flame deliberately set to burn down Chinatown.[9] However, Chinatown, which centered around Alder Street and included nearly forty Chinese laundries, suffered comparatively little damage.[10]

In 1873, warehouse stilts were left smoldering in the wake of Portland's most devastating fire. (Photo: OrHi #7666)

"The great disaster … was telegraphed far and wide and not only offers of aid but checks for money [were] sent in from San Francisco and many eastern cities. Henry Failing … promptly telegraphed the thanks of Portland for the generous offer of aid, but kindly declined them all."[11] Mayor Failing rejected this help because Portland was rich, he said, and accepting charity was unthinkable. The city needed to dig into its own pockets to help itself. The mayor personally contributed ten thousand dollars to the relief committee that he headed. "Mayor Failing's response to the emergency received mixed reviews. Few criticized his organizational talents and tireless efforts in providing shelter and food for the victims. But he was roundly condemned, especially by Holladay's *Bulletin*, for "declining all offers of financial support from outside sources. … His rejection of proposals that the city should reimburse fire victims also drew *Bulletin* criticism, especially in the fall when the Panic of 1873 affected Oregon. … [There were whispers] that Banker Failing was cruelly indifferent."[12]

A crew again attempted to blow up the sunken hulk of the brig *Duc D'Lorges* that had hampered Willamette River navigation for nearly twenty years, but this 1873 effort to get rid of the ship again proved a failure. Captain Travaillot's "gift" to the city was to remain at the bottom of the river until 1882 and beyond.[13]

Portland's newspapers urged the council to widen city streets before rebuilding started, so that fire could not leap so easily across narrow streets, but the council did not heed this advice.[14]

While the city was still dazed from the fire, a financial panic, begun on the East coast, hit Portland in mid-September. "1873 was not a good year in white America; it was the year of the Panic and the Depression that followed. Especially in the East, men lost their fortunes, businesses crumbled, and the economy was disrupted. The Northwest was not hit as badly, but it was affected. The main setback in the region was the bankruptcy of the Northern Pacific Railroad."[15]

The financial panic of September 1873 kept Ben Holladay from raising more funds to finance his debts,[16] and his reign as railroad king ended at Roseburg, 180 miles south of Portland.[17] Holladay again defaulted on interest payments to his German bondholders. They, in turn, sent an American-educated lawyer-journalist named Henry Villard to Oregon the following year to investigate what was going on.

Trouble. Trouble. Trouble. It now came from a new direction: women. Women's roles in the first twenty-two years of city governance had been confined to that of wife, prostitute, maid, or victim (e.g., falling through the sidewalks). Now a few bold ladies of Portland were about to add a fifth category: activists for moral reform. "The idea [of prohibition] was born … in Ohio and transported West, after the feminine fashion, by word of mouth and with such commendable rapidity that by the middle of February the ladies of Portland were astir, bursting with … the fire of righteous zeal."[18]

The *New Northwest*, a weekly newspaper published by fiery Abigail Scott Duniway (sister of journalist Harvey Scott), urged women's suffrage, support for anti-slavery Republicans, and temperance. Susan B. Anthony and Abigail Duniway had already spent ten weeks lecturing throughout the Pacific Northwest in fall 1871.[19] Duniway had addressed the Oregon legislature in October 1872, urging support for a women's suffrage bill which failed to make the statewide ballot by only one senate vote.[20]

"Praying Down Saloons" was the title of a Duniway editorial in March 1874: "[W]e are rejoiced to see something started which will bring the women to the knowledge they can deviate from long-established customs without bringing down the heavens upon their heads. *Thousand and tens of thousands of them will blockade sidewalks, interfere with municipal ordinances, sing and pray in the most public places to be seen by men*, and by this means be awakened to a realizing sense of their political duties."[21]

Later that month, a Women's Temperance Prayer League formed in Portland. Soon the league publicly challenged saloonkeepers to close up shop. Thus began "The War on the Webfoot Saloon," a battle between temperance ladies and popular tavern-owner and former councilman Walter Moffett, said to be an honest saloonkeeper who instructed his bartenders to "give the customer full measure." Moffett was known to have "an explosive temper equipped with a very short fuse," and to regard the temperance movement as "hypocritical humbuggery." [22]

During the first few skirmishes, the temperance ladies simply demanded entrance to saloons, were turned away, and left quietly. By the end of March, they grew bolder. A group of league members lined up in front of the Webfoot Saloon one afternoon to sing and pray. They attracted a large audience. "Moffett shortly appeared, wearing his spectacles and an expression of mock dignity, and carrying a Bible from which he proceeded to read passages 'selected with express reference to the occasion' … The ladies sang louder. Moffett shouted. In thus wise the duel continued until four o'clock, when the Leaguers withdrew."[23]

Encounters between league members and Moffett continued, each time drawing larger crowds. The police were nowhere to be seen. On April 7, while fifteen ladies sang and prayed in front of the Webfoot,

Crowds milled around the new city jail after women temperance crusaders were arrested in April 1874. (Photo: OrHi #5626)

Chief Lappeus appeared. Moffett bellowed that he was a taxpayer who had paid his one hundred dollar license fee[24] and was entitled to police protection to operate his business free of trespassers. Lappeus "approached the ladies and with grave dignity asked them to withdraw. They flatly refused. ... Whereupon he told them, with sad reluctance, that their obstinate course left him no alternative but arrest. ... [After the arrest], male relatives ... descended ... to offer bail. The ladies ... steadfastly declined."[25]

The judge who heard the complaint dismissed it on grounds that the crusaders were "merely exercising freedom of worship." Confrontations continued. On April 15, during another pray-in in front of the Webfoot Saloon, twenty-one women were arrested on charges of disturbing the peace. Mayor Failing himself had apparently ordered the arrests.[26]

Six of these women were brought to trial on April 20. City Attorney Marion F. Mulkey opened his remarks by noting that the defendants, "being women, were not accountable beings."[27] The trial lasted two days, after which the jury found the defendants guilty as charged. The ladies spent the day in jail, turning down numerous offers to pay their five dollar fines. "The remainder of the day they spent locked up in the third floor jail, holding court for the throng of well-wishers who poured in endless procession through the corridors, drinking the hot soup brought them by thoughtful friends, singing and praying at intervals, and enjoying themselves hugely."[28] That evening, after the crowds had thinned down, Chief Lappeus ordered the ladies out of jail without offering any escort to see them home.

Rather than cool their ardor, this public attention only enflamed the women's passions. They continued their sing-ins and pray-ins. The league even endorsed a slate of temperance candidates in the upcoming city election.

Things might have gone differently had it not been for an innocent-sounding broadside entitled "The Voter's Book of Remembrance," published in the league's name. This volatile publication, "rich with clinical descriptions framed in language exceedingly blunt," linked liquor and prostitution in a way that offended nearly everyone.[29] The women of the league fell off their pedestals. The league's success had been based on its high moral tone. The temperance candidates lost badly at the polls.[30]

"A more orderly and peaceable election has not transpired in this city for some years," reported the *Oregonian* of the June 1874 elections.[31] On election night, after the votes were counted: "[A] band of music commenced discoursing animated strains in celebration of the glorious victory. Sky rockets and bombs were fired off ... Later in the evening, the band, followed by a concourse of several hundred citizens, visited the residences of the newly elected Councilmen and serenaded them. … [S]hort addresses were made by the victorious candidates in response. … Mayor Failing's residence was also visited by the band."[32]

On June 17, the mayor approved yet another ordinance regarding the licensing of barrooms and drinking shops. This one prohibited females from holding licenses and made it a misdemeanor to employ any woman as "waitress, bartender, or to sing or dance or serve in any other capacity in a barroom or drinking shop."[33] The following month, the council reduced the required license fee for barrooms and drinking shops by half, from one hundred dollars a quarter to fifty.[34]

Not only were Holladay's forces depleted, but so were the advocates of prohibition, at least for the time being.

In fall 1874, Mayor Failing and the council successfully lobbied state legislators, who now had a Republican majority, to let Portland voters elect the Board of Police Commissioners.[35] The charter amendment also said that no one could serve as a police commissioner at the same time he held any other city office. The mayor would appoint the first three police commissioners, with council consent, and the voters would choose their successors. The council would decide how many police could be hired, and at what salary.[36]

The council rejected Mayor Failing's first slate of three nominees for police board positions, but accepted his second proposal. Thus former councilman Shubrick Norris returned to city government as a police commissioner twenty years after his former service ended.[37]

Again this year, the council changed its meeting room, moving council chambers to another building owned by Henry Corbett. Exactly which building is not clear, because Corbett owned at least five downtown buildings at this time.[38]

Mayor Failing sought reelection in June 1875 as a representative of the Peoples' Party. (Ben Holladay had usurped the Republican banner.) Heading the Republican ticket was another former mayor, Dr. James Chapman, Ben Holladay's personal physician and a former Democrat who had run unsuccessfully against Philip Wasserman four years before. The campaign was a bitter one. The *Oregonian* said Holladay planned to "secure by corruption the election of Chapman as mayor, so that the city government can be used for the purpose of carrying the county and state in Holladay's interest."[39]

Holladay's *Bulletin* hammered Failing's refusal to accept outside offers of assistance after the big fire, and depicted him as cold-hearted and uncaring. Saloon interests criticized Failing's handling of the temperance crusade. Some voters may even have blamed Failing for a new law the legislature passed requiring all bars to close while the polls were open.[40]

When the votes were counted, Chapman had defeated Failing by six votes.[41] Holladay's man had won. The *Oregonian* cast its disappointment in the best possible light by declaring that Dr. Chapman's election was a clear case of "a barren scepter in a gripless hand."[42]

> The People have now two-thirds of the Council, so they have not only a complete check on any jobbery the ring [Holladay's group] may wish to put through, but also sufficient strength to pass any necessary ordinance over the veto of the Mayor. Dr. Chapman will have the sublime satisfaction of presiding over the deliberations of a body of men over whom, or with whom, he has no sort of power by law. He will have to run the city in the interest of the people, whether he likes it or not.[43]

Only 1,596 citizens voted in the 1875 election compared to 2,190 the year before. Apparently the possibility of the election of temperance candidates the prior year had brought out voters en masse. The commingling of temperance and women's suffrage thus held back the granting of votes for women partly because men feared that women would tip the ballot box toward prohibition.

July 1875 - June 1877

Seven years after his first term as mayor, James Chapman returned as Portland's twenty-second mayor. In the meantime, Chapman had founded the Progress Club, a booster organization of one hundred men who favored aggressive development for Portland.[44]

Rebuilding from the big fire of 1873 was nearly complete by this time. Both the St. Vincent Hospital and the Good Samaritan Hospital and Orphanage opened in northwest Portland in 1875.[45] Soon Portland would celebrate its first quarter-century as a city, in the same year the nation observed its centennial. The city was about to throw one of its grandest parties ever.[46] Elaborate festivities were clearly in order. Mayor Chapman chaired the centennial executive committee, which included former mayor Henry Failing. Planning and advance events took place throughout the spring.

Mayor James Chapman.
(Photo: OrHi ##38385)

The water level of the Willamette River paid the planning committee no heed, however. As snow melted in the mountains, as it did every spring, the water level rose. Flooding of downtown Portland had occurred in 1853, 1854, 1861, 1862, and 1871. And now, with citizens busily engaged with arrangements for a glorious 1876 Fourth of July, the city experienced one of its worst floods to date. "Merchants on Front Street ... placed chains, kegs of nails, heavy cases of iron, grindstones, pig iron, scrap iron, and all the heaviest items they could find which were not soluble in water upon the wooden sidewalks to prevent their being floated away. ... It was necessary to dump bricks and loads of gravel on the streets themselves to prevent the Nicholson paving from floating away."[47]

On June 24, the Willamette reached a high water mark of 25.3 feet. The gasworks flooded. Most shops were closed. Boats and hastily built elevated sidewalks transported people from one building to another. The Clarendon Hotel raised its false floor higher and higher to stay above water. Fortunately, the water receded by the end of June. Preparations for the Fourth of July proceeded as planned, even as the arduous task of cleaning up mud, stench, and debris began.[48] Council committees supervised subcommittees and events; citizens from East Portland joined in. Six hundred posters were distributed throughout the Willamette Valley, eastern Oregon, and Washington Territory inviting out-of-towners to join the week-long jubilee.[49] The city's seventy-one licensed saloons stocked up extra supplies of firewater.[50] By July 3, the city's twenty hotels were filled to capacity. Steamships and boats of all sizes and shapes anchored along the waterfront for lodging. A campground was set up at Sullivan's Springs in East Portland.[51]

On the Fourth of July, cannons roared and church bells rang at sunrise. The dusty streets were sprinkled with water. Crowds gathered early, waiting for events to begin. At 10:35 a.m., the grand parade started, with bands, volunteer firemen, military drill teams, prancing horses, and decorated wagons marching past twenty thousand cheering spectators.[52] It took twenty-five minutes for the parade to pass any given point. The procession ended at the park blocks, where grandstands had been erected to seat ten thousand people. There the crowd sweltered in

The barren Park Blocks of the 1870s (center) held little resemblance to the forested terrain of 1845 or today's shady Park Blocks. (Photo: OrHi #23454)

the sun, except for dignitaries sheltered under a canopy of canvas and fir boughs. No shade existed in the park blocks at this time—the trees had apparently all been cut down for lumber.[53]

After a lengthy program of speeches, invited guests gathered at the Turn Verein Hall for a 4 p.m. banquet that included sixteen rounds of well-planned toasts and entertainment. In the evening, a dazzling display of fireworks, visible for miles around, played for the grandstands in the park blocks. The centennial committee had allocated two thousand dollars (the equivalent of thirty-one thousand dollars today) for this extravaganza, which was the largest display of fireworks ever ignited on the West Coast at the time.[54]

Events continued throughout the week. Fire companies from neighboring towns vied to see whose fire engine could throw its stream of water farthest. Contests were held in gymnastics, yachting, scull boat racing, billiards, baseball, rifle shooting, horse racing, military drilling, and pigeon shooting. The week ended with more fireworks on Friday evening and public dancing to Charles E. Bray's orchestra in the Turn Verein Hall on Saturday afternoon. The grand finale Saturday evening was by invitation only. At that time, the mayor presented cups and medals, and weary revelers danced until midnight.

The council pronounced itself well pleased. Contributions to cover expenses had been received from the business community, including three hundred sixteen dollars from forty Chinese citizens.[55] The splendid centennial celebration had cost almost fifteen

In 1876, German bondholders removed Ben Holladay from management of the O&C railroad and turned its affairs over to the man who had been sent to investigate, Henry Villard.

thousand dollars, including six hundred dollars for centennial medals, nine hundred forty-four dollars for the banquet (three hundred thirty-four dollars for wine and six hundred ten dollars for food), three hundred seventy-eight dollars for "carriage hires," over fifteen hundred dollars for six bands, and sixty-six dollars for meals for one hundred thirty-two soldiers.[56]

Council deliberations at this time dealt primarily with basic city services: improving streets, intersections, and sidewalks; installing sewers and street lamps; providing fire and police protection. City streets now extended as far west as Twelfth and as far south as Hall. Existing streets were in need of repair.

Harvey Scott, long since divested of his fascination with Ben Holladay, bought out Henry Corbett's interest in the *Oregonian* in April 1877. Scott and publisher Henry Pittock also purchased the other outstanding shares. Scott returned as the *Oregonian*'s editor, a position he was to hold for thirty-three more years until his death in 1910.[57]

Although Mayor Chapman did not stand for reelection in 1877, he would return five years later for an unprecedented third term.

July 1877 - June 1879

The most hotly contested race in the 1877 election was for police commissioner, and the most contentious issue was whether to retain James Lappeus as chief of police. The Republican candidate for the commissioner's position, "Red" Riley, pledged to replace Lappeus. Riley's opponent, Democrat Charles Sitton, was cast as the chief's defender.[58]

Riley won the police board election handily, winning two out of every three votes cast.[59] The police board wasted no time in naming a former nine-year councilman, Lucerne Besser, as new chief of police to replace James Lappeus.

The Republican candidate for mayor, William Spencer Newbury, won 55 percent of the vote over a Democratic rival with the last name of Davis.[60]

William Newbury was as close to the average profile of a Portland mayor as anyone ever has been. He hailed from the most common state of origin—New York.[61] Newbury was a member of a common mayoral profession—the law.[62] He also spent time as a merchant, the most universal occupation. At age forty-three, Newbury was close to the average age of forty-six when he took office.

Newbury had served as a lieutenant for the Union forces during the Civil War, as assistant secretary of state for Kansas, and as postmaster and mayor of Iola, Kansas. During his tenure as Portland's volunteer mayor, Newbury operated a successful farm machinery business.[63]

Mayor William Newbury. (Photo: OrHi #104366)

Newbury held strong anti-Chinese views, as did the majority of his constituents. "Newbury's attitude in regard to the exclusion of natives of China was emphatic and consistent," said a biographer of his time.[64] "The Chinese evil continues in our midst," Mayor Newbury said in his mayoral message to council. No Chinese should be employed to work on city public works projects, he added. Turning to other issues, he noted that the fire department was in a "splendid state of efficiency," and fully deserved the "high encomiums paid it." So many wharves had been built out into the river that river currents could move the river channel toward the east side if serious attention were not paid to that matter.[65]

Mayor Newbury's two-year term was relatively quiet. No major catastrophes. No charter changes. No big occasions to celebrate. Council passed four hundred sixty-nine ordinances during these two years, most of which involved streets, with fire protection a distant second.[66] The First Street Bridge across Marquam's Gulch was repaired, as was the Washington Street Bridge across Tanner's Creek.

Anyone who hitched a horse or other animal to a shade tree was to be fined for doing so. Shade trees planted along city streets were to be trimmed nine feet up from the street or sidewalk to allow free passage underneath.[67] The council appropriated two hundred dollars to light the town clock in the Odd Fellows Temple.

In June 1878, the council adopted a city seal that was to retain its form for eighty-six years, until modernized in 1964.[68] The "seal … shall consist of a female figure in the center thereof, representing commerce, and holding in her right hand a trident and pointing with her left to a sheaf of wheat and a forest, with a representation of Mount Hood in the background, and at her feet a cog-wheel and hammer, and on her right, a steamship coming into port. Said seal shall also have the words 'City of Portland, Oregon,' in the outer rim thereof; also the figures

Two Portland council members, Stephen Skidmore and Homer Sanborn,[70] represented Oregon at the 1878 Paris Exposition as part of a six-member delegation. Another member was seventy-year-old Portland pioneer James Terwilliger[71] for whom a school, park, and boulevard were later named.[72] "The 1878 Paris Fair was the most ambitious international exposition that had ever been undertaken. More than 16 million visitors attended the 66-acre site during the five months it was open, May to September. Sanborn accumulated an elaborate exhibit to publicize [Oregon's] products. Grasses, grains, fruits, and wood samples were contained in a specially made cabinet, 17 feet high and 9 feet across."[73]

The trip from Portland to Paris began with a steamship ride to San Francisco, where Oregonians boarded a transcontinental railroad, now in its ninth year, for New York. There they embarked on another sea voyage across the Atlantic. In Paris, Oregon's agricultural exhibit received favorable reviews. Stephen Skidmore spent four months viewing European cities, a visit that was to result in the Portland fountain that would one day bear his name.[74]

'1851,' the date of the incorporation of the city of Portland, and shall make an impression 2 1/4 inches in diameter."[69]

The council leased Block 132, originally designated for a public market,[75] to the Portland Mechanic's Fair Association for construction of a suitable pavilion and other buildings for holding fairs and exhibitions at least once a year.[76] The lease required no payment for the first year, one hundred dollars a year the next four, and one hundred fifty dollars a year for the second five years. The Mechanics Pavilion erected in 1879 cost sixteen thousand five hundred dollars.[77]

In spite of the mayor's warning about the possible negative effects on the river channel, council authorized the building of seven more wharves and pilings during Mayor Newbury's term.[78] Shortly before Newbury left office, the council established a Willamette River wharf line.[79]

A new charter amendment would soon be passed providing for three-year mayoral terms, making Mayor Newbury the last two-year mayor for the next fifteen years. Some time after his term ended, Newbury moved to Baker City, Oregon, where he practiced law intermittently until his death at age eighty-one.[80]

Chapter 13

The Scandalous Eighties

1879 – 1885

Mayors

No. 24: July 1879 – June 1881

David P. Thompson (two-year term)

July 1881 – June 1882

David P. Thompson (extended term)

No. 25: July 1882 – June 1885

James A. Chapman (third term, three-year term)

Republican David Thompson won the 1879 mayor's race in a close contest with Judge William Strong, a Democrat, to become Portland's next mayor.[1] As a nineteen-year-old, Thompson had walked across plains and mountains from Iowa to the Willamette Valley, driving a herd of fourteen hundred Merino sheep.[2] The entrepreneur who had hired him and eleven other sheepherders was R. R. Thompson, later a principal owner of the Oregon Steam Navigation Company[3] and who

Mayor David Thompson. (Photo: OrHi #70850)

served as a Portland councilman on two different occasions. Sources differ as to whether David and R. R. Thompson were related.[4]

David Thompson made Oregon City his base for twenty-three years, from 1853 until 1876, when he moved to Portland. He first worked as a surveyor, gaining a thorough knowledge of the northwest country. For a time, he managed the Oregon City Woolen Manufacturing Company, and later served as vice-president of the Oregon Railway & Navigation Company. He became a director of several national banks and was a member of the state legislature for seven years.[5] During his lifetime, he was a "woodchopper, blacksmith, surveyor, railroad builder, volunteer soldier, manufacturer, educator, statesman, banker and philanthropist."[6] He also was governor of the Idaho Territory (1874-76), Republican candidate for Oregon governor against Sylvester Pennoyer, and U.S. Ambassador to Turkey for four months in 1892-93.[7]

Soon after Thompson took office as mayor, the council directed the city surveyor to prepare plans for a main sewer to run from Tanners Creek and B Street (later Burnside) to the Willamette. This and other sewer projects received a good deal of council and state legislative attention during Mayor Thompson's tenure.[8]

In October, the Board of Police Commissioners dismissed police chief Lucerne Besser and hired former chief James Lappeus of the Oro Fino Saloon in his place. The city then filed suit against Besser and those who had guaranteed his performance for nine hundred thirty-seven dollars that he had collected, but failed to turn over to the city treasurer. The Oregon Supreme Court eventually awarded two hundred thirty-five dollars of that amount to the city.[9]

Responsibility for police management had proved a difficult challenge for whichever party was in power. The *Oregonian* noted that many more applicants had been promised police jobs than there were positions to fill, which led to "quarrels and jealousies." The party newly in power would take over the police force, only "to find it in their turn a thing to quarrel over and lead to their defeat, as they found it before."[10]

The contract for boarding prisoners housed in the city jail was awarded to the manager of the Burton House, payable at fifteen cents per meal served, with a maximum of two meals per prisoner a day. Two weeks later the contract was amended to allow prisoners who worked on public streets or other public property to be served three meals a day.[11]

In the financial markets of the East Coast, Europe, and Portland, deals were being negotiated that would shape Portland's transportation future. Henry Villard, the German-American who had come to Oregon on behalf of Ben Holladay's German investors, had bought out the O&C

Portlanders welcomed each arrival of a steamship from San Francisco with great anticipation. The steamer brought mail, books, visitors, new merchandise, settlers, excitement. Five days later, passengers boarded the steamer for the trip to San Francisco, from where they could catch a train eastbound across the continent. Otherwise, travel was by horseback, stagecoach, covered wagon, or a boat up or down the Willamette and Columbia rivers.[12]

> *"Steamer day" was a joyous occasion and the pomp and ceremony attending the arrival of the ocean steamer was not easily forgotten. A cannon was fired announcing its arrival and bulletins at the telegraph and newspaper offices gave out the exact time of the departure from Astoria. ... A large crowd always met the incoming ocean steamer and the usual runners were out for the (hotels). Patrick Kinney ... [buggy driver] ... was on hand and his modest and gentlemanly bearing always brought him a full load.*[13]

bondholders and was now a major financier in his own right. He had instigated an "immigration bureau" to promote Oregon in the eastern United States and Europe. Over thirty thousand people were said to have settled in Oregon as the result of this promotion.[14]

Villard assumed Holladay's domain and moved swiftly forward. Although his more dignified demeanor and higher standards of morality were in sharp contrast to the boorish behavior and corrupt morals of Holladay, Villard's ambition and single-mindedness regarding a railroad empire were much the same.[15] Villard planned a line from Portland along the Columbia River and thence southeast to Ogden, Utah, to connect with the transcontinental track there. He also put together financing to purchase that "grand monopoly of the Columbia," the Oregon Steam Navigation Company. Villard saw that "the force of gravity made the Columbia River the easiest and cheapest route to tide-water." This made Portland an ideal end-of-the-line for railroads from all over the country.[16]

A nineteenth-century version of modern graffiti captured the council's attention as they outlawed the posting, sticking, stamping, painting, or otherwise affixing of "notices, placards, bills, posters, advertisements, etc." to any "sidewalk, crosswalk, curb or curbstone, lamppost, hydrant, shade trees or tree boxes or upon any fence, gate, gatepost ... building

On January 9, 1880, a devastating windstorm hit Portland, a "frightful tornado"; an event that "would never be forgotten by any who witnessed it" according to an 1882 account: "At noon the gusts grew strong and frequent, and at one o'clock a continuous roar and clatter from the gale, and the falling signs, chimney, shutters, etc., was quite too audible in every part of the city. Half the older shade trees were ruined; church spires and solid houses were blown down; one or two persons killed and several injured by this breeze, which [was] the only such event in local history [at that time]."[19]

... bridge ... telegraph or telephone pole," without the owner's written permission.[17]

The council contracted with the O&C Railroad for use of its ferryboat and crew to help extinguish fires. The city agreed to install a force pump, hose, and other needed apparatus on this steamer ferry, and in return, the railroad was allowed to use the equipment for combating fires endangering its property beyond the city limits. However, the ferry crew was not required to fight city fires if doing so would prevent them from making connections with any passenger train.[18]

The Willamette River flooded again in late June 1880. Business virtually halted on both Front and First streets below Washington. The Clarendon Hotel dining room floor was submerged under five feet of water. The *Oregonian* moved its offices to the second floor. The Willamette reached a high water mark of 27.4 feet on July 1—two feet higher than the previous record set in 1876.

That winter, two more floods occurred. The Willamette reached 20 feet on December 2, and 21.4 feet on January 6. These high water levels prompted a thoughtful *Oregonian* editorial about the causes of such flooding: "Early settlers remember how the water, after a heavy rainfall, would spread out to great width in the swales, obstructed in its flow by the turf and the long, fallen grass, where now, since the grass has disappeared and the turf has been broken, deep and wide gullies have been worn, through which the water rushes in torrents. Thus, the tributaries of the Willamette fill more quickly than formerly, and of course the river itself rises more suddenly, and, therefore, is quite likely to rise higher. ... [A] flood is likely to occur any (year); and hence, the proper thing to do is to prepare for it. ... As the scientists would put it, we must get into harmony with our environment. It will be no great trouble to do so."[20]

Today, with the benefit of hindsight, we see that Harvey Scott's prediction of "no great trouble" to "get into harmony with our environment" was naïve and overly optimistic. By year 2000, the Bureau of Environmental Services was working to restore swales and wetlands along the river destroyed by continued dredging, contamination, and infill.[21] Flooding continued to pose problems throughout Portland's history, although the threat was reduced considerably by dams and other flood control measures undertaken in the twentieth century.

City business had now increased so much in volume that council authorized an assistant for the city auditor.[22] Soon thereafter, the auditor was directed to prepare a voluminous ordinance spelling out in minute detail the manner in which city streets were to be improved. The resulting ordinance covered permits, surveys, digging, sidewalk sills, crosswalks, box gutters, plank roadways, repairs, and testing. All lumber used in construction or repair was to be of "sound yellow fir, free from sap, shakes, or loose knots ... sawed of uniform thickness with good square edges." The exact specifications for macadamizing streets were spelled out, as were all details for maintaining city streets.[23]

In 1880, Portland boasted five school buildings and a public high school.[24] A third of city government's general fund revenue came from liquor license fees and bonds.[25] While Portland continued to dominate Pacific Northwest commerce and transportation, a lieutenant for Henry Villard noted that many Portlanders who had already accumulated wealth were neither very ambitious nor philanthropic: "There has been a lamentable lack of enterprise here. A large number of persons have made a great deal of money and live in fine houses, but they have shown so little public spirit, it is not difficult to guess their money has been made almost exclusively in trade without competition, and that with the infusion of new blood they will give way to another class."[26]

Portland was still five times larger than Seattle, and Oregon's population was more than double that of the Washington Territory, which would not become a state until 1889.[27] The 1880 census listed almost three thousand housewives in Portland, seven hundred eighty-four women "at home" (probably as unmarried relatives), three hundred sixty-nine women domestics, two hundred forty-seven seamstresses, two hundred thirty-six women in school, ninety-nine professionals, ninety-seven teachers, seventy-four women working in boarding houses, and fifty-eight prostitutes.[28]

> Abigail Scott Duniway and the state Equal Suffrage Association lobbied the legislature to grant women the vote, and a resolution was passed by the fall 1880 legislature to eliminate the word "male" from the state constitution chapter on privileges and elections. "A grand ratification meeting was held," Duniway reported, before the resolution was vetoed as unconstitutional by the governor "because of some technicality."[29] Duniway was not deterred for long by this setback.

In October 1880, the state legislature amended the city charter, extending the mayor's term to three years and giving him broad administrative powers over police matters, including hiring of the police chief. The charter also gave the mayor the right to appoint the city attorney, auditor, surveyor, street superintendent, and police judge, all of who were to serve three-year terms.[30] The provisions took effect July 1, 1881.

This new charter threw the next council into disarray. Both the mayor's race and a city council seat were contested.

Two people claimed Donald MacKay's former Ward 2 seat.[31] MacKay had resigned during the year and William Andrus had been appointed to take his place. Former county commissioner Charles Holman was elected in June to fill the remainder of MacKay's term, but Andrus insisted he was entitled to the seat until December. The new charter contained a provision—which a Multnomah County senator said was a simple clerical error—that failed to change all dates to June when the legislature was deciding between a December or June city election date. The council adjourned its initial meeting without deciding the dispute between Holman and Andrus."The absurdity of [the charter provision] is too apparent to merit serious consideration," argued Mayor Thompson. If council followed the provision, he pointed out, it could keep appointing its own members indefinitely.[32] The council, however, was not swayed by Thompson's logic, and decided, on a five to three vote, that Andrus would hold the position until January, when Holman's term would begin.[33]

Next the council addressed an even more contentious issue—who would be Portland's next mayor? Thompson's two-year term had expired, and he now sought a new three-year term.

The bruising mayoral campaign in June 1881 had ended in a virtual standoff between Thompson and a brash, ambitious politician named Joseph Simon. Both candidates were Republican, although Thompson lacked strong party loyalty. Lawyer Simon, thirty, was a powerful state senator and city councilman, a party loyalist who harbored plans to control the state Republican Party. His merchant father had brought

About this time, a legendary Portland saloon called Erickson's was built on Burnside Street. It covered nearly an entire city block and featured five bars, all in one huge room. The saloon "grew in size and magnificence until loggers, hard-rock miners and other hearty men from all over the West and sailors from the seven seas and beyond vowed they had rather see Erickson's with its gaslights in full blow than to view Niagara Falls tumbling into the Grand Canyon of the Colorado."[34]

Erickson's bartenders sported carefully tended mustaches and heavy watch chains dangling across broad white vests. A retinue of gargantuan bouncers kept crowds under control, so the saloon required little help from Portland police. "A favorite story around Erickson's ... concerned a ... troublesome Swede logger who liked to argue about the comparative abilities of different nationalities. On one such occasion ... the bouncer plucked Halverson by the collar and pants and threw him bodily out the Second Avenue entrance. Halverson presently wandered in through one of the three Burnside Street doors. Out he went again in a heap. This continued until he had been ejected through four different doors. ... [When]Halverson made his entry through the fifth and last door [the bouncer stood just inside]. Halverson stopped short. 'Yesus!' said he, 'vas yu bouncer en every goddam saloon en Portland?'"[35]

the family to Portland when Joseph was six years old. Now Simon was affiliated with the prominent Dolph law firm, and was a forceful proponent of the interests of his clients, who included railroad mogul Henry Villard. Simon focused his mayoral campaign on the need for more aggressive leadership in promoting Portland as a railroad center.[36]

Thompson was supported by a prominent citizens' committee and the *Oregonian*. The *Oregonian* charged that Simon would promote his clients' affairs and his own personal ambitions over the best interests of the city, and accused him of "stealing the levee."[37]

After the polls closed on election day, election judges first announced that Simon had won a nine-vote victory. However, when a three-member board of canvassers—the city auditor, county clerk, and justice of the peace—reviewed the ballots, they concluded that Simon had lost by one vote: 1,784 to 1,785.

Simon then petitioned the council to declare him the winner.[38] Both Thompson and the *Oregonian* charged that "gross corruption and bribery" had occurred during the election, and demanded a recount.[39]

The council met seven times over the next ten days, including all day on Saturday, in an attempt to straighten out this conundrum. In the meantime, David Thompson remained as mayor. He presided over routine council business while council president Henry Hewett took the chair whenever the mayor's race was discussed—which was most of the time. Both Thompson and Simon had taken the oath of office as mayor, and both showed up at every council meeting expecting to be named the rightful winner. A recount of votes was clearly necessary, but it took several meetings before the council could agree on the logistics.

Councilman Andrus's vote became an issue. Mayor Thompson charged that Andrus had a financial stake in the outcome of the election because he had placed bets on Simon to win. Andrus then produced an affidavit sworn before the justice of the peace that he held no pecuniary interest in the result of the election. But at the council's next meeting on July 8, four more affidavits appeared—from C. E. Sitton, Joseph Taylor, Stephen Skidmore, and Eli Morril—swearing that Andrus *had* bet money on the race. Counter affidavits were read from P. G. Baker and Mark A. Mayer, stating that the bets Andrus placed were on their behalf. The council compromised by voting to exclude Andrus from taking part in "preliminaries pertaining to the contest."[40]

The council had no guidance or precedent for deciding a contested election. Should each candidate be allowed to have lawyers make opening statements? Should outside parties be brought in as clerks and observers? Should each candidate have his own arsenal of clerks and witnesses? Should a member of the council or the city auditor preside over the opening and closing of the ballot box?

Council members finally agreed to perform most of the functions themselves, and to tally the ballots from each ward separately. All councilmen (except Andrus) would participate in the process. Councilman Gerdes removed the ballots from the string on which they had been strung; Councilman Chittenden called out the vote on each ballot, Councilman Keller restrung each ballot after it was read and counted. One clerk representing Simon and one clerk representing Thompson kept separate tallies of the votes. Councilmen Honeyman and Nicklin sat on each side of Councilman Gerdes, while Councilmen Kellogg and Raleigh sat on either side of Councilman Chittenden, to see that each vote was properly read. President Hewett retained order.[41]

The recount gave a one-vote margin to Thompson, excluding two disputed ballots for Simon, which were held out for possible reconsideration.

If the two ballots were kept in, Simon won by one vote.

If both ballots were discarded, Thompson won by one vote.

The disputed ballots were identified and labeled as "Ballot No. 100" and "Ballot No. 200." The council adjourned without deciding either ballot.

On July 11, the council gave lawyers for each side fifteen minutes to address them on Ballot No. 100. Simon's name had been written over Thompson's on this ballot. The council awarded the ballot to Simon on a five to three vote.[42] The tally was now tied at 1,783 to 1,783.

Next, the council allowed legal counsel from each side to take as much time as he liked to argue the legality of Ballot No. 200. We do not know exactly what was wrong with Ballot No. 200, but no one proposed counting it for Thompson. When the lawyers finished their presentations, four council members voted to count the ballot for Simon; the other four voted nay. One member was absent. The council was deadlocked.

The next evening, July 12, council discussion and resolutions centered around alleged irregularities concerning the entire Second Ward ballot box, of which Ballot No. 200 was part. The council again adjourned without reaching a final decision.

Two evenings later, on July 14, council voted to ask the chief justice of the Oregon Supreme Court to determine whether or not Ballot No. 200 should be counted. In the meantime, Mayor Thompson was to refrain from making any charter-mandated appointments. If the chief justice counted the ballot for Simon, then he would be declared mayor; if the judge voided the ballot, no one would be elected and incumbent David Thompson would remain in office until the following June.[43]

Understandably, the chief justice declined the invitation. So council members again had to address the issue. On August 3, they voted to record the various recount tallies in the council minutes, the first time this had been done.

President Hewett put the crucial question to his fellow councilmen: "Those in favor of counting the ballot for Mr. Simon will vote yea." Three councilmen—Andrus, Chittenden, and Gerdes—voted yea; the other six voted nay. The ballot was not counted. Simon and Thompson remained tied at 1,783 votes each.

By default, David Thompson would continue in office until the general election of June 1882 when a new mayor would be elected. By a five to four vote, the council postponed indefinitely Joseph Simon's petition to be declared mayor for the 1881-84 term.[44] Not satisfied with the council's conclusion, Simon filed suit in the state supreme court. In December, the court upheld the council's action.[45]

Henry Villard received a hero's welcome when he appeared before the Portland Board of Trade in October 1881. East Portland had granted his OR&N Railroad a "perpetual, non-compensatory franchise," and the Multnomah County commissioners had approved running a single track up Sullivan's Gulch to the Columbia River. Villard spoke of his plans to build a passenger terminal and a grand hotel on the west side of the river, as well as a freight terminal and shop facilities in Albina on the east side.[46]

Twenty-eight years later, Joseph Simon would return to Portland city government as the city's thirty-sixth mayor, after a prominent and controversial political career that included four years as a U.S. senator from Oregon (late 1898 to early 1903). During these interim years, Simon was to engage in an acrimonious battle for leadership of the Oregon Republican Party with John H. Mitchell, former city attorney and a deceitful politician, who served as a U.S. senator from Oregon in 1873-79 and 1901-05.[47]

Soon after the city's mayoral contest was decided, the council granted George Weidler a right-of-way to erect electric light lines in Portland.[48] Weidler had already erected a dynamo at his sawmill that lighted ten electric arc lamps, as well as a similar dynamo for the fall 1880 Mechanics Fair. The first electricity was soon on its way to Portland customers.[49]

That fall, the council awarded a second streetcar right-of-way grant.[50] In the next two years, the council would authorize several companies to build and operate street railroad tracks in different parts of the city, all still powered by horses.[51]

On May 6, 1882, Congress passed the Chinese Exclusion Act, which prohibited Chinese persons from entering the United States. Most Portlanders favored this legislation, as evidenced by a mass meeting that had been held in Portland in March 1879 protesting President Rutherford Hays' veto of a similar bill. That meeting, presided over by Oregon Governor Thayer and assisted by the Multnomah County District Attorney and the Chief Justice of the State Supreme Court, had produced an angry resolution: the "Chinese are … alien to every principle of American civilization, foes to the interest of our industrial population, who have not assimilated and never can assimilate with our people, who bring with them all the debasing vices of their effete social life, who contribute nothing to the wealth of our country, and

Although Chief Lappeus showed little interest in arresting prostitutes,[52] public pressure sometimes dictated otherwise. Thus it was with a floating whiskey scow anchored in the Willamette River since around 1880, on which a woman named Nancy Boggs had erected a two-story house that she had painted Nile green and screaming red.[53] "Miss Boggs' floating palace of sin was a success from the night it opened. On both east and west shores she stationed boatmen—pimps charged with seducing, then rowing, customers to the middle of the stream, where Nancy and her girls took care of the rest. … If the East Portland cops, in a moment of virtue, set out to raid the place, Miss Boggs, always forewarned, simply upped anchor and moved the scow nearer the Portland shore. … It also worked in reverse order."[54]

In 1882, during "one of those great moral waves that sweep over American cities every decade or so," Portland police teamed up with East Portland forces for a joint raid. Miss Boggs was well prepared for the onslaught. "She herself in person met the combined police forces with hose in hand, and out of the hose issued a terrific blast of steam straight from the scow's heating plant. Cursing and screaming like all the Harpies alive, Nancy poured live steam over the bluecoats, who got out of there quickly. … [Police] superiors considered what to do. … Along in the dark of the next morning, some unnamed policeman in a rowboat very quietly cut the manila ropes midway between the deck and anchor, and Miss Boggs' scow started on a wild trip downstream."[55] Eventually, author Stewart Holbrook says, the scow ended up anchored in the town of Linnton, several miles further down the Columbia River.[56]

who serve as a constant drain on our prosperity, sending away to China all the wealth they can hoard by living in hovels. … We … demand … that this bill be approved by the President."[57]

Thousands of Chinese coolies had come to the United States to perform the hard manual labor of hacking railroad lines through the mountains and desert for the Central Pacific Railroad. Depression times had aggravated anti-Chinese fervor. The 1882 Chinese Exclusion Act passed by Congress originally specified that it would apply for the next ten years, but the law was subsequently extended for another ten. Congress made the exclusion permanent in 1902. The law was not repealed until World War II, sixty years after passage.[58]

Nineteenth-century Portlanders would have been astounded to learn that, in 1998, a Chinese-born immigrant named David Wu[59] would be elected to represent Oregon's First District in Congress, a district which included downtown Portland.

❧

One of David Thompson's final official acts as mayor affected the Willamette River in a more lasting way: Portland's harbor was beginning to suffer in comparison to that of Seattle on the Puget Sound, both in the depth of the channel and prices charged to vessels and sailors. "There was a wild, tempestuous bar at the mouth of the Columbia with a natural depth of only 20 feet; the channel to Portland was only 10 feet deep and was obstructed by several islands and a particularly dangerous bar below Portland called 'the Hog's Back' … [S]ix English shipmasters … in 1881 [wrote] that 'the exorbitant prices charged at this port surpass any that have ever come before our notice.'"[60]

The council had no control over marketplace charges, but it could and would act to keep channel access open. Mayor Thompson signed an ordinance authorizing funds for a dredger, bull, dump scow, and appliances with which to remove mud, sand and gravel from the bottom of the river.[61] Sand and gravel bars had always been a challenge, but dredging did work, according to this testimonial in the *1866 City*

This stately elk fountain, located in the middle of Main Street near the county courthouse, was donated by former Mayor David Thompson in 1900. (Photo: OrHi #9550)

Directory: a "steam dredging machine for the purpose of keeping the bar at the junction of the Willamette and Columbia rivers clear of obstacles to navigation has met with the approval of a great majority of the citizens, and the machine ... has answered the purposes for which it was intended. ... [I]f its operations succeed only in silencing the croakings of the opponents of this city [regarding the Swan Island Bar] it will have achieved a glorious work."[62]

When election time neared, David Thompson again filed for mayor, hoping to win a full three-year term. The person nominated to run against Thompson had already served as mayor twice: Dr. James Chapman.

Although Joseph Simon took no visible role in the campaign, it was commonly understood that he helped Chapman defeat Thompson.[63] Vote buying also occurred, as will be seen in events of the following year.

David Thompson had been a conscientious but cautious mayor.[64] Late in life, he gave Portland the famous Elk Fountain statue located in the middle of Main Street, only a block north of city hall.[65] His family also donated the bronze statue of two "heroic-sized" Indians titled "The Coming of the White Man," placed in Washington Park in David Thompson's memory.[66]

July 1882 - June 1885

James Chapman now returned as Portland's twenty-fifth mayor, for his third and longest term[67]—a term that would bring him disgrace. He was now sixty-two years old, his private medical practice had fallen off, and he was suffering financial difficulties. He had dropped his expensive membership in the Arlington Club.[68]

Mayor Chapman's third term started out quietly enough. Street and sidewalk and sewer projects moved forward.[69] The need for a paid fire force was discussed, a topic which had surfaced regularly for several years. Whenever a fire alarm sounded, the volunteer firemen had to rush to the firehouse, then haul an engine to the fire. By the time they reached the fire, they were "exhausted from hard work hauling the engines over the rough, muddy streets and not able to do the hard work required of them, for which they receive[d] no compensation."[70] The answer was horses to pull the engines. A council committee advocated equipping at least two fire companies with horses that could be kept

Mayor James Chapman. (Photo: OrHi #38385)

ready for service at a moment's notice.[71]

In October, the state legislature created a paid fire department with a three-member Board of Fire Commissioners. The board was given complete control over Portland fire department matters, including appointment of a fire chief[72] at an annual salary of two thousand dollars.[73]

Even with a volunteer force, fire protection was expensive for city taxpayers. In 1878, Company No. 1 got a new eight thousand dollar firehouse and Company No. 5 got a new four thousand dollar fire engine, bringing total fire department expenditures to thirty thousand dollars. Regular fire expenses exceeded police department costs by two thousand dollars.[74] The new Board of Fire Commissioners appointed by the mayor soon presented the council with an estimated budget nearly double the previous year's at fifty-five thousand dollars, to be covered by a dedicated property tax.[75] Projected expenses included twenty-six thousand dollars for the salaries of forty-eight firemen, one chief, two assistants, and one secretary; thirty-five hundred dollars for fourteen horses; another thirty-five hundred dollars for a new engine; and eighteen hundred dollars for four new carts. Food for the horses was budgeted at twenty-four hundred dollars a year; and keeping them shod, another two hundred seventy-five dollars. More cisterns and hydrants would be installed.[76]

The legislature also approved a new city charter in 1882. The 1864 charter had been amended so many times that officials found it difficult to keep track of all its changes.This fifth charter[77] provided an annual salary of fifteen hundred dollars for the mayor and three hundred dollars for council members (approximately twenty-six thousand dollars and five thousand dollars, respectively, adjusted for inflation today)—a significant change for officials who had previously volunteered their services. The council would once again appoint the auditor. From now on, the superintendent of streets had to be a civil engineer. The council was authorized to suppress "places kept for smoking opium" and to "punish inmates of bawdy houses, houses of ill-fame, keepers of places kept for smoking opium and opium smokers."[78] Most importantly, the charter eliminated the Board of Police Commissioners. The mayor would again appoint the police chief and promulgate all police rules and regulations, although the council could still limit the number of officers. The police chief's salary would be three thousand dollars per year, double that of the mayor and 50 percent higher than that of the fire chief.[79]

The big news was that the Northern Pacific Railroad was coming to Portland! In December 1882, the council authorized construction of rail lines through north Portland to a westside terminus.[80] Portland had nearly a year to prepare for the arrival of its first transcontinental train.

For years, the quarterly license fee for barrooms and drinking shops had fluctuated between fifty and one hundred twenty-five dollars, depending on the council's inclination. This year, the council settled for seventy-five dollars a quarter, but added stiffer penalties for violations. Any business that sold intoxicating liquor during voting hours on election day would be fined at least one hundred dollars and be forced to forfeit its license. Any establishment which permitted a woman to act as a waitress or bartender, or to sing or dance, was to be fined twenty-five to fifty dollars *and* forfeit its license.[81] The ink was barely dry on that ordinance when council raised the quarterly fee back to one hundred twenty-five dollars, a whopping increase.[82]

Street improvements remained the council's main business. They spent entire meetings talking about streets: which ones to improve, how steep the slope should be, who should pay the cost. The council approved surveys for proposed streets and sidewalks and plans for new ones, assessed costs against the owners of benefited property, and ruled on protests by property owners asking that their assessments be reduced.

Street ordinances were so numerous that auditor R. B. Curry created two indexes in the new city ordinance journal: one index was for street ordinances, the other for all other city laws.[83] This bound ledger weighed nineteen pounds, measured twelve by eighteen inches, and was over three inches thick. It would not likely be accidentally misplaced.

In March 1883, the *Portland Weekly News* made scandalous allegations against Marshal James Lappeus. The newspaper reprinted an 1860 poster charging Lappeus with offering to free convicted murderer Danford Balch from jail for one thousand dollars. The reprinted affidavits said Mrs. Balch had attempted to raise the bribe, but had been unsuccessful.[84]

About this time, a group of well-known Portland citizens formally incorporated the River View Cemetery Association. The board included two members each from the Failing, Corbett, and Ladd families, as well as Judge Matthew Deady.[88] The cemetery would be situated on three hundred acres overlooking the Willamette River near today's Sellwood Bridge. Twelve Portland mayors would be buried there.[89]

The council now investigated these allegations, and cleared Chief Lappeus of the charges, but Mayor Chapman removed him from office anyway.[85] Lappeus had served a total of thirteen years as either city marshal or city police chief, and was Portland's "major police personality" for twenty-four years.[86] Charles Abbot Tracy III, who researched Portland's early police function, said that although Lappeus was sometimes controversial, a "majority of the historical evidence indicates that he served Portland's major commercial interest quite well at a time when their continued growth needed police protection."[87] Chapman appointed William H. Watkinds as new police chief.

As we shall see, it appears likely that these old charges against Lappeus were deliberately dug up to give Chapman an excuse to appoint a new chief of police.

❧

The council decided to move its chambers to the second floor of Frank Dekum's "new brick building" at S.W. Third and Washington, which was to house Portland's growing city government for the next eight years, and would be dubbed the "Council Building."[90]

Five blocks away, across from Pioneer Post Office, Henry Villard's workers started to build his luxury hotel in early 1883, a hotel that would be worthy of serving the Northern Pacific transcontinental passengers who would soon descend on Portland. Work was halted after a few months for lack of money, however, leaving exterior walls standing, some two stories high. This produced an annoying eyesore, complete with weeds and lowlife, which later became known as "Villard's Ruins" and "Villard's Folly."[91] Seven years later, the magnificent Portland Hotel would open on this site and would become the center of Portland's upper- and upper-middle class social life for sixty years.[92]

On September 10, 1883, three hundred dignitaries from around the world arrived at the Northern Pacific depot in East Portland, exuberant from their trek across the continent from New York to Portland on the

A grand celebration greeted arrival of the first transcontinental train on September 11, 1873. Portland is symbolically joined with Portland, Maine, by signs on either side of the arch. (Photo: OrHi #26180)

Northwest's first transcontinental train. Only two days before, the east and west lines had met in western Montana.[93] And although Villard was experiencing serious financial difficulties due to an economic recession, he refused to cut back on the grand ceremonies planned to mark this historic event. An observer later wrote of the occasion: the "evening illumination … was produced by … 20,000 gas jets employed to write in flame the initials HV [Henry Villard] on one side and NP [Northern Pacific] on the other, with fiery wreaths of gas jets, sparkling like diamonds. These wreaths were placed on either side of First Street. The word WELCOME was also written in letters of fire, arched over the street at First and A."[94]

Guests ranged from former president Ulysses S. Grant to Lord James Bryce of England to Francis Pettygrove, Portland's co-founder. City officials had been involved in the celebration process at every stage of the event—from initial permissions for decorations to the ceremonies and speeches and cleanup afterward. The transcontinental train was a triumphant, long-awaited beginning, but also the end of an era. "The celebration staged was the greatest which Portland had ever seen, the whole town garlanded with evergreens and flowers, vast bannered arches raised above the streets, thousands following the procession to its culmination. But in many ways it was a celebration of the past as much as of the future—a farewell as much as a greeting—for the town well knew that it was the end of its formative pioneer epoch."[95]

❧

The city had barely recuperated from this excitement when Mayor Chapman admitted that he had bought his election. He told the *Mercury* newspaper that he had agreed to appoint two men to top city jobs if he got elected mayor, and in exchange, these men were to assure his election over David Thompson. Chapman admitted he had signed a contract with Lucerne Besser, former councilman and former chief of police, before the election, when he "had no obligation to citizens." He had agreed to appoint Besser superintendent of streets and Connell as police chief upon "receipt of $1,000 in gold coin." However, when seven council members voted to name Watkinds chief, Chapman had to renege on the contract. He told the newspaper that Besser was blackmailing him as a result. Besser and his friends had "spent some money" to pay "election expenses," Chapman said. "You know that such bargains are made before every election … Presidents of the United States do it, too."[96]

At its October 4, 1883, meeting, the council convened a committee of three to investigate the "alleged execution by his honor, Mayor J. A. Chapman, of a certain agreement with L. Besser in May 1882." In a late November council meeting that lasted until midnight, the committee presented majority and minority reports on its findings. The *Oregonian* headlined its story the next day:

FURTHER DISGRACED
The City Council Impeaches Mayor J. A. Chapman
"Plainly the Intention Was Bribery"
Committee Appointed with Full Power to Prosecute the Case
Under the Civil Code of Oregon. [97]

James Chapman and Lucerne Besser had signed a written contract on May 16, 1882, the majority report said, in which Besser promised to nominate Chapman for mayor and to furnish the money to secure his election. Chapman in return agreed to nominate Thomas Connell for police chief and Besser for superintendent of streets. Besser pledged to pay Chapman one thousand dollars in gold coin and to use his influence with the Multnomah County legislative delegation to amend the city charter so the mayor would get an annual salary of five thousand dollars.

If the salary increase did not pass, Besser would pay Chapman an additional one thousand dollars a year to "compensate him for his time and trouble and loss of time and certain incidental expenses that will naturally occur in discharging the onerous duties of the office of mayor of this city."

During questioning of Besser by the committee, Besser had "taken possession" of the contract and refused to return it, Councilman J. B. Haley said in his minority report. Haley concluded that because the council had no jurisdiction to act on charges against the mayor, and no power to compel witnesses, it would be unfair to proceed further. The mayor was an independent branch of government, and the matter should be indefinitely postponed.[98]

While the committee found no evidence to prove that money had been paid to or by the mayor, the majority report said, in signing this contract Chapman had fulfilled the provisions of Oregon law calling for forfeiture of office. Alfred Sears, Jr., and W. L. Chittendon, the majority members, recommended that the council hire legal counsel and institute proceedings to declare the office of mayor vacant. The *Oregonian* reported what happened next this way:

> Haley (jumping to his feet)—*Can you prove that he received a bribe? Can you hang a man before he has committed a murder?*
>
> Gerdes—*The investigating committee have found mayor Chapman guilty. Where is their authority to try him? … If there has been bribery the grand jury and the district attorney should look into it and bring the guilty party to justice. … We have spent too much money already for lawyers' fees.*
>
> Honeyman—*The whole matter charged has been admitted. In a public communication the mayor admitted his guilt and attempted to justify it. The only possible defense now would be that in his communication to the Mercury he did not state the truth.*[99]

By five to three, the council voted to proceed with action against the mayor.[100] But there the matter sat.

Two months later, in early February 1884, an *Oregonian* editorial titled "The Corrupt Mayor" said the council had not acted because it had no money to hire a lawyer, Chapman would veto any ordinance which sought to authorize the funds, and the mayor's supporters on the council would sustain the veto. The editorial urged the district attorney to press charges against Chapman.[101] But Multnomah County District Attorney John F. Caples declined to do so.

A new district attorney, John Gearin, was elected in June, but the council committee did not approach him, because, reported Councilman Sears, they feared Gearin might unjustly charge that they lacked impartiality and fairness. Sears recommended that the present committee, of which he was chair, be discharged. The report was adopted.[102]

The next day, the *Oregonian* noted that Mayor Chapman had finally asserted his independence of the "Gerdes ring," and those who had protected Chapman in the past were now out for revenge.[103] Both Gerdes and Sears were now against Chapman. Again, the paper called for a grand jury investigation of Chapman's election and the Besser contract.[104] But no such investigation occurred. Mayor Chapman was to finish his term with no formal charges filed against him.[105]

City business had, of course, continued while the Chapman bribery scandal titillated the town. The council appropriated six thousand dollars for the purchase of ten dirt carts and enough horses, men, and equipment to clean the city streets.[106] Another ordinance required all new downtown buildings to have walls of brick, stone, or other noncombustible materials. Outer walls were to be at least twelve inches thick for the first story; eight inches thick for the second.[107]

Bankrupt railroad mogul Henry Villard abandoned plans for a luxury hotel in1883, leaving this ghostly eyesore, "Villard's Folly," for six years. Depicted by Francesca C. R. Grothjean's painting. (Photo: OrHi #35227)

A disorderly conduct ordinance specified prohibited offenses: trespassing on private property, defacing public property, roaming around the streets after midnight, smoking or buying opium, soliciting prostitution, killing robins, driving cattle through certain streets, riding a bicycle on the sidewalk, carrying baskets or buckets on poles across one's shoulders, hitching horses to a sidewalk, or bathing without bathing dress that covered the body from the neck to the knees.[108]

In 1884, the first black police officer, George M. Hardin, was hired.[109]

In that same year, Henry Villard's advisors declared him insolvent, and a committee of New York bankers named a career railroad man as president of the Northern Pacific Railroad.[110]

State voters turned down a women's suffrage amendment by more than two to one in June 1884. Multnomah County defeated the measure, which was supported by all the state's rural counties. Abigail Scott Duniway, who had been certain of victory, blamed defeat on Washington railroad workers who were herded to the polls "like sheep," and on prohibitionist women who got the suffragists' opponents stirred up. Immigrants were said to have been paid up to two dollars and fifty cents for each anti-suffrage vote.[111]

In February 1885, a new charter amendment prohibited the sale or circulation of obscene literature in Portland; allowed the city to license, tax, and regulate lawyers, doctors, brokers, and others; and again extended the city limits.[112]

Coal oil lamps were abandoned for lighting city streets when the council contracted to pay sixteen thousand dollars a year for five hundred gas lamps that would burn from twilight until midnight, with the option of extending the time that lamps were lit until daylight for an additional two thousand dollars.[113]

Problems continued with the city's water supply. Not only were citizens paying too much for water, but water pressure was low and quality dubious. "In 1884, customer dissatisfaction came to a head with cries of 'tainted water.' Waste matter from upstream mills and settlements posed a constant threat to the Willamette River's potability. Occasional tidal shifts backed up the Columbia, which in turn … return[ed] to Portland its riverborne wastes. Citizens held protest meetings and printed pamphlets decrying the dirty water."[114]

In June 1885, the council approved a twenty-year contract with P. F. Morey to supply the city with water from the Bull Run River. The city would pay Morey forty thousand dollars per year, to be raised from a special property tax of three mills. In addition, Morey would collect monthly service fees from customers, according to a price structure written into the ordinance:

$1 for dwelling houses and stores.
50¢ for a residential tub of hot or cold water; $1 for boarding houses.
50¢ for each residential water closet.
10¢ for each urinal.
50¢ for each cow per private stall; 25¢ for each horse.
$1.25 for a garden hose to water 250 square yards.
Metered rates of 20¢ per gallon for the first 50,000 gallons, 15¢ thereafter, applied for restaurants, bakeries, butcher shops and drinking saloons, along with other charges.[115]

Within two and a half years, Morey had agreed to build a system of pipes, pumps, and storage reservoirs to bring water from the slopes of Mt. Hood to Portland. Within five years, the city could purchase these water works at cost plus 6 percent. After ten years, the council could set new water rates, provided that Morey received a net annual 10 percent return on his investment. Mayor Chapman signed this ordinance a week before his infamous three-term mayoral career came to an end.

❧

Nothing about Dr. James Chapman's record indicates popularity with the voters. On the contrary, Chapman won his elections through vote buying and bribery. His candidacies can be summarized as follows:

- In 1867, appointed to a one-year term as mayor after Thomas Holmes died and Aaron Wait declined to serve.
- In 1871, ran for mayor; soundly defeated by Philip Wasserman.
- In 1875, won election as mayor in a close contest over Henry Failing in which Chapman was said to be the candidate of unscrupulous Ben Holladay.
- In 1882, won election as mayor in a close contest over David Thompson; later admitted signing a bribery contract with Lucerne Besser to assure this election—a low point in Portland city politics.

Less than six months after leaving office, on December 12, 1885, Dr. Chapman was yanked from his buggy by a telephone wire hanging across the street and killed. His estate owed debts totaling five hundred dollars.[116]

Chapter 14

Riots, Oligarchy, and a Presidential Visit

1885 – 1891

Mayors

No. 26: July 1885 - April 1888

John Gates (elected for three-year term)

No. 27: May 1888 - June 1888

Van DeLashmutt (appointed for two-month term)

July 1888 - June 1891

Van DeLashmutt (elected for three-year term)

The winner of the 1885 mayoral race—John Gates—bested the next governor of Oregon, Sylvester Pennoyer, by a margin of only 150 votes in doing so.[1] But Pennoyer—Harvard-educated, pro-labor, avidly anti-Chinese—was not to be discounted. He would not only wield power over Portland in his role as governor, but would be elected Portland mayor eleven years later.

The city's twenty-sixth mayor, John Gates, was a prolific inventor whose credits included nautical innovations such as a hydraulic steering gear for steam vessels and propellers for sluicing out sand bars from navigable streams. He supervised construction of numerous steamers, including the *John Gates*.[2] A 1947 *Oregon Journal* photo caption proclaims him a "steamboat genius" who was known as "the Edison of the West."[3] Born in Maine in 1829, Gates was the second-oldest mayor in the city's history thus far, at age fifty-six.[4] Gates had joined the California gold rush,[5] then came to Portland as engineer for the Reed & Abrams steam sawmill in 1853.[6] He was later chief engineer for the influential Oregon Railway and Navigation Company, a position he continued to hold throughout his mayoral term.

Statewide, the Republican Party was splintered between the Henry Corbett and Joseph Simon faction and John H. Mitchell and his allies. Gates was part of the Corbett-Simon contingent. In fall 1885, the state legislature cast sixty-nine ballots before adjourning without choosing a

Mayor John Gates (right) and Capt. John Couch. (Photo: OrHi #71187)

U.S. senator. In a special session the following month, John Mitchell won reelection to that position by one vote over Henry Corbett.[7] Intense rivalry between these camps in the Republican Party would manifest itself in city elections for years to come. The new nine-member city council generally supported the economic interests of the Corbett-Simon camp, says historian E. Kimbark MacColl, but was "jealous of Simon's political power in the legislature."[8]

A lawsuit enjoining the city from entering into the P. F. Morey waterworks contract placed that agreement in abeyance until the lawsuit was resolved.[9] In the meantime, a group of prominent Portlanders paid Judge Matthew Deady to draft legislation that would wrest control of the city's water supply and operations from the council and give that authority to an independent citizen body.[10] The council strongly opposed this measure, which was sponsored by Joseph Simon, labeling the proposed water committee an "Oligarchy of Fifteen" that would lack responsibility to the people. The legislation was flawed, council members said, because no limit was placed on the number of terms a water committee member could serve, and because the main qualification for appointment was "simply to be moneyed."[11]

Nevertheless, the legislature approved creation of the Portland Water Committee in spite of concerns raised that the city was taking on too much bonded debt—seven hundred thousand dollars for the water works in addition to the city's basic one hundred thousand dollar debt limit. The charter amendment named fifteen men who would constitute this new "oligarchy."[12] Included were Mayor Gates, former mayors Henry Failing and William Ladd, former councilmen Henry Corbett and Simeon Reed, and the council's landlord, Frank Dekum.[13]

Securing "good, pure and wholesome water" for the "comfort, convenience and well-being" of Portland citizens was the charge given this new committee. The original fifteen members were to disband after a water supply was obtained and the system became operational. Five committee members were to continue as a permanent water commission to oversee ongoing operations.[14] Membership on the Water Committee was indeed elitist and self-perpetuating, but the results obtained over the years were to create a legendary Portland success story.

Henry Failing was elected Water Committee chair, a position he would hold until his death thirteen years later.[15] Col. Isaac Smith, the new staff engineer, soon recommended that the same Bull Run water identified in P. F. Morey's proposed waterworks be pursued as the most promising source for water.[16] But it would be many years before the Water Committee acquired all the needed property and right-of-way deeds for a pipeline that would bring good, pure, wholesome Bull Run water from the slopes of Mt. Hood to Portland.

Joseph Simon won another political triumph in autumn 1885 with the re-establishment of Portland's Board of Police Commissioners. Virtually all mayoral and council power over the police force was revoked, and handed back to a new three-member police board to be selected by the governor, with subsequent commissioners to be elected by the citizenry.[17] Republican governor Zenas Moody appointed Simon and two of his allies, Byron P. Cardwell and Jonathan Bourne, Jr., as the new police commissioners. Both Simon and Bourne would later serve as U.S. senators,[18] and both would use the police board as a political tool, making the board even more controversial than before. Joseph Simon's nephew told his friends that he carried political cash from Portland to his Uncle Joe in Salem, presumably cash paid to influence police board matters.[19]

Bourne, a fast-living, ruthless, aggressive man, used his police board connection to extort "at least $10,000" in one year from Chinese gamblers and saloonkeepers in the North End, where he maintained close connections with ward bosses. While Bourne was never elected to city office, he played an influential role in municipal affairs for several years, using his wealth to great advantage. "Most everyone liked [Bourne]," said former congressman A. M. Lafferty. "He dressed well. He always had money, remittances from Bourne Mills," his family's textile plant in New England. "He entertained much at the best eating places and was a charming host."[20] Bourne was later to undergo a political transformation, and to campaign as a reformer during the Progressive era.[21]

❧

A general depression gripped the region during 1882-86,[22] but hard times did little to slow down Portland's growth. The city now boasted twenty-one millionaires.[23] Portland led all cities on the West Coast "in the number of elegant and costly dwellings as compared to her total population," according to *The West Shore* magazine.[24]

The city had a day and night police force and a paid fire department. Liquor flowed freely, and fees from licensing of saloons and drinking shops contributed a substantial share of general city government revenue. A harborful of ships and an eastbound transcontinental railroad provided connections to the outside world. Farm produce reached the harbor by rail, boat, and wagon. The telegraph, telephone, and electrical lines provided the modern technology Portland needed to expand and prosper.

The municipality boasted one hundred miles of sidewalks, sixteen miles of wooden crosswalks, two miles of stone crosswalks, two miles of stone trestles, and fifty-two miles of streets.[25] Since the cost of improving city streets and sidewalks was parceled out to benefited property owners, little general fund money was used for these projects.[26]

❧

In early 1886, widespread anti-Chinese prejudice was fanned into violence in Portland. A labor organizer named Daniel Cronin, who had recently forced three hundred Chinese out of Tacoma, arrived in late January with the avowed purpose of stirring up emotions against the Chinese.[27] "In three months," Cronin declared, "there will not be a working Chinaman in Portland."[28]

A committee of fifteen notified Chinese to "git up and git." An Anti-Coolie Club—which might have been the same entity[29]—formed on January 27, and set a forty-day deadline for all Chinese to leave Portland.[30] Mayor Gates doubled the city police force and swore in three hundred armed citizens in anticipation of trouble. In Seattle, four hundred Chinese were forcibly loaded on ships for deportation in early February. The governor of Washington Territory declared martial law.

The night of February 22, 1886, armed men forced one hundred sixty Chinese employees of the Oregon City Woolen Mills onto the steamer *Latona* and shipped them to Portland. The terrified Chinese were then paraded before a torchlight crowd of a thousand shouting men and boys. The parade instigators were arrested and brought before Judge Deady, but the violence continued. The following chronology of Portland's subsequent anti-Chinese violence was provided by Leslie Scott in an appendix to *History of The Oregon Country*: "On February 28, masked men drove Chinese out of Albina, and on March 4, from Mount Tabor. … On March 12, a Chinese colony at Guild's Lake was raided by masked robbers, and, on the same night, a dynamite attempt was made to blow up a Chinese house at North Portland."[31]

Mayor Gates called a March 13 meeting, only to have it taken over by anti-Chinese agitators who elected Governor Pennoyer as chair and passed resolutions to expel and exclude all Chinese.[32] Gates and the law-and-order contingent moved to another room to regroup and plan strategy.[33]

"An attempt was made on March 23, 1886, to blow up a Chinese wash house in Sixth Street … and the next day a Chinese shanty in East Portland was burned by rioters. Two militia companies were organized at Portland March 24. The United States grand jury indicted the Oregon City rioters March 29, and arrests followed. These displays of the power of the law had a sobering effect."[34] March 24 was the date by which the Chinese were to be out of town,[35] but the day passed and the Chinese remained. "A dynamite outrage was perpetrated at East Portland on July 7, 1886, and on August 12 an assault was committed upon a Chinese laundry at East Portland. A Chinese camp at Mount Tabor was attacked with dynamite on September 9, and a similar outrage committed against a Chinese camp of woodcutters at East Portland."[36]

Sources differ as to what finally halted the violence. The fact that arrests were made was undoubtedly a factor. Pennoyer toned down his rhetoric and urged his followers to "seek relief at the ballot boxes."[37] The salmon industry needed Chinese labor for "the bloody task of hacking up fish all day," which white laborers were loath to do.[38] Even after the violence ended, the intimidation of Chinese continued for some time. Perhaps the violence was never actually brought under control, but "simply wore itself out."[39]

Between 1880 and 1890, the Chinese population in Multnomah County doubled, even as the Northwest in general was experiencing a

Author Malcolm Clark compared 1886 conditions in Portland with the relocation of Japanese in 1942 following the attack on Pearl Harbor, noting that the anti-Chinese riots occurred during years of depression and unemployment, the organization of national and local labor groups, "grinding conditions imposed by massive corporations on laborers," and lack of integration of Chinese into western culture and customs.[44] The gradual slipping away of Chinese, he laments, left the city "poorer for their going."[45]

drop in foreign immigration.[40] Oregon's Chinese were thus more heavily concentrated in Portland than ever before. Another result of the riots was that Portland gained a large armory that was built as barracks for the militia formed to deal with anti-Chinese incidents.[41]

Although the degree of violence against the Chinese in Portland never matched that in Seattle or San Francisco, the riots represented a "large nub on the thread of bigotry which passes through the town's history."[42] On the other hand, a history of Portland's Chinese concludes that Portland, as well as the whole state, "became a refuge for persecuted Chinese looking for less hostile environs."[43]

Oregonian editor Harvey Scott explained the prevailing 1890 view of the Chinese situation this way: the Chinese "are not a particularly desirable people … but it has not been found necessary to expel them, and it is acknowledged by thinking people that the work they perform so well—laundrying, housework, wood-cutting, clearing up land and railroad construction—is no detriment but makes work of a more desirable and better rewarded kind for the American. Also, to those who believe that the race which claims the more enlightenment owes fraternal care to those inferior … it seems odious to deny an equal chance in our city."[46]

The 1885-86 council approved numerous street and sewer projects, and passed ordinances to improve City Park, prevent and suppress gambling, restrain and punish intoxication, prevent and suppress bawdy houses and places where fornication was enacted, and required that privies and cesspools located within a hundred feet of a sewer had to connect to that sewer. Rules were adopted to prevent and punish the storage of uncured hides of animals that created "a noisome or offensive smell or atmosphere." The council took steps to prevent bribery at election time by offering a reward of two hundred and fifty dollars to anyone who supplied the city with usable information about bribes. And in a much-needed effort to improve access to city laws, council appropriated up to fifteen hundred dollars to have all city ordinances codified in book form.[47]

Rules promulgated by the new Board of Police Commissioners specified that no policeman could leave the city without permission of the chief, and prohibited solicitation of funds for political purposes by or from police members (a provision that was flagrantly violated). A failure to pay indebtedness for clothing and subsistence was "cause for ignominious dismissal." A year of Portland residency and the ability to read and write English were required of all applicants for the position of patrolman.[48]

In December, the Water Committee purchased three reservoirs, thirty miles of iron water mains, and a pumping station at Palatine Hill for pumping water from the Willamette River.[49] Banking institutions controlled by committee members William S. Ladd, Henry Failing, and Henry Corbett were the high bidders on bonds to buy the private waterworks.[50]

A petition signed by forty-one citizens protested the condition of sidewalks along Alder Street, noting that merchants were storing heavy boxes and barrels on awnings that could collapse on people walking beneath them at any time. The sidewalks were "constantly crowded with a mass of idle men so as to prevent the use of this street by ladies and children," the petition said. Mayor Gates told the council that the existence of "empty boxes, garbage barrels, ash barrels, threshing machines, crockery crates, and iron grindstones" which littered the sidewalks was one of the most pressing matters facing the city.[51]

The Morrison Bridge opened April 11, 1887; it was the first bridge across the Willamette and the longest vehicular bridge west of the Mississippi River.[52] The wooden bridge was built and operated by a private company with the consent and encouragement of the city council. Portlanders on both sides of the river joined in jubilant celebration. All bridge traffic was free the first day. Afterward, the toll was five cents for foot travelers, loose sheep, and hogs; ten cents for loose horses, cattle, and a lone horse with rider; fifteen cents for a wagon with a single horse and driver; and twenty cents for a wagon with two horses and one driver.[53]

Agitation for a bridge had been especially strong on the east side. Candidates running for office had always favored such a bridge, but were dissuaded by ferryboat interests after election day. This waiting engendered a poem, "locally the most celebrated doggerel ever penned," by a printer named Stephen Maybell. The seven verses, of which the first and last are printed below, bemoaned the fate of a lad who sat on the riverbank, waiting, waiting, waiting—"through boyhood, through middle age, and into senility, chanting endlessly."[54]

Behind the pines had sunk the sun,
   And darkness hung o'er Oregon,
When on the banks of Willamette
   A youth was seen to set and set;
And set and sing unto the moon
   A wild, yet sweet pathetic tune—
"They're going to build, I feel it yet,
   A bridge across the Willamette."

***

Years pass'd—there came a trav'ler roun'
   To visit our East Portland town;
As on the river bank he stood,
   He saw a sight that froze his blood;
Right there beneath the glowing sun,
   There sat a ghostly skeleton,
Which turned its hideous, fleshless head,
   And grinned most horribly, and said:
"They're going to build, I feel it yet,
   A bridge across the Willamette."[55]

Regardless of how the name was pronounced (even then, Willamette correctly rhymed with "dammit" rather than "yet"), the river would never again be a formidable barrier to trade and communication.

But getting the bridge built had taken more than an act of Congress, because Congress had passed an enabling act seventeen years before. Numerous attempts had been made to complete plans for a bridge. Many petitions had flown back and forth. Efforts had been repeatedly thwarted over the years.[56] In 1881, Judge Deady had halted construction of the bridge, arguing that it would obstruct navigation and violate federal law.[57] Deady was overruled by the U.S. Supreme Court.

A second bridge—for trains—would be built across the Willamette the following year, with a second deck for other traffic opened a year later.[58]

Another transportation milestone was reached in December 1887, with the arrival of the first train from San Francisco.[59] No poem chronicled this waiting, but it had taken nearly twenty years, since the ground-breaking ceremonies on both sides of the Willamette in April

1868, for the line to be finished.[60] The Southern Pacific Railroad completed the Oregon - California connection.

The year 1887 saw unprecedented prosperity for the Pacific Northwest, according to the *Oregonian*, with no failure or setback of any kind. The population of Portland and adjoining suburbs, including Albina and East Portland, totaled around fifty thousand. The most important duty now facing the city, the *Oregonian* declared, was to build a first-class hotel, a project which was already in the fund-raising stage.[61]

Druggist Richard B. Knight donated a menagerie of animals to the city that year, a donation that would mark the beginning of a Portland zoo. Knight's collection included a grizzly bear purchased from a sailor for seventy-five dollars, an Alaskan bear purchased for fifty dollars, a seal, and four deer. The city housed the animals in City Park, to be looked after by a park keeper who received an annual salary of seven hundred seventy-fourdollars.[62]

In early April, the council authorized purchase of a sturdy Remington typewriter for the auditor's office at a cost of one hundred forty-five dollars. Council minutes and ordinances would henceforth be more legible.[65]

Portland experienced a "historic siege" of cold weather during the winter of 1887. Future mayor Henry Rowe drove into town in a sleigh every day for weeks from his home on the far east side. On January 15, 1888, the Willamette River froze over. The temperature dipped to two degrees below zero, forcing ice-bound Columbia River traffic to a standstill.[63] "Governor Pennoyer inaugurated the idea of carrying a long pole, so that if you broke through the ice, the pole would keep you from going under. … It was no uncommon sight to see a steady stream of people making their way over the river, and each one of them holding onto the long fir stick. … The river continued frozen for several weeks."[64]

With only two months left in his three-year term, John Gates died suddenly on April 27, 1888, the second Portland mayor to die in office.[66] At the time of his death, Gates was in the midst of a campaign for governor.[67] He was fifty-nine years old—a "kindly, hardworking, religious man."[68]

For the next five days, council president C. M. Forbes[69] assumed the duties of acting mayor while council pondered the choice of a successor. Several councilmen were nominated, but declined to serve. The final ballot delivered six of the eight votes to a political newcomer—Van B. DeLashmutt. Forty-six-year-old DeLashmutt obviously expected to be chosen for this honor, because he was waiting outside the council chambers. When informed of his appointment, he came inside, took the oath of office and delivered a brief address.[70]

May 1888 - June 1891

The new mayor received his appointment in time to campaign for the June municipal election. He easily won the mayoral title for a full three-year term.[71]

DeLashmutt brought impressive credentials to the job. He was president of Oregon National Bank and continued in that position throughout his mayoralty.[72] The three mining companies he had founded yielded one hundred thousand dollars' worth of dividends in 1890, the equivalent of nearly two million dollars today.[73] He was said to be a financial genius, although he would be in deep financial trouble two years after the end of his term.[74]

DeLashmutt was considered to be a humorous speaker,[75] a man of "unusual personal attractiveness which led to wide acquaintances and

Mayor Van DeLashmutt. (Photo: OrHi #39434)

On the afternoon of September 22, 1888, a large crowd gathered for the unveiling of Skidmore Fountain, an ornate, European-inspired fountain where "horses, men and dogs" could drink.[76] Council president Tyler Woodward accepted the fountain on behalf of the city.[77] The cooling waters of this fountain remain a city landmark today, and the message inscribed on its west side is as true now as then: "Good citizens are the riches of a city."[78]

Druggist and former councilman Stephen Skidmore had bequeathed five thousand dollars for the project, and other donors chipped in over the years to meet total project costs of nearly twenty thousand dollars (the equivalent of three hundred eighty thousand dollars today).[79] Politicians and citizens had debated where to locate the fountain for nearly five years, finally choosing the busy triangular intersection at First and Ankeny streets, in an area known today as Old Town. Nationally known sculptor Olin Warner was engaged to design and sculpt the fountain. Brewer Henry Weinhard offered to pump free beer through the fountain for opening day festivities, but cautious committee chair Henry Failing turned down the generous offer.[80]

great popularity."[81] Born in Iowa, he migrated with his parents to a farm in the Willamette Valley as a ten-year-old boy in 1852.[82] He began his career as an apprentice printer, then served in the cavalry during the Civil War. He married a southern belle, a cousin of Penumbra Kelly, a former state legislator and soon-to-be Multnomah Country sheriff. An avid sportsman and horse racer, DeLashmutt had a half-mile racetrack built on his farm. [83]

On July 10, 1888, the city's second bridge—the Steel Bridge—opened as a railroad bridge for Union Pacific trains. By the following February, a second deck had been completed for regular traffic. This bridge, like all early bridges, had to be soon replaced; the Steel Bridge was replaced in 1912, only twenty-four years after it was built.)[84]

Early in DeLashmutt's term, the city received word that the Oregon Supreme Court had dismissed a lawsuit brought by two hundred citizens against the city. The suit had challenged the city's method of spreading the cost of the Tanner Creek sewer—the largest sewer project that the city had yet undertaken. Property owners had mutinied when they received their assessment notices. Their properties did not benefit directly, they argued, and they had not been adequately notified of sewer plans. However, in *Paulson v City of Portland*, the supreme court noted that sewers benefit everybody.[85] The plaintiffs had "remained passive and indifferent spectators during all the time the city was engaged in assuming liabilities in the construction of the sewer," the court pointed out, and notices regarding the sewer's construction were published regularly in the city's official newspaper. The city's process was affirmed.[86]

Dogs running at large were a perennial problem for the council. A dog-licensing ordinance authorized the poundmaster to advertise and sell unlicensed males for one dollar each and females for three dollars. If no one wanted the dog, the poundmaster was to kill the animal and "deliver the carcass at the docks for city garbage, to be cremated." Anyone who hindered the poundmaster in his duties was subject to a one hundred dollar fine or up to twenty days imprisonment.[87]

Governor Pennoyer now vetoed a bill to add five hundred thousand dollars to the city's bonding capacity to cover the increased costs of Portland's new Bull Run waterworks. Judge Matthew Deady, who had drafted the legislation, was so incensed that he christened the governor "Silpester Annoyer." Deady also denounced Pennoyer's "impractical, cranky nature and conduct" in his diary.[88] Pennoyer said Bull Run water originated in glacial run-off and would therefore "cause goiter to the fair sex of Portland." The legislature came within one vote of overriding Pennoyer's veto.[89]

About this time, the Water Committee yielded to public pressure and reduced water rates from a dollar fifty per household to seventy-five cents a month, a rate that gave Portlanders some of the cheapest water in the nation.[90]

❧

Portland's burgeoning city government needed a permanent home. City offices and council chambers had been housed in seventeen different rented quarters during it's the council's nearly thirty-eight years of existence. In February 1889, the legislature passed a charter amendment authorizing the council to issue one hundred seventy-five thousand dollars worth of bonds for constructing and furnishing a city hall. Governor Pennoyer signed the bill.[91]

The same 1889 charter amendment gave voters back the right to elect their police commissioners. The legislature also directed the council to codify and publish all general city ordinances in pamphlet or book form every two years.[92]

Construction was halted on the city hall designed by Henry J. Hefty (at left) and a less flamboyant version adopted. The city's first city hall was opened for business January 2, 1895. (City of Portland Archives, 1890 Council Documents file)

In 1890, the council purchased a block between Fourth and Fifth streets, uphill from the river and only a block from the county courthouse, for its first permanent city hall. They were eager to start building.[93] A special council committee reported in June 1890 that four architectural plans had been selected as finalists in a design contest. The council unanimously chose Henry J. Hefty's elaborate, five-floor, five-tower design that carried an estimated cost of five hundred thousand dollars. The second-place winner received a prize of seven hundred dollars; third place, five hundred dollars; and fourth place, three hundred dollars. The council found reviewing plans and specifications so interesting that they increased the city hall committee to include the entire council. Soon the letterhead of all city officials bore an etching of Hefty's elaborate city hall design.[94]

Sewage problems were not solved by completion of the Tanner Creek sewer. In his invaluable 1890 *History of Portland*, Harvey Scott gave the sewerage system a "very unsatisfactory" rating, saying that sewer pipes ought to be thoroughly flushed and washed every day, with contents taken "far below the city, even, if necessary, to the Columbia River." A special tax to raise even a million dollars (which would be roughly nineteen million dollars today), Scott said, "would be a small outlay in comparison with the health and benefit to be derived."[95] Unfortunately, no such tax was levied. City leaders were ignorant of the extent to which contamination of both the Willamette and Columbia rivers would become an ever-increasing problem for Portland.[96]

The city's problems in 1890 were not limited to sewers. Garbage disposal had been ignored by city fathers as an unpleasant distraction. Scott declared that the city's greatest need was for a proper crematory, or incinerator, to consume its refuse and garbage.[97] An 1889 *Oregonian* article quoted a tourist from Chicago who said that Portland was the "most filthy city in the Northern states. … Any one who walks through [downtown streets] early in the morning can see the rotting vegetable matter in the gutters, can catch the odor of the seventy separate stinks."[98]

In spite of these shortcomings, Portland was a city of "civility and refinement," Scott said, whose strengths emanated from its homogeneous roots.[99] He reported that city government was employing a physician with power to quarantine and to inspect ships, trains, and buildings. City policemen served as city health officers. The city maintained a city hospital, a pest house, and a poorhouse and farm for the "indigent, incompetent and unable." The city farm was located a few miles west of town on a "beautiful and salubrious site," at which Chinese lepers (of which there had been several, said Scott) were kept.[100]

Scott's history contained a list of "those living at or near Portland prior to 1852."[101] The only woman on the entire list of over two hundred fifty people was "Mrs. Asperson and family," even though the 1850 census listed the names of over ninety women residents.[102]

❧

Two significant happenings marked the end of Mayor DeLashmutt's tenure: first, a vote to consolidate Portland with the towns of Albina and East Portland, and second, creation of the Port of Portland.

Consolidation of east- and westside governments had been virtually inevitable once the Morrison Bridge opened, especially after promoters promised free bridges as part of the consolidation package. Streetcars had created a feeling of community between neighborhoods, for electric trolleys had spread rapidly, especially on the east side. And while downtown Portland was hemmed in between the river and its surrounding hills, the wooded east side provided nearly unlimited land for expansion. Westside Portland was already home to forty-six thousand people—an average of 6,230 bodies crowded into each of its seven and a quarter square miles.[103]

Both East Portland and Albina had grown rapidly since the coming of the railroad.[104] Far-sighted William S. Ladd owned twelve hundred acres on the east side—seven hundred acres inside the proposed new city boundary and another five hundred acres to the south, later developed as Eastmoreland.[105] Two ice factories, a vinegar factory, and a cider factory were being built on the east side.[106]

In February, the legislature approved a consolidation charter to be voted on by the citizens of all three towns on June 1, 1891. Promoters touted consolidation as good common sense. Three sets of elected

A new exposition building opened in September 1889, making Portland a "sort of Mecca for the whole of the Northwest." The building at Nineteenth and Washington covered two blocks. Its three stories included a grand music hall, exhibit galleries, officers' quarters, a ladies' parlor, and a gentlemen's smoking room.[107]

Soon thereafter, construction of the city's long-awaited luxury hotel was completed. On April 7, 1890, a well-trained staff welcomed guests to the awesome Portland Hotel, built on the same Block 179 which Henry Villard had abandoned seven years before, leaving unfinished walls standing. The magnificence and size of the new hotel were beyond anything Portlanders had imagined. The Portland Hotel towered eight stories high and contained 326 sleeping rooms, a restaurant, ballroom, billiard room, bar, sitting rooms, dining rooms, sewing rooms, a reception room and ladies parlors, public rest rooms, public telephones, a news-and-cigar stand, Western Union telegraph office, and quarters for live-in staff. And, of course, elevators.[108] The price tag was over one million dollars. Four million bricks were used in its construction. Local investors included promoter George Markle and the familiar names of William Ladd, Henry Corbett, Henry Failing, and many others.[109]

For sixty years, the Portland Hotel served as a center of social, commercial, and civic activities. (Photo: OrHi #35807)

officials and three different charters were unnecessary, expensive, and confusing. State laws governing the three jurisdictions were also outdated. The most vocal opponents to consolidation were ferryboat owners, who feared they would be put out of business if the government provided free bridges.

By a whopping six-to-one margin, the voters said yes to consolidation, with 88 percent of westside voters favoring the measure, 86 percent of East Portlanders, and 71 percent of Albina voters.[110] The consolidated entity would be known as the City of Portland.

The February 1891 legislature also chartered the Port of Portland as a separate corporation with the power to tax,[111] thereby creating the most permanent and autonomous commission in the city's history.[112] Appointments to the fifteen-member port commission were to be made by the legislature (today, they are made by the governor). Two of the original port commissioners were from Albina, three from East Portland, and ten from the west side. Then as today, these appointments were deemed an honor reserved for business and community leaders. Seven of the ten westsiders named to the original port commission were members of the Arlington Club, including Henry Failing and William S. Ladd, who was named commission president.[113]

The port commission's main charge was to keep the Willamette and Columbia rivers navigable for ocean-going vessels. Competition from Seattle and Tacoma on Puget Sound had continued to increase. Portland's 110-mile shipping channel to the sea needed to be safeguarded and its seventeen-foot channel deepened. The legislation empowered the port commission to dredge and maintain the channel to a depth of twenty-five feet.[114]

U.S. President Benjamin Harrison planned a West Coast visit in early May 1891, with train stops at cities along the way. The president would start in California and head north. Portland made eager preparations for a suitable reception, but Oregon Governor Pennoyer declined to take part. Pennoyer also refused to be part of an Oregon delegation meeting the president at Ashland, near the California border.[115] Pennoyer declared: "I have no intention of going to the state line to meet the President. To do such a thing would be unbecoming to the dignity of the governor. The states are sovereign, and while in the state the governor is a higher official than the President. If he wants to see me, I'll receive him in my office in Salem."[116] Pennoyer did agree to meet the president at the Salem railroad station. Mrs. Pennoyer, however, planned to join Mrs. DeLashmutt in receiving ladies who attended a reception honoring Mrs. Harrison between 9 and 11 p.m. at the Portland Hotel. Mrs. Pennoyer also served on the decoration committee, which decorated the hotel reception room with native Oregon greenery—dogwood, wild grape, and ferns.[117]

The president's schedule called for Governor Pennoyer to meet Harrison at the Salem railroad station on May 5. President Harrison's train arrived on time, but Governor Pennoyer was not there to greet him. Salem Mayor D'Arcy ceremoniously welcomed the president, after which "Five minutes elapsed, then four minutes more and there was no sign of Governor Pennoyer. Everything was at a standstill and President Harrison paced his [train] car and now and then looked out of a window. Many thought the governor would not come. At the end of ten minutes a carriage drawn by a pair of white horses was seen coming from the state house and the word was in everybody's mouth: 'Here is the governor.' Sure enough there was the governor."[118]

The president, governor, and Salem mayor then took part in a suitably elaborate ceremony that was moved inside to the Hall of Representatives because of "inclement weather." The hall was crowded "almost to suffocation" with legislators and local dignitaries.[119]

That evening an eager crowd of fifteen thousand jammed the Exposition Music Hall in Portland to hear the president speak after Mayor DeLashmutt's lengthy welcoming address. The audience was especially pleased by Harrison's implied promise to work for further dredging of the Columbia River. The president said: "That this river of yours should be made safe and deep so that waiting commerce may come without obstruction to your wharf, is to be desired. (Cheers.) It should receive those appropriations which are necessary to make the work accomplish the purpose in view. (Cheers.)"[120]

Dignitaries invited to sit on the platform with the president and mayor included state senate president Joseph Simon, ex-U.S. Attorney-General George Williams, federal judge Matthew Deady and twenty-four others. Governor Sylvester Pennoyer was not among them. It was, the *Oregonian* said, the greatest reception the city had ever seen.[121]

Thirty years later, the *Oregonian* would recall DeLashmutt's era as a romantic time of stern-wheelers and stage coaches; a time when "social life gravitated about a few outstanding men and women" (usually including the mayor); a time when sports events centered around the race track. That was the rose-colored view of life in 1880s and 1890s Portland.

Chapter 15

Consolidation, Financial Panic, and a City Hall at Last

July 1891 – June 1896

Mayors

No. 28: July 1891 - June 1894

William S. Mason (elected for three-year term)

No. 29: July 1894 - June 1896

George P. Frank (elected for two-year term)

William S. Mason swept into the mayor's office by nearly a 25 percent margin in June 1891. He headed the Citizens' Consolidation ticket two weeks after voters had approved consolidation for Portland, Albina, and East Portland. The *Oregonian* called Mason's election "a triumph for the people against Simon's ring," writing that this election marked "the end of municipal misrule and the defeat of bossism, the sack, insolent policemen and hoodlum firemen. It was a contest of honesty and decency against boodle and slums, and honest and decency won. … Votes were bought right and left (by the ring). … The conduct of the police was positively shameful. Not only did they protect rowdies and encourage rowdyism, but became rowdies themselves. … The firemen were every bit as bad. … As they were allies of the police, they could do as they liked. … Several fights enlivened the proceedings as the day wore on."[1]

Although Mason was an ardent Republican, his main opponent was the Simon Republican candidate known as "the tall sycamore of the Willamette," former congressman M. C. George.[2] Mason had championed consolidation, both in the legislature and with the voters. His nomination by the Committee of 100[3] was a nonpartisan good-government effort to support the best possible candidate as "first chief executive of the united city."[4]

Portland's new mayor was a wholesale grocer with little formal education who had lived in Portland only ten years. Born in Virginia fifty-nine years earlier, William Mason moved with his parents as a young

Mayor William Mason (Photo: OrHi #72056)

boy from Ohio to Iowa to southern Illinois. He was employed as a store clerk from ages twelve to twenty-five, then worked for various railroads for the next twenty-five years, ending up in San Francisco. Hoping to better his situation, he migrated north. In Portland, he took an active role in the Masonic order, Chamber of Commerce, and Republican Party politics.[5] He was named president of the newly organized Portland National Bank the same year he was elected mayor. William Mason was described as a man of "commanding presence … tall and portly … quiet, thoughtful, and determined."[6]

By consolidating with East Portland and Albina, Portland had tripled its acreage and increased its population by half (from around fortyy-six thousand to an estimated seventy thousand). The city now contained nearly twenty-five square miles, a third of that on the west side of the Willamette River and two-thirds on the east. The legislature had recently expanded Albina's boundary to include a huge tract of undeveloped land stretching north to the Columbia River.[7]

Incorporated only four years before, Albina was named for the wife and daughter of lawyer William W. Page, one of the town's developers.[8] East Portland had been platted by James Stephens and laid out in 1872. The coming of Ben Holladay's railroad had generated warehouses, sawmills, steel mills, flour mills, factories, and related housing and commercial ventures. The eastside rail yards were located in Albina.[9]

The newly consolidated government was patterned after Portland's existing structure with a few changes. The 1891 charter (Portland's sixth)[10] provided for a council of sixteen councilmen, two each from eight designated wards. The voters would elect the mayor, council members, police and fire commissioners, treasurer, assessor, auditor, attorney, police judge, street superintendent, overseer of the street cleaning department, and surveyor, with the mayor and police and fire commissioners to serve three-year terms, while all others would serve two. The mayor would continue to preside over council meetings and retained veto power; in addition, he gained authority to cast tie-breaking votes. Two members were added to the Water Committee, one from East Portland and one from Albina, with the first three committee vacancies to be filled by eastsiders. The treasurer, auditor, and assessor comprised a Board of Equalization that would rule on property tax assessment appeals. All existing Portland ordinances remained in force until repealed.

> Topography was the main cause of eastside financial difficulties. Transportation there required elevated roadways, landfills, and accessways, many of which had been poorly constructed the first time they were built. Not only did West Portland boast a superior harbor with a solid bank, but it had road and rail access to Tualatin Valley farmlands. Before ships could moor on the east side, expensive trestles and wharves had to be built across its marshland and floodplains.[13]

The provision that gave eastsiders the best of the consolidation deal was this: the new entity acquired all assets and liabilities of the previous three municipalities.[11] Albina and East Portland were both overburdened with liabilities. In fact, the Albina council had deliberately taken on more debt just before the consolidation deadline.[12]

The 1891 consolidation charter named a seven-member Board of City Hall Commissioners, to whom the council was directed to turn over "the site, superstructure, books, papers, plans, specifications, contracts, rights, privileges and property of every description and nature" connected with the planned city hall. Construction work on city hall had been halted because architect Henry Hefty's plans were proving too ostentatious and expensive. Estimates of the cost to complete Hefty's design were now one million dollars—double his original projection. The charter named seven new city hall commissioners, including Henry Failing and William M. Ladd (son of former mayor William S. Ladd.) These commissioners were authorized to appoint an architect and superintendent, and to issue an additional five hundred thousand dollars of bonded debt above and beyond the one hundred seventy-five thousand dollars previously authorized for the building.[14] As soon as the building was completed, the commissioners were to assign quarters to officials and bureaus.

Mayor Mason took the oath of office July 6, 1891, the effective date of the new charter. In the absence of a real city hall, the mayor conducted daily business from his wholesale grocery, and presided over council meetings in the rented "Council Building" at Third and Washington.

But the council had nearly doubled in size—from nine members to sixteen—and needed more space for its meetings. In July, carpenters extended the rented council room as far as possible,[15] but it was not enough. Once again, city hall moved, this time to the new Bickel Building at Second and Ash, not far from Skidmore Fountain. The council leased the entire second floor for three hundred twenty-five dollars a month, with the privilege of extending the lease for a third year at the same rate.[16] For the first time in its history, the council decided to meet regularly during the day, at 2 p.m. on Wednesday afternoons, twice a month.[17]

The new mayor and council spent the month of July evaluating contracts, records, and ordinances from all three jurisdictions. The cities of East Portland and Albina had recently passed hasty legislation and Mayor Mason urged the council to conduct a thorough examination of these matters. Council committees did so, and were particularly critical of Albina street-grading contracts, East Portland water-services contracts, and East Portland street franchises which granted extensive fifty-year privileges to private companies with little or no payback to the public. The council authorized the auditor to hire a competent person to examine and write up the books of the two former cities.[18]

As far as vice and police officer conduct were concerned, Mayor Mason was frustrated by his inability to bring about change. He told the council in November 1891: "We lack the power to enforce the laws … [and have] no control … over the police force of our city. … Our police perambulate the streets day and night and we hear of no arrests for violations. … [The ordinances on gambling] are a dead letter on our statute books. … [Are the police] … sharers in the spoils?"[19]

Joseph Simon, the most powerful presence on the police board for the past six years, was now a candidate for U.S. Circuit Court of Appeals judge. Among those opposing his appointment was railroad organizer

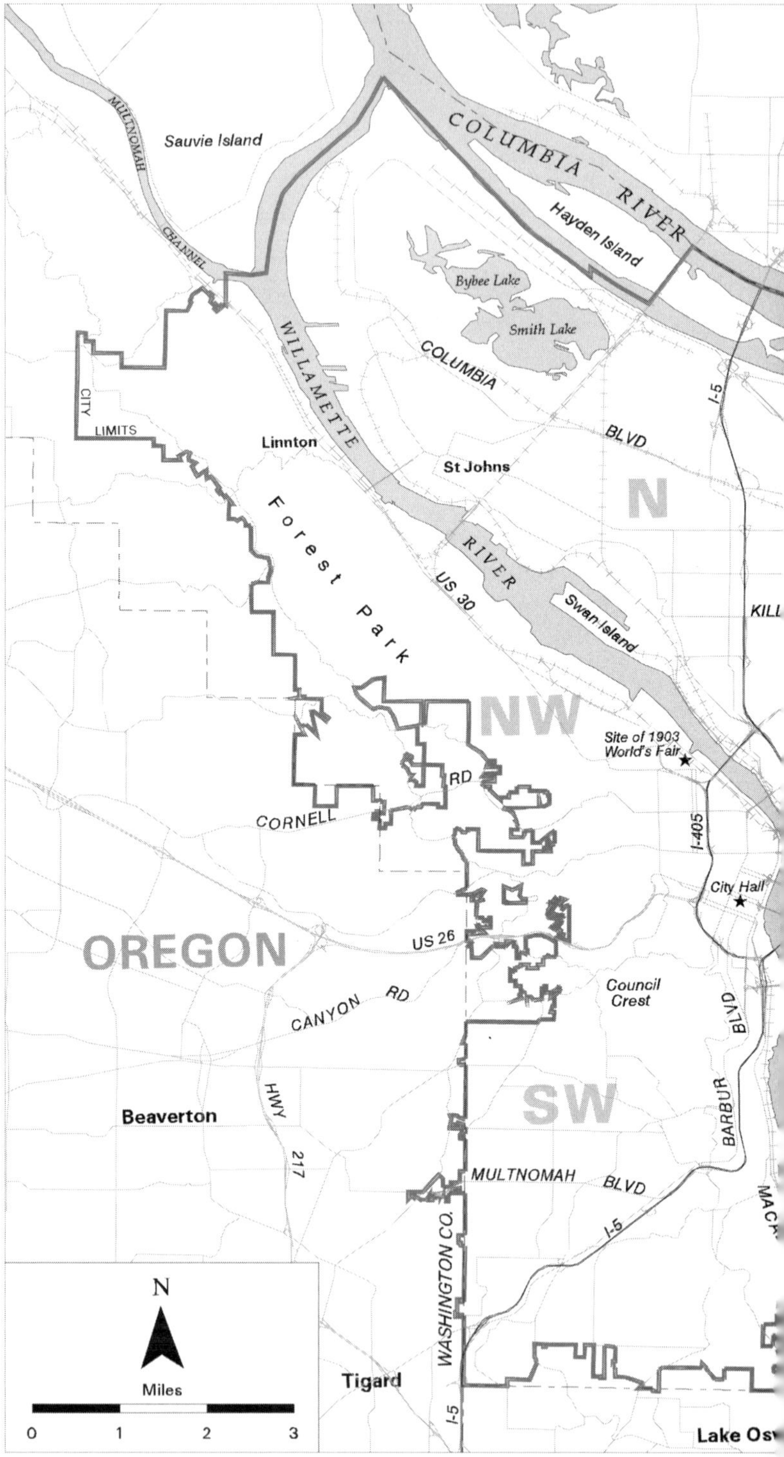
COLUMBIA RIVER
Sauvie Island
MULTNOMAH CHANNEL
Hayden Island
Bybee Lake
Smith Lake
WILLAMETTE RIVER
COLUMBIA BLVD
CITY LIMITS
Linnton
St Johns
N
I-5
Forest Park
US 30
Swan Island
KILL
NW
Site of 1903 World's Fair
RD
CORNELL
I-405
City Hall
OREGON
US 26
Council Crest
CANYON RD
BLVD
SW
BARBUR
HWY 217
Beaverton
MULTNOMAH BLVD
I-5
MAC
WASHINGTON CO.
N
Miles
0 1 2 3
Tigard
I-5
Lake Osw

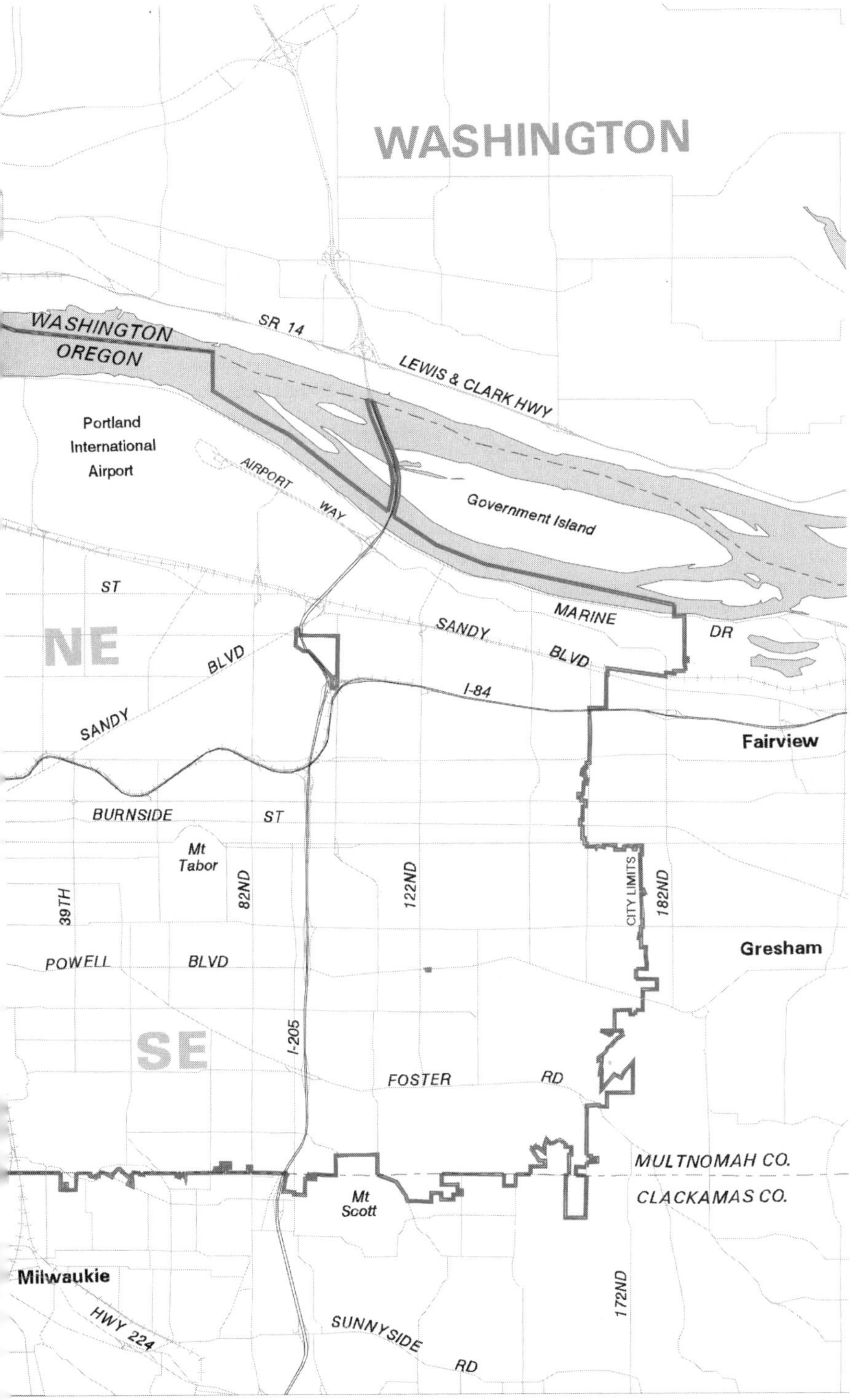

2001 map of the City of Portland and surrounding areas. (Courtesy City of Portland Planning Bureau, design by Cartographer Carmen Piekarski)

The growing city next turned its attention to the problem of duplicate street names. The city now had three Washington streets, twelve A, B, and C streets, nine Cedar streets, and many other duplications; subdivision developers had generally been allowed to choose their own street names. Mayor Mason referred the issue to the council streets committee, which in turn passed the challenge along to elected streets superintendent Douglas Taylor. Taylor proposed extending westside streets to their eastside equivalents, and renaming westside alphabet streets for men connected to Portland's history.[21] Proposed new street names were published, debated, revised. The council streets committee made further changes. Everyone had an opinion and a favorite pioneer to nominate. "Very wisely," says Eugene Snyder of the Great Street Renaming of 1891, "Taylor did not leave any records showing why or how he distinguished between those prominent Portlanders who were judged worthy of commemoration and those who were not!"[22] Alternate names considered for Davis Street, for example, were Dennison, Denny, and Dolph. Coffin Street was apparently never a viable alternative for Couch Street, but Everding Street was considered and rejected in favor of Everett.[23]

Joseph Gaston, who accused Simon, in a letter to President Harrison, of "ruining the police force by making it a political tool." Gaston said enforcement was lax, and that officers were receiving bribes. Simon, as chairman of the police board, was responsible. "Mr. Simon is not a man of honor and integrity in public affairs," Gaston said.[20]

The Board of Police Commissioners were at the center of much of the "local political corruption and bribery" of the day, according to E. Kimbark MacColl, but there was much favoritism throughout government. "The prevailing form of corruption was bribery—influence peddling—not looting the public treasury, at least directly. Many businesses received favorable treatment in municipal contracts. Tax assessments were kept low through political influence. There is no record of Portland mayors or other public officials receiving pay-offs as such. Real estate speculation and business investments were [their] primary sources of wealth."[24]

Operating independently of the council, the city hall construction committee authorized spending nearly one hundred twenty-five thousand dollars in early 1892 to tear out much of the foundation and first floor of the Hefty design already completed. They engaged architects William Whidden and Ion Lewis, recently of Boston, who had designed the popular Portland Hotel, to design a new city hall. The work would proceed with a more careful budget and realistic architectural plan, the committee said.[25] A final payment of 8,635 dollars in architect's fees was paid to H. J. Hefty.[26]

The council condemned the tearing down of partially built city hall and requested a court injunction to stop the "wanton destruction of property and consequent waste of the people's money." However, a circuit court judge held that the city hall committee was "endowed with ample power to conduct the work of destruction and construction in the manner proposed by it."[27] Mayor Mason objected strongly to the autonomous role that this committee and various other independent government bodies now held.

> [T]he mayor and common council of the city of Portland occupy a rather anomalous position. [We] are elected by the votes of a city of eighty thousand people to act as their representatives, their law makers, to see that the laws we have are enforced, to enact new ones. ... Ardently as you may desire to carry out your aspirations in this respect ... you are met with the stubborn fact, that *we are governed by commissions*, over whom you have no control, not even the right of protest, or courtesy of consultation, but the law renders it your duty to levy taxes, to raise funds, that their demands on you shall be paid, not reserving to your body the right to criticize.[28]

Free bridges, promised at election time, were a top priority for the mayor and council. A free bridge committee began negotiations to buy the Morrison and newly completed Madison Street bridges. The eleven-month-old wooden Madison bridge was poorly designed, and shuddered when the Mt. Tabor streetcar crossed over it, and the price was high. Nevertheless, the council approved its purchase for 142,500 dollars. On November 11, 1891, Portlanders had their first free bridge.

The following year, the council approved a contract to build another free bridge, the Burnside, which would be completed on July 4, 1894.[29]

Until 1887, travel from one side of the Willamette to the other was only by boat. The popular Stark Street ferry is shown above. (Photo: OrHi #12269)

In the meantime, the council purchased the Albina ferry and made it free.[30] The city also purchased the Morrison Street Bridge and the Stark Street ferry in 1895 and made them both free, though the Stark Street ferry would be closed permanently on September 30, 1895.[31]

Seven new councilmen took office in July 1892, including one council member whose qualifications were challenged on the basis of residency. The council's judiciary committee heard twelve witnesses and generated thirty-seven pages of transcript before deciding that H. J. McInnis, who ran hotels in both Portland and Vancouver, Washington, was entitled to sit on the council.[33]

> The Bull Run area was designated a "national forest reserve" by President Harrison in 1892, a designation created by Congress the year before. Most Bull Run acreage was on federal land, so Portland's Water Committee had enlisted help from the Oregon congressional delegation to gain this protected status for the wooded slopes that sheltered the city's planned water supply.[32]

Less than two years after the 1891 consolidation charter took effect, the legislature passed yet another new city charter. Joe Simon had retired from the state senate, and, in Simon's absence, a Portlander named James Lotan had gained control of the Republican Party.[34] Lotan, a bitter opponent of Mayor Mason and of consolidation (he was half-owner of the Stark Street ferry), made his influence felt through sweeping charter changes.[35]

Portland's seventh charter, passed in February 1893, expanded the city limits from twenty-five to thirty-nine square miles by adding the town of Sellwood and annexing large unincorporated areas southeast of the current city limits.[36] The number of wards was increased from eight to eleven, but council size was reduced because only one councilman was to be elected from each ward.[37]

The new charter gave the mayor more power and more salary, but only after Mayor Mason's term ended. The mayor would choose the three police commissioners and three fire commissioners, all of who would serve at his pleasure.[38] The mayor would also appoint a building inspector, plumbing inspector, inspector of steam boiler and generators, harbor master, health officer, and superintendent of street cleaning and sprinkling. Furthermore, the mayor would receive an annual salary of five thousand dollars,[39] but no person could hold the office for two successive terms. Bonded debt for the city waterworks was increased to over three million dollars.[40]

A nationwide financial panic and depression hit Portland by early summer 1893. The New York stock market had virtually collapsed.[41] Many Portland businessmen were ruined; all suffered severe reverses. Several banks closed forever. Local government resources were stretched perilously thin.[42] The builder of a "castle" later known as "Piggott's Folly" was forced to sell his splendid home after living in it for only a year. The white brick building above downtown's south hills is still a prominent landmark today.[43]

Sheriff Penumbra Kelly and two others, including Oregon National Bank president George Markle, were indicted by a Multnomah County grand jury and "arrested for misuse of $318,000 of public funds." Not only had Sheriff Kelly failed to withdraw public funds entrusted to his care from Oregon National Bank, but he had deposited an additional two hundred thousand dollars to help shore up the bank's resources when it was in financial trouble. Former mayor Van DeLashmutt, a cousin by marriage of Kelly, was said to be nearly ruined. *Oregonian* editor Harvey Scott and former mayor David P. Thompson posted the bail bonds for the three indicted men. E. Kimbark MacColl says no court records were found to indicate how the case against Kelly and Markle was resolved, and he concludes that the charges were apparently dropped.[44]

In the midst of the 1893 depression, the Ministerial Association of Portland began a vice probe to control prostitution. They identified owners of property that housed vice operations, a list that included many prominent Portlanders such as former mayors Van DeLashmutt and David Thompson, former councilmen R. R. Thompson and Henry Corbett, brewer Henry Weinhard, lawyer Joseph Simon, and the law partners of both Simon and former councilman J. C. Moreland, who was now a Multnomah County judge. The *Oregonian* largely ignored these findings because, as editor Harvey Scott later admitted, he was not willing to risk taking on "the men of wealth on whose patronage the paper relied."[45]

An ordinance passed by the council that fall specified that no home for fallen women or reform school could be built within fifteen hundred feet of a public school building. Another ordinance prohibited construction of barbed wire fences within the city, and required existing barbed wire fences to be torn down. A third limited bicycle speed to six miles an hour and required bicycle riders to sound a gong or bell when approaching and crossing intersections.[46]

❧

A new target of potential discrimination now surfaced: Scandinavians. During discussions of a contract for street cleaning, Councilman L. M. Davis said, "If the contract were let to a rich corporation, they would employ Scandinavians, Negroes and Chinese. It would be better to leave the matter as it is until spring, and let white men have the benefit of the work." A storm of protest followed. Citizens of Scandinavian ancestry held a mass meeting and delivered a stinging denunciation of Davis. They called upon the council to expel Davis "for misconduct in office and because [he is] unworthy and unfit to occupy such a position."

A special council committee concluded that Councilman Davis's language did indeed deserve severe condemnation and censure. Not only had persons of Scandinavian birth been unfairly demeaned, but Davis's comments had also been unfair to black men, who deserved a

> Two men who had played significant roles in Portland history died in early 1893: former mayor William S. Ladd and federal judge Mathew Deady, drafter of more state legislation regarding city government than any other person.[47] Ladd had suffered several strokes during his last few years, and had been paralyzed from the waist down for nearly twenty years, but this had slowed him down very little.[48]

chance to compete on merit for public works jobs. There was no comment about insult or inequity to Chinese workers. The committee nevertheless concluded that the council did not have the power to remove one of its own from office for this kind of offense. Councilman Davis was censured, but remained on the council.[49]

The Committee of 100 Portland Taxpayers reminded the council that one hundred dollars would now buy as much as one hundred fifty would have purchased two years before because of the current depression. They urged reduction of property taxes and retrenchment in all city affairs, and recommended that the council members reduce their own salaries to set a good example.[50] The Committee of Judiciary and Elections, to whom the matter was referred, concluded that further consideration of an ordinance proposing reduced council salaries should be indefinitely postponed. Council members were paid the same as they had been paid for several years before consolidation,[51] the committee said, while council duties had increased "at least four fold" since then. That meant that present council members were being paid only one-fourth of their worth. Anyone who felt his services were not worth what he was being paid could return the excess to the city treasury. The city's interests would not be well served by reducing the salaries of trained employees and risking the loss of their services.[52] Salaries for council members and the mayor would remain unchanged.[53] The committee urged all department heads to reduce the size of their work forces.

A stunning tragedy occurred on a foggy, dark morning in early November. The streetcar *Inez* plunged into the Willamette River. At least seven passengers lost their lives.

It was 6:45 and still dark, and the rails were covered with frost.

> The car … headed onto the Madison Street Bridge. Too late, the motorman made out the red light that indicated an open draw. He applied the brakes, but the wheels failed to grip the frosty rails, and the car rushed onward to disaster. The motorman and many of the passengers managed to leap to safety, but some remained trapped in the car, which [broke through the gate and] dropped upside down into the murky waters of the Willamette, narrowly avoiding the deck of the passing steamboat.[54]

The East Side Railroad Company, owner of the *Inez*, was unable to meet the cost of satisfying damage suits and went into receivership in December.

❧

In late spring 1894, a devastating flood reached Portland in the midst of the city election campaign. Democrat R. D. Inman was vying against Republican George P. Frank for mayor. On election day—Monday, June 4—the river reached a high water mark of thirty-one feet, with hundreds of boats colliding on streets as far west as Twelfth. The election proceeded, but many folks did not vote. During the worst flood in Portland's history, the city elected George Frank, who would prove to be one of the city's worst mayors.

Gas works and sewers were flooded. Train service was cut off. Fire engines plied the streets on rafts. Two drawbridges were stuck open, leaving only one Willamette bridge available. Nicholson pavement blocks and sidewalk pieces floated everywhere. Retail shops sold merchandise from the windows of their second floors. Erickson's floating saloon did a brisk business, as did floating barbershops and lumber companies selling lumber for flatboats and constructing raised sidewalks. The water reached seven feet deep at Ash and Ankeny, where the council had recently vacated its upstairs quarters.[55]

The Willamette crested at thirty-three feet at midnight on June 6.[56] Two days later, the water started receding and the city turned its attention toward repairing the damage. "[T]he brisk wind [had] made boating most laborious, and elevated sidewalks were so slippery and uncertain that foot travel was far from pleasant. … A fine bridge has been built over Third street … so that the central police station can now be reached

Willamette River floodwaters reached 33 feet in early June 1894, causing the worst flood in Portland's history. Shoppers crossed hastily constructed wooden bridges such as these at the corner of Second and Washington. (Photo: OrHi #47959)

without the aid of boats. … The flooded streets seem to be alive with suckers, chubs and carp, which have been taken in large numbers. … [A] boatman drove a 15-pound salmon into the shallow water on Front street … and with the assistance of Mr. Abpel, the drygoods dealer, managed to land it in his boat."[57]

As the water continued to go down, owners struggled to get floating docks, warehouses, stores, and dwellings back on their foundations. The aftermath was nearly as unpleasant as the flood itself.[58] "The receding flood is leaving behind it an intolerable stench which will require the wholesale use of disinfectants, to prevent general sickness … Dead rats, dead fish and sewer filth" are reported everywhere.[59]

One encouraging note did emerge from the ravages of the flood. The Chinese gained a new status because of boating skills they demonstrated during a flood-inspired regatta. "With great celerity [the Chinese] moved their boats by powerful strokes of the oars, skillfully eluding the miscellaneous craft in the way. … [H]undreds of people gathered to witness the event. … This incident, demonstrating their skill and ability, elevated the Chinese in the eyes of many Portlanders and contributed towards an increasing respect for that race."[60]

The 1894 flood reached the highest level recorded on the Willamette River at Portland[61] since the U. S. weather bureau started observations in 1879.[62] The 1894 Columbia River level at Vancouver was to be exceeded only by the Vanport flood of 1948.[63]

William Mason was not a candidate for reelection as mayor. Perhaps it was a personal choice as well as a forced one, for his tenure had been beset by troubles. In any event, the 1893 charter prohibited any mayor from holding office for two successive terms. Mason left office in the midst of flood cleanup and a deep economic depression. His reform efforts had not accomplished nearly as much as he had intended. Vice problems continued unabated, the police force had been reduced, the city was overrun with unemployed men, and independent committees and commissions tied the mayor's hands. Mason would be persuaded to run for mayor again four years later, in 1898. In the interim, he would be elected president of the local Chamber of Commerce, the only Portland mayor to ever serve in this position.[64]

July 1894 - June 1896

Vice activity centered around Portland's notorious North End. Bribery. Vote-buying. Constant drunkenness. Opium smoking. Illegal gambling. Open prostitution. Shanghaiing. (More on that later.) Crimps.

Crimps—the middlemen who provided the sailor-power for long sea voyages—usually owned sailors' boarding houses that served as a cover for various nefarious activities, including vote-buying and shanghaiing. According to *Portland Telegram* feature writer Dean Collins: "Their systemized method of controlling and delivering votes made their influence much courted by all political forces. The story of … visiting sailors and loggers … voting early and often as they were marched about the North End ward, receiving $2.50 per vote per head, is one that never grows stale in the hearing. The picture of Larry Sullivan, or Bunco Kelly … sitting above the ballot box with a sawed-off shotgun across the knees … has been preserved to us in the memory of eyewitnesses."[65]

The city's twenty-ninth mayor, George P. Frank,[66] was allied with North End political bosses. His vote-buying contacts there, combined with the great flood of 1894, had gotten Frank elected in a light turnout.[67] His opponent, Robert Inman (the "demo-populist" candidate), was a respected wealthy lumberman[68] who had served in both the Oregon house and senate. Inman lost to Frank by a 5 percent margin. Two minor candidates also received votes, so Frank was elected with five votes short of a majority.[69]

Three years before, Frank had been an unsuccessful candidate for police commissioner, a position he had previously held by appointment.[70] "Geo. P. Frank Is Snowed Under," the *Oregonian* headline had said of his loss. "All the Money That the Bosses Spent Couldn't Save Him. The ringsters went broke in their efforts to save their pet nominee, Fire Commissioner George P. Frank. … Thousands of dollars were spent in the First and Second wards for him, but the result shows that it was money poured into a rathole."[71]

The new mayor was "a man of few principles and extreme rascality," in the words of historian E. Kimbark MacColl. Future mayor George Williams referred to George Frank as "an infernal scoundrel."[72]

George Frank was born in upstate New York, and moved to Wisconsin with his family as a boy of twelve. Like Mayor Mason before him, Frank started his career as a railroad man, then switched to merchandising. He came to Portland at age twenty-four to establish a branch of the agricultural implement firm he and his brother had started in San Francisco the previous year. Frank served on the prestigious Water

Mayor George Frank (Photo: OrHi #65588)

Committee, and chaired its construction committee after the death of William S. Ladd.[73] The new mayor had allied himself with Republican Party chair James Lotan, the man who had secured the 1893 charter provision to grant the mayor a five thousand dollar salary and unprecedented powers. Mayor Frank thus began his tenure with more clout than had any previous mayor. As the *Oregonian* put it, the new charter "practically gives the mayor entire charge of the municipal government."[74]

Reneging on a campaign promise to divorce the police department from politics, Frank immediately replaced the three police board members elected by the people with his own appointees. Within three months, he ordered the board to fire police chief C. H. Hunt and hire John Minto, Jr., an activist in Republican Party politics.[75] Mayor Frank reminded police board members that they served at the mayor's pleasure.

The big flood had highlighted unhealthy living conditions, and motivated the council to create a Board of Health composed of the mayor, police chief, council health committee chair, and city physician. Among other duties, the Board of Health was to examine premises for offensive-smelling privies and under-the-sidewalk cesspools. They were to report their findings to the council and estimate the cost of draining and filling these holes. The council could then order them filled, with the cost charged to the property owner.[76]

In addition to basic street, sewer, and bridge matters, this eleven-member council passed ordinances covering subjects from cow bells to waffle vendors. Steamboats were prohibited from running faster than five miles per hour near downtown.[77] Bells on animals running at large were declared a public nuisance and the city poundmaster authorized to impound and sell any animal wearing a bell. Eight categories of vagrancy were defined, including every idle or dissolute person without visible means of support, those soliciting alms or found begging, those habitually roaming about without any lawful business, persons loitering about or found lodging in any barn, shed, outhouse, vessel, or railroad car without permission of the owner.[78] Every person who frequented houses of ill fame or habitually associated with common prostitutes was a potential vagrant, as was "every common prostitute or person found on a public street or at a window of a street opening on any public street soliciting prostitution,"[79] and every person "commonly known as a pimp."[80] The chief of police was authorized to sell unclaimed property taken from arrested persons after sixty days, with the proceeds to be credited to the police fund.[81]

Another ordinance prohibited boys and other unauthorized persons from climbing on railroad cars and trains or entering engines "to the endangering of life and limb and to the annoyance and hindrance" of employees.[82] Horses or mules were to be driven no faster than a walk in city parks and squares. Standing on, stepping on, removing, destroying, swinging on, or climbing over benches, fences, grass, flowers, shrubbery, or trees therein was prohibited.[83]

Burials within city limits were confined to the Jewish cemetery, Lone Fir Cemetery, River View Cemetery, and St. Mary's Catholic Cemetery. The scraping or cleansing of the skeleton of any dead body was prohibited except in a suitable building on cemetery grounds outside of public view.[84]

A quarterly license fee of seven dollars and fifty cents was required of any person who baked and sold waffles on the public streets.[85]

The new city hall opened on January 2, 1895,[86] the same day that the first Bull Run water reached the city from the slopes of Mt. Hood.

The council had met in eighteen different rented quarters and four interim meeting places (in offices and stores, never homes) over the past forty-four years. Now city government had its own space, and it was indeed grand. The *Oregonian* provided an elaborate description of city hall, inside and out: "No city of Portland's size in the United States claims a public building devoted to the use of the officers of the municipal government which approaches in point of beauty and finish, or in its modern convenient interior arrangements, the new city hall. ... There is not a gloomy corner in the entire structure. Two interior courts, by which light is admitted to the building, are on either sides of the staircases. ... The gallery has a seating capacity of 300. ... Connecting with [the mayor's] suite is a private staircase for use of the mayor which leads to the auditor's department."

The honor of sipping the first ceremonial taste of Bull Run water went to the very man who had once held up financing for the project, Governor Pennoyer: "[A]mid festivity and brass band music, [Pennoyer] was asked to give a toast. He raised his glass of Bull Run, tasted it, and set the goblet down. 'No flavor,' he said, 'no body. Give me old Willamette.'"[87]

Despite the governor's negative opinion, Portland now had a water supply "which for purity is probably unexcelled anywhere in the world," according to a Water Committee report. It had taken millions of dollars to complete the process, but the job was well done. Contrary to the expectations of the council, however, the Water Committee did not consider its mission completed. Many eastside citizens still received water from two other sources—the East Side Works that had been supervised by the city since consolidation in 1891, and the private East Portland Water Company.[88] A legislative act approved February 25, 1895, required the Water Committee to take over operation of the East Side Works and "to connect said waterworks with the Bull Run system ... inasmuch as there is urgent need of giving people of the east side of the city of Portland the benefit of Bull Run water."[89]

The *Oregonian's* effusive coverage of the new City Hall and Bull Run water also praised Mayor Frank for making necessary innovations during stringent times. The mayor had been allowed to make these changes "without the protest of the people who elected him" which was "more than satisfactory evidence that his course has met with the hearty approval of everybody interested in Portland's prosperity."[90] These were words the paper would later regret.

The city now had a debt of 1.2 million dollars (in addition to 2.6 million dollars of water works debt[91] plus debt incurred for building bridges). Mayor Frank warned council that garbage was still a very serious matter. He said, "We now have a crematory which cost the city very nearly $14,000. It has been in operation one year and has proven anything but a success. I am satisfied that some other arrangements will have to be made as to the disposal of our garbage."[92]

In the meantime, the police board adjusted its spending to depression-era times by reducing the salaries of police officers by 10 percent and eliminated two positions. The policemen were said to have accepted these reductions in good grace, knowing there were "over 1700 applications on file to wear a star."[93]

❧

The new mayor was not interested in cracking down on vice. By fall 1895, the newly formed Central Municipal Reform League was so disgusted with Mayor Frank's refusal to enforce anti-gambling ordinances that they considered trying to impeach him. The Committee of 100 also weighed in against Frank. Organized gambling was hurting the city's reputation, the committee said, and the mayor did nothing about it. "Even Joseph Simon now realized that his original support of Frank had proved to be a disastrous mistake," says E. Kimbark MacColl. "Frank's blustery and crude arrogance stirred up the old guard."[94]

No impeachment proceedings were ever filed against Frank, however, partly because contentious state and national political issues were diverting political attention. The question of a gold or silver standard split national Democratic and Republican ranks. The Populist Party was gaining attention and converts. Bitter in-fighting continued in statewide Republican circles.[95]

In March 1896, the *Oregonian* lashed out at Mayor Frank: "It is time to expose to public view the inspiration and facts of the organized effort being made by a number of self-seeking Portland politicians." Senate president Joseph Simon had tried, unsuccessfully, the newspaper said, to pass a worthy new city charter during the legislative session, but Mayor Frank had forced city employees to contribute one-tenth of their annual salaries to a "corruption fund" to defeat the measure: "Senator Simon, with the aid of reputable and responsible citizens, had prepared a new charter for the city of Portland … [whose] main purposes were two-fold: First, it simplified and centralized the city government; second, it effected a saving in the municipal expenditure of about $180,000 … [I]t reduced the mayor's annual salary from $5000 to $3000. … Most shameful methods were used to defeat (the measure)."[96] Furthermore, the article said, the mayor was not willing to do his part after the council ways and means committee had struggled valiantly to cut costs so they could prepare a balanced budget. "Salaries of city employees everywhere were reduced, and still the reduction was not sufficient. It was then proposed as a last resort to devise some way of reducing the salaries of city officials fixed by charter. Mayor Frank was summoned and asked if he would consent to a reduction of his $5000 salary, if the members of the council would come down on their $1000 salaries. He refused point blank, and the effort was perforce abandoned."

Frank expected to be appointed federal collector of customs as his political reward for aiding U.S. Senator John H. Mitchell, the newspaper said. Other allies of Frank's were also lined up for various government jobs. In addition: "[M]ayor Frank has seriously affronted the public sense of fairness and justice, and achieved the unquestionable distinction of committing the most egregious and stupid political blunder in the history of local politics. His removal of the board of fire commissioners ... had no other motive than politics. ... The record of the fire commission was the one admirable feature of the Frank administration; and it is, perhaps, not too much to say that it was the only branch of the administration which had and deserved the entire confidence of the public."[97]

Portland's Grand Central railroad station opened February 14, 1896. The attractive Romanesque building with its red metal-mission-tiled roof and stately clock tower had taken four years to build.[98] Henry Villard had started construction at a nearby site in 1883, but had been forced to abandon it when hit by financial reversals. Grand Central Station (later renamed Union Station) would become a busy hub of activity over the next fifty years. The terminal stood on top of former Couch Lake, now filled in, where Capt. John Couch had once sat on his front porch and shot ducks for supper.[99]

Oregon received national attention during the June 1896 election campaigns, because Oregon was seen as a bellwether state in the national struggle between Republicans, Democrats, and Populists. Issues included the silver-versus-gold standard, blame for the depression, proposals to further restrict immigration, and whether or not to enact more protective tariffs. Combatants on Portland's battlefield generated "hard-hitting newspaper editorials, torchlight parades, political oratory, band music, and excited sidewalk arguments," in which national political leaders took part.[100] "'If God Almighty should come to this city during the campaign and try to work against the schemes and combinations of practical politicians, he would lose the fight,' a prominent local citizen said of the Republican infighting that took place that year."[101]

With the Republicans brawling amongst themselves, former governor Sylvester Pennoyer captured the mayor's seat with little trouble. This time, he was nominated not only by the Democrats, but by the Taxpayers' League and the Populists in his race against David Solis-Cohen, a Simon Republican,[102] and General Charles F. Beebe, a Mitchell Republican.[103] Pennoyer was elected mayor by a substantial plurality.[104]

Chapter 16

Outrageous Conduct, Shanghaiing, and Vice

July 1896 – June 1900

Mayors

No. 30: July 1896 - June 1898

Sylvester Pennoyer (elected for two-year term)

No. 31: July 1898 - March 1899

William S. Mason (elected for two-year term)

No. 32: May 1899 - June 1900

William A. Storey (appointed for thirteen months)

Sylvester Pennoyer served eight years as Oregon's most controversial and irascible governor, then returned to the spotlight as Portland's mayor at age sixty-five. He was the only former governor to ever serve as Portland's mayor. A gifted, egotistical showman, he craved the limelight and loved playing the role of iconoclast. Even his friends admitted that Pennoyer's hyperbole was often to gain attention rather than a statement of true conviction. But no one impugned his honesty.[1] As governor, Pennoyer made statements that were "absurd in the extreme and created great merriment in the Legislature and out of it," recalled former governor T. T. Geer. Yet he never failed "to touch some sort of popular chord and win a following." Pennoyer preferred being abused to being ignored.[2]

Pennoyer had rudely refused to meet President Benjamin Harrison at the border in 1891, or to attend the president's Portland reception. He had likewise behaved boorishly toward President Grover Cleveland. Secretary of State Walter Q. Gresham had telegraphed all governors, including Pennoyer, concerning the Chinese Exclusion Act about to go into effect in 1893. The telegram said: "Apparently reliable reports indicate danger of violence to Chinese when exclusion act takes effect, and the President earnestly hopes you will employ all lawful means for their protection in Oregon."

Pennoyer replied: "I will attend to my business; let the President attend to his. Sylvester Pennoyer, Governor."[3]

Mayor Sylvester Pennoyer
(Photo: OrHi #54772)

This famous "Mind-Your-Own-Business" reply[4] was dated May 3, 1893. Pennoyer told an Associated Press reporter, "It comes with poor grace for the President to ask me to enforce the laws of the state, while he, without warrant, suspends the exclusion law." Soon thereafter, Pennoyer demanded Cleveland's impeachment.[5]

In 1877, Pennoyer had lost a famous U.S. Supreme Court case cited in thousands of future appellate cases. Marcus Neff had filed a donation land claim on three hundred twenty acres in Portland's west hills, hired attorney John H. Mitchell to do some legal work, and left for California without paying Mitchell's fee. Mitchell sued for his two hundred ninety-five-dollar bill in Neff's absence and received a default judgment. The sheriff sold Neff's claim to Pennoyer for three hundred forty-two dollars, which was used to pay Mitchell's fee. When Neff returned to Portland in 1874 and found his land gone, he sued to regain it. Judge Mathew Deady decided in Neff's favor. Pennoyer appealed to the U.S. Supreme Court. In *Pennoyer v Neff* (with the land now worth at least fifteen thousand dollars) the Supreme Court upheld Deady's ruling.[6]

Pennoyer never forgave Deady for this adverse judgment, and during his inaugural address as governor, he proclaimed that the Oregon legislature might be duty-bound to seek Judge Deady's impeachment. Deady wrote in his diary: "He has made a laughing stock of himself as I knew he would if elected."[7]

The new mayor's background was nearly as varied as were his spirited, theatrical quips. Born in New York, Pennoyer graduated from Harvard law school before he migrated to Portland in 1855 at age twenty-four. His father, a well-to-do farmer, had once served as a state legislator. In Portland, Pennoyer taught school for six years, served as Multnomah County superintendent of schools, went into the lumber business (a "life work" at which he prospered), became editor and later owner of the *Oregon Herald* newspaper, and was listed as an accountant in the *1874 City Directory*.[8]

While editor of the *Oregon Herald*, Pennoyer published a poem in September 1871 lampooning local suffragist Abigail Scott Duniway and her fellow activist Susan B. Anthony, who had stopped in Portland on a lecture tour around the Pacific Northwest.

> Along the city's thoroughfare,
> A grim old gal with manly air
> Strode amidst the noisy crowd,
> Tooting her horn both shrill and loud;
> . . .
> A meek old man, in accents wild,
> Cried, "Sal, turn back and nurse our child!"
> She bent on him a withering look,
> Her bony fist at him she shook,
> And screeched, "Ye brute! ye think I'm flat
> To mend your clo'es and nurse your brat?
> Nurse it yourself; I'll change the plan,
> When I am made a congressman—
> Women's Rights and Suffrage.[9]

Democrat Pennoyer could be depended upon to put on a good show. In today's parlance, he knew how to craft a good sound bite. Although he was aristocratic and stiff in bearing and dress, Pennoyer's appeal was strongest to the labor ranks and the downtrodden, whom he championed. However, he openly advocated exclusion and expulsion of the Chinese, sided firmly with the South during the Civil War, and was staunchly pro-slavery. He waxed eloquent on the merits of free coinage of silver. He advocated, ahead of his time, a graduated income tax, but opposed taxes for higher education as "a tax on all the people for the benefit of a few."[10]

At the time of Pennoyer's 1890 campaign against Republican challenger David P. Thompson (former Portland mayor) for reelection as governor, the *Oregonian* said: "Mr. Pennoyer is peculiar, eccentric,

> A bizarre footnote to Portland history occurred in May 1897, when grave-robbers excavated the 1893 burial site of former mayor William S. Ladd. A gardener at River View Cemetery discovered the theft. The metal inside the coffin had been cut open and the body removed. Detectives found the body a few days later, and the culprits, who had intended to collect ransom, were arrested. To prevent any possible repeat, Ladd's grave was cemented over after the remains were returned to their rightful place.[12]

demagogic; owing such celebrity or notoriety as he posses to the general unsoundness of his opinions. … His appeal is never to intelligence and manliness, but always to ignorance and discontent. … He is a wealthy man, but his wealth has been gained wholly through the system which he denounces…. Personally, Mr. Pennoyer is an amiable man, but he is a humbug … he is specious, plausible, misleading, dangerous. … [T]hey who have known him longest, never knew him to entertain sound opinions on any important public question."[11]

Pennoyer pronounced Portland's new city hall "expensive, unseemly and unhealthful." He referred to the exterior sandstone walls as discolored and inferior to stone within a few miles of the city.[13] The *Oregonian* later summed up Mayor Pennoyer's two years as the head of Portland's government this way: "While less conspicuous, Pennoyer's career as mayor was marked by the same determination and independence as his administration of the Governor's office. He appointed and removed fire and police commissioners rapidly, vetoed the ordinances of the council, and was not to be argued with about his reasons or purposes."[14] While that capsule of Pennoyer's mayoral term catches its general flavor, the degree of disruption he created in ordinary city business is overstated. Pennoyer signed the overwhelming majority of council ordinances with no comment. Of the seven hundred sixty-six ordinances passed during the twenty-month period of January 1897 to September 1898, over 60 percent were for basic services and were processed routinely—the authorizing, planning, construction, spreading costs of, and hearing complaints about street, sewer, sidewalk and bridge improvements.[15]

However, in the more visible part of his job, Pennoyer replaced the entire police force within his first year and appointed four different police chiefs during his two-year tenure.[16]

❧

On July 17, 1897, a ship arrived in Seattle's harbor carrying gold discovered in Alaska. Portland merchants immediately started advertising mining equipment and apparel for sale. Portland was better equipped and stocked than Seattle to meet the needs of the prospective miners who started pouring into the Pacific Northwest. The city was to experience a three-year economic boom centered around commodities such as wheat, lumber, mining supplies, and tents. Many adventurers who came to the Northwest seeking gold would stay on as permanent residents.[17]

"The city is again overrun with burglars and thugs," said an April 1898 *Oregonian* article. "The most barefaced and daring crimes are perpetrated every night, and as long as Pennoyer's orders to policemen not to disturb criminals till after election are allowed to stand, property owners can expect no protection."[18]

A week later, the *Oregonian* noted that, after Pennoyer had appointed a new member of the board of fire commissioners, he had requested and received resignations from another fire commissioner and a police commissioner. With these resignations in hand, however, the mayor did not accept them. "Now that they have resigned," Pennoyer said, "I will leave them suspended between heaven and earth as a frightful example to bolters from a democratic convention." The newspaper sarcastically rejoined: "The fact that no other commissioners were appointed is due entirely to the refusal of men solicited to take the places to accept them."[19]

In Washington, D. C., the United States was pressuring Spain to permit Cuban self-governance. In early 1898, President McKinley sent the battleship *Maine* to Havana harbor to protect Americans there against rioters. On February 15, the *Maine* exploded and two hundred sixty people were killed. In April, the U.S. declared war on Spain, officially beginning the Spanish-American War. A regiment of Oregon volunteer infantrymen was trained and equipped at Portland's Irvington Park under the supervision of Gen. Charles F. Beebe, a regiment that would serve with distinction in the Philippines. An armistice ended the short-lived war in August, and a December treaty granted Cuba its independence and ceded the Philippine Islands, Guam, and Puerto Rico to the United States. Eight years later, a monument to Oregon soldiers killed in the Philippines was erected east of the Multnomah County Courthouse, paid for by private contributions.[20]

Pennoyer and his wife deeded six acres to the city for a park, today known as Governor's Park, located on Robinson's Hill in Portland Heights.[21]

While soldiers volunteered for the war, miners rushed off to Alaska, merchants supplied the miners and soldiers, and politicians fought amongst themselves, other Portlanders joined the national bicycle craze. Future councilman Fred T. Merrill sold 8,850 bicycles from his shop in 1898 alone, making him the biggest bicycle operator west of the Mississippi.[22] Suffragette Susan B. Anthony had praised bicycle riding for women in a widely publicized national interview two years before: "I think it has done more to emancipate woman than any one thing in the world. I rejoice every time I see a woman ride by on a wheel. It gives her a feeling of self-reliance and independence the moment she takes her seat; and away she goes, the picture of untrammeled womanhood."[23]

Untrammeled womanhood was not always warmly received in Portland: "Two women were riding their bicycles on the sidewalk on Third street yesterday morning when something caused them to turn off into the street. One of them … remarked spitefully, 'I have to pay a $1.25 license for riding in the mud.' A man who overheard the remark [said] there was one alternative left … for her to stay at home until the mud dried up. … Another remarked that he would bet that she had put the roast for the family dinner in the stove and 'banked' the fire, and would get home just in time to get it half done for her husband's dinner."[24]

"It was a common sight of a Sunday to see a dozen wheels going down a street," author Percy Maddux says. Refreshment booths catering to cyclists were built along the roadways, while other cyclists carried picnic lunches to the country or arranged for lunch at a nearby farm. On one Sunday alone, three thousand bicycles[25] crowded the Portland-Vancouver road to take a ferry across the Columbia or simply to ride to the river and back.[26] Many bicycles were built for two, called tandems, and sometimes for three, four, and five riders, all seated in a row.

Mayor Pennoyer might have sought reelection if the charter had not prohibited successive terms. As it was, his contentious political career ended when he left city hall. At the time of his death in 1902, a council resolution said, "His political career forms one of the most interesting chapters in Oregon history. … He was persistent and fearless even to the point of eccentricity."[27]

July 1898 - March 1899

The Simon and Mitchell factions of the Republican Party vied for power in the 1898 mayoral race. "Probably no state in the union (excluding perhaps Delaware), ever witnessed party strife so malignant or so deadly," said a newspaper article a decade later.[28] Simon's candidate, former mayor William S. Mason, faced Mitchell's candidate, John Minto, Jr., former police chief under Mayor Frank.

Many downtown stores and offices closed on election day to encourage a heavy vote for Mason, the incumbent Chamber of Commerce president running on a reform platform. Mason divested himself of his wholesale grocery firm before the campaign began, but retained his presidency of Portland National Bank.[29] Mason, who had been the city's twenty-eighth mayor, won handily, and served again as the thirty-first. He was now sixty-six years old.[30]

Mayor Mason wasted no time cleaning out the ranks of police officers assembled by Pennoyer. Within eleven days, he had replaced the entire police department of eighty-four people. "City Hall was humming like a beehive yesterday morning," said the *Oregonian* of July 2. "Many heads were cut off. The ax struck well." Mason also appointed an all-new police commission[31] and a new chief of police.

Police Chief D. M. McLauchlan[32] was the first chief to enforce the city law prohibiting women from serving liquor. The mayor wanted to serve notice that things were different now.[33] "Mason instructed the Board of Police Commissioners to put regular patrolmen back on the beat in the North End. … told Chief McLauchlan to clean up the brothels and close the gambling establishments, including the Chinese games and lotteries. Board president Hunt ordered police officers 'to refrain from collecting any fees from houses of prostitution, gambling houses, or any objectionable class of people.'"[34]

Mayor William Mason (Photo: OrHi #72056)

But after an initial flurry, these efforts and ultimatums did little to clean up Portland. Habits of years past did not change overnight. Many leading Portland businessmen benefited from rents and profits from these activities, and efforts to change things met the same resistance that the Ministers' Association investigation had encountered five years before.

The police budget also had to be cut again. Portland had still not eradicated debts assumed from Albina and East Portland, or for construction of city hall, a total of over one million dollars in bonded indebtedness. Uncollected city property taxes totalled one hundred thousand dollars. Assessed property values lagged far behind reality, partly because county officials feared Multnomah County "was being required to pay too high a share of state taxes."[35]

Joe Simon returned to the state senate in 1897, and was again elected its president. This time he succeeded in getting passed a new Portland charter that he had promoted unsuccessfully two years before.[36] Soon thereafter, Simon was elected to the U.S. Senate with the unanimous support of all sixty-six Republican legislators.

This new charter (Portland's eighth) directed the mayor to appoint a new five-member Board of Public Works to review all proposed city contracts, bids, franchise applications, and purchases, and to make recommendations to the council.[37] Such boards were being used by other cities, Mayor Mason told the council, who were "highly gratified" with the results.[38]

Other portions of the new charter authorized the mayor to appoint a competent person to examine, without notice, the accounts and property of any city department or official, with a written report to be issued of each such examination.[39] The mayor's annual salary was reduced from five thousand to three thousand dollars—effective after Mason left office—and the prohibition against successive mayoral terms was eliminated. Council members were to receive no salary or compensation, while other officials had their salaries reduced about 20 percent.[40]

Theoretically, the new board of public works should have improved city government, says historian E. Kimbark MacColl, but few positive advantages were realized. No centralized purchasing occurred, purchases were dribbled out in small amounts so there was little quantity

> Former mayor Henry Failing died in early November 1898, at age sixty-four. He had played an invaluable role in Portland's history, by providing strong direction for Portland city government and long service on influential city boards and commissions. Now, within five years of the death of William S. Ladd, both these pioneer leaders were gone. Failing was buried in River View Cemetery,[41] which he had helped found sixteen years before.[42]

buying, the competitive bidding process changed little, no public notice was given of when council items would be heard. The council usually approved the board's recommendations without discussion at the same meeting that items of business were introduced.[43] The biggest city purchases were for lumber, sawdust, hardware, and hay.

> [T]he largest beneficiary of city business was Donald MacKay, president of the North Pacific Lumber Company, … who was accused publicly of being the major organizer of City Hall graft. "Not a single item enters into the consumption of the two governments (city and county) that has not paid its portion in tribute [to MacKay]. MacKay was not only accused of extorting kickbacks but of furnishing lumber to the two governments at his own price. This latter charge is not verified. … Street paving contracts … were clearly enmeshed in politics and influence peddling."[44]

Many businessmen considered the award of city contracts as their fair share of the pie; the following letter was addressed to the Board of Public Works: "Being a heavy taxpayer … and having for many years devoted a part of my time to the up-building of our good city … [I] feel justified in petitioning for … a reasonable share of insurance on public buildings."[45]

The city was back on a cash basis as required by charter, Mayor Mason told council in his January 1989 message. Portland had paid off outstanding warrants by selling four hundred and thirty thousand dollars' worth of thirty-year, 5 percent bonds. He urged the strictest economy in all city business. The crematory was working well, he said, and was an "absolute necessity" for disposing of the city's garbage. The street cleaning crew had been reduced from seventy employees to forty; private citizens would have to pay for sprinkling their own streets to keep down the dust.

Mason proposed that the council consider consolidation with Multnomah County. The county levied a tax of five to six mills, Mason said, of which nine-tenths was paid by city residents. This money paid the salaries and expenses of county government, with a "very small fraction" of that tax going for the maintenance and operation of bridges within the city. "[I]f the county and city were consolidated under, say, the title of City and County of Portland, would not the saving of one set of officers be a great gain to the taxpayers of the county? Would not much better results be obtained from the levy of 13 or 14 mills for joint use than from separate and independent governments, each spending their proportion of the above levy? … This matter is worthy of thought."[46] Perhaps if Mason had lived longer, city-county consolidation might have occurred, for Mason had the kind of power base and personal commitment that such an undertaking would have required. But no further public discussion of the issue now took place.

Less than three months later, Mayor William Mason died. His attempts to reform city government came to an abrupt halt during the early morning hours of March 27, 1899, following a six-week illness.[47] For the third time, a Portland mayor had died in office.[48]

Mason was buried in San Francisco, at his prior written request. San Francisco Chamber of Commerce members acted as his pall bearers.[49] Many Portlanders felt deprived by this turn of events, as articulated by the *Oregonian*: "[It is natural for a proud state] to desire to hold in its bosom the dust of those whom it has honored and whose lives have honored it. … Burial at San Francisco takes away from [Mason's] life the better part of its real significance, which certainly was his career at Portland. … Besides, a state feels that it never wholly possessed the hearts of those who express a wish to be buried somewhere else."[50]

The city paid for Mason's six hundred fifty-four-dollar funeral and casket expense,[51] leaving the implication that his estate lacked the funds to do so. Mason had built a splendid house seven years before.[52] Council minutes do not say why his burial expenses were borne by the city in such tight financial times.

❧

Nearly two months elapsed before the eleven-member council could agree upon a successor to Mayor Mason. Council president William A. Storey presided as the council deadlocked for fourteen meetings held between April 18 and May 16. Each time, two candidates received five votes each, with a third candidate receiving one vote. The first nominees were George W. Bates, a wealthy entrepreneur who owned several companies and banks,[53] and city councilman C. J. Jameson, whose supporters included future mayor George L. Baker and council president Storey.[54]

Coucilman Jameson never voted for himself, probably in deference to the 1867 Oregon Supreme Court ruling that had overturned Councilman Rosenheim's appointment as marshal as "contrary to the policy of law for an officer to use his official appointing power to place himself in office."[55]

On the first eleven ballots, Bates and Jameson each received one vote less than the required majority. On the next three ballots, council president Storey and former council president Tyler Woodward also tied at five votes each.

Storey, meanwhile, had replaced the poundmaster with a new appointee. Councilman Cameron protested this action, insisting that Storey had no such authority. The city attorney, however, opined that the council president did indeed have authority to perform the duties of mayor.[56]

On its fifteenth attempt to choose a replacement for the deceased mayor, the council met at 10 p.m. the evening of May 16, with Councilman Martin absent. The Bates contingent nominated Henry S. Rowe, while the other faction stayed with Storey. Storey then asked Councilman Jameson to preside over the meeting. Just before the vote was taken, Storey slipped out of the room, leaving only nine councilmen to vote so that five votes would constitute a majority. By this maneuver, he racked up five votes to four for Rowe. Even though he would still have received five votes if he had stayed in the meeting (and cast his own straw vote for a third candidate), that would have constituted only half of the ten votes cast, not a majority. Now the matter was settled. Storey became mayor by absenting himself from the meeting. He would serve out the remainder of William Mason's mayoral term, a period of thirteen months.[57]

May 1899 - June 1900

Storey came to Portland from Maine in 1877 at age twenty-three. When he became mayor, he owned and published the *Northwest Sportsman*.[58] William A. Storey started out as a woodmill worker who "rose from the ranks" by "sheer hard work," and was now a "heavy taxpayer."[59] He had served as president of the Board of Fire Commissioners in 1890-91.[60] His peers elected him council president when he first came on council, so he had less than a year's council experience when elevated to the mayor's chair.

A new challenge for the council was providing adequate bicycle paths for cyclists and keeping them in good condition. Wagon wheels, horses' shoes and cows' hoofs cut up the surfaces and made deep impressions. "When [paths are] thus used," noted the *Oregonian*, "they are practically destroyed. ... [A)] strong legislative enactment will have to be passed applying to the whole state, as the cycle path presents a new condition not provided for in the road laws."[61]

Mayor William Storey (Photo: OrHi #228)

The first automobile appeared in Portland on November 3, 1899.[62] Its owner, Henry Wemme, a German immigrant, was a realtor whose tent and awning business had prospered during the Alaska gold rush and Spanish-American War.[63] His car moved along smoothly at ten miles an hour on Sixth Street, Wemme said, but slowed to five miles an hour on the cobblestones of Front Street. He had purchased the automobile for pleasure purposes, but planned to use it to deliver small packages so people would be seeing it around the city regularly.[64] Wemme later described his new Locomobile this way: "It was a good little car. It could go as fast as you could stay in it. It was light and it jumped about a good deal, so that you were apt to be sitting in the seat one moment and by the side of the road the next if you tried to go more than ten miles an hour. My automobile was not popular either with horses or their owners. … ([T]here were more runaways the first year I had it than had occurred in Portland for the twenty preceding years."[65]

Nobody suggested building roads for such motorized vehicles; it would be another ten years before automobile roadways became an issue. In the meantime, other transportation modes were proving costly in unexpected ways. The rickety, wooden Madison Street (Hawthorne) Bridge had lasted less than ten years, so the city had to rebuild it in 1900.[66] An eight-year-old boy fell to his death under a Southern Pacific freight train in late January 1900. The city ordinance prohibiting climbing on trains[67] was clearly not being enforced. The brakeman

Portland's first automobiles bounced along cobblestoned Front Street, where horse-drawn delivery wagons are shown waiting to be loaded. Ownership of the Starr Block at far left was decided by the landmark Starr v. Stark *lawsuit. (1904 photo: OrHi #8296)*

testified that "boys were constantly climbing on the moving trains, and that hardly a train passed to and from the shops without from one to ten boys hanging on it." The trainmen said warning the boys had no effect, and the only way to keep them off the trains would be to knock them off with clubs.[68]

A host of legends has grown up about an alleged aspect of Portland life at the end of the century: the shanghaiing of sailors through underground passageways near the waterfront.[69] These tunnels were probably built originally for drainage, flood control, and hauling cargo to and from ships docked in the harbor, but for fifty years, from the latter part of the nineteenth century into the 1920s, the tunnels were also said to be used for transporting shanghaied sailors to waiting ships.[70] A possible scenario for how this might have occurred:

> A "crimp," as the men who Shanghaied sailors were known … [would] make the rounds of the bars and cardrooms where the sailors spent their time in port. … And he

> would entice the seamen to come with him … by promising them women and fine food and all they could drink. … [A]t a certain point in the evening Captain Jack would slip some knockout drops into their drinks, causing them to pass out. Then he would take them down through the basement, where there was a tunnel that led … eventually to Shanghai Dock.[71]

A notorious "crimping" episode had been reported in October 1893, in which Bunco Kelly[72] and Larry Sullivan (a boarding-house owner from the North End) were accused of passing off twenty-four dead men as drunken sailors to the skipper of the *Flying Prince* and collecting seven hundred twenty dollars for doing so. The dead sailors had apparently thought they were breaking into the cellar of the Snug Harbor Saloon, where they thought they could drink without payment, but instead stumbled into a nearby undertaker's cellar and mistook wooden kegs holding formaldehyde for beer kegs. In the words of storyteller Stewart Holbrook, Bunco Kelly was passing by on the street above when he noticed an open trapdoor in the sidewalk and decided to investigate. He beheld a scene never to be forgotten. "'My hair,' Kelly later related to Spider Johnson, 'was pretty thin, but the few hairs I had stood up and pushed my cap into the air.'"[73]

> Bunco … sent a boy on the dead run to fetch a cab. He roused four or five old friends …. and …. asked for five more cabs to hurry to Front and Morrison. … "Five dollars in gold to each of you," he told his aides, "as soon as these sailors are aboard ship." … By half-past one, fourteen corpses and ten men who were very ill had been stowed away snugly in the *Flying Prince*'s forecastle, bound out for China. … The captain … counted out $30 each for two dozen men. … At dawn the *Flying Prince* cast off and headed down the Columbia for the open sea. Long before noon the first mate made the hideous discovery in the forecastle. The ship put in at Astoria, where the corpses were removed.[74]

Federal law defined shanghaiing "as the employment of any sailor who had not signed ship's articles or who had signed unwillingly or unsoberly." The Portland Chamber of Commerce printed a handbill in 1898, when William Mason was president, declaring that captains allowed crimps to come on board their ships to entice sailors on shore, kept them there long enough to void their contracts that were soon to expire, then took on board a different crew of shanghaied sailors who wouldn't know until they reached the open sea that they had been fleeced of their money and were now in servitude for another three years. The crimps operated "too often with the knowledge and consent and even the connivance of captains and owners."[75]

Many ship captains, however, disputed these allegations, insisting that Portland was "a lawless place that gave them no assistance" in trying to keep crimps off their ships. "Captains ... expected the ports to police themselves, and complained of Portland's failure to do so."[76] Although shanghaiing gave Portland's port a bad reputation, crimps kept the traffic of commerce flowing and for this reason were not prosecuted as they might otherwise have been.[77]

Crimp Larry Sullivan boasted to a visiting consul that he "was the law in Portland." Newspaper articles written just before and after his death in 1918 recalled an election in which "Sullivan brandished a shotgun at police who arrived to investigate the polling booth located at his boardinghouse." Police waited until the polling was over, then arrested Sullivan, who, as usual, was released without any serious charges filed against him. Another account said an entire crew of non-English-speaking Dutch sailors had been given two dollars apiece for voting in that same election.[78]

Not all references to waterfront activities in 1900 were as odious as those of shanghaiing. In a backward look at Portland as the new century dawned, Barbara Bartlett Hartwell said: "[T]he river dominated our

Low tide brought out well-dressed visitors to the waterfront at the turn of the century. Note the ever-present Portland umbrella. (Photo: OrHi #28059)

The French vessel La Rochefoucauld *anchors at a Portland dock ready to load a pile of sawdust in the late 1890s. (Photo: OrHi #104302)*

In June 1900, the second statewide vote on women's suffrage overshadowed local elections. Abigail Scott Duniway and her allies had carefully laid the groundwork for this election for at least three years. Duniway was confident of victory "as a most fitting accompaniment to the dawn of the twentieth century."[80]

Every one of the two hundred twenty-nine newspapers in the state except the *Oregonian* endorsed the measure. The *Oregonian*, under the editorship of Duniway's brother Harvey Scott, ran a "twenty-day, fourteen-editorial preelection attack on woman suffrage from every angle."[81]

Women's suffrage lost by two thousand votes out of fifty-five thousand votes cast statewide, with a negative vote of 3,473 in Portland.[82] Scott's son, Leslie, later said his father's opposition to suffrage was based on the belief that women voters would double the "ignorant and irresponsible voting of taxes and governmental extravagance" by citizens who did not feel the burdens imposed on property owners by such taxes.[83] The measure's defeat was also blamed on whiskey interests who feared that women would vote for prohibition.

lives and the life of the town. What cargoes those sailing ships brought in, sandalwood, cedar, sweet white wine. What endless bunches of bananas, with an occasional tarantula stealing passage only to end his criminal career in a bottle of alcohol. ... Sailors were men of strange oaths and browned faces who wore rings in their ears. ... The whistles of river steamers, the sound of bells, the sloshing of paddle wheels turning were sweet to the ear. .... We rowed on the river, went by river to the Oregon City bluffs for school picnics, swam in the river."[79]

Mayor Storey ran as an independent in seeking another term as mayor. He was opposed by Republican Henry Rowe and Democrat G. M. Wells. A front-page box in the *Oregonian* urged readers to vote a straight Republican ticket. The *Oregonian* may have tipped the scales for Rowe, because he won with only 37 percent of the vote, one of the slimmest pluralities in city history. Storey trailed by only ninety-five votes, gaining 34 percent of the votes, and Wells pulled a respectable 29 percent.[84] One Democrat and one independent won council seats, but all other city officials were "safe" by the *Oregonian*'s standards—that is to say, Republican.[85]

> The [June 6] meeting of the Common Council ... was a very pleasant one. Everyone seemed pleased that the election was over, and even [Mayor Storey], who missed his spring for reelection, was happy over the good run he made, and jokingly asked if he could not take his chair home, so that he might sit in it as much as possible for the remainder of the month.[86]

Former mayor Storey was to launch a recall effort against Governor Oswald West after West clamped down on Portland vice twelve years later. An *Oregonian* article called it a "foolish" recall movement. Storey insisted that "no liquor interests, no houses of ill-fame, or county or city officials" were behind the recall petitions.[87] Historian E. Kimbark MacColl implies that Storey had questionable political ties during his 1902-04 tenure as Multnomah County sheriff, and says: "[H]onest Tom Ward defeated incumbent Sheriff William A. Storey."[88] MacColl also characterizes Storey's mayoral tenure as the beginning of a six-year period of "weak, ineffective government" that would not end until the election of Harry Lane.[89]

Chapter 17

More Vice, the "Oregon System," and a Dazzling World's Fair

July 1900 – June 1905

Mayors

No. 33: July 1900 - June 1902

Henry S. Rowe (elected for two-year term)

No. 34: July 1902 - June 1905

George H. Williams (elected for two-year term, term extended to odd-numbered year by 1903 charter)

Turn-of-the-century Portland boasted one automobile; thousands of bicycles; dozens of clanging, rocking streetcars and cable cars; hundreds of wagons drawn by clattering, iron-shod horses; a harborful of steamships and sailing ships; four bridges; twenty-two daily arrivals and departures of passenger trains at Union Depot; and a Southern Pacific train running down Fourth Avenue next to the county courthouse and new city hall. Whenever there was a fire, powerful horses "plung[ed] down the street with gongs ringing and firemen clinging all over the engine or hook-and-ladder vehicles."[1] Bands played concert music in the forecourt of the Portland Hotel with its potted palms and lush green vines, while townspeople gathered across the street on the lawn of the Pioneer Post Office to listen. "There were band concerts, too, in the City Park, now called Washington Park. ... Few left the Park without visiting the zoo. It had little resemblance to that of today. ... Animals were kept in cramped, stinking cages. The bear pit was an abomination. Even so, the animals were a never-failing source of interest. ... monkey cages ... owls ... guinea pigs ... great eagles ... wolves and foxes ... seals."[2]

Street hawkers plied their wares; Italian vendors[3] pushed carts overflowing with fruits and vegetables through the residential districts calling: "Nanoes! Nice ripe nanoes, ten cents a dozen. Oranges! Sweet oranges!" or in late summer, "Watermelons! Ripe watermelons!" Then from August to November, the "whanging voices" of circular saws rang out in the residential districts because all Portland homes were heated by wood fires.[4]

Women laced themselves into bony corsets and piled on as many as five petticoats to make their skirts fluff out. They wore high-button shoes along with wide, floppy-brimmed hats anchored to puffed-up hair with long, deadly hatpins. Men wore straw boaters or felt hats and suits of cotton, wool, cashmere, or silk; denim overalls for work on the farms and in the mills.[5]

The century's first Portland mayor, Henry S. Rowe, was a Simon Republican, a solid forty-nine-year-old businessman and the tenth of eleven Portland mayors born in New York State.[6] His life career, like that of Mason and Frank before him, had started with the railroad. When he first came to Portland in 1880, Rowe worked as a superintendent for the Oregon Railroad and Navigation Company. Also like Mason and Frank, Rowe then spent time in merchandising. By 1900, he owned considerable real estate. He maintained memberships in the Arlington Club, Chamber of Commerce, Commercial Club, Masonic order, Knights Templar, Elks, Woodmen of the World, and Modern Woodmen of America. Rowe had served as president of the Board of Fire Commissioners for several years, and continued to serve on the Water Committee during his tenure as mayor.[7]

The 1890s cable car route to Portland Heights from Goose Hollow passed a castle-like residence on S.W. Cable Street that is still in use today. (This is not the Piggott's Castle visible from downtown.) (Photo: OrHi #9008)

Mayor Henry Rowe. (Photo: OrHi #97629)

Rowe's major goal was to rein in the cost of city government, which he did.[8] E. Kimbark MacColl calls Rowe's regime "dull, safe businessman's government."[9]

As part of a citywide austerity program mandated by the city charter, councilmen were now serving without pay. In his inaugural message, Mayor Rowe praised the sacrifice and devotion that council members exhibited in their willingness to assume office without monetary compensation. He also urged council harmony. "In the past we have heard of the solid six and the solid seven," Rowe said, "but I am anxious now that you maintain a solid eleven; the only power of the mayor in legislation is when there is a division in the council." Rowe's inaugural message also recommended passage of an ordinance to require the removal of moss from building roofs to improve the city's appearance and to protect against fires.[10]

❧

At the same time voters elected Rowe, they approved creation of an independent city parks commission with the power to levy an annual half mill property tax for purchasing land and improving and maintaining city parks. The mayor was to chair the commission, the Multnomah County Circuit Court was to appoint the five citizen members (no more than three from one political party), and the city engineer would serve as the seventh member.[11] The commission was given authority to levy a second half mill for additional park purchases if approved by a special citizen vote.[12]

Parks commission appointees were Unitarian minister Thomas Lamb Eliot, a parks champion;[13] Brig. Gen. Charles F. Beebe of the Oregon militia; former congressman Rufus Mallory;[14] former councilman Henry Fleckenstein; and Lester Leander Hawkins, of whom more will presently be said. The board convened in October 1900 and accepted control of city park property from the Water Committee. They soon approved a parks property tax levy for 1901.[15]

The commission also took on responsibility for maintaining the elk statue and fountain donated by former mayor David Thompson and installed in late summer 1900 in the middle of Main Street.[16] An enterpriser named M. J. Walsh proposed to wire the elk's head, at the cost of a mere twenty dollars, to add "a miniature light on the tip of each horn, with a bunch of red, white and blue lights on the forehead; and one miniature light placed in each eye." A council committee quickly buried the proposal.[17]

Portland's population virtually doubled during the decade from 1890 to 1900, from a little more than forty-six thousand to slightly more than ninety thousand; at least half of the increase came from consolidation with East Portland and Albina. Seattle's population still lagged behind Portland's by ten thousand, but it was fast catching up, fueled by gold-seekers who came for the Alaska gold rush and stayed on. Portland men continued to outnumber women three to two, with over a fourth of the city's female population being foreign-born.[19]

> Mud was still a major problem. Two pedestrians waited until a team and wagon passed to cross the street at Second and Morrison, only to be caught mid-street by a team "driven at breakneck speed" which came rushing around the corner. "Both pedestrians fled for their lives," said the *Oregonian*, but one was caught and "knocked down and trampled under the horses' feet and rolled over and over in the mud, till he looked like a mud image." The man barely escaped serious injury, while the reckless driver, identity unknown, went careening on down the street.[18]

A wide disparity in population existed between city wards. Southwest Ward 7 had only 2,855 residents while downtown Ward 4 contained over six times as many. Yet both wards were represented by one council member. "One person, one vote" had not yet arrived in Portland.[20]

Streets, sewers, and sidewalks continued to monopolize the council's time. Many road projects completed earlier had to be redone, because of worn-out materials, poor workmanship, or new technology. Nicholson paving, for example, once seen as the perfect road construction for the city's rainy clime, had fallen from favor. Its wooden blocks were shaped like bricks, about fourteen inches by five or six inches. "They were not laid straight with the street, but slanted this way and that, a few one way then a few another. They had some tarry substance between them, which might ooze up on warm days. And in winter they might bulge up in spots from water in and between them freezing and expanding. On occasion, a bulge would become so severe it would burst, lifting a few blocks clear out of position. Most streets in the heart of the city, though, were paved with cobblestones."[21]

City hall now housed two popular attractions— a free public museum and a free public library. Several rooms on the fourth floor, as well as the two light courts in the center of the building, were filled with stuffed birds and animals, along with displays moved into city hall from the now-defunct exposition hall. The "father and indefatigable promoter" of the city hall museum was Lester Leander Hawkins, president of Ainsworth National Bank and member of the new parks commission. Hawkins later added dinosaur bones to the city hall museum collection. Earlier, he had built a pedestal to display a six hundred-pound stone globe measuring two feet wide that had been found in Astoria bay, where it had probably slid into the water from a soapstone cliff. Some people imagined it might be the petrified eyeball of a sperm whale.[22]

The Oregon Historical Society also had its offices in city hall. The society, incorporated only two years before, requested the use of two additional rooms in 1900, when Harvey W. Scott was listed on letterhead as president and the address as "Rooms in City Hall, top floor, N.W. corner."[23] Later that year, the society proposed honoring the one hundredth anniversary of the Lewis and Clark 1805 expedition down the Columbia with a 1905 world's fair. The idea of a fair had been floating for five or six years, but it was the historical society that proposed the specific date and theme that would catch the public's fancy.[24]

Empty rooms in city hall generated envy in the hearts of county commissioners who labored in tight quarters two blocks north in the Multnomah County Courthouse. County accommodations were "entirely inadequate," said a testy letter from the county auditor presenting the commissioners' case for low-rent use of available rooms in city hall: "[C]onsidering that the County is now required to perform much service for the city without compensation—in the collection of city taxes, the care of its boulevards and some of the streets, the maintenance of the criminal department of the Municipal Court, (the revenue from which in fines, costs, and forfeited bails all go into the City Treasury) ... the Commissioners submit that the county is entitled to the use of necessary rooms ... at a nominal rental, if indeed any charge, at all, should be made."[25]

Two public libraries were operating in Portland—one with paid memberships known as the Library Association of Portland (LAP), and a free Portland Public Library (PPL) located at city hall. The LAP had thirty-eight thousand volumes and its own building on Stark Street, whereas the free library had fewer than three thousand books and only four rooms, but was visited by an average of two hundred forty-five people a day.[26] The LAP had begun in 1864 as a successful subscription library and reading room,[27] but was now facing financial difficulties because the financial panic of 1893 had struck while they were erecting a new building.

The LAP was forced to reexamine its operations by a remarkable bequest received in September 1900. A merchant named John Wilson left eight thousand volumes and twenty-five hundred dollars in gold coin to LAP in his will, with the stipulation that the books be used as a *free* reference library. The collection was too valuable to reject. Either LAP had to open its doors to the public without fee, or find some other answer.

The state legislature cooperated by passing a law in early 1901 that authorized cities to levy an annual one-fifth mill property tax for library purposes. At LAP's urging, the bill included a provision that allowed a city to contract with a private nonsectarian group for its library function.[28] The Portland city council levied this tax and designated the LAP as the city's official public library. Soon thereafter, the free library at city hall disbanded and donated all its books and assets to the LAP. On March 10, 1902, the library doors at S.W. Stark between Broadway and Park were opened to the public without charge.[29] This library was the forerunner of today's fine Multnomah County library system.

The fact the public had approved a new half mill property tax levy for parks and had little objection to the one-fifth mill library levy might seem to indicate full recovery from the financial panic of 1893, but such was not the case. Revenues and expenditures for general city government use were still down, and the world's fair was being touted as a way to recover completely from the depression.[30]

Mayor Rowe boasted, in his January 1902 message to the council, that city government spent less in 1901 than at any time in the prior eight years. From 1893 through 1901, expenses for fire, police and general purposes had decreased nearly 40 percent, while interest charges had nearly tripled. The net effect of all economies was an overall reduction of 23 percent in city expenditures. For the first time since 1893, Rowe said, the city was starting the year with no backlog of unpaid debts. Rowe praised the board of public works and fire department efficiency, but said the police force was too small. "The expenditures of [the police] department have been less than those of any other city in the Union of like size either in population or area," Rowe said.[31]

The mayor said nothing about cracking down on prostitution, but he and the council must have been aware of how openly it was practiced. Observer Laurence Pratt tells of the "Red Light District" that stretched thirteen blocks along Fourth Street from Everett to Salmon, virtually on the doorstep of the county courthouse and only two blocks from city hall. Pratt first saw these establishments in 1902, during the tenure of Mayor Williams, but he notes that an open vice policy must have existed under Mayor Rowe for them to be so firmly ensconced, and that acceptance of such open cribs must have been supported by "influential business interests." "When I first walked north on Fourth ... I was startled to find it bordered with one- and two-story frame buildings like little shops, each with a window against the sidewalk and a woman seated inside. Over each door was a girl's name—Jennie, Lulu, May, Yvonne, The Favorite, or another. ... Later, when I had a bicycle, I rode down the street, not so close to those windows, and found the rows stretch for blocks on both sides of the street. ... It was a jolt when a girl with a skirt above her knees would venture out of her crib and wave at me as I passed on my bicycle."[32]

Contradictory messages thus survive regarding the years 1901-02. The year 1901 was "the greatest year for business in the history of Portland," according to a newspaper article of early 1902.[33] A finance company reported, "Never in the history of Portland has the real estate market been in a more healthy ... and prosperous condition than it is today."[34] A 1901 reception at the home of Mrs. Henry W. Corbett featured an orchestra which played the entire afternoon, while women "handsomely dressed in the costume of the time, veiled, gloved and with wasp-waisted skirts sweeping the heavily carpeted floors with their swishing taffeta dust ruffles, called and sipped tea."[35]

"The most remarkable, complicated and paradoxical period in Oregon's tortuous political history" is how E. Kimbark MacColl characterizes the sixteen-month period of March 1901 through June 1902.[36] For on June 2, 1902, Oregon voters approved, by the spectacular majority of 92 percent, a statewide constitutional amendment which launched the initiative and referendum process which would soon become known as "The Oregon System."[37]

> "How would you like to live in a state where the people can and do enact laws for the common good which their Legislature has failed to enact for them, where they can nullify an obnoxious measure passed by the Legislature ... a state where the party boss has been put out of business; a state in short where the people rule ... Such a state is Oregon."[38]

Surely the broad coalition of political and business establishment supporters of the initiative and referendum had no inkling of how many and diverse would be the measures placed on future statewide ballots by the initiative process.[39]

In spite of this populist victory, the power to amend Portland's charter still rested with the state legislature. In 1901, the legislature had appointed a committee of Portland citizens to draft a new charter for referral to city voters in June 1902. After voter approval, the legislature would adopt or reject the charter. A committee of thirty-three distinguished citizens had begun work immediately after its appointment in February 1901, choosing as chairman Abbot L. Mills, vice-president of First National Bank and chair of the city's board of public works.[40] The group pondered alternatives for over a year.

Portland voters were presented with a proposed new charter (the ninth) at the same election that the initiative and referendum measure was adopted statewide and they approved it by an astounding 90 percent majority. However, the charter would not become effective unless and until it was approved by both the state legislature and the governor, and that was not possible until the legislature reconvened in January 1903.[41]

Rowe did not seek reelection. He left elective politics for a position as general agent for the Chicago, Milwaukee & St. Paul Railroad. However, he maintained an interest in Republican party politics and in city affairs until his death twelve years later.[42]

Republican Party boss John Mitchell had searched for a 1902 mayoral candidate who could win, but could also be depended upon to take direction. He found the ideal candidate in one whose name was already well known to Portlanders as Portland's claim to national fame: George Williams, fondly known as the "Grand Old Man."

July 1902 - June 1905

Well-intentioned. Distinguished. Trusted. Kindly. Eloquent. Weak. Taken-advantage-of. Spineless. Past-his-prime.

Any and all of these adjectives described Portland's next mayor, George H. Williams, who, at age seventy-nine, was by far the oldest mayor ever to assume that office.[43] The new charter increased Williams's tenure to three years because all city elections were moved from even-numbered years to odd-numbered years so city campaigns would not be mixed in with partisan state and national elections. With the powerful backing of U.S. Senator John Mitchell, Williams was elected mayor over lumberman Robert D. Inman, the candidate of a Republican - Democratic coalition ticket. Inman lost by roughly the same 5 percent margin he had suffered in the disastrous flood election of 1894.[44]

The three years of Williams's mayoralty were to prove tempestuous ones.

George Williams was truly Oregon's national celebrity, albeit a controversial one. He had arrived in Oregon in 1853 at age thirty as chief justice of the territorial supreme court, appointed by President Franklin Pierce, whom he had helped get elected in Iowa. Five years later, Williams resigned from the court to practice law. He was chosen in 1857 as a delegate from Marion County to the state constitutional convention. A Democrat at that time, he opposed establishing slavery in Oregon and may have lost out in his bid to become the next U.S. senator from Oregon for this stand.[45] But in 1865, the state legislature chose Williams to represent Oregon in the U.S. Senate, where he served until 1871. While he was still in D. C., President Grant appointed him as the top lawyer in the land—Attorney General of the United States—a position he was to hold for five years, from 1873 to 1877.[46]

After Williams had served in this post for nearly two years, President Grant nominated him as Chief Justice of the United States. But Williams never made it through the approval process. He fell from grace for several reasons: his wife, Kate, treated other Washington wives arrogantly and overspent her income; Williams's legal scholarship and attainments were

Mayor George Williams. (Photo: OrHi #104367)

deemed mediocre; he either misused government funds or exercised poor judgment in commingling personal and government money. Also, while Williams was waiting for confirmation to the Supreme Court job, Oregon's Judge Deady and Addison Gibbs, U.S. Attorney for Oregon, were expediting a big voter fraud case concerning Oregon's 1872 elections. Williams, under pressure from U. S. Senator John Mitchell, forced Gibbs to stop bringing these indictments. When Gibbs refused Williams's order to desist, Williams used his authority as U.S. Attorney General to remove Gibbs from office.[47]

Williams's detractors had also started calling him "Landaulet" Williams as a result of a gossipy kind of scandal that had developed over Mrs. Williams's frequent use of a government carriage. Oregon Congressman James Nesmith moved to strike two thousand dollars from the Attorney General's appropriation bill for horses, carriages, and harnesses. Nesmith told a congressional committee, at least partly in jest: Attorney General Williams "is the only one who indulges in this gorgeous, oriental splendor of riding in a $1600 landaulet. Why, sir, lawyers of my state, of his caliber, ride upon the outside of a fifty-dollar mule, and think they are doing well at that."[48]

Harvey Scott found Nesmith's role in this scandal "one of the most disgraceful and contemptible things of which partisan malice in our country has ever been guilty."[49] However, extravagances in the Williams household went far beyond the landaulet. "The laxity with which Williams had long conducted his office had lately crossed the line of corruption," author Allen Nevins says. "Mrs. Williams was largely responsible. Expensively dressed, living fashionably … keeping a fine equipage, entertaining well, she had exceeded their means." There was also substance to other charges against Williams: "It was alleged that Judge Williams had mingled his accounts … and that during the panic, when the banks were not paying private checks … that the moneys for meeting the expenses of his house had been paid from the funds of the government . … [T]he letter Williams had written in an attempt to explain the charges [was] unsatisfactory. … [The committee was convinced that the Attorney General] had shown the most culpable negligence and indiscretion, and while his intentions might not have been criminal, his use of the contingent funds of the Department of Justice was at least a technical violation."[50]

President Grant finally decided that his presidency could not afford another public scandal like the gold speculation scandal implicating his vice president, charges that his appointees took bribes from the railroads, and impeachment of his secretary of war for conspiring to defraud the government. So Grant asked Williams to withdraw his name. But before Mr. and Mrs. Williams left Washington, Grant also became convinced of Mrs. Williams's "unconscionable viciousness" because of "anonymous" threatening letters she wrote in an attempt to keep her husband in the attorney general's office.[51]

Williams practiced law in Washington, D. C., until 1881; then returned to Oregon and joined a Portland law firm. He and his wife built a "very substantial and attractive home" at N.W. Eighteenth and Couch, in the most fashionable residential district of the city. Around 1893, Mrs. Williams became involved with a new religion and established her own faith cult. She started long-term fasting. One of her fasts lasted forty days. Another, which weakened her so drastically that she died soon thereafter, extended one hundred and ten days.[52]

Seven years later, George Williams was, for a time, a chief contender (as John Mitchell's candidate) against Henry W. Corbett for a return trip to the U.S. Senate. However, it was war-horse John H. Mitchell himself who eventually won out over Corbett in the 1901 legislative maneuvering for that seat.[53] Mitchell then backed Williams to become Portland mayor in 1902.

❧

Williams urged beautification of the city and an improved air of respectability. The subject of bawdy houses was an unpleasant one, he said, and though the council might not be able to suppress such places completely, the cribs should at least be removed from the city's main streets to more secluded quarters. If gambling and prostitution could not be banished, he said, "they can at least be controlled and be subject to a system of 'periodic fines.'"[54]

One councilman openly advocated taxing vice, rather than outlawing it. Fred T. Merrill, who had sought office on "a lark" to promote his bicycle business, said prostitution and gambling would always be with us, and suggested regulating them, simply making sure they paid their license fees and taxes. "There has never been a time during my fifty-four years in Portland when a total stranger couldn't find a gambling game or a sporting house," Merrill told E. Kimbark MacColl in an interview toward the end of his life.[55]

Oregon was now committed to hosting a world's fair in 1905 to commemorate the 1805 Lewis and Clark expedition,[56] so bringing Portland's seamier side under control during the next three years became an important goal. The idea of promoting Oregon's commerce by inviting visitors from all over the world had been percolating since 1895. "We have the natural resources, climate and everything else needed except people," said Col. Henry E. Dosch, in promoting the exposition cause in April 1899.[57]

The state legislature had endorsed the idea of a world's fair in early 1901, pledged money, appointed five commissioners, and got the bandwagon rolling. It would be the first world's fair on the West Coast and would be patterned after the successful 1876 centennial exposition in Philadelphia, the 1893 Chicago world's fair, and a 1904 fair scheduled for St. Louis. Exposition chair Henry W. Corbett chose a blue-ribbon executive board, whose membership was ratified by a mass citizens' meeting in November 1901. A stock issue of three hundred thousand dollars, the equivalent of six million dollars today, was oversubscribed within ten days, half by subscriptions of over twelve hundred dollars and the other half in amounts from two dollars to one thousand dollars, with three thousand citizens participating.[58] Anticipation was already building and the event itself was nearly three years away.

City government used these years to good advantage.

The parks commission brokered a deal with the Lewis and Clark fair board to split the ten thousand dollar cost of bringing John Olmsted from New York to design both an exposition grounds and a Portland park plan. By the time Olmsted arrived in May 1903, the fair board had already chosen marshy Guild's Lake in northwest Portland as the fair site, after seriously considering City Park (now Washington Park)[59] and several eastside locations. The exposition grounds at Guild's Lake ("pronounced with a long *i*, as in *guide*, rather than *gild*") consisted of "a grove of trees, 180 acres of pasture, and 220 acres of waist-high stagnant water."[60]

❧

Meanwhile, routine city business occupied most of the council's time. A "classic case of conflict of interest" regarding city streetcar franchises occurred between November and January (when the new charter would be ratified by the legislature). Between the time voters approved a new city charter in June 1902 and the legislature approved it the following January, the public works board and city council rushed to complete agreements which granted twenty-five- and thirty-year exclusive franchises to railway companies represented by Abbot Mills, chair of both the charter committee and public works board.[61]

The *Oregon Journal* urged the council to wait on these franchises until the new charter was approved because it specified a maximum twenty-five-year franchise award and "fair compensation" to the city. But the council granted the long-term franchises anyway. Even the *Oregonian*, which supported the council's actions at the time, was later to accuse the railway companies of fraud, claiming they had duped the newspaper in late 1902. Harvey Scott wrote in 1906: "The tricks of the franchise gang of Portland are coming to light." Eastern financiers had purchased some of these utilities by 1906, and Scott called the whole package "political jobbery, costing the city millions of dollars," because the companies were paying such low franchise fees and earning such sizeable profits.[62]

❧

In January 1903, the state legislature passed, and Governor George Chamberlain signed, Portland's citizen-drafted and voter-approved new charter. This ninth charter made substantive changes in Portland's governance.

The independent boards of police, fire, parks, water, and public works were abolished; replaced by new boards of parks, water, health, and free library; with a civil service commission of three and an executive board of ten established; all to be appointed by the mayor and to serve at the mayor's pleasure. The executive board that replaced the board of public works was to review all proposed franchises and other contracts and recommend what action the council should take.[63] Council membership was increased to fifteen, with ten councilmen elected from wards and five at-large, and council terms to last four years. The terms of the elected mayor, auditor, treasurer, city attorney, and municipal judge would all be two years. Council members would be paid five dollars for each council meeting attended, plus three dollars for each committee meeting, not to exceed twenty-five dollars a month, or three hundred dollars per year.

The mayor retained his veto power, authority to preside over council meetings, and power to cast tie votes, with the council president to exercise all powers and duties of the mayor in his absence. The term of city-granted franchises could not exceed twenty-five years, with fair compensation to be paid to the city for all franchises and a favorable two-thirds council vote required for ratification. The city was authorized to acquire a public utility if approved by a vote of the people.

All municipal officials, except women, who were permitted to serve on the library and park boards, had to be registered voters of Portland.[64] The total property tax levy allowed for city government was ten mills (1 percent, or one dollar on each one hundred dollars of property value).

An underlying charter principle was that the mayor should be made responsible for administering city affairs "in such manner that it cannot be evaded."[65] Administrative responsibility had previously been spread too thin and the mayor had become almost a figurehead. Now the mayor had real power, committee members said. The mayor was a member of, and chairman of, all boards and commissions specified in the charter.[66] He would not only appoint all department heads and members of citizen boards, but could remove them as well.

As soon as the charter was signed, Mayor Williams chose ten men, all solid Portland businessmen, to comprise his new executive board, which included Whitney L. Boise, Jr., a lawyer and realtor who would later oppose installation of water meters and usage-based water fees because of the impact on his personal finances.[67]

Williams appointed two members of the old parks commission—Thomas Lamb Eliot and Lester Leander Hawkins—to the new park board, plus new appointees Ion Lewis (the city hall architect) and J. D. Meyer.[68]

The new water board members were all former water committee members, except for the mayor. This provided continuity regarding an issue that had been a committee priority for some time concerning the Bull Run watershed.[69] In December, the water board asked Oregon's congressional delegation to seek federal legislation to keep hunters, campers, and others who might start forest fires out of the Bull Run

Reserve. With the help of President Teddy Roosevelt, the Bull Run area got that protection the following spring with passage of the Bull Run Trespass Act. This law prohibited anyone except forest rangers and official government employees from entering the reserve, and specifically excluded the grazing of stock therein.[70]

❧

The March *Century Magazine* carried a rave review of Portland, based on an extensive visit to the Northwest by reporter Ray S. Baker. Baker liked Portland's "brisk energy" and its "signs of conservatism and solid respectability. Few cities of the size of Portland can exhibit finer store and office buildings, a better streetcar service, or more comfortable residences. Unlike almost any other Western town, save San Francisco perhaps, it has … passed the stage of pioneer crudities. … Portland is noted for the solidity of its financial institutions, its fine clubs and hotels, its good schools and libraries. It is beginning to take a solicitous interest in its history, a true sign of the self-consciousness which comes of assured success."[71]

This glowing assessment set the stage for a May 1903 visit to Portland by John Olmsted, son of the designer of New York's Central Park. The younger Olmsted was hired to design the world's fair grounds as well as lay out a Portland park plan. Olmsted played no part in fair site selection, as previously noted.[72]

President Roosevelt promised to lay the cornerstone for a Lewis and Clark monument as a kick-off to construction and promotion. Planning for Roosevelt's visit involved numerous meetings and extensive organization. In April, council president Louis Zimmerman fired off a letter of protest to the centennial committee chairman about proposed carriage assignments for the president's parade. "[T]he President is to be the guest of the City … and it is therefore only proper and right that the City officials should have precedence over all others. … I hope you will therefore arrange matters so as to have at least one member of the Council and one member of the [City] Executive Board in the carriages with the Presidential party."[73]

Cheering crowds greeted Teddy Roosevelt on the bright sunny day of May 21, 1903, with one council member and one executive board representative assigned to the seventh vehicle, and Mayor Williams riding in the first carriage with the president and Governor Chamberlain.[74] A photograph of the president's triumphant Portland parade graces the front cover of Laurence Pratt's book, *I Remember Portland*. The caption says Roosevelt made five public addresses in Portland that day.[75]

City auditor Thomas Devlin reminded the executive board in early August that civil service rules established by the new city charter were not being followed: "In several departments under your control," he said, "there is now and has been for a considerable time many men employed and paid who have not been formally appointed to the positions occupied by them." The executive board was required to send an estimate of expenditures to council every month, Devlin noted, and he was not authorized to pay any bills in excess of such estimates. He would be doing less than his duty, Devlin said, if he did not refuse to pay any such bills.[76]

The new city charter required publication of an inventory of city property with the auditor's annual financial report. No such inventory had ever been made. Auditor Devlin suggested that council appoint a competent group to do so.[77] The council chose three old-timers to make the appraisal: former city councilman J. P. O. Lownsdale; pioneer photographer and former sheriff Joseph Buchtel; and Julius Kraemer.[78] The appraisal committee reported in October 1903 that city-owned property was worth 8.7 million dollars, or the equivalent of one hundred seventy million today. They reported city-owned assets and values as follows:

City Waterworks	$6,500,000
City Hall land and building	600,000
Park Blocks	360,000
Burnside Bridge	250,000
Madison Street Bridge	60,000
Morrison Street Bridge	30,000
Albina Ferry	17,000
City Park (part of today's Washington Park)	192,000
Two Public Squares near City Hall	165,000
Market Square (block 132)	50,000
Holladay's Addition parks, 4 blocks	40,000
Macleay Park, 108 acres	27,000
John Mock's 29 acres of park	19,000
Ladd's Addition parks, 5 parcels	9,000
Crematory, 5 acres north of St. Helen's Rd	21,000
City barn, 6 lots, "Davenport Tr."	21,000
Pest house property, 2 acres	2,000
East-side water company land, 3 acres	16,000
Police court lot	18,000
Fire engine houses and lots	91,000

Fire engines and other fire equipment	133,000
Street-cleaning equipment	12,000
Unimproved lots and blocks	15,000
Other	10,000
Grand total[79]	$8,657,000

Regarding the three bridges and one ferry, the committee had been advised that "while the title of the three bridges and Albina Ferry … is vested in the city, the same are for the present turned over to the county to operate and keep in repair at the county's expense."[80]

❧

Vice was still widespread in Portland. The city, "by a regular system of monthly fines … practically licensed gambling and prostitution, and under this system of official encouragement the city had become a popular headquarters for all the vicious characters in the Pacific Northwest," according to *McClure's Magazine*.[81] Mayor Williams blamed his executive board for licensing gambling. "The board had a secret meeting without my knowledge and consent," the mayor said, "in which they decided to try this system of fining gamblers." He does not mention that he had himself suggested, in his inaugural address, that gambling and prostitution might be controlled and subjected to a system of periodic fines. When the matter did come to his attention, he said, he was told that the city treasury was down to bedrock and money was needed to fix up the city for the fair.[82]

Police Chief Charles Hunt occasionally sent mixed signals concerning this fine "system." Business owners got confused between what was a real fine and what was a license to continue disobeying the law "without molestation." A group of slot machine operators who had paid fines did so because they believed they had a "special understanding and agreement with certain city officials or their agents," and complained to the council that they were now being ordered to turn the slot machines to the wall or have them removed. A council investigating committee concluded: "[I]t was tacitly understood by the police department and by the owners and operators of money paying slot machines that the slot machines were to be put upon the fine system the same as other forms of gambling and that the money was so deposited as bail by the various persons depositing same."[83]

On July 14, 1903, a group called the Portland Municipal Association organized,[84] based on the following principles: party politics should

> A twenty-five-year-old woman who arrived in Portland for the first time in late 1903 later described her walk from Union Station to the downtown post office: "The stench of stale beer and whiskey often mixed with the nauseating smell of vomit on the sidewalks, and drunken staggering men blocking my way almost turned my stomach. Portland was very much a logging, lumbering, mill city as well as a seaport with swarms of nautical men, sailors and officers alike ... [going] in and out of almost every second doorway. ... Saloons were especially prominent on corners throughout the business district. ... I could hear a jangling of voices ... inside, coupled with the slap-slap of cards on green-felted tables off to one side where gambling went on continuously day and night."[87]

have no place in municipal government; the vices of a city form the breeding-ground of graft; and the morality of a community is the foundation of its prosperity.[85] The association would grow to two thousand members, with a goal of eliminating such vices as prize fighting, open gambling, slot machine lotteries, restaurant and saloon "boxes," and dance hall and combination "houses," along with Sunday closure of saloons.[86]

Preparations for the upcoming world's fair were the highlight of Mayor Williams' January 1904 message to the council. He reported that the park board had erected a music stand in City Park at a cost of one thousand dollars. "Weather-beaten and dingy houses should be painted, dilapidated buildings removed, old fences repaired or renewed, lawns and ground cleaned up," the mayor said. A committee had secured landing places for a free ferry at Sellwood, but nothing had yet been done about the additional Albina free ferry authorized by the legislature because no reasonably priced landing place had been found. The garbage crematory had cremated 251 horses, 38 cows, and 742 dogs, along with city garbage greatly in excess of any previous year. Diphtheria and typhoid fever, with twenty-seven deaths each, were the leading causes of 1903 disease-related deaths.[88]

The postmaster warned the council that it would be "impossible for the delivery of mails to be accomplished any time in the next six months" if a plan went through to erect street signs throughout the city using a new numbering system.[89] The council deferred the program.

In 1903, the Port of Portland built its first floating dry dock— a structure from which water could be removed for repairing and cleaning ships—in the St. Johns district.[90]

The Olmsted plan for Portland parks—an ambitious, even radical proposal—was released in June 1904. The plan recommended acquisition of land that would virtually ring the city in parks.[91] Today's "forty-mile loop" of connecting trails around Portland traces its conception to the Olmsted plan.[92] While the plan received considerable publicity, little action ensued. The city's attention was consumed by preparations for the world's fair and continuing problems of open vice in downtown Portland.

❧

A statewide measure placed on the ballot by way of the new initiative system, drew a good deal of attention during the June 1904 county, state, and national elections. A controversial local option liquor law that allowed local jurisdictions to opt for or against prohibition was approved by less than a 4 percent margin. This new law engendered a "highly charged evangelical revival" in Portland, during which a Presbyterian minister accused *Oregonian* editor Harvey Scott of helping to "fasten gambling and prostitution on the city of Portland." A young Baptist minister attacked Mayor Williams in sermons titled "The Mayor of Sodom," "Our City's Crimes and Criminals," and "What Shall It Profit a City to License Crime?"[93]

A crusader named Tom Word, who pledged to close gambling houses, was elected Multnomah County sheriff. *Portland Telegram* writer Dean Collins said Portland had "five of the biggest gambling houses in the United States running wide open."[94] Reformers pointed out that these gambling houses were not the "best advertisement in the world for exposition visitors." Sheriff Word had brought with him from Alaska a certain flair for the dramatic and a willingness to take on all comers. Collins described the scenario that took place after Word took office:

> "I'm responsible for Multnomah county," said Word, and inasmuch as Portland was in Multnomah county, he sent word to the Chief of Police to clean up the gambling houses.
>
> He was notified to go to Hell.
>
> He sent word to … August Erickson on Burnside street, and … all the other pool halls and gambling houses to close.

> He was told unanimously to go to Hell.
>
> So he gathered up his deputies and moved upon the Bad Lands with wagons and axes, after having sent three warnings. Portland rocked with excitement.
>
> [Mayor] George H. Williams ... was horrified and outraged at Word's undignified methods and at Word's invasion of the Police duties of the city. He resisted with dignity but in vain. The axe campaign had captured the popular imagination.[95]

On January 4, 1905, Mayor Williams was formally indicted by a grand jury for malfeasance in office for refusing to perform the duties of his office in cracking down on gambling.[96] He had failed "to direct the chief of police or some other officer to arrest the proprietors of a certain club for running a gambling house."[97] The indictment was soon dismissed, on motion of the Multnomah County District Attorney. Multnomah County judges were said to be part of the machine.[98]

A combination of efforts—Sheriff Word's crusade, the Portland Municipal Association, pressure from the public (partly brought to bear because of increased exposure to information by the new daily *Oregon Journal* newspaper),[99] and Mayor Williams's call to beautify the city—all helped clean up Fourth Street and scatter houses of prostitution around town, where they congregated, less visibly, in the Irvington and Portland Heights areas.[100]

Drunkenness, gambling, and prostitution were not the only targets for reform. The manner in which public works contracts were bid, awarded, and carried out was less visible, but a ready target for corruption. Public construction projects such as streets, sewers, and bridges were easily manipulated to allow contractors backed by big banks to meet the bonding requirements while smaller, more competitive contractors were frozen out. Some inspectors approved low-quality workmanship, allowing businesses to line their pockets at the public's expense. The lack of quality was sometimes hidden so well it was difficult to prove. At other times, the results manifested themselves in such a way that a culprit was clearly identified. The Tanner Creek sewer was a case in point.

The bottom had been left out of the Tanner Creek sewer! Property owners protested. Seepage from sewage became such a problem that the cause was tracked to its source: the contractors had simply cut corners on the specifications. Equally as disturbing was Mayor Williams's response to the predicament. The *Oregon Journal* summed it up this way: "Finally, when the reports of two investigating committees and admissions of the [city] engineer himself no longer left any room to dispute that glaring defects existed in the work, Mayor Williams attempted to have the cost of the repairs advanced by the city. … Only the opposition of a majority of the councilmen prevented this crowning iniquity to the Tanner creek scandal."[101]

Another project that involved questionable practices was an enormous landfill on the inner east side along the river covering the equivalent of forty city blocks. Bridges and viaducts had previously criss-crossed over this marshy frog pond and swamp. Now a more permanent solution was sought. For the next two years, contractors worked on the project, which ran as deep as twenty-nine feet in places and required four million cubic yards of sand and gravel dredged from the river. The project cost over 1.3 million dollars. Historian E. Kimbark MacColl says the company was not held to any part of its contract—the bid specifications, promised dates of completion, or cost estimates.

The huge landfill also changed forever the topography of the east shore of the Willamette River. What had been a "frog pond and swamp" became solid land on which streets, businesses, and homes were built. The I-5 freeway would traverse this landfill in 1963, and an Eastside Esplanade would open along the shoreline in 2001.[102]

❧

The Lewis and Clark Centennial Exposition, officially titled the Lewis and Clark Centennial and American Pacific Exposition and Oriental Fair, officially opened Thursday, June 1, 1905, at 8 a.m. "At ten a big parade, in which thousands marched, starting at the Portland Hotel, went up to the grounds, reaching them at 11:30.[103] At noon the opening ceremonies commenced with a salute of a hundred guns and the public were admitted to all the buildings. At 2:30 a concert was held at the grand stand. At 7:30 at night there was another concert, and at 8:30 fireworks were displayed from Guild's Lake. The gates were closed for the first day at eleven p.m. The day's attendance had been 39,577."[104] The fair would run four and a half months, until October 15.

The exposition committee had done its job well. So had city government. The city had built new streets to the exposition grounds, completed a new Morrison Bridge,[105] and spruced up the town for its visitors. Private investors had built new hotels and lodgings; fair booths were ready to feed the multitudes. Fresh water was pumped into Guild's Lake from the Willamette River every day to keep the water clean and its level high. Bright lights, handsome buildings, sparkling water, remarkable exhibits, and carnival attractions for every taste greeted fair

Opening day festivities at the 1905 Lewis and Clark Centennial Exposition. (Photo: OrHi #67685)

visitors. Guild's Lake had been turned into a dazzling fairgrounds, sophisticated enough to please every level of fair-goer. Most buildings had gleaming white exteriors with red roofs and campaniles; a "Spanish Renaissance" motif.[106]

The awesome interior of the Forestry Building erected for the 1905 world's fair drew a steady stream of visitors until it burned down in 1964. (Photo: OrHi #26217)

The pride of the Northwest was the Forestry Building, a towering log cabin, the largest in the world, constructed of enormous Douglas fir logs from land on the lower Columbia River near Oak Point, Washington, owned by lumberman Simon Benson. In transporting the logs to Portland, the loggers had "carefully handled the select trees, using 'grabs' instead of 'choker' so the bark would not be damaged."[107] The massive logs were to amaze succeeding generations as old-growth timber disappeared from the Northwest. By the time the building burned down in 1964, the structure had become almost a shrine; a never-to-be-forgotten wonder to those fortunate to view its awesome, open-beamed interior.[108] "My parents never grew tired of telling of the enjoyment they received from attending the Lewis and Clark World's Fair," says an Oregon memoir. "People who came to Oregon were surprised that Indians were not lurking around each corner. They were pleased with our temperate climate."[109]

❧

Four days after the fair opened, the first city election under the new charter was held. George Williams sought reelection at age eighty-two. He had opened his campaign with a vigorous defense of his administration, denouncing his critics. The *Oregon Journal* headlined his speech this way:

> **Mayor Calls Clergy Liars and Scoundrels.**
> **"Packed Grand Jury" Indicted Him,**
> *Declares Mr. Williams in Opening His Campaign for Reelection. Says He Meant to Stop Gambling But City Couldn't Afford Loss — Dodges Every Item of the Tanner Creek Sewer Scandal. "They are a pack of liars and scoundrels," declared Mayor Williams … in speaking of the preachers who were present at the great mass meeting of 2,000 citizens held to demand a reform of the abuses in the city government.*[110]

"The most important political office in the state is the office of Mayor of Portland," said the *Oregonian* in endorsing Williams. Allegations against him were of a trifling nature, the paper said, and any serious wrongdoing was the fault of the political machine, not the mayor. The *Oregon Journal* supported challenger Dr. Harry Lane, a Democrat who had been nominated by a coalition group that included many Republicans.[111]

Future U.S. Senator John Gearin summed up Williams's term as mayor in a keynote speech kicking off Harry Lane's "integrity in office" campaign: "George Williams is an old friend of mine of thirty years standing, a man of winning personality, guileless as a child, but he's a foxy old grandpa just the same. … He has not been a bad mayor, he's not been a mayor at all."[112]

Williams was backed by the liquor and gambling interests.[113] His big weakness—"an inability to recognize insincerity and sham in those who flattered or pampered him"[114]—was to be his undoing. His friend and supporter, John H. Mitchell, had been indicted in January and February of 1905 on several charges of obtaining federal timber land through fraud. The extensive land fraud trials would expose one of the biggest scandals in Oregon's history. Mitchell's trial was set to begin two weeks after the city election.[115] U.S. Marshal Jack Matthews, who was Mitchell's power boss in Portland, was also removed from office as part of the fraud investigations.

Harry Lane defeated Williams decisively.[116] Diehard Republican Harvey Scott, who could not bring himself to credit any contemporary Democrat, declared in an editorial two months later that Lane had been elected due to Republican in-fighting. Senator John H. Mitchell had had much to do with that attitude, Scott said. "The controlling force that elected Harry Lane mayor was the purpose of large numbers of Republicans to 'get rid of Jack Matthews,' as they expressed it, and to 'clean out the last vestige of his influence and power in politics.'"[117]

Portland State University professor Gordon Dodds places blame squarely with Williams himself. "Behind Williams' distinguished appearance," says Dodds, "the city lay in the grip of business interests, gamblers, and thugs." Williams and his cronies were the front for gambling dens and houses of prostitution, which earned him a "legion of enemies who fought him on the grounds of religious morality and municipal efficiency." Dodds calls Williams a "notorious representative of the casual morality of Oregon politicians in the post-civil-war years" who was lucky to escape impeachment from his U.S. Attorney General job.[118]

But a fond recollection of Mayor Williams comes from the memoir of an ordinary Portland citizen: "One of the most familiar forms and faces on our streets was that of Judge George H. Williams, so affectionately remembered as the 'Grand Old Man.' He is the man of whom Oregon is so justly proud and whose name will go down into history linked with that of U. S. Grant and other illustrious men of his time."[119]

On the occasion of Williams's death five years after his defeat for reelection, his law partner, C. E. S. Wood, penned these lines: "[Williams's] life covers the most active part of the history of this country. When it began, there were neither railways nor telegraph lines. Travel was by river, canal and coach. Chicago did not exist. Pittsburgh and St. Louis were the western frontier and in all that has gone to the making of the country and of the State of Oregon he has had a conspicuous part."[120]

Chapter 18

Greedy Give-away Time or a Golden Age?

July 1905 – June 1911

Mayors

No. 35: July 1905 - June 1907

Harry Lane (elected for two-year term)

July 1907 - June 1909

Harry Lane (reelected for two-year term)

No. 36: July 1909 - June 1911

Joseph Simon (elected for two-year term)

He was the right mayor for his time— honest, down-to-earth, a fighter with no apparent ambition for personal wealth or status.

He was Portland's first Oregon-born mayor.

He was the first mayor who lived on the east side of the river.[1]

He rode the streetcar to work.[2]

He was the first mayor with an Oregon political heritage (his grandfather, Joseph Lane, was Oregon's first territorial governor).

He was only the second Democrat in thirty-five years to be elected mayor.[3]

He was elected as a Democrat while every other citywide position went Republican[4]—auditor, treasurer, city attorney, municipal judge, and all five at-large council positions.

He was the second medical doctor to serve as mayor. The first—James A. Chapman—left a miserable legacy in three separate mayoral terms in the late 1800s.

He ran as a reformer, on moral and humanitarian grounds. Any improvements he made would stand in stark contrast to the legacy of previous mayors who were beholden to business interests and political bosses.

It was also important that the voters and legislature had given this mayor more power than his predecessors (through the 1903 charter) to

Mayor Harry Lane.
(Photo: OrHi #28102)

make genuine change. Citizens were demanding reform. And cleanup of Portland was exactly what the city's new mayor was about.

As a boy, Harry Lane attended public schools and worked in his father's store in Corvallis, a small town on the Willamette River a hundred miles south of Portland. At age seventeen, he tried mining, then worked as a deck hand until he saved enough money to enroll at Willamette University in Salem, where he received a medical degree at age twenty-three. He did post-graduate medical study in New York and practiced in San Francisco before returning to Oregon in the 1880s to set up a medical practice. In 1887, Governor Pennoyer appointed Lane superintendent of the state insane asylum in Salem. There he gained a reputation for thrift by putting inmates to work on the asylum farm and getting rid of crooked contractors. Around 1891 Lane moved to Portland and affiliated with the "locally prominent" Coffee Sanitarium in northwest Portland.[5]

Like his grandfather, Joseph Lane, Harry Lane was a combatant who "would fight at the drop of a hat." In personal demeanor, however, Harry Lane was "genial, kindly and witty."[6] Lane had been president of the state, county, and city medical associations, and was appointed to the state board of health in 1903. His campaign for mayor was his first foray into politics—and he was rewarded by an upset victory.[7]

Dr. Harry Lane's defeat of incumbent mayor George Williams was an ironic rematch for Williams, who had sought the U.S. Senate seat won by Lane's grandfather Joseph Lane forty-seven years before.[8]

On the same 1905 ballot that elected Harry Lane mayor, voters approved measures to extend the city limits north to the boundary of St. Johns and east to Mt. Tabor.[9] The voter turnout was much lighter than expected, possibly because there was less illegal voting than usual. "Democrats asserted that many North End voters were 'scared out' by the threat made against illegal voting by Democratic District Attorney John Manning and by the presence at the polls of Democratic Sheriff Tom Word with some 80 deputies. The North End vote turned out perhaps 700 votes short of what it was expected to do, but it was said in Democratic quarters last night that many more than that number had been shut out."[10]

From the world's fair in 1905 until the beginning of World War 1 in 1917 has been termed "Portland's golden age." "The economy could hardly have been better. ... [E]thnic conflicts were rare. ... [T]he percentage of houses owned was extremely high and there was little crowding. .... Portland, with one of the lowest death rates in the nation, was a healthy place to live. ... [T]here was the town's 'balmy' air ... together with the magic elixir of ... Bull Run water. .... Almost every house had a garden."[11]

Portlanders grew thousands of roses in their gardens, and the city had planted fifty thousand sweet-smelling, pink Caroline Testout roses in city parks and parking strips for the world's fair. Varieties of plants such as rhododendrons, monkey trees, yucca and bamboo were also introduced to Portland by the Lewis and Clark Exposition.[12] Portland's climate was ideal for such flora to flourish.[13] "Portland needs a festival of roses," Mayor Lane proclaimed.[14] The Rose Festival (begun officially in 1907) was to become an annual tradition that continues to thrive today.[15]

Portland's first permanent amusement park had opened two days before the world's fair on a Willamette River peninsula called The Oaks near the southeastern suburb of Sellwood. The park was visited by throngs of world's fair visitors. The Portland Traction Company built Oaks Park as a destination for its riders, a park which today has nonprofit status and bills itself as "the oldest continuously running amusement park in the nation."[16]

Lumber, wheat, and flour were shipped out of Portland in record quantities as the world's fair progressed. Fair visitors from the East were heard to comment on the "politeness and good breeding" of the people, while investors saw Oregon as a state in which they were not likely to be induced to "invest in wild-cat propositions."[17] The finish line of the nation's first transcontinental auto race was located at the fairgrounds. The winner made the trip in forty-four days and five hours.[18]

Throughout the summer and early fall, visitors arrived from all over the country. Each day, the fair honored a different organization, person, or state. The city of Portland was feted on September 30, when crowds were dwindling. Mayor Lane urged Portlanders to turn out in record numbers for Portland Day, and a paid attendance of over eighty-five thousand was recorded—twice as many as on opening day and more than seven times the average daily paid attendance of eleven thousand six hundred.[19] A souvenir program for Portland Day told the Lovejoy and Pettygrove coin toss story about naming Portland, and included a photo of the famous 1835 copper penny.[20]

The Willamette Meteorite, the "largest meteorite ever found in North America," was displayed during the last weeks of the fair. The meteorite, discovered in Clackamas County in 1902, weighed 31,107 pounds. It took twelve horses to haul it from the Willamette Falls area to the fairgrounds.[21]

> At 5:34 a.m. on April 18, 1906, five months after Portland's world fair, a massive earthquake hit San Francisco. The earthquake was quickly followed by fires that burned for three days. The quake and fire together destroyed most of the city and shattered buildings as far away as Stanford University and beyond. At least five hundred people were killed and half a million left homeless.[22] Future Portland mayor Dorothy McCullough Lee lived through this trauma as a child, and remembered it for the rest of her life.[23] Portlanders came to the aid of the Californians, and Portland businesses benefited from increased trade while their San Francisco neighbors rebuilt their city.

Exposition president Harvey Scott, who had assumed leadership duties after Henry Corbett's death two years before and had now reconciled with his sister, designated October 6 as Abigail Scott Duniway Day.[24]

The Lewis and Clark Exposition closed October 15, 1905, ending a four and a half-month phenomenon unlike anything Portland had ever seen. It was a resounding success, and its reputation has stood the test of time. The major shortcoming historians have noted is that it left no lasting memorial because of the transitory nature of the grounds. No building or park remains there for subsequent generations to enjoy.[25] The fair took place on leased land, and its buildings were not considered permanent. Seven years later, Guild's Lake would be filled in with rock and gravel "sluiced by flume down the hill when the Westover terraces were built."[26] Today it is an industrial district, difficult to imagine as the same four hundred-acre site on which sparkling Guild's Lake, gleaming white exposition buildings, exotic exhibits, and merry carnival rides once beckoned.

One memorable structure—the Forestry Building, which had been built at state expense—lasted nearly sixty years. The building was "constructed of the largest timbers ever put into a building," an act passed by the state legislature said, and it was doubtful there would ever again be another like it. The bill authorized the centennial commission to give the structure to the City of Portland, provided the city would obtain at least one acre of ground, keep the building in repair, and allow public historic, mineral, and forestry exhibits.[27] The city acquired the Forestry Building and two acres of surrounding grounds in April 1906.[28] The stately edifice burned to the ground in 1964.

Fair income exceeded expenses by nearly eighty-five thousand dollars—an amazing accomplishment in world's fair circles. Most fairs required financial bailouts to pay off creditors. However, the Lewis and Clark Exposition did not deliver a "profit," as some accounts would have it. Investors bought stock with the understanding that their money would most likely be a contribution; instead, shareholders received back about 22 percent of their initial investment.[29] The real profit came from business generated outside the fairgrounds. In that, no one was disappointed.

Overall fair statistics were impressive: one and a half million people had paid admission fees (34 percent of these were Portlanders, 40 percent were Oregonians from outside Portland and Washingtonians, 16 percent were Californians, and 10 percent came from everywhere else.) Close to a million guests stayed at Portland hotels and an estimated eight million dollars was pumped into the Portland economy.[30]

A spectacular population explosion and building boom were ignited by the 1905 exposition. During 1906 alone, real estate values increased by 25 to 50 percent. "From 1905 though 1911, every economic indicator reflected extraordinary prosperity. .... The value of building permits jumped by 458 percent. ... [T]he new surge of growth required massive new office space ... with skyscrapers of ten or twelve or fourteen floors on Fifth and Sixth ... Portland also built a new middle-class city on the east side of the Willamette."[31]

At least forty automobiles were now driving on Portland's streets. At the behest of the Portland Automobile Club, the council increased the speed limit for autos from eight mph to ten mph downtown and fifteen mph elsewhere in the city limits.[32] Mayor Lane approved the measure.

In other matters, however, the mayor and council maintained a running battle. Mayor Harry Lane experienced the most adversarial relationship with his city council of any mayor in Portland history. Over and over, his vetoes were overridden by thirteen-to-two, fourteen-to-one, twelve-to-three council votes. The only council support Lane ever got was from eastside councilmen.[33] During his first year in office, Lane vetoed thirty-two council ordinances, and the council overrode two-thirds of those vetoes by the required two-thirds margin.[34]

Lane was particularly opposed to the "give-away" of franchises to privately owned utility companies. He clamped down on vice and championed the rights of "the little guy" over business interests at every turn. His friend, lawyer Richard Montague, was later to memorialize Lane in these words: "A fighting man with an ingrained love of humanity and a basic, uncomplicated justice is pretty sure to be a success in politics, and [Lane] was a fighting man in every fiber. ... Of the arts of the politician he had none ... for intrigue and combination he had absolutely no aptitude, and for the complicated team play and strategy necessary to carry through large political programs little enough. ... But the plain people could not be deceived as to his detestation of privilege and power based on privilege."[35]

Council overrides did nothing to slow down Lane's actions and rhetoric; if anything, they whetted his appetite for the fray. Lane's success, in spite of the standoff with the council, was partly due to the new daily *Oregon Journal* and its civic-minded publisher, Sam Jackson. Through its reportage and editorial positions, the *Journal* gave Lane's side of the story, a far different perspective from his *Oregonian* coverage.[36]

A constitutional amendment passed overwhelmingly through the initiative process in 1906 gave Oregon cities and towns exclusive power to enact and amend their own charters, an initiative which would profoundly affect the future course of Portland government.[37] So, after nine different charters and at least twenty-five separate amendments to those charters, the citizens of Portland would now set their own course. The state legislature would no longer control the city's destiny.

A women's suffrage initiative on the same 1906 ballot failed by 12 percent—ten thousand votes.[38] Abigail Scott Duniway had been isolated from the campaign by enemies in the WCTU who spearheaded Oregon's campaign effort.[39]

Fall 1906 brought two significant railroad franchise matters to the council calendar. First, the city wanted to move the Southern Pacific Railroad from Fourth Street. The track had been originally designed for passenger trains but now handled mainly freight, causing traffic tie-ups and generating irritating noises and smells. After much maneuvering between the council, the mayor, and the railroads, the railroad continued to stall by filing a lawsuit. The issue was finally resolved several years later when the railroad built a bridge across the Willamette at Lake Oswego so freight trains could connect with the eastside line without entering downtown Portland.[40] Fourth Street was then extended south from downtown to become a major highway, 99W, also known as Barbur Boulevard.[41]

The other pending railroad issue concerned access from Washington State to the main railroad terminal in northwest Portland. The Spokane, Portland and Seattle Railroad proposed making a deep cut across the huge peninsula that separated the Willamette and Columbia Rivers opposite Vancouver, Washington—a peninsula on which the settlement of St. Johns had thrived since the earliest days of Oregon history. Lane vetoed an ordinance to allow this excavation, but his veto was overridden, eleven to one. Lane called the proposal a "a defacement of property and a visual blight" and "out-and-out give-away" that would "destroy the unity of the neighborhood."[42] The council, however, was so impressed with railroad mogul James J. Hill and his willingness to invest money in Portland that they gave him virtually everything he asked for. Hill planned to spend three million dollars to carve out a ravine through which his trains could run unimpeded. The trains would cross the peninsula from a Columbia River bridge to a new Willamette River bridge, and then use surface tracks to Union Station. Not only did the council grant these franchises, but they allowed another railroad, the Oregon, Washington Railway Navigation Company, to build a tunnel under part of that same peninsula.[43]

The result was that instead of sixteen streets running lengthwise on the St. Johns peninsula, there are today only four streets that span the railroad right-of-way that the council allowed Hill to dig. Every walker, bicycle rider, bus, automobile, and truck that traverses the St. Johns peninsula has to cross this artificial ravine on one of those four viaducts.[44]

Corrupt contractors were Mayor Lane's pet peeve. He launched a one-man crusade against them. A popular story concerns his dealings with a sidewalk contractor in the Irvington district:[45] "Not being able to secure the cooperation of the other city officials, [Lane] secured a hammer, tapped the curbs and walks and wherever he found a hollow spot, broke the curbing or the sidewalk. He got schoolboys to tap the streets and sidewalks and wherever they found hollow spots to make a chalk mark. When the contractor came in and threatened him, he told the contractor that unless he tore up the defective walks and curbs and built them according to specifications, he would see that he was sent to the penitentiary. During the balance of Mayor Lane's administration, the sidewalks and curbs were built according to specifications."[46]

Harry Lane was nominated for reelection in May 1907. His campaign kick-off at the armory drew a cheering crowd of fifteen hundred people and a big brass band. His chief opponent, Republican city auditor Thomas Devlin, opened his campaign with a lengthy speech to a small group of supporters. Devlin was supported by the liquor industry, and his campaign slogan was, "The reformer ultimately fails." Lane countered with the motto, "The rights of the people come first."[47]

In spite of lukewarm support from Democratic Party leaders (Lane was headstrong and some said arrogant), Harry Lane was reelected by fifteen hundred votes—three hundred more than his margin had been two years before. However, Republicans were elected to every other position on the ballot except for one council position. Lane made a clean sweep on the east side, especially his own southeast ward, while Devlin won all six westside wards.[48]

Several city money measures passed, an indication of the prosperous mood the world's fair had engendered. Voters approved a one million dollar bond issue for parks and boulevards; a five hundred thousand dollar issue to buy land for a public dock; four hundred fifty thousand dollars for a new Madison (Hawthorne) bridge; and two hundred seventy-five thousand dollars to acquire a new fireboat, hydrants, and water mains. Failed measures included salary increases for the city engineer, attorney, treasurer, municipal judge, and council. A three million dollar measure to build a new Bull Run pipeline and two new reservoirs eked out a one hundred thirty-one-vote favorable margin out of 14,363 votes cast.[49]

This second Bull Run pipeline was sorely needed, for the city's population had nearly tripled since construction had started on the first pipeline in 1893—from sixty thousand people then to one hundred seventy-two thousand only fourteen years later.[50] The system's storage and delivery capacity were tripled by 1911. Although the city waterworks then accounted for half of Portland's bonded debt, citizens were pleased with their water system.[51]

Mayor Lane's relationship with the new council was no better than it had been with the last. Nearly half the 169 ordinances Lane vetoed during his four-year tenure were overridden by the council.[52] Even though Lane appointed his own executive board, the charter stipulated that the council had to authorize all appropriations and approve contract terms, which created a balance of power that held Mayor Lane and his executive board in check.

❧

A Corrupt Practices Act was added to the Oregon System in the June 1908 statewide election. This measure had failed to pass the 1907 legislature, so its passage as an initiative provided proof that citizens could take matters into their own hands. The Act required all future

An early rose parade winds its way south along Fidth Avenue. Meier and Frank department store balconies (far left) provide prime viewing spots. (1907 or 1908 photo: OrHi #104063)

candidates, measure supporters, and measure opponents to submit sworn statements regarding how much money had been spent. The Act also spelled out prohibited use of money and influence, banned campaigning on election day, and provided for publication of a Voters' Pamphlet in which candidates could place a photograph and statement for a nominal fee.[54]

In other statewide measures, the legislature was required to vote for the U.S. Senate candidate that citizens had awarded the most votes;[55] the general election date was changed from June to November; and a process was added for recalling elected officials. Women's suffrage was once again defeated, and by an even wider margin than before—twenty thousand votes.[56]

Another oft-told anecdote concerned Mayor Lane's efforts to supervise city employees.

Mayor Lane conducted an investigation to determine if water mains and meters had been properly installed. On Wednesday, August 29, 1907, he personally went out to West Park and Glisan and began digging. A man coming by asked him what he was doing.

"We have to look at this meter," Lane explained.

So the man inquired if he worked for the city. Lane replied in the affirmative.

"I used to do that kind of work," the man volunteered, "but I got a better job, and it's a good thing, too, what with the mayor's program to make city employees work harder. If he'd quit sitting in his office and come down here and try it himself, he'd see that this is hard work."[53]

Portland's population more than doubled in the ten-year period 1898 to 1908. The 183,570 inhabitants now averaged 4,420 people per square mile. The total area of the city had increased from thirty-seven to forty-two square miles.[57] More city municipal building projects were underway in 1908 than ever before in the city's history: the Broadway Bridge; nearly one hundred miles of street improvements; the second Bull Run pipeline; sewers; and park improvements. Half a dozen ten-story office buildings were in the process of construction, as were four hundred residences. The volume of garbage also increased steadily.[58] "The garbage crematory … has been a bone of contention ever since its erection. No one wanted it for a neighbor. And well they might object. For the year 1909 the crematory cremated 480 horses, 2,434 dogs, 31 cows, 23 calves, 2 hogs, 1 donkey, 1 sheep, 7 colts and 2 goats, using up 1,761 loads of sawdust and 369 cords of wood, and costing $22,182 to do the work."[59]

During his last three months in office, Lane continued to veto franchises. The final vote on a new franchise for the Portland Railway

> The first woman police officer in the United States was hired to head up Portland's new "Women's Division" in 1908. Lola Greene Baldwin was a crusader against vice who would lead the "ragtime drive" for "social hygiene" in Portland.[60]

Light & Power (PRL&P) occurred in April 1909. The proposed contract required the city to keep all switches, elevated roadways, and bridges in good repair for PRL&P use, with the city paying 75 percent of that cost. No common-user clause was included as required by charter. Franchise fees paid by the corporation over the next twenty-five years would total only twenty thousand dollars—an incredibly low figure for a fifteen-million-dollar company. The railroad was given "the guaranteed right to abandon any one of or all forty streets" anytime it wished. Lane objected strenuously: "I do not remember ever before having heard of a case where an incorporated municipality so far lost its self-respect as to voluntarily consent to being assessed and taxed by a private corporation which was its own creature. ... [A city which acts in this fashion] surrenders its sovereign rights [and] ... is unfit to exist."[61]

The council's override of his veto, by a thirteen-to-two margin, may have been a factor in Lane's decision not to seek reelection. He was tired. In addition, the Democratic leadership would not support him again.[62]

After Harry Lane decided not to seek reelection, future governor Oswald West urged him to become the 1910 Democratic candidate for Oregon governor. West arrived in Portland by train late one night, and discovered that his favorite hotel was entirely booked by Republicans who were holding a nominating convention. West found another hotel, put down his luggage, and phoned Lane to tell him that he had an important political matter to discuss right away. West made his way to the mayor's home via streetcar and trails across vacant lots and through woods to find the mayor already in his nightshirt, with a friend there to monitor the conversation. Oswald West describes what happened next in his "Reminiscences": "I stated the purpose of my visit; spoke of recent trips over the state; that I had found he had many admirers—both Democrats and Republicans; and, as a champion of the initiative and referendum and the direct election of U.S. Senators, he could be elected. He feared, however, that he couldn't make it; that he couldn't stand the expense of such a campaign. ... I told him he could have an hour in which to decide; that we had to have a candidate by morning."[63]

Oswald West received no return phone call from Lane, and decided during the night to become the candidate himself. West would be elected Oregon's next governor. He later said that Lane soon realized he had "made a political mistake in not following my advice. He could have been elected hands down."[64]

Three years after Harry Lane completed his four years as Portland's crusading mayor, he was elected to the U.S. Senate.

Oregon historians Terence O'Donnell and Thomas Vaughan, writing in 1984, considered Harry Lane "one of the most distinguished mayors in [Portland's] history."[65]

July 1909 - June 1911

The Portland business community breathed a collective sigh of relief when Joseph Simon was elected the city's next mayor. Simon defeated councilman and future mayor Allen Rushlight in the Republican primary, then won an easy victory in the fall over four opponents—Democrat Judge M. G. Munley; independent ("anti-machine" and future mayor) H. Russell Albee; T. S. McDaniel, a prohibitionist; and W. Noffke, a socialist.[66]

Joe Simon and Harry Lane presented a sharp contrast. Simon was ambitious for power, a back-room operative of the shrewdest order, a man who understood the businessman's perspective, a manipulator who

Mayor Joseph Simon. (Photo: OrHi #CN009532)

calculated his goals and planned a course to reach them. Lane, on the other hand, was a man of the people, a bull-in-a-china-shop, a blunderer unskilled in the finer nuances of negotiation and compromise for which politics has always been known.

This was not Simon's first race for Portland mayor. His first try, twenty-eight years before, had ended in a recount and tie that left his opponent in office. That 1881 race was the biggest setback of Simon's political career—a career that saw him as the dominant power broker in Oregon politics for over thirty years. A lawyer by profession, Simon promoted his clients' interests by using his political positions to further theirs. He was one of the most influential state legislators in Oregon's history, was elected president of the Oregon senate five times, and served a total of twelve years as a state senator. He also represented Oregon in the U.S. Senate from 1898 to 1902. His most bitter rival was lawyer and sometime U.S. Senator John H. Mitchell. Their acrimonious infighting within the Republican Party was legendary.[67]

Born in Germany the same year that Portland was incorporated as a city, fifty-eight years before his mayor's duties began, Joe Simon immigrated with his parents to Portland when he was six years old. He worked in his father's store during his growing-up years, and took an interest in political issues as a young man. His first political office was that of Portland city councilman, a position he held from 1877 to 1880. He headed the state Republican Party organization for six years. In the state legislature, he lobbied actively for Portland issues, and was the brains behind many changes in Portland's city charter.[68] He was Portland's third Jewish mayor, and the fifth of six mayors who were foreign-born.[69]

☙

No less than thirty-five local ballot measures faced city voters in 1909, most of them city charter amendments. A one hundred fifty thousand dollar bond measure to build a new incinerator passed handily, as did a two million dollar bond measure to build a Broadway bridge. Voters rejected a two million dollar bond issue for a municipal light and power plant. A measure to set up a commission form of nonpartisan city government failed two-to-one. A referendum to require licenses for vehicles lost by only eight hundred votes out of fifteen thousand cast.[70]

Mayor Simon greeted President William Howard Taft on behalf of the city when the presidential train pulled into Union Station at 7 a.m. on Saturday, October 2, 1909.[71] For two days, the president immersed himself in city activities. He rode in a military parade, addressed a gathering of twenty thousand school children (whom he declared to be Portland's fairest roses), played a golf game at Waverly links (he won), gave a speech before five thousand at the armory, and attended three church-related activities on Sunday.[72]

Today's Wildwood Trail had its beginnings in September 1909 when the park board asked park superintendent Emanuel T. Mische to find a "suitable path" between the Forestry Building and the top of the hill in Macleay Park (near where Henry Pittock would later build his famous mansion).[73] The path Mische plotted began under today's Thurman Street bridge and is still a popular access route to the main Forest Park trail today.

The statewide election of November 1910 saw little slackening in the number of initiative petitions. Of thirty-two measures on the ballot, twenty-six were instigated by citizens. Oregonians voted to give cities and towns exclusive power to regulate liquor traffic within their boundaries. They also established a direct primary vote for U.S. president and eliminated poll taxes, but voted down women's suffrage by an even bigger margin than before.[74] Two measures that would have added parts of Clackamas and Washington counties to Multnomah County were resoundingly defeated, and two measures that would have limited or prohibited the sale of alcohol also lost.

Nevertheless, the prohibition movement was gaining strength in Oregon, as elsewhere, with a saloon-smashing, Bible-thumping woman named Carrie Nation drawing national attention. By 1911, there were "a hundred prohibitionists now to the one who preached to empty benches forty years ago."[75]

The one million dollars—the equivalent of eighteen million today—approved for parks and boulevards two years before finally became available after a court case was resolved. Real estate prices had skyrocketed in the meantime, and the purchasing power of the bonds was considerably reduced. Land in Portland Heights that had been purchased for two hundred fifty dollars an acre in 1888 was selling for five thousand dollars an acre by 1910.[76] One-fourth of the parks money—two hundred fifty thousand dollars—was spent to construct three miles of a parkway called Terwilliger Boulevard along a ridge south of downtown. The rest of the money bought acreage for neighborhood parks in Mt. Tabor, Laurelhurst, Sellwood, Peninsula, and Kenilworth—a total of about two hundred acres.[77]

The following year, the park board built a swimming tank at Sellwood Park "to replace the unhygienic public baths in the Willamette."[78] A

A woman who signed herself "A Working Girl" asked the park board to re-establish one of the two public squares near city hall for women only. Five years before, the board had informally designated the south plaza block for women, children, and their escorts because men were bothering women who came to the park. Now Working Girl said men still hogged all the benches of the south block at lunch and break times, and there was no place for women to sit when they got off work or simply wanted to relax. The board granted her request, and the south plaza block known today as Chapman Square was officially designated "Women's Square."[79]

swimming instructor was hired, and use of the swimming tank was free. The park board also installed several playgrounds for children, all of which were segregated by gender.

The Committee of One Hundred[80] had metamorphosed into the Civic Improvement League and Mayor Simon was on its executive committee. The group now urged follow-up to the 1904 Olmsted report, calling for private donations to a City Beautiful Fund so a comprehensive Portland plan could be modeled after those of Chicago, San Francisco, and Washington, D. C.[81] The twenty thousand dollar fund to hire an expert was soon fully subscribed. Edward Bennett of Chicago was chosen to create the plan, a task that would be completed by fall 1912.[82]

❧

Although voters had approved half a million dollars to acquire waterfront land for public docks, Mayor Simon vetoed a 1910 council ordinance to sell the bonds, and the council failed to override his veto. Simon later admitted that he didn't believe in municipal ownership of docks; his railroad clients were heavily invested in Portland's existing docks. The *Oregonian* supported Simon, saying: "Every city should leave to private enterprise the active industries on which development depends" or else waste, corruption and politics would result.[83] Yet Simon's veto was a clear case of special-interest politics.

But Simon's veto backfired. In a special November 1910 election, voters approved a docks bond measure for five times as much—two and a half million dollars. An independent dock commission was created to issue the bonds and to pay for them by levying taxes, thereby bypassing the council and the mayor.[84] The Oregon System of initiative and referendum had once again proved its value.

That such an expenditure was needed at all was a decades-old Portland scandal concerning ownership of the levee. "The enormously wasteful consequences of earlier decisions ... made with total lack of foresight" had made this expenditure necessary. Much of the money would be spent to buy back 1850 levee land that "had been taken from the public domain by political skullduggery," says E. Kimbark MacColl.[85]

Lawyer Joseph N. Teal, son-in-law of former mayor David Thompson, had been a tireless advocate for the cause of public docks. Teal produced a report for the Chamber of Commerce showing that all Portland's working docks belonged to railroads. Teal had traveled extensively in Europe and observed the operation of their harbor facilities, coming away convinced that Portland could attract shipping from every corner of the world with adequate public docks. A Federal Corporation Commissioner analysis had downgraded Portland's harbor because it had no city dock, and noted that Portland's waterfront was privately owned, almost entirely by the railroads.[86]

Wooden sidewalks could no longer be constructed in Portland, according to a new council ordinance, signifying the passing of another era. From now on, sidewalks had to be made of concrete, artificial stone, asphalt, or brick (although existing wooden sidewalks could still be used if kept in good repair). The construction company's name, the date, and street name were often imprinted at the corner of these early concrete sidewalks. Some are still visible today. At N.E. Twenty-seventh

Bustling traffic awaited ferry transport at the foot of Alder Street on the east side of the Willamette River in 1905. (Photo: OrHi #5897)

In August 1910, Portland lost one of its most influential citizens. Harvey Scott, though never elected to public office, had been intimately involved for forty years with state and local politics as editor of the *Oregonian*. His conservative, business-oriented, clearly articulated, often strident views, had kept the *Oregonian* on an unflagging Republican course.[87] His 1890 Portland history was to prove a valuable historical resource, as would the six-volume Oregon history published in 1924 that would be compiled by his son, Leslie Scott, based on Harvey Scott's writings.[88]

and Hancock, for example, the firm of Miller & Bauer left its imprint in 1908. The street name was still embedded in the cement at the corner of N.E. Twenty-eighth and Hancock in year 2000; a triangular imprint noted that the sidewalk was constructed by Oregon Hassam Paving Company in 1910.[89]

Another sign of the changing times occurred when Meier & Frank started making home deliveries by gas-powered trucks instead of horse-drawn wagons.[90]

The city's prosperity was evidenced by a "turbulent, noisy, clamorous jam of humanity which flooded the principal thoroughfares" to ring in the new year of 1911. Fifty thousand people thronged the downtown streets, the *Oregonian* reported.[91]

❧

In his exhaustive city history published in 1911, Joseph Gaston lashed out at city government, sharply criticizing the fifteen-member council for its lack of efficiency. The executive board and the city's myriad of other boards and commissions made city government "a hit and miss affair." Responsibility was so divided that it was "a matter of great difficulty in locating the blame for unsatisfactory service," Gaston said, proposing instead "a board of five men, each in charge of a separate department of the city service … and each held responsible for the conduct of the business of his own department." Under such a system, "responsibility could be attached to the person rightly subject to praise or blame."[92]

Gaston was describing the "Galveston plan," a commission form of government recently introduced in Galveston, Texas, and being implemented in many other cities, including Baker City in Eastern Oregon. A ballot measure to adopt a commission form of government for Portland had failed two years before, but the idea was gaining converts.

Gaston's book includes an inventory of city parks and playgrounds, which totaled four hundred fifty-seven acres then compared to ten thousand acres in city ownership by year 2000.[93] About half of the 1910

> A painful tragedy struck the fire department on June 26, 1911. Chief David Campbell was killed while fighting a fire. Campbell had been fire chief for sixteen years, and he was widely respected as a capable and career-oriented leader. On the morning of June 26, 1911, Campbell was fighting alongside his men to control a one hundred thousand dollar fire at the Union Oil plant in southeast Portland when the building he had entered exploded, killing him immediately.[96] A David Campbell Memorial dedicated to all firemen killed in the line of duty was erected on a small triangular lot on Burnside Street between S.W. Eighteenth and Nineteenth, where it can still be seen today .[97]

city park properties had been donated.[94] Parks consultant L. H. Weir said in 1912 that Portland was far behind Seattle, Tacoma, and the cities of California in parks acreage.[95]

In June 1911, voters approved six hundred thousand dollars for a public auditorium; two hundred thousand dollars for a new jail, police headquarters, and emergency hospital; seventy-five thousand dollars for a garbage collection system; and backed regulations regarding billboards and signs.[98]

The *Oregon Journal* and the Municipal Association were hurling a "steady barrage of criticism" at Mayor Simon. They charged that street paving costs had soared (to the paver's profit) because of Simon's "hard surface" policy, and blamed him for the malfeasance of his police chief, A. M. Cox, who was indicted for "permitting certain disorderly houses to operate without molestation." E. Kimbark MacColl says Simon "compromised away the rights of city government for the benefit of private enterprise" in signing off for payment of two contracts in which the work had not been done according to specifications. The first was a lighting contract, the other a Brooklyn sewer in southeast Portland that, because the bottom was of substandard materials, was to cost taxpayers many repair bills when parts of the bottom washed away.[99]

Joseph Simon was undecided about seeking reelection. He finally ran, but was defeated almost two-to-one in the 1911 Republican primary by councilman A. G. Rushlight, in spite of strong support for Simon from the *Oregonian.* The election marked the end of Simon's political career.[100] He would live for another twenty-four years, but never again would he play a major role in Oregon politics.

Chapter 19

The "Tin-Plate Law," a New Beginning, and an Unsuccessful Recall

July 1911 – June 1917

Mayors

No. 37: July 1911 - June 1913

Allen Golden Rushlight (elected for two-year term)

No. 38: July 1913 - June 1917

H. Russell Albee (elected for four-year term)

Dramatic changes occurred during the two-year term of Mayor Allen Rushlight. He would be the last mayor to serve under the mayor-council form of government.

Three shocking reports were released during Rushlight's term—two vice investigations and a critique of city operations. These exposés were to bring the governor to town on a clean-up crusade, and cause a transformation in city government. But a benchmark report that included the city's first comprehensive plan was also delivered during Rushlight's tenure.

Perhaps it is no wonder, then, that contrary images emerge concerning Rushlight. He was termed "the last of the mayors whose type savored the old regime," by *Evening Telegram* reporter Dean Collins, who attributed Rushlight's motivation in appointing a vice committee to "a wholesome fear of what the reform forces and puritan thought of the community might do to him" as well as "a forlorn hope" of keeping such forces at bay. Although it was Rushlight himself who convened a charter revision committee, Collins saw this as nothing more than an attempt to forestall other efforts, rather than a personal interest in reform.[1]

"Unmarried and something of a sport," is how a 1966 University of Oregon doctoral dissertation describes Mayor Rushlight, although Rushlight had been previously married. "The stench of corruption

Mayor Allen G. Rushlight. (Photo: OrHi #97535)

[hung] over Rushlight's administration concerning paving contracts," the dissertation said.[2]

On the other hand, another historian says of Rushlight: "He carried forward the fight for honest government."[3] A supporter of the mayor at the time maintained that Rushlight had reduced the cost for road oiling from fifty-four dollars a mile to twenty-three. "How did he do this?" the supporter shouted to a campaign crowd. "He told the contractors that they would have to make their bids reasonable or the city would buy its own apparatus and oil its own roads."[4] The *Oregonian* later said of Rushlight: "In confidential moods, of late years, he stated that he could have received one hundred thousand dollars by approving 'extras' on one large [city paving] contract and twenty-five thousand dollars if he would allow 'extras' on another. He also caused the price of paving to go down as low as $1.45 a yard, saving large sums to the property owners who had to pay for the improvement."[5]

The *Oregonian* spoke glowingly of Rushlight, a Republican, in a 1930 obituary, calling him a practical man who saved the taxpayers "many thousands of dollars," and who later served effectively in the Oregon legislature., where he chaired the ways and means committee and held down appropriations as an opponent of "freak legislation."[6]

Whatever his motivations, the fact is that Rushlight aided and accommodated change. E. Kimbark MacColl considers him a "dedicated public servant" (albeit a "colorless figure") whose two years in office would "prove to be turbulent as a result of conditions and problems that were not really of his making and over which he could exercise little control."[7]

Allen Golden Rushlight's unusual middle name came from his birth city—Golden, Colorado. When he was three years old, his parents moved from Colorado to southeast Portland, where he lived out the rest of his life in the same ward that Harry Lane lived. Rushlight trained to be a plumber, but for some years he ran an auto dealership before starting his own plumbing shop. His business grew until it was handling "some of the largest plumbing contracts in the state and northwest," using as much as twenty thousand dollars of supplies in a month.[8]

Before his election as mayor, Rushlight had served six years on the city council. In his first year on the council, he had accused powerful William M. Ladd of "using his influence with the city water committee" to provide water service to undeveloped Ladd's Addition while existing eastside residents were more needy and deserving. Rushlight also criticized the water service provided to Holladay's Addition, charging that it got preferential treatment while hundreds of requests by ordinary citizens were denied.[9] Perhaps these prior criticisms were the reason all four water board members resigned when Rushlight took office as mayor. They assumed, the *Oregonian* said, that the new mayor would want to "clean house." Mayor Rushlight summoned these prominent businessmen to his office and "chided them for leaving him in the lurch when he needed their cooperation, and appealed to their civic loyalty." They withdrew their resignations.[10]

The public was clamoring for clean-up of the city's vice situation when Mayor Rushlight took office. Now the *Oregonian* joined the chorus: "The trains are loaded with gamblers, macquereaux, touts, pimps, confidence men, common women … who have heard that the town is wide open, the pastures green, and the feeding good."[11] The council authorized the mayor to appoint an investigating committee in August 1911.[12] Mayor Rushlight immediately named fifteen citizens, including four ministers and four doctors. This was the first vice probe sanctioned by city government, so the group began its inquiry with more status and clout than had any previous study. The committee pursued its work diligently, with little fanfare.

The mayor used his plumbing background to taxpayer advantage. When the city's "balky" crematory kept acting up, Rushlight donned his old overalls and climbed inside to repair it: "The mayor ... in a few minutes discovered the fault. All that was needed were a couple of fans and a little ventilation, changes which were made at a cost of a few dollars. After this the incinerator's daily capacity increased from 100 to 200 tons and no fuel was required. Prior to the mayor's personal investigation the fuel bill for the incinerator was $600 a month. The 700 cords of wood on hand when Mr. Rushlight crawled into the crematory were no longer needed, so the city sold them."[13]

> That fall, the city's first institution of higher learning was founded: private, nondenominational Reed College. The establishment opened September 17, 1911, funded by a bequest from Amanda Wood Reed, widow of financier Simeon G. Reed, who had served as a city councilman for a short time. Reed College would develop into a nationally known campus noted for its high scholastic standards and its decision to eschew intercollegiate sports and college fraternities.[14]

The vice committee appointed by the mayor reported back to the council in January 1912.[15] Their five-month investigation found: "[O]n the west side alone there were more than 400 'immoral' places, by which [the committee] meant mainly brothels, but also hotels and rooming houses welcoming short-term guests. Many of these places were in the city's 'aristocratic section,' while between the court house, the police station and the river there was an average of three to every block. And somewhat disconcerting to 'a city of churches' was the quaint fact that 'a person might stand on the roof of one of the principal churches of the city and throw a stone into any one of fourteen immoral places, ten of which are wholly immoral!'"[16]

Few publications in the city's history have stirred the degree of attention afforded this famous 1912 vice report. A full page map, published as part of the report, "with the street lines carefully erased, showed in variegated dots the relative location" of four hundred thirty-one of the four hundred fifty-seven investigated apartment houses, hotels, rooming houses, "and what not" which were "wholly given up to immorality."[17]

> An hour after the report was published, draughtsmen in most of the architects' offices around town had reconstructed the streets on the map. Portland guffawed and gobbled up the reports as fast as it could lay hands on

> them. ... One of the leading concerns in the city, having to do with building administration and rentals, emerged roaring for the scalp of the Mayor and threatening damage suits by the score, because the committee report had plastered red spots on the majority of apartment houses under that company's jurisdiction."[18]

Owners of properties in which vice activities were conducted were profiting by an outrageous 84 percent to 540 percent return on their investments, the commission found. Venereal disease accounted for at least 25 percent of all diseases treated by city doctors, without counting any untreated cases or occurrences treated by home remedies.[19]

That summer, another important report was published: the Greater Portland Plan, a comprehensive city plan designed by Edward Bennett "to guide Portland's growth to a city of two million residents."[20] The mayor, park superintendent, and city engineer were all members of the Greater Portland Plan Association (GPPA), successor to the Civic Improvement League, the group that had hired Bennett's services. City government paid for publication and distribution of twenty-five

By 1912, the Rose Festival parade had become a popular annual event. A bevy of young women ride in the Rose City Park float. (Photo: OrHi #5696

thousand copies of a summary of the plan, with the auditor's semi-annual report appended.[21]

Bennett's plan recommended rebuilding Portland's harbor in preparation for the large marine business that completion of the Panama Canal would bring. Rebuilding was to include deepening the Willamette River channel, constructing fireproof, publicly owned docks, and installing a waterfront belt-line railroad. Wide radial traffic arteries would be superimposed on the city's gridiron of streets, with more bridges and tunnels for the Willamette River; the Union railroad station would be "re-constructed" and moved closer to the river; Burnside Street would be the city's primary east-west axis, with the intersection of Burnside and the Park Blocks as a new focal point for downtown.[22] A civic center for public buildings and a recreation center with public auditorium, academy, and museum of fine arts were to be created, and significant additions made to the city's system of parks and boulevards through "great woodland or forest reserve areas" as well as neighborhood parks. Portland should be linked to the surrounding region by a better suburban highway systems for quicker transit.[23]

GPPA members took to the lecture circuit to promote a ballot measure that would designate the Bennett plan as the city's official growth guideline. "The plan involves no extraordinary expenditures, but simply seeks to adapt the units of improvement to a coherent plan as the city grows," advocates argued. "The cost will be measurably less than in haphazard growth," Bennett said.[24]

A wealthy lumberman named Simon Benson now donated ten thousand dollars to the city for twenty bronze drinking fountains to be installed on the sidewalks of Portland. Benson said the reason many working men patronized saloons was because there was nowhere else to quench their thirst. "I came to the conclusion that if a workman could get a drink of cold, pure water on a street corner, without any obligation, he probably wouldn't go into a saloon so often," Benson said.[25] Since 1896, the Portland water bureau had been providing water for public fountains at no charge. The distinctive Benson bubblers were now included in that service.[26]

A grand jury investigating charges of vice activity issued a final report in late August. "We found the city practically an open town. Gambling

Norwegian immigrant Simon Benson donated money for public fountains so that sailors would have someplace other than saloons to quench their thirst. (1913 photo: OrHi #83848)

and vice flourished under the very eyes of the mayor and chief of police. The north and south ends of the city were infested with dissolute women who plied their trade from open doors, windows and on the streets. … [H]ordes of them … are operating in parlors and under the guise of dressmakers, manicuring, etc. … The evidence that we have acquired … leads this body to believe that graft has permeated nearly all departments, involving a great many of our public officials."[27]

No city crackdown on vice had occurred by then, so Governor Oswald West proclaimed his intention of ridding Portland of its debauchery. In addition, he said, the railroads were shipping liquor into dry counties in violation of state law. West sent directives to the sheriff, district attorney, police, liquor outlets, and railroads, among others, regarding actions they should be taking.[28]

> The city's first introduction to aviation occurred on June 11, 1912, when the components of a "push-plane" were lifted to the top of the Multnomah Hotel. There the parts were assembled, and the plane "pushed down a runway off the roof." The pilot made his historic flight across the Columbia River to Vancouver in twelve minutes.[29]

On the evening of September 4, 1912, before a crowd of thirty-five hundred gathered at the Gypsy Smith Tabernacle in Portland, Governor West declared: "I may be … here a week or ten days, or I may be here for two years, but I'm going to keep hammering away all the time I am here until a lot of this law breaking has been cleaned up. … I am not here to get these poor unfortunate women. … I'm here after the men crooks. … [If the newspapers will not print the names] I am going to get out on a soapbox in the streets and do a little publishing of my own."[30]

West vowed to bring down the political and corporate officials who profited from vice and allowed it to continue.[31] The *Oregon Journal* supported his crusade, calling the current arrangement a double standard, a classic struggle between two systems of government: "One system holds that the law means what it says and says what it means, the other system holds that the law is only to be enforced sometimes."[32]

Governor West, whose father had "a serious addiction to alcohol," blamed Rushlight and Portland's breweries for the continued influence of the North End on Portland politics.[33] Before West returned to Salem, he brought in a visiting judge to hear vice cases, empanelled a special grand jury, and replaced the district attorney."[34] He accused a member of Rushlight's executive board named Waldemar Seton of representing an indicted saloon keeper and, in Seton's capacity as a member of the police board, of disciplining two officers who had attempted to curb vice in the past. West pledged to seek a statewide abatement law during the 1913 legislature to get at the owners of vice property.[35]

Now came the city's famous "tin plate law." On October 24, 1912, the council passed an ordinance requiring every owner of a "hotel, apartment house, rooming house, lodging house, tenement house or saloon" to post a conspicuous plate or sign bearing the name and address of the owner(s) large enough to be easily read by persons passing by on the street. A fine of one hundred dollars a day would be levied for noncompliance.[36]

Many old-established families saw this as tantamount to a Scarlet Letter "pinned upon the bosom of their most remunerative properties, while the peasantry smacked its thighs and roared with laughter."[37] "This was meant to shame the patricians of the city, the principal owners of these 'immoral places,' into evicting their tenants. Some well-bred squirming did take place but in the end a loophole was found. The ordinance neglected to specify that the owner's name must be in the English language. As a result some plates went up in Urdu, Arabic, Chinese and Hebrew."[38] After the novelty wore off, the tin plates got little more than "passing notice."[39]

The village of Lents, on the east side of the river in the Mt. Scott area, was annexed to Portland in 1912. The city now covered fifty square miles.[40]

In the same year, the federal Rivers and Harbors Act gave sole responsibility for maintaining Portland's harbor to the Port of Portland, specifying a project depth of thirty feet and a minimum width of three hundred feet for the Willamette channel. The Port was to work with the U.S. Corps of Engineers in maintaining the Columbia River channel. Under provisions of the Act, the federal government would build two dredges patterned after the hydraulic pipeline dredge already in use by the Port of Portland.[41]

Dredging and filling were now big businesses in Portland. Builders started filling in Guild's Lake, site of the 1905 world's fair. Rock, sand, and earth were carried a mile downhill in an elaborate flume, by means of a sluice and pump system, from ninety acres of previously inaccessible hillside, to create a housing development called Westover Terraces.[42] Over the next few years, Guild's Lake would be converted to fifty acres of dry land. The *Oregon Journal* noted:"For many years the consensus of Portland opinion has been that some day Guild's lake would be the manufacturing district of Portland. … [T]hat it would be done someday nobody doubted. … [N]o one who is at all familiar with the difficulty … [of] securing desirable manufacturing and industrial sites, will deny [the importance of this development]."[43]

❧

The national and state elections of 1912 brought Teddy Roosevelt to town on a return visit as the (unsuccessful) Progressive (Bull Moose) Party candidate[44] for president. Harry Lane campaigned, successfully, as the Democratic candidate for the U.S. Senate from Oregon.[45]

By less than a 4 percent margin, Oregon voters finally approved women's suffrage that November.[46] Abigail Scott Duniway, now seventy-eight and crippled with arthritis, wrote and signed the state's equal suffrage proclamation at the request of Governor West. She then became Multnomah County's first registered woman voter.[47]

Another 1912 statewide initiative proposed a method by which cities and counties could consolidate and create new counties, but voters rejected the measure by fifty-seven thousand no votes to forty thousand yes.[48]

On the local level, Portland voters approved adoption of the Bennett plan as Portland's guideline for future growth by a two-to-one margin. The council was to be guided by the Bennett plan "as far as reasonable and practical."[49] There was no organized opposition, but a two million dollar park bond measure that would have implemented part of the plan was defeated. Many saw additional parks as an unnecessary taxpayer burden.[50] In spite of this loss, planning advocates were encouraged—Portland was ahead of other cities on the Pacific coast in adopting an official plan for growth.

In a simple ceremony at the mayor's home, Allen G. Rushlight wed Agnes O'Connor Ingram on February 2, 1913. The event merited a four-column photo in the next day's *Oregonian*, showing the newlyweds with a few relatives and friends, including the mayor's young children, Juanita and Willard Rushlight, and friends, Mr. and Mrs. George Baker. The bride's father was a prominent Central Oregon stockman. The newlyweds left for California that evening, the photo caption said, and hoped to extend their honeymoon to the Hawaiian Islands.[52]

> City workers excavating ground for a road on Mount Tabor discovered an extinct volcano. Rumors started that the old crater contained gold, and a mini-gold rush was on. With shovels, buckets, and other paraphernalia, "over a thousand persons began carrying away the volcanic ash until they had removed a ton of it." Some years later the city decided to use the ash and cinders for surfacing park paths and other city projects, and continued to do so until the late 1920s. Later, the crater was filled in and signs forbidding further removal of the lava rock were posted.[51]

The New York City Bureau of Municipal Research released partial results of an evaluation of Portland city government in April 1913. The New York Bureau had been commissioned "to make a preliminary survey of the organization and business methods of Portland's City government" by a group of Portlanders that included Sam Jackson of the *Oregon Journal*, who was promoting the possibility of a new city charter.[53] As surveys of various city bureaus were completed, the New York experts released their findings to the press, extending the drama over days and weeks. The final report, over a hundred typed pages long, examined virtually every city department—police, fire, buildings, health, garbage, street cleaning, public works construction and maintenance, paving and sewer assessments, water, budgeting, ordinances, expenditure control, purchasing, revenue, bonded debt, parks, municipal court, civil service commission, and departmental reporting.[54]

The New York researchers lambasted the city's operations in meticulous detail. In effect, they said the city was back in the dark ages, "still managing its affairs in much the same manner" as it had in 1891 when the city was less than a quarter of its present size.[55] Highlights of the final report, dated May 5, 1913, included:

- Police department—"[T]here is practically not one single earmark of proper organization or efficient method." Vice control is "vicious for its irresponsibility."
- Fire department—Portland has good fire-fighting equipment, but is doing "practically nothing on prevention," which is the keynote of any "modern efficient fire department."
- Building department—"[E]xcellently organized and efficiently operated," but it is unable to obtain desirable results because there is "no executive backing, frequent overruling by the council, and lack of definite jurisdiction lines."
- Health department—"There is scarcely a record … which gives the information necessary to intelligent supervision … [and] practically all of the totals published … are of doubtful accuracy."
- Garbage collection and incineration—"Whereas the present incinerator is ably operated under the direction of a competent superintendent, the garbage collection is a disgrace to any city. … [C]ollection of garbage by private scavengers [as in Portland] has proved to be a failure wherever tried."
- Street cleaning—"Portland's streets are clean." Local conditions, such as lack of congestion, smooth surface pavements, and evenly distributed rainfall help keep them so. Suggestions are to help decrease the cost.
- Public works—Reorganization is needed within and between departments and jobs regarding jurisdiction, assignments, and inspections. Accounting systems are inadequate and economy in purchases is virtually disregarded.
- Water department—A difference of 238,000 dollars between revenues reported and consumption measured is a discrepancy no one has tracked down; it could be a leak or present flat rates may be inequitable.
- Auditor—Several boards are "making a clerk out of the independently elected auditor, who should be equal to and not subordinate to the water and other boards in matters pertaining to financial method, regularity, etc."
- Budgeting—"[T]he public has not been adequately informed … even the Council itself in passing appropriations has labored largely in the dark." Budget preparation is "seriously defective from almost every point of view—in fact, the city has no real budget."
- Expenditures—"[T]he auditor's financial control is no control. It consists of his being informed of what has been done after it has been done."

A horse-drawn fire engine emerges from Engine #2 Firehouse around 1915. The building, at the northeast corner of N.W. Third and Glisan near Union Station, is still standing.(Photo: OrHi # CN006288)

- Purchasing—"The city … might save $100,000 a year by the adoption of correct organization and methods for [centralized] purchase."
- Reporting—"[C]itizens of Portland have been left almost completely in the dark concerning their city government. They have known little of what was going on at the City Hall and their government has afforded them no means for becoming informed."[56]

The May 1913 election was destined to be a historic one, if for no other reason than that women would cast their ballots for the first time.[57] In Portland, however, the novelty of women's first vote took a back seat to a highly charged mayoral contest and passionate campaigning about the proposed charter amendment which would "revolutionize" Portland's government.[58]

A charter committee of nine, headed by Mayor Rushlight and including council president George L. Baker, had produced a charter patterned after the Galveston plan.[59] Under the proposed commission form of government, there would be only six elected officials—a mayor,

In the state's capital, a historic bill was signed by Governor Oswald West in early 1913 designating Oregon's beaches as public highways. West cleverly convinced the legislature they would be making "a huge addition to the state highway system at no cost." Future generations would use this law to provide protection and public access to the state's ocean shore.[62]

four commissioners, and an auditor—instead of the current twenty.[60] The mayor and commissioners would pass laws and administer city bureaus. The auditor would be the city's independent accountant and clerk, and was required to be "an expert accountant." The mayor could switch the bureaus assigned to various commissioners if he felt that the public service would be "benefited thereby." The mayor would chair council meetings and participate as a voting member. He would be paid six thousand dollars annually, while commissioners would receive five thousand dollars, and the auditor, "not less than $3,600." All terms were for four years, except that the new auditor and the two commissioners gaining the least number of votes would stand for election again in 1915, putting these three positions in alternating four-year cycles with the mayor and the other two commissioners.[61]

This new government would be more efficient, said promoters, because it would be easier to pinpoint responsibility. Other cities were pleased with the results of similar systems. The current ward system pitted neighborhood against neighborhood, and the fifteen-member council was too big for clear accountability. "It now takes 30 men to kill a fly," said councilman George Baker.[63]

Although Mayor Rushlight had initially considered the commission form of government "extravagant and weak in centering responsibility,"[64] he now supported it. Other advocates included mayoral candidates H. Russell Albee and C. L. McKenna, lawyer C. E. S. Wood, William M. Ladd, Joseph Teal, William Brewster, R. L. Glisan, Will Daly, D. Solis-Cohen, Rabbi Jonah Wise, and the Reverend Thomas Lamb Eliot. The *Oregonian* remained neutral. Although admitting the need for change, editor Edgar Piper criticized the way the charter had been presented to the public and did not like its provision for nonpartisan elections.[65] The entire proposal generated extensive public interest and debate.

The draft charter had "smooth sailing at the outset," but three weeks before the election, former councilman Gay Lombard went on the attack.[66] Lombard was president of the Pacific Grain company, an ally of Joseph Simon, a millionaire, and now a candidate for mayor opposing

Rushlight in the Republican primary. Lombard's arguments ran like this: "The existing charter was not to blame for criticisms in the [New York] Research Survey ... Mayor Rushlight was to blame, as was council president George Baker. ... The new charter would grant too much power to the mayor. ... The mayor's ability to transfer departments would threaten civil service procedures. [The problem was] the people's apathy, not the instrument of government. How naïve to believe that with the new charter, 'lions will lie down with lambs in the streets of Portland,' and that 'all of a sudden, badly run departments will blossom,' and 'Nirvana' will be attained."[67]

Lombard also accused seven members of Mayor Rushlight's administration of "failure to perform their duties."[68] Rushlight, in turn, accused Lombard of making personal profits by organizing a bonding company while he was a member of the council.[69]

Others joined Lombard in opposing the charter, including vehement objections from the aging Abigail Scott Duniway, who argued that women had been excluded from the committee which drafted the charter amendment and that the proposed language created a hodgepodge rather than a true commission form of government.[70]

The astounding reality of the May 3, 1913, vote was the slim margin of the amendment's passage. The commission form of government was adopted by a mandate of only two hundred ninety-two votes out of more than thirty-four thousand cast.[71] Eastsiders approved the amendment by a fifteen hundred-vote margin; westsiders defeated it by slightly less than the same number.[72] Less than half the city's registered voters cast ballots,[73] which meant that only 24 percent of eligible voters adopted the extensive revision of the 1903 charter, most provisions of which would survive for at least ninety years.[74] Based on this longevity, one might assume a more enthusiastic reception at the inception of the charter revisions. But change never comes easily, and this charter mandated dramatic change.

A mad rush to file for city offices now ensued, for nominees already chosen in the May 3 primary no longer had standing. The June 2 election would be a nonpartisan free-for-all. Names were to be printed on the ballot in the order received, so a premium was placed on speedy action. Some candidates filed their petitions, which had to be signed by one hundred voters, immediately after the polls closed on May 3, creating uncertainty over the legality of signatures obtained before results of the charter balloting had been determined.[75]

Two women—L. Victoria Hampton and Maria L. T. Hidden—filed for commission positions, along with seventy-two men.[76] Incumbent auditor Asbury L. Barbur, for whom present-day Barbur Boulevard was named when he later served as Commissioner of Public Works,[77] was the leading candidate for auditor.

Mayoral candidates were incumbent mayor Allen Rushlight, who had handily defeated Guy Lombard in the Republican primary, although that no longer mattered; H. Russell Albee, who had easily won the Progressive Party's nomination over Dan Kellaher; C. L. McKenna, who had been the Democratic nominee for mayor; Dan Kellaher, now running again in this nonpartisan race; and W. J. Smith, Socialist (although that designation would not be allowed on the June ballot).

The June 2 election brought out nine thousand more voters than had taken part in the May primary, but turnout was still low.[78]

Even though his primary victory did not count, Albee had gained status and publicity during his campaign for the Progressive Party nomination. He had also served on the city council for three years—1902-05—representing eastside Ward 10. But ward representation was now, of course, history—all four commissioners would be elected citywide.

H. Russell Albee won election as the city's new mayor. A controversial preferential voting system (today called "instant runoff") allowed voters to select first, second, and third choices for mayor, so if no candidate received a majority, second and third choices would be tallied to avoid a run-off election.[79] Albee failed by 1,108 votes to win a majority based only on first-choice votes, so all choices were counted.[80]

Four commissioners were elected: Robert Dieck, C. A. Bigelow, William Brewster, and incumbent councilman Will Daly. Men with well-known names who lost council bids included council president George Baker,[81] *Oregon Journal* editor Marshall Dana, former county treasurer A. W. Lambert, and incumbent councilmen Ralph Clyde and James Maguire.[82]

Failed measures included an eight hundred fifty thousand dollar Willamette River bridge; a ninety thousand dollar Council Crest park; a two hundred fifty thousand dollar historical society and museum building; and a second try for a two hundred thousand dollar park bond issue.[83] In addition:"Planning advocates suffered major losses in 1913. ... [T]hey failed to win locations prescribed by the plan for a new art gallery and public auditorium. ... Even more serious was the defeat of the Bennett plan's proposal to widen Burnside Street—an avenue chosen to become one of Portland's major traffic arteries. Burnside Street property owners, working through their local improvement organization, successfully opposed the GPPA's plans to alter Burnside. Any changes, they feared, might injure their property values."[84] Today,

Burnside Street is still a bottleneck of traffic congestion, especially West Burnside, even though the street was widened in the 1930s.

July 1913 - June 1917

Harrison Russell Albee[85] seldom used his first name, choosing simply the initial H. and his middle name: H. Russell Albee. He had been born and raised in Illinois, where he worked for some years as a blacksmith's helper in his father's machine shop. At age seventeen, he moved to Michigan and worked as a clerk in a hardware store, then in a railroad freight office, then in a lumberyard. Before he came to Portland at age twenty-eight, he had already owned and operated a lumber mill. In Oregon, he worked for Northwestern Mutual Life Insurance Company, and was promoted to the position of general manager for the company's Portland territory at age thirty-eight. In the meantime, he had been elected to the city council. He was elected Portland mayor at age forty-six. He was a strong advocate of public ownership of utilities.[86] Writer Fred Lockley wrote that he "dances, skates, swims, plays football and baseball and is an outdoor man. In describing him the adjectives that come first to one's mind are genial, kind, sympathetic, affable, chivalrous and witty."[87]

Mayor H. Russell Albee. (Photo: OrHi #55108)

The four new commissioners boasted impressive backgrounds. Will Daly, the only commissioner with prior council experience, was manager of the Portland Monotype Company and president of the Portland Central Labor Council.[88] C. A. Bigelow was a "well-regarded department store official." Robert Dieck had a civil engineering degree from the University of Pennsylvania and took a keen interest in planning. William Brewster was a Columbia Law School graduate active in civic affairs and a member of Joseph Teal's law firm.[89]

Albee had barely taken office when, on July 1, his chief of police ordered strikers at the Oregon Packing Company to "quit picketing, quit speaking, quit parading, or else face a jail sentence."[90] The company had an all-woman labor force, and strikers were protesting low wages and unsanitary working conditions. By July 16, ten strikers had been arrested and jailed. Within three weeks of his inauguration, Albee had "banned all street speaking except religious speeches." More arrests and violent police responses to strike activities occurred that summer and fall. Local union officials started a drive to recall the mayor. Under pressure, Albee lifted many restrictions in early November, but his handling of union activists and his intolerance of free speech were proving much harsher than the policies of Mayor Rushlight.[91]

Portland voters had approved building a city auditorium two years before, and a lengthy controversy had ensued over its location. Mayor Simon, who was leaving office just as the measure passed, had appointed a committee to select a site and an architect. Businessmen's organizations on both sides of the river engaged in bitter dispute. The Portland Symphony Orchestra insisted it would not play on the east side. Now the council had to decide where to place the new auditorium. Daly and Bigelow voted for the proposed site on the east side, while Dieck and Brewster were for the west.[92] Albee cast the tie-breaking vote for the west side site, largely because the city already owned Block 132, the compromise site on the west side, and the money thus saved could be spent on the building itself. Block 132 had been designated as a public market square on the first Lownsdale townsite map. A grand Mechanics Fair Pavilion had been built there, rebuilt and enlarged into the Metropolitan Public Market.[93] Today's Keller Auditorium sits on Block 132.[94]

Water meters were also a contentious issue. Thirty percent of city customers already had meters installed, which meant they paid for actual water consumed. Flat-rate customers paid a basic fee each month regardless of usage. Mayor Albee insisted that all users should be metered. He was supported in this by Commissioners Brewster and Daly.[95]

Daly, in his capacity as Commissioner of Public Utilities, discovered an outrageous fact—the outgoing water committee had agreed to lay a seventeen thousand dollar water main (equivalent to two hundred sixty-five thousand dollars today) half a mile outside the city limits to wealthy *Oregonian* publisher Henry Pittock's new mansion above Macleay Park. Daly found a copy of this contract in the files and immediately cancelled it. Pittock thus became one of the chief opponents of metered water systems, and from then on treated Will Daly as the "devil incarnate."[96]

In a special election held December 9, 1913, all fifteen Portland measures on the ballot were rejected by the few voters who turned out, including a two hundred thousand dollar parks measure supported by only 16 percent of the voters, a measure on its third try in thirteen months.[97]

In February 1914, recall petitions began circulating against Mayor Albee and commissioners Robert Dieck and William Brewster. Although enough signatures were obtained to initiate a recall election by mid-March, the petitions were not filed for another six months, possibly because the circulators were trying to find viable candidates to supplant the three incumbents. The *Oregon Journal* was vehement in its objection to the entire process: "We cannot conduct government if we get up a recall movement every time an official does something which some of us do not approve. Nor can we get anywhere with government if we start a referendum on every city ordinance with which some of us are not suited. These foolish proceedings only more and more discourage desirable men from entering public

> Also in February, the Ford Motor Company started producing ten cars a day from its new three-story assembly plant at S.E. Eleventh and Division, a brick building that would later house Multnomah County's archives and other county offices.[98]

The city's first public dock, covering 663 feet along North Front Street, was dedicated in March. Pier A was part of a municipal dock one-fifth of a mile long under construction at the foot of Upshur Street.[100]

life. It is getting so in Oregon that the moment a man assumes high public position all the malignity, all the malevolence and all the vials of abuse are uncorked and referendums, recalls and floods of invective turned upon him. ... The best thing to be done with the petitions is to throw them into the river."[99]

The recall petitions were filed on October 2. The petition against Mayor Albee, signed by 9,796 voters, charged him with violating the city charter by retaining his position as general manager of an insurance company, and with dismissing competent city employees without just cause. Commissioners Brewster and Dieck were charged with extravagance, inefficiency, and bad judgment. The unstated issues were the westside location of the city auditorium, Albee's handling of the labor strike, and efforts to install water meters for all customers.

Nearly 56 percent of registered voters turned out for the recall election of October 27, 1914—three times the number who had voted the previous December. By more than a two-to-one margin, voters rejected Mayor Albee's recall. While the margin of support was smaller, 62 percent voted to retain William Brewster and 58 percent to retain Robert Dieck.[101]

Giddy with the power of the initiative and referendum, Oregon voters approved prohibition in November 1914 (although liquor could still be "imported" from out of state for consumption in private homes).[102] Only three others of twenty-nine statewide issues passed: requiring voters to be U. S. citizens, allowing merger of adjoining cities and towns (sought by Portland and St. Johns), and abolishing the death penalty.[103]

Voters in St. Johns and Linnton, incorporated cities north of Portland near the mouth of the Willamette River, soon decided to "commit municipal suicide" by giving up their city charters to merge with Portland.[104] This merger expanded Portland's boundaries by 25 percent, to a total of sixty-six square miles. Portland increased its access to the Columbia River by its merger with St. Johns, and added nearly four thousand acres of undeveloped forestland by its merger with Linnton. Thirty years later, that forestland would become a major part of the city's Forest Park Reserve. Portland's population now approached a quarter million, at 232,500 people.[105]

"One of the most important trials of the age," was how silver-tongued attorney C. E. S. Wood characterized the trial of Margaret Sanger that began in Portland on June 30, 1916. Sanger was a national birth-control advocate who had already been jailed in New York. She and six of her associates had been arrested for selling family limitation pamphlets when Sanger spoke at Portland's Heilig Theater. C. E. S. Wood defended Sanger, arguing that the anti-obscenity ordinance under which she was arrested was an unconstitutional restriction of free speech. Wood declared: "If Portland's statute is legal then the Holy Bible is obscene."[106]

The judge found in favor of the city. The pamphlets were obscene, he said, because "general distribution by those 'not having the high and lofty motives of Margaret Sanger' would produce thoughts 'of impure and libidinous character.'"[107] The city had a right to censor materials that the majority of Portland's citizens would find objectionable, the judge said. However, he levied fines of only ten dollars each, which he then suspended.[108]

Councilman Bigelow was reelected in June 1915, but William Brewster, who had voted to locate the city auditorium on the west side, was edged out by former councilman George Baker. A referendum to purchase water meters failed, as did a measure to prohibit stores from opening on Sundays.[109]

The same month, pioneer logger Simon Benson donated scenic Wahkeena Falls in the Columbia Gorge to the city, along with 380 acres of land. The council accepted the property with "hearty thanks" and named the property Benson Park in his honor.[110]

In July, the new Columbia River Gorge Highway opened.[111] Multnomah Falls—a spectacular waterfall with a sheer drop of 620 feet that was now accessible by automobile—became city property in September, another gift from Simon Benson.[112] Multnomah Falls and its surrounding parkland, including Benson Park, twenty miles east of Portland, would eventually be taken over by the state of Oregon because the city lacked the resources to maintain the popular areas.[113]

About this time, Simon Benson made headlines for a totally different reason. He had visited several city departments, Benson said, and now advocated adoption of a city manager form of government. "I find, upon casual examination, that I could save at least $1,000 a day," Benson said at an August 1915 public meeting at city hall. "I could save twice that

> In fall 1916, a group of "forward-looking young men" founded a weekly luncheon group called the City Club of Portland, patterned after similar organizations in eastern cities. The group would evolve into an influential research body and the state's foremost public forum for issues and candidates.[116]

much ... by getting rid of the present form of government ... that gives us actually, five mayors." Hiring a professional manager who would be paid at least twice what the mayor or commissioners were getting would bring the kind of professional management the city needed to rid itself of the "terrible waste" Benson saw in "almost every channel of the city's activity."[114]

"Spokane is considered the best and Portland the worst commission-managed cities in the West," Benson later declared. An *Oregon Journal* editorial responded with a challenge to Benson that he should submit a bill of particulars backing up this "sweeping indictment": "In this bill of particulars, why not make some mention of the fact that there never was a time in the history of Portland and that there never was a city in the United States in which there was such complete freedom from public scandal and charges of graft as is true of Portland under commission government?"[115]

Oregon's "bone-dry" liquor law, forbidding any sale or importing of alcohol, passed by a 51 - 49 percent vote in November 1916. Although Multnomah County voters firmly rejected the measure, the rest of the state overcame that margin to give the measure a five thousand-vote victory.[117] The day of the bootlegger, moonshine, and speakeasies had begun!

The first interstate bridge across the Columbia River opened with great fanfare on Oregon's fifty-eighth birthday—February 14, 1917. Mayor Albee and the mayor of Vancouver, Washington, shook hands, and signaled for a mile-long procession of Oregon automobiles to cross the bridge. A few horse-drawn vehicles took part.[118]

Despite this sign of progress, Portland's economy was not living up to the bright promise that had seemed inevitable after the 1905 world's fair. The price of both wheat and lumber had collapsed, starting in 1913. Local construction was severely curtailed. "City spending on streets and sewers fell from $7 million in 1911 to an average of $600,000 in 1915, 1916, and 1917."[119] Great Britain declared war on Germany in 1914; Italy joined the fray in 1915 and 1916; international trade was severely restricted. The entire Northwest economy was depressed. The Panama

Canal had suffered a giant landslide and was closed for repairs. The result of all these economic downturns was that the Bennett plan never got off the ground. One exception was completion of the city's first public docks—one on each side of the Willamette—and construction of a third terminal now underway in the newly added St. Johns area near the Columbia River.[120]

One result of the depression, fortunate for future Portlanders, was that, because planned housing developments in northwest Portland never took place, private owners forfeited hundreds of acres of forest land to the city. "[I]n 1914, the city of Portland started a wood-cutting camp on Tualatin Mountain to provide work for the unemployed. At the same time, in hopeful anticipation of a great land boom, developers proposed and laid out large subdivisions throughout the [area]. ... By 1915 ... Leif Erikson Drive was completed. ... In its first year, a winter's landslide closed the road. ... It was a realtor's nightmare. ... [B]etween 1915 and 1931, hundreds of lots, totaling fourteen hundred acres, were forfeited to the city of Portland for nonpayment of the assessment."[121]

These forest lands had been identified by both the Olmstead report of 1903 and the Bennett plan of 1912 as ideally suited for a "Forest Park." Although it would be nearly thirty years before the potential was realized, individual ill-fortunes at this time would ultimately benefit the public.

On April 6, 1917, Congress declared war on Germany, marking American entry into World War I. "The United States today accepted Germany's challenge to war and finally abandoned its place as the greatest neutral country in a world in arms," the *Oregonian* said. The same day, a Portland special patrolman who uttered a remark considered disloyal to the United States was forced to resign immediately.[122]

Now Oregon's "vast supply" of timber, wheat, and other foodstuffs was in great demand. The *Oregonian* opined that five regiments of troops would be raised in Oregon, and that the Northwest's "inexhaustible" waterpower would be harnessed for electrical processes used to manufacture nitrates. By June 26, American troops had begun landing in France.[123]

Only six U.S. senators opposed entering the war. One of them was former Portland mayor Harry Lane. The reaction at home in Oregon was so fast and vicious that future senator Richard Neuberger later summarized it as a hatred campaign "without parallel in the history of the far west."[124] Harry Lane died of a stroke six weeks later, on May 23,

Crowds swarmed to the south shore of the Columbia River after a streetcar line opened in 1916. The first interstate bridge to Washington State opened near this site the following year. (Photo: OrHi #47051)

1917, at age sixty-one.[125] His casket lay in state at city hall for four hours the day before his funeral. At least fifteen congressmen came to Portland by special train from Washington, D. C. to honor him.[126]

But the war was still far away from Oregon. The May issue of *Collier's Weekly* magazine contained an article sure to capture Portland's attention. Titled "Portland the Spinster," the article poked fun at the reigning F. F. P. (First Families of Portland), implied that Oregon's reforms had sneaked through only because of an *Oregonian - Oregon Journal* rivalry, mocked the "$60,000 cow pasture" in a side yard of the Corbett mansion,[127] and eulogized the city's physical setting. The Corbett mansion was only three blocks from city hall on valuable downtown property, land on which the Greyhound bus depot would later stand, and which, by April 2001, was scheduled to be occupied by the Pacific Building and a new, 20-level Hilton Executive Tower, an annex to the existing Hilton. *Collier's Weekly* said:

> (H)ow sweetly this city lies, as it were, in the hand of the land; the river washing serenely through it in a great slow S; the hills and mountains girding it about protectingly; and the peaks of everlasting snow—Hood and St. Helens and Mount Jefferson, and the others—standing high in the distance like sentinels looking afar, stately and majestic in

> their proud guardianship. … [The] city reminds [one] more than anything else of a prim, rather human old maid set down in the midst of a group of distinctly hoydenish and frivolous sister cities, viewing them through nose spectacles with an air of frank and rebuking disapprobation. …. Portland thinks Seattle forward, pert, and radical. She thinks San Francisco quite impossible." [128]

After a four-year trial, citizens gave a resounding show of confidence to the commission form of government. Voters in June 1917 turned down two measures to do away with it (one was a measure to repeal, the other to abolish) by better than two to one. By an even greater margin, voters approved a three million-dollar bond issue for grain elevators, docks, wharves, and warehouses. They also supported a special levy for parks and playgrounds.[129]

Mayor H. Russell Albee decided one four-year term was enough. If the fate of the two other targets of the 1914 recall is any indication, he made the right choice in bowing out. Both Robert Dieck and William Brewster were defeated for reelection by city auditor Asbury L. Barbur and newcomer John M. Mann in an at-large field of sixteen candidates.[130]

Portland's "Golden Age" was at an end and a new era about to begin.[131]

Chapter 20

World War I, Politics as Theater, and the Great Depression

July 1917 – December 1940

Mayors

No. 39: July 1917 – June 1921

George Luis Baker (elected for four-year term)

July 1921 – June 1925

George Luis Baker (elected for four-year term)

July 1925 – June 1929

George Luis Baker (elected for four-year term)

July 1929 – June 1933

George Luis Baker (elected for four-year term)

No. 40: July 1933 - Dec 1936

Joseph Kirtley Carson, Jr.
(elected for three and a half-year term)[1]

Jan 1937 – Dec 1940

Joseph Kirtley Carson, Jr. (elected for four-year term)

Two days before the 1917 election, George Baker was running second in the race for mayor. Former mayor Allen G. Rushlight wanted the job, as did city commissioner Will Daly,[2] the same Will Daly who had cancelled Henry Pittock's water main because it was outside the city limits. Baker was supported by the *Oregonian* and the Republican hierarchy; front-runner Daly was supported by the unions and the *Oregon Journal*; Rushlight had always been a poor public speaker and was left at the starting gate by the other two men.[3]

With the vote scheduled for the next day, the *Sunday Oregonian* of June 3 triumphantly revealed that Daly had joined the Socialist Party in 1910.[4] The timing left Daly and his supporters no way to inform voters that Daly had re-registered as a Republican two years later and had been attacked repeatedly by radical Socialist leaders since that time.[5]

Mayor George Baker, known as a ladies' man, is shown here with three "Lady Elks" in 1928. As mayor, Baker provided the public with "color and dash" for sixteen years—an unparalleled record of service at the time. (Photo: OrHi #75222)

Baker won in 177 precincts, while Daly won in 175.[6] Thus began the colorful, sixteen-year mayoral career of George Luis Baker.

Physically, George Baker was a "giant of a man"—topping six feet and weighing more than two hundred pounds.[7] Thick craggy eyebrows and a bulbous nose dominated his face. The *Oregon Voter* magazine titled this boisterous man the "champion loud noise of the Pacific Northwest south of Seattle."[8] By the time he left office, Baker was a legend, a character fondly referred to as "Our George."

A native-born Oregonian whose father had immigrated from Germany, Mayor Baker was born at The Dalles in 1868 and spent most of his boyhood moving up and down the West Coast, always in poverty.[9] His formal education ended at age nine.[10] At age twenty-one, Baker migrated to Portland.[11] After several business misfortunes, he found success with the Baker Stock Company, a resident Portland stock theater that also performed in Seattle, Spokane, and Los Angeles, and became known as far away as the eastern seaboard.[12]

George Baker joined every organization in sight. "If you want to get elected to any public office," he said, "join 'em all, those votes are all in the bag."[13] As a ward leader, Baker had operated like an old-time political boss distributing patronage jobs. The Ministerial Alliance had accused him of representing liquor and brewery interests located in his ward.[14] During his thirteen years on the council, Baker had sponsored popular programs like municipal band concerts, bathing beaches, rifle ranges, and golf courses.[15]

Forty-nine-year-old Baker was to serve longer than any previous mayor in Portland's history.[16] During the entire span of Baker's mayoralty, from 1917 until 1933, all council members lived on the east side of the river.[17] Four other city officials who served at the same time as Baker served record-breaking tenures. City auditor George R. Funk was the elected auditor for twenty and a half years (1917-37), the longest tenure ever logged in that office.[18] C. A. Bigelow, who served seventeen years on the council, resigned his seat in 1930, and subsequently served nine years on the Multnomah County Board of Commissioners.[19] Asbury Lincoln Barbur had already served ten years as the elected auditor before his sixteen years on the council.[20] John M. Mann, a liberal on the issue of public power, ended nearly fifteen years on the council when he was accused of larceny and recalled from office in 1932.[21]

Other commissioners who served on the council for varying lengths of time during Baker's tenure included Dan Kellaher,[22] an outspoken advocate of public power, state legislator, and two-time candidate for mayor who frequently clashed with Baker and other conservative members of the council.[23] He was defeated in his reelection bid by Sylvester C. Pier,[24] for whom Pier Park near the confluence of the Willamette and Columbia rivers was named.[25] Sylvester Pier's son, Stanhope S. Pier, was a former state legislator turned out of office by the voters in 1930 after eight years on the council.[26] The father served from 1919 to 1923; the son from 1923 to 1933. Ralph Clyde won reelection to the council on his third try in 1930, and thereafter served nearly sixteen years before dying in office in August 1943.[27] Earl Riley was first appointed to a vacant council seat, and would later be elected as Portland's mayor. Harvard-educated engineer A. G. Johnson served only six months, filling John Mann's vacant seat, before losing his bid for a full council term.[28]

The most controversial council member to serve under Mayor Baker was J. E. "Jake" Bennett, who accumulated nearly ten years on the council in two separate segments and was recalled in 1952. He continued to run (unsuccessfully) again and again for a council seat and (successfully) several times for the state legislature until his death in April 1970 at age seventy-nine.[29]

Zealous patriotism was the mood of the day when Mayor Baker assumed office. The U.S. had entered the Great War less than three months before. Mayor Baker hosted farewell breakfasts for departing World War I soldiers. "Goodbye and God bless you, boys," Baker would call to the soldiers at the train station as they left for Europe, a gesture that many soldiers remembered all their lives.[30]

The mayor was part of a prestigious committee that led the city's war effort, including the sale of liberty bonds.[31] Portland outdid her Pacific Coast rivals in such sales. Passions ran so high that an assistant librarian in Portland who refused to buy a war bond finally resigned over the furor that her refusal caused.[32] The council changed the names of Germanic-sounding streets: Frankfurt became Lafayette; Bismark became Bush; Karl was changed to Haig.[33] Police focused on ferreting out subversive activity by German-born "enemy aliens."[34]

One home-front wartime success story concerned recycling of garbage, which the city collected, segregated, and sold. Food waste was sold for hog swill, while paper, dried bones, rags, tin cans, and scrap metal were retrieved and sold by the ton. A private paper drive collected nearly sixty thousand dollars' worth of salvageable paper in two years.[35] Another council success was the sale of fresh fish to the public at low cost, a project led by Commissioner Kellaher. The city leased a boat,

In a single weekend, volunteers erected this World War I Liberty Temple in mid-street between the Portland Hotel and Pioneer Post Office. (Photo: OrHi #4497-a)

hired fishermen, and rented a stall at the city-owned public market on S.W. Yamhill. The popular program lasted more than a year, until a court ruled that the practice was unconstitutional.[36]

Volunteers erected a Grecian-style Liberty Temple in the middle of the street near the Portland Hotel and Pioneer Post Office. The structure was dedicated on April 6, 1918, the first anniversary of America's entry into the war.[37]

❧

That fall, the "greatest single epidemic in human history," struck Portland.[38] The deadly so-called "Spanish" flu was spread by military troops converging on Europe to fight the war,. The city's health officer, Dr. George Parrish, warned in a front-page *Oregonian* article on October 5 that while only a few Portland cases had been reported, an influenza epidemic was already raging in Boston and Philadelphia. Parrish asked theater owners to eject anyone who coughed or sneezed. Six days later, Mayor Baker ordered all public meeting places closed. On October 17, the newly dedicated Civic Auditorium was converted into a city hospital. But Portland did not suffer the ravages long. Less than a month later, by November 11, 1918—Armistice Day—the death rate had leveled off enough for the city to lift its meeting-place ban even though the State Health Office considered the action premature.[39] Churches and schools reopened November 15. Mayor Baker organized a huge celebration for November 16 to mark the end of World War I.

However, the flu was not really over. In the first week of December, new cases rivaled the initial outbreak. The council passed a resolution requiring quarantined houses to place large red cards in their windows. The flu raged into January. The council considered requiring people to wear masks. After two weeks of discussion, they compromised, passing an ordinance that required masks, effective thirty days later. But by that date, the flu had left Portland "as rapidly as it had arrived."[40]

❧

The wartime shipbuilding boom had created a serious housing shortage. In response to public pressure, the council had turned to California planner Charles Cheney, who recommended that the newly formed Cooperative Housing Association build two thousand "cheap" homes for needed family housing. With war's end, this changed to an "Own-Your-Own Home" campaign. Cheney urged adoption of a housing code to guard against shoddy home construction, which in turn led to creation of the City Planning Commission in late December 1918.[41]

Early in 1919, a national "Red Scare" focused on the "Wobblies" (Industrial Workers of the World). This motivated Portland police to stage a series of raids on the local IWW headquarters, smashing furniture and carrying off literature and records. Mayor Baker threatened to prosecute the building's owner if he failed to evict the union.[42] But the Wobblies devised effective retaliation: "The IWW wrote letters to the city fathers, the W.C.T.U. and all of the city's leading ministers telling them exactly 'where all of the speakeasies and bootleg joints' were located. They then began to picket the thirteen outlets, carrying banners proclaiming, 'This place sells poison bootleg liquor—All good IWW's will not patronize.' Within 24 hours, persecution of the Wobblies ceased."[43]

Prohibition was now a fact of life in Portland—on paper. The entire nation had embraced prohibition with ratification of the Eighteenth Amendment to the U.S. Constitution in January 1919.[44]

Prohibition reduced the incidence of alcohol-related crimes, thereby decreasing municipal court fees by about one hundred seventy-five thousand dollars a year. It also shrank city general fund revenues by three hundred fifty thousand dollars annually because of lost liquor license fees.[45] A Portland vice squad member, Floyd R. Marsh, later said Prohibition was violated so often around city hall and the police station that he took it for granted. "Portland was a central distribution point for bonded liquor coming in from Canada as well as moonshine made in the woods nearby. … At least $100,000 a month was paid out in protection money to authorities of Multnomah County and the City of Portland."[46]

Ten whiskey dealers did a brisk business in Portland, Marsh said, along with at least twenty stills, a hundred speakeasies, and a hundred beer and wine parlors, with the profits "funneled into the gambling racket. In the late 20s, there were about 40 gambling places operating in Portland. … They paid the man on the beat $10 per month, and the City Hall got theirs through two plainclothesmen who hung around the Station. … The gambling pay-off in Portland was about $50,000 a month. … At one time there were 35 'sporting houses' with madams, and from 2 to 6 girls in each house. … Over all, the 'Tenderloin District' paid about $20,000 a month for protection, in addition to the legal pinch they took every so often."[47]

In fall 1920, the *Oregon Journal* publicly accused the police department of conspiracy with the bootleggers.[48] Officer Marsh insisted that Police Chief Leon V. Jenkins himself was honest, but that (unnamed) others in city hall were not.[49]

❧

Mayor Baker sought reelection in November 1920.[50] He won enough first-place votes to defeat all three opponents (including former Commissioner Dan Kellaher) without having to count second- and third-place votes.[51]

Boom times followed the war. Portland's per capita income was "probably greater than that of any city west of the Mississippi," according to a 1921 *Oregonian* article.[52]

❧

The Ku Klux Klan gained many Oregon converts in the early 1920s. While southern Oregon was the Klan's most fertile ground, Portland was also a regional center of Klan activity. "Fiery crosses frequently were burned on such nearby hillsides as Mt. Tabor and Mt. Scott," says historian David Horowitz.[53]

An oft-reprinted photo taken August 1, 1921, shows Mayor George Baker and Police Chief Leon Jenkins, along with seven other Portland-area public officials, standing with two hooded members of the Ku Klux Klan. However, historian E. Kimbark MacColl says the photograph was a frame-up, a photo manipulated by the KKK at a Multnomah Hotel social event. Officials were asked to line up for a photo, and just before the camera clicked, the two hooded men stepped out from behind a curtain. The two district attorneys present were infuriated by this trickery, but the damage had been done. MacColl says of the photograph: "Unfortunately for the record, historians were to use this as evidence that the Klan had taken over the 'capital, city hall and the courthouse.' This was far from the truth, at least in August of 1921."[54]

An ex-Klan editor later claimed that Mayor Baker was an enrolled Klansman.[55] No other documentation is known to prove such membership, but it is a matter of record that Baker was an inveterate joiner. Baker did nothing to repudiate the Klan; on the contrary, he and Governor Walter Pierce participated in a "patriotic" dinner honoring the KKK Grand Dragon,[56] and he solicited its support in his unsuccessful bid for the U.S. Senate seat in 1923, a race he lost to incumbent Charles McNary in the Republican primary.[57] Shortly after that, the Klan's

Hooded Klansmen stepped from behind a curtain to catch several local politicians unaware at an August 1921 social event. Mayor George Baker, who courted Ku Klux Klan support in his unsuccessful 1923 race for the U.S. Senate, is third from right, and Police Chief Leon Jenkins, third from left. (Photo: OrHi #54338)

influence in Oregon virtually disappeared, in part due to the indictment and recall in May 1924 of all three Multnomah County Commissioners for "gross irregularities in the award of contracts for the construction of the Burnside and Ross Island Bridges."[58] All three had been KKK protegés.[59]

After Mayor Baker lost his U.S. Senate bid in 1923, rumors circulated that he might not file for reelection because the six thousand dollar mayor's salary, the equivalent of sixty-one thousand dollars today, was not enough to live on. So a committee of businessmen raised seventy-one hundred dollars to pay off Baker's home mortgage. The *Oregon Voter*, which investigated the matter, decided that the payoff was of little concern because thousands of dollars "would have flowed" in for this purpose if others had known of the mayor's circumstances. At least one candidate for mayor, former Multnomah County commission chair Rufus Holman, saw the matter differently. "They may call it a tip; a gratuity, or explain it any way they can," he said, "but I call it a bribe." Among those who solicited contributions to make up Baker's "swag" was Franklin T. Griffith, president of Portland Railway Light & Power Company, whose city-granted franchise was soon to expire.[60]

In addition to questions about the propriety of his mortgage payoff, Baker was accused of showing favoritism to his stepson in city insurance

Times were good. In 1924, the old county poor farm was converted into a nine-hole golf course under the aegis of the Portland park bureau. This West Hills Golf Course would later become the site of today's popular Washington Park Zoo.[64] Five years later, the assistant superintendent of parks was suspended for thirty days because he was betting with players at the city golf links about "sinking the ball." Thereafter, city employees were prohibited from playing golf with patrons.[65]

matters. But although it was a bitter campaign,[61] the mayor easily won reelection over six opponents.[62] His endorsement by the *Oregon Voter* helps explain why Baker enjoyed such longevity as mayor: "In spite of his press-agented grandstanding, in spite of his sporadic and political police raids, and in spite of his issueless senatorial campaign … Mr. Baker has given Portland an administration that compares favorably with … other large cities. … [H]e has assisted in keeping Portland in a favorable light before the country. That has come to be a function of American mayors. The people expect it from their mayor. Mr. Baker has supplied the color and dash which a more prosaic but nevertheless efficient business man might not possess."[63]

❧

Zoning had been a hard-fought issue in Portland for several years. A proposal to create eight zones was derailed by the Portland Realty Board, whose members saw zoning as "a ruthless interference with property values that would raise rents by limiting apartment construction." Voters had rejected a zoning measure four years before by only five hundred forty-six votes out of over sixty thousand cast.[66] In June 1924, voters passed a watered-down measure that divided the city into four zones: 1) single-family houses; 2) duplexes and apartments; 3) commercial and residential; and 4) unrestricted (intended primarily for industrial use).[67] This four-tiered zone plan was drafted by a committee headed by realtor Fred German—an opponent of zoning—who made sure nothing more than this weak proposal made it to the ballot. The result, says E. Kimbark MacColl, was a "realtors' dream."[68]

In a comprehensive rating of large cities, the *American City* magazine gave Portland a high score of 84 for city services overall, compared to the national average score of 78.[69] Portland's highest ratings were for its schools, library services, and low death rate. Rated "above average" were parks, street paving, and garbage collection." Street cleaning was average. Sewer services and fire losses were rated below average.[70]

Sewer projects required a petition signed by the owners of 50 percent of affected property owners, so they were not a high council priority. Mayor Baker later boasted that he had "consistently followed the policy of not burdening the property owners or taxpayers with unnecessary expenditures."[73] He apparently considered sewers, with their low public appeal, an unnecessary expenditure.

The voters approved a bond issue in May 1926 for widening streets.[74] The city saved more than 50 percent on paving costs by operating its own municipal plant, a project championed by Commissioner Asbury Barbur.[75]

Radio came into its own during the 1924 election. President Calvin Coolidge broadcast two speeches over a nationwide network of twenty-seven stations, including Portland's KGW. Half a million people in Oregon, Washington, Idaho, and Montana heard these KGW broadcasts beamed from the *Oregonian* building—an impressive performance by a fledgling radio station only two and a half years old.[71]

The "moving picture show" was another new Portland entertainment that had begun a decade earlier with nickelodeons and "shanty theaters." Audiences were soon enchanted by characters such as the "zany Keystone Cops."[72]

Mayor Baker continued to demonstrate his knack for showmanship. He led every annual Rose Parade. When New York's famous mayor, Jimmie Walker, came to visit in 1926, Baker "picked the little guy up in his big arms and rocked him on his lap like a baby. Anything for a joke and another picture in the papers." Baker was a "publicity hound, period," a reporter said.[76]

At a Progressive Business Men's club luncheon about this time, Baker overshadowed the official speaker with his "fiery oratory" as chairman of the day. The mayor chastised the Law Enforcement League for its criticism of Police Chief Jenkins, and reprimanded the British, whose "inexhaustible supply of liquor was making criminals out of a large percent of American citizens." His remarks were met with vigorous applause until a judge took offense at Baker's censure of the circuit court and told the mayor he didn't know what he was talking about.[77]

Baker knew how to conjure up "public displays of puritanical virtue." He once loudly protested a speaker's use of the word *virginity*: "Mr. Chairman," Baker said, "I object to the use of this insidious word in the presence of women."[78]

Consolidation of Portland and Multnomah County governments again emerged as an issue after the 1925 state legislature convened a Government Simplification Committee to study Portland's metropolitan government. The group—chaired by lawyer Richard Montague, a member of both the 1902 and 1913 Portland charter commissions[79]—studied the issue for two years. They then proposed a state constitutional amendment to enable city and county voters to adopt a consolidated government.

Before that proposal made it to the ballot, however, a twenty-five-member committee led by Mayor George Baker proposed lengthy charter changes. The amendment, titled "Simplify and Retain Commission Form of Government," was turned down by a 3 percent margin in November 1926. The council resubmitted the amendment the following June, only to have it rejected again, this time by a five-to-one margin. "Taxes Go Up If Charter Is Adopted," warned a front-page *Oregon Journal* headline before the election. The amendment included a twenty-six-year tax levy to pay for 50 percent increases in the mayor's and council members' salaries, and pensions for police, fire, and civil service employees. Favorable treatment for utility franchise holders was also criticized by the *Journal*, as was the vacating of streets for private use; reducing from two thousand to one thousand feet the amount of public domain street footage required at river access points; and inclusion of other unneeded matters.[80]

Supporters of legislation to enable city-county consolidation fought an onslaught of objections. In an impassioned, three-page response to arguments published in the *Voters' Pamphlet*, Richard Montague labeled the existing structure "complex, ill-adjusted, expensive and inefficient," and arguments against the measure as ill-founded. Opponents, he claimed, declare "flatly that the whole thing is a scheme by designing interests of Portland to bankrupt the farmers of Multnomah County by bringing them into the city and thereby increasing their tax burdens to the point of confiscation. ... [An] intelligent consolidation system ... most certainly would provide a zoning system by which taxes are graduated [based on whether] the property is urban or rural. ... The charge that the consolidation would create bureaucratic control is sufficiently refuted by the fact that the entire bureaucratic force of county and city job-holders ... is fighting tooth and nail against the amendment."[81]

The June 1927 statewide measure to enable consolidation was opposed by 58 percent of voters, with nearly one hundred thousand statewide voters casting ballots.[82] Portland-Multnomah County consolidation was again a dead issue for nearly fifty years.

On September 14, 1927, four months after his famous solo flight across the Atlantic, Charles Lindberg landed his *Spirit of St. Louis* at Portland's newly constructed Swan Island airport. There he was met by a tumultuous welcoming crowd, whisked across the Willamette aboard a yacht, welcomed in a rousing parade, honored by many speeches, and feted at a formal banquet. He seemed most touched by the cries of "Lindy! Lindy! Lindy!" from schoolchildren in the audience at Multnomah Stadium.[83]

The Port of Portland had acquired 250-acre Swan Island in 1921, and subsequently received permission from Congress to connect the island to the mainland by filling in part of the east channel. By summer 1928, the Swan Island airport was completely operational.[84]

At about the same time, the Port hired a lobbyist to convince Congress that a planned private toll bridge across the Columbia River halfway between Portland and the ocean at Longview, Washington, would be too low because its proposed 135 feet of clearance was not adequate for ships to pass underneath. Congress increased the required clearance to 190 feet. With the Panama Canal mostly completed by 1914 and its official opening on July 12, 1920, Portland's trade potential had increased, the Port said, and unrestricted river passage was essential to the city's shipping industry.[85]

The prosperous 1920s allowed the city water bureau to undertake two huge construction projects. A "great pipe line" that doubled the city's capacity to transport water from Bull Run was completed between 1923 and 1925. Then, between 1927 and 1929, a massive concrete dam was built on the Bull Run River for water storage. No popular vote was needed to finance these projects because voters had approved a charter amendment in 1910 that allowed the council to issue water bonds without a special vote of the people.[86] The new Bull Run reservoir stored ten billion gallons of water, and provided capacity that would serve the city without major improvement for the next twenty-five years. The dam and reservoir cost nearly three million dollars, to be paid for from future water usage fees.[87]

The 1928 election saw Rufus Holman challenging George Baker for the mayor's seat for a second time, and losing again, this time by a solid 12 percent.[88]

The accumulation and backup of sewage during low water, coupled with frequent flooding at high water, had forced businesses to locate on higher ground away from the waterfront. "The feculence of the river was so great that people were repelled rather than attracted to the area."[89] So another major construction project—a combined sewer-seawall that included the city's first harborwall—was begun, and completed in 1929. Because the city charter did not allow local improvement districts (LIDs) to fund flood-prevention programs, the sewer and riverwall were built together as a sewer LID, with the entire two-million-dollar cost billed to property owners benefited by the sewer. The "seawall," built of solid concrete eighteen feet wide at the base and thirty-two feet high, stretched for twenty riverfront blocks, from S.W. Jefferson to N.W. Glisan Street.[90]

Westside civic groups soon urged the council to improve the waterfront even further, but Mayor Baker declared that they should not

Portland's waterfront was a smelly repository for debris and sewage before rotting old docks were torn out to make way for a massive harborwall and interceptor sewer project in 1928. (City of Portland Archives photo)

promote any such plan because they had "fathered" too many projects already and did not want "any more babies left on our doorstep." However, the council in December 1929 did authorize five thousand dollars for a waterfront study.[91] In spite of this study, the only waterfront development undertaken for many years was a public market building (later known as the *Journal* building) that would prove to be one of the worst "boondoggles" in the city's history.[92]

An interesting tiff occurred between Auditor George Funk and Commissioner Stanhope Pier about this time. Funk publicly threatened to quit the tax delinquency committee on which both men sat because the committee was not paying attention "to the business of handling millions of dollars worth of property." The committee did not meet half of the time it was supposed to, Funk charged, and Commissioner Pier was usually not there. When a newspaper reporter told Pier of Funk's threat to resign, Pier said, "Good! You tell Mr. Funk that I am generally on the job, but when I am called on to attend to the funeral of my best friend I shall attend the funeral whether Mr. Funk likes it or not."[93]

An outspoken, determined man, Auditor Funk used his law school studies to good advantage. At least three lawsuits were filed against him in his capacity as auditor that went to the Oregon Supreme Court. Two cases concerned demands against the city that Funk refused to pay; the third concerned a measure he refused to put on the ballot. In each instance, the court sided with Funk.[94]

In late October 1929, the New York stock market crashed. The Great Depression had begun, although most Oregonians did not yet realize it. The depression would not bottom out until summer 1932, nearly three years later.[95]

The *Oregonian*'s annual review section of January 1, 1930, presented a glowing picture of city prosperity. Portland had experienced increased automobile sales, bank clearings, income tax collections, postal receipts, water connections, expenditures for public works projects, power demand, telephone installations, new industrial plants, and other successes in 1929.[96] Yet, despite the newspaper's optimism, businesses were now failing, loans were being foreclosed on big buildings, and unemployment was spreading.[97] "Hoovervilles" appeared beneath bridges and in uninhabited areas, particularly along the Sullivan's Gulch railroad tracks in east Portland. Hoovervilles were named in mocking reference to the "do-nothing" policies of President Herbert Hoover. They were shanty towns where hundreds of the homeless lived in hovels built from discarded or pilfered scraps of lumber, boxes, metal, and tarpaper.[98]

The national predicament was put this way by Will Rogers, "It beats all what you can buy with the dollar you haven't got."[99]

❧

In February 1930, a Citizen's Recall League announced a signature-collection drive to recall the entire city council—Mayor Baker and all four commissioners: John Mann, Asbury Barbur, Stanhope Pier, and C. A. Bigelow. As local government officials, the five were handy targets in a depression era. "Stop the non-enforcement of laws, the waste of public funds, the mismanagement of city affairs, the betrayal of public trust, waste and mismanagement of public affairs," the petitioners said.[100] While none of the petitions gained the necessary twenty thousand signatures, the attempt was a forewarning of difficult times ahead. Bigelow resigned in August; Pier was defeated at the polls in November; Barbur lost his bid for reelection two years later; and Mann was later recalled.

The council appointed Robert Earl Riley as Bigelow's replacement. Three months later, former council member Ralph Clyde ousted Riley for the short-term vacancy on the ballot, but both Clyde and Riley beat out incumbent commissioner Stanhope Pier to top a field of ten candidates for full four-year terms starting in July 1930.[101]

The Independent Merchants Association of Portland soon placed blame for the Depression "squarely on the shoulders of the chain store system." Chain stores were "destroying the very economic structure of our nation," the association director said. Five thousand merchants signed petitions to the council insisting that, in fairness, store owners should be taxed "according to the number of outlets each owner operated in the city." The council thereupon passed an ordinance levying such a tax, the first one in the country. Safeway and Piggly Wiggly, with seventy-two and twenty-two stores respectively, took the lead in opposing the tax. Their businesses were "the poor man's stores," they said, because prices were cheaper there. However, both the voters and the Oregon Supreme Court upheld this new Portland law.[102]

❧

The most volatile Oregon issue during the mid-'20s and '30s was private versus public ownership of utilities.[103] Public power advocates fared far better in Washington State than in Oregon, partly because former Oregon governor Oswald West, a popular Democrat, was a paid lobbyist for private power. Public power was basically a Democratic issue, and the Democratic Party and Democratic-leaning newspapers were weak in Oregon. The *Oregon Journal* was the "only large-circulation newspaper generally supporting Democrats."[104]

In February 1931, the Portland city council approved a resolution, by a three-to-two vote, for "The City of Portland to declare itself in favor of a municipally owned and operated power and light system for the City of Portland."[105] Sponsor Ralph Clyde told his colleagues that the city was eligible for a twenty-five thousand dollar appropriation from the state public utility commissioner to study the feasibility of such a system. Clyde was joined by Barbur and Mann in supporting the resolution, with Baker and Pier opposed. Baker said Portland should not take "independent action" when the governor was expected to introduce legislation regarding state public power and Congress was considering a power project on the Columbia River, although neither of these possibilities was to materialize.[106]

The City of Tacoma, in Washington State, had been chosen over Portland for a three-million-dollar factory two years before because Tacoma's municipal power rates were nearly 30 percent lower.[107] Now the firm that undertook the Portland power study reported back favorably, proposing three options by which the city could establish a municipal system, ranging in cost from fifteen to fifty million dollars.[108]

In spite of projected lower power rates and three viable options for implementation of a municipal system, council declined, by a three-to-two vote, to refer the matter to the voters. Not only was the private power lobby strong, but one of the initial three affirmative votes, that of Commissioner Mann, was lost when he was recalled by the voters as will soon be seen. Mann's replacement, A. G. Johnson, was an anti-public power vote.[109] Author E. Kimbark MacColl, writing in 1979, declared: "Today, it seems almost ludicrous to imagine that Portland might have been able to develop a municipally owned electric power system for just over $50 million, or that it might have been able to purchase the power facilities of Portland General Electric for approximately $25 million [roughly 255 million in today's dollars]. The city council had the opportunity at least to place the issue before the voters, but it failed to do so."[110]

The public versus private power issue would be debated for many years, and return in various forms in modern times.[111]

In May 1931, Mayor Baker headed a delegation of twenty-five American mayors attending an international exposition in Paris. The French government paid Baker's round-trip expenses from New York to France. His journey was widely publicized, and was said to have spread the "name and fame" of Portland throughout the world. Baker had been urged to participate by the Portland Chamber of Commerce. At one point, however, Baker caused "what almost turned out to be an international incident: At the tomb of the French Unknown Soldier beneath the Arc d'Triomphe, Baker made a speech. According to custom, one didn't make a speech at this spot. It was a hallowed place in the eyes of the French where silence was golden. But Baker spoke out in true Baker style and for fifteen minutes said what he had to say. He laid a wreath on that tomb, a wreath from Portland post of the American Legion."[112]

Mayor Baker's much-publicized European trip made the front page again in 1932, this time unfavorably. A group of taxpayers sued the mayor for illegal expenditure of city money, arguing that his sixty-five days of absence from the city amounted to a pleasure trip at city expense.[113] The Oregon Supreme Court agreed, noting that Portland's charter made no provision for such an excursion.[114]

Baker had departed the city on May 8, 1931, and returned July 13. While he was still in France, the council passed an ordinance directing the mayor "to remain in Europe for an additional thirty days … for the purpose of visiting other sections of Europe."[115] However, neither the council nor the mayor specified what city business was served by this trip extension. The court noted that municipal corporations had no implied authority to assume ambassadorial relations with another state or foreign power,[116] and directed Baker to pay the city back six hundred ten dollars for the thirty-five days his absence had exceeded the thirty-day limit imposed by the city charter.[117]

"Just another of the things that discourages one from trying to accomplish things for the good of the community," Mayor Baker said when told of the court's decision. "I have never worked harder than on that trip to Europe. … If I had known I was going to lose my pay I would have stayed home." Baker said the money he owed would have to be withheld from his future salary because he didn't have the money available to pay it. Friends had recently offered to cover any required payback by Mayor Baker, the *Oregonian* reported. "Whether those offers will be renewed, no one was in a position to say."[118]

While the mayor was at turns shocking and wowing Europe, the area's northernmost and most beautiful bridge across the Willamette—the St. Johns suspension bridge—was dedicated during the 1931 Rose Festival. County voters had approved a bond issue for this bridge before the Depression started.[119]

The *Oregonian* ran an article around this time that mentioned "rats in the basement" of a Fred Meyer store. The first Fred Meyer grocery had opened downtown on S.W. Yamhill in 1922. Meyer also opened a "one-stop shopping center" in the Hollywood district in May 1931. After the rat story ran, Meyer pulled all his advertising from the *Oregonian* and gave the *Oregon Journal* his exclusive patronage—a move that helped the *Oregon Journal* surge ahead of the older daily in both circulation and advertising revenues. Entrepreneur Fred G. Meyer would continue building his popular one-stop-shopping stores—cash and carry stores utilizing innovative concepts of prepackaging, self-service, and selling drugs, variety items, and groceries under one roof—throughout his lifetime. Not only would the corporation he founded become one of the Portland metro area's largest employers, but 128 "Freddy's" shopping centers were operating in five western states by year 2000.[120]

Another Portland institution, the Jantzen Knitting Mills, shipped "nearly a million dollars worth" of swimming suits in 1930, principally to Europe.[121] At the same time, multimillionaire California oilman Ralph B. Lloyd started acquiring fifty or sixty contiguous blocks near eastside Holladay Park.[122] It would be another thirty years, however, before the famous Lloyd Center would open.

In late October 1931, a lawsuit charged Commissioner John M. Mann with "malfeasance, corruption, and delinquency." Specifically, petitioners accused Mann of appropriating lumber and a motor belonging to the city for his own personal use and gain; "willfully and corruptly" requiring city employees to perform work on his personal property; and allowing employees to convert city property to their own "use, profit and pleasure." The lawsuit was filed under a state law providing that a public officer could be removed for committing acts of malfeasance which "constituted forfeiture of office."[123] While the suit against Mann was dismissed,[124] the publicity it generated undoubtedly contributed to his subsequent recall.

The renaming of streets, and need for a renumbering system, kept resurfacing as a council issue. The city's confusing street names and numbers frustrated everyone, especially newcomers, visitors, and the post office. Federal funds were available for projects of this kind, so the council decided the time was right. In September 1931, the council divided the city into five districts: N, NE, SE, NW and SW.[125] At the postmaster's urging, the council decreed that these geographical designations must be placed before the street names (instead of after, as in some cities), so they would not be inadvertently left off the address. A system of one hundred numbers to a block was established. Roadways running east and west would now be called "streets" while those running north and south would be "avenues."[126] The Willamette River generally separated east from west, with Burnside Street designated as the north-south divider.[127] By 1933, all city street signs had been replaced and buildings had been renumbered, and many unemployed men had been put to work in doing so.

The city's waterfront area had fallen into such disuse and disrepair that the council agreed study was needed. Bartholomew and Associates of St. Louis reported to the council and Multnomah County commissioners on January 19, 1932, that because the city's population was spread so thin, sewers, roads, and water mains were being built too far from the downtown core, causing financial resources to flow to these new developments to the neglect and blighting of the old.[128] The Bartholomew report also addressed past recommendations regarding the waterfront: "Bartholomew ... accepted the [proposed] widening of Front Street but opposed a belt-line railroad. ... [He] suggested an underground garage for 2,500 cars to free land for [a waterfront] esplanade, park, and formal plaza. ... [These] recommendations may seem reasonable to people [today] but the city council of 1932 was unwilling even to publish the report, let alone to act on its suggestions. ... [The plan] faded from public attention because of political neglect."[129] In cities like Portland, "the problem is not one of congestion but rather one of how much can we afford to spread out," Harland Bartholomew warned.[130]

In April 1932, recall petitions were filed against Mayor Baker and commissioners John Mann and Earl Riley. The same day the recall petitions were filed, a circuit court trial for malfeasance and negligence had begun against Baker, Mann, Riley, city engineer Olaf Laurgaard, and contractor C. Lee Wilson. For four months, a grand jury had investigated the planned public market on the waterfront, a new edifice that was to replace the popular, but congested, farmers' market at Fifth and Yamhill.[131] Indictments against the three elected officials alleged that they had taken bribes and had paid two hundred thousand too much for the waterfront site.[132]

Although the indictments against all five men were dismissed, the prospect of a trial had cast a dark cloud over upcoming elections. But none of this stopped construction of the grandiose municipal market. The machinery had already been set in motion. Federal Reconstruction Finance Corporation (RFC) funds had been approved. Commitments had been made, contracts signed. Construction of the public market began during Mayor Baker's last month in office, June 1933.[133]

The petition against Riley failed to gain the necessary signatures, but the other two succeeded. Auditor Funk set a recall election date and gave Baker and Mann the required five days specified by charter to resign. Both declined to do so.[134] The recall petition against Mayor Baker said that by his "failure to enforce the laws against various social evils … he has given aid and comfort to denizens of the underworld and to official graft and corruption connected therewith. His solicitude for the public utilities has been evidenced by his tactics of obstruction." The petition against Commissioner Mann claimed that he had "used his position of trust as a means of private profit. … His acts of malfeasance have been numerous, open and unashamed. … Clean, honest and efficient management of civic affairs demand his immediate removal."[135]

Baker asserted that a grand jury had spent four months investigating "every phase of these charges of underworld graft" and found nothing. As for public utility matters, his voting record "disproved this charge." John Mann's official response railed against the "vague, general and unspecific" reasons given for his recall, and labeled the recallers "an unscrupulous group of self-seeking malcontents and schemers" who were angry because Mann had "refused to bow to" their wishes, coercion, threats and demands.[136]

By nearly a two-to-one vote, John Mann was recalled in May 1932 after fifteen years of service. Mayor Baker survived his recall, although 47 percent of the 82,500 citizens who went to the polls voted to remove him from office[137]—hardly a soaring mandate for a mayor whom some historians have painted as one of Portland's most popular mayors.

The council chose a Harvard-educated engineer named Albert G. Johnson to fill Mann's vacant seat until the next election.[138]

The Mann recall and Baker's near-recall must have stifled council ambitions, because not a single past or present council member sought the mayor's seat when Baker announced he would not seek reelection.

Fifteen mayoral candidates surfaced, including county commissioner Frank Shull, a young lawyer named Joe Carson, and communist Dirk DeJonge (whose 1934 suit regarding the right of peaceable assembly and of free speech would eventually win in the U.S. Supreme Court).[139] In a close election, newcomer Joe Carson was the man chosen for the mayor's job.[140]

In a field of twenty-six candidates, with two seats up for grabs, persistent Jake Bennett and former commissioner Ormond Bean ousted incumbent commissioner Asbury Barbur and newly appointed Albert Johnson, and outpolled former commissioner Stanhope Pier.[141] A significant shift in council makeup was about to take place.

The hiatus between a November election and a July swearing-in was a small matter when council members were succeeding themselves, but the eight-month lag now seemed onerous. To change that for the future, a 1932 ballot measure specified that officials elected in 1932 and 1934 would serve only three and a half years, after which all city officials would serve four years, with terms beginning with the calendar year.[142] The preferential "instant runoff" voting system that allowed second and third choices was also eliminated.[143]

❧

During summer 1932, the council utilized federal unemployment grants to hire four thousand laborers to improve Portland's streets and parks. These temporary employees paved roads in Washington and Mt. Tabor parks, cleared land and planted specimens in Hoyt Arboretum, drained the swampy area of Eastmoreland, and cleaned up the "jungle" between the highway and the river at Benson Park along the Columbia River.[144] Nearly eighteen thousand men had competed for the jobs. By March 1933, the money ran out, and the city started paying the men in scrip.[145]

By the winter of 1932-33, banks all over the country had closed.[146] By 1933, in Portland "two of every three small businesses were behind on their property taxes."[147]

Immediately after he took office on March 4, 1933, President Franklin D. Roosevelt embarked on a program of recovery and reform called the New Deal. Three days later, he declared a national week-long "bank holiday" to allow the treasury department time to examine banks for the soundness of their financial condition and to loan money to those strong enough to reopen. The nation's banking crisis was stabilized by June, but other effects of the Depression were longer lasting: "Portland economic life was in a state of trauma during much of 1933. Lumber, Oregon's largest industry, was "dead." Portland's three largest mills were shut down during the winter months. Wheat prices were far below cost of production, and a cold spell in early February froze out all the winter seeding. .... [T]he welfare rolls exceeded 40,000 people."[148]

George Baker retired in June 1933. At the time, he was said to be the best-known mayor in the world.[149] Some future writers would call him Portland's "most colorful" mayor.[150] He was also nicknamed the "kissing mayor" because of his "over-friendly greeting of womenfolk" visiting Portland. When Queen Marie of Rumania paid a visit, Baker gave her "a pat on the fanny, but she took it in stride."[151] Baker had met eight U.S. presidents—McKinley, Teddy Roosevelt, Taft, Wilson, Harding, Coolidge, Hoover, and Franklin Roosevelt. He had attended 2,500 council meetings and given 8,320 speeches (an average of ten per week) during his sixteen years as mayor.[152]

After he left office, Baker was involved in several private Northwest developments.[153] When he died in May 1941, a hundred honorary pallbearers were named and his body lay in state in council chambers

Erected in 1933 as a municipal market, this two-block concrete behemoth later housed the Oregon Journal *for fifteen years, then served as a parking garage before being sold back to the city for demolition in 1968. Today, both the building site and Harbor Drive (next to the seawall) are part of Waterfront Park. (Photo: OrHi #90827)*

all morning the day of his funeral.[154] "Our George" would have loved those final touches.

July 1933 - December 1940

The city's fortieth mayor, Joseph Kirtley Carson, Jr.,[155] assumed his mayoral duties in the most difficult of times. It was the depths of the Depression, a time of discontent and turmoil, "the beginning of the greatest economic change in the history of the nation."[156] Joe Carson's seven and a half-year tenure as mayor spanned the Great Depression, the 1934 Portland dock strike, and construction of Bonneville Dam (1935-37).

Professor Carl Abbott described Carson as "a states' rights Democrat who worked hard to keep the New Deal out of Portland."[157] Historian E. Kimbark MacColl rates Carson's administration as "undistinguished in both accomplishment and spirit" and writes that it aimed "to please the business establishment."[158] However, a contemporary of Carson's said Carson entered city hall "quite unaware of the huge task he was undertaking," but "did a good job."[159] The *Oregonian* called Carson "the kind of man who naturally was called Joe, a man with a friendly grin on a cherub face."[160] At age forty-one, he was Portland's third-youngest mayor to date in the twentieth century.[161]

Born and raised on a farm in Kentucky, young Joe moved with his family to Hood River, sixty miles east of Portland on the Columbia River, when he was twelve years old. Joe's father, convinced that the upcoming world's fair in Portland would be the "making of this part of the country," took up merchandising in Oregon. Joe finished his schooling in Hood River, playing on its championship high school basketball team. In 1914, he moved to Portland to attend night law school at age twenty-three.[162]

Carson was admitted to the bar a month after the U.S. entered World War I, and immediately enlisted in the army, along with most of his law school classmates.[163] When Joe returned home from France after the war, he ran unsuccessfully for the state legislature in 1922.[164] He then served as a Democratic Party precinct committeeman, and later as secretary of the state Democratic central committee. He twice attended national Democratic Party conventions (1928 and 1932) and played an active role in getting the party to include repeal of Prohibition in its 1932 national platform.[165]

Mayor Joseph Carson, Jr. (Photo: OrHi #104368)

Immediately after the 1932 Democratic convention, Carson announced his candidacy for mayor. His ballot slogan said: "Consolidate functions, eliminate non-essentials, cut all expenses, pay as we go."[166] He proposed cutting the salaries of all city employees, which, he said, had not been reduced in proportion to wages in "other lines."[167]

Carson threw himself into campaigning so heartily that he gave little thought to preparing for the job. Then, between his November election victory and July inauguration day: "Job seekers stormed his apartment and office and he was forced to move. Favor-seekers followed him and the first few weeks after election his rooms became a madhouse. To escape, he took … a cruise to the Orient. Home again, it was the same, so he resolved to see everyone who wanted to talk to him, no matter what the subject. … He has tried hard to study the city hall situation, but the callers took nearly all his time. However, he is gradually concluding his preliminary studies and will know what he intends to do when he takes over the new task."[168]

Carson's army commanding officer, Col. Burton K. Lawson of Cottage Grove, Oregon, had come to Portland to help him campaign for mayor. Carson now appointed Lawson as his new chief of police.[169]

The city council that convened in July 1933 bore little resemblance to the "good ol' boy" character of its predecessor. "On one extreme was

> In late August 1933, a disastrous fire raced through Tillamook County forests forty miles west of Portland. A heavy smoke pall hung over Portland for days, while the temperature climbed into the nineties. The "Tillamook Burn" lasted eleven days, leaving behind a blackened forest. In spite of later reforestation projects, the results of that fire are still visible today along Oregon Highway 6.[172]

the Red-baiting councilman J. E. (Jake) Bennett, described even by the conservative *Oregon Voter* as contentious and obnoxious. At the other extreme was Councilman Ralph Clyde, a strong and persistent advocate for municipal ownership of electric utilities. Joseph Carson … was a special friend of the private utilities and an enemy of organized labor. Proposals for new government programs such as public housing often lost three votes to two, with future mayor Earl Riley joining Carson and Bennett in opposition. The liberal Ralph Clyde was joined in the minority by architect Ormond Bean."[170]

The new council had barely begun its deliberations when a Portland City Club report proposed changing to a city manager form of government. "Portland's twenty years of experience with the commission form of government have demonstrated that this system is basically defective," said the report, arguing that the city manager plan was "inherently superior."[171] The study created a flurry of interest, but ended up on the shelf.

Oregonians overwhelmingly voted to repeal Prohibition in 1933. Prohibition ended formally on December 5, 1933, with ratification of the Twenty-first Amendment to the U.S. Constitution. Governor Julius Meier appointed a committee headed by Dr. William Knox of Portland to recommend how liquor sales should be handled in Oregon. The committee proposed a system, subsequently known as the Knox Plan, that eventually evolved into the state's present structure of state liquor stores and licensed premises.[173]

Even though voters approved six million dollars in sewage system bonds in a special July 1933 election, the bonds proved unsaleable because they lacked general fund backing.[174] The city tried for federal sewer funding the following year, but was turned down because Oregon had already received its quota of federal funds. Next, the council asked the voters to approve sewer bonds *with* general obligation backing, but the voters again said no.[175]

The sanitary condition of the Willamette River was already "appalling" in 1934. A test demonstration in 1937 showed that fish dropped into the river next to downtown Portland lived less than seven minutes.[176] The following year, a City Club investigation of Willamette River oxygen levels found the water dangerously polluted all the way from Portland's northernmost city limits to Oregon City.[177] In spite of such overwhelming evidence of hazardous sanitary conditions, it would be eighteen years after that first 1933 vote before a major Portland sewage treatment plant would be built.[178]

On November 20, 1933, between 8:30 and 9 a.m., a professional auditor who had investigated alleged wrongdoing at the Port of Portland was shot and killed in his home.[179] Frank Akin had accused the port's general manager, James A. Polhemus, of mismanagement, charging that the port had unnecessarily "lost revenues totaling $8.5 million during the previous 11 years."[180] In public committee hearings, Akin said one of the main reasons the Port lost revenues was because certain customers received reduced rates.[181] But the *Oregonian*, on the day before Akin's murder, insisted these were trumped-up charges and that the "whole Port investigation from the first has smelled of dirty politics."[182] Years later, historian E. Kimbark MacColl concluded, after extensive study, that Akin had been told "to do a hatchet job of the whole Port of Portland operation."[183] Akin's murder was never solved.

"Dirty Liar, Mayor Yells at Bennett," a front-page *Oregonian* headline announced in February 1934. "Mayor Carson yesterday halted in what appeared to be a movement to punch Commissioner Bennett in the nose and called the commissioner 'a dirty liar' in the course of a clash over an ordinance which the mayor declared Mr. Bennett agreed to vote for but which Mr. Bennett killed. … The … clash was brought about over an ordinance to authorize a contract … for the annual city audit. … Several conferences were held over the contract … [and] members had agreed to the terms. … [Bennett's negative vote, which killed the contract for the time being] so angered the mayor that he bit his lips and turned white."[184]

The council's internal strife thus stopped short of violence, but events on the waterfront did not. "One of the least civil and ugliest periods of Portland's history," is how E. Kimbark MacColl characterizes the waterfront strike of 1934.[185] For nearly three months, from May 9 to July 31, Portland's docks were immobilized in a longshoremen's strike, part of a West Coast union struggle to force employers to submit labor demands to binding arbitration. When employers refused to do so, the unions went out on strike.

The Portland Chamber of Commerce sought to break the strike locally through secret backing of a Citizens Emergency Committee (CEC) and Citizens Emergency League. Mayor Joe Carson, as police commissioner, authorized the deputizing of extra policemen recruited and paid for by the CEC. He also allowed several thousand vigilantes to be used as police backups. On July 5, 1934—a day thereafter known as "Bloody Thursday" because of the "notorious police killing" of two San Francisco strikers—employers up and down the West Coast moved to open their ports and break the unions by attacking picket lines. Police fired shots at President Roosevelt's emissary to Portland. No one was killed in Portland, but many men were injured. Only the planned arrival by steamer of the president himself to dedicate the Bonneville Dam site brought waterfront employers to the table. They agreed to submit all issues to federal binding arbitration, and the strike was soon over.[186]

During the dock strike, a campaign had been launched to collect signatures on petitions to recall Mayor Carson, citing his priority for industrial use of Bonneville power,[187] authorization of violence against striking dock workers, failure to reduce taxes as promised, and his appointment of Police Chief Lawson (who soon left the job), who had "three times been indicted for crime by the grand jury of Curry county."[188] The recall effort failed to gain enough valid signatures.[189]

While all this discontent and agitation was occurring in Portland, a book published in New York City laid laurels at Portland's feet: "In temper, like Philadelphia, Portland is solid, strong, venerable, dignified, and self-sufficient. Freeman Tilden once wrote that in order to know how Portland, Oregon, would react in any given situation, it was only necessary to know how Calvin Coolidge would react. But with all her dignity and conservatism and respectable calm, Portland is beautiful. [She has been called] the Cinderella of the Pacific Coast, the loveliest of the sisters and the least appreciated."[190]

Workers for the New Deal Civil Conservation Corps (CCC) and Civil Works Administration (CWA) improved city parks again in 1934. These workers could not be used for routine maintenance, so they built long-lasting trails, bridges, picnic areas, stone buildings, picnic fireplaces, golf course improvements and drainage systems, both in Portland and in Benson and Oneonta parks in the Columbia Gorge.[191]

Also through the use of federal funds, the council renovated city hall in 1936 to provide more office space. Commissioners authorized closing the interior light courts, sealing the windows of the council chamber,

The main entrance to city hall had been moved to Fifth Avenue (above) by the time this 1940 photo was taken. The Multnomah County Courthouse is in the background. (Photo: OrHi #92072)

and removing the stuffed-animal museum. The main city hall entrance was changed to Fifth Avenue, with space on the Fourth Avenue side to be used for automobile parking by city officials.[192] Prior to the renovation, "The lobby was full of life-sized animals, including a rampant polar bear; and all the corridors were lined with glass-topped cabinets filled with relics of the pioneers and of the Indians—old pistols, tomahawks, peace pipes, and fascinating collections of arrowheads."[193]

Four candidates challenged Mayor Carson in his 1936 reelection bid: Commissioner Ralph Clyde, insurance agent Dewey Rand, and two others.[194] An *Oregonian* news story summarized the issues and personalities this way:

> Mayor Carson … is campaigning on the issue of a world's fair for Portland and by urging the city to capitalize on Bonneville power. He claims certain financial savings and, last but not least, is a good greeter. He will get the conservative vote.
>
> Commissioner Clyde is acknowledged to be at the helm of the greatest political machine the city or county have known in a decade. He is continually telephoning and writing letters on stationery which bears this imprint:

> "Not printed or mailed at public expense." ... Clyde ... advocates public ownership and municipal power from Bonneville.[195]

Candidate Dewey Rand insisted that a world's fair would be too costly, that the mayor knew about vice conditions and payoffs in the city, and that the mayor was claiming financial savings for which the public itself was responsible.[196] But Carson's opponents made little headway against popular Joe. Both Mayor Carson and Commissioner Bean each received over 50 percent of the primary vote and were spared general-election campaigns.[197] Incumbent Jake Bennett was forced into a November runoff after seven candidates filed against him, but he won the runoff handily.[198]

Portlanders now made history by electing Nan Wood Honeyman to Congress in an upset campaign victory.[199] Honeyman was Oregon's first congresswoman and the only new woman seated in the seventy-fifth Congress of 1937-39. The daughter of lawyer-poet C. E. S. Wood, Honeyman represented east Portland's Third District for only one term before being defeated for reelection.[200]

At the same 1936 election, Portland voters agreed that future candidates for city office should limit their campaign expenditures to 15 percent of the yearly salary for that office in the primary election, and to another 10 percent of that salary in the fall election. Itemized statements of campaign contributions and expenditures would have to be filed with the city auditor under oath.[201]

The mighty Bonneville Dam on the Columbia River forty miles east of Portland was now completed. The eighty-two million dollar federal project (or one billion in today's dollars), over three years in the building, was seen as government waste by some—a vast oversupply of unneeded electricity. Unlike many other dams, Bonneville had nothing to do with irrigation; its purposes were to generate electricity, put unemployed men to work, and control the devastating floods that rampaged after winters of heavy snow in the mountains. President Franklin Roosevelt came to Oregon to dedicate Bonneville Dam on September 18, 1937, and on the same day, also dedicated Timberline Lodge.[202]

By the time the president's motor cavalcade reached Portland for a parade through downtown streets that afternoon, the party was behind schedule, hurrying to make a train connection in Vancouver. Consequently, the crowds that thronged Portland's streets caught only a brief glimpse of Franklin and Eleanor as they sped through town in an open car.[203]

Even before the dam was finished, the contentious question of rates to be charged for various classes of electricity engendered furious lobbying in both Portland and Washington, D. C. The Bonneville Power Act passed by Congress in 1937 was not as far-reaching as a proposed Columbia Valley Authority that would have given the Bonneville Power Administration (BPA) authority to acquire privately owned utilities.[204] Still, the act was "one of the most striking pieces of social legislation in the history of the United States."[205] The act specified that the BPA should "give preference and priority to public bodies and cooperatives."[206] The proposed Columbia Valley Authority had been so controversial that a Portland City Club report on the subject was shelved as just "too hot a potato."[207]

"Good-bye to Bachelor Days," chirped an *Oregonian* headline of June 1937 when Mayor Joe Carson took marriage vows for the first time at age forty-five.[208] In doing so, Carson became the third Portland mayor to be married while in office.[209]

The public versus private power debate came to a head in May 1940, with a ballot measure to create a Public Utility District (PUD) that would buy out Portland's private electrical companies. A like measure appeared in nearly every county in Oregon. "Liberal activists like journalist Richard Neuberger and consumer groups like the Oregon Grange supported PUDs with the expectation of lower rates. … With the Northwest Electric Company [later Pacific Power and Light] and Portland Electric Power [later Portland General Electric] in the lead, the state establishment (including mayor businesses and the *Oregonian*) worked especially hard to defeat the Portland PUD, which would be the essential link in a statewide public power system."[210]

The Portland measure failed decisively, with only 24,729 votes for and 57,964 against. The vote represented a "crushing defeat for public control of electric power."[211] Because three members—a majority—of city council members vigorously opposed municipal ownership of power facilities, the council missed the opportunity to provide leadership that could have established a municipal power system for Portland ratepayers at low cost.[212]

Commissioners Clyde and Bean pushed for creation of a local housing authority so the city would be eligible for 90 percent federal matching funds under the U.S. Housing Act of 1937. They cited a 1934 U.S. Department of Commerce study showing six thousand Portlanders living in 1,372 dwellings "unfit for human habitation," and urged fellow council members to see conditions for themselves. After months of debate, Mayor Carson, Commissioner Riley, and Commissioner Bennett, although they opposed creation of a housing authority, agreed to refer the proposition to a vote of the people, where it was roundly defeated.[213]

Three months later, Commissioner Bean took Mayor Carson and Commissioner Riley on a tour of substandard housing. They saw "rooms with little if any ventilation, kitchens with wood stoves but no water, buildings with 30 or more families using one toilet, families living in 20 foot square confinement, and garbage piled high on fire escapes." The *Journal* headline said, "Slum Squalor Shocks Council."[214] This publicity brought passing embarrassment, but no change of heart to the council majority.

Portland therefore lost out on a good deal of federal funding that was available for the asking in the 1930s. E. Kimbark MacColl calls this "dramatic failure to achieve federal funding and loans for its various public works projects" an indictment to be laid squarely on the shoulders of Joe Carson, Earl Riley, and Jake Bennett,[215] the same public officials who had opposed a municipal power system.

An urban planner-philosopher of national repute named Lewis Mumford gave Oregonians a passionate wake-up call in 1938.[216] In an address before the Portland City Club, Mumford chastised Oregonians for their failure to protect the state's natural resources, specifically citing the Columbia River. Industrial parks needed to be developed "not immediately on the river," he said, and new areas designed for this purpose before all available land disappeared. "Neglect of this," Mumford said, "is nothing short of a public disgrace."[217]

In a pamphlet Mumford wrote about his Oregon visit, he called for strong *regional* planning, a concept that would not gain favor in Oregon for another thirty years. Portland had been short-sighted, Mumford said, concentrating "too much attention on its own growth" and not enough on the region. He scorned those who took the two paths of least resistance—the "congestion-for-profit school" or the "spread-to-everywhere school."[218] Of freeways, Mumford said, "Instead of curing congestion, they widen chaos."[219]

Not long thereafter, Ormond Bean resigned his council seat to serve as Oregon Public Utilities Commissioner under Governor Charles Sprague.[220] The council appointed printer William A. Bowes to fill the vacant city commissioner position, thus launching a thirty-year council career for Bowes, who was to make city hall the focus of his life until his death in 1969.

Two major transportation projects received a good deal of publicity during Mayor Carson's last year in office, one a beginning and the other a completion. The beginning was that of Harbor Drive, a six-lane expressway along the seawall with underpasses at all four bridges that required seventy-nine buildings and houses to be razed before construction took place. The state highway commission paid 2.8 million dollars of the cost (nearly 70 percent) and Portland taxpayers funded the remaining one and a quarter million dollars.[221] The project included a concrete esplanade along the top of the seawall and a "narrow strip of park land" between Front Avenue and Harbor Drive.[222]

A new airport was dedicated on October 13, 1940. The DC-3 twin-engine airplanes of the mid-thirties had made the Swan Island airport obsolete. The marshy seven hundred-acre site east of the city, on which today's Portland International Airport stands, required dredged materials from the nearby Columbia River to make building there possible. According to a Port of Portland history, "It took four years, $3 million and the assistance of the Works Progress Administration" to complete construction of this new Portland-Columbia Airport.[223]

Meanwhile, in Central Europe, a madman named Adolf Hitler was waging a lightning war *(blitzkrieg)*. Great Britain and France had declared war on Germany in September 1939 after Hitler invaded Poland. By the end of 1940, Germany had occupied Austria, Czechoslovakia, Poland, Denmark, Norway, Belgium, Luxembourg, The Netherlands, and France. The first local awakening to this gigantic struggle reached Portland through Henry J. Kaiser of Spokane, Washington, who had contracted with the British to build thirty-one cargo ships. With encouragement from the Portland Chamber of Commerce and key businessmen, but little or no involvement by the mayor or council, Kaiser chose Portland as his site for building these ships. The dock commission quietly agreed to sell Kaiser eighty acres of land it owned in St. Johns, a Kaiser site that would eventually expand to over three hundred acres.[224]

Joe Carson did not seek reelection at the end of his eight years as mayor, perhaps on the assumption that the United States would soon be drawn into another global war. He volunteered again for World War II military service and returned to Portland as a lieutenant colonel. He then took up the private practice of law. In 1947, President Harry Truman named Joe Carson a U.S. maritime commissioner, in spite of resistance to his nomination by some labor unions.[225] Carson served on the commission for three years,[226] then practiced law in Washington, D. C. for a few years before returning to Oregon.[227] He was an unsuccessful candidate for Oregon governor in 1954.[228]

Chapter 21

World War II, More Vice, and No Sin Lee

January 1941 – December 1952

Mayors

No. 41: Jan 1941 — Dec 1944

(Robert) Earl Riley (elected for four-year term)

Jan 1945 — Dec 1948

(Robert) Earl Riley (elected for four-year term)

No. 42: Jan 1949 — Dec 1952

Dorothy McCullough Lee (elected for four-year term)

At the beginning of 1941, U.S. entry into World War II was still a matter of debate. Nazi forces occupied Paris; Londoners suffered nightly air raids; Franklin Roosevelt sought possible ways to aid the Allies. Henry J. Kaiser and his son, Edgar, announced publicly in mid-January that they had acquired eighty-seven acres in north Portland on which to build Liberty ships, starting immediately.[1]

Mayor Earl Riley had won an acrimonious campaign over attorney Frank Hilton, who attacked council member Riley as a "friend of both the 'over-world' and the underworld."[2] "Until 1939, Frank Hilton said, forty brothels with neon signs had advertised their business on the blocks between the business district and Union Station, operating as 'boarding houses' under licenses issued by Riley's city bureau. Although the lights had come down, Hilton and his supporters in the Ministerial Association were convinced that it was business as usual in the city's seedy hotels and back alleys, and … managed to get Riley into a run-off election."[3]

Hilton's crusade was not strong enough to overcome Riley's support base, however, and Riley won by a 2 1/2 percent margin. In the same November election, pharmacist Fred Peterson ousted "curmudgeon's curmudgeon" Jake Bennett in a close contest for Bennett's city commission position.[4] Kenneth L. Cooper won an eighteen-way, winner-take-all election to fill Riley's council seat (the position had been placed on the ballot in case Riley won his race for mayor). Cooper, who

Mayor Earl Riley. (Photo: OrHi #55800

had been a member of the vigilante committee seeking to break the 1934 dock strike, captured a scant 15 percent of the vote,[5] thus winning a council seat by the lowest percentage ever recorded.[6] Cooper was a former gridiron star at Oregon Agricultural College in Corvallis and a World War I veteran who had organized the Oregon Veteran's Bureau after the war.[7]

Commissioner Ralph Clyde now became the lone remaining council voice for a progressive agenda, with Mayor Riley and Commissioner Bowes solidly in the conservative camp, and Fred Peterson and Kenneth Cooper likely to join them. Former Multnomah County auditor Will E. Gibson now occupied the city auditor's chair, having been elected to that position after the death of George Funk in 1938.[8]

❧

Earl Riley was the first and only native-born Portlander to serve as mayor during the city's first one hundred fifty years. In 1929, Mayor Baker had appointed Riley to the city civil service commission, and a year later, the council had chosen him to fill C. A. Bigelow's vacant council seat. Riley's father was a captain in the Portland Fire Bureau[9] and his grandfather had helped build the original Canyon Road.[10] Riley's background included work as a newsboy, attendance at Oregon State College, military service in World War I, and business connections to general contracting as well as auto, trucking, and machine shop businesses. He was a partner in a Portland tire shop when he was appointed to the council. Perhaps taking a cue from George Baker, Riley belonged to nearly every organization in town: the Masons, Rotary, Lions, Grange, Woodmen, Moose, Pythian, NAACP, Optimists, American Legion, Multnomah Athletic Club, Shriners Hospital for Crippled Children (a major interest for Riley), two Commercial Clubs, two golf clubs, and many more.[11]

Riley was a capable administrator who "disliked public intervention in the private economy, opposed public housing, and showed little interest in land-use planning."[12] E. Kimbark MacColl says of him: "'Business as usual' was the guiding theme of the mayor's office during the 1940s. Leadership was defined in narrowly selfish terms: Give the people—usually one's friends—what they want. ... Mediocrity and indifference at the top produced equally mediocre and indifferent enforcement of the law, particularly in matters related to vice. ... The double standard of public morality that selectively enforced the law infected the standards of private morality that governed business and financial affairs."[13]

Folk balladeer Woody Guthrie, who was living in Los Angeles, was hired to compose lyrics about Bonneville and Grand Coulee dams.[14] In Oregon, Guthrie was assigned a chauffeur-driven government car to travel the nearly five hundred miles between the two dams and to visit the Washington and Oregon countrysides. In thirty days, Guthrie wrote lyrics for twenty-six songs, for which he was paid a month's salary by the Department of Interior.[15] One of his songs—"Roll On, Columbia, Roll On," parts of which are based on the music of "Good Night, Irene"—became an enduring hit.[16] Two memorable lines of the song proclaimed: "Your power is turning our darkness to dawn/So roll on, Columbia, roll on!"[17] In 1941, little thought was given to the long-term impact of these dams on the environment. The prevailing view of nature was "as servant and handmaiden to humankind."[18]

The *Star of Oregon*, Portland's first Liberty Ship, was launched with appropriate ceremony from the Kaiser shipyard in September 1941.[19] Long before the ship hit the water, a housing shortage had developed in

> Several invaluable Oregon history projects undertaken by the Works Progress Administration with local sponsors were published in 1940 and 1941, including a thirty-page history of Portland that was researched through the WPA Writers' Program.[21] Several histories prepared under WPA grants were used in the preparation of this book.[22] Archival inventories were compiled for every Oregon county,[23] along with indexes of such resources as the *Oregon Spectator* newspaper (1846-54)[24] and a guide to the manuscript collections of the Oregon Historical Society.[25]

Portland. The vacancy rate had fallen from 6 percent to 2 percent, with the flood of new workers and their families just beginning. In 1941, the number of new Portland and Multnomah County residents was almost double that of the entire previous decade.[20] However, the council did nothing to address the issue of housing.

On December 7, 1941—"a date which will live in infamy," in the words of President Roosevelt—Japanese forces bombed Pearl Harbor. Immediately, United States neutrality in World War II ended.

Four days later, the council created the Housing Authority of Portland (HAP) as a wartime emergency measure. Mayor Earl Riley led the effort. His reason for doing so, he said, was to protect the city from action by federal "carpetbaggers."[26] The city was now eligible for a full range of federal housing funds. The newly appointed housing authority began debating and drafting plans immediately, but little concrete action occurred. Nothing happened fast enough to meet wartime needs, and shipyard workers started leaving town because they couldn't find a decent place to live.[27]

In March 1942, hundreds of Japanese left Portland, "presumably to avoid the newly imposed 8 p.m. - 6 a.m. curfew"[28] and because evacuation or detention was impending. By the first week in May, the remaining 1,707 Japanese and Japanese Americans who had not already left "were removed from their homes … and placed temporarily at the North Portland Assembly Center."[29] By the end of the war, some forty-five hundred Japanese and Americans of Japanese descent from Oregon and Washington had been removed from the West Coast, and placed in inland internment camps.[30]

On June 21, 1942, a Japanese submarine shelled Fort Stevens, a hundred miles west of Portland, near Astoria on the Oregon Coast.[31] Fortunately, the submarine was out of range and the seventeen shells fired caused little damage. However, the incident gave Portlanders a heightened sense of vulnerability. As a leading shipbuilding center, Portland was a logical target for bombing. As it turned out, Fort Stevens would be the only target of such a shelling during the war, and gained the distinction of being "the only mainland installation on the continental U. S. to be fired on since the war of 1812."[32] That August, with neither HAP nor council involvement, Edgar Kaiser announced plans to build a gigantic Portland housing project of six thousand units (soon increased to ten thousand) on a square mile of Columbia River floodplain just north of the Portland city limits. Tenants started moving in four months later. A total of 9,942 houses and apartment units were built, eventually occupied by an estimated forty-two thousand men, women, and children, making Vanport the "largest wartime housing project in the United States and the second-largest city in Oregon."[33]

The Kaiser shipyards set a national record for speedy shipbuilding by assembling a Liberty ship in fourteen days during September 1942. President Roosevelt visited Portland to watch the launching of the *Joseph N. Teal*, but word of the president's visit did not leak out until a few days later because of voluntary media censorship.[34] The combination of Kaiser shipyards, a deep harbor, good port facilities, and cheap Bonneville electricity made Portland a wartime hub. After the war, then-president Truman said that winning the war "would have been impossible" without the hydroelectric power provided by Grand Coulee and Bonneville dams.[35]

Thousands of recruits thronged to Portland for work in the St. Johns Kaiser shipyards during World War II. (Photo: OrHi #68767

> Kaiser workers throughout the Portland-Vancouver region gained prepaid health insurance coverage under a plan that later became the country's largest not-for-profit health maintenance organization. By year 2000, Kaiser Permanente had eight million members in eleven states and the District of Columbia.[39]

War activities pervaded every aspect of Portland life. Industrial workers came from all over the country to fill high-paying jobs, and they needed food, clothing, shelter, transportation, entertainment—a complete array of services. Women, minorities, and teenagers were sought after in the job market as never before. Rosie the Riveter was a fact of life. Teenagers helped roll bandages for the Red Cross, worked in restaurants, grocery stores, gas stations, and the fields, and gathered scrap metal, paper, rubber, tinfoil, and grease for war uses by bicycle and on foot.[36] Retailers collected ration coupons for sugar, coffee, meat, gas, and shoes, though some citizens had hoarded sugar and coffee and other staples before rationing began. "Sixth Avenue between the Portland Hotel and what was then called the Pioneer Postoffice was 'victory center' during World War II. Every noon huge crowds would fill the street to hear a famous entertainer or war hero give a pep talk for war bonds or the scrap metal drive."[37]

The Portland Park Bureau expanded its recreation program "to increase the morale and reduce the absenteeism of workers in the war industries." Juvenile delinquency rose because children lacked supervision, and because "consistent blackouts meant evening sports could not be played."[38]

The boilermakers' and shipbuilders' unions strongly resisted hiring African Americans, which created a big problem for the Kaisers. The impasse was broken only by a federal executive order of May 27, 1943, forbidding discrimination in war industry employment based on "race, creed, color, or national origin."[40] Even so, the closed-shop boilermakers' union (which had mushroomed from one hundred seventy-five members before the war to more than fifty thousand) stalled its compliance with the order to keep blacks relegated to lower ranks.[41]

Portland's long pattern of discrimination against blacks and other minorities was continued in wartime housing.[42] A staff memo spelled out HAP's policy: "It has always been our impression that the [HAP] Commissioners' desire in the matter of housing Negroes was to segregate them, and this policy has been followed by the staff from the beginning."[43] This segregation policy was adhered to at Vanport, as well as at Guild's Lake, Portland's second-largest temporary housing project.[44]

In 1943, the prestigious City Club admitted its first black member, the distinguished physician Dr. DeNorval Unthank who had founded the local Urban League and for whom a city park was later named.[45] At the time of his admission to the City Club, however, three members of the board voted against welcoming Unthank into the club on grounds that it would "hurt the club." The membership was polled, with one hundred sixty-six members voting in favor of admitting Unthank and forty-seven against.[46]

The following year, a national Urban League official called Portland "the most prejudiced [city] in the west," a place that discriminated "just like any Southern town." While Mayor Riley was a strong segregationist, he admonished his fellow citizens that the city needed to "forget some of [its] previous ideals" in the name of patriotism and wartime exigencies.[47]

By war's end, Portland's African-American population had grown from an estimated two thousand before the war to around twenty-one thousand—a ten-fold increase.[48]

On August 15, 1943, Commissioner Ralph Clyde, with more than sixteen years of city council service to his credit, died. The council appointed Clark D. Van Fleet in his place. However, Van Fleet's residence turned out to be 150 feet outside the city limits, so he was ineligible to serve. He therefore set a record for brevity of council tenure—two days.[49] Dorothy McCullough Lee, a long-time state legislator, was then named to fill Clyde's seat. She was nominated by Commissioner Fred Peterson, a recommendation he would later come to rue. Lee closed her private law practice, gave up her state senate position, and became the first woman to serve on the city council.[50] About the same time, the council granted Auditor Will Gibson extended military leave and named John O. Bredemeier acting auditor in Gibson's two-year absence.[51]

Portland's economic base had now undergone substantive change, with 50 percent of the population employed in industry, as compared to 17 percent before the war. In 1943, to address problems and opportunities arising from this shift, the council appointed the Portland Area Postwar

Development Committee (PAPDC), a group which included no blacks or women, even though Portland's mainstream work force had been dramatically altered by their addition. "The chief power and influence [of PAPDC] resided in six people: [David] Simpson, [L. T] Merwin, E. C. Sammons, Harry Banfield, Chester A. Moores and Aaron Frank. These men literally ran the city of Portland. … Mayor Earl Riley seldom made a move without consulting Meier & Frank president Aaron Frank. When Frank would return to the city from a business trip, he would call Riley's office and inform the secretary, 'I'm back in town.'"[52]

The PAPDC hired Robert Moses, New York City's nationally heralded Park Commissioner,[53] to draw up a plan for local postwar public works projects.[54] The PAPDC in turn persuaded the school board, city, county, Port of Portland, and Docks Commission to share the one hundred thousand dollar cost—a million of today's dollars—of hiring Moses and his team.[55]

"Portland Improvement," the resulting Moses plan, was widely circulated and endorsed by both Portland daily newspapers and the City Club. The plan called for spending sixty million dollars during the first two years after the war, which would put twenty thousand men to work. Moses proposed building a freeway loop around the downtown core, a loop which would eventually be built, though in tighter configuration, as interstate highways I-5 and I-405. His plan included improvements to sewers, schools, public buildings, and the airport; upgrading of parks and streets; and constructing more highways outside the city. A twenty-block civic center in the vicinity of city hall and the county courthouse was part of the proposal, as were a modern railroad depot to replace Union Station and waterfront landscaping. Commissioner Bowes promoted the Moses plan in a radio address, presenting the proposal as one that would provide Portland the opportunity "to build the wartime boom into permanent prosperity."[56]

Some Portlanders were later to blame Moses for subsequent "excesses" of freeway construction in Portland, but E. Kimbark MacColl insists that "the record does not support such contentions. … All of the freeway routes that were to be constructed in Portland had been tentatively selected by the state highway commission prior to June 1943."[57] However, Professor of Urban Studies Carl Abbott notes that it took almost thirty years for downtown Portland to shake off the notion that big construction projects were the "solution to any problem."[58]

Portland voters gave enthusiastic approval to parts of the Moses plan in May 1944 by approving a twenty-four million dollar package composed of twelve million dollars in sewage bonds; three million dollars in docks bonds; a county roads and bridges measure totaling four million dollars; and a five million dollar special school levy. The package excluded parkways and arterials because those problems were considered too complex for immediate solutions.

At the same election, voters handily returned Earl Riley, Fred Peterson, and Dorothy Lee to council office. An opponent of Dorothy Lee used the slogan "Elect a qualified man for a man's job," but she had established solid credentials with voters when she convinced the U.S. Army to loan the city a bomber to spray twenty-five thousand acres of ponds and sloughs for mosquitoes along the Columbia and Willamette rivers, dramatically reducing the city's "mosquito menace."[59] In the fall, Bill Bowes won his run-off against persistent candidate Jake Bennett.[60]

The following year, Portland voters firmly rejected another part of the Moses plan by turning down a two mill property tax to build a civic center and thereby reduce downtown blight. In 1946, the council again placed a civic center proposal on the ballot, only to see it again rejected. An initiative ballot measure asked voters to choose between the west- and eastside for a civic center site, and the result favored an eastside location by a 4 percent margin: 38,018 votes for the eastside to 34,541 for the west.[61]

Another of Moses' propositions addressed a long-time dream many Portlanders held for a wilderness park. "The City has not taken full advantage of its great natural assets such as the wooded hills and river front," Moses said. "We believe that the steep wooded hillsides located on the westerly border of the City should be in public ownership." Other priorities claimed the council's attention, however, and no action was taken at this time to do anything about those wooded hills.[62]

As part of the war effort, the Forest Service granted Crown Zellerbach permission to cut down timber inside the Bull Run Reserve, contrary to the 1904 Bull Run Trespass Act. This endangered Portland's water supply and prompted a 1944 council resolution urging Oregon's congressional delegation to gain federal legislation that would prohibit further logging in the reserve. Congress, however, declined to do so, thereby supporting the Forest Service logging policy.[63] "While the city managed to stave off large-scale commercial logging within the Bull Run reserve and watershed until 1958, [the city's] stubborn protectionist attitudes inevitably lost ground to the Forest Service's "multiple-use" policies throughout the 1940s. … [S]everal sales of government-owned timber within the Bull Run reserve took place during these years."[64]

> Among other wartime problems, Portland experienced a high incidence of venereal disease. Late in the war, after the military threatened to brand Portland off-limits for service personnel because of VD, the Portland City Club undertook a study of the issue. Their report, issued in January 1945, did not paint a pretty picture. The reaction was swift in city hall. "The hard-hitting report struck a sensitive chord with Mayor Riley and his colleagues. When ... the City Club president ... took the report to him, the mayor blew up. He accused the City Club members of trying to "get him." ... Mayor Riley and Chief Niles, both obviously embarrassed by the expose of laxness, issued firm denials as to the truth and accuracy of the study."[65]

On April 12, 1945, three months after being sworn in for an unprecedented fourth term as president, Franklin Delano Roosevelt died. His poor health and physical handicap had been downplayed to the public. While the nation mourned, Vice-President Harry Truman was sworn in as the nation's new commander-in-chief.

Less than a month later, the war in Europe ended—"V-E Day."[66] Portland's ecstatic rejoicing was restrained only by thoughts of loved ones still fighting in the Pacific, a war even closer to home for those living on the West Coast. On August 6, the United States dropped an atom bomb on Hiroshima, Japan, unleashing destructive power previously undreamed of. Newspaper photos of the event showed a giant mushroom cloud rising high into the sky. On August 9, a second atomic bomb was dropped, this time on the city of Nagasaki. Portlanders breathed a collective sigh of relief that the horror of war was finally near an end. Only later would second thoughts and doubts arise about the morality of nuclear warfare, a spiritual soul-searching that continues today.

August 14, 1945, was "V-J Day." In a frenzy of wild jubilation, Portland celebrated the end of World War II. "Crowded downtown Portland streets went from tense expectancy to joyous bedlam in a matter of seconds Tuesday afternoon, as cheers, laughter, the wailing of auto horns and cascading confetti welcomed announcement of the end of the Japanese war. Electrified crowds surged into the street, as confetti and paper of all kinds, including government forms, rained down from taller buildings to meet the roar that arose from the spontaneous celebration."[67]

An enormous weight had been lifted. The shores of the continental United States had not been breached. Portland had not been bombed. Air raid drills, lights-out curfews, rent controls, price controls, and rationing were now (or soon would be) things of the past. Brothers, uncles, cousins, and neighbors would be coming home from the service—all but the 4,694 Oregonians who had given their lives.[68]

The *Oregonian* of August 15 bespoke another reality: the navy had cancelled orders for twenty-seven Kaiser ships, in addition to the eight aircraft carriers already canceled the previous Saturday.

Statewide, an innovative program was ready for returning veterans—a revolving farm and home loan fund approved by voters the previous year. The program was to prove enormously popular, providing low-interest loans for veterans to acquire housing or farms, and injecting capital into the economy. The loans were guaranteed by the State of Oregon for up to 8 percent of the true cash value of all property in the state.[69]

The aftermath of World War II was harder in some ways than had been the war. During wartime, people had pitched in with patriotic feelings and worked toward a common goal. That goal was now history, and new goals had to be set. For some, the goal was simply to return to normal, even though what was normal would never again be the same. In a 1944 survey, over half the ninety-one thousand Kaiser shipyard workers had said they wanted to live in the Portland area after the war. Nearly thirty-two thousand planned to stay in Portland with or without a job, while another twenty thousand said they would remain if work were available.[70]

The future of Vanport was a divisive question. Some people advocated converting the site to permanent low-cost housing, and Edgar Kaiser proposed building "several hundred permanent dwellings" there. However, Mayor Riley and HAP chairman Chester Moores wanted Vanport to be demolished immediately and the land used for industrial development.[71] Their private reason was simply that they didn't want African Americans staying in Portland. Period.[72] The majority of African Americans who came during the war had "quietly settled" in Vanport, where over 10 percent of the population was black.[73]

In mid-1946, the State Board of Higher Education opened a college extension center at Vanport.[74] After a series of ups and downs, a new spirit of community had been generated at Vanport and the population stabilized at around eighteen thousand.[75]

In July 1947, a citizens' "Committee of Fifty" asked the council to dedicate all public lands in a six thousand-acre area of the west hills for a municipal forest park. The potential for such a park had long been a dream of many far-sighted citizens, dating back to at least 1900 when voters approved creation of an independent city parks commission with power to levy a small annual property tax for parks.[76] Now the council unanimously approved the creation of a forest park to be composed primarily of land the city and county already owned from property tax foreclosures during the Depression.

The city's assessment collection division transferred fourteen hundred acres in Forest Park boundaries to the park bureau as the first stage in the process. The following year, Multnomah County deeded another eleven hundred acres for the park, overcoming various legal hurdles to do so. When Forest Park was formally dedicated on September 25, 1948, additional gifts of land and tax foreclosures had brought the total size to forty-two hundred acres.[77]

By this quiet, unheralded process, Portland's unique and lovely Forest Park ensured that these unspoiled wooded hills would remain as parkland. A fifty-mile network of trails would later be added.[78] This postwar action by Mayor Earl Riley and commissioners Peterson, Bowes, Lee, and Cooper, as well as the Multnomah County commissioners,[79] was far-sighted, and constituted a wonderful gift to future generations. Forest Park also represented a triumph for citizen involvement, for it was the groundwork laid by the Committee of Fifty that convinced the council that this hodgepodge of land ownership could be brought together as a unified whole. "Forest Park ... stretches for seven miles along the flanks of the Tualatin Mountains, the largest wilderness park within the confines of an American city. [T]his park ... [is] rich with a variety of trees—hemlock, spruce, and alder, dogwood, willows, pine and fir. There is also much wildlife—bobcats, beaver, grouse and quail, flocks of mourning doves and on occasion elk and deer."[80]

Two eye-popping reports grabbed the public's attention in early 1948, both dealing with the age-old problem of vice.

The first report was commissioned because of a grisly murder that had occurred the previous year. Three employees of an after-hours club located "within shooting distance of police headquarters" were found guilty of murdering Captain Frank B. Tatum, the skipper of a merchant marine ship.[81] With public pressure forcing some action, council members hired a retired Berkeley, California, chief of police—August Vollmer—to study Portland's police bureau and report his findings. Mayor Riley, who had supervised the police bureau for seven years, reluctantly assented to Vollmer's review.

The "Vollmer report," released in mid-January, depicted the Portland police as "overcostly, underproductive, poorly organized, inadequately supervised and underpaid," adding that it was little wonder Portland's crime rate was above average compared to other American cities and little wonder that the crime rate had increased over the past ten years.[82] The *Oregonian* noted that the doorways of downtown businesses were constantly "used at night as convenient toilets, receptacles for empty liquor bottles and for illicit sex purposes."[83]

A month later, the City Club released its report on law enforcement in Portland and Multnomah County. "No City Club study for a long time has stimulated so much curiosity and aroused so much speculation," said the club's bulletin, "nor has any been awaited more anxiously by a variety of people."[84] Under the heading "Wide Open Town," the report described the current Portland situation: "Gambling, prostitution, bootlegging and other forms of vice have been carried on openly and notoriously throughout the city for a period of several years past. … Gambling and bootlegging "clubs" or "joints" are the habitual rendezvous for a considerable assortment of safe burglars, stick-up men, dope peddlers and other underworld characters, and are a principal field of operation for pimps and prostitutes. … Several police officers … stated that they found it difficult, if not impossible, to enforce laws which they felt the general public was not interested in having enforced."[85]

Vice activities had been operated so "openly and notoriously and on such a scale" that "no police officer or public official competent enough to do his job at all could be unaware of the situation." Furthermore, these establishments were operating under a system of police protection that collected around sixty thousand dollars per month.[86] A chronological list of ninety-five newspaper headlines and editorial titles dealing with vice (dated 1934 through 1945) was included in the report. The main author of the report was a union official named Stanley Earl, who would be elected to the council four years later.[87] A summary of the City Club's previous venereal disease recommendations was attached as a reminder that those problems remained unaddressed.[88] At the time of the original report, Portland had had "the second-highest incidence of venereal disease in the nation."[89]

Much of the protection money collected by police was said to be "skimmed off by Riley and stored in a special vault installed in the room adjacent to his city hall office."[90] The system was "common knowledge among his closest aides," Dorothy McCullough Lee later told E. Kimbark MacColl, a system in which "the mayor got the loaf and two other commissioners got the crumbs."[91]

In the wake of these scathing reports, Mayor Earl Riley met ignominious defeat at the polls three months later. Councilwoman Dorothy McCullough Lee, motivated by the Tatum murder, was the only person willing to take on Riley. She won a stunning victory in the May 1948 primary, eliminating the need for a fall run-off. Her pledge to clean up government and enforce the law found a receptive audience, in spite of Riley's continued backing by the Portland business establishment.[92] E. Kimbark MacColl says of these businessmen: "Few periods in Portland's history have witnessed as corrupt, morally insensitive and generally impotent a mayorship as Earl Riley's, and the business community had to bear some of the blame. By supporting, let alone condoning, such leadership in city hall, Portland business and banking executives revealed a high degree of ethical myopia."[93]

In the same election, Jake Bennett forced Commissioner Bill Bowes into a repeat run-off in the fall by garnering eighteen more primary votes than Bowes.[94]

On a warm Memorial Day weekend in 1948, while Mayor Riley was still reeling from his humiliating defeat at the polls and Portlanders had taken to the beach and mountains for a first joyous round of summer, tragedy struck Vanport City. A heavy spring snow melt was expected to trigger flooding on the Columbia River,[95] but Vanport residents had been assured they were in no danger. When the rising Columbia River breached a railroad fill at Smith Lake late Sunday afternoon, the people of Vanport had scant warning.[96]

"A wall of water 10 feet high roared through [the break], knocking down buildings like a bulldozer, crumbling some, and popping the walls out of others. … One report described showers of spray 50 feet high upon impact with the slough water. … [C]ars were sent careening, houses wrenched apart. … Buildings floated like slow moving giants, sometimes turning in whirlpools being created."[97] Floodwaters quickly destroyed the entire city. Residents received a few minutes of warning—somewhere between 10 and 40 minutes, depending where people were at the time. Without this reprieve, the loss of life would have been even more tragic. As it was, chaos reigned, but most people got out alive. Emergency housing was established at Swan Island, and in schools, churches, community centers, and private homes.

But the flooding waters were not yet finished. Downtown Portland was next: "As the Columbia washed into the Willamette, the river waters flooded through the Union Station and over the railroad yards on the west side of the Willamette. A fifteen-pound steelhead was caught in Union Station. … The crest of the flood struck Portland that Monday, but the sea wall and the temporary dikes which had been built held well, and on Tuesday, the flood began to drop."[98]

Within a few days, the federal government had sent in trailers for emergency use, trailers that HAP placed at Guild's Lake and other locations around town. President Truman personally viewed the ruins of Vanport and approved a ten million dollar relief bill.[99] It took weeks before the floodwaters receded from Vanport completely, and only then was an official toll of fifteen dead reported by the Multnomah County Coroner's office. Another seven persons were listed as missing and never located.[100]

By the time of the flood, approximately 25 percent of Vanport's population of about eighteen thousand was black. Nowhere in Portland was housing readily available to a person of color except the Albina area, so uncomfortable overcrowding now occurred there.[101] "[M]iddle-class Portland by the end of World War II associated public housing with undisciplined war workers and blacks. Vanport in 1946 and 1947 had a whispered reputation for crime, dissipation, and welfare clients. Although the recorded crime rate was no higher than that for Portland, Earl Riley spoke for many citizens when he called Vanport a "great headache" and a "monstrosity." Except for the victims, many of whom were blacks, few Portlanders were upset … [when the flood] swept away Vanport's flimsy buildings."[102]

Rushing floodwaters destroyed the World War II city of Vanport after a dike on the Columbia River broke during Memorial Day weekend 1948. (Photo: OrHi #67766)

Today, the Portland International Raceway and Heron Lakes Golf Course occupy the West Delta Park, an area once the bustling city of Vanport.

❧

In November 1948, Commissioner Bowes bested Jake Bennett by a comfortable margin, and former commissioner Ormond Bean was easily elected to complete Dorothy McCullough Lee's term as commissioner.[103]

Influenced by both the Vollmer and City Club reports, voters gave strong approval to a ballot measure that created a "pay-as-you-go" pension system for police officers and firefighters. The Vollmer report had noted that Portland police received "disgracefully low salaries."[104] The City Club had said that "decent retirement provisions would go a long way toward improving the general effectiveness of the police department."[105] The city's new Fire and Police Disability and Retirement Fund gave uniformed personnel protection in case of accidental injury or death, and extended benefits to their widows and dependent minor children.[106] Benefits were to be paid from an annual property tax levy of between one and two and a half mills, depending on annual estimated needs, along with a contribution of 6 percent of salary by police officers and firefighters.[107] A reserve fund of seven hundred and fifty thousand dollars was to be built up and maintained.[108]

"Pay-as-you-go" meant that Portland taxpayers covered only the out-of-pocket cash paid to officers already retired or disabled. Nothing was contributed toward future retirement costs for current members of the force.[109] Many public employee retirement systems of the mid-1900s, such as Multnomah County's, started out as pay-as-you-go, but were later converted to fully funded systems by spreading the cost of their accumulated unfunded liabilities over a number of years. In such systems, accumulated assets earned interest, dividends, and capital gains, making them less costly in the long run than pay-as-you-go.[110]

January 1949 - December 1952

Striking similarities are evident between Portland's two most reform-minded mayors of the twentieth century, Henry Lane and Dorothy McCullough Lee. Both came to office when fundamental change was sorely needed. Both were loners—smart, well educated, moralistic, stubborn, inflexible, lacking in negotiating skills, and dedicated to the public good. Both ended their elective careers in public disfavor. Their roots were quite different, however. Lane's were firmly planted in Oregon with the "common man," while Lee's were more worldly, more patrician. An only child, she grew up in California and metropolitan areas around the world, and attended an eastern finishing school.[111]

Dorothy Lee was a slender woman, five and a half feet tall. Her father had been a lieutenant commander in the navy (later a rear admiral in the Navy Medical Corps) who led Dorothy and her mother on a "globe-trotting odyssey" to "both odd and familiar parts of the world." Flora McCullough was a "feisty and colorful" lady who passed along her "independent spirit" to her only child. Young Dorothy McCullough received her undergraduate and law degrees from the University of California at Berkeley, then moved to Portland the following year when her fiancé of four years, engineer W. Scott "Scottie" Lee, was transferred there in 1924 by his employer, Standard Oil.[112]

Local law firms offered her stenographer work, but would not consider hiring a woman practitioner, so Lee set up a small private legal practice and joined a few women's clubs.[113] Two years after her arrival in Portland, she threw her hat in the ring as a Republican candidate for the Oregon legislature. Out of a field of forty-six candidates, she came in twenty-second, her first political loss. Two years after that, however, she placed third and won a House seat at a time when all Multnomah County legislative candidates ran at large. Her success was noteworthy:

The 1949-50 city council, left to right: Ormand Bean, Kenneth Cooper, Mayor Dorothy McCullough Lee, Fred Peterson, William Bowes. (Photo: OrHi #CN008915)

only one woman had previously represented Multnomah County in the legislature, and no woman had served in the Oregon legislature for the past three years.

After two terms in the Oregon House of Representatives, Lee was elected to the Oregon Senate. Although she was a conservative Republican, she supported free textbooks, state-sponsored kindergarten, and old-age pensions. She opposed a sales tax and blocked a bill that would have allowed hard liquor to be served in hotel dining rooms.[114]

Lee's second ballot loss came when she ran for reelection to the state senate in 1936. Fellow-Republican Homer Angell ousted her in the primary, the same Homer Angell who would defeat another female incumbent, Democratic Congresswoman Nan Wood Honeyman, two years later. When Angell left to serve in Congress, the Multnomah County commissioners appointed Lee to complete the remaining two years of his state senate term.[115] After that, she was reelected continuously to the senate (with sessions in Salem lasting only about two months once every two years)[116] until her appointment to the Portland City Council in 1943.

As a state senator from Oregon's most populous county, Lee had sought the state senate presidency in 1942 and almost got elected. "The legislators deadlocked; fifteen supported Lee and fifteen supported William H. Steiwer of Fossil. The political maneuvering was frantic. … Behind the scenes those backing Steiwer argued that Lee was not qualified … because that office was next in succession to the governor, and no woman could possibly make a good wartime governor. The voting went on for more than fifty ballots over two days." [117]

The deadlock was broken only when Dorothy Lee withdrew her candidacy after gaining a concession from her opponent that gave her an equal voice in naming committees. Scottie Lee later contended that his wife lost the office of senate president "but won the battle,"[118] although that interpretation seems naive.

❧

No mayor in Portland's history came to office with a more stunning landslide victory over an incumbent than Lee. For every vote incumbent Mayor Riley received, Lee had racked up four.[119]

By winning in the primary, Lee gained seven months to prepare for the mayor's job from the vantage point of a city commissioner. With that margin of victory, that much time to prepare, and a citizenry clamoring for reform, one might expect Mayor Lee to have laid the groundwork for popular success, as Harry Lane had forty-four years earlier. Yet Lee would be turned out of office four years later. Among the forces that contributed to her downfall were traditional concepts about the role of women. The *Oregon Voter*, in its endorsement of Lee, had, in effect, apologized for supporting a woman, noting that "no man of outstanding reputation would make the sacrifice" to run, and the electorate should therefore "Vote for the courageous little woman."[120] Powerful private organizations were closed to Lee because of her sex, organizations in whose meetings important business, civic, and political matters were debated, negotiated, and sealed. "Anything that people did not like" after Lee was elected, says author Percy Maddux, "was generally attributed to 'a woman mayor.'"[121]

Lee was also to misjudge the strength of her vote as a mandate for more than it was. She had little flair for showmanship and lacked the "color and dash" which people had come to expect from their mayor, as the *Oregon Voter* had put it so succinctly in its 1924 endorsement of the ebullient Mayor Baker. Furthermore, the citizenry lacked a common goal or vision for the future beyond cleaning out the stink at city hall. The two vice reports that propelled her into office were soon forgotten, overshadowed by the hue and cry over Lee's focus on "petty" vice.

Lee was a tireless worker who spent hours reading reports and drafting memos. In her first one hundred days as mayor, she set the town on its ear. She switched commissioners' duties, transferred the current chief of police to a night relief supervisor's job, and hired an out-of-towner as her new police chief. She ordered a crackdown on vice as promised, targeting slot machines and punchboards offered in taverns and men's social, civic, and athletic clubs.

In those earliest acts, Lee threw down the gauntlet to all the city's most powerful forces—city council members (with whom she had not conferred over bureau assignments); the police department, by bringing in a surprise outsider; and business, professional, and blue-collar men who enjoyed a little "harmless" vice in the form of pinball machines and punchboards at their clubs and taverns. Slot machines, along with the income they generated, now disappeared from the Press Club, the Multnomah Athletic Club, and American Legion, Eagles, Shrine, Veterans, Woodmen of the World, and Aero clubs. Many of these organizations relied on these revenues for a healthy portion of their budgets. The Press Club, for example, reported fifty thousand dollars in gambling income for 1948.[122]

Prior to her swearing-in, the forty-eight-year-old mayor-elect had visited several other cities and had concluded that "the most effective attack on organized crime would be at its roots, with ... slot machines and punchboards."[123] Lee's attack on vice, therefore, did not focus on the underworld, but on the most visible components of illegal gambling.[124]

Punchboards[125] that awarded merchandise as prizes were legal in 1949, but cash-prize punchboards were not. Lee argued that "having to separate the legal from the illegal was a time-consuming burden for city officials," and sought to make all punchboards illegal.[126] Tavern owners hotly protested, arguing that "the city's crackdown had already cost between 140 and 150 employees their jobs, and some establishments had actually closed." Lee's proposed ordinance failed, three votes to two, at a jam-packed council session.[127]

Sports pools, and horse and dog racing, were legal, however, and Lee expressed no concern about this. When a bogus ordinance to outlaw sports betting was leaked to the press, she was furious, calling it a "clear effort to paint her as a radical reformer in the Carrie Nation tradition."[128] But a radical reformer was exactly what she was. Unfortunately for Lee, a crusading Multnomah County sheriff associated himself with her in the public's mind so successfully that some of his bad press rubbed off on her. "'Mike' Elliott … had been elected Multnomah County Sheriff in the November 1948 balloting. … [He was] supported by gambling interests … [but] proved to be a questionable choice. … Elliott … took to headline grabbing with raids on taverns and confiscations of unlicensed pinball machines … [and] linked his anticrime crusade to Mayor Lee's efforts in the city, calling it a 'Dual Drive on Vice.'"[129]

After the *Oregonian* exposed egregious false claims by "two hundred-pound extrovert" Elliott (who had received a bad conduct military discharge and never attended the college he claimed), and after Elliott fired key employees, turning the sheriff's office into a "circus," a recall effort against him was initiated and supported by both major newspapers. Elliott was recalled on October 21, 1949, after nine months in office. Future mayor Terry Schrunk, a Portland fire captain, was appointed sheriff by the Multnomah County commissioners to take Elliott's place.[130]

The lawyer who had headed up the Elliott recall, Maxwell Donnolley, also initiated a recall against Dorothy Lee. Her recall got nowhere, however, and Donnolley sent her a dozen red roses when the effort folded, with a note saying, "I was only fooling." Lee declined to accept the offering.[131]

Lee was not intimidated by the many threats against her, and publicly chastised applicants for liquor license renewals. When the license of a night spot called the Music Hall came up for renewal the following March, for example, Lee scolded the owners of the Music Hall for featuring female impersonators. She attached a condition to the license renewal that "men who act like unladylike ladies must go," or the license would be revoked. 'These people were run out of San Francisco,' Mayor Lee said sternly. 'They have got to get out of Portland along with the undesirable persons they attract.'"[132]

Lee's predecessor, Mayor Riley, had declined to raise taxes even though the city's reserves (built up through the sale of tax-foreclosed properties) had dwindled to nothing by the time he left office. Therefore, the city was in tight financial straits. The council had passed a 1 percent business license tax to balance the budget in Lee's first year, but it never took effect because a referral petition gained enough signatures to put it on the ballot in 1950.[133] Voters defeated the fee resoundingly, as well as a tax levy proposed by the council "for increased city services." At the same time, the electorate approved a four-tenths mill levy for parks and one hundred fifty thousand dollars for municipal auditorium bonds, but turned down financing for two thousand units of low-income housing.[134]

In January 1950, the *Oregonian* asked Portland's businessmen what factors had most influenced the city's growth since 1900. "Harbor and river improvement" received the most first-place votes, with "hydroelectric power" gaining an honorable mention.[135] Portland had more than quadrupled its population in that half-century, from 90,426 in 1900 to 373,628 in 1950.[136] The 1940-50 decade alone had seen a net increase of 20 percent in population with virtually no annexations.[137] Geographic size had doubled, from thirty-six acres in 1900 to seventy acres in 1950, as the city had annexed and merged with surrounding areas. For the first time, more Oregon voters were registered as Democrats than Republicans. The 1950 Oregon workforce was 74 percent male, 26 percent female. Of the state's 1.5 million people, 98.4 percent were white.[138]

Lee received little support from her fellow council members for programs she proposed.[139] While she sometimes had support from Ormond Bean,[140] an example of their differences came in early 1950, when Bean warned the council that the city would "go in the red" by more than nine hundred thousand dollars by the end of the fiscal year if they didn't make a 10 percent cut in budgeted city expenditures. The mayor blocked Bean's proposal, and instead, pushed through a resolution asking for "strict economy," which Bean insisted was "merely a gesture."[141]

Lee is sometimes credited with "revitalizing" and strengthening HAP, the city housing authority, with the appointments she made in the wake

The color guard for the Benson High School band carried a new city flag in the 1950 Rose Festival parade, a flag created by the school art department so the then all-boys school could compete more "colorfully" with the drum majorettes boasted by other schools. The flag was white, bearing the city seal, with "City of Roses" and "Portland, Oregon" emblazoned across it in "loud, red letters." Lee gave the flag an enthusiastic reception and promised to "adopt it officially as the city's flag by any necessary legal hocus-pokus." Eight years later, Commissioner Bean was to say, "Mrs. Lee may have 'hocussed'—but she forgot to 'poke us' as far as getting official city approval of that flag."[144] Today's official city flag is of soft yellow, blue and white against a green background.[145]

of the Vanport flood.[142] Planning expert Carl Abbott sees her performance on behalf of both housing and planning differently: "The reform drive sputtered to a halt in part because Dorothy Lee was not a credible executive. … [She] failed to effectively utilize her influence on the Housing Authority. She also stirred open controversy and marred her image as a nonpolitical crusader by replacing four of the nine Planning Commission members during her first months in office, but then offered no leadership, no guidance, and no attention to her new appointees, and no new program for the Planning Commission to pursue."[143]

❧

In fall 1950, perennial candidate Jake Bennett defeated incumbent Kenneth Cooper for a seat on the council, a change that would constitute a mixed blessing for the mayor. For while Lee frequently won Bennett's support for her proposals, he was "a Bible-thumping fundamentalist, an avid prohibitionist and all-around gadfly."[146] Council sessions often fell into disorder as Bennett shouted at the other commissioners and Lee had to adjourn meetings for tempers to cool. Bennett's antics helped rob Lee's anti-crime effort of its momentum and credibility. An *Oregon Journal* survey in April 1951 delivered bad news to the mayor. "Whether true or not, the public felt that the mayor was harassing minor offenders while serious gamblers and out-of-town racketeers went unscathed, and that the whole effort had become something of a circus. Furthermore, with horse and dog betting legal, many citizens wondered at the inconsistency of the laws in the first place. … [Lee's efforts] brought only minimal results while housing problems and the city's economic dilemmas went unresolved."[147]

Portland's narrow streets had finally reached the point of impossible congestion. When Lovejoy and Pettygrove had hired Thomas Brown and James Terwilliger in 1845 to lay out the original grid with eighty-foot north-south streets and sixty-foot east-west streets, they anticipated nothing like the stream of automobiles, busses, trains, trolley cars, and pedestrians which now vied for right of way. In early 1950, the council established a one-way traffic grid for downtown.[148]

Lee's study of other cities had convinced her that a strong-mayor form of government would be best for Portland, but her proposal for such a change made little headway. Her only support on the council came from Commissioner Bean, and a 1950 citizens' signature drive fell three thousand short, in part due to lack of support from the *Oregonian*.[149] Lee also tried, unsuccessfully, to outlaw racial discrimination. She convinced the council to create a Portland Intergroup Relations Commission[150] and to pass an ordinance that assured equal rights to all persons, regardless of race, in "public places in the city."[151] However, opponents gained enough signatures to put the equal rights measure on the ballot, where it was defeated by a 12 percent margin.[152]

By the end of her first year as mayor, Dorothy McCullough Lee was named Outstanding Woman in the Field of Government by the National Women's Press Club and awarded honorary Doctor of Law degrees from both California's Mills College and Pacific University in Forest Grove, Oregon. Western Airlines named its new airliner "The Dorothy McCullough Lee."[153]

Her most common nickname was "Dottie,"[154] but Dorothy Lee was known by many other nicknames as well. She was "Portland Portia" to the *Oregon Journal* during a short stint as an interim municipal judge. As a city commissioner, she became "Dauntless Dottie" when she froze more than two and a half million dollars of Portland Traction Company funds after they failed to remove antiquated streetcars that were tying up traffic.[155] *Life* magazine christened Lee "Dottie-Do-Good" in its March 21, 1949, issue, and the "No Sin Lee" sobriquet came after Lee ordered Chinese gambling establishments raided. She was derisively dubbed "Mrs. Airwick" by C. S. Jackson's widow after she refused to meet with Mrs. Jackson to discuss a possible compromise over slot machine raids on private clubs.[156]

In December 1950, after nearly a hundred years of local ownership, the *Oregonian* was sold to the eastern Newhouse chain on behalf of Pittock and Scott heirs for five million dollars, with radio station KGW thrown into the bargain for another six hundred thousand dollars. Samuel Newhouse promised that he would leave the *Oregonian*'s editorial policy totally in local control.[157] He also expressed interest in buying the *Oregon Journal*, but C. S. Jackson's widow and son Philip, the *Oregon Journal* publisher, were not ready to sell.[158]

As Lee was the city's first female mayor, it was inevitable that her family life and mode of dress would receive a good deal of public scrutiny. Lee's husband, Scottie, was her solid supporter.[159] The couple had adopted a son and daughter in 1936 and 1937 after Dottie lost her first senate reelection bid. They employed a housekeeper "who got the children up, cooked and became more or less a part of the family." When the children were twelve and thirteen years old, in September of Mayor Lee's first year in office, the Lees received phone calls threatening harm to their children. They made the difficult decision to send both children to private boarding schools, a decision that would later cause estrangement between the Lees and their children, especially Dorothy and her daughter. The mayor was also criticized for "not educating her children" in public schools at home.[160] When Lee was first elected mayor, she told the press that she was "unable to boil water, that her husband did much of the family cooking."[161]

The mayor's hats were also a subject of idle contemplation. A June 1949 letter to the editor said Lee's hats were "audacious 'blobs' of felt or straw which always seem to be on the verge of falling down over her honor's eyes," and implored the newspaper to either spare the public from so many pictures of Lee or else ask that she refrain from wearing such hats. That letter engendered others. An *Oregonian* editorial by author Ben Hur Lampman called a halt to the flurry by declaring there were "few women in the world who could wear the hats" Mayor Lee wore, but that Lee carried it off with "serene regality" above her "calm yet provocative face."[162]

Lee's chief of police retired in May 1951 after more than two years on the job. As a former Oregon State Police supervisor, Charles Pray had come out of retirement to take on the challenge. He was widely respected for his honesty, knowledge of police work, and clean slate as far as Portland's past police problems were concerned, but the Portland police force had resisted him from the beginning. Pray repeatedly complained that "everybody at the police station seemed to know where gambling was conducted" but him, and nobody would tell him things "that were common knowledge."[163] Lee replaced Pray with insider Donald I. McNamara.[164]

Councilman Jake Bennett faced a recall on the same day that Lee's name appeared on the ballot for reelection as mayor (May 16, 1952). Reasons cited on the official ballot for his recall included these: "[H]e has been discourteous, abusive, uncouth, insulting, with personal, scandalous attacks, insults, ridicule and abuse toward respectable citizens of the City ... he has expressed personal prejudice and hatred for certain of our law-abiding citizens ... he has caused Portland to be disliked and unpopular with the citizens of the rest of the State by vicious, personal attacks ... thereby injuring Portland's business goodwill ... he has attempted to supplant law by his own personal whim."[168]

> During Portland government's one hundredth birthday year, 1951, the venerable Portland Hotel was torn down to make way for a two-level Meier and Frank parking garage, surely one of the worst tumbles from glory any spot in Portland ever suffered.[165] Also late in 1951, television arrived in Portland.[166] The city's first television station, KPTV, began broadcasting as a UHF station the following year.[167]

Because council meetings were now being broadcast over radio station KGW in the evenings (having been prerecorded during the day), the public had heard Bennett's outbursts for themselves.[169] Bennett's official justification for his conduct said:"[I]t would be unnatural and dangerous to have all Commissioners of one mind or to deny them or the public the right of free speech ... Beware of propaganda and name-calling when only one side of the story is told. Their charges against me are untrue and meant to mislead honest persons. ... I have ... followed the dictates of my conscience and fought for what appeared to me to be in the best interests of the public."[170]

The citizenry, at least 58 percent of the one hundred fifty-two thousand who voted, said it was time for Jake to go. He also filed as a candidate for mayor at the same election, but drew only 5 percent of the vote. The council appointed Nathan "Nate" Boody of the Retail Trade Bureau[171] to Bennett's vacant seat.

For Lee, the primary election results brought disappointing news. She received nearly three thousand fewer votes for mayor than Commissioner Fred Peterson, even though she won enough votes to force him into a fall rematch.[172] That fall, Fred Peterson won election as mayor by a 6 percent margin. Lee had paid scant attention to the race, perhaps assuming that the same voters who had propelled her into office would recognize and reward her hard work and good intentions.

Nate Boody, the businessman friend of Peterson's whom the council had appointed to Jake Bennett's seat, was elected to complete Bennett's four-year term. A newcomer named Stanley Earl, running for Peterson's commission seat, received 77 percent of the vote in his fall runoff, thereby becoming one of the few city commissioners of that era to gain a council seat by election rather than appointment.[173]

Voters overwhelmingly approved a two and a half million dollar sewage disposal bond measure, but turned down a four million dollar bond measure for the zoo in spite of Commissioner Bean's warning that the physical condition of "caged animals" at the Portland zoo was deplorable. "The animals cannot get the exercise which is essential to them and normal outside of captivity," a committee sponsored by Bean reported.[174] Also rejected were urban redevelopment bonds and the creation of a transit and parking commission.[175]

❧

When Lee left office at the end of 1952, she was honored for her civil rights activism by the National Association for Advancement of Colored People, and awarded three additional honorary college degrees. She was subsequently appointed to the U.S. Board of Parole by President Dwight Eisenhower, then served for five years as chairman of the controversial Subversive Activities Control Board which ferreted out Communist-front organizations.[176] The Lees lived in Washington, D. C., for ten years. In 1962, Dorothy Lee and her husband returned to Portland,[177] where the former mayor practiced law and taught classes in government and world politics at three area colleges.[178]

An *Oregonian* article written at the time of her death in 1981 says Dorothy Lee "erased the city's reputation as a 'wide open town.'"[179] Many people credit her with breaking the mold from the "good-old-boy," corrupt government of her predecessors to the "clean" political climate of today. Certainly her administration operated in marked contrast to that of Mayors Baker, Carson, and Riley. Historian Paul C. Pitzer, who researched Dorothy Lee's tenure and wrote of it for the *Oregon Historical Quarterly*, summed up the impact of her successes and failures this way: "Portland was maturing … [and] Portland's citizenry became more and more uneasy with the cozy relationship between the city establishment [and the vice industry] … In the long run this trend, more than anything accomplished by Dorothy McCullough Lee, changed the nature of Portland. The mayor served the city by providing for four years positive support on which those trends could build."[180]

"She was a real lady," Governor Tom McCall said of Dorothy McCullough Lee. "But she had an iron will. … She sanitized the city, and she was kicked out in the next election. People don't want a perfect city."[181]

Chapter 22

An Exposé, Sixties Turmoil, and a Visionary Plan

January 1953 – December 1972

Mayors

No. 43: January 1953 - December 1956

Fred L. "Pete" Peterson (elected for four-year term)

No. 44: January 1957 - December 1960

Terry D. Schrunk (elected for four-year term)

January 1961 - December 1964

Terry D. Schrunk (elected for four-year term)

January 1965 - December 1968

Terry D. Schrunk (elected for four-year term)

January 1969 - December 1972

Terry D. Schrunk (elected for four-year term)

"Portland needs a businessman" was Fred Peterson's winning slogan in his campaign against incumbent Dorothy McCullough Lee.[1]

Pharmacist Fred Peterson would be the last Republican elected to head the city's nonpartisan government in the twentieth century.[2] Mayor Peterson misread his win over Lee as a message to trash her reforms, much as Lee had misconstrued her landslide victory over Riley as a mandate to clean out every nook and cranny of illegal gambling. But Lee was a harbinger of change, whereas Peterson reached back toward the past.

Peterson, who liked to be called "Pete," owned and operated a drugstore in the Hollywood District for twenty-two years before becoming a full-time city commissioner. Born in Minnesota, he was six years old when his family moved to the Lents area of Portland in 1902. His pharmacist father introduced Fred to the family drugstore business. When World War I broke out, young Peterson was serving in the National Guard and studying pharmacy, and was soon sent to France. There he gained the froglike voice that would become a lifelong trademark by inhaling too much gas after an ammonium tank exploded.

Mayor Fred Peterson. (Photo: OrHi #CN013370)

Back home, Peterson passed his pharmacy exam and settled into comfortable Portland middle-class life. He was a strong supporter of the Shriners Hospital for Crippled Children, and belonged to several Masonic organizations, as well as the American Legion, Elks, and military and pharmacist organizations. At the time of his death at age eighty-nine in 1985, he had been a regular attendee at Portland East Side Breakfast Club meetings for fifty-five years.[3]

The new mayor's political career had begun with a successful challenge to incumbent Jake Bennett for a 1940 council seat. As a twelve-year council member, Commissioner Peterson had gained his biggest headlines by staging an early morning raid on a restaurant supply house that was selling horsemeat. He was rewarded with front-page coverage for this surprise attack on "horseburgers."[4]

The council was now a chorus line of five aging Caucasian males: Nate Boody, seventy-four; Ormond Bean, sixty-eight, who often played a dissenter role;[5] Bill Bowes, fifty-nine; Mayor Peterson, fifty-six; and new commissioner Stanley Earl, forty-two. Council meetings were rebroadcast by radio late Saturday nights, and a Portland State college student of the time remembers listening to the council's roll call echo out of the darkness: "Bean, Boody, Bowes, Earl, Peterson."[6]

The Korean War, begun three years before, ended in 1953 with 269 Oregon casualties reported.[7] At the state level, the Oregon legislature struck a blow for civil rights by passing the 1953 Public Accommodations Law, making it illegal for restaurants and hotels to refuse service to anyone because of race, religion, or national origin.[8]

Portlanders needed a diversion from the postwar doldrums, and it came in the form of an enormous gray-colored bundle named Rosy. The four-year-old Asian elephant arrived at the zoo in September 1953, creating an immediate sensation. Attendance at the zoo burgeoned, and Peterson gained the nickname "elephant mayor" for founding the zoo's elephant herd.[9] The following year, Rosy helped motivate voters to pass a five-year, 1.2 mill levy for building a modern zoo in Washington Park above Sunset Highway.[10]

On the same ballot, the electorate approved eight million dollars in general obligation bonds for an Exposition - Recreation Center (Memorial Coliseum), and six and a half million dollars in bonds to rehabilitate and modernize harbor facilities. That fall, however, voters firmly rejected a transit levy, a ten-year capital improvement levy, and a 17 percent increase in the city tax base.[11]

In terms of housing, it was "dog days, as far as progress was concerned."[12] Peterson packed the Housing Authority of Portland with commissioners who opposed the concept of public housing.[13]

In 1954, construction began on interstate freeways. North-south Interstate 5 was to stretch from Canada to California, crossing the Columbia River between Vancouver and north Portland, proceeding southbound east of the Willamette River before crossing below downtown on a new Marquam Bridge. East-west Interstate 80 (now I-84) was to follow Sullivan's Gulch eastward, roughly tracing the Oregon Trail along the Columbia River to Idaho and beyond.

The placement of I-5 on the east bank of the Willamette River, with a dangerous curve onto the Marquam Bridge, has been cited as one of the council's biggest mistakes of the past fifty years. The I-5 alignment was a state highway proposal, affirmed by a council majority (with Mayor Schrunk and Commissioner Bean opposed).[14] Many people "welcomed the removal of blight" along the east waterfront and few considered how valuable such riverfront property would be in the future.[15] While ships could pass easily underneath the Marquam Bridge without need of a drawbridge after it opened in 1966, and the top eastbound deck commanded marvelous views, the bridge was "almost universally" reviled as ugly.[16]

The eight million-dollar Exposition-Recreation (E-R) Center bonds represented a major triumph for Mayor Peterson. He was so eager to get the project going that he convened an E-R Commission meeting before the council had formally approved his nominees.[17] Peterson spoke to the newly appointed commissioners of their broad authority to act: "It is your obligation and yours alone to determine the location of this facility ... [Y]ou will let the contract. You will be the authority after the contract is let and completed to operate the facility. Your obligation is to operate as you see it to be operated. If you want a manager, this you choose. It is to be free from any so-called political pressure."[18]

Two members of this powerful E-R Commission are mentioned elsewhere in this book. One was James H. Polhemus, former Port of Portland general manager (1923-36), who had been charged with mismanagement and use of his Port position for personal gain twenty years before. The independent auditor who made the charges, Frank Akin, was found murdered on November 20, 1933, and the murder was never solved. In 1940, Polhemus had been elected president of Portland General Electric Company. E. Kimbark MacColl, who examined available Polhemus records, concluded that some of Akin's charges against Polhemus "were indeed valid."[19] The other E-R commissioner whose name would surface publicly less than two years later was that of Clyde C. Crosby, a Portland Teamsters union representative.[20]

The impending coliseum construction pleased Mayor Peterson, who loved building nearly anything.[21]

A newspaper exposé launched April 19, 1956, shook Portland to its core. Two *Oregonian* reporters, flush with success over an Indian land fraud exposé, investigated possible bribery and police payoffs in an alleged attempted take-over and expansion of Portland-area vice operations by the Teamsters union.[22] In a copyrighted series, reporters Wallace Turner and William Lambert laid out allegations against the Teamsters, who were supporting Sheriff Terry Schrunk for mayor over incumbent Peterson in the upcoming election.[23] Other players in the ensuing drama included:

- "Big Jim" Elkins, an ex-convict and Portland racketeer who was the *Oregonian*'s principal source of information;
- Clyde Crosby, ex-convict and Oregon's top Teamsters union leader whom Mayor Peterson had appointed to the E-R Commission nearly two years before;[24]

- Multnomah County District Attorney William Langley (who was the only person convicted of a crime in this matter, but later investigated and reinstated to practice by the Oregon State Bar);[25]
- Police Chief Jim Purcell;
- City Commissioner Stanley Earl;
- Oregon Governor Paul Patterson;
- Oregon Attorney General Robert Thornton;
- *Oregon Journal* reporters Brad Williams, Rolla Crick, and Doug Baker;[26]
- Robert Kennedy (brother of future president John F. Kennedy), attorney for the U.S. Senate Select Committee on Improper Activities in the Labor or Management Field, searching for evidence of labor misdeeds;[27]
- U.S. Senators Joe McCarthy, John McClellan, Karl Mundt, and other members of the above U.S. Senate committee;
- Nationally syndicated columnist Drew Pearson; and
- At least fifty various other characters.[28]

The *Oregonian* articles touched off the most contradictory, convoluted, controversial, inconclusive, overblown, and sensationalized scandal in Portland's history. So many different activities, agendas, and cross-purposes were involved that, even years later, there was no consensus in Portland as to what really happened, or the validity of various charges.[29] The *Oregon Journal* attacked the accuracy of the *Oregonian* stories and undertook its own investigation. The bitter rivalry between the two newspapers produced a good deal of information as a result of their "ruthless advocacy" and circulation war.[30] The *Oregonian* series was to earn a 1957 Pulitzer Prize for reporters Lambert and Turner.

The first *Oregonian* stories were based on "five or six" tape recordings made by Big Jim Elkins, purportedly supporting his allegations that Teamster racketeers from Seattle were moving into Portland. *Oregonian* publisher Robert C. Notson later said the paper's decision to pursue the story was motivated both by the Elkins tapes[31] and by a warning from Howard Morgan, head of the Oregon Democratic Party,[32] that Teamsters were attempting to take over law enforcement and government in Multnomah County, and eventually, in Oregon.[33] The *Oregonian* had also heard rumors of "hanky-panky by speculators dealing in properties being blocked out for Portland's new coliseum."[34]

The staunchly Republican *Oregonian* supported Mayor Peterson, while the *Journal* backed Sheriff Schrunk. Republican fears that the Democrats were becoming too powerful in Portland politics may have been a factor in the *Oregonian*'s decision to publish the series just a month before the Peterson - Schrunk mayoral primary.[35] Even so, Terry

Schrunk bested Peterson by nearly seventeen thousand votes, but fell 2 percent short of a majority, propelling the two candidates into a fall rematch.[36]

On the same May 1956 ballot, a city measure to outlaw pinball machines passed by a 13 percent margin.[37] Pinball machines were devices much like the electronic arcade games children play today. A pinball machine of the fifties released a small steel ball that bounced around until it fell in a hole marked with a score. A flipper controlled by the player could influence the ball's direction. The player who won a big score was awarded a free game, and many free games could be accumulated. Players who fed twenty or so nickels into the machine, one right after the other, could increase their odds of winning. The difference between these pinball machines and today's games—in addition to electronic wizardry—was that in 1956 an attendant could turn a toggle switch and pay off a player in cash.[38] The machines were a vice activity only because they were prohibited by law. "Making desired acts illegal does indeed create crime," noted Joe Uris, a Portland State University assistant professor in his doctoral study of the vice probe. Pinball operations that did not pay cash were legitimate businesses until banned by the council ordinance.[39] Voters also approved—by a bare three hundred and three votes—an initiative petition requiring the coliseum to be built on the east side of the city. Voters handed Commissioner Stanley Earl a four-to-one victory over his challenger, County Auditor Jack O'Donnell, but Commissioner Bill Bowes faced a fall run-off against the indefatigable Jake Bennett. In November, Bowes easily retained his seat.[40]

Both Attorney General Thornton and District Attorney Langley convened special grand juries to investigate charges made by the two newspapers concerning vice in Portland. "It was with horror and a dawning sense of doom that Thornton discovered that much of the *Oregonian*'s famed Elkins tapes were unintelligible to the average listener. … Witnesses were scared. Some had disappeared. Reporters wormed their way in everywhere, even into the Grand Jury waiting room. It was a circus."[41]

During grand jury presentations that summer, an Elkins employee "unexpectedly fingered Terry Schrunk as a bribe recipient."[42] Witnesses said Schrunk had picked up an envelope containing five hundred dollars—the equivalent of three thousand dollars today—in bribe money at the 8212 Club in north Portland. The incident allegedly took place by an outdoor fountain during a late-night raid in September 1955. Schrunk vehemently denied any such bribe taking, and offered to take a lie detector test, which he failed.[43]

All through the summer and fall, the *Oregonian* printed new charges of vice activities and competition between racketeers to dominate Portland's vice scene. In August, District Attorney Langley was arraigned, based on a state grand jury indictment, for "willfully neglecting" to prosecute after he had visited, for twenty minutes, a charity function benefiting the Junior Chamber of Commerce at which gambling had occurred.[44]

The mayoral contest between Peterson and Schrunk grew more heated as summer turned to fall. September headlines blared: "Mayor, Sheriff Hurl Charges Following Raid; Interference in Law Enforcement, Political Trickery Allegations Made." "Portland's mayoralty candidates were at each other's throats Saturday as charges of 'politics' were hurled back and forth in the aftermath to the Tuesday night raid by deputy sheriffs on a gambling and drinking establishment. [Schrunk] accused the city police department of 'destroying our chances' to raid a 'fairly sizable' poker game just outside the city. Peterson accused Schrunk of 'vicious' political trickery."[45] Peterson said Schrunk was "passing-up brothels" in the county to stage a sensational raid in the city. Schrunk responded that the Keystone Club raid had been initiated by the district attorney's office, and that he knew nothing about the planned raid in advance.[46]

In the fall election of 1956, Schrunk trounced Peterson by nearly forty thousand votes to be elected mayor.[47]

The same electorate overwhelmingly reaffirmed the outlawing of pinball machines,[48] a ban that was to last twenty years.[49]

❧

At the end of December, Mayor Pete Peterson left city hall to return to the pharmacy business. For many years, he ran the Grant High Pharmacy. After retirement, he received a city pension of fifty-eight dollars a month for his sixteen years of service.[50] Of his successor, Peterson said, "Terry Schrunk beat the hell out of me. I'd have stayed there for the rest of my life. But I should be glad he beat me. It would have killed me. I will be ever grateful to him for that."[51]

January 1957 - December 1972

Terence Doyle Schrunk was forty-four years old during his first year as mayor. He was to serve for sixteen years, tying the all-time record. Schrunk was the first liberal Democrat (if we rate Joe Carson as conservative) to be elected mayor since Harry Lane in 1905. In fact,

The six elected officials who served during 1971 and 1972 are pictured after the November 1970 election. Left to right: Commissioner Lloyd Anderson, Commissioner Frank Ivancie, Auditor George Yerkovich, Mayor Terry Schrunk, Commissioner Connie McCready, and Commissioner Neil Goldschmidt. (Photo by David Falconer, © 1970, The Oregonian)

Schrunk was only the fourth Democratic mayor of any kind in eighty-five years.[52] This resurgence of Democratic Party hopefuls was echoed statewide in the 1956 election of Democratic governor Robert Holmes. A Democrat was also chosen to head the state senate for the first time in more than twenty years.[53]

"Farm Boy to Fireman to Mayor of Portland," was how the *Oregon Journal* later summed up Schrunk's personal history. A photo accompanying the story showed Schrunk opening a 1961 midget-auto race, with the caption "Virile and Popular Mayor." Born sixty miles south of Portland of an Irish-born mother and Oregon-born father, Schrunk called the St. Johns area of North Portland home from the time he was eight years old.[54] The *1961 Who's Who for Oregon* summarized his background as follows:

> b. Stayton, Oreg. March 10, 1913; … grandparents early Oregon pioneers; educ, public schools of Portland, Univ. of Portland, Univ of Oreg B. A.; … Fire Dept, capt to 1949; apptd Sheriff, 1949; mayor, 1956-; vet, World War II;

> Legionnaire; VFW; mem, City Club, Military Order of Purple Heart, Mult. Anglers & Hunters Club; active, Red Cross, Boy Scouts, Pal Inc., YMCA; Mason; Eagle; Woodman; address, City Hall, Portland, Ore.[55]

Soon after Schrunk took office, the U.S. Senate Select Committee on Improper Activities in the Labor or Management Field subpoenaed him and others to testify in Washington D. C. The hearings, led by counsel Robert Kennedy, were intended to find "a sensational way to excite public concern against alleged abuses by organized labor."[56] Several Portland witnesses were poorly treated.[57] Columnist Drew Pearson summed it up this way: "[S]enate inspired hearings smeared Portland, Or., as the vice capital of the West and made a convicted dope peddler the hero of Capitol Hill."[58]

Two days after Schrunk returned from Washington, D. C., a state grand jury convened by Oregon Deputy Attorney General Arthur Kaplan, later referred to as the "run-away" grand jury because of all the indictments it brought, grilled Schrunk concerning accusations about the taking of a bribe at the 8212 Club. On March 29, the grand jury indicted Schrunk for bribery and perjury, charging that he had lied to them.[59] A citizens' group called "Committee to Defend Our Mayor" organized a fund drive to help pay court and attorney costs. Former Chamber of Commerce president Sidney Woodbury gave two hundred and fifty dollars, with this testimonial: "[I]n the whole United States there aren't enough investigators and lawyers and grand juries and senators … to make a single Pal Club member believe that Terry Schrunk is other than honest, God-fearing, [and] good."[60] An *Oregonian* editorial called for Schrunk to resign.[61]

Schrunk's perjury trial took place during June 1957. By then, several witnesses had changed their stories. Schrunk's attorneys argued that it made no sense that the sheriff would take bribe money in full sight of witnesses. Senate Committee Counsel Robert Kennedy came to Portland to testify during the rebuttal period, but his testimony "added little to the case."[62] "Yet the … young lawyer impressed courthouse observers—Judge Crawford included. As Kennedy rose to leave the witness stand at the end of his testimony, he extended his right hand toward Judge Crawford. The veteran judge of twenty-six years extended his arm across the bench and shook Kennedy's hand as the jury sat watching. In Judge Crawford's chambers, [the defense attorneys]… demanded a mistrial. The next day … Crawford [told the jury]: '… it was purely instinctive reaction and is not to be regarded as any personal or judicial expression of approval or disapproval of the witness.'"[63]

The jury listened to testimony for two weeks, then deliberated for only an hour and fifty minutes before pronouncing Schrunk "Not guilty."[64] Among those watching the trial was Schrunk's fifteen-year-old son, Michael, today Multnomah County's district attorney, a position he has held since in 1981.[65]

Citizens living in Portland at the time still argue the merits of the case against Terry Schrunk. "*Nobody* in the sheriff's office believed the charges, regardless of whether or not they supported Schrunk politically," says former sheriff and county executive Don Clark, a deputy sheriff at the time. "Everyone at the sheriff's office was convinced it was a frame-up."[66]

In all, one hundred fourteen indictments were brought by special grand juries against 41 defendants.[67] The only conviction obtained was of District Attorney Langley, as previously noted, for "neglect of duty," for which he was fined one hundred dollars and removed from office. One madam pleaded guilty to operating a bawdy house and was fined two hundred and fifty dollars, and an organization called the Coin Men also pleaded guilty.[68] A federal wiretapping conviction of Jim Elkins was later thrown out by the U.S. Supreme Court.[69]

Police Chief Jim Purcell had been indicted on charges of "incompetence, delinquency, and malfeasance,"[70] but the indictment was dropped when Purcell left office at the end of Mayor Peterson's term. Attorney General Thornton listed eighteen after-hours, bootleg, gambling, and whorehouse operations that Purcell and Mayor Peterson both must have known about, some of which were located "within a half-block of the police station." Thornton was convinced that payoffs were made by madams, bootleggers, and others through Jim Elkins to the police.[71] While Mayor Fred Peterson was not indicted, *Journal* stories implied that Peterson had been "involved in bribery." The *Oregonian* ignored evidence of police corruption, the *Journal* said, "that could have been embarrassing" to Elkins and Peterson.[72] However, researcher Joe Uris concluded there was "no evidence to indicate that Peterson himself gained financially by the policy of vice tolerance then customary in Portland." Peterson denied that any "policy of tolerance" existed.[73]

Commissioner Stanley Earl's role in the vice scene is even more difficult to evaluate. As the principal investigator for the 1948 City Club study that lambasted Mayor Riley's government, Earl had taken a firm stand against vice.[74] The *Oregonian* later eulogized Earl as a "plain-spoken, stubbornly principled man" who gave material assistance to the *Oregonian* "in exposing a gambling-oriented conspiracy."[75] A future fellow commissioner was to say of Earl that he had a keen mind and assessed problems in a constructive way, but that he had a little problem with the bottle.[76]

Prior to his service on council, Earl had been a CIO and IWW union leader, a federal labor advisor during the Korean War, and a bouncer for Fred Elkins, brother of Big Jim. When Earl first came on the council, he voted to license pinball machines because, he said, it presented a good revenue source for the city. Earl told the U.S. Senate committee that he changed his mind about pinball machines after a working man's wife told him her husband had "lost all his salary in one week" playing pinball.[77] Investigators for columnist Drew Pearson, however, linked Earl's stands on pinball machines back to Big Jim Elkins.[78] *Oregon Journal* reporter Brad Williams said Earl's position on pinball changed because Elkins got shut out of the business.[79] Teamster official Clyde Crosby, who had by this time resigned his E-R Commission position, said Earl was cozy with Elkins and the *Oregonian* reporters, who were all trying to smash the Teamsters.[80] A police officer interviewed by Uris later claimed that Earl was "up to his neck in crooked activities."[81]

National columnist Drew Pearson wrote in an April 1957 column: "Big Jim and his friend, Stanley Earl, are using the McClellan hearings as a publicity megaphone to help take control of the city of Portland." Earl sued the Coos Bay, Oregon, newspaper that ran the column for libel. Earl lost, engendering the following Pearson column: "It has now been one year since … I reported that Big Jim Elkins actually was 'out to retaliate against the elements that knocked him out of the pinball racket' … Last week a Coos Bay jury found Stanley Earl to be a friend of Underworld Leader Elkins."[82]

Besides the Pulitzer, the *Oregonian* series earned other national honors for reporters Turner and Lambert.[83] Libel suits totaling four million dollars were filed against the *Oregonian*, but all were eventually dismissed without payment.[84]

The Senate committee's badgering treatment of Mayor Schrunk and others caused Portlanders to close ranks against those who cast aspersions at their mayor and their city. When Senator Karl Mundt said, "If I lived [in Portland], I would suggest that they pull the flags down at half-mast in public shame,"[85] it engendered a backlash. "[T]he U.S. Senate Committee created a situation in which the local Portland leadership perceived itself as under external attack from outside forces which it saw as far more dangerous than any local threat at the time," says then-graduate-student Joe Uris in his doctoral thesis. "[T]he danger represented by an alleged Teamsters takeover was ended."[86]

Schrunk's long-time friend and campaign advisor, lawyer Ray Kell, said the "negative publicity, humiliation and expense of the trial" changed Terry Schrunk from an "open, easy-going liberal" to a "much more suspicious, cautious, and conservative" person.[87]

An end-note to the drama occurred in 1964, when Big Jim Elkins was convicted of a narcotics charge based on evidence collected by Portland police officer Dick Bogle,[88] the same Dick Bogle who would later become a KATU-TV reporter and whose mother, Kathryn, had written a 1937 *Oregonian* article describing discrimination against her as a Negro in Portland.[89] Dick Bogle would be elected to the city council in 1984.[90]

Schrunk's sixteen-year mayoralty saw enormous sociological change, not only in Portland, but across the nation. Notable national events occurred. Young president John F. Kennedy had barely launched the Peace Corps and authorized the botched Bay of Pigs invasion of Cuba before he was cut down by an assassin's bullet. Schrunk's tenure spanned the time of the Vietnam War; Vietnam War protests; San Francisco Haight-Ashbury hippies, potheads, and flower children; the Peace Corps; the "New Frontier"; a civil rights march from Selma to Montgomery, Alabama, led by Martin Luther King; killing of Kent State students by the National Guard; President Lyndon B. Johnson; the "Great Society"; passage of the Civil Rights bill; assassinations of Martin Luther King and Robert Kennedy; the Woodstock rock festival; Ken Kesey's yellow bus, marijuana, and LSD; ascendancy of the Beatles; publication of influential books such as *Silent Spring*, *The Feminine Mystique*, and *Future Shock*; launching of *Ms.* magazine; introduction of the computer age; referral of the Equal Rights Amendment to the states by Congress; founding of the National Women's Political Caucus and NOW; President Richard M. Nixon; the Cold War; the War on Poverty; and Neil Armstrong's walk on the moon.

Statewide, historic legislation was passed during this period: a Fair Housing Act (1957),[91] the Oregon Beach Bill (1967), and the Oregon Bottle Bill (1971). A crusading television journalist named Tom McCall, who would take office as Oregon governor three years later, produced a 1964 documentary called "Pollution in Paradise" that awakened Oregonians to the ugly contaminated state of the once-pure Willamette River. The Willamette Greenway concept proposed in the late '60s emerged in the 1970 landmark Oregon Scenic Waterways Bill.[92] Governor McCall uttered a now-famous admonition to outsiders: "Visit Oregon, but don't stay." This did nothing to deter newcomers, for Oregon's population grew to two and a quarter million by 1974, a 25 percent gain during McCall's eight years as governor (1967-74).[93]

Portland voters in 1958 approved creation of the Portland Development Commission (PDC) as a "development and civic promotion department."[94] Urban renewal, through PDC, became the central theme of Schrunk's administration.

The South Auditorium Renewal area, where today massive high-rise apartment towers and modern office buildings stand, was a major urban renewal target. The area encompassed eighty-three and a half acres, roughly four blocks wide and fourteen blocks long, from Front Avenue to Fourth, and Market Street to Arthur. The project, begun under Mayor Peterson, displaced hundreds of people from their homes and businesses, and was always controversial. "UR Area Property Owners Hold Noisy Meeting, Plan New Protest," said a September 1959 headline.[95] The city's urban renewal staff considered the area "blighted and economically isolated," and basically unsalvageable.[96] But those who lived in the area and did business there said it was the city's actions that had caused the depressed conditions. "[F]or the past five years, [we] have been the victims of rumor, propaganda, indecision, threats and promises. ... No one could sell, lease or trade property. It was unwise to repair or build. So ... by edict of our city, the area has become the slum that the do-good bunch behind urban renewal so heartily desired."[97]

The project went forward, however, and eliminated an entire old Jewish and Italian neighborhood.[98] The southern part of the area was later bisected by the I-405 freeway loop that circled downtown and connected to eastside I-5 via the Marquam and Fremont bridges. "The eighty-four acres of dilapidated and abandoned buildings, storefronts, and homes of the old ethnic neighborhoods were bulldozed clear and replaced by ... parks, gardens, fountains, office towers and high-rise apartment blocks. Designed by Skidmore, Owings and Merrill, it was a breakthrough in urban design that complemented the natural landscape."[99] High-quality improvements and a "lush and creative" landscape design by Lawrence Halprin and Associates included three large parks—Forecourt Fountain Park; grassy, hilly Pettygrove Park; and Lovejoy Fountain Park—all connected by tree-lined pedestrian walkways.[100] North-south Second and Third avenues were vacated for six blocks, as were four cross streets (for three blocks), thus creating solid pedestrian-only areas in which people could work, live, and play.

Critics questioned, in retrospect, the heavy-handed approach the city used to accomplish all these changes, and bemoaned the loss of a colorful ethnic neighborhood. Don Sterling, former *Oregon Journal* editor, reminisced about the project in year 2000: "Many say that you couldn't build the South Auditorium Renewal Area today the way it was built in the '60s. ...[Y]ou couldn't go in and bulldoze a neighborhood and lay it flat. But I don't know what we would have gotten [if that hadn't been done.] I don't know that we would have been smart enough to reinforce the old housing, and I don't know that we would have wanted to."[101]

The man most responsible for Portland Development Commission actions was Chairman Ira Keller, a wealthy businessman.[102] Keller was comparatively new to Portland when Terry Schrunk appointed him as PDC chair, and Keller did not disappoint. "More than any other factor, it was Keller's enormous energy that made urban renewal work in Portland," says Carl Abbott. "He chaired the PDC as a sometimes enlightened autocrat."[103] Keller's admonition to PDC members was: "There will be no dissent in this commission."[104] His influence with Mayor Schrunk "became so great that the mayor was perceived by many to be Ira Keller's puppet."[105] The Forecourt Fountain, completed in 1971 as part of the South Auditorium urban renewal, became Keller's permanent memorial. The fountain, a full-block, waterfall park with thirteen thousand gallons of water a minute cascading over "terraced, concrete platforms," was renamed for Ira Keller after his death.[106] The civic auditorium, also renamed for Keller, overlooks the fountain. In

The Forecourt (Keller) Fountain was completed in 1970, and later renamed to honor Ira Keller, prime mover of Mayor Schrunk's urban renewal program. (Portland Development Commission photo)

summertime, children of all ages immerse themselves in the fountain's joyous waterfalls and pools.

With freeways enormously popular and parking much in demand, Rose City Transit, operator of the city's bus and trolley lines, was struggling to make ends meet.[107] Regionwide, passenger travel dropped sharply during the 1950s and '60s, from approximately sixty million riders annually in 1950 to eighteen million in 1969.[108] Voters had turned down a municipal transit system in 1962. When the council renewed Rose City's franchise in January 1963, it included a provision that, should it wish to, the city could acquire the company's real property, plant, and equipment at "fair value."[109] When the transit company applied for a fare increase in 1968 to meet labor demands, the council granted a partial increase on an interim basis. Mayor Schrunk then appointed an emergency Mass Transit Advisory Commission composed of well-known businessmen to lobby the legislature for a new public entity to succeed Rose City Transit.[110] A new federal Mass Transit Administration had been created to help fund such public takeovers.

> Mayor Schrunk helped found a national "Sister City" organization, and persuaded council to adopt Sapporo, Japan, as Portland's first Sister City in 1958.[111]

In response, the 1969 Oregon legislature created Tri-Met, an independent governmental entity with limited taxing powers.[112] Assets of Rose City Transit were transferred to Tri-Met on December 1, 1969, in time to avert a threatened driver walkout. Within three weeks, the new Tri-Met board, composed mainly of the same seven men who had served on Schrunk's emergency committee, enacted a payroll tax on employers within Tri-Met's boundaries, because passenger fares alone were inadequate to cover personnel, pension, and equipment costs.[113]

Creation of Tri-Met was a major breakthrough for regional mass transit. The year after it began, Tri-Met also took over the suburban Blue Lines.[114] In other ways, the agency started out timidly, but later asserted itself to become a major player in regional transportation matters.[115] More recently, two main criticisms have surfaced about Tri-Met: first, that board members appointed by the governor are not directly accountable to the voters, and second, that Tri-Met should be doing more to solve traffic congestion problems. Metro, a regional planning and land-use entity that began operations in 1979, has the authority to take over Tri-Met operations by vote of its board, which is an elected body. No such takeover has yet occurred.

The third Morrison bridge opened the same year, while a 1958-59 recession "brought real estate development to a virtual standstill and put another nail in the coffin of the central downtown retail merchants."[116]

In 1959, a strike began against the *Oregonian* and *Oregon Journal* newspapers that was to spell the end of the *Oregon Journal*'s local ownership. The strike would ultimately last five and a half years. In 1961, the *Journal* was sold to the Newhouse chain for eight million dollars, a price that included the two-block *Journal* building on the waterfront originally built as the city marketplace and eventually converted to a parking garage.[117]

At age seventy-five, Councilman Ormond Bean challenged forty-eight-year-old Terry Schrunk for the job of mayor in the 1960 primary.[118] Bean's hopes were dashed when Schrunk tallied more than a two-to-one primary victory, precluding a run-off.[119] In Schrunk's two subsequent mayoral elections, in 1964 and 1968, no serious challenger opposed him. He "came to be regarded by many would-be candidates as virtually unbeatable," said the *Oregon Journal.*[120]

Bean would serve another six years on the council until his retirement in 1966 at age eighty-one, becoming "an increasingly crotchety, isolated figure who enjoyed the role of dissenter and who liked to clarify issues with pedantic memos to his colleagues."[121]

In 1960, the following events occurred:

- Mayor Schrunk cut a ribbon to open eastside Lloyd Center, then the world's largest indoor shopping center;[122]
- Pioneer Church was donated to Portland and moved by barge from Milwaukie to Sellwood;
- The eastside Memorial Coliseum (E-R Center) opened with a performance of "Holiday on Ice;"[123]
- Maurine Neuberger was elected to represent Oregon in the U.S. Senate, where she was Oregon's first woman senator and only the third woman ever to so serve;[124]
- John F. Kennedy was elected president of the United States after an acrimonious race against Vice-President Richard M. Nixon.

Bill Bowes, the only commissioner to surpass Bean in council longevity, "suffered from the arrogance of success. … [He] modeled himself after Robert Moses and argued the engineering solution to every problem."[125] Lloyd Anderson, the commissioner later appointed in Bowes' place, noted that in spite of Bowes' tough-guy image, he was unwilling to face up to the unpopular task of raising sewer rates and simply withheld design work already prepared to correct serious sewerage problems. By the time Anderson took office, sewer rates had to be tripled in order to finance these improvements.[126]

Portland's commission form of government was the target of reform ballot measures twice during Mayor Schrunk's tenure. The first referendum, in 1958, proposed a "council-manager" government, with administrative responsibility assigned to an appointed city manager who would answer to the council. Opponents called the concept undemocratic, because a manager appointed by and answerable to the council would not be directly accountable to the voters. The measure lost by only 6 percent, an outcome close enough to encourage its supporters.[127]

Three years later, the City Club published a forty-seven-page report decrying the "lack of initiative" inherent in the existing city government, and recommending that one, and only one, elected official be given sole responsibility for city administrative matters. The City Club then drafted a "strong-mayor" proposal, and a coalition of groups called the Citizens League for Effective City Government collected 30,351 signatures to put the measure on the 1966 ballot.[128] An elected executive—the mayor—would run the city and preside over council meetings; the elected city auditor would be replaced by appointed personnel; and an eight-member, part-time council would set policy and pass laws.[129]

"Portland has become a grown up city since 1913," a campaign brochure said. "It's time to help our elected officials tackle Portland's 'big city' problems by giving them modern tools of government." Problems cited were "sewage, traffic tangles and freeway chaos." Supporters cited the combination of legislative and administrative authority in the hands of council members as a basic flaw. "A football player doesn't referee his own game. A butcher shouldn't be his own meat inspector. Five city administrators should not sit in judgment on their own budgets and operations. The city council which passes ordinances and approves budgets should be separated from the five city departments. Councilmen (who are legislators) should not be commissioners (who are administrators). Portland's 1913 form of government is INADEQUATE and OBSOLETE."[130]

The present city council had not done anything "outrageously bad," an *Oregon Journal* editorial said, but the council was too often guilty of "doing nothing much at all to deal with increasing urban problems." Examples given were "the long and still unsettled wrangle over location of the East Side [I-205] freeway; the lack of a capital improvements plan with an orderly list of priorities; the failure to do anything effective to provide for a park on the east bank of the Willamette River, and for other civic beautification projects."[131] Supporters noted that eight cities had recently abandoned the commission form and that no city had adopted it since 1917. Most other large cities operated under some variant of a strong-mayor structure.[132]

Opponents called themselves Citizens for Good Government. "New 'Dictator-Mayor' Plan Could Cost Taxpayers Fortune," proclaimed their campaign brochure. "SAVE YOUR CITY! VOTE NO CHANGE." A four-page flyer showed photos of Memorial Coliseum, the Rose Festival, city zoo, police and fire departments, and other views of "one of the most beautiful and well administered cities in the United States."[133] The flyer pointed out that Portland had already tried a strong-mayor form of government between 1903 and 1913, and had unceremoniously thrown

Voters firmly rejected a 1966 "good government" initiative to replace Portland's commission form of government with a strong mayor. (Cartoon from opposition campaign flyer; author's file)

> While attention was focused on this controversial initiative to change city government, voters passed a home-rule charter for Multnomah County, effective January 1967, which eliminated a host of elective offices and created a five-member county commission with authority to make its own laws without going through the state legislature. In 1971, the state legislature would establish a city-county charter commission to draft a consolidated Portland - Multnomah County charter for submission to the voters in 1974.[138]

it out. City Attorney Alexander Brown issued a twenty-three-page opinion sharply critical of the ballot measure: "The adoption of the proposal would result in municipal chaos, a heavy increase in costs, ... and an era of uncertainty which would handicap, if not make impossible, the orderly conduct of City business for an indefinite time in the future."[134]

All five council members opposed the measure, including Ormond Bean, who had previously worked for a change in the form of government. Also complicating the situation was that a thirty-eight-member Metropolitan Study Commission had been appointed by area legislators in 1963 to study governmental structures in Multnomah, Washington, Clackamas, and Columbia counties.[135] Critics said the commission's work would be hampered if Portland changed its form of government in the middle of that commission's deliberations. Others scoffed at the notion.[136]

The strong-mayor proposal went down to decisive defeat, rejected by 62 percent of the voters.[137] The old adage "If it ain't broke, don't fix it," had once again prevailed.

Another important governmental body, Columbia Region Association of Governments (CRAG), was also created in 1966, but without a vote of the people. CRAG replaced the Metropolitan Study Commission, and was created in response to the commission's efforts, as well as federal government threats to withhold highway, housing, and urban development grants unless a voluntary association of elected officials representing 90 percent of metropolitan area residents banded together. CRAG's role was that of regional land-use and transportation planning, a role that would be shifted to Metro in 1979.[139]

A second new governmental entity, the Metropolitan Service District (MSD), whose main purpose was to oversee solid waste disposal, was approved by voters of Washington, Clackamas, and Multnomah counties in May 1970. Portland officials had expressed fear that MSD might try to take over the city's water supply, and the city had fought passage of the MSD bill in the legislature. However, Multnomah County voters solidly backed the measure at the polls, overcoming its loss in both Clackamas and Washington counties.[140] MSD was administered by an executive director and governed by seven directors, all elected officials from cities and counties in the region.[141]

A major stumbling block to effective city government still remained: the votes of three council members were required to get anything passed.[142] Mark "Buck" Grayson, a former assistant to Ormond Bean, had been elected to the council in 1958[143] to fill the seat held by Nate Boody for eighteen years,[144] and Frank Ivancie, Schrunk's former administrative assistant, was elected in 1966 (over former mayor Fred Peterson) to the vacancy created when Ormond Bean retired. Neither of these new commissioners changed the conservative council majority, for Grayson's vote was much like Boody's, and Ivancie's vote was more conservative than Bean's. After January 1967, the council consisted of Terry Schrunk, Bill Bowes, Stanley Earl, Buck Grayson, and Frank Ivancie—still a council of aging Caucasian males, with Ivancie the youngster of the group at age forty-two.

> When he joined the council … commentators described [Ivancie] as the voice of the next generation, even as a bit of a liberal. … If you came to Portland as the 60s were ending, you might easily have concluded that Frank Ivancie *was* Portland. As the loudest voice on the City Council and the presumptive next mayor, Ivancie exemplified a xenophobia that pervaded city hall—a fear and loathing of foreign ideas as well as people.[145]

While the I-5 freeway between Salem and Portland had been nearing its 1961 completion,[146] two additional freeways had been debated: one to run almost due east toward Mt. Hood from a point just south of downtown, and one to bypass downtown in a west semicircle to connect with I-5 at the north and south ends. The downtown bypass debate was settled in favor of a four- to six-lane "concrete walled box canyon"[147] dug out between S. W. Thirteenth and Fourteenth. This "Sunset-Stadium Freeway," today's I-405, was to cut neighborhoods in half, displace seventeen hundred residents, and dead-end at the north end until the Fremont Bridge opened four years later, in 1973.[148] Aesthetic appearance was given a high priority for the planned Fremont Bridge because of the severe criticisms leveled against the "erector-set" design of the Marquam Bridge. The Fremont Bridge ended up costing eighty-two million dollars—five times as much as the Marquam.[149]

In 1968, Governor Tom McCall called for closure of Harbor Drive as soon as I-405 was finished, in keeping with the Willamette Greenway concept.[150] Harbor Drive, a six-lane highway along the seawall, had opened as a downtown bypass with great fanfare only twenty-six years before.[151] Now McCall proposed replacing it and the old *Journal* Building adjoining it (which the city had purchased and decided to raze)[152] with green open space. He appointed an intergovernmental Harbor Drive Task Force to study various alternatives for the area, but that group recommended a plan quite different from McCall's. Task Force members Frank Ivancie and State Highway Commission Chair Glenn Jackson decided that a ten-lane expressway was needed for Front Avenue and Harbor Drive. McCall did not stand in their way. Ivancie made plans to announce this new expressway publicly in July 1969.

But before the announcement occurred, the Portland City Club stepped in. The City Club board notified the state that it would issue a three-page press release protesting this "bilateral" decision by Jackson and Ivancie if the plan to pave over the *Journal* site was announced without public hearings. The Ivancie - Jackson decision contradicted the intent and previous statements of Governor McCall, the City Club said, as well as policies adopted by the Portland Planning Commission.[153]

This maneuver by the City Club resulted in a revised announcement by Ivancie. Three alternatives were being considered, Ivancie now said, for "improving traffic conditions and scenery" along Harbor Drive: widening Harbor Drive only, with no emphasis on establishing a "green strip" (minimum treatment); a "cut and cover" approach, in which Harbor Drive would be depressed, then covered over with a park-like pedestrian green strip; and realignment of Harbor Drive west of its present location, with a green strip along the harbor wall.[154]

In August 1969, the City Club released an interim *Journal* Building study, and in October, Governor McCall called for a full public hearing on proposed development of the west bank of the Willamette River.[155] The topic received wide public discussion, with citizen response favoring a waterfront park along the Willamette.[156] By September 1971, the city council had approved a resolution introduced by Commissioner Lloyd Anderson committing the city to complete closure of Harbor Drive when the Fremont Bridge opened two years hence. An extensive Downtown Plan was already in process, and Anderson's resolution allowed those working on the plan time to complete it before Harbor Drive closed.[157]

The furors over the Marquam Bridge and Harbor Drive were warm-ups for the public uproar generated by plans for an eastside freeway headed toward Mt. Hood.

> In early 1969, the highway division announced the alignment for a multi-lane, controlled access highway. … This road would have moved 5,520 people, bulldozed thousands of homes—1% of the houses in the entire city—plus schools, stores and churches. It had been approved by the City Council, by the County Commission, by the State Highway Commission, and by the Federal Highway Administration. Every level of government had approved—except the one level called "the people." … [Regarding possible neighborhood objections] the Chair of the State Highway Commission said, "We'll worry about that if and when it happens."[158]

The so-called Mt. Hood Freeway, which actually stopped far short of Mt. Hood, was to parallel S.E. Division and S.E. Powell, running almost due east from a new bridge to be constructed south of downtown, across the north-south "circumferential" highway, I-205, with a possible later extension to the suburban city of Gresham. While an environmental impact assessment was underway, grassroots opponents organized themselves.[159] By the time Schrunk left office, neighborhood voices were loudly protesting the proposed freeway. The Multnomah County Board of County Commissioners passed a resolution placing a moratorium "on condemnation and construction of the Mt. Hood Freeway and the interchange with I-205," and asked the state highway department to include bicycle and pedestrian paths for I-205.[160]

While freeway battles raged, daily life in the city went on.

In April 1962, Portlanders welcomed Packy, a baby male elephant weighing at least 150 pounds. Packy, born of Big Belle at the Washington Park Zoo, made a big hit with the public and was the nation's first native-born elephant.[161]

A replica of Philadelphia's Liberty Bell was placed in the city hall rotunda beneath the council chambers with elaborate ceremony in May 1964. The bell, purchased by public contributions to a trust fund, had arrived eleven months before; it simply took eleven months for the council to agree where the bell should be located.[162] Also in 1964, the Portland Park Bureau gained custody of Henry Pittock's mansion in the west hills, along with sixty-four acres of surrounding property. The mansion, which commanded gorgeous views and overlooked downtown, was later converted to a public museum.[163] A beautiful Japanese Garden, opened in 1967 near the Rose Gardens in Washington Park, was "generally acknowledged to be one of the finest of its kind in the United States."[164] Between 1965 and 1968, the old civic auditorium was gutted and rebuilt at a cost of nearly four million dollars. Only 17 percent of the old structure built in 1917 was salvaged.[165]

Other new amenities included a downtown sports stadium approved by the voters in 1966;[166] two-block Unthank Park in northeast Portland; Delta Park raceway; Heron Lakes golf course on the former Vanport site, designed to handle large crowds of spectators;[167] six hundred fifty-acre Tryon Creek State Park, two-thirds in southwest Portland and one-third in Lake Oswego, a park created as a result of citizen initiative and involvement;[168] and private development of Johns Landing, the first example of Portland riverfront property converted from industrial to residential use. Included in the Johns Landing development was a shopping center of small specialty shops, offices, and restaurants, remodeled in 1971 out of the former Biltwell Furniture factory with its picturesque Johns Landing Water Tower.[169]

In the first half of the 1960s, Mother Nature struck three devastating blows. Winds peaked at one hundred sixteen miles an hour on Columbus Day 1962, causing well over one and a half million dollars of local damage, the equivalent of nearly ten million dollars today, and taking forty-eight lives in western Oregon.[170] Some called it "the worst natural disaster to hit the West Coast since the 1906 San Francisco earthquake."[171]

Two years later, fire destroyed the popular, irreplaceable Forestry Building originally built for the Lewis and Clark Exposition.

That same winter, the Willamette River flooded and breached the downtown seawall. Front-page *Oregon Journal* photos on December 25, 1964, showed water breaking over the seawall sidewalk and a houseboat smashing against the Morrison Bridge.[172] Harbor Drive closed when the big dip between the seawall and the *Journal* Building flooded. The northwest industrial district also flooded, as did the south waterfront renewal area.[173] On the slopes of Mt. Hood, a conduit bearing Bull Run water to the city broke.[174]

One positive aspect of the 1964 Christmas Flood was that the seawall proved its worth—it kept water out of downtown and "sewage out of basements."[175] The Willamette crested at 32.45 feet in Portland, two and a half feet higher than the level of the 1948 Vanport Flood, and only six inches shy of the all-time record of thirty-three feet set in 1894.[176]

Portland got caught up in the sixties unrest sweeping the rest of the country. On July 30, 1967, race riots shook Albina after a peaceful Black Arts and Culture Rally in Irving Park. The park director was assaulted and suffered five broken teeth, mouth lacerations, and bruising of his face and hips. Only the decisive action of an African-American summer park employee prevented further assault. The following year, Commissioner Frank Ivancie sponsored a controversial midnight-to-dawn curfew that limited night usage of city parks in response to a "growing fear of a hippie invasion" of Portland.[177]

On May 4, 1970, after President Nixon ordered the invasion of Cambodia, four Kent State University protesters were killed by the Ohio National Guard. Students all over the nation, including Portland, blockaded city streets and occupied campus buildings, bringing campus life to a standstill and disrupting downtown businesses. After a weekend when Portland activists "blockaded streets and erected large tents, for which they had obtained permits from the city,"[178] Mayor Schrunk and Parks Commissioner Ivancie decided the protesters needed a harsh lesson. "Shortly after noon, a one-hundred man police riot squad moved in on the Park Blocks, where they found about one hundred students milling aimlessly in the park. With little warning, the police moved in, attacking without provocation. ... The officers clubbed and punched anyone in the park not wearing a police uniform. ... Thirty-one protesters, many with head and face injuries, later required medical care. ... [Later] a small group of student leaders talked of a retaliatory march—payback for the police beating suffered in the Park Blocks."[179]

In late May, the national American Legion announced that President Richard Nixon would keynote its late-August convention in Portland. In June, the FBI informed Governor Tom McCall that fifty thousand young people were expected to descend on Portland for anti-Vietnam demonstrations organized by the People's Army Jamboree. Word of this threat leaked out through the Portland dailies in early July. "Portland's newspapers made the jamboree and its leaders front-page news as they applied to use Washington Park ... as an encampment for protestors. Soon, local Legion officials swaggered before television cameras to declare they would confront anti-American protesters. ... Oregonians soon had an inescapable impression: violence in the streets of Portland was a certainty, and only its intensity remained unknown."[180]

It was the hippies themselves who came up with a solution to the potential problem. A small group of flower children decided that a peaceful gathering would draw young people away from Portland and avert confrontations. They envisioned a festival with free admission, music, and food—a vortex of peace patterned after the Woodstock rock concert on the East Coast the year before. "The name stuck, and the group soon called its festival 'Vortex I.'"[181]

Portland officials declined to listen to such wild-eyed schemes, but Governor McCall's chief of staff, Ed Westerdahl, eventually met with two hippie representatives. Westerdal recognized a good idea when he heard it, and quickly followed up. He located an ideal site for such a happening at rural McIver State Park, thirty miles southeast of Portland, and started enlisting support for the plan. The state would have to sponsor the event for the festival to succeed, Westerdahl argued. Police would have to allow attendees to indulge in drugs and nudity without interference, because a police presence in the park would "inspire people to flee the festival and return to downtown Portland."[182]

Governor McCall, a candidate for reelection that fall, endorsed the plan with trepidation, fearing as he did so that he had just put an end to his political career. He was in a no-win situation, as he saw it, for a Portland mêlée would end his career just as surely. Opposition to the Vortex festival exploded immediately, including resistance from some state and local officials. An outraged Commissioner Frank Ivancie sputtered, "You're telling these people, 'You can get stoned at this state park … but please don't do anything violent. We will exempt you from our laws and rules.'"[183]

McCall sent Oregon National Guard divisions to Fort Lewis, Washington, for riot training. Westerdahl sought to impress Jamboree leaders by exaggerating the number of troops available, and not informing them that the state was planning to ban the use of loaded guns and to have helicopters ready to drop rose petals on protesters while loudspeakers broadcast a tape of Gov. McCall urging peace.

"Downtown businesses boarded up their windows. … The city and county emptied their jails, sending inmates to the state penitentiary to make room for mass arrests."[184] When the first day of Vortex dawned clear and warm, organizers held their collective breaths. But attendance exceeded all expectations. By the end of the first day, more than thirty-five thousand people had shown up to take part. "[I]nside McIver, Vortex blossomed into a gigantic, peaceful gathering. Many people at Vortex were local folks who had come to the park simply to see what a rock festival looked like. They saw what they had expected to see: young people openly smoking marijuana and strolling around naked."[185]

When the Legionnaires arrived in Portland for their national convention two days later—on August 30—they were met only with peaceful demonstrations by a small number of protesters. Vice President Spiro Agnew spoke in place of President Nixon, but even that substitution may have been unnecessary, for the threatened hordes of outside agitators simply failed to materialize. The crisis was over. No lives or property—except for one broken window—had been lost.

The conventional wisdom was that Governor McCall had averted "certain violence" for Portland through Vortex I. But McCall biographer Brent Walth concludes that FBI forecasts were faulty from the beginning, and that the impact of Vortex was highly exaggerated. Even so, McCall's decision had been a risky one. But positive public reaction was clearly evident in November, when McCall handily won reelection over his opponent, Oregon State Treasurer Bob Straub.[186] Concerns over McCall's tendency to waffle, as in his early willingness to compromise over the closing of Harbor Drive, had been put to rest.

The only woman to play a visible role in Portland city government thus far in its history had been Mayor Dorothy McCullough Lee. Nearly sixteen years after Lee's departure, Marian C. Rushing was appointed city attorney in 1968. She had been the first woman appointed as a deputy city attorney in 1944, then the first woman chief deputy city attorney in 1950. Now, with the retirement of opinionated, long-term city attorney Alexander Brown, fifty-seven-year-old Rushing assumed the city's top legal office for the next five years, the only woman yet to serve in that capacity.[187]

The election season of 1970 saw more council positions on the ballot than at any time since the 1913 adoption of the commission form of government. Bill Bowes had died in office the previous November at age seventy-four, and the council had appointed engineer Lloyd Anderson to take his place. The process that catapulted Lloyd Anderson into city hall was quick, informal, and secretive. Anderson was interviewed first by PDC Chair Ira Keller, then by a lobbyist for Pacific Power and Light, then by Commissioner Ivancie, who "wanted somebody from the outside, because the papers were blasting him about everybody on the council had just been appointed by their friends and bosses." While Schrunk was out of town, Commissioners Ivancie, Grayson, and Earl met with Anderson in a basement room at the Congress Hotel, at which time one of them said, "I make a motion we approve Anderson for being on the council." By the time the council met in formal city hall session later that week, "there was hardly any discussion at all." Just, "Call the roll." The mayor said he wished they had a bit more time to pick someone, and thought maybe his assistant, Howard Travor, ought to be appointed, but in the end, he made the choice unanimous for Anderson. So, from "a standing start on Monday," Anderson says, he was officially designated as a new council member by Friday.[188]

Five months later, in March 1970, Commissioner Stanley Earl died after a heart attack. The council appointed the second woman to ever serve on the council, state legislator Connie McCready, to fill that vacancy. She had served as a Republican state legislator for two terms. At the legislature, she was named Legislative Conservationist of the Year, and backed environmental and civil rights bills.

Both Anderson and McCready sought election in 1970. Well-known *Oregon Journal* columnist Doug Baker filed against McCready, who was herself a former *Oregonian* reporter married to the *Oregonian*'s managing editor, Al McCready.[189]

Commissioner Buck Grayson planned to retire, and a young legal aid lawyer named Neil Goldschmidt led the pack of fifteen candidates who filed for his seat. Rounding off the cast of candidates was a contractor named Tom Walsh who challenged Commissioner Frank Ivancie. All four council seats were therefore contested, with only the mayor and auditor escaping the hard-fought campaign battles of 1970. The mayor's term was not up, and Auditor Ray Smith had no opponent.

None of the council races was decided in the primary, so all four campaigns carried into the fall.

The Ivancie-Walsh campaign became especially bitter and personal. Ivancie and his allies dubbed Walsh the "King of the Hippies." Walsh mounted a grassroots campaign that drew more than a thousand volunteers, many of whom avidly opposed Ivancie's pet project, the Mt. Hood Freeway.[190] Walsh bested Ivancie in the primary by 726 votes, forcing Ivancie "into a desperate campaign that touched the boundaries of legality."[191] The final result in November favored Ivancie by only a 1 percent margin.[192]

Ivancie relied heavily on city employee unions for financial support—relied so heavily that he "gave away the store." Former fire chief Kenneth

Owens later said Ivancie was "largely responsible for the good deal firefighters have" because he needed union support in his council and mayoral campaigns. "The city is still paying for that," Owens said.[193] Part of the reason city employee unions in general gained so much strength in the 1970s was because they contributed so generously to winning city council and mayoral campaigns.

McCready and Anderson handily retained their seats.[194] "Carpetbagger" Goldschmidt, a Portland resident for less than three years, ran an impressive campaign focusing on neighborhood coffees and an army of volunteers for door-to-door canvassing, a campaign planned and managed by Goldschmidt's University of Oregon college buddy, Ron Buel.[195] Among Goldschmidt's campaign volunteers was a housewife named Vera Katz, the same Vera Katz who would one day lead Portland as its mayor.[196] Goldschmidt's opponent in the fall was Republican attorney and former four-term state representative Shirley Field, who had won 48 percent of the vote against Bill Bowes two years before. This time, Goldschmidt garnered a solid 60 percent to win the seat.[197]

Adding further excitement to the fall campaign, Auditor Ray Smith had died in office three months after the primary, the third city official to die within less than a year. Smith was a former Jefferson High basketball star and teammate of Commissioner Buck Grayson, and a devoted Golden Gloves promoter. The council appointed an interim auditor, while thirteen candidates filed for the November election to fill the vacancy. Front-runners were Ross Hall, a certified public accountant, and George Yerkovich, an avid sports enthusiast and boxing promoter who had formerly operated a downtown tavern called Mike's Place,[198] and had been Auditor Smith's administrative assistant. The charter specified that the elected auditor had to be an "expert accountant," but there were no guidelines for determining what constituted such expertise.

"[I]t has generally, albeit facetiously, been accepted in City Hall that anyone who could balance his wife's checkbook at year's end would be considered an expert accountant [said Acting Auditor James Hamill]. ... Hamill, who will ultimately have to work for the winner of the Nov. 3 election, is reluctant to pursue the matter."[199] The *Oregonian* had no such reluctance. In a front-page story with a banner headline, the *Oregonian* noted that only three of the thirteen auditor candidates would meet "expert accountant" qualifications in a court test. Yerkovich was not one of the three. But in spite of strong editorial support for CPA Hall from both the *Oregonian* and *Journal*,[200] the better-known

On November 21, 1970, a bomb damaged city hall, destroying the Liberty Bell replica hanging in the rotunda beneath council chambers and shattering windows in buildings as far as two and a half blocks away.[202] "The blast's power was underscored by the discovery that a piece of metal, apparently from the bell, had been hurled down a 50-foot hallway (in city hall) and through a 3/4-inch steel vault door, shearing off a chrome steel lock bolt. Once in the vault, the metal shard went another 20 feet through a cardboard box, and struck a rigid cardboard file on the vault's opposite end."[203]

Most city records escaped harm from the blast. A replacement Liberty Bell was later purchased with donations by schoolchildren and others, and was mounted on a pedestal resting on green grass at the northeast corner of the city hall block in April 2001. The bomb was generally assumed to be the work of Vietnam War protesters.

Yerkovich won 29 percent of the vote in the November general election to Hall's 21 percent. Since there was no charter provision for a run-off, Yerkovich won election with less than a third of the popular vote.[201]

Before the end of Schrunk's term, the Dock Commission and Port of Portland were consolidated; the municipal and district courts were consolidated; and a city hotel-motel transient lodging tax was adopted. In 1972, for the first time since 1905, there were no city measures on the ballot.[204]

During this period, citizen involvement played a major role, with many volunteers serving on boards and commissions. The two bodies that had the greatest impact during the Schrunk years were the Portland Development Commission and the City Planning Commission. The PDC, through the visible presence and actions of Ira Keller, has already been discussed.

In January 1970, planning commission members took the courageous step of denying a permit for downtown's biggest department store, Meier & Frank, to build a twelve-story parking structure as a replacement for its two-level parking lot across the street from the store. The ensuing struggle over the future of this central city block would personify a change in public attitude that would mark 1970s Portland.[205] Former *Journal* editor Don Sterling captured the essence of this decision in later reminiscences: "I was truly amazed that the Portland Planning Commission and the City Council would turn down that parking garage proposal by Meier & Frank. … They actually tabled that proposal while they started the Downtown Plan. That was an amazing act, I think, by a city. I certainly don't know another example of that. Under all that kind of pressure and the concern about having parking, that they were able to sort of ward that off … that was an amazing act."[206]

Portland received a one-year federal grant to plan improvements for northeast Portland in 1968, as part of a Model Cities program aimed at improving conditions for African Americans. Portland's application had been developed by several city agencies. Portland's chances of obtaining the grant were enhanced by Mayor Schrunk's position as president of the National Conference of Mayors. Even so, the federal government criticized the citizen-participation component of Portland's application because it relied more on informing residents than on involving them. So the first Model Cities plan director, Paul Schulze, "made a key decision … to base the planning more heavily on input from citizens than from public agencies,"[207] a decision that would make the program more workable and valuable in the long run, but that made it controversial with other city agencies. The PDC strongly opposed the plan. Citizen groups and then-director Ken Gervais overcame agency opposition, however, and gained council approval. This led to a five-year Portland Model Cities grant for the years 1970 to 1974.

Throughout the sixties, neighborhood groups had been organizing in response to dissatisfaction with the way city government was handling problems in their areas.[208] Representatives of several southeast neighborhoods "argued angrily at city council hearings in February 1968 that their communities had the same type of problems and needed the same sorts of help as the Model Cities area."[209] In 1969, the Northwest District Association packed meetings regarding a planned Good Samaritan Hospital expansion, and insisted on a comprehensive plan for the district before any urban renewal projects were approved.[210]

Several city problems seemed to worsen all at once: a deteriorating downtown, declining transit service, lack of parking space, an ugly waterfront (where the massive old concrete marketplace "loomed like a beached whale"), and not enough office space. "The planning process that produced the downtown guidelines emerged with the realization that choices in one issue could as easily hurt as help on the other problems."[211] The biggest single impetus for an overall plan was the high-rise Meier & Frank parking garage proposal.[212]

The 1972 Portland Downtown Plan was adopted during the last month of Mayor Terry Schrunk's tenure. The plan culminated three years of effort, and, as subsequently implemented and expanded upon, represented one of the greatest achievements in the city's history.[213] A crucial difference between this proposal—"Planning Guidelines: Portland Downtown Plan"—and previous plans was that this one was home-grown, built step by step by local professionals[214] with input from top-level businessmen, architectural and engineering firms, and an active Citizens' Advisory Committee.[215] Six outside experts had previously offered advice and specific proposals for Portland: the John Olmsted plan of 1903-05; the Edward Bennett plan of 1910-12; Charles Cheney's housing and planning advice of 1918; the Harland Bartholomew and Associates' plan of 1931-32; Lewis Mumford's advice delivered in a City Club speech and follow-up pamphlet in 1938; and Robert Moses' grand highway proposals of 1943. In addition, numerous city planning studies had laid valuable groundwork for the 1972 Downtown Plan.

The current process brought together divergent views: "Bill Roberts [downtown businessman and head of the Tri-Met board] was always down in the mouth, you know, 'all we need is parking, we don't need all these maps and all these pictures, what we need, God damn it, we need some parking!' Pete Mark ... thought that the downtown was going to die on the vine because Harbor Drive was closed. ... Glenn Jackson was wonderful and whenever things started to get out of control, he would bring them back into control. He wanted a plan."[216]

Professor Carl Abbott presents a thorough discussion of the 1972 Downtown Plan's development in his book, *Portland—Planning, Politics, and Growth in a Twentieth Century City*.[217] The plan "offered integrated solutions to a long list of problems that Portlanders had treated piecemeal for fifty years. It was technically sound, because it dealt simultaneously with transportation and the possibility of land-use changes. It was also a viable political document, because it prescribed tradeoffs among different public agencies, private interests, and competing uses as part of a coherent strategy."[218]

Personal recollections by planners Richard Ivey, Bob Baldwin, and Richard Brainard, reflecting on how the plan got put together, are available today on an internet web site.[219] "[T]he plan was just ... a plan of what exists, what are the attributes of downtown that we want to protect and build on, and what kind of other additional things do we need that we don't have, and that became the plan. It wasn't a plan for the 21st century ... but ... a plan for what we need today. [That was] why it was so easy for everybody to agree on it."[220]

The basic underpinnings of all city projects accomplished during the '70s were present in that Downtown Plan. Goals included striving for a pedestrian atmosphere with "interesting and active streets," auto-free zones, pedestrian malls, more open space, recreation opportunities, new downtown housing, better access to the river, and density that would step down from a high-density office corridor (along the transit mall) to the waterfront.[221] The future transit mall, often credited entirely to the next council, was already planned before Schrunk left office.[222]

All council members supported adoption of the plan, although early on, Commissioner Frank Ivancie was said to consider it a lot of folderol. "Give me a blackboard and a piece of chalk," he purportedly once said, "and I'll give you a downtown plan." However, as commissioner in charge of planning, Ivancie had assigned a full-time city planner and other assistants to the project throughout the process.[223]

In April 1972, Terry Schrunk suffered a heart attack and never fully recovered. New council member Neil Goldschmidt had already filed for election as mayor, and Schrunk did not seek reelection. Goldschmidt immediately started planning to assume the reins of government after a strong primary victory in which he racked up a thirty-three thousand-vote edge over his nearest competitor, businessman Bill DeWeese, giving him an outright victory in the primary, even though his name still appeared, unopposed, on the November ballot. Goldschmidt made good use of the seven-month interval between his May election and January swearing-in, while continuing to play a lead role on the council.[224]

Terry Schrunk's last year in office was marred by poor health and absenteeism, a sad way for a dedicated man to leave office after sixteen years as mayor.[225]

The city of 1972 was a far cry from the city of 1956 that Schrunk had inherited. Much progress had been made toward today's Portland, and Terry Schrunk deserves due credit. His tenure headed downtown Portland toward its renewal. He "repeatedly assumed a leadership role in selling local taxpayers on the idea of lending support to civic improvements such as street lighting and park levies, airport and river development, new bridges, creation of the Coliseum and reconstruction of the Civic Auditorium."[226]

Today, a lovely park and outdoor amphitheater bear Mayor Schrunk's name. The Terry Schrunk Plaza, located between city hall and the Edith Green - Wendell Wyatt Federal Building, adjoins the Chapman and Lownsdale Plaza blocks that were designated for public squares more than 150 years ago. Schrunk Plaza was called Federal Plaza when it was completed in 1975. Oregon's legislative delegation introduced a bill in

Congress in 1976 to have the park honor Schrunk's name.[227] The federal General Services Administration maintains the plaza and its underground federal employee parking.[228]

During the forty-year period of 1930 to 1970, two council members had been recalled: John Mann (1932) and Jake Bennett (1952). Five elected officials had died in office: Auditor George Funk (1938), Commissioner Ralph Clyde (1943), Commissioner Bill Bowes (1969), Commissioner Stanley Earl (1970), and Auditor Ray Smith (1970).

Schrunk's tenure ended a council era. The makeup of city council was already changing from the "aging Caucasian male" model, and was about to become even more diverse in age, gender, and race. Four of the five mayors who succeeded Schrunk were still living when the city government reached the one hundred fiftieth year of existence in April 2001,[229] as were most council members who served after Schrunk's tenure. Most of these elected officials were known personally to most of the sources for the contemporary history that follows.

Chapter 23

A Renaissance: The River, Downtown, and Neighborhoods

January 1973 – November 1980

Mayors

No. 45: Jan 1973 — Dec 1976

Neil Edward Goldschmidt (elected for four-year term)

Jan 1977 — Aug 1979

Neil Edward Goldschmidt (elected for four-year term)

No. 46: Sept 1979 — Nov 1980

Constance Averill McCready
(appointed, fourteen months)

Not only was Neil Goldschmidt the city's youngest mayor in more than a hundred years,[1] he was also the youngest big-city mayor in the United States at the time.[2] He was thirty-two years old when he was sworn in as mayor in 1973.

The Goldschmidt era would be one of solid accomplishment. He inherited a "politician's dream"—a plan on which consensus had been reached, ready for execution.[3] He enjoyed a receptive council majority, hired outstanding staff, and had enough council experience to know his way around city hall. The public was ready for change, and both federal money and local urban renewal dollars were readily available. Goldschmidt himself was articulate, energetic, charismatic, and champing at the bit to get things done.

Despite his youth, Goldschmidt's background was broad. Born and raised in Eugene, Oregon, of second-generation German-Jewish parents, Goldschmidt spent a year abroad during his college years, which included a stint in an Israeli kibbutz. At the University of Oregon, where he majored in political science, he was elected student body president.[4] After college, he traveled to the South and returned home to recruit Oregon college students for the 1964 Mississippi Summer Project during which three young civil-rights workers died. He completed law school

Mayor Neil Goldschmidt. (Photo: OrHi #89972)

at the University of California's Boalt Hall, then worked as a legal aid attorney in Portland for three years before being elected to city council at age twenty-eight. In 1972, he was named Portland Junior First Citizen and one of America's Ten Outstanding Young Men by the U.S. Jaycees. *Time* magazine would include Goldschmidt in its roster of two hundred outstanding young Americans in 1974.[5]

Less well known is the fact that Goldschmidt worked for Maurine Neuberger in the U.S. Senate for several months, dabbled in Berkeley city government politics while at law school, worked for a short while on Bob Straub's staff, and as a volunteer on Wayne Morse's ill-fated 1968 U.S. Senate campaign against Bob Packwood.[6]

❧

The council took a long time to fill the vacancy created by Goldschmidt's election as mayor. All four council members—Neil Goldschmidt, Frank Ivancie, Lloyd Anderson and Connie McCready—had strong views, and none relied on lobbyists to screen their candidates. Goldschmidt and Anderson agreed on lawyer Hardy Myers, but they couldn't get a third vote. Ivancie wanted lawyer Mildred Schwab, and McCready clung to her nomination of labor leader Ed Whelan "through thick and thin." Finally, says Anderson, "I went to Connie and said, 'Look, months have gone by now and we haven't ended up appointing anybody. We're having all of these secret meetings, which is creating just a tremendous uproar. We ought to … make a decision. But … I'm not going to vote for Ed Whelan.' … Well, Connie hated Mildred Schwab with big, unbridled passion. … I told Connie, 'Unless you get off Ed Whelan and we pick someone that we can agree on and get Neil to vote with us, I'm going to bag it and vote for Mildred.'"[7] When McCready wouldn't budge from Whelan as her choice, Anderson joined Ivancie and Goldschmidt in voting for Schwab. "And it was a cat and dog fight between Connie and Mildred from the word go," says Anderson.

Mildred Schwab would prove enormously popular with the public. Her "tight-fisted approach to municipal fiscal matters made her one of Portland's most popular city commissioners ever."[8]

The public perception of Schwab was that of a kindly, but firm, Jewish spinster aunt. Her general untidiness and lack of fashion added to that image. She loved music and once considered a career as a classical pianist; she also gloried in chasing fires, riding in police cars, and attending sports events. She sometimes brought her two German Shepherds, Ranger and Blitz, to city hall, where her staff members and other hapless city employees were commandeered to take them for walks.[9] The backseat of her city-owned car got torn apart by her dogs. A city hall staff member who accepted a ride from Schwab later recounted the experience:

> Mildred was driving and smoking, I was in the passenger seat in a dark blue summer-weight suit, and Blitz was in the backseat, moving constantly from the open window on the left of the car to the open window on the right side of the car (all the car windows were wide open). As we entered the tunnel, a draft blew cigarette ashes in my direction, just before Blitz began barking furiously at a dog in the backseat of a car that was passing us on our left. I all but jumped out of my seat with the initial outburst from good old Blitz. The dog continued to bark all the way through the tunnel and Mildred never batted an eyelash. ... We arrived a few minutes later at the CRAG offices. I got out of the car to discover that the back of my suit coat and my suit trousers were covered with dog hair, left over apparently from Blitz's last ride in the passenger seat.[10]

Schwab was a stickler for budget details and, as such, became much beloved by the general populace for her ability to spot errors in staff work, giving the appearance that she was guarding the privy purse. But many insiders saw her as a nitpicker who bore grudges and treated her employees poorly; staff turnover in her office was legendary. A temperamental politician with an unerring sense for what would sell with the public, Schwab was nevertheless paranoid, from the first time she stood for reelection to the last, that a strong candidate might run against her. But from an outsider's point of view, watching "Mildred"—as everyone called her—was jolly entertainment. "I just loved it when she picked departmental budgets to pieces," a contemporary told the author. "We should have someone like her around today. She was human. Public officials today are far too self-conscious."[11]

Every year the American Cancer Society designated a day for smokers to kick the habit, and Schwab was perennially featured as a heavy smoker. But each year as the Great Smoke-Out rolled around, Schwab was said to shut herself in her office to smoke up a storm. Twice during her tenure, the fire department was called to put out fires in her wastebasket.[12]

Statewide, 1973 was a pivotal year. Land use planning was approved with passage of Senate Bill 100, creating Oregon's oft-vaunted and oft-reviled Land Conservation and Development Commission (LCDC). The LCDC had broad powers to limit urban growth and control land use.[13] A new Public Records and Public Meetings Law was also passed in 1973, requiring public bodies to make their meetings public anytime a quorum was present to make or deliberate toward decisions.[14] No more secret votes to choose city council replacements. The Oregon legislature also ratified the U.S. Equal Rights Amendment that had been referred to the states by Congress.[15] Future mayor Vera Katz began her first term in the state legislature that year, and a new wave of women made its mark on state government.[16] In October 1974, the City Club of Portland admitted women to membership after energetic and extended picketing by a group of politically oriented women.[17]

During winter 1973-74, a critical gas shortage developed and Governor McCall adopted an innovative solution: automobiles with odd-numbered license plates could purchase gasoline only on odd-numbered days, and those with even-numbered plates on even days.[18]

In Portland, Goldschmidt left no doubt who was in charge during his debut as mayor. Council members were told to surrender the reins of their bureaus, which he reshuffled, a task clearly within his charter prerogative. He also asked for the resignations of PDC, HAP, and Planning Commission members, for which there was no charter authority. Some commission members, knowing they had been appointed for a designated term and hence did not serve at the pleasure of the mayor, angrily declined his request to resign, leaving some wondering just how far this young man was prepared to go to force his own agenda.[20] Goldschmidt then reorganized the city planning office and staff to give him greater control, and hired a new planning director named Ernie Bonner.[21] Goldschmidt took charge of city affairs so completely through personal diplomacy and dynamic leadership that his governance was close to a strong-mayor form of government without need of a charter change.

The Downtown Plan that awaited Goldschmidt and his staff outlined a prioritized agenda "for which there was wide approval and deep support and to which most opposition had been neutralized."[22] Projects included O'Bryant Square (completed in 1973 with a parking garage underneath),[23] a bus Transit Mall on Fifth and Sixth avenues, a public square on the Meier & Frank parking block, two parking garages in key locations to serve downtown, a government office building core, and many other amenities.[24] The Downtown Plan "urged that new buildings be built out to the sidewalks, preferably with street-level retail, in order to reproduce a sense of 'enclosure' and high levels of activity which make downtowns special. ... [T]he Plan proposed a public square, ... a north-south spine of high density offices adjacent to the Transit Mall, ... [and] districts of lower density buildings ... two historic districts adjacent to the waterfront,[25] preserving the remaining cast iron buildings, an apartment house district west of the Park Blocks."[26] Nearly everything in the original plan was eventually realized, except that planned skybridges were scuttled because they detracted from street and sidewalk activity.[27]

U.S. troops were withdrawn from Vietnam in 1973, ending an unpopular war in which fifty-seven thousand Oregonians had fought, with 799 killed or missing in action.[19] Plans were made for an International Women's Year Conference to be held in Mexico City in 1975. U.S. Vice President Spiro Agnew resigned after a scandal over income tax evasion, and Rep. Gerald Ford took office as the nation's new vice president. Watergate became a household word as five defendants pleaded guilty to the Watergate break-ins and all eyes turned toward the televised Senate Watergate hearings. After secret tape recordings made in the Oval Office were discovered, serious impeachment talk began. On August 9, 1974, President Nixon resigned. Gerald R. Ford was sworn in as the thirty-ninth U.S. president.

Sparks regularly flew at council meetings between Ivancie and Goldschmidt, and between McCready and Schwab. It made a good show for council watchers and for city employees who listened to audio broadcasts from their offices. "[T]he philosophical and personality clashes of the Ivancie/ Schwab/ everybody else days ... enlivened council deliberations. ... Ivancie the dogmatic conservative, Goldschmidt the progressive liberal, complemented by Schwab's bean-counting, prosecutorial approach to everything provided delightful entertainment—the best show in town. ... Goldschmidt was able to charm Schwab to his side often, but never Ivancie."[28]

Goldschmidt's nationwide search for a new police chief ended with the selection of Bruce Baker in January 1974. Because Baker was an outsider from California, he failed to get the kind of cooperation from insiders that make for the most comfortable tenure, even though he remained in charge of the Portland police for over seven years.[29] In 1974, the first black woman police officer, Carmen Sylvester, was hired.[30]

Commissioner Lloyd Anderson resigned in early 1974 to become Executive Director of the Port of Portland; he would run for mayor in 1988. To fill his vacancy, the council chose its first African-American member, Charles Jordan, former director of Portland's Model Cities program. Goldschmidt had previously appointed Jordan to head the city's new Bureau of Human Resources, and thirty-six-year-old Jordan had won praise for his leadership potential and ability to work with people.[31] Goldschmidt appointed Jordan as the Police Commissioner, an unprecedented move. While the charter gave the mayor authority to change bureau assignments at any time, Goldschmidt was the first mayor to hand over control of police to another council member.

Polls showed that voters favored city-county consolidation in concept, and the state legislature had passed a bill enabling creation of a consolidation charter commission in 1971.[32] By the May 1974 election, that commission had prepared a consolidation charter for the Multnomah County ballot.[33] When "nobody really stepped forward to pick up the ball," Mayor Goldschmidt threw himself and his volunteer resources solidly into the effort for passage. His support turned out to be both a blessing and a curse, because many saw consolidation as a Goldschmidt power grab.[34]

The Portland - Multnomah County consolidation charter provided for a strong mayor and eleven council members, eight by districts and three at large, with the votes of seven council members required to override a mayoral veto. The specifics of the charter doomed it to failure. Portland police officers strenuously objected to a uniform benefit plan for all sworn law enforcement officers because they would lose the generous pension and disability provisions in the existing city charter. Other unions joined Commissioner Ivancie, police and fire unions, and the Chamber of Commerce to defeat the measure.

Opponents distributed a four-page color tabloid featuring a cartoon character wearing dark glasses and a lapel rose, smoking a big cigar, with paper money sticking out of his pockets in every direction—money obviously stolen from gullible taxpayers. The tabloid warned of high tax bills, a sales tax without a vote of the people, ward politics, and a "mayor so powerful that not even council" could require him to justify his actions.[35] The measure bit the dust by a 71 to 29 percent margin. The *Oregon Journal* noted: "The experience of consolidation in the country indicates that it fails unless proposed during a crisis or outrageous scandal in local government. There was none such here, and there will be no consolidation."[36]

Commissioners Schwab and Ivancie easily won reelection that May. Charles Jordan garnered nearly 35 percent of the vote out of a field of sixteen in the primary, and captured 58 percent of the vote in the fall.[37] At a time when no woman had previously been elected to Multnomah County office, two women broke that barrier.[38] Women had likewise been missing from statewide state office, and State Senator Betty Roberts of Portland made a pioneering bid for the governor's chair, but lost to former state treasurer Bob Straub in the primary.[39]

City and county elected officials had taken part in several joint endeavors, expecting consolidation to pass. Most of these projects subsequently fell apart.[40] One such undertaking was a joint computerized accounting system. A massive IBM mainframe located in the county's Penumbra Kelly Building in northeast Portland constituted the hardware, and two different national firms custom-designed the software.[41] July 1, 1973, was the target date for start-up of the online Financial Management System (FMS), and the computer started processing transactions as of that date. However, city employees soon found that the codes and category descriptions for cash disbursements did not match those in the budget because they were part of two different computer systems, and there was no cross-reference guide to identify or reconcile differences. Many city expenditures were never accurately identified by budget category.[42] A newspaper account put it this way: "After spending more than $400,000 to develop a sophisticated computerized accounting system, the city of Portland has been notified by its independent auditor that the city's fiscal 1973-74 budget cannot be balanced. The imbalance has caused the city to delay paying its bills in some cases, losing the normal discounts for prompt payment. It also could have an impact on the city's bond and credit ratings and its ability to apply for federal grants."[43]

The bungled start-up was an embarrassment for the Goldschmidt administration. The financial officer resigned. Commissioner Schwab forced employees who appeared before council to admit that more than six hundred forty thousand dollars had been charged to the contingency account of the general fund to balance the books.[44] The FMS system logic was redesigned, the mayor saw to it that the accounting division got the resources it needed to correct problems, and no permanent damage ensued.[45]

The computer problems were the result both of underestimating the complexity of switching computer systems and of the pressure employees felt to have a system up and running for the new consolidated entity. Once consolidation failed, the potential savings possible through a joint endeavor were soon overlooked.

❧

In 1974, the council established the Office of Neighborhood Associations (ONA) to formalize a working partnership between the planning bureau and the city's neighborhoods. Sixty-eight neighborhood associations were already operating throughout the early 1970s, and the ONA gave them permanent status and a guaranteed place at the table in the planning decision process.[46] To obtain Schwab's vote, Goldschmidt promised that she could add the ONA to her personal portfolio. The program proved both valuable and popular, and increased citizen participation. The first ONA director, Mary Pedersen, brought hands-on experience from the Northwest District Association (NWDA). Petersen later became Portland's best-known Rajneeshee—a follower of the controversial Bhagwan Shree Rajneesh. Pedersen was one of hundreds of young and middle-aged people who donned bright red clothing as followers of the Bhagwan during the group's short and controversial stay at the sixty-four thousand-acre Big Muddy Ranch in central Oregon in the early eighties.[47]

❧

No issue of the 1970s was debated more hotly than the east-west Mt. Hood Freeway proposed for southeast Portland. The I-205 route (a north-south bypass east of Portland) adopted by the state highway commission in July 1965 had included an agreement that gave Portland "its long-sought highway through the southeast."[48] In 1974, by a contentious four-to-one vote (with Ivancie in the minority), the council reversed the city's long-time support for that southeast freeway. Led by Goldschmidt, the council voted to divert funds earmarked for the Mt. Hood Freeway to improve east-west I-84 along the Columbia and to install mass transit. Mt. Hood Freeway supporters led a successful initiative drive to challenge the council's decision, but a judge kept the petition off the ballot. The council's decision was administrative, rather than legislative, the court said, and therefore not subject to voter approval.[49]

Enemies of the freeway later boasted that "nothing shaped Portland so much as the murder of the Mount Hood Freeway. ... The story of the freeway's demise is a tale of urban America after World War II and a lesson in what distinguishes Portland from other West Coast cities. It gave us strong neighborhoods, proud schools and MAX. It cemented the region's commitment to ecology. ... [I]t also established Portland's philosophy of urban livability—the idea that cities are for people, not

With completion of the Fremont Bridge in 1973, an inner freeway loop surrounded downtown Portland. (Photo: OrHi #62574)

just for commerce and cars. . . . 'Our quest,' [said one crusader], 'was for policies that would stem the tide of people fleeing to the suburbs.'"[50]

The trump card that won the day for Goldschmidt was assurance that killing the freeway would not deprive Portland of its promised five hundred million dollars of federal highway funds. Instead, this money could be used for "other transportation options." A 1973 environmental-impact statement also concluded that the Mt. Hood Freeway "would not relieve congestion and would be obsolete by the time it was completed."[51] Behind the scenes, a Governor's Task Force on Transportation headed by Goldschmidt was developing a regional transportation plan which called for a public transit system "that would be competitive with the freeway network."[52] All these maneuvers paved the way for a future fifteen-mile rapid transit line called MAX that would roughly parallel the east-west I-84 freeway.

Due credit or blame for terminating the Mt. Hood Freeway also belongs to the Multnomah County commissioners who requested delay of the final I-205/Mt. Hood Freeway interchange design in May 1972, and who placed a moratorium on construction and condemnations for the entire Mt. Hood Freeway in November 1972.[53] These county actions gained valuable time for Goldschmidt to marshal his forces. The Oregon Department of Transportation (ODOT) had already been purchasing and condemning land in the freeway path for some time.[54]

❧

To the wonder of Portlanders who doubted it would really happen, jackhammers started tearing up Harbor Drive in 1974. The following year, the federal Environmental Protection Agency declared Portland the most livable city in the United States,[55] placing Portland at the top for every criterion used in rating livability—economic, political, social, environmental, and health/education.[56]

The removal of Harbor Drive and the addition of Waterfront Park influenced the character of today's downtown and inner eastside Portland more than any other single twentieth-century governmental act. Along with rejection of the Mt. Hood Freeway, closure of Harbor Drive represented a checkpoint in the steady ascendancy of the automobile. The famous lawsuits that settled the levee's public versus private ownership question had taken place a hundred fifteen years before. During the intervening years, the levee had gradually been reacquired for public use for docks and Harbor Drive. Ironically, the high priority given the automobile by business and government made construction of Waterfront Park possible by keeping that valuable

The RiverPlace development of the late 1980s provided pleasing amenities and increased pedestrian access to the waterfront. (Portland Development Commission photo)

riverfront property in the public domain as Harbor Drive from 1942 to 1974.[57] When Tom McCall claimed the right of way for a waterfront greenway, he relegated the automobile to second place. The 1869 band of irate citizens who, led by Mayor Stephen McCormick, had torn down a warehouse built on the levee would have been proud.[58] Finally, in 1974, the levee truly belonged to the people. There would be no further challenge to that ownership.

The first section of Waterfront Park opened in 1978; it was the initial installment of a recreational area that would stretch for twenty-two blocks and cover thirty-six acres from S.W. Clay Street to the Steel Bridge by 2001. Also in 1978, the council added ten acres at the south end of Waterfront Park as an urban renewal project. Here, RiverPlace was developed. The plans called for "500 residences, a small luxury hotel, restaurants, retail shops, a small boat marina and a riverfront park and esplanade," all of which met with enthusiastic public approval.[59] Waterfront Park was later renamed Tom McCall Waterfront Park in honor of the man who, more than any other single individual, had made it possible.

Not all Portlanders found the council's everyday antics to their liking. In a Bardsley and Haslacher poll conducted for the *Oregonian* in September 1975, voters rated the council's performance "mediocre." Pollsters heard comments such as, "council spends too much time bickering" and "too little time solving people's problems." For every four voters who commended the council, five "found fault with their efforts." While 40 percent of the sample said the council was doing a good job, 41 percent said "only fair," and 13 percent, poor.[60]

The innovative bus Transit Mall proved to be a key ingredient in reviving Portland's downtown.[61] During the nearly two years it took to build, first northbound Sixth Avenue was closed, then southbound Fifth Avenue, for Operation Big Switch.[62] The mall stretched eleven blocks, from city hall on the south to Burnside at the north end. Intersections and sidewalks the entire length of the mall were lined with bricks, while sidewalks were festooned with fountains, sculptures, banners, huge basins of flowers, kiosks, and trees.[63] Dedicated in 1978, the Transit Mall cut the time required for busses to travel through downtown from thirty minutes to fifteen.[64] A Fareless Square was instituted in 1975, in which passengers could ride for free if they both boarded and debarked within the downtown area. This gave office workers, store employees, and customers a popular way to get around downtown.[65]

While the Transit Mall was under construction, Goldschmidt faced reelection. His chief opponent was his arch-rival Commissioner Ivancie, the man whom many, including Ivancie himself, had considered the natural heir to the throne for many years. Goldschmidt ran a fairly quiet campaign, but Ivancie blundered badly. He made the Mt. Hood Freeway a major issue, posting billboards that said, "If Ivancie were mayor, you'd be home now," failing to consider that most commuters, to whom the message would appeal, could not vote in a city election.[66] Ivancie vowed

On July 4, 1976, the nation celebrated its two hundredth birthday. This time, Portland's celebration was much more subdued than it had been a hundred years earlier when the whole town turned out for week-long festivities. In 1976, automobiles carried many Portlanders to the mountains and beaches; others stayed home for back-yard barbecues. The *Oregonian* collected a sampling of 1976 memorabilia items, sealed them in a metal time capsule, and placed it in Battleship Oregon Park to be opened a hundred years later.[69]

to end "rat-a-tat-tat" government, a statement many people took as an unnecessary personal remark ridiculing Goldschmidt's rapid-fire speech delivery.[67] An Ivancie billboard showed a hairy fist in the "thumbs up" position, with IVANCIE in big block letters, regarded by many women as a sexist message. Overall, Ivancie came across as stiff and bureaucratic, while Goldschmidt was smooth and public oriented; it was a classic case of the old guard versus the new. Even with half a dozen other contenders in the race, Goldschmidt won 53 percent of the primary vote, thus eliminating a fall campaign.[68]

In May 1978, voters in the tri-county area approved a new metropolitan government for the urban portion of Multnomah, Clackamas, and Washington counties. The officers of the new organization, soon to be called "Metro," were to be elected directly by the people. Effective January 1979, Metro's jurisdiction covered land use planning, solid waste disposal, transportation planning, operation of the Washington Park Zoo, and authority to take over the operation of Tri-Met. These same functions had been previously assigned to its predecessor organizations—the Columbia Region Association of Governments (CRAG) and the old Metropolitan Service District (MSD). The Metro measure was aided by a ballot title that promised to abolish the CRAG, a controversial land-use-planning body composed of elected officials from each of several cities and five counties.[69] The actuality was that the CRAG had been merged with the MSD with none of its basic purposes abandoned.

Goldschmidt made several trips to Seattle to convince Nordstrom department store owners to build a new store in Portland. Nordstrom did so. They built on Broadway, across from the planned public square where the Meier & Frank parking lot still stood—"absolutely the ugliest block in downtown and ... one of the most central and most visible."[70] In 1978, Goldschmidt lured a German electronics firm to Portland's northwest industrial area. Wacker Siltronic Corporation employed eight hundred workers, providing a welcome addition to the city's economic base.[71]

Portland voters turned down a 19.7 million dollar parks ballot measure in 1978 that would have provided new indoor pools, community centers, and a performing arts education center. Thirty park restrooms were closed that year because of "undesirable activity" around the restrooms and problems with vandalism. Surprisingly, the Parks Bureau said, no one called to complain about the closures.[72]

Enthusiastic fans cheered Trailblazer coach Jack Ramsey after the basketball team's triumphant June 1977 world championship win at Memorial Coliseum. (Photo: OrHi #91147)

Portland's professional basketball team, the Trailblazers, was now wowing the city. Red-head center Bill Walton was the team leader. Blazermania swept the state. On June 5, 1977, the last game of the National Basketball Association world championship finals was played in Memorial Coliseum. The Blazers held on to a narrow lead to win in the final two seconds of the game.[73] Many Portlanders today consider winning this championship the highlight event of the 1970s. "[T]he city erupted. Thousands filled Portland's streets for an all-night celebration. The next day, tens of thousands more clogged downtown Portland for a parade honoring the team. Walton tried to ride his bike through the parade before abandoning it when the enthusiastic crowds mobbed him."[74]

In August 1979, Neil Goldschmidt resigned as mayor to become Secretary of Transportation for President Jimmy Carter in Washington, D. C.[75] "By any standards, Neil Goldschmidt was a political success," says author Carl Abbott. Columnist Gerry Frank allowed as how, in different circumstances, Goldschmidt could have been a United States vice president. The *Oregonian*'s art and architecture reporter, Randy Gragg, later stated flatly: "Goldschmidt is widely acknowledged as

Portland's greatest mayor who, after stints as governor, secretary of transportation and, now, private lawyer, is the city's most powerful behind-the-scenes deal-maker."[76]

Certainly Goldschmidt was a hard act to follow. As Portland's mayor, he was the right person for the right job at the right time.

September 1979 — October 1980

The power struggle among council members to succeed Goldschmidt as mayor was intense. The process took five weeks. Ivancie made no secret of his interest in the job, nor did Jordan, who had talked of running for mayor in 1980.[77] The council deadlocked between the two, with McCready supporting Jordan, and Schwab supporting Ivancie. McCready continued her long enmity toward Schwab, while Jordan and Schwab "disliked each other from the get-go and never worked it out. Mildred in real life was far different from her much-loved public image."[78]

Public pressure started mounting for action, and McCready announced that she herself would be a candidate. About the same time, Schwab proposed the name of former commissioner Lloyd Anderson, whom McCready said she would support if her own bid failed. While Jordan was meeting with Anderson, Ivancie announced he was switching his vote to McCready. Ivancie thought he could beat McCready at the polls, and assumed she would vote for herself. He also guessed correctly that Jordan would support her, in return for the vote she had earlier given him.[79]

Suddenly Constance Averill McCready was Portland's new mayor. No one raised the constitutional issue that had deprived Councilman Rosenheim of the marshal's position in 1867, when the state supreme court ruled that it was "contrary to the policy of law for an officer to use his official appointing power to place himself in office."[80]

"Miss Schwab accused Ivancie of agreeing to vote for Mrs. McCready now in order to deny Anderson the advantage of a mayoral incumbency during the next campaign," the *Oregonian* reported. Ivancie announced his intent to seek the mayor's seat at the ballot box the following spring, and both Schwab and Jordan told the newspaper they might also enter the race.[81]

As the city's second woman mayor, Connie McCready was to serve the shortest mayoral term in the twentieth century, only four hundred fourteen days. She took office on September 5, 1979. A month later, the Federal Reserve Board raised interest rates, ending the boom years of the 1970s. "A dwindling timber supply and high interest rates shattered

Mayor Connie McCready. (City of Portland Archives photo)

the Oregon economy. ... The free and easy times of the 1970s ... deflated overnight."[82] McCready had unfortunately hit the downside of that spiral.

The council chose insider Mike Lindberg, former public works director and administrator of planning and development, as McCready's replacement on the council.[83] Lindberg was a Phi Beta Kappa graduate in economics from the University of Oregon, and a former commissioner's assistant to Lloyd Anderson. Lindberg would be known not only for his tenure as the public works and water bureau commissioner, but for his advocacy for the arts.[84]

Born in Pendleton, Oregon, fifty-eight-year-old McCready attended Portland public schools and was a graduate of the University of Oregon journalism school.[85] As a former *Oregonian* reporter and sometime society editor, she had sat next to fellow-reporter Tom McCall in the newsroom.[86] Her husband was *Oregonian* managing editor Al McCready. This relationship concerned some who wondered if the newspaper would slant its news and editorial coverage in her favor, but the *Oregonian* editor insisted that the newspaper would view her administration with critical detachment.[87]

Connie McCready was a fiercely independent person, as evidenced by her banning travel by city employees to states that had not backed the Equal Rights Amendment and her subsequent endorsement of Democrat Jimmy Carter over Republican Ronald Reagan in the 1980 presidential campaign.[88] She also had a busy home life. Her friend and neighbor Peg Bracken, who authored the wildly popular *The I Hate to Cook Book* that featured short-cut recipes and a humorous style, dedicated her book this way: "Dedicated, with mixed emotions, to Constance Averill McCready, who got me into this, and helped me get out."[89]

During McCready's first month on the job as mayor, the council began the process of choosing a public services building design; it was a process that would prove nearly as factious as that surrounding the elaborate Hefty city hall design of 1890. A selection committee chose three teams of architects and contractors as bidders; these choices were ratified by the council in early October 1979. However, Ivancie then decided to enlarge the group to five teams so that local contractors could be included. The *Oregonian* criticized this delay, bringing an angry retort from Ivancie that the *Oregonian* had engaged in a "political smear" and "slanted journalism." The *Oregonian* stood by its story, however, and Ivancie declared to a news conference, "I'm not going to take this without a fight."[90]

The following May, the council accepted the controversial design of architect Michael Graves, the lowest-cost proposal submitted for the Portland Building. The structure was to house city and county operations, and would occupy the block between city hall and the county courthouse that was then occupied by a small annex and a surface parking lot. After extensive debate, including "biting disdain from architect Pietro Belluschi," council members accepted Graves' motif. Work could now begin on "the nation's first large-scale post-modern building."[91]

Two months later, the council made another difficult choice in accepting the design of Willard Martin's team for a planned Pioneer Courthouse Square. Design teams had submitted 161 proposals for the public square that was to replace the ugly Meier & Frank parking lot with its orange and blue Union Oil sign.[92] Winning architect Will Martin was a local artist and all members of his team were local men.[93] Meier & Frank contributed five hundred thousand dollars toward the new square, and several sources of government grant money were identified. Federal matching funds would be available if an additional one and a half million dollars (the equivalent of three and a half million today) could be raised. The task of finding this money began, a task made more difficult by slow economic times and the planned open-air design of the square.[94]

On May 18, 1980, two days before the 1980 primary election, Mt. St. Helens erupted. Mt. St. Helens was a 9,677-foot, snow-capped peak in the Cascade Range of Washington state, forty miles north of Portland. Seventy-five people were missing and presumed dead.[95] The explosion was "500 times more powerful than the Hiroshima bomb." A DC-9 airplane was forced to land after only four minutes in the air because its engines clogged. The "eruption blanketed Portland in an eerie post-apocalyptic layer of gritty gray ash that settled on trees and puffed up from the ground with every step. ... [D]istant friends called to see if we, too, had become part of the 75 tons of ash that was ejected 16 miles into the air and is still circling today."[96]

Despite the ash still swirling in the air, Portlanders went to their polling places on May 20 to choose between Mayor McCready and Commissioner Ivancie for mayor. (Neither Schwab nor Jordan had entered the race.) Both candidates waged hard campaigns, but Ivancie's long-time name familiarity and blue-collar/business support base won out. He polled a comfortable twelve thousand-vote margin, eliminating the need for a fall campaign. However, he still had to wait until the general election results were certified in late November to take office, because his name would still appear on the fall ballot, albeit uncontested.[97]

In the same 1980 primary, new commissioner Mike Lindberg bested his closest competitor, anti-government activist Clyde Brummel, by better than three to one. A charter amendment on the same May ballot specified that future council and mayoral vacancies would be filled by election rather than council appointment. The measure was wholeheartedly endorsed by the citizenry.[98] From now on, city voters, rather than council, would decide who their new officials would be.

A fall bond measure backed by Ivancie to renovate the civic stadium passed easily.[99] At the same election, Ronald Reagan ousted Jimmy Carter as president of the United States.

In McCready's last month in office, the council adopted the city's first Comprehensive Land Use plan.[100] The plan had been in process for many years, and a preliminary draft had been published in January 1979. The final plan "continue[d] the Goldschmidt policies by encouraging reliance on public transportation and allowing increased density and diversity of population."[101] By accepting the existing mix of housing and commercial ventures in inner neighborhoods, it put pressure on more affluent, automobile-oriented suburbs to increase their density in accordance with an urban growth boundary set by Metro. The plan represented "the capstone ... of neighborhood involvement, neighborhood zoning, neighborhood planning."[102]

A farewell roast and toast banquet for Mayor Connie McCready was attended by approximately five hundred Portlanders. The master of ceremonies joked that mayor-elect Frank Ivancie, who was in attendance, "graciously consented to pick up the tab for the evening's festivities." McCready told the audience that her ten years in city government had been "without a doubt one of the most wonderful experiences of my life."[103] A former staff member later said of McCready: "Connie's success in leadership was due in good part to her personal strength and virtues, and a wonderful style she brought to conducting a political office and managing city agencies. ... Connie was well-known for her genuine friendliness, her great smile, her graciousness. People who knew only that charm of hers might think she was an easy mark. But she was tough, courageous, did her homework."[104]

During McCready's short tenure, decisions were made which led to the downtown performing arts center and inauguration of a 911 emergency phone system; a thirty million-dollar cable television franchise was awarded after years of conflict; gay rights legislation was introduced; and the city started replacing street intersection curbs with wheelchair ramps.[105]

Chapter 24

From Suit and Tie to Casual Dress Day

November 1980 – December 1992

Mayors

No. 47: Nov 1980 - Dec 1980

Francis J. "Frank" Ivancie (elected for thirty-eight days)

Jan 1981 - Dec 1984

Francis J. "Frank" Ivancie (elected for four-year term)

No. 48: January 1985 - Dec 1988

John Elwood "Bud" Clark (elected for four-year term)

January 1989 - Dec 1992

John Elwood "Bud" Clark (elected for four-year term)

Francis J. Ivancie, now age fifty-six, had had the longest mayoral apprenticeship of any Portland mayor——nine years as Mayor Schrunk's executive assistant and fourteen years as a member of the council. Ivancie's first career had been as a schoolteacher, administrator, and principal. Born and raised in Minnesota, he did his undergraduate work at the University of Minnesota, served in the air force during World War II, and in between was employed as a miner and dockworker.[1] He was a registered Democrat, although some assumed otherwise.[2]

With Ivancie's elevation to mayor, his vacant commission seat now had to be filled by election. The contest drew eighteen candidates for a special February primary, and a replacement would not be seated until April. Two candidates were young progressive Democratic former legislators—Earl Blumenauer and Stephen Kafoury—and two were citizen activists—Margaret Strachan and Bill Sizemore. State Representative Vera Katz considered the race, but decided against entering.[3] In the February 1981 primary, Strachan won 11,202 votes; Blumenauer, 10,758; Kafoury, 9,268; and Sizemore, 6,868.[4] No candidate had received a majority, so a runoff between Strachan and Blumenauer was set for March 31, six weeks away. The two held numerous debates and joint appearances, and Blumenauer outspent Strachan nearly two to one.[5] Blumenauer had countywide name familiarity as an incumbent county commissioner, but Strachan had a strong home base in the Northwest District Association, one of the most active neighborhood associations in the city, where she had been a staff member for three years. She had also coordinated Charles Jordan's successful 1974 city council race, and worked in Commissioner Mike Lindberg's office for a year.[6] When the ballots were counted, Strachan claimed victory with a margin of ten thousand votes out of seventy-seven thousand cast in a light voter turnout. On the same ballot, Portland voters approved bonds for construction of a Portland Performing Arts Center, in spite of tight financial times.[7]

In April 1981, Margaret Strachan was sworn in as the fourth woman to serve on the council, the first to join the council by election rather than appointment,[8] and the first woman Democrat to serve. (Neither her sex nor party had been a campaign issue; her election was seen as a victory for grassroots neighborhood activism.)

Strachan assembled the strongest contingent of women staff members that city hall had ever housed. These women staffers would continue to serve in visible governmental and political roles for years to come.[9]

The city council that Mayor Ivancie presided over was a loud and raucous one. Strachan had ties to Lindberg and Jordan, but battled continually with Ivancie and Schwab, although she and Schwab actually related well to each other off camera. Schwab cut Ivancie considerable slack, but loved to pick on Lindberg and Jordan. Ivancie could turn the charm off or on, depending on his mood, sometimes bullying city employees and citizens who appeared before the council.[10] Commissioner Lindberg acted as peacemaker. Jordan was generally reserved and considerate, although sometimes his annoyance with the discourteous behavior of his colleagues showed.

In April 1981, Portland officers Craig Ward and Jim Galloway, young police officers from the Northeast Precinct, tossed four dead opossums in front of the Burger Barn, a black-owned restaurant. The incident shook the community. "Portland's black and liberal activist communities marched through downtown and swamped the Police Bureau with protests. Politics dictated that Charles Jordan, the city commissioner in charge of the Police bureau, fire the two officers, sparking an angry

The 1981 city council, left to right: Mike Lindberg, Charles Jordan, Mayor Frank Ivancie, Margaret Strachan, and Mildred Schwab. Jordan was the first black member of council; Strachan the first woman elevated to council by popular election. (Photo by Randy Wood, © 1981, The Oregonian)

counter-demonstration as hundreds of cops marched on City Hall. ... The Burger Barn filed a $3.4 million civil rights suit against the city but eventually settled for $64,000."[11] An arbitration process reinstated Ward and Galloway with a thirty-day unpaid suspension, but their careers "were stunted." The following year, the council passed an ordinance, crafted by Jordan, to establish a citizens' police review committee. The police union fought the measure, gathered enough signatures to refer the ordinance to the voters, and outspent supporters three to one. In spite of those efforts, the measure won by a narrow seven hundred-vote margin out of one hundred forty-eight thousand votes cast.[12] The review committee was established.[13]

Two months after the opossum incident, Police Chief Bruce Baker resigned. The previous fall, he had suffered a heart attack and had been off the job for nearly four months. He insisted that the current turmoil had nothing to do with his leaving.[14] Ivancie chose local insider Ron Still as the new chief and soon assigned Commissioner Schwab to the police oversight role, a responsibility she relished.[15]

"Pioneer Square Is Dead," blared an *Oregonian* banner headline in January 1981.[16] Newly installed Mayor Ivancie maintained that big donors would not support the project as proposed. Businessmen were convinced the planned open-air design would create a gathering place for transients and other undesirables. Ivancie and former Tri-Met president Bill Roberts (owner of Lipman & Wolfe department store and the new PDC board chair)[17] were particularly outspoken in their opposition to Pioneer Square as planned.[18] The one and a half million-dollar federal matching funds would have to travel elsewhere.

Portland citizens came to the rescue of Pioneer Courthouse Square much as citizens had rescued a railroad terminus for the west side 110 years before.[19] Now, under the aegis of a group called Friends of Pioneer Courthouse Square,[20] Portlanders rallied. They purchased 47,432 bricks at fifteen dollars each (the equivalent of thirty-five dollars today), raising more than seven hundred thousand dollars.[21] The remaining money needed for the one and a half million-dollar federal match came from donors who underwrote specific items, such as drinking fountains, park benches, and statues.[22]

Pioneer Square was dedicated April 6, 1984,[23] and soon became a popular city landmark. For the first time, Portland had a true town

Crowds gather for a noon-time concert in Portland's "living room:" popular Pioneer Courthouse Square. (2000 photo by Duane Morris)

square. It included a grand amphitheater and a waterfall. Although old-timers still mourned loss of the beloved Portland Hotel, no one could deny that the new square was more readily accessible to all comers, regardless of ability to pay or mode of dress, than a hotel could ever be.

"Allow Me," the statue of a man under an umbrella with his hand outretched, soon became a popular subject for amateur and professional photographers alike.[24] On the Sixth Avenue side of the square, parts of the original wrought-iron railing and the pedestrian arch from the old Portland Hotel were placed in the same approximate location they had formerly claimed. Columns along Morrison Street recalled the "romance of the ruins" of Villard's Folly, the hotel that was started, but never finished, on this same block.[25]

Today, Portland loves its living room.[26] Every noon, a weather machine performs, "forecasting upcoming weather by displaying one of three metal figures amid a show of fanfare, mist and flashing lights."[27] The square is a delightful place for people watching and for eating lunch outdoors on warm summer days. A coffee shop beckons on the Broadway side, other stores and offices are located below ground, and a new Portland Visitors Center opened in June 2001. The Transit Mall runs northbound along the east side of the square, with light-rail lines running eastbound and westbound along the north and south perimeters. Approximately two and a half million people visit the site every year, and three hundred special events are held there annually.[28] The open-air, whimsical design has proven to be a popular choice.

Portlanders' love of the outdoors was also demonstrated by the 1981 founding of a private, non-profit land trust to raise funds for a forty-mile loop trail much like the Portland Park Plan proposed by John Olmsted in 1904.[29] Today, a network of connecting trails reaches nearly one hundred forty miles from Sellwood Bridge at the south; Forest Park on the west; St. Johns Bridge, the Columbia River, and Blue Lake on the north; and Troutdale, Gresham, and Boring on the east; connecting again at the south end with Milwaukie via a 16.5-mile Springwater Corridor trail in an old railroad bed.[30] A two-mile stretch between Milwaukie and the Sellwood Bridge is still unfunded, but trail advocates are determined that this "missing link" will eventually be connected.[31] The 40-Mile Loop Land Trust is in the process of tying up a few loose ends to fully connect the region's dozens of hiking and biking trails.[32]

❧

On December 28, 1981, Mayor Ivancie dedicated two Bull Run hydroelectric power plants. He had worked hard to bring the projects to fruition. After extensive debate and study of several water-quality impact statements during the 1970s, the council had approved bond sales totaling fifty-five million dollars for construction of the power plants in 1979 and 1980. Portland General Electric (PGE) contracted to buy all power generated under a thirty-eight-year agreement. Ivancie was convinced that the plants would provide ongoing revenue to the city after construction costs were recovered.[33] In year 2000, the hydro plants were contributing an average three hundred thousand dollars per year to the city's general fund (of which approximately two hundred thousand dollars was earmarked to pay off interest on Performing Arts Center bonds). This amount was far less than the profit originally projected, due to revised energy forecasts and other market factors. The plants are scheduled for complete pay-off by 2016, when the PGE contract will expire. Whether or not the hydro plants will become a bigger future source of revenue depends on energy supply and demand.[34]

Ivancie also gave priority to development of a groundwater backup system for Bull Run water. Groundwater wells that tapped into the aquifer[35] near the Columbia River, were completed at a cost of forty million dollars in 1984 and 1987.[36] These wells were intended as an emergency source in case of drought, or in "the unlikely event of a breakdown in service from Bull Run." The project was also supposed to generate hydroelectric power during periods of excess supply through a turbine system involving the Powell Butte Reservoir (where well water is mixed with Bull Run water), but this potential has never been realized.[37]

Since activation of the groundwater wells in 1985, the wells had been used eleven times as of December 2000; six times for water shortages, four times because of turbidity in the Bull Run supply, and once because of a landslide and conduit failure at the Bull Run watershed.[38]

In 1986, trichloroethylene (TCE) was discovered in some privately owned wells located just south of the city's well field.[39] By 1992, contamination in two of the city's twenty-three wells raised fears that using the others might draw pollutants into them. The city continued to use the wells, however, with both the water bureau and the state Department of Environmental Quality monitoring groundwater quality and safety.[40]

The controversial Portland Building was completed in 1982. Designed by architect Michael Graves, it has been called "poetry, a jukebox, adventurous, a turkey, innovative, punk."[41] "Post-modernism is ornament, expression, pastiches, the frivolous, and the bizarre. The Portland Building is all of these things. Cream-colored terra cotta brick, and aquamarine-colored tile base, two chocolate pilasters running up the middle of the facade ending at an inverted pyramid design, also chocolate, that runs to the roof. In a way, it does look like a juke box, a favorite term used by the building's detractors."[42]

Architects and magazines across the country showered the Portland Building with both praise and disdain. Few were neutral about Graves' design.[43] "Critics of his post-modern play on classicism are legion, and many of their complaints are valid. ... But the sheer exuberance of [Graves'] design delighted many who were exhausted by the bargain glass-and-concrete aesthetic that prevailed until the early '80's. ... Its completion ... generated tremendous publicity and gave the city a singular structure that immediately distinguished its skyline from the dull, corporate piles of Raleigh, Denver or Fort Worth."[44]

Structural problems associated with this building that surfaced later were blamed on compromises the council made during construction because money was tight. Poor-quality materials were used, which eventually required expensive repairs.[45] The Portland Building served as "the launching pad" for post-modernism, and helped make architect Graves "the Frank Gehry of the '80s."[46]

*Satirized as a giant juke box, the Portland Building designed by Michael Graves received national attention as a controversial example of post-modernism. (*Oregonian *cartoon by Jack Ohman)*

Portland voters elected three women to city office in the 1982 May primary for terms beginning the following January: incumbent commissioners Mildred Schwab and Margaret Strachan, and incoming city auditor Jewel Lansing. The advent of three women in city hall at one time was a novelty, as only two other women (Lee and McCready) had ever served as city elected officials. Retiring auditor George Yerkovitch testified at a city budget hearing that a sex change was about to take place in the auditor's office, so his magnificent old walnut furniture would probably be discarded and frilly pink curtains hung in the windows. Amused onlookers opined that the biggest change in atmosphere would likely be airing out the layers of smelly cigar smoke from Yerkovich's office.

With pomp and ceremony, construction began on the fifteen-mile Portland-to-Gresham light-rail line called MAX in 1982. Funds for the project came from the now-defunct Mt. Hood Freeway and another derailed freeway project from the northwest Portland area (I-505), plus other state highway funds.[47] The route ran east from downtown across the Steel Bridge, along I-84 through Sullivan's Gulch, then branched southward to Gresham, giving eastsiders a speedy alternative to the clogged automobile arterials into Portland.

In September 1982, the eighty-year-old *Oregon Journal* ceased publication. Circulation had been cut in half since its peak in 1948. Readership of afternoon dailies was down all over the country. Owner Samuel Newhouse combined the *Journal* staff with that of the *Oregonian.* A farewell editorial on the *Journal*'s front page noted city and state accomplishments since its founding—clean milk, the direct election of U.S. senators, improvement of the Columbia shipping channel, and statewide adoption of the initiative, referendum, and recall. Issues still outstanding were protection of the environment, wise use of the land, vigilance against abuse in government, a sound transportation system, and providing for human needs.[48] Twenty years later, that list is still valid. The presence of a second daily newspaper in Portland is still missed, although the *Oregonian*'s editorial policy moved toward the center after the *Journal*'s demise.

As if to fill part of that void, a public-access television station began gavel-to-gavel coverage of council sessions in fall 1982.[49] Previously, council deliberations had taken place in comparative privacy, with Neil Goldschmidt occasionally flicking paper clips at the council clerk to wake him up. Commercial television stations had sometimes covered parts of council meetings, bringing in their big lights and cameras when controversial issues were on the agenda. Gavel-to-gavel coverage would be different. Now, television cameras were omnipresent and council members began to pay more attention to demeanor—unless, of course, they forgot the cameras were there.

To the delight or dismay of listeners tuning in to the new live television broadcast, Commissioner Strachan engaged in verbal sparring with a lawyer who represented a client against a zoning code variance that had been before the council three times. The exchange went something like this:

> Lawyer: *Well, if these people are willing to give up their hot tub, they wouldn't need a variance.*
>
> Strachan: *Let's be real here, it's not just a fucking hot tub, it's the whole house.*

As soon as the expletive left her mouth, Strachan realized that her words were picked up by the television audio and carried into people's living rooms. She immediately called the station manager and asked to have the word bleeped from the rebroadcast, which, after some debate,

> In sharp contrast to the hullabaloo over the Portland Building, a new Justice Center designed by the local architectural firm of Zimmer, Gunsul, Frasca, received complimentary reviews. The building, dedicated in 1983,[50] faced the Portland Building across Chapman Square, and housed the county jail, courtrooms, central police precinct, retail shops, and cafes.[51]
>
> The following year, 1984, the elegant 1928 Paramount Theater was opened as the refurbished Arlene Schnitzer Concert Hall—"The Schnitz." Its vertical sixty-five-foot "Paramount" neon sign was changed back to its original "Portland" name,[52] and the sign remains today as a distinctive Broadway Avenue landmark. The Schnitz, with a seating capacity of 2,776 (nearly the same as the civic auditorium),[53] was the first of three theaters comprising the Performing Arts Center[54] authorized by the voters three years before.[55] Responsibility for management of all four performance halls was transferred to Metro in 1990.[56]

the manager consented to do. Later that day, Mildred Schwab happened to be at Rogers Cable office when the manager got a call from KGW-TV wanting a copy of Strachan's blooper to run on their six o'clock news. The manager asked Mildred what he should do, and Mildred told him not to give out the tape. So he didn't.[57]

Increased trade with Alaska and Asian Pacific Rim countries was a major Ivancie goal. He traveled to foreign ports and mainland cities as a salesman for the city.[58] Portland played host to a major international conference in 1985 largely through his efforts. He encouraged a leading Japanese precision-machinery manufacturer to open a distributorship in Portland, and fostered Japanese financing for the eighty million-dollar PacWest Center near city hall.[59] In 1984, Ivancie had Bull Run water bottled for display and tasting at the Louisiana World Exposition in New Orleans. He took along copies of a soft-cover book he had commissioned called *Water, Portland's Precious Heritage.*[60]

Auditor Jewel Lansing, the first certified public accountant to hold that position, arrived at city hall in January 1983 fresh from eight years as Multnomah County auditor, in which position she had successfully implemented performance auditing.[61] She immediately convened a ten-member Citizens' Advisory Task Force to help determine the appropriate function and structure of the auditor's office, a review never before undertaken.[62]

The auditor's task force interviewed council members and major bureau heads, as well as previous city administrators. Mayor Ivancie at first agreed to meet with the task force, then cancelled his appearance. The group soon learned that, nearly ten years before, Mayor Goldschmidt had moved accounting duties assigned to the auditor by charter to the city finance office without seeking a charter change, albeit with Auditor Yerkovich's consent. Goldschmidt had also convened a performance auditing group reporting to him, but the effort had quickly turned into a management assistance office, then disappeared altogether.

Task force members enthusiastically advocated performance auditing as a function of the city auditor. Mildred Schwab championed the cause. Commissioners Lindberg, Jordan, and Strachan had reservations, afraid that Lansing might use the audits for personal political gain or to portray employees (and by extension, council members) as bad managers.

Commissioners were especially nervous about the fact that Lansing always made her audit reports public.[63] Mayor Ivancie was adamantly opposed to this invasion of his turf.[64] "'The city has survived a long time without performance audits,' [said] Jim Kuffner, executive assistant to Mayor Ivancie. 'The mayor has the authority to initiate an investigation at any time without council approval.' However, he does not exercise that authority and doesn't want Lansing to do so, either."[65]

After various stalling tactics by the mayor, the council by a four-to-one vote approved funding for Lansing to conduct performance audits of city bureaus on an eighteen-month trial basis. "This has become an issue of the openness of this government," Lindberg said in supporting the allocation. Public pressure, through the media, was the deciding factor. The public liked the idea of an independent auditor evaluating how well programs were meeting their goals, and whether public dollars were being spent efficiently.

The *Oregonian* termed it a major victory for Lansing, and gave the controversy a banner headline in its afternoon edition.[66] Auditors in other parts of the country were astounded that a daily newspaper could be that interested in a governmental audit operation. Ivancie probably did Lansing and the public a favor by drawing attention to this new adaptation of the auditor's traditional financial watchdog role.[67]

A new bridge over the Columbia River, the Glenn L. Jackson Bridge, opened to traffic December 15, 1982, with four lanes each direction and a separate pedestrian/cyclist lane in the middle. The bridge was under construction for five years and cost an estimated one hundred seventy-five million dollars. It was designed high enough to allow ships to pass underneath and low enough to clear the flight path of airplanes from nearby Portland International Airport. Three months later, the final segment of Interstate 205 was completed, connecting the Glenn Jackson Bridge with Interstate 5 in a loop that bypassed the downtown districts of Vancouver and Portland on their eastern flanks. The bridge drew twelve thousand runners for a twelve-kilometer "Run Between the States" on May 15, 1983.[68]

❧

Taxpayers were the beneficiaries in 1983 when the city and county agreed to eliminate much duplication and overlap of functions. The governing bodies of Portland and Multnomah County ratified a policy commonly referred to as "Resolution A." Portland was to be the major provider of "city-level services"—police, fire, transportation, parks, water, and sewer[69]—and the county would specialize in state-mandated county roles and countywide "human and justice services"—corrections, social services, assessment, taxation, libraries. The city hoped to annex unincorporated areas, but agreed to provide some services on an interim basis by intergovernmental service agreements. The east-county city of Gresham later became a third partner in this allocation of service areas and types of services.[70]

During implementation of Resolution A, the most difficult accomplishment for both jurisdictions was that of prying loose the entrenched bureaucracies already handling these functions. "As each agency came under the ax, the feathers flew; and, what was intended to be straightforward division of services, often became a battle royal ending finally in a complex series of compromises."[71]

The bottom line, however, was a laudable consolidation and reorganization based on function, with reshuffling based on common sense and carried out by contract and negotiation, rather than by the ballot box. And because properties and personnel were formally transferred from one jurisdiction to the other, the chance that this reorganization would backslide to square one, as many previous cooperative attempts had done, was small. County Commissioner Earl Blumenauer, who spearheaded the effort, considered Resolution A his major accomplishment during the eight years he served on the county commission. On the city side, Mayor Frank Ivancie had "broken the log jam" on early negotiations to make agreement possible.[72] Two-thirds of Resolution A reshuffling was complete by the time Ivancie left office.[73]

Multnomah County deputy sheriffs were transferred to the Portland police force, but the county sheriff retained responsibility for corrections and jails. The county also transferred three hundred ninety-one miles of roads and maintenance responsibility to Portland.[74] All county parks within the city limits were eventually transferred to the city,[75] while the county assumed responsibility for social services of all kinds.

The troika of traditional "vice" areas—alcohol, prostitution, and gambling[76]—caught the public's attention in 1984. First, the city banned consumption of alcoholic beverages in all downtown parks except for special events, such as the Northwest Brewers' Festival.[77] Second, the Portland City Club recommended that prostitution be legalized in zoned areas of Portland. The report "created a heated civic debate," but nobody gave it serious consideration.[78] Third, by nearly a two-to-one vote, Oregon voters approved state sponsorship of lottery games and video poker, with profits to go for economic development.[79]

Mayor Ivancie sought reelection in 1984. Several well-known potential candidates considered the race, but opted out of doing so because he was viewed as virtually unbeatable.[80] Five months before the primary, a tavern owner named Bud Clark decided to take on the challenge.

Polling done in mid-March showed Ivancie 35 percentage points ahead of Clark, an almost insurmountable lead. Clark's campaign consultant, pollster Tim Hibbitts, and campaign manager Ben Padrow, a former Multnomah County commissioner, did everything they could to lull Ivancie into complacency. "Hibbitts and Padrow proceeded to pull off Portland's first stealth campaign. Padrow, whom Clark paid in packs of Tarreytons, would 'confide' in City Commissioner Mildred Schwab, telling her what a shambles the campaign was in, knowing that the news would reach Ivancie. 'It was basically a sandbag job,' says Hibbitts. In reality, the campaign had rounded up nearly 400 volunteers who blanketed the city for Bud."[81]

Not until a couple of weeks before the May election did Ivancie finally realize he could lose the election. Clark says he knew he was going to win when, a week before the election at the St. Johns parade, people watching from the sidewalks booed Ivancie and cheered him. "I had campaigned several Saturdays on Lombard, going from business to business, and tavern to tavern, talking to the people," Clark said. "It paid off."[82]

Shortly before the election, Ivancie resorted to negative campaign tactics and printed a mean-spirited brochure for distribution door-to-door:

WE ALL LIKE A GOOD JOKE, BUT …

Portland's Future Is At Stake!

No matter what you think of Frank Ivancie … Do you want to put a self-proclaimed "born-again pagan" in the Mayor's Office, someone whose claim to fame is exposing himself to a downtown statue? Surely, our City's fate is more important to you and your family than that.[83]

Bud Clark had worn a pair of shorts underneath a raincoat to pose as a flasher for a famous poster captioned, "expose yourself to art." His back was to the camera, and his raincoat was thrown open as he stood in front of a female statue on the Transit Mall. The poster, generally regarded as whimsical and humorous, if in questionable taste, proved popular around the globe.[84]

By 2001, this Bud Clark photo published as a poster in 1978 boasted eight hundred thousand copies in print around the world. (© 1978 E. Michael Beard "expose yourself to art"™ www.errolgraphics.com)

Ivancie's billboards said: "Keep the Mayor Who Will Keep Portland Growing" at a time when the public was no longer convinced growth was a good thing. Clark's billboard showed him with a friendly smile and a red rose in his lapel. A much better image.[85]

Bud Clark toppled Ivancie from his throne in the May primary, not only capturing more than 50 percent of the vote, but piling up a fourteen thousand-vote lead as well.[86] There would be no fall rerun, no second chance for Frank Ivancie.

Some pundits insisted that people were just trying to teach Ivancie a lesson, and voted for Clark because he didn't have a chance to win and Ivancie was getting too arrogant. Yet others said Bud's upbeat manner and one-on-one campaigning won him the race. "In the good old days, Ivancie's public side would not have been so sorely tested. But the social ferment of the '70s tested anyone in public office. There was new emphasis on planning, which Ivancie shunned, and on such innovations as community policing, which he scorned. … There were, in fact, two distinct sides to Ivancie's personality. In private, he was smiling, chipper and unfailingly courteous. In public forums, however, he was a bully."[87]

On the same ballot that propelled Clark into office, Commissioner Mike Lindberg was challenged by Carl Piacentini, owner of a chain of convenience stores, in an expensive campaign that may have brought out Lindberg supporters who also voted for Clark.[88] Lindberg held off Piacentini's challenge by a fifteen thousand-vote margin and thus was also spared a fall campaign.[89]

Charles Jordan had no serious competitor, and easily won reelection in May. Three months later, however, he announced that he would leave his council seat at the end of September for a job in Austin, Texas, as administrator of public parks. This precipitated a special "primary" election on the November ballot to replace Jordan.[90]

Nineteen candidates——sixteen men and three women—filed for Jordan's seat. Two African Americans won the right to compete in a run-off election: Dick Bogle and Herb Cawthorne.[91]

In the rematch held December 18, Bogle won by a seven thousand-vote margin in a light turnout.[92] Bogle was best known for his fifteen years as a reporter and anchor for KATU-TV. He had also been Commissioner Schwab's executive assistant the year prior to his election. Bogle was a third-generation Portlander who had attended Portland public schools and served as a Portland police officer for eight years.[93]

Mayor Ivancie served another seven months after his defeat until his term ended December 31, 1984. His wife Eileen filed for divorce in January 1985, and was granted a dissolution decree the following year.[94] Ivancie was appointed to the Federal Maritime Commission in Washington, D. C.,[95] where he served multiple terms. He remarried while in D. C., and is now living with his new wife in southern California.[96]

Ivancie is fondly remembered for his mangled metaphors—"You buttered your bread, now lie in it" or "The ball is in your park."[97] He often warned those who questioned his grasp of affairs: "I didn't just fall off the turnip wagon."

Three critical decisions of the 1970s and early '80s were opposed by Frank Ivancie as commissioner or mayor—closure of Harbor Drive, completion of Pioneer Courthouse Square, and rejection of the Mt. Hood Freeway.

"History belongs to those who adapt," notes an epitaph for the Ivancie city hall years in *Willamette Week* newspaper. "The times changed. Ivancie did not."[98]

January 1985 - December 1992

The city's new mayor, J. E. "Bud" Clark, wore a suit, tie, and freshly trimmed beard for his *Voters' Pamphlet* photo. But the public remembers Bud Clark in casual clothes, perhaps riding a bicycle or paddling his canoe on the Willamette.

"As Mayor," Clark promised in the *Voters' Pamphlet*, "I will be the city's police commissioner. My top priorities will be preventing burglaries and violent crime; providing help for crime victims; having police work more directly with neighborhood organizations." He pledged to expand the use of city schools to better serve the community, to strengthen neighborhood associations, and to strive for the very best police agency in the nation.[99]

Clark was the owner of Goose Hollow Inn and other properties,[100] and founder of *The Neighbor* newspaper.[101] He attended Vanport College, Oregon State University, and Reed College (but never long enough to earn a degree). He was a former Marine Corps staff sergeant, and his community credentials included neighborhood associations, the Planned Parenthood Association, a precinct police advisory committee, and volunteer work for Meals on Wheels.[102] Early in his campaign, the *Oregonian* reminded voters of Clark's "memorable one-man protest that drew national attention" when Clark refused to serve

Mayor J. E. "Bud" Clark. (City of Portland Archives photo)

Budweiser beer in his tavern because Budweiser was trying to defeat an Oregon-style bottle bill in California.[103]

"Bud's Ball," a gala inaugural event held at the Memorial Coliseum in early January 1985, paid off his campaign debt.[104] The event featured thirty-three bands, the Youth Symphony, the Imperial Brass, a bagpiper, and fireworks. "Yes, it was chaos," said Billy Hults, one of the organizers.[105] Hundreds of people volunteered their time,[106] and ten thousand people paid ten dollars each to attend the memorable festivity.[107]

The media loved Mayor Bud Clark at the beginning—not just the local press, radio, and television, but national news services and commentators as well. He was everyone's favorite uncle. A Santa-Claus look-alike. Quotable. He was frequently photographed in lederhosen with his bushy beard and a rose in his lapel or paddling his canoe in the Willamette River or hoisting a brew in his tavern. The saga was appealing: unknown tavern owner comes out of nowhere to become mayor of one of the largest cities in the country. His trademark exclamation was a jolly, "Whoop, whoop!" Bud was light hearted and fun to be around. But could he handle the job of mayor?

"Bud Clark was like a breath of fresh air," says historian E. Kimbark MacColl, who put a lot of money into Clark's campaign to help rid the city of Frank Ivancie. "But when Bud got to city hall, he was like a steamboat captain who suddenly gets put in charge of the Queen Elizabeth. He was well-intentioned, but over his head."[108]

❧

Joining Clark on the council were veteran commissioners Mildred Schwab, Mike Lindberg, and Margaret Strachan, along with rookie Dick Bogle. Bogle often voted with Schwab, and was usually a conciliatory voice on the council.

Mayor Clark's first major decision was to choose insider Penny Harrington as his police chief, an act widely hailed as farsighted and egalitarian. Clark said he wanted to shake up the bureau, and this appointment signaled real change. Harrington was the first female police chief in any major U.S. city, and as such, received nearly as much national publicity as did Mayor Dorothy McCullough Lee in 1949. She was invited on national talk shows and was named a *Ms.* Magazine woman of the year.[109] She laid plans almost immediately to reorganize the bureau.

The first serious problem came three months after Harrington's swearing-in, when black security guard Lloyd Stevenson died at the hands of white police officers on April 20, 1985.

> That night the black 31-year-old Fred Meyer security guard entered a Northeast Portland 7-Eleven … just as white store clerks were detaining an African-American man suspected of shoplifting. … [A] large crowd gathered … Stevenson tried to contain the melee until the police arrived. … [A] gas station attendant … started arguing with Stevenson. … [A police officer] stepped between them. Another officer … applied a "sleeper hold" to Stevenson and maintained pressure for 15 seconds. Stevenson went into cardiac arrest. None of the officers administered CPR. … Stevenson was pronounced dead on arrival at a nearby emergency room.[110]

The incident stunned Portland. Bureau policy specified that CPR should be administered after application of the sleeper hold, but no officer had made a move to do so. Making matters worse, two East Precinct officers had T-shirts made up showing a smoking gun and the slogan, "Don't Choke 'Em, Smoke 'Em." The officers sold at least thirty of the T-shirts to their colleagues in the East Precinct parking lot the very day of Stevenson's funeral. The message they sent was that Officers Gary Barbour and Bruce Brantley hadn't erred in killing Stevenson, they just hadn't done it the smartest way.

An inquest panel found Officer Barbour guilty of criminally negligent homicide in applying the sleeper hold, but a grand jury declined to file criminal charges. Chief Harrington, backed by Mayor Clark, fired the officers who sold the T-shirts. Both men were later reinstated by a federal arbitrator.[111]

"Bud" Clark and the members of his 1985-86 council. Left to right: Margaret Strachan, Dick Bogle, Mike Lindberg, Mayor Clark, and Mildred Schwab. (City of Portland Archives photo)

Workers transported the copper statue Portlandia *downtown by barge in 1985. (Photo by John C. Neeley)*

A new city symbol arrived in the form of a six and a half-ton statue called *Portlandia* in fall 1985. From its assembly point in the Northwest Industrial District, the thirty-eight-foot, hammered-copper figure was floated up the Willamette River accompanied by a flotilla of admirers, including the mayor. Once *Portlandia* reached land, crowds on foot followed her progress along the street. Parents lifted their children to touch *Portlandia*'s outstretched hand. At the Portland Building, *Portlandia* was hoisted to her second-floor perch above the main entrance.[112] She was an instant and lasting hit with residents and visitors alike.[113]

❧

Mayor Clark next conceived a plan for cutting down on prostitution. He would read aloud at city council meetings the name of every man and woman who had been arrested for prostitution, a modern version of the pillory and stocks and a revival of Governor Oswald West's threat: "If the newspapers will not print the names [of crooks]," West had said in 1912, "I am going to get out on a soapbox in the streets and do a little publishing of my own."[114] An *Oregonian* editorial urged Clark to move with caution: no names should be read until after a person had been found guilty, and the mayor should include enough identifying information so that innocent people were not defamed.[115] Soon a judge found the mayor's plan unconstitutional. An African-American newspaper accused Clark of proposing the idea only because he knew it would fail. A panel of five out-of-town consultants had told Albina business owners that it was imperative to reduce prostitution there if they wanted to foster economic development.[116]

A twelve-point plan Clark proposed to break the cycle of homelessness became a key agenda item for his administration.[117] The plan included housing for the city's homeless, a center for troubled teenagers, longer hours for the detoxification center, a ban on the sale of fortified wine in Old Town, and putting all homeless-advocate agencies under one roof.[118]

Bud Clark was angered by a letter that surfaced in February 1986 inviting businessmen to a fund-raising lunch for Multnomah County Commissioner Earl Blumenauer, a candidate for Schwab's council position. (She was not seeking reelection.) The letter, signed by businessman Blake Hering, said: "I think we have all experienced some degree of frustration with City Hall over the past few years. In fact, if you feel as I do, City Hall is a disgrace. Council meetings turn into a three ring circus led by Clown Clark."[119]

Downtown merchants were annoyed with Clark's new ban on the sale of fortified wine in Old Town. Edward Hamilton, owner of Edward Hamilton Furrier, solicited five- and ten-dollar donations from other business owners to charter a bus that would gather up a load of derelicts around O'Bryant Square and haul them to Bud Clark's Goose Hollow Inn. There Hamilton promised to treat them to five hundred dollars' worth of free drinks, the equivalent of an eight hundred dollar bar tab today. "'The transients who are chronic alcoholics are creeping up into our area, and no one can do anything about it,' [Hamilton] said. 'Chief Penny Harrington says the police don't have the time or the manpower and that it's not a priority.' He added that he's attended several council meetings and 'they don't see it as a priority, either.' ... Clark acknowledged ... that street alcoholics who once inhabited Old Town were moving into other parts of the city, apparently so they could buy fortified wine."[120] The bus ride never happened.

"Whether he wishes to or not," Historian E. Kimbark MacColl said in a March 1986 opinion piece, "Clark must take the initiative to provide firm leadership and coordinated planning for city projects." MacColl spoke of fractured authority and divided responsibilities inherent in the commission form of government, and cited the controversy over a proposed Fred Meyer complex at N.E. Thirtieth Avenue and Halsey as an example of what happens "to an inexperienced mayor who is thrust unwittingly into a no-win situation."[121] MacColl was not alone in feeling uneasy about the lack of focus and disorganization evident in Clark's regime. More bad press was in store for Clark over the next few months.

First, the media revealed that one of Clark's top administrative aides had been under investigation in a cocaine-trafficking case for about eight months. A grand jury was expected to consider the case the following week.[122] The same staff member had also been interviewed "at least four times" regarding a major embezzlement case involving his former wife. The aide was not charged, but immediately took a leave of absence from his job while the investigation continued.

Rumors were also circulating that Police Chief Penny Harrington and her husband, Officer Bruce Gary Harrington, had tipped off the owner of a restaurant called Rickshaw Charlie's about a planned drug raid and the investigation of a prior shooting. Clark appointed a special committee to monitor an internal police investigation of these allegations against the Harringtons. He was asked at his weekly news conference about the Harrington investigation and his aide's cocaine trafficking case: "'The things that have been brought up, the things against the Harringtons, for instance, I think are just ridiculous,' Clark said. 'Everybody likes to convict people before they're guilty. … Somebody's out there trying to get us, I guess. … I think maybe they thought that it was impossible for a businessman to come out of the community and be the mayor of Portland.'"[123]

In April 1986, former U.S. Attorney Sidney Lezak convened the special committee appointed by Clark to monitor the Harrington investigation.[124] They took public testimony regarding allegations about Chief Harrington's relationship with the owner of Rickshaw Charlie's as well as her decision to disband the police drug and vice division and her management style in general. Deputy Chief Tom Potter "asked for and got" a demotion to captain, then testified that Harrington's reorganization had not been part of any deliberative planning process, and that Harrington had misled the committee in implying that it had.[125]

By mid-May, Clark was so frustrated and displeased with his media coverage that he cancelled his regular weekly news conferences. His press secretary, Jack McGowan, explained that Clark felt his time would be better spent elsewhere. "Clark believes the media have given too much attention to 'ongoing concerns with the police' and to just two segments of his 12-point plan for the homeless, the city purchase of hotels and the ban on fortified wine. 'The mayor believes the media failed to pay enough attention to other elements of the homeless plan and to his accomplishments in restoring city finances,' McGowan said."[126]

Sigrid Clark, Bud's wife of twenty-two years, gave a newspaper interview soon thereafter. She discussed her life since Bud was elected mayor, which included her taking over management of Goose Hollow Inn. Sigrid was an accomplished violinist who still played regularly with the Oregon Symphony, and who still managed Mother Goose Antiques. Bud worked about ninety hours a week as mayor, she said, and the two of them were working on the problem of finding time for each other.[127]

In the May 1986 primary, County Commissioner Earl Blumenauer racked up 55,500 votes to 5,500 for his nearest competitor to replace Mildred Schwab on the council. In a contested four-way race for the city auditor position (Lansing having earlier announced she would not seek reelection), CPA Barbara Clark received more than 50 percent of the vote.[128] The names of both successful candidates would appear uncontested on the fall ballot, and they would take office the following January.

One contested election remained for the fall. Commissioner Margaret Strachan missed winning a majority in her reelection bid by two thousand votes, and therefore faced city police officer Bob Koch in a November run-off.[129]

On June 2, 1986, Bud Clark announced the resignation of Police Chief Penny Harrington, sixteen months after her much-ballyhooed appointment. The Lezak committee had issued a "scathing 38-page report on the chief's management style, recommending her ouster."[130]

A storm of publicity and protest followed. The *Oregonian* editorialized that "the flailings of a well-meaning amateur in the mayor's chair at City Hall [had] greatly undermined the administration of his own appointee." The editorial charged Clark with enlarging the scope of inquiry after hearings started to include Harrington's reorganization of the bureau and to consider every gripe her subordinates could raise. Clark's budget had forced Harrington to cut seventy-two positions.

"Clark should examine his own management and maneuvering," the editorial said. "Then he should follow Harrington's example and step down as police commissioner."[131]

Columnist David Sarasohn said the Lezak report cited no violation of the law or departmental rules by Harrington. Her "deviousness" was apparently nothing more than implying that her decisions were better thought-out than they actually were. "If this is a reason for moving out public officials," Sarasohn said, "most of the people in the Portland Building should start preparing resumés." The real reason for her ouster was probably the dissatisfaction of police officers with her budget cuts and her firing of the cops who sold the "Smoke 'Em" T-shirts, Sarasohn said. Many officers felt she was too responsive to the black community. Furthermore, police officers didn't like her "no-smoking" edict for bureau personnel, nor were they interested in participating in her proposed sensitivity training.[132]

Harrington's firing captured media attention across the country. Soon a committee was formed to recall Mayor Clark, even as he declared his intent to seek reelection two years later. Commissioner Schwab announced she was strongly considering a mayoral race herself because she felt "a little nervous" about how the city was administered by Mayor Bud Clark. However, she opposed his recall, stating that the recall process should only be used in cases of malfeasance.[133]

In mid-August, Clark hired veteran police officer James T. Davis as his new police chief. A poll taken by the *Oregonian* showed Clark's approval rating had suffered a sharp drop during the fifteen-month period May 1985 to August 1986, from 67 percent to 46 percent. His performance as police commissioner rated especially low: 63 percent of respondents graded him fair or poor, with only 25 percent giving him good or excellent marks. This was almost an exact reversal of his approval ratings four months after Harrington's appointment. His highest marks were for outgoing personality and involvement with citizens. In a potential mayor's race against Schwab, she led by 4 percent. Clark predicted that his appointment of Chief Jim Davis had marked the beginning of his administration's "come-back" and that six months from now public opinion of his accomplishments would be brighter.[134]

A month later, Clark was in trouble again. Speaking off the cuff to NBC-TV anchorman Tom Brokaw, Clark said: "The only time Mildred [Schwab] ever has an orgasm is in the middle of a budget meeting." Clark apparently believed this to be a private remark. However, Brokaw repeated the comment to an audience of over seven hundred people at a Portland Advertising Federation luncheon that day, and the remark was taped by local radio and rebroadcast later.[135] The next day, a mayor's office staff member brought Clark a greeting card with a cartoon of a dog with a head at each end, the two heads looking at each other. One of the heads said to the other, "One of us is an asshole."[136] Clark apologized to Schwab, who graciously commented later in the day, "If he has learned his lesson, to think before he talks, then all is forgiven."[137]

MAX light rail service from downtown Portland to Gresham via Lloyd Center and the Gateway shopping mall—fifteen miles—began September 5, 1986. Neil Goldschmidt was now running for governor against popular Secretary of State Norma Paulus. His campaign manager, Bill Scott, later admitted to being "chicken" about putting Goldschmidt on the inaugural MAX run because it wasn't at all clear how MAX would be received. Worry was needless, however, because citizen response to MAX was gratifying.[138]

An October *Oregonian* article gave Clark and his staff a pat on the back regarding their progress: "Veteran observers of city government say Clark is growing into the job, is putting his stamp on city government and may turn out to be a surprisingly effective mayor—despite the problems that have plagued his second year." Former Goldschmidt staffer Len Bergstein noted: "It takes a while to understand that not every power you have is written down and not every power that's written down, you've got." It was Clark's "casual, forthright manner" that was both his biggest strength and the trait that got him into the most hot water. Clark and staff were now focusing in closer on specific goals: To create a safer city, preserve jobs and promote investment, and deliver "maximum service at minimum cost."[139]

The mayor's executive assistant, Christine Tobkin, was chosen for that position by her peers at a mayor's staff retreat in July 1985, and received a vote of confidence from them in September 1986 at another retreat. The staff developed a stubborn esprit de corps, an *Oregonian* article said, based partly on Clark's loyalty to staff. When his aide's cocaine-trafficking case was withdrawn from the grand jury, Clark brought him back on staff. Furthermore, he had provided the aide with paid administrative leave while he was under investigation.[140]

In a surprise upset, police lieutenant Bob Koch defeated Commissioner Margaret Strachan in the November election. An August poll had given Strachan a commanding 27 percent lead.[141] The Central City plan she had worked so hard on was not something that caught the public eye, so probably did not help her at the ballot box.[142] In a press conference

Long-held suspicions by both incoming and existing residents that annexations were costing each group more than the other were assuaged by an urban services audit released by Auditor Lansing in September. After extensive examination of a vast array of tradeoffs, her auditors found that newly annexed and long-time city residents were being affected almost equally. New financial burdens were placed on city residents to bring annexed areas up to city standards of service, while new Portlanders were helping to pay old city obligations such as the annual police and fire pension fund levy.[144]

after the election, Strachan attributed her loss to a fabricated last-minute accusation by Koch that she planned to impose fees for street maintenance and other city services if elected. Her hairstyle may also have contributed to her loss; she now wore it pulled back severely from her face into a pigtail or bun in back, whereas her earlier *Voters' Pamphlet* photo had shown her long hair in soft curls around her face. Campaign staffers agreed that Strachan's hairstyle came up frequently on the doorstep, noting that women candidates were still held to different standards than men. Strachan polled 49 percent to Koch's 51 percent—a difference of three thousand votes.[143]

Meanwhile, Mayor Clark had been out stumping for passage of a measure to be voted on by citizens throughout the metropolitan area: funding for a regional convention center to be built in Portland. All three counties passed the property tax measure by margins ranging from 50.7 percent in Clackamas County to 52.6 percent in Multnomah County, and 54.5 percent in Washington County; this was gratifying news to Mayor Clark and others who had worked hard for its success.[145] Supporters now turned their attention to Salem, looking to governor-elect Neil Goldschmidt to help gain the fifteen million dollars of state money needed to complete the funding package.[146]

With a parting shot at the Police and Fire Disability and Retirement Fund, Jewel Lansing completed her four years as Portland's auditor on December 31, 1986. The fund was overly generous, she said, and Portland's police officers and firefighters were disabled more often and for longer periods than other uniformed employees statewide. She noted their retirement benefits were higher than those paid to most other public employees.[147] An *Oregonian* article credited Lansing with transforming the job of auditor from that of "an invisible bean-counter" to a "high-profile, independently elected official with the staff and power to monitor the performance of local government operations, and to let the public in on the findings."[148]

An *Oregonian* banner headline in April 1987 proclaimed: "Mayor fires Police Chief Davis." Not only had Clark fired Davis less than a year after he had hired him, but he had done so at the Fat City Café, a place that captured the public's imagination. The mayor and chief had met to iron out accumulating tensions. Davis insisted that he needed one hundred twenty new police officers, but reconciled himself to only thirty more. Then he learned that Clark's proposed budget included none. About the same time, City Auditor Barbara Clark's office prepared a draft audit that said, among other things, that the police bureau could do away with at least sixteen sworn-officer positions by using non-sworn personnel for routine office work. Davis demanded that copies of all audit work papers be sent to his office, and threatened to sue the city if his request was not met.[149] The dialogue at Fat City Café went something like this:

> Chief Davis: "*Read my lips, I want the Auditor's files delivered to my office.*"
> Mayor Clark: "*Read my lips: You are no longer the Chief of Police.*"[150]

According to the *Oregonian*, that last line by Clark was even simpler: "Read my lips. Goodbye."[151]

Davis announced immediately that he would run for mayor in 1988. Fat City, a small Multnomah neighborhood restaurant, enjoyed a surge in business. The owner put up a plaque above the booth where the two warriors had sat: "Fat City Massacre. Lip Reading Done Here." The café became an unofficial headquarters for Davis's campaign.[152]

Clark appointed insider Richard Walker as new police chief. Walker would remain on the job for three and a half years.

Soon thereafter, Clark cancelled an invitation the city had extended to the International Police Chiefs' Association to hold their convention in Portland the following year. He explained that the city didn't have enough money in its budget to cover security costs for such a large convention. His decision caused such adverse reaction that Clark changed his mind a week later, "asserting he had found the needed money."[153]

Despite his trouble keeping a police chief, Bud Clark garnered sixty-three thousand votes in his May 1988 reelection bid against ten primary opponents, only seven hundred eighty-five votes shy of a majority.[154] In the fall, Clark faced former police chief Ron Still, who had placed second in the primary. Ex-chief Still garnered strong support from the downtown business establishment, but he was no match for Bud at the ballot box. Election day in November saw Clark winning by an impressive 18 percent margin, a difference of thirty-four thousand votes.[155]

❧

The Portland City Club still harbored doubts about the efficiency and effectiveness of the commission form of government, and had appointed a study committee to take a fresh look two years before. Now the study committee concluded that Portland's present governing structure was not so bad after all. In a fifty-five-page draft report that the board declined to publish, the committee, headed by lawyer Barnes Ellis, said that major problems facing the city were being addressed as well as in cities with other forms of government. The prospect of an improved city government was not great enough to "warrant the years of turmoil and uncertainty reorganization would cause," the draft said, even though the committee took note of "turf protection, buck-passing and lack of clear leadership" often evident with "five virtually co-equal city commissioners" under the present system. The committee reminded its board that attempts to revamp city government were defeated in 1958 and 1966, and that nothing had happened since then to change the public's mind.[156]

❧

Nationally, Portland received many accolades. In 1985, *The New Yorker* hailed Portland's "closely controlled new building, the carefully monitored rehabilitation of worthy old buildings, [and] the vigorous creation of open space," calling Portland a city of "individuality and distinction." An informal 1988 poll of national planning experts rated Portland's efforts to deal with urban design among the best in the nation. Downtown Portland won a City Livability Award from the U.S. Conference of Mayors the same year, and the following year, the Bruner Foundation awarded the city its Award for Urban Excellence. These awards were based primarily on the city's "strong and vibrant" downtown.[157]

> The Oregon Vietnam Veterans' Living Memorial, located near the World Forestry Center and Oregon Zoo, was dedicated in 1987.[158]

All during 1987 and 1988, while an all-male city council held forth in city hall, an all-female county commission deliberated in the Multnomah County Courthouse two blocks north. The point was not lost on observers that the pay scale for city officials far exceeded that for the county, whose office-holders were now hobbled by a charter amendment requiring voter approval of any increase in salary—a formidable obstacle.[159]

Around this time, a controversial Mid-County Sewer Project got underway, a task mandated by the state Department of Environmental Quality and fought by area residents. The project would eventually take eleven years, utilize three hundred ninety-four miles of pipe, and cover twenty-eight square miles of the city east of the Willamette River, mostly newly annexed areas.[160]

Also during the Bud Clark years:

- the council banned the use of Styrofoam containers for take-out food from restaurants located in Portland city limits;[161]
- Clark accepted Governor Neil Goldschmidt's offer for Oregon National Guard assistance in containing the city's gang problem in summer 1989;[162]
- the council voted against adding a southbound ramp onto the Interstate 5 freeway near the Marquam Bridge and against moving I-5 off the east bank of the Willamette;[163]
- the council changed the name of N.E. Union Avenue to Martin Luther King Boulevard (having decided against naming Front Avenue for King after downtown business leaders strenuously objected);[164]
- city voters approved a 7.3 million-dollar levy for park improvements, including funds for acquiring green spaces, natural areas, parks, trails, and other projects;[165]
- Goodyear started advertising on the tower overlooking the racetrack at the Portland International Speedway for twenty-five thousand dollars per year;[166]
- and across the globe, Central Europe's Berlin Wall came down in 1989, marking an end to the Cold War with the Soviet Union.

After a short period of comparative calm in city hall, the atmosphere turned stormy in fall 1989, near the beginning of Mayor Clark's second term. The whirlwind centered around "an angry, stubborn side" to Mayor Clark's personality of which most people had been previously unaware.[167] It started around the time a negative *Sunday Oregonian* feature about Clark appeared as part of a series on crime.[168] An *Oregonian* columnist said it documented "how badly" the mayor had "failed to respond to the problems that have faced his administration."[169]

A sprightly new fountain opened in Waterfront Park in 1988, named Salmon Street Springs through a contest held the following year. Water in the fountain was propelled through 185 jets and danced in three different cycles of changing patterns known as "misters, bollards and wedding cake."[170]

Since 1988, the Salmon Street Springs fountain at Waterfront Park has delighted children of all ages. (Author's photo)

Clark had recently dismissed press aide Kathy Dimond and his black community liaison Ollie Smith. He had threatened to pull the parks bureau from Commissioner Mike Lindberg's control after learning that Lindberg planned to hire Charles Jordan, a potential mayoral rival, as parks director. He engendered a storm of protest when he told black leaders that he wanted to be his own liaison to them, then angered them by saying he would try to get a better suntan.[171] A group of black leaders condemned Clark's actions and demanded an apology. Two weeks after the fact, Clark appeared in front of *The Skanner*, a black-owned weekly newspaper, to publicly apologize for his remark about getting a suntan. It took him a while to understand why the comment was offensive, Clark said, and he had not meant it as a joke. He promised to hire another liaison to the black community, and said that aide would probably be black, as Ollie Smith had been.[172]

Clark's actions were widely seen as evidence of a siege mentality, which appalled many of his supporters. [173] Historian E. Kimbark MacColl publicly voiced his displeasure with Clark, saying Clark might face a recall effort if his uneven leadership continued. *Oregonian* columnists Steve Duin and Phil Stanford jumped on the bandwagon rolling over Clark.[174]

Clark's popularity continued its steady decline, according to an *Oregonian* opinion poll taken in February 1990. Now almost three-fourths of Portland voters viewed Clark's mayoral performance as fair or poor. "This 'whoop, whoop' stuff has got to stop," said a plumber from Linnton interviewed by a reporter. "It just seems like he's in over his head but won't admit it. … I wouldn't vote for him again."[175]

Former police chief Penny Harrington filed a sex discrimination suit against Mayor Clark and the city, which went to trial in February 1990. Harrington said she had had a difficult time finding a job in police work after leaving the city. At the time her suit went to trial, she was employed by the investigative division of the California State Bar Association. City Attorney Jeff Rogers, called as a defense witness, testified that Clark had been "under great pressure" to remove Harrington before the Lezak committee was even appointed, pressure which a reporter understood to come from the police union and news media.[176] Clark's executive assistant, Chris Tobkin, told the court that growing public and press criticism of Harrington for eliminating the police drug and vice unit had motivated Tobkin to recommend that Clark appoint a special review committee.[177]

Chuck Duffy, Clark's police liaison at the time of Harrington's termination, said Harrington had not been fired, but rather had quit. According to Duffy, after Clark showed her the Lezak Commission report recommending that she be replaced, Harrington declared, "I cannot continue as chief of police in light of this report." Harrington's attorney insisted that Harrington had no choice at that point but to resign.[178] It also came out in the trial, as *Willamette Week* had previously informed its readers, that Clark's soothing words to Harrington after she resigned were: "Tits up!"[179]

Harrington's civil rights suit was unanimously rejected by the jury. After the verdict came in and Clark was walking back to

> The all-male city council unanimously agreed to ask the all-male Arlington and University clubs to open their doors to women. Both clubs maintained facilities in downtown Portland. If the two clubs did not allow women as members by January 1, 1990, council members warned that they would enact a law banning such discrimination. Both clubs "voluntarily" changed their admissions rules, and no ordinance was needed.[180]

Mayor Bud Clark's hiring and firing of police chief Penny Harrington, and his earthy comments after she lost her sexual discrimination suit, inspired this 1990 Oregonian *cartoon by Jack Ohman*

city hall with his lawyers and staff member Chris Tobkin, Clark "shook hands with each attorney, clapped each one on the back and said, 'Tits up.'" The following week, Clark issued another public apology. "For those people who are offended, I'm sorry," he said at a televised news conference. "That's about all I can say. My family and my children are upset that people are upset." He did not consider his exclamation to Harrington sexist, he said. It was a phrase he had often used.[181]

Although Harrington lost her lawsuit, the city's defense had cost taxpayers over three hundred thousand dollars in legal fees, as the *Oregonian* informed its readers in a six-column headline.[182] Harrington was awarded a full pension for her time on the city police force,[183] and later in the summer dropped her appeal of the jury verdict.[184]

❧

The heady days of Mayor Bud Clark's campaign and his first exciting year in office were almost forgotten by now. Clark's exuberance and love of the city were laudable at first, his colorful language charming. But the bloom had been off the rose for nearly five years, in the words of a city hall reporter.[185] Since the previous fall, Clark had limited his regular media contact to weekly cable-television broadcasts where he could talk directly to the people without a reporter. Although he liked and respected some reporters, he said, he was bitter because the "institutional news media had turned against him." In spite of this, Clark made no move to fill his press secretary's position, now vacant for six months.[186]

Without a press secretary, Clark held an open-air news conference at Pioneer Courthouse Square in April 1990. He was surrounded by members of a forty-member policy committee of respected community leaders he had appointed to guide a year-long strategic planning process called Portland Future Focus. "The committee will examine trends in Portland," Clark announced, "following specific issues, such as crime, transportation, housing, parks and social services. It will then set a vision for the city and spin out specific work plans to get to that vision. … The city is investing $400,000 and staff time to the job … [and] businesses are expected to make in-kind donations."[187]

Soon thereafter, another council member drew the spotlight from Clark. An assistant to Commissioner Dick Bogle filed a sexual-harassment complaint citing more than a dozen inappropriate actions and comments by Bogle.[188] The claim was settled two months later, and Bogle agreed to pay the twenty thousand-dollar settlement from his own pocket.[189] Only a month later, Bogle had more bad press, this time for his failure to itemize or document fifteen hundred dollars' worth of travel expenses for a city business trip to Asia two years before. Bogle insisted that there had been no misuse of funds, but agreed to reimburse the city for the questioned amounts.[190]

In the May 1990 primary election, County Commissioner Gretchen Kafoury, a former state legislator, ousted former police officer Bob Koch after he had served only one term on the council.[191] Kafoury was a popular liberal and an outspoken political activist who had served three terms in the state legislature and six years on the county commission.[192]

Decorative twin spires now rose on the east side of the river, adding a distinctive new landmark to the Portland skyline. The handsome Oregon Convention Center opened in September 1990.[193] On the west side of the river, a Japanese-American Historical Plaza was dedicated, commemorating both internment of Japanese Americans during World War II and their reintegration into Portland life.[194] Pioneer Place shopping mall in downtown Portland also opened in 1990.[195]

When Police Chief Richard Walker retired in November 1990,[196] Clark named Captain Tom Potter, a strong advocate of community policing, as his next chief. Potter said he had watched a succession of chiefs during his career. "I've seen a lot of people walk in the front door smiling," he said. "I've seen a lot of people leave the back door without a smile. My personal goal is to walk out of this with a smile."[197]

A second Clark aide was now being investigated for alleged use of cocaine. This aide resigned abruptly after the investigation became known, although no charges had been filed against him. When reporters reached Clark at his home for comment, Clark responded in anger: "You're going to say what you want to say, and I can't compete with that."[198] On his weekly cable-TV show,[199] Mayor Clark urged his audience not to drink and drive, noting that twenty-eight years before, in mid-November, his first wife had been killed by a drunken driver.

Barbara Roberts was sworn in as Oregon's first woman governor in January 1991, the same month that Clark announced that he would not seek a third term. Clark was confident he would win if he did run, he said, although polls indicated otherwise. Key staff from prior campaigns had also made it clear they would no longer be part of his team.[200]

That summer, Commissioner Mike Lindberg asked residents not to water their lawns because the city's water supply was so low. A severe drought continued through most of September, and back-up ground wells were used to augment Bull Run water for forty-five days.[201] Mayor Clark admonished fellow Portlanders to conserve. "You don't have to flush every time you wee-wee," he said.[202]

In answer to a 1992 poll asking respondents if Portland was better off, worse, or about the same after Clark's eight years in office, 46 percent felt the city was about the same, while "better off" received a 5 percent edge over "worse off."[203]

Oregon voters passed Measure 5, a restrictive 1-1/2 percent property tax limit measure, in November 1990, in spite of opposition by virtually every state and local public official. Measure 5 capped all school and local government levies combined at fifteen mills, or fifteen dollars for each one thousand dollars of the lesser of real market value or assessed value.[204] More will be said about Measure 5 later.

Clark's planned exit from the political scene had encouraged strong candidates to enter the 1992 mayoral race. The two leading contenders were veteran councilman Earl Blumenauer and the first woman speaker of the Oregon House of Representatives, Vera Katz.[205] Vera projected a warm, motherly image, while Earl appeared cerebral and efficient, somewhat stern. Both were seasoned public figures who knew how to raise campaign funds and how to articulate their agendas. *Willamette Week* termed their race, "Battle of the Bleeding Hearts."[206] In the fall, Katz won decisively with a 14 percent edge.

The race between Commissioner Dick Bogle and his challenger, neighborhood association activist Charlie Hales, was much closer. With only a 3 percent margin, Charlie Hales unseated Bogle from the position he had held for eight years.[207] A Republican and vice-president of the Metro Homebuilders Association when elected,[208] thirty-seven-year-old Hales would sever both those ties before leaving office after nine and a half years of service on council.[209] Hales was to gain a reputation as a bold planner and advocate for transportation and parks issues, and would likely have run for mayor in 2000 had Mayor Katz not sought reelection.

OMSI, the popular Oregon Museum of Science and Industry, moved from its old location near the Washington Park Zoo to spacious new quarters on the southeast riverfront in 1992. The impressive new facility was renovated from an abandoned power plant.[210]

Bud Clark left office at the end of December 1992 as one of the most accessible mayors in modern history—accessible to everyone but the media by the end of his tenure. Clark treated citizens and city staff members who appeared before the council with courtesy and respect. Unfortunately, he never learned to handle media criticism, and was unwilling to hire strong staff members who could compensate for his weaknesses. Nevertheless, the city survived and thrived under his stewardship. All council members contributed significantly to the city's welfare in their various spheres of responsibility.

Clark introduced community policing, managed budget cuts under a statewide property tax limitation measure, guided Portland through a difficult financial slump, made inroads against drug-dealing and prostitution, drew community leaders together for the Portland Future Focus, and helped assure successful passage of the Oregon Convention Center measure. His twelve-point plan for the homeless was an important step in the right direction.[211]

As for his "casual dress, beard, and cheerful 'Whoop, Whoop' greeting," *Willamette Week* noted that Bud Clark was more in step with Portland than "almost any mayor that preceded him."[212]

Chapter 25

Today's Decisions — Tomorrow's History

January 1993 – April 2001

Mayor

No. 49: January 1993 - December 1996

Vera Katz (elected for four-year term)

January 1997 - December 2000

Vera Katz (elected for four-year term)

January 2001 - present

Vera Katz (elected for four-year term)

When Mayor O'Bryant governed Portland in 1851, the town was a remote outpost reachable only by water, a frontier settlement of boarding houses and transients, gold dust and whiskey. Women's roles were limited to those of housewife (of whom there were few),[1] prostitute (of whom there were fewer), or maid (of whom there were even fewer).

As Portland government celebrated its one hundred fiftieth year,[2] the person at the helm represented a turn-about from that earlier day. Vera Katz was the third woman to serve as mayor,[3] the fifth Jewish mayor, and the sixth mayor who was foreign born.[4] She was the forty-fourth person to claim the mayor's seat; four other mayors had served nine interspersed terms.[5]

Born of Russian heritage in Dusseldorf, Germany, Vera Pistrak was a year old when her politically oriented parents gathered up Vera and her older sister to flee the Nazis for France in 1934. Six years later, the family escaped France on foot across the Pyrenees Mountains into Portugal. They arrived in New York essentially penniless. When Vera was eleven, her father abandoned the family, leaving her mother to earn money however she could—knitting sweaters, making beaded bags, laboring in garment sweat shops, taking in laundry. It was a childhood of poverty and constant moving from one disadvantaged neighborhood to another.

Vera found her refuge in work and study. She graduated from Brooklyn College with a degree in sociology and anthropology, and

Mayor Vera Katz. (Photo by Joseph Grimes)

married a young artist named Mel Katz. She was employed as a market researcher for eight years in New York before she and Mel and their two and a half-year-old son Jesse moved to northwest Portland in 1964. Jesse started school about the time presidential candidate Bobby Kennedy established a campaign headquarters in Portland, and Vera Katz made her first foray into politics by licking stamps and soaking up the atmosphere of the highly charged Kennedy campaign. (She also taught dance, part time, at the private Catlin Gabel Lower School.) When Neil Goldschmidt ran for city council in 1970, Katz joined his cadre of volunteers. By 1972, she was challenging incumbent state representative Fritzi Chuinard, a Republican, for a seat in the legislature. Katz walked door-to-door throughout the district, and won that first campaign with a two-to-one edge.[6]

Following this initial victory, Katz served ten terms in the Oregon House. During three of these sessions, she served as the first woman speaker, the second woman in the entire country to so serve. At the beginning of her legislative career, Katz voted an ultra-liberal Democratic line, but became more conservative after she served on the ways and means committee, where she grew proficient at analyzing state budgets. In the 1983 session, she favored a 5 percent sales tax dedicated to schools, a position that put her at odds with traditional Portland liberals.[7]

Vera and Mel Katz were divorced in 1985, but Vera continued to live in northwest Portland, where she still resides today. She does not drive, and uses the city transit system when not utilizing a city car and driver.

Her physical presence "sets her apart and makes her rise to influence particularly curious in a state as distinctively Western as Oregon," said *Oregonian* reporter Foster Church in 1990. "She stands 5 feet 3-1/2 inches tall and varies grandly in weight—50 pounds or more, from svelte to zaftig—depending on the pressures of the season. … [S]he is a striking woman, beautiful in her fashion: prominent cheekbones, dancing eyes, a broad, prominent mouth. The looks contribute to her aura of command. In a photograph, a joint appearance, attention fastens on Vera Katz. She wears bright colors and bold, fashionable jewelry. And then there is her speech, startling in Oregon: a heavy, laid-on-with-a-trowel New York accent, acquired in her youth."[8]

After her election as mayor in 1992, Katz sailed through two reelections with no serious challenge; she was immensely popular with the voters. She was elected in 2000 to her third four-year term,[9] and became the third-longest-serving mayor in Portland's history.[10] She announced in July 2003 that she would not seek a fourth term.

As an outsider to city hall, Mayor Katz had definite ideas about how city government ought to be run, and was committed to the use of modern management tools. With political skills honed in partisan legislative halls, her style was considerably more authoritarian than that of her predecessor. Even so, this council—composed of Vera Katz, Earl Blumenauer, Charlie Hales, Gretchen Kafoury, and Mike Lindberg—was to work together creatively, albeit with internal tensions, for the next four years.

"That's the way we've always done it" was not a justifiable bureaucratic response to either Katz or Hales, neither of whom had any previous experience in city government. Although Katz and Blumenauer had waged a hard-fought mayoral campaign and came down on opposite sides over the contentious issue of moving the Eastbank Freeway (Katz, for; Blumenauer, against), they were remarkably civil to each other in their public dealings. The council meetings were more orderly and polite under Katz than under most previous mayors, and therefore less interesting as a spectator sport. The two most frequently at odds behind the scenes were Katz and Kafoury, in spite of similar basic philosophies and having served together during three legislative sessions. Kafoury maintained that the mayor did not involve other council members enough in crucial city decisions[11] and several budget decisions were three-to-two, with Hales and Lindberg supporting the mayor.

1996 council members, left to right: Charlie Hales, Mike Lindberg, Mayor Vera Katz, and Gretchen Kafoury. Commissioner Earl Blumenauer had left for another meeting before the picture was taken. Council chambers underwent extensive renovation soon after this picture was taken. (Photo by Aubrey "Al" Smith)

In 1995, Blumenauer was elected to represent Oregon's third congressional district in congress, and resigned his council seat in mid-term.[12] Blumenauer was to champion livable communities in congress, utilizing his solid grounding gained in twenty-two years as an elected official in state and local government.[13] Since Lindberg had already decided not to seek reelection, two council seats opened up at almost the same time.

A quirk of fate helped propel Erik Sten into office at age twenty-eight. After losing in a hot primary contest for Lindberg's seat to Jim Francesconi and Gail Shibley, Sten filed for a special September primary being held for Blumenauer's seat. With a strong campaign organization still intact, Sten then bested a primary field of sixteen and won a November run-off against Chuck Duffy, a former member of Mayor Clark's staff.[14] Sten, a product of Portland public schools and Stanford University, was chief of staff to Commissioner Kafoury and had played a lead role in X-Pac, an organization that worked to get young voters more involved in politics.[15]

Jim Francesconi, an attorney in private practice, won the fall contest against Shibley with a nine thousand-vote edge. Francesconi was a graduate of the University of Oregon law school in Eugene, and co-founder of the Jesuit Volunteers' Youth Employment and Empowerment Project of the Portland Organizing Project.[16]

Two years later, in 1998, Kafoury, after two terms in office, declined to run for a third term, leaving a record of passionate advocacy for affordable housing and progressive causes.[17] Her seat was won by Dan Saltzman, an environmental engineer and a graduate of Beaverton High School, Cornell University, and M. I. T.[18] Saltzman gained his seat after a fall run-off against fellow-Multnomah county commissioner Tanya Collier. Auditor Barbara Clark retired the same year, after twelve years in that position.[19] Gary Blackmer, the incumbent Multnomah County auditor and a certified internal auditor with seven years experience as a performance auditor for the city of Portland, drew no opponents when he filed to replace her.[20]

When city government celebrated its sesquicentennial in 2001, the average age of its six elected officials was sixteen years older than the first seven officials to serve the city. In 1851, ages had ranged from twenty-three to forty-four; in 2001, the range was from thirty-three to sixty-seven.[21] No powerful personality clashes were evident between council members as the new century began, and continuous cable TV coverage of council meetings kept many council squabbles out of the council chambers.[22]

❧

The most influential position in city hall was held by thirty-seven-year-old Sam Adams, the "confidant, political strategist and chief of staff" to Mayor Katz. Lured from his position as political director of the House Democratic Caucus to run Katz's 1992 mayoral campaign, Adams also directed her political and administrative affairs as her "exec" from the time she arrived in city hall.[23]

Three police chiefs served under Katz in her first ten and a half years as mayor. Police Chief Tom Potter resigned six months after Katz took office, leaving a two and a half-year legacy of good police-community relations. Potter championed the rights of gays and lesbians, and let the public know how proud he was of his daughter Katie, "an openly lesbian police officer."[24] The mayor chose Charles Moose, a veteran of the local force, as Portland's first and only black chief of police to date. Moose, who remained on the job for six years before accepting a chief's job in Maryland, once publicly chastised local TV stations for showing live coverage that endangered officers' lives, embarrassing the stations into reforming their ways.[25] After a nationwide search, the mayor hired Mark Kroeker, a former Los Angeles deputy chief of police, in late 1999.[26] Kroeker's salary was the highest in city government in 2000, at one hundred thirty-four thousand dollars.[27] As an outsider to the force,

Kroeker's settling-in period was rocky,[28] but he earned respect by sincere apologies for previous remarks, an approachable demeanor, and frequent public appearances.

State politics played a defining role in Portland's fortunes during the last decade of the century as citizen activist Bill Sizemore championed statewide ballot measures that curtailed school funding, cut social services, limited civic improvements, and restricted civil liberties.[29] Sizemore, an unsuccessful city council candidate in 1981 and 1984, received prominent news coverage as a sponsor of Measure 47, passed in November 1996, and Measure 50, passed in May 1997. Together, the measures reduced statewide assessed property values to their 1995 value less 10 percent, and limited future increases in value to 3 percent annually.

Under these constitutional amendments, local option levies were possible only when a majority of those casting ballots approved the levy *and* when a majority of registered voters actually voted—the so-called "double majority" rule–that could be avoided only in November elections in even-numbered years. The 1-1/2 percent property tax limitation imposed by Measure 5 in 1990 was retained, with 1/2 percent specified for schools and the remaining 1 percent allocated to all other government functions combined. Every local taxing district suffered a cut in its 1997 operating levy, with levies for bonded debt excluded. Portland's Fire and Police Disability and Retirement Fund was excluded from the Measure 50 cut, but had to be included in the 1 percent property tax levy total, thereby serving to "compress" other governmental levies in the Portland area. Portland government lost over two million dollars in property tax revenue in 1997-98 because of compression required by

National issues and events during the Katz tenure included the near-impeachment of President Bill Clinton; the proliferation of Indian casinos and state-run lotteries; Y2K—a widespread fear of computer failures throughout the nation that proved to be more hype than premonition when internal computer clocks turned from 1999 to 2000; a spectacular rise and subsequent fall of stock market prices; an increase in the number of women U.S. senators from four in 1993 to thirteen in 2001;[30] and a tight presidential election in November 2000 between George W. Bush and Al Gore, finally settled in Bush's favor after extended legal skirmishes in Florida and the U.S. Supreme Court.

Measure 5, in addition to twenty million dollars in cuts engendered by Measure 50.[31]

In 1993, Oregon held the nation's first statewide vote-by-mail election, celebrated the one hundred fiftieth anniversary of the Oregon Trail; and decisively rejected a sales tax for the umpteenth time in state history. In 1994, state voters approved a pioneering assisted suicide law to allow terminally ill adults to obtain prescriptions for lethal drugs (reaffirmed at the ballot box in 1997 but subject to possible federal intervention).[32] In 1998, Oregon voters endorsed the medical use of marijuana. In 2000, the Oregon electorate passed Measure 7, requiring Oregon governments to compensate property owners for decreases in property value caused by government action, a measure later ruled unconstitutional.[33] Voters rejected ballot measures aimed at restricting the civil rights of homosexuals three times in nine years—Measure 9 in 1992; Measure 13 in 1994; and Measure 9 in 2000. In 2001, thirty women sat in the Oregon state legislature, tying Oregon for fifth place in largest percentage of women legislators in the nation.[34]

❧

In Portland, the council adopted a special funding mechanism to pay for uniformed employees of the private Association for Portland Progress (APP) to improve downtown security, cleanliness, and incidence of crime. This property-management license fee was challenged and upheld by the Oregon Tax Court.[35]

Cadres of volunteers, led by Mayor Vera Katz, stacked sandbags along the shores and banks of the Willamette River when it flooded in February 1996. City employees and volunteers erected a four-foot high, mile-long plywood barrier along the downtown seawall to keep out flood waters. Fortunately, the water crested at 28.6 feet before it topped the wall, nearly four feet lower than the 32.45 feet crest of Christmas Day 1964, and four and a half feet lower than the all-time high of 33 feet in June 1894.[38] A plaque along the seawall designates the spot where President Clinton viewed devastation caused by the flood and praised the city's volunteer efforts.[39]

> The city celebrated its first Cinco de Mayo festival in 1995,[36] and welcomed the first games played in the Rose Garden, a sports arena complex built largely by software billionaire Paul Allen, owner of the Portland Trailblazers professional basketball team.[37]

Even more potentially dangerous than the possibility of water breaching the seawall, however, was the undrinkable muddy water that emanated from the Bull Run water shed. "On Feb. 7 [1996], city officials quietly took a risky step. As the Bull Run ran muddy, they started drawing water from two dozen wells along the Columbia River, including wells unused since 1987 because of the threat of contamination. … [P]ast logging partly is being blamed for the muddy debris that washed out the [Bull Run] water supply."[40]

At the Oregon Symphony, conductor James DePreist, nephew of "legendary contralto Marian Anderson," was bringing national recognition to Portland's music scene. The Portland Art Museum prospered under the leadership of husband-and-wife team John and Lucy Buchanan, who attracted four hundred thirty thousand people to the "The Imperial Tombs of China" exhibit, expanded the museum's space and doubled its budget, completed an impressive 13.3 million-dollar capital campaign, and more than doubled membership.[44]

Also in 1996, the council changed the name of Front Avenue to Naito Parkway to honor Bill Naito, a local visionary and businessman who had recently died.[41] The "rush to rename" violated a city law requiring a five-year wait after a person's death before honoring that person with a renaming, an ordinance passed after a furor caused by the council's process for changing Union Avenue to Martin Luther King, Jr. Boulevard in 1989.[42] In the case of Naito Parkway, the council waived the waiting period with no objection from the Portland Chamber of Commerce.[43]

A measure to establish term limits for city elected officials was soundly defeated in 1996,[45] and a similar effort in 2000 failed to gain enough signatures to get on the ballot.[46] Off-leash dog areas were established in 1996 on a trial basis at Chimney, Gabriel, and Mt. Tabor parks, but continued to be a source of conflict.[47]

A newly refurbished city hall opened in April 1998 after a sorely needed, two-year renovation of the one-hundred-three-year-old structure.[48] The combination of old and new features created a majestic interior and brought the building into compliance with city codes. During the makeover, city hall employees occupied temporary quarters in the old state office building two blocks south. Final project cost: more than twenty-nine million dollars.[49]

An important downtown block escaped fate as a twelve-story parking garage when developer Tom Moyer bought one of the "missing" park blocks in 1998 and turned it over to the city.[50] Two years later, the city's long-time dream of reclaiming all the park blocks was reawakened with

MAX West, an eighteen-mile light-rail line from downtown Portland to Washington County, began service in September 1998, utilizing a three-mile tunnel dug through the West Hills,[53] the same West Hills that had presented such a formidable barrier to transportation in 1851.

the announcement by former mayor Neil Goldschmidt that four additional properties were being bought or donated, and that eighteen patrons had agreed to donate twenty-five thousand dollars each toward acquiring such property. A pedestrian promenade of shops, restaurants, and trees with generous underground parking was proposed, then scaled back when opposition ensued.[51] Work toward a long-term goal of joining the north and south park blocks continued.[52]

Consolidation of Portland and Multnomah County was again given serious consideration when an eleven-member citizens' task force undertook a year-long study of pros and cons. A task force majority concluded that study of consolidation should be continued.[54] This so alarmed east county officials that they looked at possible ways to secede from Multnomah County.[55] A measure to allow new counties to form failed on the 2000 statewide ballot, but the idea of Portland - Multnomah County consolidation had already been shot down by city and county officials shortly after the task force report was released.[56] Some observers thought that burgeoning Washington County with its high-tech industries would be a more logical community of interest for Portland to pursue than east Multnomah County.[57]

Urban renewal again played a major role in upgrading the city's infrastructure at the end of the twentieth century. Tax increment financing for urban renewal projects had increased substantially after passage of statewide property tax limitation Measures 5, 47, and 50 in 1990, 1996, and 1997, respectively.[58] "While the city's general fund stagnates," an October 2000 *Oregonian* article noted, "the PDC budget has more than quadrupled in just three years to $230 million, restoring it as one of the most powerful local government agencies in Oregon."[59] In October 1998, the council approved a three-hundred-nine-acre River District urban renewal project in northwest Portland that included plans for fifty-five hundred new housing units, four parks, and retail and commercial development.[60] The area included abandoned railroad yards, contaminated former industrial sites, underutilized buildings, and surface parking lots. The unsightly Lovejoy Ramp onto the Broadway Bridge was to be torn down as part of the project. Although the League of Women Voters and others protested that one hundred million dollars would be lost to other local taxing districts during the life of the district, supporters successfully argued that property taxes would be increased manyfold after the renewal period was completed.[61]

In August 2000, the council approved creation of the Interstate Corridor Urban Renewal area in north and northeast Portland, the city's largest renewal area ever, at 3,710 acres. The area included large industrial areas, ten neighborhoods, the I-5 freeway, and the Columbia Slough. One of its key elements was a 5.4-mile light-rail line. A three-story Paul Bunyan statue of steel and stucco in the Kenton neighborhood was moved as part of the project.[62]

An estimated twenty-five to fifty thousand Portlanders whooped it up with the mayor and other dignitaries to welcome in the new millenium at Pioneer Courthouse Square on New Year's Eve 1999.[63] The city spent fifty thousand dollars for the once-in-a-lifetime event, and a quarter-million dollars on Y2K preparedness.[64]

In April 2000, Mayor Vera Katz announced that she was on the road to recovery after an operation for breast cancer two weeks before, a malignancy detected through a routine mammogram. Katz stressed that her "workaholic ways" would not change. "I put in about 14 hours a day," she said, and this will slow me down "maybe—maybe—to 12."[65]

In May 2000, council voted to invest eight million dollars for building a seventy-mile fiber-optic network to serve the city. The network would also provide "relatively cheap access" for schools and local governmental agencies across the region. Commissioner Erik Sten declared that fiber-optic networks were "at least as important as roads."[66]

A beautiful Classical Chinese Garden debuted on a full block in northwest Portland in fall 2000, cementing a friendship and trade bridge with Portland's sister-city of Suzhou, China.[68] Rave reviews met the garden's debut.[69]

A new Eastside Esplanade that joined the east and west banks of the Willamette River in a three-mile riverside loop opened to the public in May 2001 as a one hundred fiftieth birthday gift to the city (paid for by federal,

For the first Rose Festival of the twenty-first century, San Diego-based U.S. Navy warships with more than twenty-two hundred sailors from all fifty states and around the world converged on Portland for the ninety-second annual Rose Festival in June 2000. Seven Navy ships were opened for public touring. "It's all about the 3 R's," said a Navy press release. "Roses, receptions, and recreation—as the U.S. Navy makes the most of its four-day Pacific northwest visit to one of the most popular ports of call in the country."[67]

The Eastside Esplanade along the Willamette River opened in 2001. (Author's photo)

state, and local government funding). The long, thin park boasted a grand view of downtown, the Portland skyline, and north harbor. Its one and a half-mile trail and floating walkway, squeezed between the river and busy Interstate 5 Freeway, was lighted for twenty-four-hour use. Steps connected downtown bridges to esplanades on both sides of the river so that pedestrians and bicycle riders could cross the river over four different bridges to access the three-mile loop.[70]

A new computer system launched by the water bureau in February 2000 was to cause the biggest snafu in contemporary city government history. As of April 2001, the billing system was still unfinished, and system problems of undelivered and erroneous water bills unresolved. The public was outraged. The over-budget costs and lost collections were later estimated at between twenty and thirty million dollars,[71] to say nothing of the erosion of public confidence that the disruption caused. Just how much damage this caused the political fortunes of Erik Sten, commissioner in charge of the water bureau, only time would tell.

Portlanders received a wake-up call when a 6.8 magnitude earthquake struck Olympia, Washington, one hundred thirty miles north of Portland, on Wednesday, February 28, 2001, causing an estimated two billion dollars in damage. Portland scientists and officials alike agreed that Portland was "woefully unprepared" for earthquakes, and that much more seismic retrofitting was needed for the city's buildings and bridges.[72]

Between 1990 and 2000, Oregon's population increased 20 percent to 3.4 million, nearly matching Washington State's 21 percent growth rate and surpassing both California's 14 percent growth and the national average of 13 percent.[73] Clark County, Washington, grew 41 percent; Oregon's Washington County, 31 percent; Clackamas County, 21 percent; and Multnomah County, 8 percent.[74] The trend toward a more diverse Portland population was demonstrated by the proliferation in the number of families with the Hispanic surname "Gonzales" and the Asian surname "Nguyen." In eight years, the number of households listed in the Portland metro phone book with these names had more than doubled.[75]

Total Portland population density was 3,500 persons per square mile in year 2000 compared to 5,375 density in 1950, and 600 per square mile a hundred years earlier. The geographic size increased from two square miles in 1851 to seventy square miles in 1950, and doubled to one hundred forty-seven square miles as the century ended.

By 2000, privately owned property within city limits was valued at an estimated forty-three billion dollars. Largest property holders were three utilities, three airlines, Fred Meyer grocers, Freightliner truck manufacturing, and two real estate companies. For the fiscal year ended June 30, 2001, the city expended more than a billion dollars for general government purposes, collected two hundred thirty million dollars in property taxes, and had net bonded debt of fifty-two million dollars. The city boasted eighty-three hundred employees, two thousand miles of water mains, twelve thousand seven hundred fire hydrants, four thousand lane miles of streets, ten thousand acres of parks, four golf courses, thirteen community centers, and fifteen swimming pools. Total population within Portland city limits was 529,121.[76]

> In February 2001, *The Portland Tribune* was launched, a free bi-weekly newspaper to be published every Tuesday and Friday morning. Funded by wealthy Portland businessman Robert Pamplin, Jr., the mainstream newspaper was the first to appear in Portland since the *Oregon Journal*'s 1982 demise. *The Tribune* hired well-known staff away from other Portland media to jump-start its debut.[77]

Out-of-state ownership of the city's largest businesses continued to grow. Other trends included public commitment to preservation of the environment; voter registration shifts from major political parties to "independent" or unaffiliated; polarization of the citizenry on social and ethical issues; low voter turnout; decreased participation in community organizations (including neighborhood associations recognized by the city); and an inclination by the populace to approve restrictive financial measures. The city again experienced a flight to the suburbs by families with young children.[78]

Oregon's economy shifted dramatically during the second half of the twentieth century from its lumber and agricultural base to that of electronics, high-tech manufacturing, and services. Tourism became big business. Vineyards and Christmas tree farms found a special niche. Portland retained its position as a shipping center for products to and from the Columbia Basin. "The french fries that McDonald's serves up in Tokyo move through Portland. So have many of the Toyotas and Hondas that populate American roads. ... [T]he value of Oregon's manufacturing exports exceeded the value of farm and forest exports for the first time ever in the early 1990s."[79]

Even though the last decade of the twentieth century was a time of relative prosperity and political calm, major challenges faced the city as the new century began. Problem areas included rivers, transportation, growth and livability, schools, drinking water, and police. A slowing economy and decreased property tax revenues meant tight budgets and strong competition for revenue dollars.[80]

River(s). Six miles of the Willamette River were placed on the federal Superfund list of most polluted sites in the nation in 2000.[81] Tests showed a high level of dangerous chemicals in Portland-area fish.[82] The federal Environmental Protection Agency planned to seek funds for cleanup from industries located around the harbor. City government itself was dumping sewage into the Willamette River every time it rained, with 60 percent of the city's population served by a sewer system carrying both domestic sewage and stormwater runoff.[83] The Bureau of Environmental Services estimated a price tag of 4.7 billion in future dollars over the next twenty years to fix the combined sewer overflow problem and "operate, maintain and improve sewer and stormwater management systems," a cost that would require nearly tripling current monthly residential rates from an average of thirty-three dollars to ninety in future dollars.[84] At the end of the 1990s, the city had embarked on a cleanup program mandated by the state to correct past damage, keep the river clean for the future, and restore wetlands along the shorelines.

Deeper dredging of the Columbia River also threatened water quality. In 1866, when army engineers first began limited dredging, the Columbia River's one-hundred-three-mile shipping channel to the ocean was only ten to fifteen feet deep in several places.[85] In 1891, the state legislature created a port commission and gave it authority to dredge to twenty-five feet.[86] By 2001, the Port of Portland was lobbying for a forty-three-foot depth, arguing that the current forty-foot depth was not deep enough to keep Portland globally competitive. Congress appropriated 183.6 million dollars for this purpose in 1999, but the governors of both Oregon and Washington denied water quality permits to the Corps of Engineers.[87] Possible adverse environmental impacts included damage to salmon and other wildlife habitats; disturbing contaminated sediments already in the river; and erosion of sand from the state's beaches.[88]

Better access to the Willamette River was also needed for recreational and transportation purposes. Even though the river had always been the heart of Portland, its recreational and short-run transportation potential had yet to be fully realized.

Transportation. Traffic congestion, speeding on residential streets,[89] parking shortages, disruption from continual tearing up of city streets,[90] the need for sidewalks in neighborhoods that lacked them, and the long-range possibility of removing Interstate 5 from the east bank of the river[91] were among transportation issues facing the council. While Portland was noted for its forward-thinking transportation policies and bicycle-friendly milieu,[92] the backlog for street maintenance was at a ten-year high.[93] Carbon monoxide levels had "increased significantly" in 1999.[94]

Plans were underway at the turn of the century for three additional environment-friendly transportation alternatives—a central city streetcar, an airport rapid light-rail system, and an Interstate Avenue MAX.[95] The Port was considering a third runway at the airport. Oregon Health Sciences University proposed building a controversial sky tram from the riverfront to the top of Marquam Hill.[96] It would take innovative thinking and careful decision making by the council to reach the best choices with limited resources in the transportation arena.

Growth and livability. As Portland continued to grow, retaining the qualities that made the city a desirable place to live and raise children became a challenge. Issues included providing jobs friendly to the environment; retaining neighborhood character while increasing housing density; preventing sprawl; preserving central core areas; curtailing houses that presented only garages to the street; providing affordable housing; making the city more family- and pedestrian-friendly; maintaining and expanding parks and hiking, biking, and walking trails; and fostering growth of culture and the arts. Reclaiming the park blocks. Capping two and a half blocks over I-405.[97] Economic development. Deciding where "telco hotels" should be allowed to locate.[98] Encouraging more recycling. Providing for the homeless and the have-nots. Dealing with the effects on planning and the urban growth boundary by increased pressure to provide compensation to property owners for governmental "takings."

Schools. Adequate funding for quality public education was a major dilemma in Oregon.[99] The "double majority" requirement for school option levies was especially restrictive. In essence, it gave a "no" vote to registered voters who failed to cast ballots. A property tax measure lost, regardless of its approval rate, unless 50 percent of registered voters cast ballots, as provided in Measures 47 and 50 passed in 1996 and 1997.

As a visiting lecturer reminded Portlanders, a more productive workforce would be possible only if the Portland area considered education "its most important economic strategy."[100] While experts and the public alike agreed that large class sizes and and shortened school years were detrimental to a good education, finances were the big hurdle. In addition, more non-school-hour activities for both children and their parents were needed.

The area's institutions of higher learning had special needs, including provisions for study in emerging technological fields.[101] The lack of a major research university in the Portland area was sometimes cited as a competitive business disadvantage.

Drinking water. An "abundance of good, pure and wholesome water" reached the city from the slopes of Mt. Hood on January 2, 1895.[102] By year 2001, neither the quantity nor quality of that water supply could be taken for granted. Underground wells along the Columbia River had been threatened with contamination,[103] but were nevertheless being tapped for emergencies.[104] Ongoing discussion centered on the need for a third Bull Run dam and reasons why building such a dam would be unwise. Portland was selling a good deal of water to neighboring cities, which in turn helped pay for the system's capital costs. However, other jurisdictions were exploring the possibility of reducing their future reliance on Portland water in favor of treated water from the Willamette and Clackamas rivers.[105] Portland's water supply was adequate for the next twenty years, the city water bureau said, with a "modest expansion of the city's well fields"—if water users would cut their consumption by 11 percent.[106]

Police. Among police issues were community-police relations; police conduct; containing the cost of the Fire and Police Disability and Retirement Fund; financing the pension fund's one billion-dollar unfunded liability;[107] reining in drug users and gangs; curtailing prostitution; extending equal protection and respect to minorities; and police use of deadly force. A Police Internal Investigative Auditing Committee (PIIAC), created in 1982 as an arms-length citizen oversight group, had not satisfied citizens' demands for a more open and hands-on process for investigating police conduct.[108]

By 2001, Portland's Fire and Police Disability and Retirement Fund had accumulated an unfunded liability of approximately one billion dollars, and was paying disability and pension benefits of approximately fifty-six million dollars per year. City financial staff warned that this unfunded liability could cause great hardship to future Portland generations if the fund's millage rate did not cover mandated payouts, thereby requiring general fund revenues to make up the difference, as guaranteed by a 1989 charter amendment.[109] The council's failure to deal with the unfounded liability issue when presented with a long-term plan in 1998 and 1999 was short-sighted.[110]

By 2001, all large U.S. cities except Portland had abandoned the commission form of government adopted by voters in 1913.[111] In spite of several attempts to change it, Portland's commission form had lasted eighty-eight years.[112]

Critics complained that this "five-mayor" form of government resulted in costly inefficiencies; that no one person was "in charge."[113] Some citizens and members of the business community felt that their interests were not adequately heeded by the council. Fragmented responsibility permitted unglamorous issues such as a decaying infrastructure and employee benefits to grow into bigger problems with no one person accountable. Powerful employee unions too easily played the game of "divide and conquer." Citywide election campaigns were increasingly expensive, and district representation was touted as a way to improve that. Yet past proposals for basic change had failed, as the *Oregon Journal* pointed out in 1974—"unless proposed during a crisis or outrageous scandal."[114]

Portlanders defending the commission form of government said it gave citizens good service; had been relatively free of scandal for the past fifty years; provided several lines of access to city hall; kept too much power out of the hands of one individual; and enhanced citizen participation.[115] The council had attracted intelligent and civic-minded members partly because it provided autonomy and the opportunity to exercise initiative. Having elected officials responsible instead of bureaucrats forced elected officials to experience the results of policies first-hand and held them accountable. The elected auditor played a valuable role in this system of checks and balances.[116]

A 1991 Portland League of Women Voters study concluded that Portland's commission form was "accountable, flexible and responsive to citizens," and preferable to other alternatives.[117] In year 2000, a notable 84 percent of city residents responding to a citizen survey rated their neighborhoods' livability good or very good, and thought that public safety had increased significantly over the preceding decade.[118]

☙

The final thirty years of the twentieth century were city government's most efficient and productive to date. City managers were well paid, experienced, and professional. Portland was viewed as a model for other jurisdictions. *Financial World* magazine rated Portland the third-best-managed city in the U. S. in 1992 and again in 1995 (the last year they did such ratings), based on accounting, budgeting, program evaluations, and infrastructure controls.[119]

In 1995, *Forbes* magazine said of Portland: "A good quality of life, high immigration levels, and computer smarts helped make this rainy town a winner … a town that's far better than most for a young company to be in." In 1997, the cover of *Time* magazine featured Portland as one of the nation's fifteen hottest spots for new kinds of job growth.[120]

Planners and dignitaries from around the country visited Portland to see for themselves how the urban growth boundary worked. In one month of 1999 alone, Portland was praised for its livability by *USA Weekend*, *Outside Magazine*, *Parade Magazine*, and National Public Radio. *The Economist* of Great Britain concluded that Portland was "the nation's darling of urban correctness."[121]

In winter 2000, *Money* magazine chose Portland as the "Most Livable City" in the nation: "Portlanders are deeply passionate about their city—and rightly so. There's plenty to be proud of, especially the city's successful transformation from old timber town to high-tech hub … Three decades of keen planning have reined in urban sprawl and given rise to a mini-metropolis with short, easy-to-stroll blocks renowned for java joints, brewpubs and bookstores. A superb light rail network and a new streetcar system are helping to make it a cinch to get around. … Its stellar location [is] in the heart of the beautiful Pacific Northwest.

It's an area of unparalleled natural beauty, abundant with recreational opportunities."[122]

One hundred and fifty years ago, Oregon pioneers took six months to cross the continent, doubted that there would ever be a bridge built across the Willamette, and were convinced that no railroad could make it over the Northern Rockies.[123] Today, jets traverse America in less than six hours, ten bridges span the Willamette,[124] and transcontinental trains have served the city for nearly one hundred twenty years.

One hundred and fifty years ago, nine out of ten residents were in their twenties and Portland was, for the most part, an all-male frontier town.[125] Today, Portland is a city of neighborhoods and gardens, equally peopled by women and men, with more than a third of the population either under eighteen or over sixty-five.

One hundred and fifty years ago, the territorial governor's first tour of Portland was cut short by vast quantities of mud and water, and irrepressible Captain O. Travaillot was fined twenty-five dollars for riding his horse at a furious rate through Portland's muddy roadways.[126] Today Tri-Met busses, light rail, automobiles, pedestrians, skateboarders, bikers, and scooters all lay claim to Portland's inviting downtown streets.[127]

From Stumptown to *Portlandia* and Mrs. Corbett's cow to MAX light rail, change in Portland has been an endless becoming. The dense woods and mosquito marshes of yesteryear have changed to "city"—the twenty-eighth largest in the nation.[128]

Downtown Portland from the Rose Gardens; snow-capped Mount Hood in the background. (1981 photo by C. Bruce Forster)

Appendix A

Portland City Charter

AN ACT
To incorporate the City of Portland In Washington County

SECTION 1. *Be it enacted by the Legislative Assembly of Oregon Territory,* That so much of the county of Washington as is comprised in the land claims, known as the "Portland claim," and "John H. Couch's claim," and bounded as follows, viz.: Commending at the north-east corner of Finis Caruther's land claim, thence down the middle of the Wallamet River two miles, to the north line of Couch's claim; thence west along said line, one mile; thence south, along the line of said Couch's and Portland claims, two miles; thence east to the place of beginning; shall be, and the same is hereby erected and constituted a city corporate, by the name of the "City of Portland." *Provided,* That that part of the incorporation, within the limits of said incorporation, known as the Tannery property, be exempt from taxation for city purposes.

SEC. 2. That for the good government of said corporation, and the citizens thereof, it shall be lawful for the white male inhabitants, who shall have resided in said corporation three months, next preceding any election held by virtue of this act, and having the qualifications of electors of members of the Legislative Assembly, to meet at some public place in said corporation, on the first Monday of April next, and annually, on the same day thereafter, at such place as the City Council may direct, and then and there proceed, by a plurality of votes, to elect by ballot, one Mayor, one Recorder, and five Councilmen, who shall reside within the limits of said corporation, and who shall be entitled to vote at elections under this act, who shall severally hold their offices until the first Monday of April following, and until their successors in office shall have been elected and qualified: said Mayor, Recorder, and councilmen shall constitute a City Council, any five of whom shall constitute a quorum for the transaction of business pertaining to their duties under this act; but any less number shall have no power, other than to adjourn from time to time, till a quorum be convened.

SEC. 3. That at the first election held under this act, there shall be chosen, *viva voce,* by the electors present, three judges, and a clerk of said election, who shall each take an oath or affirmation, faithfully to discharge the duties required of them by this act; and at all subsequent elections, the councilmen, or any two of them, shall be judges, and the Recorder shall be clerk of the election; and at all elections to be held by virtue of this act, the polls shall be opened at, or before the hour of nine, before noon, and closed at four o'clock in the afternoon, and at the close of the polls, the votes shall be canvassed and counted by the judges, in the presence of such of the electors as choose to be present, and an accurate statement of the result shall be proclaimed in an audible voice to the electors present, by one of the judges, and the clerk shall make a true record thereof, and within three days thereafter, said clerk shall give notice to the persons so elected, of their election; and it shall be the duty of the City Council, at least ten days before each and every annual election, to cause notice of the same to be posted up in three of the most public places in said corporation.

SEC. 4. It shall be the duty of the Mayor, or in case of his inability of absence, the Recorder, to preside at all meetings of the City Council; and it shall be the duty of the Recorder to attend all such meetings, and keep a fair and accurate record of their proceedings.

SEC. 5. The City Council shall have power to fill all vacancies which may happen in their Board, from the qualified voters in said corporation, whose appointment shall continue until the next annual election, and until their successors are chosen and qualified; and whenever it may happen that the Recorder is not present at such meetings, the council shall appoint one their number to perform the duties of the Recorder, *pro tempore.*

SEC. 6. The Mayor, Recorder and Council of said corporation shall be a body corporate and politic, with perpetual succession, to be known and designated by the name and tile of the "City Council of the town of Portland:" and shall be capable, in their corporate name and capacity, to acquire property, real, personal, and mixed, for the use of said corporation, with power to sell and convey the same; may have a common seal, which they may alter, break, amend, or renew at pleasure; may sue and be sued, plead and be impleaded, defend and be defended, in any court of competent jurisdiction, whether of law or in chancery; and when any suit shall be commenced against said corporation, the first process shall be a summons, an attested copy of which, left with the Recorder, or at his usual place of abode, not more than twenty, nor less than ten days before the return day thereof, shall be considered lawful service.

SEC. 7. Each member of the City Council shall, within ten days next after his election or appointment, and before he enters upon the discharge of his duties, take oath or affirmation to support the constitution of the United States; and also an oath of office.

SEC. 8. The said City Council shall have power to ordain and establish such by-laws and ordinances not inconsistent with the constitution and laws of the United States, and of the Territory, as they may think necessary for the good government of said corporation, and the health, morals, and safety of its citizens; and repeal, alter, amend, revise, or modify the same at pleasure; to provide in such by-laws, for the appointment of a treasurer, marshal, and such other subordinate officers as they may deem necessary for the convenience of said corporation; to prescribe their duties, and the duration of their appointment; to establish and regulate the fees said officers shall be entitled to receive (except in so far as they are provided for in this act). and may require said subordinate officers to take an oath of office, and such of them as the City Council may think proper, to give bond for the faithful performance of their duties, in such sums and with such securities as the Mayor may approve:

the City Council shall have power to fix to the by-laws and ordinances of the corporation, such reasonable fines and penalties as they may deem proper and necessary to enforce obedience to the same; and to provide for the disposition and appropriation of said fines and penalties, when collected. No by-laws or ordinances of said town shall take effect, and be in force, until a copy of the same shall have been posted up at least six days in three of the most public places in said corporation; or published in some newspaper published in said county.

SEC. 9. The City Council shall, at the expiration of each and every year, cause to be made out and posted as aforesaid, or published in some newspaper published in said county, a fair and accurate schedule of the receipts, disbursements, and expenditures of the preceding year.

SEC. 10. The City Council shall have power to lay out, regulate, and improve the streets, lanes, alleys, sidewalks, and public levees, within said corporation, and to fix and determine the width thereof; they shall have power to provide for the removal of all nuisances within said corporation, and all obstructions in the streets, lanes, or alleys, or on the public levees thereof; and to do all things which a corporation of a similar nature can do to secure the peace, and preserve the health of the citizens of said corporation, and preserve good order within the same.

SEC. 11. That whenever, by the by-laws and ordinances of the city of Portland, the owner or owners of any lot, or part of lot, situated in said city, shall be required to repair, improve, pave, or gravel a sidewalk, alley, or gutter adjacent to such lot or part of lot, and if the owner or owners thereof shall neglect or refuse to repair, improve, pave, or gravel the same, according to the provisions of such by-laws, ordinance or ordinances, the same may be improved, repaired, paved, or gravelled, at the expense of said city.

SEC. 12. That whenever the City Council shall require any owner or owners of any lot, or part of lot, to pave in front of the same, or otherwise improve the same, as is provided for in the preceding section of this act, the owner or owners of the same, if residents of said city, or of said county of Washington, shall have written personal notice of the same; and to any owner or owners of a lot, or part of a lot, not resident of said city or county, notice shall be given by publication, for six consecutive weeks in some newspaper published in said county, and such notice shall contain a pertinent description of such lot, or part of lot, and a statement of the time within which such improvement is required to be made, which, in the notice to be made by publication, shall be made at least three months after the first publication, and if the notice is personal, at least two months after the service of such notice; and the expenses of such publication shall be assess upon said lot, or part of lot, and be collected in the same manner, and at the same time that the taxes are collected upon such lot, or part of lot.

SEC. 13. The City Council are hereby empowered to license or prohibit shows and exhibitions; and to levy a tax upon real estate and personal property, subject to taxation for territorial and county purposes, within the limits of said corporation: *Provided, however,* That the tax shall not exceed, in any one year, for corporation purposes, one-fourth of one per centum on the aggregate of all such taxable property, within the limits of said corporation; and the City Council shall annually, between the first Monday of April, and the last Monday in June, determine the amount of tax to be assessed and collected for the current year.

SEC. 14. It shall be the duty of the Recorder of said corporation to make out duplicates of taxes, charging each individual within said corporation, and amount of tax in proportion to the aggregate value of taxable property belonging to said individual within the limits of said corporation, as appear from the books of the probate clerk of Washington county; and the Recorder of said corporation shall have access to the books of the probate clerk, for the purpose of making our such duplicates, free of expense; and the duplicates, when made out shall be certified by the Mayor and Recorder, and one of said duplicates shall be delivered to the marshal, or to such other person as shall be appointed collector, whose duty it shall be to collect said tax, in the same manner, and under the same regulations as the collectors of territorial and county taxes, are required by law to collect territorial and county taxes; and the said marshal or collector shall immediately after collecting said tax, pay over the same to the treasurer of said corporation, and take his receipt therefor; and the said marshal or other person charged with the collection of taxes of said corporation, shall have the same power to sell property, real or personal, as is given by the laws of this Territory, to county collectors: and when necessary, the Recorder shall have power to make deeds for real estate so sold, in the same manner that county auditors are authorized by the laws of this Territory, to make deeds for lands sold for taxes by the county collector; and the marshal or other person charged with the collection of the taxes of the said corporation, shall receive for his collection services, such sum, not exceeding seven per centum on all moneys by him collected and paid over, as the City Council may direct, to be paid by the treasurer on the order of the Mayor, duly attested by the Recorder.

SEC. 15. The treasurer of said corporation shall not pay out any moneys belonging to said corporation, to any person for any purpose, except upon the written order of the Mayor, duly attested by the Recorder, and the said treasurer shall keep, in a book or books, to be provided at the expense of the corporation, a fair and accurate account of his receipts and disbursements, which books shall, at all times, be open to the inspection of the Mayor, or any other member of the City Council, and any committee appointed by the City Council to examine the same, and which book the treasurer shall deliver over to his successors in office.

SEC. 16. The City Council shall have power to appropriate any moneys remaining in the treasury of the corporation, to the payment of the lawful fees of the officers of the corporation; to the purchasing of such blank books, and other things of a like nature, which may be necessary for the use of said corporation; to the improvement of the streets, alleys, lanes, and sidewalks of said corporation; to the erection of a market house, and to the making of any and such other public improvements in said corporation, as the City Council may think conducive to the convenience and prosperity of said corporation; all payments, however, to be made by the treasurer pursuant to the requirements of the fifteenth section of this act, and in no other manner whatever.

SEC. 17. The Mayor of said corporation shall be a conservator of the peace throughout said corporation, and is authorized to do and perform, within said corporation, all things which, by the laws of this Territory, a Justice of the Peace may do and perform within the county wherein such Justice of the Peace is elected, and may reside; and said Mayor shall do and perform all the duties required of him by the by-laws and ordinances of said corporation, and appeals may be made from the decisions of said Mayor, and writs of *certiorari* allowed, to revise, reverse, or correct his proceedings and judgments, in the same manner as is provided by the laws of this Territory, for appeals from and writs of *certiorari*, to correct the judgments and proceedings of Justices of the Peace in similar cases.

SEC. 18. The marshal shall be the principal ministerial officer in said corporation, and shall have the same power within said corporation that constables have in their various townships, and in criminal cases his jurisdiction shall be co-extensive with that of constables in similar cases; and in serving subpoenas on witnesses in civil cases, his jurisdiction shall be co-extensive with the county, and he shall receive the same fees for his services that constables are entitled to for similar services by the laws of this Territory.

SEC. 19. That in all cases of absence or inability to serve of the marshal, the Mayor shall have power to appoint, temporarily, any person to serve as marshal: *Provided*, That said person so appointed, be a resident and voter in said corporation, and a certificate of such appointment, officially signed by the mayor, shall authorize such person to act, and make his acts legal: *Provided further*, The said appointment shall continue no longer than the duration of the absence or inability of the marshal aforesaid.

SEC. 20. The Mayor shall receive the same fees for his services that Justices of the Peace are entitled to by law, for services of a similar nature; and the Recorder shall receive such fees as may be provided by the by-laws and ordinances of said corporation.

SEC. 21. The Mayor and City Council shall have power to require, by ordinance, each able-bodied male person, over the age of twenty-one years, resident within said corporation, to perform labor upon the streets and alleys of the same, not exceeding two days in any one year, which shall be in lieu of one day's labor required under the present laws regulating roads and highways; and upon refusal or neglect to perform such work under the proper supervisor, the delinquent shall be liable to the same penalties as are provided by law, against persons refusing or neglecting to perform the two days labor required in said law.

SEC. 22. The Mayor and Council shall have exclusive authority to form one or more road districts within the limits of said corporation, and they shall appoint a suitable supervisor or supervisors for such district or districts, when formed, who shall be governed, in the performance of their duties, by the by-laws of said corporation; and all road tax charged upon the county duplicate, on property within the limits of said city, shall be worked out under the direction of the proper supervisors within said city, as said authorities may, by resolution or ordinance, designate and point out; and all taxes charged for road purposes, as aforesaid, on property within the limits of said city, and collected by the county collector, shall be paid into the hands of the treasurer of said city, as aforesaid, to be appropriated especially, by the City Council, to road purposes within said town.

SEC. 23. The City Council shall have power, if authorized to do so by a majority of all the electors of said city, at any election held for that purpose, to levy a special tax, in addition to the taxes authorized to be collected by authority of this act, sufficient for the purchase of an engine hose, and other necessary apparatus, for the extinguishment of fires in said city: public notice of which election, and the object thereof, shall be given, by posting up written or printed notices thereof, in at least six of the most public places in said city, at least fifteen days before the time of such election.

SEC. 24. The City Council shall have power to erect a suitable building for the imprisonment of such persons as may be lawfully imprisoned by the officers of said corporation, under the by-laws and ordinances thereof; and all persons so imprisoned, shall be kept in charge of the marshal, or other person having charge of the jail, until lawfully discharged.

SEC. 25. The City Council shall not pass any ordinance or by-laws whatever that will, in any wise, preclude any citizen of this Territory from bringing into, and selling, any article of produce raised on their farms.

SEC. 26. The Legislative Assembly reserves the right to repeal or amend this act, at any time they may think the public good requires it.

SEC. 27. The Mayor shall deliver over to his successor, all dockets, books, papers, and other property of the corporation in his custody.

SEC 28. This act to take effect, and be in force, from and after its passage.

Passed the House of Representatives, January 14th, 1851.
Passed the Council, January 23d, 1851.
RALPH WILCOX,
Speaker of the House
WM W. BUCK,
President of the Council

I certify the foregoing to be a true copy of the original roll on file in my office.
E. HAMILTON,
Secretary of the Oregon Territory

Dated March 16, 1851
(Oregonian Press, Portland)

Only two copies of this 1851 Portland charter "broadside," as it was termed in Belknap's *Oregon Imprints,*[1] were known to exist as of April 2001.[2] One was framed and mounted on the east wall of the Rare Book Room of the Multnomah County Library. The other was owned by an unknown private collector, with a photostat of that copy filed at the Bancroft Library, University of California, Berkeley. The text of the charter presented here is taken from records of the 1850-51 territorial legislature.[3]

The charter broadside was printed on newsprint, approximately fourteen by twenty inches in size. The document contains no flourishing signatures and no official seal. The broadside was set in type by the newly founded weekly *Oregonian* in its print shop six weeks after the territorial legislature adjourned, then posted around town so that citizens would be ready to elect, three weeks later, volunteers to run this new government.

The April 1969 auction catalog titled "The Celebrated Collection of Americana of the Thomas Winthrop Streeter Collection of Americana," presents this description of the document: "Broadside, 55.5 X 40.5 cm, printed in 5 columns, within double border of type ornaments. Margins browned and stained, side margins and 3 corners frayed. Provenance: Edward Eberstadt & Sons, 1937. Reference: McMurtrie, OREGON, 29 [locates one other copy]."[4]

The Multnomah County Library obtained its copy of the charter broadside for three hundred fifty dollars at the 1969 Streeter auction in New York City.[5] The Multnomah County librarian had apparently learned from a New York friend that the broadside was being sold.

Historians often confuse Portland's charter of 1851 with its second charter, passed by the 1853 legislature, and even with later laws. Copies of the 1851 charter were not readily available, and because 1854-55 city officials started numbering their ordinances at Number 1, without repealing City Ordinances 1-23 already passed by city councils elected in 1851, 1852, and 1853, it is easy to understand how the confusion came about.[6]

Nine Portland charters were adopted between 1851 and 2001. New charters were passed by the territorial legislatures of 1851, 1853, and 1854, and the state legislatures of 1864, 1882, 1891, 1893, 1898, and 1903. Amendments to those charters were passed by the legislatures of 1858, 1860, 1862, 1866, 1868, 1870, 1872, 1874, 1880, 1885, 1887, 1889, 1893, and 1895.[7] A state constitutional change adopted in June 1906 gave cities and towns exclusive power to enact and amend their own charters.[8] The citizens of Portland have adopted many amendments to the 1903 charter, most notably a 1913 amendment to adopt the commission form of government that is still in force today.

Appendix B

Portland's First Public Library: 1850

Portland's first mayor, Hugh O'Bryant, has often been credited with founding Portland's first public library in 1850, but this credit is either vastly overstated or completely misplaced. At least five historical references say that O'Bryant founded Portland's first public library by renting a library reading room at the northwest corner of Front and Alder streets "paid for out of his own pocket,"[1] and that he solicited others to join him in donating books, magazines, and papers.[2] None of the five publications gives any indication what their source for this information was. The first reference giving O'Bryant this credit was written by newspaper reporter Fred Lockley around 1925. Later writers most likely relied on Lockley as their source.

The real credit for Portland's first public library belongs to a group of pioneer Portland businessmen.

The Portland Library Association founded in June 1850 is not to be confused with the Library Association of Portland founded in 1864 as precursor of the present Multnomah County Library. The 1850 group raised twelve hundred dollars to buy library books and entrusted William P. Abrams, a member of Portland's second city council, to purchase the volumes while he was on a trip East to secure parts for his sawmill and to bring his family back to Portland.

A summary of Abrams' 1850-51 diary compiled in 1910 by Seth L. Pope, an Abrams descendant, with Abrams' words in quotes includes the following pertinent passages:

> May 17, 1850. A friend called and said Mr. Coffin [a silent partner in the Reed & Abrams sawmill and father-in-law of partner C. A. Reed] had given notice through the Oregon City Paper that Mr. Abrams would leave for the States about June 15. … As the time for his departure drew near, Mr. Reed, Hastings and others started a subscription to purchase books for a Public Library. Subscriptions were liberal, and about twelve hundred dollars [about twenty-five thousand dollars today] was raised and placed in Mr. Abrams' hands, with results shown later.

> June 26. "I reached the steamer just in time & at 7 A.M. proceeded down the river and found myself at last on my way to my loved ones."

> [August—in New York.] The funds received for the purchase of library [were] placed in the hands of Messrs. Harper Bros. [who were asked] to make the selection which they did to about twelve hundred volumes and packed in boxes ready to ship.

> November 7, 1850. He [Abrams] sailed from New York [with his wife, two children, and a sister and brother].
>
> January 27, 1851. They passed Cape Horn—eighty-one days from New York. They had access to some of the library books so they were enabled to find plenty to read. … It being summer time here they could see by daylight to read until half past nine at night.
>
> April 14, 1851. They arrived in Astoria after a long passage of one hundred fifty-eight days. Being a sailing vessel she was dependant on the winds, and Portland was not reached until April 22.[3]

Fifty years later, the *Oregonian* printed a story about the Portland Library Association's founding.[4]

> An event of interest in those early days was the forming of the "Portland Library Association" in 1850. A meeting was called on June 12 of that year and a committee appointed to solicit subscriptions. They were successful in their undertaking and a few days later a constitution was adopted and the following officers elected: W. W. Chapman, president; Horace Lyman, vice-president; C. A. Reed [partner of William Abrams], secretary; W. S. Caldwell, treasurer; C. A. Reed, librarian. Board of Directors: A. P. Dennison, L. B. Hastings, W. S. Caldwell, Stephen Coffin and Shubrick Norris. Later on the names of T. J. Dryer, W. P. Abrams, Simon B. Marye, J. H. Wilbur, J. W. Davis, W. S. Ogden, W. L. Higgins, W. B. Otway, C. S. Kingsley, H. Failing, P. A. Marquam and others appear as officers and directors.
>
> The first meeting was held in the schoolhouse, the next in Norton & Dennison's store. One of the annual meetings was held in the Methodist Church and another in the Carlton House. The Library Association owned as many as 1100 books at one time, and when the present library was formed about 600 of the old books were collected and turned into it.[5]

Note that Hugh O'Bryant's name is not mentioned in the above story, but that many other early city officials are. O'Bryant moved south to Douglas County, Oregon, in early 1852, so had no further connection to Portland.

Whether or not the original records of the Portland Library Association are still in existence is unknown. However, the Oregon Historical Center has a document dated April 26, 1904, in Portland, Oregon,[6] with the following introduction in handwritten notes about the organization:

> *Geo L. Story showed me this day in his office the original Record Book of the Portland Library Association from which I make the following transcript.*
>
> *s/ S. L. Pope*

> Portland, Oregon Territory, June 18, 1850.
>
> A meeting of the citizens was held at the school house (First Street west side just north of Oak, next to DeWitts Hotel) for the purpose of forming a Library Association. Dr. McKenny called the meeting to order, W. S. Caldwell acting as Sec'y. By resolution the chair appointed the following persons as a committee to draft a Constitution, viz.: W. S. Caldwell, Horace Lyman, and W. W. Chapman. T. J. Hobbs moved to appoint a committee to solicit subscriptions. The chair appointed Shubrick Norris, Dr. McKenny, W. H. Berry, Ani P. Dennison.
>
> June 19, 1850. Meeting was held. Committee on Constitution submitted report, which was adopted subject to revision, then proceeded to elect officers as follows …
>
> June 21, 1850. Meeting was held, and on motion, "Resolved that anyone who subscribes $10 shall be a member of the society for one year." Constitution as amended was adopted and the following signed the 12 articles: W. W. Chapman, S. Coffin, Horace Lyman, W. P. Abrams, C. A. Reed, W. L. Higgins, W. S. Caldwell, Shubrick Norris, F. H. McKenny, A. P. Dennison, J. M. Rowell, J. S. Clinkenbeard, Elisha Hill, James H. Wilbur, Franklin Matthias, Dennis Harty.
>
> June 24, 1850. Meeting was held, and following resolutions made and adopted. "Resolved that W. P. Abrams have full power to make a selection of such books as may be fit, or appoint a suitable person to make such selection, unless he receive further instructions from the Board of Directors," and "Resolved that the Board of Directors pay over to W. P. Abrams the sum of nine hundred dollars, to be appropriated to the purchase of books according to the above resolutions.
>
> Record ends March 30 1854 when a new constitution was adopted, and in back of the book were the names of the subscribers of the first fund, and later date, appended hereto.[7]

A list of sixty-five contributors and amounts paid by each is attached to the document, a list headed by contributions of one hundred dollars each from Stephen Coffin and Daniel Lownsdale, a total of eight hundred ninety-four dollars paid by January 20, 1850, and another two hundred sixty-five dollars collected by February 20, 1850, for a grand total of 1,159 dollars.

This first Portland library was apparently maintained until 1856, then disbanded. The 1903 *Oregonian* story about the organization notes that about six hundred old books were collected for "the present library," that opened to the public in March 1902.[8]

Appendix C

City of Portland Mayors

Mayor No.	Name	Dates served	Place of Birth	Occupation	Dates of birth-death
38	Albee, H. Russell	1913-17	Rockford, IL	Insurance executive	1867-1951
39	Baker, George L.	1917-33	The Dalles, OR	Theater owner and manager	1868-1941
2	Bonnell, Allison C.	1852-52	New Jersey	Accountant	1801-1875
18	Boyd, Hamilton	1868-69	New York	Accountant, bank clerk	1820-1883
12	Breck, John M.	1861-62	Philadelphia, PA	Merchant, steamship agent	1828-1900
40	Carson, Joseph K., Jr.	1933-40	Kentucky	Lawyer	1891-1956
17	Chapman, James A.	1867-68	Friendship, NY	Doctor	1820-1885
22	Chapman, James A.	1875-77	Friendship, NY	Doctor	1820-1885
25	Chapman, James A.	1882-85	Friendship, NY	Doctor	1820-1885
48	Clark, John Elwood "Bud"	1985-92	Nampa, Idaho	Tavern owner, landlord	1931-
27	DeLashmutt, Van B.	1888-91	Burlington, IA	Banker, investor	1842-1921
15	Failing, Henry	1864-66	New York City, NY	Merchant, banker	1834-1898
21	Failing, Henry	1873-75	New York City, NY	Merchant, banker	1834-1898
4	Failing, Josiah	1853-54	Fort Plain, NY	Merchant	1806-1877
13	Farrar, William H.	1862-63	New Hampshire	Lawyer	1826-1873
29	Frank, George P.	1894-96	Granville, NY	Owner, implement company	1853-1896
26	Gates, John	1885-88	Mercer, Maine	Engineer, inventor	1829-1888
45	Goldschmidt, Neil	1973-79	Eugene, OR	Lawyer	1940-
19	Goldsmith, Bernard	1869-71	Germany	Merchant, investor	1832-1901
16	Holmes, Thomas J.	1866-67	Norfolk Co, England	Shoemaker, landlord	1819-1867
47	Ivancie, Frank	1980-84	Marble, MN	Teacher, administrator	1924-
49	Katz, Vera	1993-2001	Dusseldorf, Germany	Legislator, citizen lobbyist	1933-
5	Ladd, William S.	1854-55	Holland, VT	Merchant, banker	1826-1893
8	Ladd, William S.	1857-58	Holland, VT	Merchant, banker	1826-1893
35	Lane, Harry	1905-09	Corvallis, OR	Doctor	1855-1917

Mayor No.	*Name*	*Dates served*	*Place of Birth*	*Occupation*	*Dates of birth-death*
42	Lee, Dorothy McCullough	1949-52	Oakland, CA	Lawyer, legislator	1901-1981
14	Logan, David	1863-64	Springfield, IL	Lawyer	1824-1874
3	Marye, Simon B.	1852-53	Shenandoah Co, VA	Lawyer	1825-1868
28	Mason, William S.	1891-94	Virginia	Railroad employee, grocer	1832-1899
31	Mason, William S.	1898-99	Virginia	Railroad employee, grocer	1832-1899
10	McCormick, Stephen J.	1859-60	Ireland	Printer, bookseller	1829-1891
46	McCready, Connie	1979-80	Pendleton, OR	Journalist, legislator	1921-2000
23	Newbury, William S.	1877-79	Ripley, NY	Lawyer	1834-1915
1	O'Bryant, Hugh D.	1851-52	Georgia	Carpenter	1813-ca 1885
7	O'Neill, James	1856-57	New York	Wells Fargo agent	1824-1901
30	Pennoyer, Sylvester	1896-98	Groton, NY	Lawyer, editor, governor	1831-1902
43	Peterson, Fred	1953-56	Minnesota	Pharmacist	1896-1985
41	Riley, Earl	1941-48	Portland, OR	Tire shop owner	1890-1965
11	Robbins, George Collier	1860-61	Troy, MO	Jeweler, miner	1824-1907
33	Rowe, Henry S.	1900-02	Boliver, NY	Railroad agent, banker	1851-1914
37	Rushlight, Allen G.	1911-13	Golden City, CO	Plumber, auto dealer	1874-1930
44	Schrunk, Terry D.	1957-72	Stayton, OR	Fireman, sheriff	1913-1975
36	Simon, Joseph	1909-11	Germany	Lawyer, state senator	1851-1935
9	Starr, Addison M.	1858-59	New York	Tinsmith, distiller, banker	1828-1891
32	Storey, William A.	1899-1900	Maine	Woodmill worker, publisher	1854-1917
24	Thompson, David P.	1879-82	Cadiz, OH	Surveyor, investor, executive	1835-1901
6	Vaughn, George W.	1855-56	New Jersey	Merchant, investor	1809-1877
20	Wasserman, Philip	1871-73	Germany	Merchant	1828-1895
34	Williams, George H.	1902-05	New Lebanon, NY	Judge; Senator; Atty General	1823-1910

Appendix D

Elected Portland Officials, 1950-2001

Year	Mayor	Comm #1	Comm #2	Comm #3	Comm #4	Auditor
1950	Lee, Dorothy	Peterson, F.	Cooper, K.	Bean, O.	Bowes, Bill	Gibson
1951	Lee, Dorothy	Peterson, F.	Bennett, Jake	Bean, O.	Bowes, Bill	Gibson
1952	Lee, Dorothy	Peterson, F.	Bennett, Boody	Bean, O.	Bowes, Bill	Gibson
1953	Peterson, F.	Earl, Stanley	Boody, Nate	Bean, O.	Bowes, Bill	Gibson
1954	Peterson, F.	Earl, Stanley	Boody, Nate	Bean, O.	Bowes, Bill	Gibson
1955	Peterson, F.	Earl, Stanley	Boody, Nate	Bean, O.	Bowes, Bill	Gibson
1956	Peterson, F.	Earl, Stanley	Boody, Nate	Bean, O.	Bowes, Bill	Gibson
1957	Schrunk, T.	Earl, Stanley	Boody, Nate	Bean, O.	Bowes, Bill	Gibson
1958	Schrunk, T.	Earl, Stanley	Boody, Nate	Bean, O.	Bowes, Bill	Gibson
1959	Schrunk, T.	Earl, Stanley	Grayson	Bean, O.	Bowes, Bill	Smith, Ray
1960	Schrunk, T.	Earl, Stanley	Grayson	Bean, O.	Bowes, Bill	Smith, Ray
1961	Schrunk, T.	Earl, Stanley	Grayson	Bean, O.	Bowes, Bill	Smith, Ray
1962	Schrunk, T.	Earl, Stanley	Grayson	Bean, O.	Bowes, Bill	Smith, Ray
1963	Schrunk, T.	Earl, Stanley	Grayson	Bean, O.	Bowes, Bill	Smith, Ray
1964	Schrunk, T.	Earl, Stanley	Grayson	Bean, O.	Bowes, Bill	Smith, Ray
1965	Schrunk, T.	Earl, Stanley	Grayson	Bean, O.	Bowes, Bill	Smith, Ray
1966	Schrunk, T.	Earl, Stanley	Grayson	Bean, O.	Bowes, Bill	Smith, Ray
1967	Schrunk, T.	Earl, Stanley	Grayson	Ivancie	Bowes, Bill	Smith, Ray
1968	Schrunk, T.	Earl, Stanley	Grayson	Ivancie	Bowes, Bill	Smith, Ray
1969	Schrunk, T.	Earl, Stanley	Grayson	Ivancie	Bowes, Bill	Smith, Ray
1970	Schrunk, T.	Earl, McCready	Grayson	Ivancie	Anderson, L.	Smith, Yerkovich
1971	Schrunk, T.	McCready	Goldschmidt	Ivancie	Anderson, L.	Yerkovich
1972	Schrunk, T.	McCready	Goldschmidt	Ivancie	Anderson, L.	Yerkovich
1973	Goldschmidt	McCready	Schwab	Ivancie	Anderson, L.	Yerkovich
1974	Goldschmidt	McCready	Schwab	Ivancie	Jordan	Yerkovich
1975	Goldschmidt	McCready	Schwab	Ivancie	Jordan	Yerkovich
1976	Goldschmidt	McCready	Schwab	Ivancie	Jordan	Yerkovich
1977	Goldschmidt	McCready	Schwab	Ivancie	Jordan	Yerkovich
1978	Goldschmidt	McCready	Schwab	Ivancie	Jordan	Yerkovich

Year	Mayor	Comm #1	Comm #2	Comm #3	Comm #4	Auditor
1979	Goldschmidt	McCready	Schwab	Ivancie	Jordan	Yerkovich
1980	McCready	Lindberg	Schwab	Ivancie	Jordan	Yerkovich
1981	Ivancie	Lindberg	Schwab	Strachan	Jordan	Yerkovich
1982	Ivancie	Lindberg	Schwab	Strachan	Jordan	Yerkovich
1983	Ivancie	Lindberg	Schwab	Strachan	Jordan	Lansing
1984	Ivancie	Lindberg	Schwab	Strachan	Jordan	Lansing
1985	Clark, Bud	Lindberg	Schwab	Strachan	Bogle, Dick	Lansing
1986	Clark, Bud	Lindberg	Schwab	Strachan	Bogle, Dick	Lansing
1987	Clark, Bud	Lindberg	Blumenauer	Koch, Bob	Bogle, Dick	Clark, Barbara
1988	Clark, Bud	Lindberg	Blumenauer	Koch, Bob	Bogle, Dick	Clark, Barbara
1989	Clark, Bud	Lindberg	Blumenauer	Koch, Bob	Bogle, Dick	Clark, Barbara
1990	Clark, Bud	Lindberg	Blumenauer	Koch, Bob	Bogle, Dick	Clark, Barbara
1991	Clark, Bud	Lindberg	Blumenauer	Kafoury, G.	Bogle, Dick	Clark, Barbara
1992	Clark, Bud	Lindberg	Blumenauer	Kafoury, G.	Bogle, Dick	Clark, Barbara
1993	Katz, Vera	Lindberg	Blumenauer	Kafoury, G.	Hales	Clark, Barbara
1994	Katz, Vera	Lindberg	Blumenauer	Kafoury, G.	Hales	Clark, Barbara
1995	Katz, Vera	Lindberg	Blumenauer	Kafoury, G.	Hales	Clark, Barbara
1996	Katz, Vera	Lindberg	Blumenauer	Kafoury, G.	Hales	Clark, Barbara
1997	Katz, Vera	Francesconi	Sten, Erik	Kafoury, G.	Hales	Clark, Barbara
1998	Katz, Vera	Francesconi	Sten, Erik	Kafoury, G.	Hales	Clark, Barbara
1999	Katz, Vera	Francesconi	Sten, Erik	Saltzman	Hales	Blackmer
2000	Katz, Vera	Francesconi	Sten, Erik	Saltzman	Hales	Blackmer
2001	Katz, Vera	Francesconi	Sten, Erik	Saltzman	Hales	Blackmer

Appendix E

City of Portland Officials: A Chronological List

Mayors

O'Bryant, Hugh D.	1851-52
Bonnell, Allison C.	1852-52
Marye, Simon B.	1852-53
Failing, Josiah	1853-54
Ladd, William S.	1854-55
Vaughn, George W.	1855-56
O'Neill, James	1856-57
Ladd, William S.	1857-58
Starr, Addison M.	1858-59
McCormick, Stephen J.	1859-60
Robbins, George Collier	1860-61
Breck, John M.	1861-62
Farrar, William H.	1862-63
Logan, David	1863-64
Failing, Henry	1864-66
Holmes, Thomas J.	1866-67
Chapman, James A.	1867-68
Boyd, Hamilton	1868-69
Goldsmith, Bernard	1869-71
Wasserman, Philip	1871-73
Failing, Henry	1873-75
Chapman, James A.	1875-77
Newbury, William S.	1877-79
Thompson, David P.	1879-82
Chapman, James A.	1882-85
Gates, John	1885-88
DeLashmutt, Van B.	1888-91
Mason, William S.	1891-94
Frank, George P.	1894-96
Pennoyer, Sylvester	1896-98
Mason, William S.	1898-99
Storey, William A.	1899-1900
Rowe, Henry S.	1900-02
Williams, George H.	1902-05
Lane, Harry	1905-09
Simon, Joseph	1909-11
Rushlight, Allen G.	1911-13
Albee, H. Russell	1913-17
Baker, George L.	1917-33
Carson, Joseph K., Jr.	1933-40
Riley, Earl	1941-48
Lee, Dorothy McCullough	1949-52
Peterson, Fred	1953-56
Schrunk, Terry D.	1957-72
Goldschmidt, Neil	1973-79
McCready, Connie	1979-80
Ivancie, Frank	1980-84
Clark, John Elwood "Bud"	1985-92
Katz, Vera	1993-

City Assessors

Slater, Seth S.	1852-54
Bacon, Charles P.	1854-54
Starr, Addison M.	1854-55
Ogden, William Seton	1855-55
Holmes, Thomas J.	1855-55
Stansbury, Z. N.	1856-57
Breck, John M.	1857-58
Kapus, William	1859-59
McCoy, J. F.	1859-60
Going, James W.	1860-62
Risley, Orville	1862-63
Ladd, R. J.	1862-62
Pomeroy, F. C.	1863-64
Going, James W.	1864-65
Moreland, S.A.	1865-68
Johnston, H. H.	1868-69
Kilburn, Oscar	1869-71
Breck, John M.	1871-73
Going, James W.	1874-75
Hill, Andrew	1875-76
Chapman, W. S.	1876-77
Love, R. H.	1877-79
Kelley, W. J.	1879-82
Flower, James	1891-92
Stearns, David S.	1892-93

City Attorneys

Marye, Simon B.	1851-52
Office abolished for 2 yrs	1852-54
Farrar, William H.	1854-55
Chinn, Mark A.	1855-56
McEwan, M. L.	1856-57
Logan, David	1857-58
Shattuck, Erasmus D.	1858-59
Douthitt, David W.	1859-61
Mitchell, John H.	1861-62
Logan, David	1862-63
McGraw, E.W.	1863-64
Holbrook, Amory	1864-64
Dolph, Joseph N.	1864-66
Upton, William W.	1866-67
Freidenrich, D.	1867-68
Trimble, W. F.	1868-69
Dolph, Cyrus A.	1869-71
Ball, C. A.	1871-72
Mulkey, Marion F.	1872-74
Gibbs, Addison C.	1874-75
Gearin, John M.	1875-76

Showers, William	1876-78
Moreland, Julius C.	1877-82
Rice, S. W.	1882-83
Dement, R. M.	1883-84
Tanner, A. H.	1884-87
Adams, W. H.	1887-91
Muir, Wm. T.	1891-93
Beach, J. V.	1893-94
Giltner, R. R.	1894-96
Cake, W. M.	1896-98
Long, J. M.	1898-1902
McNary, Lawrence A.	1902-07
Kavanaugh, John P.	1907-10
Grant, Frank S.	1910-13
LaRoche, Walter Paul	1913-20
Young, John	1920-20
Grant, Frank S.	1921-38
Latourette, Lyman	1938-47
Brown, Alexander	1947-68
Rushing, Marian	1969-73
Carlsen, Clifford N.	1973-73
Osburn, John	1974-77
Thomas, Christopher	1977-85
Rodgers, Jeffrey	1985-

City Auditors

Meeker, H. R.	1865-66
Wilcox, Ralph W.	1866-66
Caldwell, William S.	1867-78
Durham, R. L.	1878-82
Spencer, M. F.	1882-82
Curry, R. B.	1883-85
Norden, Ben L.	1885-87
Wood, W. H.	1887-90
Matthews, W. F. "Jack"	1890-91
Branch, W. T.	1891-93
Gambell, A. N.	1893-1900
Devlin, Thomas Clarke	1900-07
Barbur, Asbury Lincoln	1907-17
Funk, George R.	1917-37
Jones, Edward W.	1938-38
Gibson, Will E.	1939-43
Bredemeier, John O.	1944-45
Gibson, Will E.	1946-58
Smith, Ray	1959-70
Hamill, James	1970-70
Yerkovich, George	1970-82
Lansing, Jewel	1983-86
Clark, Barbara	1987-98
Blackmer, Gary	1999-

City Council Members

Barnes, George H.	1851-52
Hastings, Loren B.	1851-52
Norris, Shubrick	1851-52
Robinson, Thomas G.	1851-51
Thompson, Robert	1851-52
McDonald, Harley	1851-51
Slater, Seth S.	1851-52
Abrams, William P.	1852-52
Dennison, Ani P.	1852-53
Pritchard, Thomas	1852-53
Tripp, Abel	1852-52
Failing, Josiah	1852-53
Norris, Shubrick	1852-53
Marquam, Philip A.	1852-53
McLaren, R. N.	1853-53
Abrams, William P.	1853-54
Couch, John H.	1853-54
Davis, H. W.	1853-54
Field, Richard M.	1853-54
Ladd, William S.	1853-54
McLaren, R. N.	1853-54
Pillow, Charles B.	1853-54
Williams, Jonas	1853-54
Thompson, Robert	1853-53
Northrup, Nelson	1853-53
Steinberger, Justus	1853-53
Norris, Shubrick	1854-55
Backus, O. J.	1854-55
Carter, Thomas J.	1854-54
Field, James, Jr.	1854-54
Fitch, A. D.	1854-55
McMillen, William	1854-55
Shipley, A. R.	1854-55
Starr, Addison M.	1854-54
Turnbull, James	1854-55
Kittredge, George	1854-55
Leland, Alonzo	1854-54
Jacobs, H. S.	1854-55
Waterman, J. Orvis	1854-54
Calhoun, E. B.	1855-56
Carson, John C.	1855-56
Hartness, Thomas M.	1855-56
Kittredge, George	1855-55
Love, Lewis	1855-56
Patton, Mathew	1855-56
Robbins, George Collier	1855-55
Slater, Seth S.	1855-56
Clark, Ranson	1855-55
Smith, Samuel M.	1855-57
Besser, Lucerne	1855-56
Harbaugh, F.	1855-56
Failing, Henry	1855-56

Beck, William	1856-57
Davis, H.W.	1856-56
Porter, Robert	1856-57
Shelby, A. D.	1856-57
Starr, Lewis M.	1856-57
Burk, James	1856-57
Seymore, H.	1856-57
Masters, William	1856-57
Goodwin, Benjamin F.	1856-57
Coon, N. S.	1857-58
Couch, John H.	1857-58
Hallock, Absalom B.	1857-58
Hardenburg, Peter D.W.	1857-58
Hutchins, Chas	1857-58
Reed, Simeon Gannett	1857-58
Holmes, Thomas J.	1857-59
Hamilton, Edward	1857-58
Coffin, Stephen	1857-58
King, William M.	1857-59
McEwan, M. L.	1857-58
Wilson, R. B.	1857-58
Ankeny, Alexander P.	1858-59
Lakin, T. N.	1858-59
Porter, Robert	1858-59
Carson, John C.	1858-59
Kingsley, C. S.	1858-59
Robbins, George Collier	1858-59
Vansycle, J.M.	1859-60
Blanchard, John	1859-60
Hawthorne, J. C.	1859-60
Shaw, Alva Compton R.	1859-60
Shelby, A. D.	1859-60
Davidson, J.	1859-61
Lucas, M. M.	1859-61
Shattuck, Erasmus D.	1859-61
Hallock, Absalom B.	1859-69
Sitzel, Jacob	1860-61
Ainsworth, J. C.	1860-61
Higgins, William	1860-62
Harbaugh, F	1861-62
Hull, W. C.	1861-62
King, William M.	1861-62
Masters, William	1861-62
McCracken, John	1861-62
Scott, Emsley R.	1861-62
White, John S.	1861-62
Barr, S. E.	1861-62
Holmes, Thomas J.	1861-62
Breck, John M.	1862-63
Coffin, Stephen	1862-63
Holmes, Thomas J	1861-62
Risley, Orville	1862-63
Silver, Clieve S.	1862-63
Walling, Albert G.	1862-63
Dennison, Ani P.	1862-63
Williams, Nathan	1862-63
Austin, I. A.	1863-64
Dodge, Alex	1863-64
Knott, Joseph	1863-64
Monastes, David	1863-64
Saxer, H.	1863-64
Sherlock, Samuel	1863-63
Sutton, John W.	1863-64
Watson, P. S.	1863-64
Lucas, M. M.	1863-64
King, William M.	1863-63
Zieber, Al	1863-64
Bennett, Wm	1864-65
Cook, James W.	1864-65
Frazar, Thomas	1864-65
Graden, Israel	1864-65
Hoffman, J. J.	1864-65
Robertson, Thomas	1864-65
Starr, Addison M.	1864-65
Gilmore, S. M.	1864-66
McCracken, John	1864-68
Clarke, S. A.	1865-66
Morgan, E. S.	1865-66
Plummer, Orlando P. S.	1865-66
Schuyler, P.C.	1865-66
Thompson, Robert R.(RR)	1865-66
Lownsdale, J. P. O.	1865-67
Rosenheim, A.	1865-68
Carson, John C.	1866-67
Carter, Thomas J.	1866-67
O'Connor, M.	1866-67
Zieber, Al	1866-67
Fechheimer, C. H.	1866-68
Mulkey, Marion F.	1867-68
Burch, C. D.	1867-69
Porter, Robert	1867-70
Ripley, A. C.	1867-70
Besser, Lucerne	1867-76
Hopkins, Chas	1868-70
Breck, John M.	1868-71
Cree, Wm	1868-71
Lewis, D. C.	1869-70
Bills, Cincinnati	1869-71
Moffett, W.	1869-72
Drake, J. M.	1870-71
Congle, J. B.	1870-73
Hallock, Absalom B.	1870-73
Hill, William Lair	1870-74
Combs, R. G.	1871-72
Burton, E. M.	1871-74
Caywood, J. M.	1871-74
Story, George L.	1871-74
Moreland, Julius C.	1872-75

Russell, Edwin F.	1872-75
Lyon, J. H.	1873-75
Hoyt, George W.	1873-76
Thompson, Robert R.	1874-75
Catlin, John	1874-76
Corbett, Elijah	1874-77
Sanborn, Henry D.	1875-76
Skidmore, Stephen G.	1875-78
Stemme, E. J.	1875-78
Wiley, J. R.	1875-78
Andrus, Wm H.	1875-81
Blumauer, Simon	1876-77
Harrington, D. F.	1876-77
Lambert, Noah	1876-79
Stephens, Thomas	1876-79
Yocum, G. W.	1877-79
Opitz, F.	1877-80
Simon, Joseph	1877-80
Payne, J. W.	1878-80
Stolte, E. H.	1878-81
Weber, H.	1878-81
Nichlin, T. L.	1879-80
Watson, James Finley	1879-80
Keller, J. S.	1879-82
Gerdes, R.	1879-91
Nicklin, T. L.	1880-82
Raleigh, J. S.	1880-82
Hewett, Henry	1880-83
Kellogg, John Beldon	1880-83
Holman, Charles	1881-83
Chittenden, W. L.	1881-84
Honeyman, W. B.	1881-84
Mackay, D.	1882-83
Adams, W. H.	1882-85
Scoggin, W. A.	1882-85
Smith, J. E.	1882-85
Hailey, J. B.	1883-84
Andrus, Wm H.	1883-86
Sears, A. F. Jr.	1883-86
Holland, J. J.	1884-87
Fliedner, Wm	1884-93
Forbes, C. M.	1884-93
Gallagher, J. J.	1885-88
Hacheney, Frank	1885-88
Farrell, Sylvester	1885-91
Schwab, R. H.	1886-89
Woodward, Tyler	1886-92
Castendieck, G.	1887-93
Hoyt, Richard	1888-91
Showers, William	1888-91
Scoggin, W. A.	1889-94
Crowley, D. W.	1891-92
Dent, W.	1891-92
Hansen, H.	1891-92
Pittenger, J.	1891-92
Watson, James Finley	1891-92
Hobkirk, P.	1891-93
Myers, John	1891-93
Nicholas, H. B.	1891-93
Parker, J.	1891-93
Merrick, W. H.	1891-94
Shelby, Eugene	1891-94
Mason, S. R.	1892-93
Dalgleish, D.	1892-94
Davis, L. M.	1892-94
McInnis, H. J.	1892-94
Richardson, S. G.	1892-94
Monks, J.	1892-96
Mock, John	1893-94
Terwilliger, J. M.	1893-96
Malone, T. C.	1893-98
Armstrong, W. H.	1894-96
Burnside, D. W.	1894-96
Fleckenstein, H.	1894-96
Hall, W. B.	1894-96
Jones, T. J.	1894-96
Menefee, J. P.	1894-96
Moffett, J. P.	1894-96
Rumelin, C. E.	1894-96
Martin, John A.	1896-1900
Cole, L. D.	1896-98
McBrien, J.	1896-98
Mead, W. H.	1896-98
Nicholas, M. L.	1896-98
Nickum, J. M.	1896-98
Peery, L. T.	1896-98
Spurrier, W. E.	1896-98
Strowbridge, George H.	1896-98
Woodward, S. L.	1896-98
Baker, George L.	1898-1900
Belding, Henry A.	1898-1900
Beutgen, N. D.	1898-1900
Cameron, George J.	1898-1900
Hanson, Fred W.	1898-1900
Jameson, J. C.	1898-1900
Luckel, J. C.	1898-1900
Meyer, J. D.	1898-1900
Showers, William	1898-1900
Storey, W. A.	1898-99
Harris, W. E.	1899-1900
Bronaugh, E. C.	1900-01
Glisan, Rodney L.	1900-01
Holbrook, F. B.	1900-01
Masters, W. Y.	1900-01
Nealond, P. G.	1900-01
Nichols, A. F.	1900-01
Walker, F. P.	1900-01
Branch, W. T.	1900-02

Mulkey, Frederick M.	1900-02
Merrill, F.T.	1900-05
Sherrett, D.T.	1900-05
Cardinell, B. P.	1902-03
Albee, H. R.	1902-05
Bentley, A. K.	1902-05
Flegel, A. F.	1902-05
Foeller, Mart	1902-05
Rumelin, C. E.	1902-05
Sigler, B. D.	1902-05
Zimmerman, L.	1902-05
Sharkey, John P.	1902-07
Whiting, Sanford	1903-05
Masters, W.Y.	1905-06
Sheppard, George S.	1905-06
Gray, Thomas	1905-07
Preston, Robert A.	1905-07
Kellaher, Dan	1905-08
Bennett, Frank S.	1905-09
Vaughn, W.T.	1905-09
Wills, A. N.	1905-09
Annand, J.	1905-11
Belding, Henry A.	1905-11
Rushlight, A. G.	1905-11
Dunning, George L.	1905-13
Menefee, R. E.	1905-13
Wallace, Hugh W.	1905-13
Boothe, J. F.	1906-07
Baker, George L.	1906-17
Cottell, W. I.	1907-09
Cellars, George B.	1907-11
Concannon, T. J.	1907-11
Driscoll, M. J.	1907-11
Heppner, H. A.	1908-09
Devlin, Thomas Clarke	1909-11
Ellis, J.T.	1909-11
Kubli, K. K.	1909-11
Lombard, Gay	1909-11
Watkins, F. E.	1909-13
Clyde, Ralph C.	1911-12
Monks, Tom N.	1911-12
Burgard, John H.	1911-13
Jennings, J. J.	1911-13
Joy, Allan R.	1911-13
Maguire, James	1911-13
Montag, John	1911-13
Schmeer, Wm	1911-13
Wilhelm, F. S.	1911-13
Daly, Will H.	1911-17
Parks, Tom N.	1912-13
Brewster, Wm L.	1913-15
Dieck, Robert G.	1913-17
Bigelow, C. A.	1913-30
Kellaher, Dan	1917-19
Mann, John M.	1917-32
Barbur, Asbury Lincoln	1917-33
Pier, Sylvester C.	1919-23
Pier, Stanhope S.	1923-33
Riley, Earl	1930-41
Clyde, Ralph C.	1930-43
Johnson, A. G.	1932-32
Bennett, J. E.	1932-41
Bean, Ormond	1933-39
Bowes, Wm A.	1939-69
Cooper, Kenneth	1941-50
Peterson, Fred	1941-56
Van Fleet, Clark C.	1943-43
Lee, Dorothy McCullough	1943-48
Bean, Ormond	1949-66
Bennett, J. E.	1951-51
Boody, Nathan	1952-58
Earl, Stanley	1953-70
Grayson, Mark A.	1959-70
Ivancie, Frank	1967-80
Anderson, Lloyd	1969-74
McCready, Connie	1970-78
Goldschmidt, Neil	1971-72
Schwab, Mildred	1973-86
Jordan, Charles R.	1974-84
Lindberg, Mike	1979-96
Strachan, Margaret D.	1981-86
Bogle, Dick	1985-92
Koch, Bob	1987-90
Blumenauer, Earl	1987-95
Kafoury, Gretchen	1991-98
Hales, Charlie	1993-2002
Sten, Erik	1996-
Francesconi, Jim	1997-
Saltzman, Dan	1999-

City Marshalls

Wilbur, Hiram	1851-51
Higgins, William	1851-53
Grooms, William	1853-54
Higgins, William	1854-54
Perkins, R. S.	1854-54
Holmes, Thomas J.	1854-56
Higgins, William	1856-57
Holcomb, S. R.	1857-59
Lappeus, James Henry	1859-61
Grooms, William	1861-63
Clark, W. B.	1863-64
Hoyt, Henry L.	1864-67
Jacobi, D.	1867-68
Lappeus, James Henry	1868-69
Saunders, Joseph	1869-70

City Police Chiefs

Lappeus, James H.	1870-77
Besser, Lucerne	1877-79
Lappeus, James H.	1879-83
Watkinds, William	1883-84
Parrish, Samuel B.	1884-92
Spencer, Ernest W.	1892-92
Hunt, Charles H.	1892-94
Minto, John W.	1894-96
Robertson, D.W.	1896-97
Myers, John	1897-97
Barry, Patrick J.	1897-97
Clohessy, Michael J.	1897-98
McLauchlan, Daniel M.	1898-1903
Hunt, Charles H.	1903-05
Gritzmacher, Charles	1905-09
Cox, A. M.	1909-11
Slover, Enoch A.	1911-13
Clark, John	1913-17
Johnson, Nelson F.	1917-19
Jenkins, Leon V.	1919-33
Lawson, Burton K.	1933-34
Niles, Harry M.	1934-46
Jenkins, Leon V.	1946-48
Flemming, James	1948-48
Pray, Charles P.	1949-51
McNamara, Donald I.	1951-53
Purcell, James T., Jr.	1953-57
Hilbruner, William J.	1957-60
Johnson, David H.	1960-64
McNamara, Donald I.	1964-74
Baker, Bruce R.	1974-81
Still, Ronald R.	1981-85
Haynes, Gary M. (Interim)	1985-85
Harrington, Penny	1985-86
Tobin, Robert M. (Interim)	1986-86
Davis, James T.	1986-87
Walker, Richard D.	1987-90
Potter, Thomas J.	1990-93
Moose, Charles A.	1993-99
Berg, Lynnae C. (Interim)	1999-99
Kroeker, Mark	1999-

City Recorders

Caldwell, William S.	1851-52
Slater, Seth S.	1852-52
Pillow, Charles B.	1852-53
Bonnell, Allison C.	1853-53
Wisenthal, Andrew	1853-54
Dennison, Ani P.	1854-55
Limerick, Lamden	1855-55
Davis, Anthony L.	1855-58
Leland, Alonzo	1858-59
Huber, Noah	1859-60
Risley, Orville	1860-62
McCoy, J. F.	1862-65
Hoffman, J. J.	1865-68
Risley, Orville	1868-69
Anderson, Levi	1869-70
Sherlock, William	1854-54
Hallock, Absalom B.	1854-55
Holmes, Thomas J.	1855-56
Higgins, William	1856-58
Wright, George	1858-59
Lappeus, Joseph H.	1860-61
Grooms, William	1861-61
Thornton, H. G.	1861-61
Stewart, A. B.	1862-63
Northrup, Nelson	1864-65
Simmonds, Samuel	1865-66
Davis, H. W.	1866-67
McMillen, William	1867-68
Tucker, Joseph	1868-69
Sloan, Joseph	1869-69
Shartle, J. F.	1869-71
Marshall, A. J.	1871-73
Habersham, Robert A.	1873-74
Davis, Perry W.	1874-76
Showers, William	1876-77
Budd, D. E.	1877-78
Braden, W.	1878-81
Kelley, W. J.	1881-82
Braden, W.	1882-83
Sears, A. F. Jr.	1883-84
Vaughn, F. E.	1884-87
Chapman, W. S.	1887-91
Taylor, Douglas W.	1891-93
Gradon, H.D.	1893-96

City Surveyors

Hallock, Absalom B.	1854-57
Henry, A. G. (Dr.)	1857-58
Leland, Alonzo	1858-59
Hallock, Absalom B.	1859-64
Burrage, Charles W.	1862-67
Belden, Geo. W.	1867-68
Morris, W. S.	1868-69
Stevenson, H. J.	1869-72
Chapman, W. S.	1872-74
Taylor, Douglas W.	1874-78
Chapman, W. S.	1878-87
Taylor, Douglas W.	1881-83
Pagett, E.W.	1887-91
Gillham, Frank E.	1896-98
Austin, Robert H.	1898-99
Chase, W. B.	1899-1900

City Treasurers

Flanders, George H.	1851-53
Barnhart, William H.	1853-54
Vaughn, George W.	1854-55
Frazar, Thomas	1855-56
Savier, Thomas A.	1856-57
Lakin, T. N.	1857-58
Corbett, Henry W.	1858-59
McCracken, John	1859-60
Wasserman, H.	1860-61
Morse, H. B.	1862-63
Risley, Orville	1863-64
Morse, H. B.	1864-65
Ferry, C. P.	1865-69
Backenstos, Edwin D.	1869-73
Lewis, L. H.	1873-75
Bachman, Joseph	1875-81
McKercher, D. C.	1881-87
Monnastes, H. W.	1887-90
Hacheney, Frank	1890-1900
Werlein, J. E.	1900-11
Adams, William	1911-13

Note: A number of city officials were first appointed, then elected as incumbents when their terms expired. Many council members served only a couple of months, or even less, particularly during the first 20 years of the all-volunteer governing body.

Appendix F

Portland City Halls[1]

Interim City Hall A	No record of location	April 14, 1851
City Hall Number 1	Councilman Robinson's building	April - October 1851
City Hall Number 2	Schoolhouse and public building at First and Oak built by Stephen Coffin and William King	mid-October 1851 - mid-June 1852
City Hall Number 3	Mayor Bunnell's office	June 1852
Interim City Hall B	Josiah Failing's store	November 1852
City Hall Number 4	Simon Marye's office	January 1853
Interim City Hall C	Law office of Philip Marquam	April 1853
City Hall Number 5	Second floor of Coffin's Building	1853
Interim City Hall D	Ani Dennison's office	March 1854
City Hall Number 6	Anthony L. Davis's room	March 1854
City Hall Number 7	Abram Waltz's room	September 1855
City Hall Number 8	Building owned by Jacob Kamm adjoining J. L. Atwood's Saloon	Spring 1857
City Hall Number 9	Second-story room in Wasserman Building	July 1862
City Hall Number 10	Second-story room in brick building owned by Blumauer and Rosenblatt	August 1866
City Hall Number 11	Second floor, Corbett's building between Washington and Alder	November 1870
City Hall Number 12	93 First Street	1872
City Hall Number 13	Building owned by Henry Corbett	Fall 1874
City Hall Number 14	Offices "scattered in buildings all over town"—Mayor D. P. Thompson	1879
City Hall Number 15	91 First Street, Corbett Building	1880
City Hall Number 16	First National Bank Building on First Street between Washington and Alder	1882
City Hall Number 17	"Council Building" at Third and Washington; second floor of Frank Dekum's "new brick building"	August 1883
City Hall Number 18	Bickel Building at Second and Ash	July 1891
City Hall Number 19	City Hall, SW Fifth and Madison	1894

Notes

Guide to Footnote Abbreviations:

C.P. Arch. = City of Portland Archives
CUE = Center for Urban Education
OBB = *Oregon Blue Book*
OHQ = *Oregon Historical Quarterly*
OHS = Oregon Historical Society
OJ = *Oregon Journal*
ONS = *Oregon Native Son* magazine
OPAT = *Oregon Pioneer Association Transactions*
Oreg. = *Oregonian*
ORS = Oregon Revised Statutes
OS = *The Oregon Story*
OSA = Oregon State Archives
P.C. Dir. = *Portland City Directory*
P. Trib. = *Portland Tribune*
Proc. C. C. = *Proceedings of the Common Council*
PSU = Portland State University
Spec. = *Oregon Spectator*
UO = University of Oregon
WW = *Willamette Week*

Chapter I

[1] *Oregon*, Federal Writers Project, 208; Purdy, 58. See also Maddux, 11.
[2] Lovejoy related his story to historian Hubert Bancroft in 1878. *OHQ* v 31 (1930), 237, 253; Scott, *Portland*, 81.
[3] Four different sites for this historic Oregon City coin toss have been postulated—the homes of Francis Ermatinger, Asa Lovejoy, Francis Pettygrove, and A. E. Wilson. An article by E. L. Meyers (a descendant of Pettygrove) says in a 1968-69 Clackamas County Historical Society publication, "The 'Firsts' of Clackamas County," p 30, that the coin toss took place "at a dinner in Pettygrove's house." Fred Lockley, *Columbia* (1928), v 1, 410, says Mr. Pettygrove and his wife and another guest, Mr. Wilson, "were eating dinner at the home of Mr. and Mrs. Lovejoy." Vera Martin Lynch, in *Free Land for Free Men, A Story of Clackamas County* (1973), p 76, says, "The story goes that they were arguing about a name at the dinner table of A. E. Wilson." F. H. Saylor, at *ONS*, Dec 1900, p 331, says the name was decided "during the course of a dinner at Oregon City." A description of Ermatinger House published in the 2000 edition of U.S. West's Clackamas County telephone book, p 6, says, "The structure, built in 1845, is the oldest house in Clackamas County. It was here that Asa Lovejoy and Francis Pettygrove flipped a coin to name Portland." Marge Harding of Ermatinger House told this author on April 8, 2000, that an early 1860s publication titled *Willamette Crossings*, which disappeared from Ermatinger House in 1999, contained diary excerpts stating that the coin toss came about during a men's politics and book club meeting at Ermatinger's home. This group would likely have been the Pioneer Lyceum & Literary Club formed in 1843, to which Lovejoy, Pettygrove, and Ermatinger all belonged. Lockley, *Oregon's Yesterdays*, 283-84; Turnbull, *Newspapers*, 25.
[4] Scott, *Oregon*, v 1, 173-76.
[5] The same year, 1845, that the coin toss occurred, thirty-seven-year-old Asa Lovejoy married sixteen-year-old Elizabeth McGary of Kentucky. They had met on the Oregon Trail in 1843 when Elizabeth came west by wagon with her mother and brother. *OHQ* v 31, 241; Lacy, 6; Corning, 152; Scott, *Oregon*, v 5, 231-2.
[6] Francis Pettygrove, thirty-three, operated a prosperous store owned and supplied by a New York firm. By 1845, he and his wife Sophia Roland Pettygrove, twenty-one, were already the parents of two children, the birth of the first having been registered in the Sandwich Islands (now Hawaii) when the Pettygroves were en route to the Oregon country by boat. Corning, 195; Lacy, 13.
[7] Lockley, *Columbia*, v 1, 410; Snyder, *Early Portland*, 31; Gaston, v 1, 198.
[8] Indian names were frequently used for Northwest sites. The county in which the Lovejoy – Pettygrove 640 acres were located was known variously as Tuality, Quality, Qualatin, and Tualatin, but was changed to Washington County by the 1849 territorial legislature. Scott, *Oregon*, v 2, 180.
[9] Pettygrove's copper penny was "no doubt then the only one in Oregon," according to F. H. Saylor, *ONS*, Dec 1900, p 331. A sketch of the Matron Head coin at Gaston, v 1, 200, shows a woman's profile, stars, and the year 1835. Pettygrove bequeathed this copper penny to the OHS by his will. *OHQ* v 31, 255.
[10] Maddux, 16; *Portland, Our Community*, 25; Lockley, *Columbia*, v 1, 410.
[11] *Portland, Our Community*, 21-26.
[12] Scott, *Oregon*, v 2, 197; www.census.gov/population/cen2000 [accessed April 5, 2001].
[13] *Oregon: End of the Trail*, 198. See also Gaston, v 1, 60-1, 641; Corning, 13; Morrison, 116-21.
[14] Morrison, 355, 420; Lockley, *Oregon Folks*, 3, 8-10; *1997-98 OBB*, 403; Collins, 18; Corning, 162, 186.
[15] Robbins, 59.
[16] Leslie Scott, *OHQ* 29 (June 1928), 152-53; *OHQ* 1928, 253-54.
[17] Leslie Scott, *OHQ* 29 (June 1928), 144.
[18] Horn, 123.
[19] Corning, 33.
[20] Scott, *Oregon*, v 1, 173-76.
[21] John Quincy Adams was arguing for Congress to settle the Oregon boundary question in 1846. *Congressional Globe, 29th Cong., 1st session, 1846*, p. 342, as quoted in Robbins, 49.
[22] Each parallel of latitude is divided into sixty minutes, with zero degrees latitude at the equator. The halfway point between the equator and the North Pole, the 45th parallel, is about forty miles south of the Willamette River mouth.
[23] Morrison, 401; Lyman, Horace, v 3, 407.
[24] Corning, 33, 103, 120, 177; Castor, 14-15; Scott, *Oregon*, v 1, vi-viii, 184-87.
[25] Castor, 5; *Oregon Law Index*, iii.
[26] In 1853, Congress designated all land north of the Columbia River and 46th parallel to the border with Great Britain as the Washington Territory. Oregon became the thirty-third state in the Union in 1859 with today's boundaries—95,607 square miles—leaving the southern portions of present-day Idaho and Wyoming as part of Washington Territory.

[27] Pioneer F. X. Matthieu also said, "I believe, of all the men I knew when I came to this country, I feel most kindly toward Dr. John McLoughlin, for I never knew a man more just, more charitable or more kindly." Matthieu to Lockley, *Oregon Folks*, 3, 8-10. Matthieu was a founder of the Oregon Pioneer Association, predecessor organization to the OHS. *OHS Spectator*, Winter 2000-1, p 2. Also see Clark, *Eden*, 158-60; *Oreg.*, Feb 4, 2001, A18.

[28] "Lovejoy's Pioneer Narrative," Henry E. Reed, ed., *OHQ*, v 31 (1930), 252; Wills, 22; Morrison, 360, 392.

[29] The Oregon City church, opened in 1844, was the first building erected exclusively for religious purposes in Oregon. Carey, 340; Clarke, v 1, 228; Gaston 407; *Oregon: End of the Trail*, 191.

[30] Gaston, 120; Morrison, 387-91.

[31] Morrison, 394, 419-25, 429, 468. For more about McLoughlin's bitter fall from power, also see O'Donnell, *1997-98 OBB*, 403; Collins, 18; Corning, 162; Aikman, 157-58.

[32] Morrison, 478.

[33] A bronze statue of Clark, his black slave York, and their Indian guide—all participants in the exploring party—was placed on Waud's Bluff at the University of Portland above the river in the mid-1980s. A Clark diary entry describes passing a "high bold shore" on the right, "to a bend under the high lands" again on the right, passing a left point. An editor's footnote to the Thwaites' Lewis and Clark journals for April 3, 1806, says, "Clark ascended to a point at or near the present site of Portland, Ore. A writer in the Portland *Oreg.*, July 25, 1902, claims that it was within the city limits, near the railroad bridge which crosses the Willamette." Clark's diary says, "When I left it [the river], it was bending to the East of S.E." Thwaites, 238-40, 243. This indicates he did not reach "The Clearing," where the river ran southerly. Two researchers in early 2000 concluded that Clark's party made it only as far as Cathedral Park at present-day St. Johns, about a mile and half north of Waud's Bluff and six miles north of downtown Portland. *Oreg.*, May 26, 2000, C1, C7.

[34] *Oregon: End of the Trail*, 208.

[35] William Johnson built Portland's first log cabin on a small stream in an area later annexed to Portland. A plaque erected by the U.S. Daughters of 1812 on today's busy S.W. Macadam Street near S.W. Curry proclaims the spot. Johnson was "an old British sailor who had become a citizen of the United States, entered the navy and was one of the crew of the frigate *Constitution*—'Old Ironsides'—on August 12, 1812, when she had her famous battle with the English frigate *Guerrière*," according to Scott's *History of Oregon*, 266. Howard Corning's *Dictionary of Oregon History*, 129, says Johnson had "an Indian wife and two children, also two Indian slaves.... [A]s settlers began to move in around his claim he either abandoned it or sold to Finice Caruthers ... and disappeared." Johnson was well-known to other settlers, and was one of the fifty-two who stood with Joe Meek at Champoeg in 1843 to seek American government instead of British rule. Also see OHS Mss 5166-1, William L. Higgins papers; Scott, *Portland*, 88; Lyman, Horace, v 3, 263-64.

[36] The filing fee for the Lovejoy-Overton claim would have paid for the services of a recorder, the elected official whose job it was to write down the boundaries of claims filed. The fee set by the provisional government for recorder's services was twelve cents for each hundred words. Thus the fee paid for recording the Lovejoy-Overton claim was probably between twenty-four and thirty-six cents. *ONS*, December 1900, 329-30. Also see Snyder, *Early Portland*, 31, 34.

[37] Snyder, *Early Portland*, 31.

[38] *ONS*, Dec 1900, 330; Quiett, 342; Scott, *Oregon*, v 2, 319-20.

[39] Snyder, *Early Portland*, 32; MacColl, *Merchants*, 8.

[40] Gaston, 200.

[41] Corning, 152, 195; Lacy, 6, 13, 83.

[42] Snyder, *Early Portland*, 32-33; *ONS*, Dec 1900, 332. Terwilliger Boulevard, which today provides a commanding vista of the Willamette River and East Portland, was built on the James Terwilliger claim in the southwest hills.

[43] Hawkins, *Grand Era*, 24; MacColl, *Merchants*, 8-9; Snyder, *Portland Names*, 15; Snyder, *Early Portland*, 32-33; communication between former city planner Ernie Bonner and the author, Feb 28, 2001.

[44] Most western cities of the mid-nineteenth century provided eighty-foot widths and more. City blocks in similarly sized cities "usually stretch anywhere from 250 to 400 feet," says Randy Gragg in "Grid Look," *Oreg.*, Nov 29, 1998, D1. Gragg notes that Portland's two-hundred-feet blocks preclude "the easy building of behemouth skyscrapers."

[45] Lockley, *Columbia*, v 1, 410; MacColl, *Merchants*, 9.

[46] Recollections of Mrs. Mary Aplin, daughter of Peter Wagner, in Lockley, *Oregon's Yesterdays*, 18, 21.

[47] Maddux, 17; Snyder, *Early Portland*, 43.

[48] Bancroft, v 2, 717.

[49] Assuming the typical floor-to-ceiling measurement of today's home at less than eight feet, a trimmed 130-foot tree would reach over sixteen stories high.

[50] "Pioneer Reminiscences of George Collier Robbins," *Magazine Miscellany*, v 6, 348.

[51] Gaston, v 1, 198-99.

[52] Lovejoy's gravestone is located in the Masonic plot of thirty-acre Lone Fir Cemetery at S.E. 21st and Morrison in Portland. Corning, 152; Maddux, 56b; *Oreg.*, Aug 1, 1998, p D1.

[53] *Josiah Parrish v Thomas Stevens*, 1 Or 62 (1853); *OHQ*, v 31 (1930), 255.

[54] Although Pettygrove commissioned a house built in Portland (Snyder, *Early Portland*, 35-36; Snyder, *Portland Names*, 182), he could not have lived there for long. The Pettygroves were living in Oregon City at the time of the 1850 census (Lacy, 13) and moved to Port Townsend in 1852. McCurdy, 25-28. Pettygrove served as chair of the May 1850 Cayuse Indian trial held in Oregon City. Lansing, *Juggernaut*, 26.

[55] Lovejoy died in Portland in 1882 at age seventy-four. Scott, *Oregon*, v 2, 319; Corning, 152. Lovejoy was an unsuccessful candidate against George Abernethy for provincial governor in 1847. Turnbull, *Governors*, 13.

[56] McCurdy, 25-28.

[57] "Captain Couch brought a cargo of goods from New York in a ship commanded by Captain George H. Flanders, and the two captains then went into business together and remained in Portland for the rest of their lives." Quiett, 341.

[58] Bancroft, 16.
[59] *Oregon: End of the Trail*, 208. Writer Stewart Holbrook describes Couch as "a weather-beaten deep-sea skipper who wore thumping great earrings and who pounded the floor with his gold-headed cane." Photos of Captain Couch show no earrings, however, and Holbrook does not tell us whether his verbal portrait is based on fact or whimsy. Holbrook, 5, 6, 8, 31. O'Donnell and Vaughan, 12, also refer to Couch as "the earringed captain."
[60] Gaston, v 1, 196-97; Maddux, 24; Quiett, 341; *OHQ* v 31 (1930), 255.
[61] Empire builder and railroad king Jim Hill was to say, at the Lewis & Clark Exposition in 1905, that "gravity built this town." *Oreg.*, Dec 4, 1950, A10, c 5. In his 1934 book, historian Glenn Chesney Quiett dubbed Portland "The City Gravity Built." Quiett, 341.
[62] Gaston, v 1, 239.
[63] MacColl, *Merchants*, 17. Couch laid out his grid at an angle to Burnside Street, lining the streets up with true north rather than magnetic north. See Snyder, *Portland Names*, 27-28.
[64] Gaston, v 1, 214, 239.
[65] Snyder, *Early Portland*, 36.
[66] In addition to Lownsdale's tannery, Maddux says, the other two most important factors in Portland's development were the discovery of gold in California and the opening of Canyon Road. Maddux, 24.
[67] Scott, *Portland*, 98.
[68] Cartwright, "Early Days," 59.
[69] Snyder, *Early Portland*, 36; *Oreg.*, March 3, 2001, B1, 7.
[70] Stark actually paid Lovejoy $1,215, but most of this cash was for cattle. The net price paid for Lovejoy's half of the claim was $390. Snyder, *Early Portland*, 34; MacColl, *Merchants*, 9.
[71] MacColl, *Merchants*, 9-10; Corning, 231; *OHQ* v 31, 256. Benjamin Stark served as U.S. Senator from Oregon, Oct 1861 - Sept 1862. *1997-98 OBB*, 387. Stark moved his family back to Connecticut in 1863. He at first opposed establishment of public schools in Portland because jails were more needed. Worchester, 22; Corning, 231. Francis and Sophia Pettygrove's child born in 1846 was named Benjamin Stark Pettygrove. Lockley, *Columbia*, v 1, 196, says this was the first white boy born in Portland.
[72] Pettygrove hired Oregon City carpenter John L. Morrison to build a house for the Pettygrove family in Portland on what would later be named Morrison Street. Snyder, *Portland Names*, 182; Snyder, *Early Portland*, 35-36. But at the time the 1850 census was taken, Pettygrove and his family were residing in Oregon City. Lacy, 16.
[73] Gaston, v 1, 206, 492.
[74] MacColl, *Merchants*, 7.
[75] Diary of Mrs. Elizabeth Dixon Greer, January 20, 1848, and February 24, 1848; *OPAT*, 1907, as recounted in Carey, *History of Oregon*, v 1, 775.
[76] Snyder, *Potpourri*, 124; Gaston, v 1, 206
[77] Clark, *Eden*, 241.
[78] Ibid., 241.
[79] Gaston, v 1, 220.
[80] The southernmost of these park blocks today form part of the PSU campus. Snyder, *Potpourri*, 129-33.
[81] Bancroft, 43.
[82] Lockley, *Columbia*, v 1, 415; Snyder, *Early Portland*, 50.
[83] Abbott, *Gateway*, 29; MacColl, *Merchants*, 73. Lownsdale later sold the public squares to Lansing Stout. MacColl, *Merchants*, 56-57. Public ownership of the squares was not assured until they were purchased from W. W. Chapman in 1870. Snyder, *Potpourri*, 130-31; Snyder, *Portland Names*, 244, 249.
[84] One of six "missing" park blocks was dedicated as O'Bryant Square in 1973. Snyder, *Potpourri*, 132. A second of these Lownsdale blocks was regained in 2000, and private efforts to acquire the remaining four blocks for public use were underway in 2001. *Oreg.*, July 17, 1999, B1; *Oreg.*, Dec 16, E8. *WW*, Jan 3, 2001.
[85] *James P. O. Lownsdale v City of Portland*, 1 Or 397 (1861); Scott, *Portland*, 134-35; Corning, 223; *OHQ*, 1930, 255; Leeson, 18; Abbott, *Gateway*, 29; MacColl, *Merchants*, 73, 76.
[86] The names of most early prominent pioneers are preserved through the naming of some kind of Portland landmark—Lovejoy Fountain, Lovejoy Street, Pettygrove Park, Pettygrove Street, the Lovejoy and Pettygrove conference rooms in City Hall, Stark Street, Couch Street, Terwilliger Boulevard, Chapman and Lownsdale squares. But nowhere will today's visitor find the name of early Portland proprietor Steven Coffin. Coffin himself is said to have requested that no landmark or institution bear his name. Understandably, one might be hesitant to start a business on Coffin Street or to live next door to Coffin Park. Scott, *Oregon*, 200-201; Snyder, *Portland Names*, 68.
[87] MacColl, *Merchants*, 13; Snyder, *We Claimed*, 36-37; Gaston, 209.
[88] Scott, *Portland*, 474; MacColl, *Merchants*, 15; Snyder, *We Claimed*, 32-33; Corning, 51.
[89] Scott, *Portland*, 88; Snyder, *Early Portland*, 64-66; Gaston, 209.
[90] Carey, 775.
[91] Snyder, *Early Portland*, 30-43, 64-67; Gaston, v 1, 206.
[92] Maddux, 195; Snyder, *Potpourri*, 125.
[93] MacColl, *Merchants*, 17.
[94] Corning, 75.
[95] Snyder, *Potpourri*, 124-27; Scott, *Portland*, 118.
[96] Land claims under the Homestead Act required five years of continuous residence and payment of a twenty-four- to thirty-four-dollar registration fee. Bowman, 180.
[97] "Population of Oregon Cities," UO Bureau of Municipal Research, Bulletin 106, Table 1; Clark, *Eden*, 248.
[98] *Spec.*, Dec 19, 1850, p 2, c 6; Gaston, 499.
[99] Lyman, Horace, v 4, 146.
[100] Ibid., 146; Scott, *Oregon*, v 3, 226.
[101] The Luellings crossed the plains in 1847. Robbins, 97; Snyder, *We Claimed*, 172; Dimon, 12.
[102] 1850 and 1910 prices are from Gaston, v 1, 629. Ordinary wages did not go far. In October 1852, laborers on a farm outside Portland earned three dollars a day. *OPAT* 42nd Annual Reunion, June 25, 1914, p 192.
[103] Cartwright, "Early Days," 58.

Chapter 2

[1] OHS Mss 2105, undated letter from Oregon Congressional Representative Joseph Showalter Smith, a candidate for mayor in Portland's first election.

[2] "U.S. 26 charted from sunrise to sunset," by Don Hamilton, *Oreg.*, July 6, 1999, p C2.

[3] The trail had been blazed by Joseph S. Smith, Daniel Lownsdale, and others in 1849. J. S. Smith letter to the *Oreg.*, OHS Mss 2105, undated letter.

[4] This planned plank roadway, also known today as Canyon Road and Sunset Highway, would one day be designated as U. S. Highway 26 from Portland to the Oregon coast.

[5] Abbott, *Gateway*, 19, 27.

[6] *Spec.*, March 13, 1851, 2:1.

[7] Gaston, 202; *1964 Portland Handbook*, 103. William King served in the 1849, 1850, and 1851 territorial legislatures, and the 1857 state legislature. He was elected president of the 1851 House of Representatives. Edwards, Cecil, 74. King also served on the Portland city council in 1857-59 (during which time he was council president for a term), again in 1861-62, and for a couple of months in 1863 before he resigned. He died November 8, 1869. *Oreg.*, Nov 9, 1869, 3; Cole 37-39; Bancroft, 143-45.

[8] OHS Mss 1142, Biography of William M. King.

[9] Handbill for July 4, 1850, celebration, OHS Neg #26614. The 1850 territorial census lists King with a thirty-three-year-old wife named Mary and five children aged three months to twelve years. Lacy, 62-63.

[10] OHS Mss 1142, Biography of William M. King.

[11] Gaston, v 1, 368.

[12] OHS Mss 1142, Letters to William M. King, 1849-1862.

[13] The Portland incorporation petition is preserved in the OSA as Doc #4246, 1850-51 Oregon territorial legislature. Hastings's letter to William King is preserved in OHS Mss 1142, Letters to William King.

[14] Scott, *Oregon*, v 5, 97.

[15] Other names on the Portland charter petition included Thomas Carter, Lewis M. Starr, Shubrick Norris, William H. Barnhart, Charles B. Pillow, William S. Caldwell, William Higgins, William M. King, Loren B. Hastings, Stephen Coffin, and Allison C. Bonnell. The legislative title was: "Petition from S. A. Clarke & 144 others praying for charter for Portland." The names "King," "Matlock," and "Deady" were signed on the petition back. —Doc #4246, 1850-51 Oregon territorial legislature, OSA. See also Bancroft, 143.

[16] Scott, *Portland*, 92.

[17] *OPAT* 1876, p.29; Scott, *Portland*, 91-92; Adams (Belknap), 81.

[18] Portland landmarks designated "King" are *not* named for Colonel William M. King. Early Portland boasted at least three prominent citizens with the last name of King. King's Hill neighborhood and King's Heights above northwest Portland are named for Amos King, who in 1871 sold forty acres of his land—the original Lownsdale claim—to the city for part of what is today's Washington Park. Amos King purchased Daniel Lownsdale's tannery and 513 acres from Milton Apperson, who sold out to Amos King in May 1949 and took off for the California gold rush. *Timeimage*, Oct 1978, p 4; *Genealogical Material in Oregon Provisional Land Claims*, v I-VIII, 91, 250; Snyder, *We Claimed*, 148-50; Lockley, *Columbia*, v 1, 513-14. A third King family—not related to either Amos or Colonel William—was associated with the well-known dry goods store of Olds and King, co-founded by S. W. King and later led by his son, Charles Willard King. Lockley, *Columbia*, v 3, 380; Gaston, v3, 232-35.

[19] Scott, *Oregon*, v 2, 307. Marshal Joe Meek, who was born in Washington County, Virginia, claims credit for originally suggesting the name of Washington County to the Oregon territorial legislature. Tobie, 189. General Francis Marion, for whom Marion County was named, was a hero of Revolutionary War fame. McArthur, 471.

[20] The territorial legislature of 1849 considered various spellings of the name Tuality, Quality, Qualatin, Tualatin, for the county which appeared in most legislative bills and maps as Twality County. McArthur, 178. Harvey Scott describes Col. King's role in changing this name: "At last William King, of Portland, arose and said something like this: 'I move that we do away with all this Indian bosh and call it Washington County.' … On the same day the naming of what is now Marion County came up. It had formerly been called Champooick district, and the pleasant Indian name no doubt would have been retained [except] that a difference arose as to the spelling of it. Some said Champoeg, and some said that it should be spelled with an 'S' [Shampoeg]. … Then old King's gorge rose so as almost to choke him, and, after mastering his disgust sufficiently to recover speech, he said: 'Mr. Speaker, I move that we drop all these names and spells, that no one knows for certain, and call it Marion County which there will be no difficulty in spelling'; and the thing was fixed without further ado."—Scott, *Oregon*, v 2, 180.

[21] OHS Mss 1142, Letters to William M. King, 1849-1862.

[22] Abbott, *Gateway*, 23.

[23] OHS Mss 1142, Letters to William M. King, 1849-1862.

[24] Scott, *Oregon*, v 5, 188-90.

[25] Oregon City's second charter, granted September 25, 1849, is printed in its entirety at Lockley, *Columbia*, v 1, 714-18. Oregon City's third charter was passed by the House on January 16 and by the Council on January 28, 1851.

[26] No evidence was located to identify the drafter(s) of the Portland and Oregon City charters. The handwriting does not match that of Judge Matthew Deady in his diaries. Clark, *Pharisee*, v 2, 383(d). William King, William T. Matlock, and Matthew Deady were all lawyers, so a legal apprentice may have done the drafting based on their instructions. The handwriting on Oregon City's charter is different than that of Portland's; it is probable that both were transcribed or copied by legal clerks at the committee's direction.

[27] As originally drafted, men in both towns would have been excused from both days of required labor on territorial roads in exchange for their two days spent on city streets. But the numbers got changed in behind-the-scenes negotiations.

[28] See Appendix A for details regarding the printing and preserving of Portland's first charter.

[29] *Oregon Special Laws, 1850-51*, 5-10, 16-22.

[30] "See House Journal, 2nd Sess., pp. 73, 76, 80-81," Adams (Belknap), 81; Clark, *Eden*, 245.
[31] An Act, to incorporate the Portland and Valley Plank Road, *Oregon Special Laws, 1850-51*, 10-12.
[32] *Spec.*, Feb 27, 1851, p 2.
[33] Ibid., p 2.
[34] Lincoln said that he turned down the job of governor of the Oregon Territory after it was proffered because his wife refused to move west. In early 1849, "Secretary of State John M. Clayton offered [Lincoln] the office of secretary to the governor of the Oregon Territory, which he promptly declined. Then Interior Secretary Ewing, realizing the snub ... tendered him the governorship of the Oregon Territory. Lincoln briefly toyed with the possibility but quickly concluded that it led nowhere. Oregon was strongly Democratic, and once it was admitted to the Union, it would hardly choose a Whig like Lincoln as governor or senator." Donald, 140-41. Also see Carey, v 2, 468-69.
[35] MacColl, *Merchants*, 88; Corning, 43-44.
[36] William L. Adams, who already had considerable newspaper experience, originally wrote "Treason, Stratagems and Spoils" anonymously. He acknowledged his open-secret authorship sixteen years later. [Sometimes the word "Breakspeare" occurs at the beginning of the title, sometimes not.] The play lampoons the Democrats' battles with Governor John Gaines, a Whig, as well as purporting to show behind-the-scenes plotting by the Democrats concerning the location controversy. It attributes corruption, drunkenness, and bribery to the territorial legislature, while adding a fictional treasonous intrigue with Mormons. Adams (Belknap) 20-21; Belknap, *Imprints*, 48-49; Nelson, 33-34.
[37] Adams (Belknap), 2.
[38] The melodrama first appeared serially in the February 7, 14, 21, and March 6, 13, 1852, issues of the *Oreg.*, one act per installment. Belknap, 48.
[39] Adams (Belknap), 20.
[40] Nelson, 34; Elwood Evans, *History of the Pacific Northwest: Oregon and Washington*; North Pacific History Company, Portland, 1889, v 2, 187.
[41] The scene at Grub's Grocery is depicted in cartoon image in the woodcuts included in two pamphlet editions of the melodrama printed six weeks after the serialized version. Clark, *Eden*, 254. Adams (Belknap) shows reprints of these woodcuts.
[42] In "An Act Regulating Grocery License" passed Sept. 27, 1849, by the territorial legislature, a grocery was defined "to include any house ... where spirituous liquors are retailed by less than one quart."—Adams (Belknap), 80, 104, note 42.
[43] Adams (Belknap), 70.
[44] Scott, *Oregon*, v 2, 312; Corning, 43-44.
[45] OHS Mss 1142, King biography and King and Kittredge papers, Penitentiary Company. A lawsuit between King and Kittredge was settled on May 29, 1860, with each party agreeing to "stop all suits now commenced and each to pay his own cost."
[46] MacColl, *Merchants*, 57. Bancroft says in a footnote at page 323: "William M. King, president of the board, charged $10 per day as commissioner, and $5 more as acting commissioner. He speculated in lots, paying Lownsdale $150 each for four lots, on condition that two lots should be given to him, for which he received $300." "In this way,' says the *Oreg.* of Feb. 4, 1854, 'King has pocketed $925, Lownsdale $600 ... of the penitentiary fund. Add to this between $1,100 and $1,200 for his [King's] invaluable services for letting all the prisoners run away, and we have a fair exhibit of financiering under democratic misrule in Oregon."
[47] Corning, 232.
[48] OHS Mss 1142, William M. King papers, Box 2, "Portland & Valley Plank Road" envelope.

Chapter 3

[1] Abbott, *Gateway*, 27.
[2] Scott, *Portland*, 414; Gaston, 499.
[3] *Oreg.*, March 22, 1851, 2.
[4] *Spec.*, Feb. 27, 1851, 2.
[5] Turnbull, *Newspapers*, 47.
[6] Lockley, *Columbia*, v 1, 450; Corning, 264.
[7] The Cayuse war ended with the May 1850 trial and hanging of five Cayuse Indians offered up by their tribe, professedly as the murderers. One of Portland's co-founders, Francis Pettygrove, served as jury foreman for the 1850 Oregon City Cayuse trial. Lansing, *Juggernaut*, 26.
[8] Although sources differ on Hugh O'Bryant's age, his birth year is listed as 1815 on both the 1850 and 1860 federal censuses. Lacy, 63; U. S. Census for Walla Walla County, Waitsburg Precinct, July 29, 1870, p 6.
[9] Jackson, *1870 Census Index*, 200; *1880 Census Index*, 123; Gilbert, 98.
[10] Lockley, *Oregon Journal*, Nov 28, 1932, 6; Scott, *Portland*, 91; Lockley, *Columbia*, v. 1, 414; Gaston, 202.
[11] O'Bryant's name appears, followed by the abbreviation "J. P.," on the June 1850 Washington County election rolls along with those of the Washington County Sheriff and Clerk of the Probate Court. These three men certified the 1850 election results. Washington County election records, June 1850, OSA.
[12] MacColl, *Merchants*, 108.
[13] Gaston, v 1, 663, 669; *Willamette Lodge*, 10, 26.
[14] This "library reading room" was said to be located at the northwest corner of Front and Alder streets. The two-story residence where O'Bryant lived, according to the 1850 territorial census, was located at Front and Alder, the home of Job and Hannah McNamee and their seven small children. Lacy, 63. If O'Bryant donated a "library room," it may have been the quarters in which he sometimes slept, since he might also have had a cabin on his land claim. Space was critically short in booming Portland.
[15] William Abrams purchased the books for Portland's first library in New York City. Information from Pope Family Papers, OHS Mss 701, Folder 25; *Oreg.*, Nov 8, 1903, p 40.
[16] The first reference about O'Bryant's "library room" was written by Fred Lockley, circa 1925, typed on onionskin paper, as a lead-in to information about founding of the Library Association of Portland in 1864. The other three references to O'Bryant's "library" —Corning, 178; *OHQ*, Dec 55, 354; Maddux, 51-52— were published in the 1950s, and may have relied on Lockley as their source.

[17] Furs were not the only commodity which provided rich rewards to early trappers and settlers. "The Hudson's Bay company … did a profitable business in the breast skins of swans, for swans-down comforters and pillows were much in favor with the well-to-do in the Old World." Collins, *Stars*, 49.
[18] Even before O'Bryant came to the Oregon Country, enterprising pioneers had used the east side of Swan Island for building an ocean-going ship. The *Star of Oregon* was launched from Swan Island in 1841 and sailed under the command of Captain Joseph Gale to San Francisco in 1842, where it was traded for much-needed cows—350 head—that were driven up through the mountains to waiting Willamette Valley settlers in 1843. Collins, *Stars*, 11-14, 48-49; S. A. Clarke, v. 2, 618; Maddux, 12-15; McArthur, 304.
[19] Maddux, 186.
[20] In the early 1930s, a landfill eliminated the east channel next to Swan Island, and the west channel was dredged, by permission of Congress, to accommodate ocean-going commerce. Price, 49-50.
[21] An abstract of O'Bryant's 1847 land claim application reads: "O'Bryant, H. D., … 640a. An island in Willamette River known as Swan Island abt 3 mi below Portland, said island being abt 2 1/2 mi long and 1/2 mi wide; designates his lines by claiming entire island to the waters edge. Intends occupancy, 10 Sept 1847." O'Bryant's claim was filed with the Oregon provincial government in Oregon City. *Genealogical Material in Oregon Provisional Land Claims, 1845-1849*, 136. Later sources say Swan Island had only 250 acres, not 640. Price, 49-50; Maddux, 186.
[22] The formal donation land claim to Swan Island was filed by Lemuel Hendrickson, who married Sarah Ann Doane at his cabin on the island in August 1853. The guests arrived by boat. Snyder, *We Claimed*, 105.
[23] Humphrey O'Bryant is listed in the Oregon territorial census of 1850 as H. P. O'Brien, shown as boarding in a Portland home with a couple and their six children. Lacy, 65. Humphrey also voted in the April 1852 Portland city election. *Proc. C. C.*, 1851, 54. He is listed in the federal census of 1880 as living in the far northwest corner of the Washington Territory. U. S. Census for Ship Harbor Precinct, Whatcom County, Washington Territory, June 5 and 7, 1880, p 6.
[24] Tansy Point is two miles north of Warrenton, only three miles from the Pacific Ocean, and near Fort Clatsop, home of the Meriwether Lewis and William Clark expedition during the winter of 1805-06. The abstract of Humphrey O'Bryant's February 24, 1846, claim says, "Held without occupancy." *Genealogical Materials in Oregon Provisional Land Claims*, 17. A 1958 history of Clatsop County speaks of Tansy Point, but does not mention Humphrey O'Bryant's abandoned claim. An historic Indian treaty was signed at Tansy Point on August 5, 1851, and a grand Flavel Hotel was built there in 1896, which was, for a time, the site of festive social activities. Miller, 121, 129-30.
[25] Scott, *Portland*, 93.
[26] Purdy, 12; Maddux, 29.
[27] OHS Mss 2202.
[28] Gaston, 554. Smith contacted "Plains Fever" on the Oregon Trail, wintered at Brown's Hole, and reached the Whitman Mission in March 1845, where he stayed about six weeks. *OHQ*, Fall 1983, Claire Smith Taylor, 291.
[29] Also residing in the Carter home were two brothers of Thomas Carter, four other children of Thomas and Minerva, and two other adult males. Lacy, 64-65.
[30] The four lawyers practicing in Portland before 1852 were Joseph Smith, Col. William King, Col. W. W. Chapman, and Frank Tilford. Gaston, 217. Smith was admitted to the bar in 1847. OHS Mss 2202, Joseph S. Smith letter to Charles Lanman, March 29, 1869.
[31] OHS Mss 2202, Joseph S. Smith letter to Charles Lanman, March 29, 1869.
[32] Balcomb, 133.
[33] Scott, *Portland*, 93.
[34] *Oreg.*, July 13, 1884, as referenced in Scott, *Oregon*, v 2, 278.
[35] In an 1884 letter to the *Oreg.*, Smith credits Daniel Lownsdale (instead of Francis Pettygrove, as the *Oreg.* had stated) with exploring Canyon Road, a route to the farmlands of the Tualatin Plains. OHS Mss 2105; Maddux, 19; Corning, 43.
[36] Portland's first private school, held for a few months in 1847, was taught by Dr. Ralph Wilcox, who was speaker of the Oregon territorial house of representatives in 1850-51, in which capacity his name appears at the bottom of Portland's first charter. Carey, *History of Oregon*, 720; Maddux, 39; *Oregon Territory Special Laws 1850-51*, 22; Gaston, 202, 367.
[37] Gaston, 367.
[38] Today the First Methodist Church at Southwest 18th and Jefferson is located where the Carter farmhouse once stood. Thomas Carter was a principal in the original Portland and Valley Plank Road company, and was to serve on the Portland City Council in 1854 for three months, and again for two years in 1866-67. Both Joseph Smith and a second Carter son-in-law, Lafayette Grover (future Oregon governor and U.S. senator) later built homes on the Carter claim in Portland Heights. Snyder, *We Claimed*, 28.
[39] Abbott, *Gateway*, 27.
[40] Maddux, 26; Gaston, 221; *ONS*, Dec 1900, 351.
[41] Smith lived on Whidby Island for five years. *OHQ*, Fall 1983, 289; Scott, *Portland*, 549.
[42] Smith stayed in Salem for twelve years before moving back to Portland permanently. MacColl, *Merchants*, 150, 184; Scott, *Portland*, 549.
[43] Scott, *Portland*, 549-50; Carey, *History of Oregon*, 656; *OHQ*, Sept 1943, 256.
[44] Joseph Smith and his brother William built Smith's Block in 1872; it was worth approximately fifty thousand dollars by 1879, the equivalent of eight hundred eighty thousand dollars today. Joseph also constructed another half-block commercial building in 1877, valued at seventy-five thousand dollars by 1879. MacColl, *Merchants*, 183; Scott, *Portland*, 549.
[45] The 1882 governor's race was won by Zenas F. Moody, a Republican from The Dalles, by 1,412 votes. Scott, *Portland*, 549-50; Carey, *History of Oregon*, 827.
[46] *Spec.*, April 10, 1851, 2.
[47] Portland co-founder Asa Lovejoy, who had already served as Oregon City mayor, speaker of the territorial house, and Supreme Judge for the Oregon Territory, again served as an Oregon City council member. Corning, 152.

[48] Scott, *Portland*, 191; *1857-58 Oregon Special Laws*, 14 and 32.
[49] Corning, 178; Gilbert, 341.
[50] *1874 P.C. Dir.*, 9; Gilbert, 229, 234, 239, 244.
[51] *Walla Walla Statesman*, May 18, 1866, p 2; Dec 28, 1866, p 2; March 29, 1867, p 3; April 5, 1867, p 2; and May 3, 1867, p 2.
[52] U. S. Census for Walla Walla County, Waitsburg Precinct, July 29, 1870, p 6.
[53] *1874 P.C. Dir.*, 9.
[54] Hugh O'Bryant's California family included his wife Matilda (age fifty-six) two sons (aged fifteen and seventeen) one daughter (age twenty-six) one son-in-law (age thirty-two) and one grandchild (age two). O'Bryant's sons were named Wilson and Sherman. His daughter is listed on the census record as Rachel Hendricks; his son-in-law as William G. Hendricks. The men and boys are all listed as laborers. 1880 census of Merced County, CA (v 5, ED43, sheet 25, line 44.) Today Merced County is a rich farm area that advertises itself as the "Gateway to Yosemite."
[55] Letter to the author dated Feb 25, 2000, from Rick Sherman, Research Assistant for the California Genealogical Society. In a letter dated Dec 11, 1999, Sherman reported that the Soundex for the 1900 U.S. census of California lists Hugh's daughter Rachel Hendricks in Santa Barbara County as the only member of the O'Bryant family still in California.
[56] *1882 P.C. Dir.*, 49.
[57] The two blocks north of O'Bryant Square were part of Benjamin Stark's claim, which Stark refused to donate for public use. Maddux, 195; Snyder, *Potpourri*, 125.
[58] Snyder, *Potpourri*, 132.

Chapter 4

[1] The charter specifies that the auditor's presence is to be counted for purposes of a quorum. Sec 2, 1851 city charter (see Appendix A).
[2] Lacy, 64.
[3] In detailed notes about Portland's early sea-trade history with New England, Caldwell gives March 7, 1850, as the date of his arrival in Portland. OHS Mss 448, William Sutton Caldwell.
[4] Nearly twenty years later, at the time of the 1870 census, William Caldwell owned real estate valued at $800, and a personal estate valued at $600. By contrast, former-mayor Henry Failing's estate was valued at $125,000; merchant Henry Corbett's at $225,000; lawyer P. A. Marquam's at $49,000; and bank clerk/former-mayor Hamilton Boyd's at $15,000. Caldwell, then age forty-five, lived with his wife, Rosalie, forty-one, born in Maine, and children aged four, six, and eight, all born in Oregon. 1870 U. S. Census, Multnomah County, City of Portland, p 81, 203, 209.
[5] That first council journal (1851-1858) is fifteen inches long by ten inches wide by two and three-quarter inches deep, and weighs nearly ten pounds. The covers are three-eighths of an inch thick and are sheathed with worn, heavy cotton canvas. Page numbers are written lightly in pencil only on the first 350 pages.
[6] 1853 census, OSA, Doc #5290, p 2.
[7] William Caldwell was appointed auditor in 1867 (when the recorder's duties were separated into two positions—auditor and police judge) and elected as auditor when the position was made elective by an 1868 charter amendment. He maintained an accounting office at 9 Alder Street in 1870. *1870 P.C. Dir.*, 109.
[8] *1863 P.C. Dir.*, 8; *Oreg.*, Apr 15, 1851, p 2, c 2.
[9] Loren Hastings was the only married councilman, assuming that George Barnes was no longer married, based on the wording of his 1912 handwritten autobiography preserved as OHS Mss 1500.
[10] Councilman Barnes was *not* the person for whom Barnes Road in northwest Portland is named. That was William Barnes, over whose tract of land a county road was built, early called "Barnes County Road." Snyder, *Portland Names*, 92. "The roads leading into Portland were well nigh impassable during the winter months and the farmers had a hard time bringing in their produce to market. Barnes Heights road was straight up in the air, very steep, abrupt and dangerous to travel." Hays, 48.
[11] Scott, *Oregon*, v 2, 248.
[12] OHS Mss 1500, Handwritten autobiography of George A. Barnes dated 1912; Scott, *Oregon*, v 2, 248.
[13] *OPAT*, 1923, 26; *ONS*, Dec 1900, 354; 1870 Jefferson County, Washington Territory, census, p 115.
[14] *OPAT*, 1923: 12.
[15] The 1850 territorial census, probably taken in spring and summer, shows Hastings and his family living in Linn County, seventy miles south of Portland. Why Hastings was living there is unclear; it may have been simply part of his search for a permanent place to set down roots. Lacey, 29.
[16] McCurdy, 23.
[17] Dr. William R. Allen as quoted in *OHQ*, September, 1960, 284.
[18] *OPAT*, 1923: 12; OHS Mss 660, 10.
[19] *OPAT*, 1923, 12; OHS Mss 660, 1.
[20] *ONS*, Dec 1900, 354. Mrs. Hastings' first name, Lucinda, was found only in the federal 1870 Port Townsend census.
[21] McCurdy, 23; 1870 Jefferson County, Washington Territory, census, p 115.
[22] *1870 P.C. Dir.*, 109.
[23] *OHQ*, Fall 1979, 320.
[24] "Names in the Paper, Advertisers & Other Persons Whose Names Are in the First Oregonian," *Oreg.*, Dec 4, 1900, p 24.
[25] Gaston, 371.
[26] Ord #11, passed May 23, 1854, created the Portland fire department. On the first Monday in September, H. W. Davis was elected as chief engineer by a vote of fire company members, and Shubrick Norris was elected assistant engineer. *Proc. C. C.*.
[27] MacColl, *Merchants*, 107.
[28] Letters to Asahel Bush, OHS Mss 851.
[29] MacColl, *Merchants*, 71.
[30] Lockley, *Columbia*, v 1, 662, 668-69.
[31] *Willamette Lodge*, 20.
[32] Thompson was born in 1810, according to this compiler's note by Leslie Scott. Scott, *Oregon*, v 2, 76, 268. However, the 1850 territorial census lists Thompson's age as thirty-eight, which would make his birth year 1812.
[33] Lacy, 64. The abbreviations for Iowa and Ireland are very similar (IA and IR) in the compilation of 1850 census records made by Ruby Lacy.

[34] *Oreg.*, Dec 1850; Edwards, Cecil, 129; Carey, *Constitution*, App C, 497; Scott, *Oregon*, v 2, 76.
[35] "Names in the Paper," *Oreg.*, Dec 4, 1900, p 24. This 1900 *Oreg.* article featuring advertisers in the first *Oreg.* describes Robert Thompson's death as occurring in winter rather than summer, and as taking place ten years earlier than does Leslie Scott , who says Robert Thompson was drowned at Portland, Oregon, June 21, 1865. Scott, *Oregon*, v 2, 268. Scott must have made a typographical error, because Thompson's estate matters were considered in 1860. OHS Mss 1275-1, Estate of Robert Thompson, intestate.
[36] The administrator filed notice in June 1860 that all persons having claims against the Robert Thompson estate must present them within one year.
[37] The two heirs were both women. OHS Mss 1275-1, Estate of Robert Thompson, intestate. 1853 map from Hawkins, *Grand Era*, 11.
[38] Scott, 194; *Genealogical Material in Oregon Provisional Land Claims*, v I-VII, 7, 44.
[39] The wedding took place on October 4, 1852. Snyder, *We Claimed*, 218-19; Scott, Portland, 193.
[40] *Proc. C.C.*, 1851, 4, 47; Bill presented to council by Stephen Coffin, Nov 21, 1851, for rent of a new meeting room at fifteen dollars per month.
[41] Robinson's first claim, filed in 1845, was "about 2 1/2 miles from Multnomah City [today's West Linn] on Twality Road," and was later sold to a William Day. The second was a 640-acre claim on the Willamette River above the falls at Oregon City, filed August 1846, and voided "at the request of claimant" three months later. *Genealogical Material in Oregon Provisional Land Claims*, v I-VII, 7, 44.
[42] Snyder, *We Claimed*, 219; Beach, Ryan and Stein, 31; Scott, *Portland*, 194; Gaston, 1908 photo opposite p 240.
[43] Lacy, 62.
[44] The first part of Councilman Harley McDonald's log chronicles his trip aboard the ship *Hopewell* from Rhode Island to San Francisco in 1849. The handwriting in the initial pages is so tiny that the words are illegible. Inside both covers are small sketches—a bird, a flag, a houseboat, a ship. McDonald relates each day's weather, starting January 25, 1849, and records daily longitude and latitude—perhaps to reassure himself that the vessel was indeed progressing. At the back of this journal, McDonald describes his trip from Portland to San Francisco in late 1851. He describes fights aboard ship and confrontations between the captain and mate, sailors, and dissatisfied passengers. OHS Mss # 948B.
[45] Nov 4, 1857 election. Election folder, 1856-57 Council Documents file.
[46] Slater lived two houses away from Councilman Thompson, Recorder Caldwell, and Treasurer Flanders; and three houses away from Councilman Norris. Lacy, 64.
[47] *Oreg.*, Mar 19, 1859, p 1.
[48] *Proc. C. C.*, April 21, 1855, 10.

Chapter 5

[1] The author's surmise that Thomas Robinson dealt in real estate was based on Robinson's age (forty-four), his two previous land claims, his ownership of the company which rented a house to the council for three months, his subsequent claim on view property in Portland's west hills, and the lack of mention of him in the *Oreg.*'s 1900 article about early Portland merchants. "Names in the Paper, Advertisers & Other Persons Whose Names Are in the First Oregonian," *Oreg.*, Dec 4, 1900.
[2] The city contained 2.14 square miles. The 1850 Portland population, according to the territorial census, was 821. That number would probably have been increased by immigrants arriving that fall.
[3] Milner, O'Connor, and Sandweiss, 537.
[4] Aikman, 157.
[5] These excerpts from April 1851 are quoted in a 1962 *Oreg.* article, "Portland's Early Mayors Busy Men," William Swing, *Oreg.*, May 6, 1962, Sports Sec, 10.
[6] "History Shows Portland Council Changed Meeting Sites Often," Don Holm, *Oreg.*, Mar 1, 1964, p 36.
[7] All council business recorded in this chapter, unless otherwise noted, has been taken from the journal titled *Proc. C. C.*, v 1, 1851-1858, preserved at the C.P. Arch., 9360 N. Columbia Blvd, Portland, OR 97203.
[8] "The location of this first City Hall is still a mystery, but it probably was in the vicinity of Front and what is now Washington," reporter Don Holm said in 1964 regarding the Thomas Robinson house that the council rented. "History Shows," 36: 1. Handwriting on the back of an OHS photo (Neg #945), taken about 1851, implies that the city hall was located in the first schoolhouse and public building on First Street at Oak, built by William King and Stephen Coffin. This was probably the second city hall, rented from Coffin in mid-Oct 1851 (see Nov 21 minutes) until mid-June 1852 (see June 10, 1852, minutes).
[9] *Oreg.*, Sat, April 19, 1851, p 2.
[10] ONS, Dec 1900, 353; Lockley, *Columbia*, v 1, 737; Gaston, v 1, 496.
[11] This and subsequent ordinances are summarized and paraphrased, except for words in quote marks.
[12] *Josiah Parrish v Thomas Stevens*, 1 Or 62 (1853); *Lownsdale v Parrish*, 62 U.S.290 (1858). See Leeson, 18; MacColl, *Merchants*, 73-74; Scott, *Portland*, 133-34.
[13] The argument was similar to the present-day controversy about merchandise sold over the internet without any tax being paid to the governments in which the purchasers reside. The petition was presented to the council in late April. The businessmen who signed the petition included many men who would serve as city officials in the future—Stephen Coffin, George Flanders, William Barnhart, Alonzo Leland, A. D. Fitch, John Couch, Nelson Northrup, John Breck, Charles Pillow, Thomas Pritchard, and William Ladd. C.P. Arch., 1851-52 Council documents file.
[14] C.P. Arch., 1851-52 Council documents file.
[15] Holm, "History Shows," p 36.
[16] The thirty-three voters who cast ballots in the May 1851 fire-engine-purchase vote, as recorded in the council journal were: S. Norris, R. Thompson, W. S. Caldwell, T. J. Holmes, H. Wilbur, P. D. W. Hardenburg, G. H. Barnes, J. Talbot, S. Coffin, F. A. Clark, F. Mathias, G. Freeman, J. C. Goodwin, S. Hayes, D. H. Lownsdale, J. McNamie, L. May, E. B. Comfort, W. H. Barnhart, W. McDonald, N. Delain, G. W. Higgins, C. B. Pillow, W. B. Otway, T. J. Dryer, W. S. Ogden, W. M. King, L. B.

Hastings, S. F. Likens, J. W. Davis, A. L. Davis, and L. Day.

[17] Marshal William Higgins was the artist who drew an oft-copied sketch of William Johnson's log cabin—the first home built in Portland. Higgins apparently visited the Portland townsite in May 1843 when employed as carpenter aboard the brig *Chenamus* captained by John Couch. Higgins returned to Oregon in 1849 and worked as a contractor in Portland for many years, superintending the construction of the Pioneer post office (1873-74) and the First Presbyterian Church. Scott, *Oregon*, v 5, 231; OrHi Neg. #73210.

[18] Lacey, 66.

[19] This one-room log-cabin jail was later burned down by "disgruntled prisoners." "Significant Events and Dates Relating to Police Functions," Portland Police Historical Society, compiled circa 1989, p 2.

[20] The mammoth spikes needed to build Portland's plank road were probably made by Portland blacksmith James Terwilliger.

[21] Gaston, v 1, 221; Lockley, *Columbia*, v 1, 428.

[22] O'Donnell and Vaughan, 14; Dodds, *Oregon*, 73.

[23] *Oreg.*, May 22, 1960; *Oreg.*, June 2, 1957; *OJ*, July 14, 1960, p11.

[24] MacColl, *Merchants*, 52.

[25] Clark, 249.

[26] MacColl, *Merchants*, 52-53.

[27] Scott, *Oregon*, v 3, 219; Gaston v 1, 369; Corning, 82 (Josiah Failing entry); Snyder, *Early Portland*, photos between pp 6 and 7; OHS photo, Neg #945.

Chapter 6

[1] Doc #4509, OSA.

[2] *Proc. C.C.*, 1851-1858, p 98-100.

[3] "Narrative of the Life of William P. Abrams, 1820-1873," by Seth L. Pope, 1910. OHS Mss 701, Folder 25.

[4] *1874 P.C. Dir.*, 9-10; *1882 P.C. Dir.*, 51; Scott, *Portland*, 191-92.

[5] Snyder, *We Claimed*, 50-51.

[6] *Oreg.*, Dec 4, 1900, p 24.

[7] *OHQ*, issue not identified, cited in Snyder, *Early Portland*, 71.

[8] Letter dated September 17, 1855, as printed in Snyder, *Early Portland*, 163.

[9] Gaston, v 1, 217; "Names in the paper," *Oreg.*, Dec 4, 1900, p 24, c 1.

[10] All council business recorded in this chapter, unless otherwise noted, was taken from the journal titled *Proc. C. C., 1851-1858*, preserved at the C.P. Arch..

[11] *ONS*, Dec 1900, 344.

[12] Abrams kept a diary from age eighteen until his death at age fifty-three. The five volumes later placed in the Bancroft Library at Berkeley by his granddaughter contain the following entry concerning a trip he made during the California gold rush (1849) to investigate possible sites for a mill to furnish lumber for mining camps: "Reamer and I saw a grizzly bear tracks and went out to hunt him down getting lost in the mountains and not returning until the following evening, found our way to camp over an Indian trail that led past a valley enclosed by stupendous cliffs rising perhaps 3,000 feet from their base and which gave us cause for wonder. Not far off a waterfall dropped from a cliff below three jagged peaks into the valley while farther beyond a rounded mountain stood, the valley side of which looked as though it had been sliced with a knife as one would slice a loaf of bread which Reamer and I called the Rock of Ages." This diary entry describes the Yosemite Valley, Bridalveil Falls, and Half Dome in what is today Yosemite National Park. *Westways* magazine, March 1954; S. Pope papers, OHS Mss 701.

[13] See chapter on Mayor Hugh O'Bryant and Appendix B for more information about Abrams's part in setting up Portland's first library. Information from Pope Family Papers, Mss 701, Folder 25; *Oreg.*, Nov 8, 1903, p 40.

[14] Map-maker Brady manufactured gentlemen's boots, made to order, and repaired boots and shoes "with neatness & dispatch." Advertisement, *1870 P.C. Dir.*, 70.

[15] MacColl, *Merchants*, 73-74; Scott, *Portland*, 133-34.

[16] *James P. O. Lownsdale v City of Portland*, 1 Or 397 (1861). A hand-drawn Lownsdale plat map dated Dec 16, 1852, is still on file in an old volume of deeds, p 190-91, at the Washington County Recorder's office in Hillsboro.

[17] Scott, *Portland*, 134-35; MacColl, *Merchants*, 76; Corning, 223.

[18] MacColl, *Merchants*, 73-74; Scott, *Portland*, 133-34.

[19] Judge Deady said in 1861 that proprietors Lownsdale, Coffin, and Chapman had agreed in August 1850 to release seven blocks of the waterfront on condition that the Parrish lawsuit be dismissed, but that it was never dismissed. *James P. O. Lownsdale v City of Portland*, 1 Or 397 (1861).

[20] *1882 P.C. Dir.*, 50. A *simoom* is a hot dry African sand-wind.

[21] Captain O. Travaillot's legacy includes a detailed map he drew in 1853 of Portland, which was to prove of considerable benefit to his peers and subsequent generations. Edward Failing copied the original Travaillot map in 1854, and Failing's map was reprinted in 1976 as a definitive resource for locating architectural buildings of the period. See Hawkins, *Grand Era*, 11.

[22] 1855-56 Council documents file at the city archives; O'Donnell and Vaughan, 18.

[23] *Proc. C. C.*, June 16, 1855, 287-88; 1855-56 Council documents file.

[24] *Oreg.*, Oct 15, 1853.

[25] Charles Pillow served the following year as a councilman. After a few years, he relocated to Eugene, more than one hundred miles south. He served as a first lieutenant in the Indian Wars. *Oreg.*, Dec 4, 1900, p 24.

[26] 1853-53 Council documents file, C.P. Arch..

[27] *Proc. C. C., 1851-1858*, p 85-86.

[28] Simon Marye's photo was originally missing, along with those of two other mayors, from a 1998 wall display in Mayor Vera Katz's office in the newly renovated city hall. Marye's photo was located by a distant relative, Elaine Lionberger of Milwaukie, Oregon, in a genealogy book titled *The Maryes of Virginia*. *Oreg.*, April 26, 1998. Mayor Marye was also omitted from the narrative descriptions of early Portland mayors in the 1874 and 1882 Portland city directories, probably because he was appointed in mid-year. He was born on a plantation in Shenandoah County, Virginia.

[29] Portland's fifth mayor, William Ladd, was only a few days younger than Marye when he assumed office. Ladd was twenty-seven years, five months and six days old when the council convened under the city's third charter on March 24, 1854. Simon Marye was born on June 7, 1825, and thus would have been twenty-seven years, five months, and eight days old when he took office. Eberhart and Robertson, 103.
[30] Simon Marye was the first lawyer-mayor and the first of three city attorneys who would serve as Portland mayors. The other two former city attorneys were William Farrar and David Logan, both of whom served as Multnomah County delegates to the 1857 Oregon constitutional convention. Carey, *Constitution*, 77.
[31] Lacy, 62; Maddux, 27; Scott, *Portland*, 192.
[32] Eberhart and Robertson, 104.
[33] Ibid., 104.
[34] Marye was one of three mayors who served only half a year: Allison Bonnell (1852) and T. J. Holmes (1866-67) were the other two. William Ladd served a half-year term in 1857-58, but he had already served a full-year term (1854-55). Scott, *Portland*, 557; Lockley, *Columbia*, v 1, 454.
[35] *ONS*, Dec 1900, 346. Gaston, v 1, 216, says Judge Marquam, "now at the age of 87, enjoys the homage and respect of every good citizen. "
[36] *Oreg.*, Nov. 27, 1852, 2.
[37] Doc #4504, OSA.
[38] Doc #4509, OSA. The petition is dated Jan 21, 1853. A legislative notation on the petition says twenty-four of the signers may not have been Portland citizens.
[39] No reference to any "E. Ely" was found in the indices of either the OSA or the OHS. However, there was a nationally known divine of the period named the Rev. Ezra Stiles Ely who authored a history of the temperance movement in the United States. He was probably the "Hon. E. Ely" referred to by the mayor.
[40]MacColl, *Merchants*, 53.
[41] Proposed Portland Charter #2 passed the territorial council on Jan 31, 1853. *1853 Oregon Special Laws*, 5-12.

Chapter 7

[1] Carey, *Oregon Constitution and Proceedings and Debates of the Constitutional Convention of 1857*.
[2] Charter #2, as printed in *Special Laws of Oregon, 1852-53*, 5-12, was ratified by Portland voters March 19, 1853.
[3] Ayes and nays were to be entered in the council journal. Ordinances would be deemed signed if not returned by the mayor within ten days.
[4] Throckmorton, 133; Scott, *Portland*, 192; Corning, 82; *1874 P.C. Dir.*, 10.
[5] Corning, 82; *1882 P.C. Dir.*, 51.
[6] *Proc. C. C.*, Meeting #4, April 29, 1853, 118.
[7] The mayor's handwritten message is preserved in 1853-54 council documents file; Meeting of April 29, 1853, 118.
[8] Meeting #6, May 9, 1853.
[9] An amended ordinance passed at a subsequent meeting, according to the minutes, but is not listed in the council ordinance journal. Meetings of May 25, June 6, and July 13, 1853, p 126, 128, 130.
[10] Meeting #14, Aug 18, 1853, 134.
[11] MacColl, *Merchants*, 69.
[12] Ibid., 69.
[13] "Narrative of the Life of William P. Abrams, 1820-1873," by Seth L. Pope, 1910. OHS Mss 701, Folder 25.
[14] *Portland Charter 1854*, Oregon Supreme Court Library, 1-9.
[15] In 1854, Oregon cities were governed by a territorial legislature of nine council members and eighteen representatives; after 1859 by a state legislature of sixteen senators and thirty-four representatives. That number was gradually increased to today's thirty and sixty members, respectively. Art IV, Sec 4, Oregon State Constitution. Carey, *Constitution*, 407; *1997-98 OBB*, 436.
[16] Political party labels and politics in the 1850s differed markedly from political parties in the twenty-first century. The Whigs were the precursors of the Republican party, but were "town-oriented," whereas the Democrats "tended to be agrarian." Heider and Dietz, 15. Politics in the 1850s usually focused on local issues, such as where the state capital should be located and what individual person should be elected. The August 1850 appointment by President Millard Fillmore of an unpopular Whig governor for the Oregon Territory, General John P. Gaines, marked the beginning of political parties in Oregon in a national sense. Woodward, 39. Strong personalities hurled libelous accusations and verbiage at each other in the writings of Democratic party boss Asahel Bush of the *Statesman* and Whig-partisan T. J. Dryer of the *Oreg.*. Carey, v 2, 500-503.
[17] The vote was 261 for Ladd to 197 for Abrams. Snyder, *We Claimed*, 55.
[18] Gaston, v 1, 371; Scott, *Portland*, 503-6; Throckmorton, 126-29; Lange, 738; Corning, 138.
[19] Ladd and Elliott were married October 17, 1854, in San Francisco. Gaston, v 3, 518. *OHQ* v 89, No 2, 131; Snyder, *Portland Names*, 41.
[20] Throckmorton, 128-29.
[21] Scott, *Portland*, 504-5.
[22] The Library Association of Portland occupied quarters in the Ladd & Tilton Bank building from 1869 to 1893. Anderson, 7-8.
[23] Fines for violation of city ordinances were still limited to one hundred dollars, but imprisonment for any one offence was lengthened to twenty days. The council was prohibited from incurring any debt beyond the estimated revenue for the current fiscal year. *Portland Charter 1854*, Oregon Supreme Court Library.
[24] Ord #1-15 (new number sequence), dated April 7 – June 16, 1854.
[25] Ord #11, May 23, 1854, created the fire department; #13, June 10, 1854, authorized purchase of equipment. This was the era when big eastern cities were replacing volunteer fire companies with professional firefighters.
[26] Pope, "Life of William P. Abrams"; Maddux, 67-68.
[27] A history of Oregon sheriffs says, "Not much is known about William L. McMillen." McCarthy, 172.
[28] *Proc. C. C.*, June 30, 1854.
[29] A further example of strict economy advocated and practiced by Councilman Norris was his full-page memo specifying that $1.50 should be deducted from a stationery bill for purchases made by Ani Dennison, city recorder. Norris said fees were provided to the

recorder by law "for all his service in making out papers, etc., for which said stationery will be used by him." Letter dated August 25, 1854; 1854-55 Council Documents file, Finances folder.

[30] Original 1851 ordinances numbered 4, 6, 7, 8, 9 and 10 were copied into the ordinance journal by 1851-52 Recorder Caldwell, presumably because they were laws governing public actions, whereas those numbered 1, 2, 3 and 5 concerned internal governance matters and were not entered in the ordinance journal.

[31] The last ordinance for year 2000 was #175211, according to Council Clerk Britta Olson in a letter to the author dated Jan 16, 2001.

[32] Two sets of 1855 ordinances were numbered 35 through 42.

[33] Ord #16-32, July 7 through Oct 27, 1854.

[34] Maddux, 48; Worchester, 26; Scott, *Portland*, v 2, 302-3.

[35] *Proc. C. C.*, Sept 22, 1854.

[36] Lewis M. Starr, brother of future mayor Addison Starr, was later a silent partner in the founding of Tacoma in Washington Territory, along with Morton McCarver, the on-site proprietor, and another silent partner, James Steel, both of Portland. Prosch, 88, 158, 172.

[37] *Proc. C. C.*, Oct 23, 1854.

[38] Ibid., Nov 11, 1854.

[39] Letter from Mayor W. S. Ladd, dated December 1, 1854, to the council. 1854-55 Council documents file, C.P. Arch.

[40] Mayor Ladd and Treasurer Vaughn were leaders in urging the legislature to create Multnomah County. MacColl, Merchants, 70. Ladd was to serve a one-year term as a Multnomah County commissioner, 1859-60.

[41] Multnomah County was carved out of east Washington County and a portion of north Clackamas County. "An act to create the County of Multnomah," Doc #6139, OSA.

[42] The jail was "burned down by disgruntled prisoners" according to a Portland Police Historical Society history, p 2.

[43] The owners of the Eureka Saloon apparently got no reduction in rates, because another petition by the same persons, filed in May 1855, noted that the license on each and every billiard table and ball alley was $121 per quarter, "a license levied by the late council when business was good and the times would justify it." The May petition again asked that council reduce that amount to "say, $5 per quarter, which with our present number of tables and alleys would make the entire license for our house amount to $75 per quarter." If these figures are correct, the Eureka Saloon had a total of fifteen billiard tables and ball alleys, and would have been paying $1,815 per quarter, a monumental difference between the actual and requested rates. 1855-56 Council documents file, May 9, 1855 petition from Reed and Pfaff.

[44] *Oreg.*, May 1, 1891, p 8.

[45] Scott, *Oregon*, v 3, 187.

[46] Scott, *Portland*, 193; Snyder, *Portland Names*, 222; Lockley, *Columbia*, v 1, 452.

[47] An *Oreg.* editorial of 1909 explained that Vaughn and others dared to publish such "blacklisting" advertisements without fear of a suit for damages. This was because the Pacific Coast states adhered to gold currency, and there was "universal detestation" of those who paid debts with paper because of its devaluation. A suit for libel "would have been thrown out of court; perhaps the jury would have ridden the plaintiff out of court on a rail." Scott, *Oregon*, v 3, 62.

[48] *Oreg.*, March 13, 1865, as reprinted in Scott, *Oregon*, v 3, 167-68.

[49] "The assessed valuation of city property in 1855 had reached $1,195,034 and there was a population of 1,209, which gave color to its boast." Carey, *History of Oregon*, v 1, 779.

[50] *Proc. C. C.*, June 11, 16, 26; July 30; and Aug 13, 1855.

[51] The Patton Home in North Portland was originally a land gift from Matthew Patton to the Union Aid Society of Albina, organized in 1887, whose object was to "provide food, clothing and fuel for the poor in our midst." OHS Mss 2309B. In 2000, Ecumenical Ministries of Oregon invested $6.6 million to renovate the 700,000-foot historic mansion. Patton reportedly gained his wealth during the California gold rush. *Oreg.*, Oct 25, 1999, E2 & Nov 20, 2000, C3.

[52] Ord #46 was passed June 30, 1855. The city collector was directed to collect this additional tax by August 15. The city collector would be paid 1 percent of amounts collected and the city treasurer 1 percent of amounts disbursed. Mayor Vaughn signed the ordinance July 7.

[53] Fire Department folder, 1855-56 Council Documents file, C.P. Arch..

[54] Ord #39, Aug 14, 1855.

[55] Scott, *Oregon*, v 3, 187; Lockley, *Columbia*, v 1, 452.

[56] Gaston, *Portland*, v 1, 240.

[57] Ord #42, Nov 3, 1855.

[58] *Proc. C. C.*, Nov 10, 1855.

[59] MacColl, *Merchants*, 70-71.

[60] George Abernethy was an Oregon City merchant and former governor under Oregon's provisional government.

[61] *Proc. C. C.*, Apr 12, 1856.

[62] Ibid., Apr 16, 1856.

[63] Scott, *Oregon*, v 2, 278; MacColl, *Merchants*, 52-53.

[64] Carey, v 2, 729.

[65] Ibid., 1851-58; *City Ordinance Journal #1.*

Chapter 8

[1] Scott, *Oregon*, v 2, 86-92; *Oreg.*, Oct 7, 1906.

[2] Governor Walter M. Pierce proclaimed Edwin Markham as Poet Laureate of Oregon in 1923 "because the poet was Oregon born." Corning, 156.

[3] Lockley, *Oregon's Yesterdays*, 338.

[4] Confusion over James O'Neill's name is evident in histories about Oregon, because there was another prominent James O'Neil (one "l") living not far from Portland. James O'Neil of Polk County was born in Georgia in 1800 and came to Oregon with Andrew Wyeth in 1834. He took part in the historic Champoeg meetings which led to the formation of a provisional government, was the owner of a copy of the Iowa statues used as a basis for the organic law of the provincial government, the builder of the first grist mill in Polk County, and a justice of the peace and judge in Yamhill County. Dobbs, *Men of Champoeg*, 51-54; *ONS*, Feb 1900, 510; Carey, *History of Oregon*, v 1, 322, 377-78, 381. This James O'Neil was not the person who served as Portland's mayor.

[5] Scott, *Portland*, 193; *ONS*, Feb 1900, 510.
[6] Elections folder, 1856-57 Council Documents File.
[7] *ONS*, Feb 1900, 510.
[8] *OHQ*, Fall 1985, 233; Scott, *Portland*, 193; Corning, 179; *ONS*, Feb 1900, 510.
[9] Corning, 179; Purdy, 12.
[10] The four levee blocks between Washington and Taylor streets were specified in Ord #51, passed June 7, 1856.
[11] "A Brief History of Your Portland Fire Department," City of Portland Fire Bureau, ca 1946; "History of Portland's Volunteer Fire Department," by Andrew C. Sherbert, date unknown, p 3.
[12] Stephen Coffin, Finice Caruthers, and Jacob Cline were granted permission, as Pioneer Water Works, to lay pipes (ditches to be sunk two feet deep) for conducting water. Ord # 54, Sept 6, 1856; Short, 2-3.
[13] Ord # 57. *Proc. C. C.*, Jan 26, 1857. This ordinance was amended in May of 1857 and again in Sept 1858, and superseded by yet another ordinance in Dec 1858, etc. *Laws of the City of Portland, 1886*, p 380-82.
[14] 1856-57 Council Documents file. In 1855, owners were given three years to redeem their property; in 1856, four years.
[15] *Proc. C. C.*, v 1, Jan 17, 1857.
[16] MacColl, *Merchants*, 74; Snyder, *Early Portland*, 32-33.
[17] MacColl, *Merchants*, 76-77.
[18] 1857-58 Council Documents file.
[19] *Proc. C. C.*, June 3, 10, and 16, 1857.
[20] MacColl, *Merchants*, 71.
[21] Stephen McCormick, William Farrar, and David Logan represented Multnomah County at the convention, and George Williams was an elected delegate from Marion County, seat of the territorial capital in Salem. Levi Anderson, future Portland city recorder (1869) and Erasmus Shattuck, both a future city attorney (1858) and council member (1859), served as two of Washington County's three delegates. Portland co-founder Asa Lovejoy was the convention president *pro tem* who participated on behalf of Clackamas County. Carey, *Constitution*, 24-27, 77; Bancroft, *Oregon*, v 2, 423; *OPAT*, 1912, 626-28.
[22] Dryer was one of the more vocal members of the convention. "He was a ready speaker, full of wit and humor, and often went into debates 'for the fun of things.' … Dryer's ambition … induced him to oppose anything that could be used to favor the Democrats. … Dryer was not a great editor, but he was well adapted to the rough and tumble of the times. " Address of Hon. John R. McBride, Yamhill County convention representative, to OHS, 1902, Carey, *Constitution*, 491.
[23] Bancroft, *Oregon* v.2, 441.
[24] *Proc. C. C.*, April 21, 1855; Administrative folder, 1855-56 Council Documents.
[25] 1854 City of Portland charter, Article III, Section 12.
[26] *City of Portland v. James O'Neill. 1 Oregon Reports, 1853-62*, 218-19.
[27] In 1862, O'Neill was appointed U.S. Indian agent for the Idaho Territory by President Lincoln and served in that position for six years. He then spent nine years back in New York before returning to the Northwest as sub-Indian agent for the Coeur d'Alenes. In 1887, he was elected auditor of Stevens County, Washington, and in 1889 to represent Stevens and Spokane counties in the Washington legislature. *Oreg.*, July 22, 1901, p 1.
[28] The territorial legislature passed a *viva voce* measure in 1854, providing that all votes should be "cried out in an audible voice by the officer attending and noted by the clerk in the presence and hearing of the voters." The purpose was to force members of a secret political group known as the "Know Nothings" into the open. The Know Nothings opposed Catholics and any candidate who was not a third-generation American. Carey, *History of Oregon*, v 2, 500-503. Nov 1857 poll results are from the Elections folder, 1857-58 Council Documents. Neither Dryer nor Ladd cast a mayoral vote, though both voted on the two ballot measures.
[29] *Oregon Weekly Times*, Nov 7, 1857, 2.
[30] *Proc. C. C.*, Oct 13, 1857.
[31] City voters did approve, by nearly four to one, entry of the 320-acre Portland townsite with the U.S. government to procure a land patent. Nov 4, 1857, Elections folder, 1957-58 Council Documents file.
[32] MacColl, *Merchants*, 74. This suit was decided for Parrish by a three-judge panel, with Judge Deady dissenting. *Parrish v. Stevens*, 1 Or 62 (1853).
[33] Finances folder, 1857-58 Council documents file.
[34] *Proc. C. C.*, Nov 24, 1857. The dead bodies were probably moved from near Ankeny, Pine, and Front streets where the Skidmore fountain would later be built to the Terwilliger/Caruthers cemetery site in the vicinity of today's S.W. Macadam, Hood, Abernethy, and Lowell streets, and underneath the I-5 freeway. Two other cemeteries were also in use: the half-acre cemetery on John Couch's land near today's S. W. 11th and Burnside, and a Jewish cemetery near the Terwilliger/Caruthers ten acres under today's approach lanes to the Ross Island Bridge at S.W. Hood, Corbett, Meade, and Porter streets and under the I-5 freeway. All of these sites were later closed. Researcher Leslie Scott says, "[A]lthough many of the graves were moved, a considerable number were obliterated, so that some pioneers repose in unknown places beneath the city." Scott, *Oregon*, v 5, 311.
[35] MacColl, *Merchants*, 54-55.
[36] *Proc. C. C.*, Dec 28, 1857. Article IV, Sec 2 of the 1854 charter says, "The members of the Common Council … may determine rules for their sure proceedings, punish any member for disorderly conduct at any meeting of the council, and by a vote of two-thirds of all the members, expel any member."
[37] *Proc. C. C.*, Jan 5, 1858. Charles Hutchins was one of several well-known Portlanders suspended from Masonic Lodge membership, probably for intemperance (liquor excess or drunkenness.) Others suspended included *Oreg.* editor Thomas J. Dryer, master politician William King, and townsite proprietor Daniel Lownsdale. Scott, Leslie, "Grand Lodge of Oregon, 1851-61," *Masonic Papers*, v 2, 342, 352-55, 362-63.
[38] Charter changes adopted Jan 1858; Ord #72, March 2, 1858.
[39] All three of these 1858 city charter amendments were signed by Hugh O'Bryant, Portland's first mayor, in his capacity as president of the territorial council, the equivalent of today's state senate. O'Bryant represented four southwestern Oregon counties.

[40] Elections folder, 1858-59 Council Documents File.
[41] Two other Portland mayors in addition to Addison Starr served as Multnomah County sheriffs. William A. Storey, 1899 mayor, was elected sheriff in 1902 and served three years. Terry D. Schrunk was county sheriff for nearly eight years prior to his election as Portland mayor in 1957. McCarthy, 172-74.
[42] McCarthy, 172.
[43] *Oreg.*, May 1, 1891, 8.
[44] The 1850 census lists A. M. Starr as twenty-two years old (Lacy, 66), which this author assumes to be a mistake. Addison Starr's obituary gives his age as seventy-one, which would make 1820 his birth year. *Oreg.*, May 1, 1891.
[45] *Oreg.*, Nov 15, 1903, 40; Nov 22, 1903, 40.
[46] The distillery building was later used by the Oregon Railway and Navigation Company as its commissary department. *Oreg.*, May 1, 1891, 8; Winther, 241; Purdy, 19; Lockley, *Columbia*, v 1, 453; MacColl, *Merchants*, 72.
[47] The date and placement of this advertisement are unknown. Purdy, 19, says, "The Starr brothers, being interested in their bank as well as the distiller, advertised," followed by the cited quote.
[48] Addison Starr served as first president of the new bank. Another incorporator was future mayor Philip Wasserman. An early bank cashier was James Steel, who, along with Lewis Starr, was one of the founders of Tacoma, Washington Territory. In 1869, the Starr brothers sold their controlling interest in the bank to Henry Corbett and future mayor Henry Failing. Purdy, 102-3; Gaston, v 1, 519; Scott, *Oregon*, v 5, 185-86. First National Bank subsequently became First Interstate Bank, and in 1996, was merged with, and took the name of, Wells Fargo Bank.
[49] The first 1864 court ruling was overturned in 1867 by the United States Supreme Court (*Starr v Stark*, 2 Oregon Reports, Sept 1865, 118-22), but the Starrs won the day with a revised plea and a second trip to the state supreme court. Mooney, *Oregon Benchmarks*, Summer 1989, v 5, no 3, 3-4.
[50] The Starr block faced Front Street between Oak and Pine and backed on the Willamette River. Hawkins, *Grand Era*, 120, 204-5; Scott, *Portland*, 193.
[51] Snyder, *Early Portland*, 66-67.
[52] Opinion written by Justice Stephen Field. Mooney, *Oregon Benchmarks*, Summer 1989 (v 5, no 3), 3-4.
[53] *Proc. C. C.*, v 1, Aug 6, 1858.
[54] Ord #73, passed April 29, 1858, amending Ord #51 of June 10,1856.
[55] *Lownsdale v Parrish*, 62 US 290 (1858), as quoted in Leeson, 18.
[56] Judge Deady was to interpret this 1858 ruling in *James P. O. Lownsdale v City of Portland*, 1 Or 397 (1861).
[57] Undated letter, Administrative folder, 1858-59 Council Documents file.
[58] *City of Portland v Alonzo Leland*. The Civic Auditorium was eventually built on Block 132 and the Pioneer Courthouse on Block 172. *Oreg.*, August 20, 1859, 2; MacColl, *Merchants*, 56-57.
[59] "Records Recall Early Lot Sale," *Oreg.*, Feb 5, 1939; Conversation with Pat Thompson, Operations Supervisor, Multnomah County Assessment and Taxation, by the author, Sept 15 and 19, 2000.
[60] *Proc. C. C.*, Oct 29, 1858; MacColl, *Merchants*, 74.
[61] *Oreg.*, May 2, 1892. Patterson was later acquitted by a jury, but was killed by a man named Donahue while seated in a barber's chair in Walla Walla, Washington. Donahue was a special policeman in Portland at the time Patterson shot Captain Staples. For a full account of the event, see *OHQ*, Summer 1979, 141-42.
[62] Henry W. Corbett, a well-to-do hardware merchant, chaired the committee on landings and wharves to whom the task of notifying Vaughn and others was given. Corbett also served as city treasurer during Addison Starr's term, and replaced N. Lakin on the council when he was chosen on the fourth ballot. *Proc. C. C.*, Nov 5, 1858.
[63] *Oreg.*, May 1, 1891, 8; Jan 7, 1859.
[64] Addison Starr married "an Eastern lady" early in the 1860s, but he left no children. He was one of the largest stockholders of the Pacific Iron & Nail Company of San Francisco. *Oreg.*, May 1, 1891, 8.
[65] Lewis Starr and brother E. A., who had "amassed a fortune in the manufacture of rye whiskey" (Winther, 251), financed transportation between Seattle and Victoria, British Columbia. Winther, 241; Lockley, *Columbia*, v 3, 645-46.
[66] Prosch, 88, 158, 172.
[67] MacColl, *Merchants*, 153, 222; Winther, 241-42.
[68] Alexander Ankeny built the historic New Market Theater that featured an exhibition match by champion prize fighter John L. Sullivan in 1884. A narrow street in Portland's old town still bears Ankeny's name. Hawkins, *Grand Era*, 68; Maddux, 124-25.
[69] The 1859-60 council included "a physician, a steamboat captain, the penitentiary superintendent, a builder, and a house painter," according to MacColl, *Merchants*, 77. Also see Maddux, 27.
[70] Four of the six mayors born outside the United States were from Germany: Bernard Goldsmith, 1869-71; Philip Wasserman, 1871-73; Joseph Simon, 1909-11; and Vera Katz, 1993-present. The sixth, Thomas J. Holmes, 1866-67, was born in England.
[71] Scott, *Portland*, 193; Snyder, *We Claimed*, 219; *Oreg.*, May 6, 1962, Sports section, 10. Information about Mayor McCormick's Catholic education is from the back of his photo at OHS.
[72] Snyder, *We Claimed*, 218-19; Gaston, v 1, photo opposite p 240.
[73] Keynote address at the Oregon Pioneer Association's 44th annual reunion by William M. Colvig of Canyonville, OR. *OPAT*, 1916, 345.
[74] Scott, *Portland*, 193; *Oreg.*, May 6, 1962, Sports section, 10.
[75] This author viewed the first seven years of McCormick's city directories on microfilm at the Multnomah County Library. The 1863 directory was microfilmed from OHS holdings and 1864 through 1869 from the holdings of the Beinecke Rare Book Library at Yale University (except for 1866, which was filmed from the holdings of the American Antiquarian Society). The C.P. Arch. had original hard copies of the directory for the years 1870 and 1872 through 1882. Publisher A. G. Walling produced the 1876 edition, but McCormick again edited the 1877 directory. J. K. Gill took over publication of these city directories in 1882.
[76] Hallock, a Quaker from Milton Ulster County in New York, was born in 1827. Hawkins, *Grand Era*, 28.

[77] "Names in the Paper," *Oreg.*, Dec 4, 1900, p 24.
[78] Hallock later retired to the Oregon coast. On April 2, 1862, Multnomah Fire Engine Company #2 presented Hallock with a silver trumpet made of fifty hammered silver dollars in recognition of five years as their foreman. Hallock's foster daughter, Mrs. Cotter, had the trumpet in her possession in 1911. Gaston, v 3, 109. Also see Scott, *Portland*, 185.
[79] Absalom Hallock was one of the two "most important of the architects in early residential design in Portland." Hawkins, *Classic Houses*, 16. Hallock was also architect for the city's first brick building, commissioned by William Ladd, and for the Ladd & Tilton Bank building. Gaston, v 3, 109; Hawkins, *Grand Era*, 28.
[80] *OHQ*, Fall 1979, 289.
[81] MacColl, *Merchants*, 72; *OHQ*, Summer 1979, 134. In 1859, Lappeus racked up a two-to-one margin of victory over incumbent marshal S. R. Holcomb, 146 votes to 71.
[82] *OHQ*, Summer 1981, 180.
[83] For complete details of the Mortimer Stump murder and its aftermath, see Snyder, *We Claimed*, 9-15.
[84] In his mayoral message, McCormick had told the council the city needed better police protection and needed to appropriate more money if the newly completed city jail was to be put into usable condition. *OHQ*, Summer 1979, 29, 134-36.
[85] Snyder, *We Claimed*, 11-12; *OHQ*, Spring, 1979, 28-29.
[86] *Oreg.*, Aug. 20, 1859, 27; *OHQ*, Summer 1981, 180.
[87] *Oreg.*, Oct 22, 1859; *OHQ*, Summer 1981, 180.
[88] Snyder, *We Claimed*, 14. The jail was then at Second and Taylor streets.
[89] Ibid., 13.
[90] One entry to the Wildwood Trail starts near the Daniel Balch homesite, a trail that began as a route from the Forestry Building to Upper Macleay Park in 1909. Draft *Portland Parks and Recreation, A Chronological History*, Dec 1998, 5-6.
[91] The *Weekly News* article ran on March 8, 1883. *OHQ*, Summer 1981, 180; *OHQ*, Summer 1979, 134.
[92] Fire folder, 1859-60 Council Documents file.
[93] *Oreg.*, Aug 13, 1859, as quoted in Clark, Hugh, p 3.
[94] *OHQ*, Summer 1979, 136.
[95] *Oreg.*, Mar 24, 1860, 2. See also MacColl, *Merchants*, 74.
[96] Alonzo Leland served for three months on the council in 1853; as city recorder for a year in 1858-59; and as city surveyor for nine months during the latter period.
[97] MacColl, *Merchants*, 74-75.
[98] Scott, *Portland*, 134; Gaston, v 1, 225.

Chapter 9

[1] Scott, *Oregon*, 332-35; Carey, *History of Oregon*, v 1, 779; Bennett, 56; Corning, 101.
[2] *Oreg.*, March 31, 1860; Corning, 243; MacColl, *Merchants*, 122-24.
[3] *Oreg.*, March 3, 1860, 2.
[4] Ibid., March 31, 1860, 2.
[5] MacColl, *Merchants*, 153.
[6] Out of 741 votes cast, Robbins defeated R. R. Thompson by a 54-vote margin. *Oreg.*, Apr 7, 1860, 2.
[7] *OHQ*, Summer 1979, 134, 137; *OHQ*, Summer 1981, 180.
[8] *Oreg.*, Apr 7, 1860, 2.
[9] Ibid., Dec 29, 1860, p 1, c 3; *OHQ*, Summer 1979, 137.
[10] *Proc. C. C.*, April 12, 1860.
[11] Personal papers of W. S. Caldwell, Miscellaneous folder, City of Portland archives.
[12] These 1860 certificates were issued under a mistaken interpretation of what federal law applied. Official land patents were issued to Coffin and Lownsdale in 1865. MacColl, *Merchants*, 55, 75.
[13] *1859-60 Oregon General Laws*, 104.
[14] Ibid., 88-92; *1863P.C. Dir.*, 91-92.
[15] Dryer held his position as commissioner to the Sandwich Islands for several years, then returned to Portland, where his daughter, Mrs. W. S. Ogden, lived. The *Oreg.* of Nov 15, 1903 (p 40) said, "Mrs. W. S. Ogden was a prominent leader in society, and displayed much ingenuousness and originality in planning new things in the way of entertaining the young folks." T. J. Dryer is buried in Portland's Lone Fir Cemetery. Corning, 76; Scott, *Oregon*, v 5, 93; Gaston, v 1, 500. See also address by John R. McBride at Carey, *Oregon Constitution*, 491, and Oregon's U.S. presidential vote at *1997-98 OBB*, 345.
[16] Pittock had worked for Dryer for seven years. Dryer assigned *Oreg.* ownership to Pittock in November 1860. Gaston, 500-501; Scott, *Oregon*, 93-94.
[17] Corning, 202.
[18] The city purchased the forty-six-acre Pittock estate in April 1964. *1964 Portland Handbook.*
[19] The four lawsuits identified were all important land-title cases for Portland: the city against McEwan and Holmes; the city against Leland and Stout; George W. Vaughn against the city; and J. P. O. Lownsdale against the city. Money from the city treasury for payment of the Cartter contract was appropriated by Ord #102, passed March 20, 1861.
[20] "The Pioneer Reminiscences of George Collier Robbins," a magazine article in four installments, was reprinted in a bound volume, *Magazine Miscellany*, v 6, p 347-49, The volume carries no date, publisher or other identification. Articles in this volume were originally published in *The Century Magazine, Pacific Monthly, Harper's Monthly*, and other unidentified sources circa 1910.
[21] MacColl, *Merchants*, 153.
[22] Robbins's reminiscences do not say where his wife was during most of his mining years. While Robbins lived in Portland, Mrs. Robbins "made quite a fad" of putting on afternoon lunch parties. "She was hostess of many a delightful and enjoyable dance, too, and the young folks loved to go there." *Oreg.*, Nov 15, 1903, 40.
[23] Possibly Mrs. Robbins stayed on at their Portland residence while Mr. Robbins was elsewhere mining.
[24] *Magazine Miscellany*, v 6, 365, 369.
[25] A public notice by Robbins, thanking his nominators and declining to serve as mayor, appeared in the April 1, 1861 *Oreg.*, p 3, c 2.
[26] Mayor Robbins camped on the Payette River in April 1861. *Magazine Miscellany*, v 6, 358.
[27] *Oreg.*, April 1, 1861, p 3, c 1.
[28] Ibid., April 5, 1861. Three candidates were nominated by both groups and won easy victory: council

candidates Absalom Hallock and John McCraken from the 1st Ward, and assessor candidate J. W. Going. *Oreg.*, April 1, 1861, p 3, c 1.

[29] *OHQ*, Summer, 1979, 137.

[30] Mayor John Breck was city council clerk, 1856-57; Multnomah County assessor, 1857-59; city assessor, 1859-60 and 1871-73; Multnomah County clerk, 1862-63; city councilman, 1862-63 and 1868-71.

[31] Breck lived in California from 1873 to 1877, then returned to Portland where he worked for Meier & Frank Company, retailers, for twelve years. After that he became a money broker. Lockley, *Columbia*, v 1, 453; Scott, *Portland*, 194.

[32] Ord #106 passed Sept 27, 1861, repealed by Ord #110, May 10, 1862.

[33] For a detailed account of Mitchell's involvement in the land fraud cases, see *Rose City Justice*, by Fred Leeson, 30-31 and 67-72.

[34] Ord #103 passed June 14, 1861. Breck argued that repealing the ordinance could leave the city open to litigation. Councilman King's motion to override the veto passed seven to one. The lone vote against override was that of Councilman John S. White.

[35] The second ordinance referenced by Deady passed the council on August 6, 1861, and was attached to the Deady case file as Exhibit E. *James P. O. Lownsdale v City of Portland*, 1 Or 397 (1861).

[36] Deady would probably have ruled for private ownership of the levee even without the two 1861 ordinances. He had *dissented* from the original 1853 Josiah Parrish case that decided in favor of public ownership. *Josiah Parrish v Thomas Stevens*, 1 Or 62 (1853); *Lownsdale v Parrish*, 62 U.S. 290 (1858); *James P. O. Lownsdale v City of Portland*, 1 Or 397 (1861).

[37] *James P. O. Lownsdale v City of Portland*, 1 Or 397 (1861); Leeson, 18; MacColl, *Merchants*, 75-76.

[38] *OHQ*, v 31, 255; MacColl, *Merchants*, 13, 75-76; Scott, *Portland*, 134-35.

[39] *Josiah Parrish v Thomas Stevens*, 1 Or 62 (1853).

[40] *Lownsdale v Parrish*, 62 US 290 (1858).

[41] Gaston, v 1, 225-26. In the 1907 general election, voters approved a five hundred thousand dollar bond measure to buy land for public docks, but Mayor Simon vetoed an ordinance to sell the bonds. Council ordinance, May 25, 1910; www.ci.portland.or.us/auditor/Elecarchives2/GEN07.htm. Both the 1910 and 1918 ballots contained further docks bond measures.

[42] Scott, *Portland*, 135.

[43] *History of the Bench and Bar*, 27-28.

[44] Address to the December 1902 annual meeting of the OHS by John R. McBride, a lawyer who represented Yamhill County at the state constitutional convention. Carey, *Constitution*, 493-94.

[45] The other mayor with no photograph is Hamilton Boyd (1868-69). Mayor Vera Katz issued an appeal to the public for photos of Simon B. Marye, W. H. Farrar, and Boyd *Oreg.*, April 26, 1998. A photograph of Marye was subsequently found, but no likeness of either Boyd or Farrar has yet been found.

[46] Address to Dec 1902 OHS annual meeting, John R. McBride. Carey, *Constitution*, 493-94.

[47] Lansing Stout had purchased this property from Daniel Lownsdale. *City of Portland v Leland and Stout.*

[48] *Oreg.*, 1862, as quoted in Hawkins, *Grand Era*, 32.

[49] Snyder, *Potpourri*, 127.

[50] Ibid., 124-33.

[51] Scott, *Portland*, 525.

[52] Handwritten letter from Mayor Farrar to the Common Council dated May 7, 1862. Council documents file, 1862-63, Administrative folder.

[53] Ord #109, approved May 10, 1862 by Mayor Farrar, declared void by the Oregon Supreme Court in 1863. *Laws of the City of Portland, 1886*, 383.

[54] *Oreg.*, July 13, 1861, p 3, c 1.

[55] Hawkins, *Grand Era*, 32.

[56] Ord #113 passed June 11, 1862.

[57] Letter from Mayor Farrar to the council, July 9, 1862. Council documents file, 1862-63, Finance folder.

[58] Address to Dec 1902 OHS annual meeting, John R. McBride. Carey, *Constitution*, 493-94.

[59] *OHQ*, Summer 1979, 144-45.

[60] J. F. McCoy was elected city assessor in 1859 and 1860, and as recorder in 1862, 1863, and 1864.

[61] Ord #125, approved by Acting Mayor McCoy Sept 18, 1862.

[62] Ord #126, approved October 11, 1862.

[63] "An Act to amend An Act entitled 'An Act to Incorporate the city of Portland,' and to amend An Act amendatory of such Act, passed January 15th, 1858," signed by Gov Addison C. Gibbs, Oct 17, 1862.

[64] Ord #109-136 passed in 1862-63.

[65] Carey, *Constitution*, 489.

[66] "[Logan] has been beastly drunk and gambling since the first day. … [H]e flourishes his revolver and says that he will shoot me on the bench, that he came out here to shoot me down himself." Judge Matthew Deady, as quoted in Leeson, 15.

[67] Judge Matthew Deady's allegation that Logan had raped an Indian woman in Jacksonville while intoxicated was first printed by Alonzo Leland in his *Democratic Standard* newspaper. Deady said Logan was observed by a number of eyewitnesses. Clark, *Eden*, 270-71.

[68] Anderson, 5.

[69] *OHQ*, Sept 1943, 254-56; Leeson, 15-6, 19, 28; Scott, *Portland*, 195; Lockley, *Columbia*, v 1, 454.

[70] *Oreg.*, March 28, 1874, as quoted in Leeson, 16; Clark, *Eden*, 270-71.

[71] *Proc. C. C.*, April 16, 1863.

[72] McAdam lived from 1756 to 1836. Pietsch, 6.

[73] The thirty-two company stockholders of the PMMRC included former mayors and council members Lewis Starr (who was company president), Addison Starr, William S. Ladd, R. B. Wilson, R. R. Thompson, D. W. Burnside, Henry W. Corbett, M. Patton, and Henry Failing. Auditor/W. S. Caldwell personal papers, C.P. Arch.

[74] Ord # 143, passed by council July 15, 1863. Macadam Road was taken over by Multnomah County sometime in the 1870s, according to Pietsch, 6-9.

[75] Scott, *Oregon*, v 3, 188-89.

[76] Auditor/W. S. Caldwell personal papers, C.P. Arch.; MacColl, *Merchants*, 188; Pietsch, 6-9; Dimon, 36, 40.

[77] Gaston, v 1, 551.

Chapter 10

[1] Short, 12-13; Scott, *Portland*, 188-89.

[2] Lockley, *Columbia*, v 1, 454.

[3] *Portrait and Biographical Record of Portland*, 27-28; Gaston, v 1, 214; v 2, 66-71; Scott, *Portland*, 521-23.

[4] Gaston, v 2, 70.
[5] *Proc. C. C.*, v 2, 566.
[6] Ibid., v 2, 564.
[7] "[T)]he city attorney's office provided a launching pad for politically ambitious young lawyers. Dolph soon became U. S. district attorney, the state senator and two-term Republican U. S. senator." MacColl, *Merchants*, 165.
[8] Other 1864-65 officials were councilmen William Bennett, James W. Cook, Thomas Frazar, S. N. Gilmore, Israel Graden, J. J. Hoffman, John McCraken, and Thomas Robertson; H. B. Morse, treasurer; J. W. Going, assessor; H. R. Meeker, auditor; Nelson Northrup, street commissioner; C. W. Burrage, surveyor; Henry S. Hoyt, marshal.
[9] *OHQ*, Summer 1979, 146.
[10] Ibid., 141, 149-51.
[11] Ibid., 147-49.
[12] Ord #159, 162, 170, 172-4, 176, 187, 190-91, 207, 209, 216, 219, and 222.
[13] Former mayor George Vaughn owned eleven pieces of property in this project, with a total value of $22,300. Ord #210, passed June 15, 1865.
[14] Letter from Auditor Gary Blackmer to the author dated Dec 7, 2000.
[15] The new charter was approved by the council September 8, 1864 (*OHQ*, Summer 1979, 146), and was passed by the state legislature, with little debate, on October 14, 1864. *1864 Oregon Special Laws*, 3-29.
[16] Sec 136-7, *1864 Oregon Special Laws*, 27.
[17] *1864 Oregon Special Laws*, 3-29. The marshal was also formally assigned the collector's duties.
[18] Ibid., 132-36.
[19] *Portrait and Biographical Record of Portland*, 28; Gaston, v 2, 70; Scott, *Portland*, 523; Maddux, 28.
[20] The council overrode a mayoral veto to pass this sewer ordinance. Mayor Failing said it was an unwise general fund expenditure not warranted by the city charter. *Proc. C. C.*, Oct 13, 1865, v 3, 183.
[21] A Front Street improvement project between Pine and Morrison was passed over the mayor's veto. Ord #235, Aug 15, 1865.
[22] Ord #225-7, 234-35, 269-76, 283, 310, 311.
[23] Ord #334 became law on May 18, 1866, without the mayor's signature, as provided by Charter Section 45, which said that a bill became law if the mayor did not return it within ten days. *Laws of the City of Portland, 1886*; *Proc. C. C.*, v 3, 433-36; *OHQ*, Summer 1979, 152.
[24] Scott, *Oregon*, v 5, 310-13.
[25] By 2000, Lone Fir was the oldest existing graveyard in the city. It had begun as the burial place for two young men killed in the explosion of the steamer *Gazelle* as it prepared to leave from Canemah, near Oregon City, for a trip upstream on the Willamette River to Corvallis, on April 14, 1854. Seven Portland mayors are buried at Lone Fir.
[26] *Proc. C. C.*, v 3, 372-74, June 13, 1866; *OHQ*, Summer 1979, 152.
[27] 1866-67 council members were Absalom Hallock, John McCraken, J. P. O. Lownsdale, A. Rosenheim, John C. Carson, Thomas J. Carter, M. O'Connor, Al Zieber, and C. H. Fechheimer.
[28] *Proc. C. C.*, Nov 29, 1866.
[29] Shubrick Norris had dropped out of visible politics at this time, and was associated with the Oregon Steam Navigation company. He was in the process of acquiring considerable property. *Oreg.*, Dec 4, 1900, 24. Norris would be named to the Board of Police Commissioners eight years later. *OHQ*, Fall 1979, 320.
[30] Hawthorne, v 1, 348-52; Scott, *Portland*, 557-58.
[31] Scott, *Portland*, 393.
[32] Ord #387, "To repeal ordinance ... and to regulate certain places of amusement," was approved Dec 8, 1866.
[33] *Proc. C. C.*, v 3, 499-503; *OHQ*, Summer 1979, 153.
[34] Ord #407, Apr 10, 1867; Ord #408, Apr 10, 1867; *OHQ*, Summer 1979, 154-55.
[35] *Oreg.*, June 13, 1867, p 2, c 1.
[36] Prior to 1867, county court sessions were held in a building at the northwest corner of Front and Salmon. *OJ*, Nov 5, 1911, sec 6, p5. Construction of the federal Pioneer Courthouse began two years later, in 1869. It was built on Block 172, originally designated for a federal customs house. MacColl, *Merchants*, 57; Long, 53.
[37] MacColl, *Merchants*, 75.
[38] Scott, *Portland*, 525; Lockley, *Columbia*, v 1, 468; *Multnomah County 1965 Annual Report*, 96.
[39] *Oreg.*, June 13, 1867, p 2, c 1.
[40] Ibid., June 14, 1867, p 2, c 2.
[41] Mayor Holmes died on June 19, 1867. Scott, *Portland*, 525, 557; Hawthorne, 351-52; Maddux, 28; *Proc. C. C.*, June 19, 1867, v 3, 592-94.
[42] Carey, *History of Oregon*, v 1, 779; Maddux, 28; *Mayor's Annual Report, 1923*, 4;
[43] Gaston, v 1, 491-92, 551.
[44] Administrative folder, Council document files, 1867-68, C.P. Arch.
[45] *Proc. C. C.*, July 24, 1867, v 4, 8. Aaron Wait was selected on the council's fifth ballot. Others who received council votes were Asa Lovejoy, Hamilton Boyd, and former council president John C. Carson.
[46] *Proc. C. C.*, July 31, 1867, v 4, 13.
[47] Gaston, v 1, 247; Scott, *Portland*, 195; Lockley, *Columbia*, v. 1, 455.
[48] MacColl letter to the *Oreg.*, September 17, 1998; MacColl, *Shaping*, 201.
[49] 1867-68 council members were Absalom Hallock, William Cree, A. C. Ripley, Robert Porter, A. Rosenheim, C. D. Burch, Charles Hopkins, former-mayor John Breck, and future police chief Lucerne Besser. *Proc. C. C.*, v 4, 4.
[50] *Proc. C. C.*, v 4, 8-11; *OHQ*, Summer 1979, 156.
[51] It then took eighteen votes to select William Caldwell, the city's first recorder, as city auditor.
[52] *OHQ*, Summer 1979, 156.
[53] The penalty for refusing to yield possession of city property was up to two hundred dollars or twenty days of imprisonment. City Ord #419, approved Aug 16, 1867.
[54] *OHQ*, Summer 1979, 156-57.
[55] Ibid., 157-58.
[56] Ibid., footnote 158, p 156-57.
[57] *OHQ*, Fall 1979, 291.
[58] *Proc. C. C.*, Aug 7, 1867, v 4, 15.
[59] *1866 City Directory*, 8.
[60] *Proc. C. C.*, August 7, 1867, v 4, 14.
[61] *Arlington Club*, 3.
[62] Ibid., 47-48, 61. Also see Gaston, 554-55.
[63] Ord #423, Aug 30, 1867; Ord #492, Apr 24, 1868.

[64] Ord #492, approved April 24, 1868; Ord #502, approved May 29, 1868.
[65] Letter from street commissioner William McMillan filed August 14, 1867. Administrative folder, 1867-68 council files.
[66] Finances folder, 1867-68 council documents file.
[67] Scott, *Portland*, 267-68; Bancroft, 695-700. See also Scott, *Portland*, 263.
[68] Bancroft, 697-98.
[69] Scott, *Portland*, 263-70.
[70] Ord #468, approved Feb 6, 1868.
[71] Gaston, v 1, 214.
[72] Scott, *Portland*, 272-73; Scott, *Oregon*, v 4, 347; Gaston, 288; Maddux, 60, 130.
[73] Boyd won election as county commissioner over three opponents: E. J. Northrup, H. Hanson, and E. L. Quimby. *Oreg.*, June 3, 1868, p 3, c 2.
[74] Several elected city officials served concurrently as elected county officials, listed here in chronological order: Shubrick Norris, A. D. Fitch, William McMillen, George W. Vaughn, Absalom B. Hallock, Lewis M. Starr, John M. Breck, Addison M. Starr, Z. N. Stansbury, David W. Douthitt, John S. White, R. J. Ladd, J. P. O. Lownsdale, Marion F. Mulkey, Hamilton Boyd, Cincinnati Bills, and George L. Story.
[75] The *Oreg.* of April 26, 1998, contained an appeal from Mayor Vera Katz for photos of three mayors whose pictures were missing from a wall display set up in newly renovated city hall. She was seeking photos of Simon B. Marye (of whom one was found), W. H. Farrar and Boyd (neither found.)
[76] Hamilton Boyd died at age fifty-two. *Oreg.*, March 26, 1883, p 5, c 1.
[77] 1870 Census, Multnomah County, Portland, p 81.
[78] Scott, *Portland*, 196; Lockley, *Columbia*, v 1, 455; Maddux, 28-29.
[79] *Oreg.*, August 15, 1868, p 2, c 1.
[80] Petition filed in papers of Fifth Regular Session of the Oregon House of Representatives, 1868, OSA.
[81] *Oreg.*, Sept 3, 1868, p 2, c 2.
[82] Ibid., p 2, c 2.
[83] Carey, *Constitution*, 415-16.
[84] Ibid., 424.
[85] Ibid., 428.
[86] The petition for consolidation is filed with papers of the Fifth Regular Session of the Oregon House of Representatives, OSA. The House Journal for Wednesday, September 23, 1868, says, "Mr. [W. W.] Chapman offered the petition of the citizens of Portland to amend the corporate law of the city of Portland, by consolidating the city government with that of the county of Multnomah. On motion of Mr. Chapman, The petition was referred to the Multnomah members of the house." No tracking number was assigned to the petition, and the petition back simply says, "Referred to the members from Portland."
[87] *Oregon Special Laws, 1868*, 90-4; *OHQ*, Summer 1979, 160-61, 165-66.
[88] Corning, 116; Scott, *Oregon* v 4, 347; Scott, *Portland*, 282-84; Quiett, 353-54.
[89] Quiett, 353.
[90] Ibid., 356.
[91] Bancroft, 700; Quiett, 356; Scott, *Portland*, 282-83.
[92] Bancroft, 702; Quiett, 357.
[93] Quiett, 353-54.
[94] Joseph Gaston was president of the westside railroad company in Mayor Boyd's time, and integrally involved in political affairs. The quotation was taken from Gaston, v 1, 633. See also Scott, *Portland*, 272-73, re Joseph Gaston.
[95] Hays, 54.
[96] None of the nine 1868-69 councilmen were listed in the *1870 Portland Directory* under the category of Grocers, Liquor Saloons, or Licensed Liquor Dealers, although William Moffit, a councilman the following year, was listed with a saloon at the corner of First and Morrison. Of the 1868-69 council, Absalom Hallock was an architect; John Breck ran a general merchandise store; a Charles Burch is listed in the *1870 Portland Directory* as a blacksmith; Charles Hopkins is listed twice in the *1870 Portland Directory*, once as a wagon-maker and second as running a hardware store; Robert Porter was a partner in a sash factory doing business as Carson & Porter. These men could also have been part-owners of a saloon, but no evidence of this was found. Lucerne Besser worked in various sawmills, but may have also worked in a saloon. The occupations of the other two council members—A. C. Ripley and William Cree—are unknown. The ninth council member, C. S. Fechheimer, was in the last year of a three-year term, and attended only the first meeting of the year. The *1869 City Directory* shows his council seat as vacant.
[97] "Autobiography of Edward Chambreau" (Reed College Library, Portland) p 217-18, as described by Charles A. Tracy III in *OHQ*, Summer 1979, 159-60.
[98] Ord #599, approved Jan 11, 1869.
[99] Ord #599, approved Jan 11, 1869. In 1910, a federal judge was to rule that the "noise, vibration, smoke, cinders and soot from the moving trains" seriously interfered with the transaction of public and private business, and was a "constant source of danger and inconvenience to the public." Leeson, 91.
[100] Bowman, 200.
[101] Ord #619, approved Feb 27, 1869.

Chapter 11

[1] Scott, *Portland*, 453.
[2] MacColl, *Merchants*, 174.
[3] Ibid., 164.
[4] Ibid., 153.
[5] The five Jewish mayors were Bernard Goldsmith (1869-71), Philip Wasserman (1871-73), Joseph Simon (1909-11), Neil Goldschmidt (1972-79), and Vera Katz (1993-present.) All except Neil Goldschmidt, Portland's forty-fifth mayor, who was born in Eugene, Oregon, were born in Germany (Lowenstein, 61). Both Katz's parents were Russian "Just Like a Woman," by Foster Church, *Governing* magazine, Sept 1990, 26. Goldschmidt's mother was born in Portland of German parents, and his father was born in Portland of a German mother and Russian father; they were married at the Benson Hotel in Portland in 1937. Letter to the author dated Jan 10, 2000, from Lori Vickers, assistant to Neil Goldschmidt. Bernard Goldsmith's birth name was Goldschmidt, the same as that of Neil Goldschmidt, although the two were not related. Lowenstein, 17. Lowenstein obtained most of his Bernard Goldsmith information from an 1889

Goldsmith interview by Hubert Howe Bancroft. *The Chronicles of the Builders*, Bancroft Library, U of C, Berkeley.
[6] Lowenstein, 18.
[7] MacColl, *Merchants*, 153.
[8] *Portland, Our Community*, 55-56; Scott, Portland, 196; Hawthorne, v 1, 328-29; MacColl, *Merchants*, 143, 153-54.
[9] Robbins, 100.
[10] Lowenstein, 21; MacColl, *Merchants*, 168.
[11] *OHQ*, Summer 1979, 161.
[12] Lowenstein, 21.
[13] Section 127 of the Portland city charter (added in 1864) said, "the city of Portland is not liable to any one for any injury to the person ... growing out of the condition of any streets." *O'Harra v. the City of Portland*, 3 Oregon Reports, Sept. 1869, 525. The Oregon Tort Claims Act effective 1968 changed the law regarding civil claims against public bodies.
[14] This doctrine of government immunity from tort liability dated back to the Divine Right of Kings, under which the king could do no wrong.
[15] *OHQ*, Summer 1979, 161-63.
[16] Holbrook, 12.
[17] Corning, 116.
[18] Quiett, 357; Bancroft, 702.
[19] Scott, *Oregon*, v 4, 348.
[20] Holbrook, 12; Snyder, *Portland Names*, 149; Lyman, *History of Oregon*, v 4, 266.
[21] Scott, *Oregon*, v 4, 353.
[22] *1870 Oregon Session Laws*, 141-58.
[23] Scott, *Oregon*, v 4, 348.
[24] *The Value of a Dollar*, edited by Scott Derks, Greyhouse Publishing, Lakeville, CT, 1999; Amtrack ticket office.
[25] Calculated by the Inflation Calculator, www.westegg.com/inflation/infl/cgi.
[26] Ord #810 approved June 17, 1870.
[27] *1870 Oregon Special Laws*, 131-35; MacColl, *Merchants*, 168-69.
[28] *OHQ*, Summer 1979, 168-69.
[29] *Proc. C. C.*, Sept 28, 1870, v 4, 512; *OHQ*, Summer 1979, 166-67.
[30] *OHQ*, Fall 1979, 289-90.
[31] Ibid., 289.
[32] The board's first meeting was held Nov 1, 1870. *OHQ*, Fall 1979, 288.
[33] *OHQ*, Fall 1979, 293.
[34] *1870 Oregon Special Laws*, 128-29.
[35] Ord #893, approved Nov 11, 1870. The following July, the council leased a fifth room in the same building for an additional twenty dollars a month. Ord #1036 approved July 28, 1871.
[36] Scott, *Oregon*, v 4, 353.
[37] Scott, *Portland*, 549-50.
[38] Scott, *Oregon*, v 4, 353.
[39] Open letter from the solicitation committee. *Oreg.*, Jan 5, 1871, p 3, c 3.
[40] Flanders and Couch had long before donated ten blocks in north Portland for a future railroad terminus. Gaston, v 1, 214.
[41] Scott, *Oregon*, v 4, 352-54.
[42] Ibid., 354-57.
[43] *Oreg.*, Jan 2, 1888, as quoted in Robbins, 123.
[44] *Portland, Our Community*, 55-56.
[45] These two public squares are now known as Lownsdale and Chapman squares, located between Third and Fourth streets, Salmon to Madison. Snyder, *Potpourri*, 130-31; Snyder, *Portland Names*, 244, 249; MacColl, *Merchants*, 57.
[46] Snyder, *Potpourri*, 130-31; MacColl, *Merchants*, 169.
[47] The forty acres that comprised the nucleus of Washington Park (today encompassing 145 acres) were purchased from tanner Amos King, who had bought the Daniel Lownsdale tannery and land claim from Milton Apperson in 1849. See King footnote 18 to Chapter 2 of this book and MacColl, *Merchants*, 170.
[48] Ord #917, January 6, 1871; Lowenstein, 21; MacColl, *Merchants*, 170.
[49] MacColl, *Merchants*, 169.
[50] Snyder, *Potpourri*, 132; MacColl, *Merchants*, 170.
[51] The ordinance suppressing brothels was introduced by Councilman Cincinnati Bills, who was also the county sheriff. Councilman Bills apparently had personal experience with the vice he sought to curtail. He died in December of that year, and Judge Matthew Deady says in his diaries: "[Bills] was naturally a good fellow, but the office of sheriff brought him in contact with vicious influences that he had not the stamina to resist. The newspapers and societies say that he died of inflammatory rheumatism, but I know that he died of a putrid fever which was brought on by the virus of clap getting into his blood and poisoning it, and his wife came pretty near dying from the same cause. " Clark, *Pharisee*, v 1, 39.
[52] Ord #959, approved March 4, 1871; *OHQ*, Fall 1979, 294-95.
[53] Ord #922, approved Jan 27, 1871.
[54] Lowenstein, 20; "Willamette River Recreation Guide," 1998-99 Edition, 17, 27. Goldsmith died in 1901 and is buried at Beth Israel cemetery. Mayor Wasserman, who died in 1895, was moved from Beth Israel to the Portland Crematorium with other family members in Oct 1935. Phone call, Beth Israel Cemetery caretaker, Mar 7, 2000.
[55] Philip Wasserman served in the Oregon house in 1862 and 1864, and in the senate in 1865. Edwards, Cecil, 136; Carey, *Constitution*, 510-11.
[56] Wasserman tallied 801 votes to Chapman's 536. *1872 City Directory*, 34.
[57] Scott, *Oregon*, 268.
[58] Wasserman served on the five-member board 1883-86. Scott, *Portland*, 196; 393.
[59] *1870 P.C. Dir.*, 76; Lockley, *Columbia*, v 1, 455.
[60] *Proc. C. C.*, June 14, 1871, v 5, p 3.
[61] John Green was the grand-uncle of controversial communist John Silas Reed, born in Portland, the only American to be buried in Moscow's Kremlin. "Portlander John Reed Remembers Lee Sing, His Family's Chinese Servant," *OHQ*, Fall 1996, 356-57; Short, 4-6; Lockley, *Oregon Folks*, 39-45; MacColl, *Merchants*, 40.
[62] MacColl, *Merchants*, 174; *Oreg.*, Sept 21, 1871, p 2, c 1.
[63] Ord #1060, approved Sept 9, 1871.
[64] Short, 4-7; *1870 Oregon Special Laws*, 128-29.
[65] *Oreg.*, June 14, 1873, p 2, c 4; *Oreg.*, June 17, 1873, p 2, c 1.
[66] Ord #1065, approved September 12, 1871, amended January 8, 1872, by #1126; Maddux, 95-96.

[67] Maddux, 96; *OHQ*, Dec 1941, 279; Labbe, 23-25; Holbrook, 12. Labbe says the line was managed by Ben's brother, Joseph Holladay. Holbrook says Ben Holladay was the "promoter, sole owner and president of the first local streetcar line," which ran along First Street from Glisan to Carruthers, and that a round trip required two hours. Maddux says the round trip took an hour.
[68] Maddux, 95-96.
[69] *Proc. C. C.*, Feb 21 & March 6, 1872, v. 5, p 1211/2, 126; *1870 P.C. Dir.*, 35.
[70] "History Shows Council Changes Meeting Sites Often," by Don Holm, *Oreg.*, March 1, 1964, 36.
[71] The June elections were for the city of Portland; the October elections were federal.
[72] Ned Wicks, owner of the American Exchange saloon, reported the encounter. MacColl, *Merchants*, 172.
[73] Clark, *Pharisee*, v 1, 189.
[74] Scott, *Oregon*, v 5, 98-102; MacColl, *Merchants*, 172-73; Corning, 113-14.
[75] Clark, *Pharisee*, v 1, 154.
[76] Ibid., 155.
[77] Leeson, 38-39; *OHQ*, Fall 1979, 299.
[78] *OHQ*, Fall 1979, 297.
[79] Ibid., 300. Governor Grover did approve two minor city charter amendments. One provided that the mayor should serve as the acting police judge in case of the judge's absence, and the other detailed street commissioner duties, processes, and powers. *1872 Oregon Special Laws*, 171-72; 198-202.
[80] Maddux, 68-70.
[81] Lyman, *History of Oregon*, v 4, 265.
[82] Scott, *Portland*, 288.
[83] Ibid., 288.
[84] This ordinance passed council June 11, 1873. OHQ, Fall 1979, 304-5.
[85] Clark, Hugh, p 3.
[86] Ibid., p 9-10.
[87] Ibid., p 10-13.
[88] Corning, 42, 44, 168.
[89] *Proc. C. C.*, April 14, 1873, v 5, 296.
[90] Ord #1347, approved June 19, 1873.
[91] *OHQ*, Fall 1979, 305-6; MacColl, *Merchants*, 167-68.
[92] *Oreg.*, June 14, 1873, p 2, c 4.
[93] Clark, Hugh, p 3-4.

Chapter 12

[1] *Oreg.*, June 10, 1873, p 2, c 3; June 16, 1873, p 2, c 1; MacColl, *Merchants*, 173.
[2] *Oreg.*, June 16, 1873, p 2, c 1; MacColl, *Merchants*, 174.
[3] *Oreg.*, June 16, 1873, p 2, c 2.
[4] MacColl, *Merchants*, 174.
[5] *Oreg.*, June 17, 1873, p 2, c 1.
[6] *Old Portland Today*, circa May 1975, a monthly newspaper published in Old Town. See also Maddux, 70-72; Scott, *Portland*, 447-50.
[7] Little had been done to improve the city's fire response after the big fire of 1873 except for the purchase of a 4,200 pound bell, sent from the East Coast around the Horn, which was hung in a tower at First and Morrison. The clapper weighed fifty pounds, and the bell could be heard for miles around. Snyder, *Skidmore*, 30. Author Maddux says the bell was placed in the tower of the fire hall at Fourth and Taylor. Maddux, 74.
[8] Scott, *Portland*, 447-50.
[9] "Specifically, the *Oreg.* referred to two letters written before the fire that had threatened the destruction of the Chinese core." *Oreg.*, Aug 9, 1873, 1:3, as quoted in Clark, Hugh, p 13.
[10] Clark, Hugh, p 12-14; MacColl, *Merchants*, 174-75; Maddux, 70-73; *OHQ*, Fall 1979, 307-9.
[11] Gaston, v 1, 249.
[12] MacColl, *Merchants*, 175.
[13] *1882 City Directory*, 50.
[14] Maddux, 113.
[15] Clark, Hugh, p 13.
[16] Corning, 116.
[17] The O&C line to California would not be completed for another fourteen years. Robbins, 114.
[18] Clark, "The War on the Webfoot Saloon," *OHQ*, March 1957, 49.
[19] Moynihan, 92-96.
[20] Twenty-one votes for a suffrage amendment; twenty-two opposed. Moynihan, 178.
[21] *New Northwest*, March 6, 1874, as quoted by Malcolm Clark, *OHQ*, March 1957, 49; *OHQ*, Fall 1979, 314.
[22] Clark, " Webfoot Saloon," 51-52.
[23] Ibid., 52
[24] OHQ, Fall 1979, 316.
[25] Clark, " Webfoot Saloon," 55-56.
[26] *OHQ*, Fall 1979, 315.
[27] Clark, " Webfoot Saloon," 59.
[28] Ibid., 59-60.
[29] Ibid., 61; MacColl, *Merchants*, 192.
[30] Clark, " Webfoot Saloon," 61.
[31] MacColl, *Merchants*, 176.
[32] *Oreg.*, June 16, 1874, p 3, c 2.
[33] Ord #1489, approved June 17, 1874.
[34] Ord #1512, approved July 17, 1874.
[35] MacColl, *Merchants*, 176-77.
[36] The police judge was to turn in all fees he collected to the city treasury and receive a salary instead. The police chief was allowed to keep a third of state fees he received, in addition to his salary. *Oregon 1874 Special Laws*, 210, 212, 218-19, 222; *OHQ*, Fall 1979, 319-20.
[37] Shubrick Norris served as president of the 1874-75 police board. *1875 P.C. Dir.* The other two new police commissioners were hardware dealer John Foster and William Wadhams, a "prosperous wholesale businessman active on the board for only five months." *OHQ*, Fall 1979, 320-21.
[38] "History Shows Council Changes Meeting Sites Often," Don Holm, *Oreg.*, March 1, 1964, 36.
[39] *Oreg.*, June 21, 1875, as quoted in Snyder, *Skidmore*, 61-62.
[40] Snyder, *Skidmore*, 64.
[41] *New Northwest*, June 1875, as quoted in Snyder, *Skidmore*, 64; *Oreg.*, June 22, 1875, as quoted in MacColl, *Merchants*, 177.
[42] *Oreg.*, June 22, 1875, p 2, c 2.
[43] Ibid., p 2, c 1.
[44] MacColl, *Merchants*, 177; *Arlington Club*, 2.
[45] St. Vincent was opened July 19, 1875; and Good Samaritan on Oct 9, 1875. *Oreg.*, 1875, as cited in "Portland of Years Past," *Oreg.*, June 22, 2000, E3.
[46] Huffman, 154.
[47] The Nicholson paving was also wooden. Maddux, 120-21.
[48] Ibid., 120-21; Huffman 128-29, 133.
[49] Huffman, 126, 139.

[50] Aikman (Collins), 171. Chief Lappeus listed seventy-one saloons operating in January 1876. MacColl, *Merchants*, 196.
[51] Huffman, 133.
[52] Ibid., 133-36.
[53] Ibid., 126, 138.
[54] Ibid., 129, 141-43.
[55] Ibid., 151.
[56] *Oreg.*, July 31, 1876, p 3, c 2.
[57] Scott, *Oregon*, v 5, 98; MacColl, *Merchants*, 173; Corning, 218.
[58] The "Citizens' Party" and "People's Party" labels for candidates had been dropped, and the national two-party system again prevailed openly in city elections. Snyder, *Skidmore*, 65-66.
[59] The vote was 1,126 for Riley to 698 for Sitton. Ibid., 65-66.
[60] Candidate Davis's first name is illegible. *Oreg.*, June 18, 1877, p 2, c 1; June 19, 1877, p 2, c 2 and p 3, c 2.
[61] Eleven of Portland's forty-four mayors were born in New York state, six in Oregon, four in Germany, two each from Illinois, Maine, Minnesota, New Jersey, and Virginia. One each was born in California, Colorado, England, Georgia, Idaho, Iowa, Ireland, Kentucky, Missouri, New Hampshire, Ohio, Pennsylvania, and Vermont. Statistics compiled by the author from numerous sources.
[62] Ten mayors were lawyers, twelve were merchants. Statistics compiled by the author from numerous sources.
[63] *History of the Bench and Bar*, 198; Scott, *Portland*, 196-97; Hawthorne, v 2, 317-18, 321.
[64] Hawthorne, v 2, 317-21.
[65] *1879 P.C. Dir.*, 49-52.
[66] *Laws of the City of Portland, 1886*, published hard-bound by the *Morning Oreg.*, 467-87.
[67] Ord #2060, approved October 1, 1877.
[68] *WW*, Whiplash column, Aug 26, 1993.
[69] Ord #2184, approved June 6, 1878.
[70] Skidmore served on the Portland council for three years, 1875-78; Sanborn for the year of 1875-76. Scott, *Portland*, 201.
[71] Snyder, *Skidmore*, 74.
[72] Corning, 240.
[73] Snyder, *Skidmore*, 69.
[74] Ibid., 75-76.
[75] The Civic Auditorium, today's Keller Auditorium, was eventually built on Block 132. MacColl, *Merchants*, 57.
[76] Ord #2458, approved June 10, 1879. Originally, Block 132 was to include a public park twenty feet wide on both the north and south sides of the Mechanics Pavilion, but that provision was repealed July 22, 1880, by Ord #2748.
[77] Scott, *Portland*, 165.
[78] City Ord # 2046, 2122, 2211, 2228, 2273, 2316, and 2387, dated, respectively, Sept 13, 1877; Jan 17, 1878; July 19, 1878; Aug 7, 1878; Sept 28, 1878; Nov 22, 1878; and Feb 21, 1879.
[79] Ord #2463, approved June 20, 1879.
[80] *History of the Bench and Bar*, 178; Scott, *Portland*, 197.

Chapter 13

[1] Thompson garnered 1,404 votes, Strong, 1,358. *Oreg.*, June 17, 1879, p 3, c 3; Snyder, *Potpourri*, 6.
[2] Corning, 243; Lockley, *Columbia*, v 3, 890; MacColl, *Merchants*, 89; Snyder, *Potpourri*, 2.
[3] Throckmorten, 250, 271.
[4] Corning, 243, says David and R. R. Thompson were brothers, but Gaston, v 1, 215, says, "R. R. Thompson was born in Harrison county, Ohio, not far from the birthplace of David P. Thompson, another prominent capitalist of this city, but they were in no way related to each other." MacColl, *Merchants*, 216, also says the two were not related.
[5] Scott, *Portland*, 197; Lockley, *Columbia*, v 3, 893.
[6] *Oreg.* editorial, circa December 15, 1901, as quoted in Lockley, *Columbia*, v 3, 894.
[7] Snyder, *Potpourri*, 6-8; Scott, *Oregon*, v 5, p 73; MacColl, *Merchants*, 217, 220; Scott, *Portland*, 393.
[8] Ord #2558 and #2938, approved Oct 30, 1879 and Dec 21, 1880, plus thirteen ordinances passed between Sept 16 and Nov 30, 1881.
[9] The change in chiefs occurred on Oct 27, 1879. 10 Oregon Reports, *City of Portland v Besser, et al.*, October 1882; *OHQ*, Spring 1979, 22; *OHQ*, Fall 1979, 295.
[10] *Oreg.*, June 17, 1879, p 2, c 1.
[11] Ord #2557 and #2566, approved Oct 30 and Nov 19, 1879.
[12] *OHQ*, Dec 1941, 279; Hays, 14; Maddux, 118.
[13] Hays, 14-15.
[14] Corning, 254-55.
[15] MacColl, *Merchants*, 211-12.
[16] Quote is from Quiett, 363. Also see MacColl, *Merchants*, 211-13.
[17] Ord #2710, approved June 3, 1880.
[18] Ord #2726, approved June 11, 1880.
[19] *1882 P.C. Dir.*, 53.
[20] *Oreg.*, Jan 19, 1881, as quoted in Scott, *Oregon*, v 5, 138-40. See also Maddux, 122.
[21] www.enviro.ci.portland.or.us.CPR.htm [accessed Aug 20, 2000].
[22] Ord #2742, passed over the objection of the mayor, July 1, 1880.
[23] Ord #2839, approved Sept 29, 1880.
[24] Wright, 19.
[25] MacColl, *Merchants*, 213.
[26] Letter from Thomas Oakes to Villard written December 1880, as quoted in Quiett, 367.
[27] Census figures for 1880 were: Portland 17,577; Seattle 3,553; Oregon 174,768; Washington Territory 75,116. Tenth Census of the United States, Department of the Interior, 1880, as quoted in *U of O Information Bulletin No. 106*, Table I; Edwards, G. Thomas, 169.
[28] 1880 Federal Manuscript Census Schedules, Multnomah County, City of Portland, as quoted in Wright monograph, Table XXXI.
[29] Duniway, 90.
[30] *1880 Oregon Special Laws*, 96, 109.
[31] Council first met on July 4, 1881.
[32] *Proc. C. C.*, July 6, 1881, v 7, 188.
[33] Ibid., 187.
[34] Stewart Holbrook, as quoted in Booth, 217.
[35] Ibid., 220-21.
[36] MacColl, *Merchants*, 218-19.

[37] Ibid., 219.
[38] *Proc. C. C.*, July 8, 1881, v 7, 190.
[39] MacColl, *Merchants*, 219.
[40] *Proc. C. C.*, July 8, 1881, v 7, 192.
[41] Ibid., July 9, 1881, v 7, 201.
[42] Ibid., July 11, 1881, v 7, 203-4.
[43] Ibid., July 14, 1881, v 7, 205.
[44] Ibid., Aug 3, 1881, v 7, 224-25.
[45] MacColl, *Merchants*, 219.
[46] MacColl, *Merchants*, 221-22.
[47] Leeson, 36, 55, 60-61; Corning, 224.
[48] Ord #3191, approved August 5, 1881.
[49] *OHQ*, Dec 1941, 279-83.
[50] Ord #3346, approved Dec 23, 1881. The First Street railway was still operating; it was to add new passing tracks and more cars for more frequent service the following year. Labbe, 25.
[51] Labbe, 25-34; Ord #3637, 3639, 3672, 3684, 3687, 3773, 3829, 3884 approved 1882 and 1883.
[52] For nearly a four-year period, November 1879 to July 1883, Lappeus "prosecuted 42 cases of prostitution, a record his replacement, William H. Watkinds, surpassed only after two months in office." *OHQ*, Fall 1979, 295.
[53] Holbrook, 16; Booth, 134; O'Donnell and Vaughan, 31. However, the *1880 P.C. Dir.* (p 309) lists Mrs. Nancy Boggs as operating a saloon at 46 Pine Street.
[54] Stewart Holbrook, as quoted in Booth, 134-35.
[55] Ibid., 135.
[56] Holbrook, 16-17.
[57] *Oreg.*, March 3, 1879, as quoted in Clark, Hugh, p 15-16.
[58] The law was repealed December 17, 1943. *47th Congress, Session I, 1882*, Chapter 126; *78th Congress, Session I, 1943*, Chapter 344.
[59] Congressman David Wu, born in Taiwan, emigrated to America when he was six years old.
[60] Quiett, 367.
[61] Ord #3482, approved June 24, 1882.
[62] *1866 P.C. Dir.*, 8.
[63] MacColl, *Merchants*, 219.
[64] Not all Thompson's contemporaries fully trusted him, including federal judge Matthew Deady. Deady speculated in 1871 that Thompson would hide assets rather than pay off on a forty thousand dollar bond he had guaranteed. In 1881, Thompson was accused in the council of failure to list the New Market Theater on his 1879 county assessor's return. Thompson bought 80 percent of the building in 1879 and paid the remaining 20 percent off in January 1880. He maintained that because he didn't take final possession until January 1881, he was not required to list the property for 1879. Clark, *Pharisee*, v 1, xxix; MacColl, *Merchants*, 216-17.
[65] Snyder, *Portpourri*, 1, 9-16. The bronze elk statue sits on a granite base surrounded by a fountain "where horses could drink," and was created by Roland Perry, dedicated in 1900. A color painting of the fountain and its environs graces the cover of *Portland Potpourri: Art, Fountains and Old Friends*, by Eugene Snyder. See bibliography.
[66] The statue group in Washington Park was designed by American sculptor Herman A. MacNeil and dedicated in 1904. "The Coming of the White Man" depicts "two Indians, of heroic size, standing on a great unhewn stone, gazing with intense interest up to the gorge of the Columbia river, down which the pale faced strangers are coming," says Fred Lockley, *Columbia*, v 3, 895. Also see Hawkins, *Grand Era*, 120; Gleason and Orloff, 53; and Snyder, *Potpourri*, 12-15.
[67] Chapman's previous terms were 1867-68 and 1875-77.
[68] MacColl, *Merchants*, 219-20.
[69] Matters related to street, sidewalk, and sewer projects included surveys, permits, digging, foundations, drainage, crosswalks, sidewalk sills, box gutters, plank roadways, repairs, and testing.
[70] *Proc. C. C.*, January 7, 1880, as quoted in "History of Portland's Volunteer Fire Department," by Andrew C. Sherbert, date unknown, p 7.
[71] Ibid., p 7.
[72] Thomas A. Jordan was appointed as Portland's first paid fire chief (1882). He served but one year. *Portland Fire Bureau Year Book, 1976*, 21.
[73] *1882 Laws of Oregon*, 73 - 80, An Act to Establish a Paid Fire Department for the City of Portland, approved Oct 9, 1882.
[74] Eighteen thousand dollars was expended for regular expenses from the fire department fund as compared to sixteen thousand dollars from the police fund. Auditor's annual report, *1879 P.C. Dir.*, 50.
[75] *1882 Laws of Oregon*, 73 – 80, Section 11.
[76] "History of Portland's Volunteer Fire Department," by Andrew C. Sherbert, date unknown, p 8.
[77] City charters passed to date were: #1, 1881; #2, 1853; #3, 1854; #4, 1864; and #5, passed by the legislature in late Oct 1882.
[78] Section 37, *1882 Oregon Special Laws*, 144-51.
[79] Section 72, *1882 Oregon Special Laws*, 160-61.
[80] Gaston, v 1, 214.
[81] Ord #3720, approved March 8, 1883.
[82] Ord #3744, approved April 6, 1883.
[83] *Ordinance Journal*, Volume 7, was started in March 1883.
[84] The *Weekly News* article ran on March 8, 1883. *OHQ*, Summer 1981, 180; *OHQ*, Summer 1979, 134.
[85] *OHQ*, Fall 1979, 290.
[86] Ibid., Summer 1979, 134.
[87] Ibid., Fall 1979, 290.
[88] Information provided by the River View Cemetery Association, 8421 S.W. Macadam Avenue, Portland.
[89] The twelve mayors buried at River View Cemetery are H. Russell Albee, John Breck, Van DeLashmutt, Henry Failing, Josiah Failing (moved there when River View opened), John Gates, William S. Ladd, Dorothy McCullough Lee, Sylvester Pennoyer (moved from Lone Fir), Allen Rushlight, David Thompson, and George Williams. Information furnished by River View Cemetery.
[90] Ord # 3912, approved August 24, 1883. The lease covered a five-year period at 160 dollars a month. The three-story, cast-iron-fronted building was also known as the Breeden Building. Located on the northeast corner of Third and Washington, it was torn down in 1978. It is not to be confused with the historic gray stone Dekum Building on the southwest corner of Third and Washington constructed in 1891-92. Norman, 73; Hawkins, *Grand Era*, 204-5; Dekum Building nomination form for National Register of Historic Places, Item 7 and Item 8, p 3.

[91] An 1890 painting by Francesca C. R. Grothjean titled "Villard's Folly" was hanging at Jake's Famous Crawfish Restaurant in downtown Portland in April 2001. Villard's purchase of Block 179—today's Pioneer Courthouse Square—had required voter approval because it was the site of the city's first public school, opened in 1858. *OHQ*, Fall 1998, 302-6.
[92] *OHQ*, Fall 1998, 298-99, 305-6.
[93] The east and west lines of the northern transcontinental railroad were joined at Gold Creek, Montana, sixty miles southeast of Missoula. Quiett, 368-69; MacColl, *Merchants*, 225.
[94] The information regarding twenty thousand gas jets was taken from *The West Shore* magazine, Dec 1883, according to O. B. Coldwell. *OHQ*, Dec 1941, 284.
[95] O'Donnell and Vaughan, 34.
[96] MacColl, *Merchants*, 219; *Oreg.*, Sept 27, 1883. Soon after this article appeared in the newspaper, Chapman denied talk around town that city offices were still for sale. But former policeman Hickey told the *Oreg.* he would not have been removed from his police duties if he had paid the Chapman campaign donation he was asked for. *Oreg.*, Sept 27, 1883.
[97] *Oreg.*, Nov 22, 1883.
[98] Ibid.
[99] Ibid.
[100] Ibid.; *1880 P.C. Dir.*, 310.
[101] *Oreg.*, Feb 3, 1884.
[102] *Oreg.*, Sept 18, 1884.
[103] Saloon keeper Richard Gerdes served a total of twelve years on the council, from 1879 to 1891. Source: Council member lists compiled by this author.
[104] *Oreg.*, Sept 19, 1884.
[105] MacColl, *Merchants*, 219.
[106] Ord #4074, approved Dec 21, 1883.
[107] Ord #4130, approved Jan 26, 1884.
[108] Ord #3983, approved Oct 13, 1883.
[109] Portland Police Historical Society list of significant events and dates, compiled circa 1989.
[110] MacColl, *Merchants*, 225.
[111] The 1884 vote was 28,176 against and 11,223 for women's suffrage. Moynihan, 181.
[112] *1885 Oregon Special Laws*, approved Feb 25, 1885, 408-15.
[113] Ord #4538, passed over objections of the mayor March 18, 1885.
[114] Short, 7-9.
[115] Ord #4621, approved June 24, 1885.
[116] Lockley, *Columbia*, v 1, 455; MacColl, *Merchants*, 219-20.

Chapter 14

[1] John Gates received 2,495 votes to Sylvester Pennoyer's 2,345. Maddux, 114.
[2] Scott, *Portland*, 197-98; OHQ, 1915, v 14, p 349.
[3] *OJ*, June 1, 1947, Pacific Parade Section, 8.
[4] James Chapman was sixty-two when he started his final mayoral term in 1882, making him the city's oldest mayor at that time. Sylvester Pennoyer was sixty-five years old when elected in 1896; W. S. Mason would be sixty-six when he began his second term in 1898; and George Williams was seventy-nine when elected in 1902.
[5] Maddux, 114.
[6] *OHQ*, 1915, v 14, p 349.
[7] MacColl, *Merchants*, 244; MacColl, *Shaping*, 61.
[8] MacColl, *Merchants*, 244; MacColl, *Shaping*, 62.
[9] City Ord #4699, approved Oct 26, 1885.
[10] Deady's diary says, on Dec 22, 1885, "Mr. Corbett for the committee paid me $300 for preparing the water commission act. It ought to have been $500, but as I said to him, I ought to contribute something to the general good as well as the committee." Clark, *Pharisee*, v 2, 481-82.
[11] MacColl, *Shaping*, 64.
[12] *1885 Oregon Special Laws*, 97-102; Short, 9-13.
[13] The other nine men named to the original Water Committee were F. C. Smith, C. H. Lewis, L. Fleischner, W. K. Smith, J. Lowenberg, R. B. Knapp, L. Therkelson, Thomas M. Richardson, and A. H. Johnson. *1885 Oregon Special Laws*, 98.
[14] Bill approved Nov 25, 1885. *1885 Oregon Special Laws*, 97-102.
[15] Short, 12, 135.
[16] Bull Run Lake and River, today part of a 102-acre watershed, were said to have been named by pioneers whose cattle, while being driven over the Cascade Range, "broke free in the area, escaping through the dense forest in all directions." The cattle were lost, and "were seen only occasionally in years to come, drinking from the river whose name they had inspired." Short, 13.
[17] *1885 Oregon Special Laws*, 74-75 and 103-4.
[18] Simon in 1898-1903; Bourne in 1907-13.
[19] MacColl, *Shaping*, 209.
[20] Amidon W. Lafferty letter of January 12, 1949, to E. B. McNaughton, in A. M. Lafferty papers, OHS; MacColl, *Merchants*, 245-46.
[21] Schlup, Leonard, "Republican Insurgent: Jonathan Bourne and the Politics of Progressivism, 1908-1912, *OHQ*, Fall 1986, 238-39; MacColl, *Shaping*, 238.
[22] Clark, Hugh, 16; MacColl, *Merchants*, 237.
[23] The number of millionaires was estimated by *The Northwest*, Nov 1885. MacColl, *Merchants*, 236.
[24] MacColl, *Merchants*, 236. *The West Shore*, "the first illustrated paper published west of the Rocky mountains," was published in Portland from 1875 to 1890, and attained a circulation of fifteen thousand. Gaston, v 1, 508.
[25] Thirty miles of streets were macadamized, sixteen miles graded but unsurfaced, three miles planked, and three miles laid with Belgian basalt blocks quarried near St. Helens. Scott, *Portland*, 206-7; *History of Portland*, WPA Writers, 19.
[26] City charter, Chapter IX; *1882 Oregon Special Laws*, 162-6.
[27] Scott, *Oregon*, v 3, 225, lists the lead Portland agitators as Burnette G. Haskell, "an agitator from California," Nat L. Baker, Al White, and J. H. Cradlebaugh.
[28] MacColl, *Merchants*, 239.
[29] Scott, *Oregon*, v 3, 225.
[30] Clark, *Pharisee*, Appendix A, v 2, 508.
[31] Scott, *Oregon*, v 3, 225. See also *Oreg.*, March 5, 1886, p 3, c 3.
[32] Clark, *Pharisee*, Appendix A, v 2, 509.
[33] Scott, *Oregon*, v 3, 225.
[34] Ibid., 225.

[35] Clark, Hugh, p 16.
[36] Scott, *Oregon*, v 3, 225-26.
[37] Clark, *Pharisee*, Appendix A, v 2, 509.
[38] Dean Collins in Aikman, 182-83.
[39] *OHQ*, June 1974, 128-30; MacColl, *Merchants*, 240.
[40] Foreign immigration to the Northwest decreased by 50 percent between 1882 and 1885. MacColl, *Merchants*, 237; Clark, Hugh, p 16.
[41] Scott, *Oregon*, v 3, 226. Many American cities were building armories at this time, often as a base for operations in case of labor strife.
[42] O'Donnell and Vaughan, 30.
[43] Chinatown section, *Potential Historic Conservation Districts*, Portland Bureau of Planning, 1978, p 35.
[44] Clark, *Pharisee*, Appendix A, v 2, 508.
[45] O'Donnell and Vaughan, 31.
[46] Scott, *Portland*, 438.
[47] City Ord #4634, 4678, 4706, 4710, 4802, 4848, 4857, and 4875: approved July, 1885 - June 1866.
[48] Police rules #17, 24, 25, 26, and 43. *Laws of the City of Portland, 1886*, xxiv-viii.
[49] Short, 8. The remains of the Palatine Hill works were still visible one mile south of the Sellwood Bridge as of April 2001.
[50] These waterworks were owned by the Portland Water Company. The Water Committee paid the company $464,551, a little over half of what the owners insisted the works had cost. MacColl, *Shaping*, 65.
[51] *Old Portland Today*, circa May 1975, a monthly newspaper published in Old Town.
[52] Long, 125.
[53] Purdy, 42.
[54] Holbrook, 9.
[55] Gaston, v 1, 344-45.
[56] Scott, *Oregon*, v 3, 205-8.
[57] *Oreg.*, March 29, 1881, and *Hatch v Willamette Iron Bridge Company*, 6 Fed. Rep. 780, as quoted in Carey, *History of Oregon*, 780; Lockley, *Columbia*, v 1, 536.
[58] Scott, *Oregon*, v 3, p 205-8; Maddux, 179.
[59] Scott, *Oregon*, v 1, 125.
[60] Ibid., v 4, 359.
[61] *Oreg.*, Jan 2, 1888, p 1, c 1 and p 18, c 1.
[62] Maddux, 192; Draft, *Portland Parks and Recreation, A Chronological History*, Dec 1998, p 1.
[63] Scott, *Oregon*, v 5, 130.
[64] Newspaper article headlined, "Ex-Mayor Rowe, Commenting on Cold Snap, Recalls the Siege of 1887." *Oreg.*, Jan 14, 1911.
[65] Ord #5540, approved April 4, 1888. Some council minutes were typed up retroactively, starting with the minutes of Oct 6, 1870. *Proc. C. C.*, v 9.
[66] The first mayor to die in office was Thomas J. Holmes, who collapsed the day following his election as mayor in 1867. Mayor Gates is buried at River View Cemetery.
[67] Conversation by this author with Sylvia Gates, wife of Stuart Gates, a grandson of John Gates, on April 5, 2000.
[68] MacColl, *Shaping*, 62.
[69] C. M. Forbes owned a "stupendous mansion of circa 1887, located at the northwest corner of Vista Avenue and Park Place" which was of "quintessential Eastlake design." Hawkins, *Classic Houses*, 177-78. See also Maddux, 214.
[70] Maddux, 114-15.
[71] Scott, *Portland*, 535.
[72] DeLashmutt had helped organize that bank's predecessor organization in 1882, along with *Oreg.* editor Harvey Scott, Judge Erasmus Shattuck, and Governor William W. Thayer. Scott, *Portland*, 534; MacColl, *Shaping*, 91; MacColl, *Merchants*, 262; *1890 P.C. Dir.*, 60.
[73] MacColl, *Shaping*, 91; Scott, *Portland*, 534.
[74] MacColl, *Merchants*, 308; MacColl, *Shaping*, 101-6.
[75] Van DeLashmutt "made one of his characteristic humorous speeches." *OPAT*, 21st annual reunion, 1893, p 10.
[76] There was nothing as beautiful as the Skidmore Fountain westward from Chicago, according to *Century Magazine*, 1889, as quoted in the *Oreg.*, Sept 21, 1987, B7. Also see Snyder, *Skidmore*, 143-44.
[77] Mayor DeLashmutt was attending a state fair executive committee meeting. Snyder, *Skidmore*, 14, 124, 130.
[78] Ibid., 137. According to his son, it was lawyer and poet C. E. S. Wood who composed the famous words on the Skidmore Fountain. Wood, Erskine, 55.
[79] Snyder, *Skidmore*, 13-15; 123-24.
[80] *Oreg.*, Feb 9, 1999; Snyder, *Skidmore*, 112-21, 131.
[81] *Oreg.*, Oct 6, 1921, p 13, c 1.
[82] Scott, *Portland*, 533; Corning, 71.
[83] *Oreg.*, Oct 6, 1921, p 10, 13; MacColl, *Merchants*, 262; Scott, *Portland*, 535; Corning, 133; Hawthorne, v 1, 432;
[84] Maddux, 179.
[85] The court said that when a sewer was necessary, the benefits to property it was intended to accommodate would be assumed to exceed the expense of the sewer's construction. *Paulson v City of Portland.*
[86] *Paulson v City of Portland*, Oregon Supreme Court, July, 1888, 450-64; City Ord #5088 and 6162.
[87] Ord #5926, Sept 23, 1889.
[88] The bill was vetoed in February 1899. Clark, *Pharisee*, Feb 23, 1889, v 2, 550-51, 571; Short, 20.
[89] Pennoyer's real reason for vetoing the bill was probably that members of the Republican-dominated Water Committee would corner any profits to be made from tax-free interest on this project. Short, 20-21.
[90] MacColl, *Shaping*, 67-68; Short, 19.
[91] *1889 Oregon Special Laws*, filed Feb 25, 1889, 448-49.
[92] Ibid., 435-52.
[93] The city purchased the block bounded by S.W. Fourth and Fifth, Madison and Jefferson streets, previously occupied by St. Helens Hall for girls, for one hundred thousand dollars. MacColl, *Shaping*, 146; *OJ*, Oct 11, 1925, 4; *Proc. C. C.*, June 18, 1890, v 11, p 88-89.
[94] *Proc. C. C.*, June 19, 1890, v 11, p 90-91; Reports of special committee dated March 5, 1890, and June 1890; various official city letterheads, Administration folder, 1890 Council Documents file.
[95] Scott, *Portland*, 209-12.
[96] The entire Portland harbor would be listed as a federal Superfund site in 2000. The cost of correcting Portland's combined sewer overflow problem was by then projected at around one billion dollars. *Oreg.*, Mar 20, 2000, A1 & 4; Dec 17, A1, 14-15; Dec 21, 2000, C8; "Managing the Costs of Environmental Responsibility, Fact Sheet 4," www.enviro.ci.portland.or.us/CPR.htm - [accessed Aug 20, 2000].

[97] Scott, *Portland,* 207.
[98] *Oreg.,* June 19, 1889, p 6, c 1.
[99] MacColl, *Shaping,* 182.
[100] Scott, *Portland,* 187. However, author Howard Corning casts doubt on Scott's statement about leprosy. "At some date near the turn of the century," Corning says, "a single Chinese, Wong Luey, was isolated on a portion of the Multnomah County Poor Farm, near Portland, where he was doubtfully diagnosed as suffering with leprosy. ... In 1920, a second 'leper,' Louis Poy, was transferred from care of the Multnomah County Hospital, to Federal medical attention, after being picked up on Portland streets in 1919." Corning, 53.
[101] Harvey Scott edited the *History of Portland Oregon,* published in 1890 by D. Mason & Co. of Syracuse, New York, printed and bound in Portland. Scott acknowledges the contributions of O. F. Vedder, H. S. Lyman, and C. H. Carey. Scott did some original writing himself, he says, and revised others' work with "as much diligence as possible." Scott, *Portland,* 5-6. Harvey Scott's thick one-volume Portland history should not be confused with the six-volume compilation of his writings edited by his son, Leslie Scott, and published in 1924, titled *History of The Oregon Country.*
[102] Lacy, 60-66; Scott, *Portland,* 116-17.
[103] These figures represent revised 1890 census figures. MacColl, *Merchants,* 283. See also Labbe, 79; Snyder, *Portland Names,* 17-18.
[104] Maddux, 130; MacColl, *Merchants,* 283.
[105] Ladd's holdings were through Ladd and Tilton Bank. "He created his vast holding out of forfeited mortgages and defaulted loans. ... [H]is larger tracts were used for farming, grazing prize dairy herds, and raising pure-bred cattle, horses, sheep, and hogs. The shrewd and patient banker had correctly assumed that the acreage would eventually be worth millions." MacColl, *Merchants,* 283.
[106] *Oreg.,* May 2, 1891, p 12, c 1.
[107] The expositions of 1889, 1890, and 1891 were profitable, but those of 1892 and 1893 ran deficits. The mortgage was foreclosed in 1894 and the building burned down July 14, 1910. Scott, *Oregon,* v 3, 215. Also see Scott, *Portland,* 434-36.
[108] Elevators had been in public use nationally since 1857. Somerset Fry, 362.
[109] *OHQ,* Fall 1998, 306-11; Scott, *Oregon,* v 3, 211-13; O'Donnell and Vaughan, 38-39.
[110] "Consolidation carried by the following vote: Portland for, 7165; against, 954; East Portland for, 1823; against, 298; Albina for, 1138; against, 462; total for, 10,126; against, 1714." Scott, *Oregon,* v 3, p 213-14, as quoted from the June 2, 1891, *Oreg.* Albina Mayor McLauchlan opposed consolidation because he feared a decline in property values, including his own investments, and possibly because it would curb his ability to "wheel and deal." MacColl, *Shaping,* 140.
[111] *1891 Oregon Special Laws,* 791-95.
[112] The three existing independent citizen bodies were the three-member Board of Police Commissioners, the three-member Board of Fire Commissioners, and the fifteen-member Water Committee.
[113] MacColl, *Merchants,* 292-93.
[114] "Partners in Progress: Port of Portland Celebrates 100 Years, 1891-1991," 1-2, 6; MacColl, *Merchants,* 292.
[115] *Oreg.,* May 1, 1891, p 1.
[116] Maddux, 132-33.
[117] *Oreg.,* May 2, 1891, p 3, c 3.
[118] Ibid., May 6, 1891, p 1, c 2.
[119] Ibid., p 1, c 2.
[120] Ibid., p 3, c 4.
[121] Ibid., p 1, c 2, 3.

Chapter 15

[1] Total votes cast were 12,312; with Mason winning "nearly a 3,000 majority." *Oreg.,* June 16, 1891, p 1.
[2] Maddux, 132; MacColl, *Merchants,* 288; MacColl, *Shaping,* 143.
[3] The Committee of 100 supported candidates in various city campaigns over the years. A newspaper article three years later mentions Chairman Corbett and Vice-Chairman Tyler Woodward; with C. H. Woodard and Messrs. Goldsmith, Thompson, Teesdale, Teal, Myers, and Strong as members. *Oreg.,* April 21, 1894, p 12, c 1, 2.
[4] Hines, 590.
[5] Hawthorne, v 2, p 265-67; Hines, 589-91; *Republican League Register,* 239.
[6] Hawthorne, v 2, p 266.
[7] *1892 P.C. Dir.*; Snyder, *Portland Names,* 18; MacColl, *Merchants,* 283; Maddux, 132; *1891 Oregon Special Laws,* 796-853.
[8] Along with Edwin Russell and future mayor George Williams, William Page developed the Albina townsite. Although today's contemporary pronunciation is with a long "i," the Page family pronounced the name Albina as Al-BEAN-ah. MacColl, *Shaping,* 126-27; Gaston, 254-55; McArthur, 8. Page was a supreme court justice for six months in 1862. Leeson, 22-23. He was a founder of the Arlington Club, and represented Nancy Lownsdale's heirs in their successful park blocks suit. *Arlington Club,* 47-48.
[9] MacColl, *Shaping,* 124-40; Historical summary of East Portland, *Potential Historic Conservation Districts,* Portland Bureau of Planning, 1978, 58.
[10] *1891 Oregon Special Laws,* p 796-853, passed by the legislature Feb 19, 1891; approved by voters June 1, 1891.
[11] Ibid.
[12] MacColl, *Merchants,* 284-89; MacColl, *Shaping,* 139-44, 149.
[13] A chapter titled "East Portland" concludes, "Consolidation in 1891 in all likelihood saved the economic welfare of East Portland." *Potential Historic Conservation Districts,* Portland Bureau of Planning, 1978, 57-58.
[14] Sec. 182-197, 1891 City charter; MacColl, *Shaping,* 146; *OJ,* Oct 11, 1925, 4. Other debt limits in the consolidation charter included a basic debt limit of $150,000 plus $2,500,000 for the city water supply, $250,000 to purchase and improve city parks, and $500,000 for free bridges across the Willamette River — a grand total of $4.1 million.
[15] *Oreg.,* July 7, 1891, p 1.
[16] The Bickel Building lease began Oct 15, 1891. Ord #7186, Nov 27, 1891, *Ordinance Journal,* v 10, p 659. Building owner Fred Bickel was a partner of Frank

Dekum in Dekum & Bickel, "Portland's first confectionery business which also included a restaurant and sales of retail and wholesale fruit." Dekum Building nomination form for National Register of Historic Places, Item 3, p 3. The Bickel Building was still in use as of April 2001, with the second-floor quarters formerly leased by the city occupied by several offices. At the time council meetings were held there, upstairs entrances were probably available from Ash, Ankeny, and Second. Dan & Louis' Oyster Bar, a family restaurant facing on Ankeny Street, has been located on the ground floor since 1907. Phone call by the author on April 7, 2000, to Tucker Wachsmuth, grandson of restaurant's co-founder Louis Wachsmuth.

[17] *Proc. C. C.*, July 15, 1891. The council still meets on the same day at the same time more than one hundred ten years later.

[18] *Proc. C. C.*, July 9 and 15, 1891, v 11; Letter to Council from Mayor Mason dated July 22, 1891, Administration folder, 1891 Council Documents file.

[19] Message from Mayor Mason to council dated Nov 11, 1891, as quoted in MacColl, *Shaping*, 193.

[20] Letter from Joseph Gaston to President Benjamin Harrison dated Dec 8, 1891, as quoted in ibid., 193-94.

[21] *Evening Telegram*, Nov 3, 1891, as quoted in Snyder, *Portland Names*, 54.

[22] Snyder, *Portland Names*, 53-55.

[23] Ibid., 55, 68.

[24] Ibid., 192.

[25] *Oreg.*, April 12, 1998, Sec F; MacColl, *Shaping*, 146; *OHQ*, Fall 1998, 306.

[26] Report of Council Committee on Judiciary and Elections, April 27, 1892. Administration folder, Council documents file, 1892.

[27] The council meeting protesting the tearing down of the Hefty city hall occurred April 6, 1892. City attorney William Muir then advised, "It is useless to appeal because the injury, if any, will be completed before the cause can be heard before the Supreme Court." Letter from Muir to the mayor and council dated May 4, 1892. Administration folder, Council documents file, 1892.

[28] Letter to Common Council from Mayor Mason dated April 20, 1892. Administration folder, Council documents file, 1892.

[29] MacColl, *Shaping*, 154, 275.

[30] By 1903, the free Albina ferry was still operating, but under the auspices of Multnomah County. Report of Appraisement Committee, Oct 26, 1903. Administration folder, 1903 Council Documents file.

[31] *Oreg.*, Jan 1, 1895, p 40, c 1. The council approved the Burnside Bridge contract in Oct 1892, and the Albina ferry purchase in April 1893. The price paid for the original Morrison Bridge in 1895 was $150,000. MacColl, *Shaping*, 151-55; Maddux, 178-81.

[32] The congressional act was passed in March 1891. Short, 26-27.

[33] Testimony before the Judicial Committee of Council, Aug 1 and 4, 1892. Administration folder, 1892 Council Documents file.

[34] Simon did not seek his state senate seat for the 1892-94 term. Gaston, v 3, 199; MacColl, *Merchants*, 320.

[35] R. L. Polk and Co.'s *1893 P.C. Dir.*, 111.

[36] Sellwood, incorporated in 1887, was named for Episcopal clergyman John Sellwood. The legislature increased the size of Multnomah County slightly, by moving the border a bit south and east in order that Portland's city limits could encompass all of Sellwood. Snyder, *Portland Names*, 18; MacColl, *Shaping*, 122-23; *History of Portland*, WPA Writers' Project, 1941, p 11-12.

[37] The sixteen-member council had lasted only two years, from July 1891 through June 1893.

[38] Portland charter, Sec 75 and 168, *1893 Oregon Special Laws*, p 810-70.

[39] The mayor's salary of five thousand dollars (Sec 39) was generous in comparison with other salaries specified by the 1893 charter: three thousand dollars each for the city attorney (Sec 56), police chief (Sec 77), and city treasurer (Sec 47); as well as twenty-four hundred dollars each for the chief engineer of the fire department (Sec 174) and police judge (Sec 69.)

[40] Portland charter, Sec 167-1/2, *1893 Oregon Special Laws*, p 810-70.

[41] MacColl, *Merchants*, 307.

[42] Gaston, v 1, 515; MacColl, *Shaping*, 100-108, 195; MacColl, *Merchants*, 308-9.

[43] Piggott's Castle, 2591 S.W. Buckingham Terrace, commands a magnificent view of downtown Portland and Washington State. Builder Charles Piggott owned Consolidated Brick Company and other enterprises. Norman, 57.

[44] MacColl, *Shaping*, 101-4.

[45] Ibid., 195-96.

[46] Ord #8541, approved Oct 5, 1893; #8491, approved Sept 9, 1893; #8561, approved Oct 21, 1893.

[47] MacColl, *Merchants*, 305-6; Clark, *Pharisee*, v 2, 628.

[48] Ladd told an oft-repeated story regarding a woman who visited his private bank office to demand a $25,000 unsecured loan. She threatened to ruffle her hair and scream that he was trying to ravish her if he didn't authorize the requested money. "Ladd leaned back in his chair and began to laugh. 'Madam,' he said, 'I want to thank you for the first merry moment I have had in this rather dull day. If you can get anybody in this whole town to believe that I have had a hard-on any time in the last 20 years, I'll give you fifty thousand dollars.'" Wood, Erskine, 47-8.

[49] Petition dated Dec 6, 1893, and Report of Special Committee adopted by council Dec 20, 1893. Administration folder, 1893 Council Documents file.

[50] Letters from the Committee of 100 dated Dec 8, 1893; Jan 24, 1894; May 3, 1894; June 9, 1894. Administration folders, 1893 and 1894 Council Documents files.

[51] Ord #6105 approved Feb 14, 1890, set the mayor's salary at $1,500 and council members at $1,000.

[52] Report filed Dec 19, 1893. Administration folder, 1893 Council Documents file.

[53] *1893 Oregon Special Laws*, 826-50; Ord #8653 passed Jan 4, 1894.

[54] Labbe, 101. The *Inez* tragedy occurred November 1, 1893. Maddux, 100-101.

[55] Maddux, 134-37; MacColl, *Shaping*, 168-73; *Oreg.*, June 10, 1894, p 3, c 2.

[56] MacColl, *Shaping*, 169; MacColl, *Merchants*, 319; Maddux, 137. MacColl says the Willamette River crested at 33.5 feet, but Maddux and the USGS sources listed in note 63 cite 33 feet.

[57] *Oreg.*, June 9, 1894, p 8, c 2-4.
[58] Ibid., c 3.
[59] *Albina Weekly Courier*, as quoted in MacColl, *Shaping*, 172.
[60] Maddux, 94.
[61] "A line on the inner side of the most northern arch of the Haseltine Building (at 133 S.W. Second Avenue) marks the level of the flood; it is 12 feet above the street level east of the Skidmore Fountain. The current was small and caused unusually little damage." Taylor and Hatton, 97.
[62] Scott, *Oregon*, v 5, 306.
[63] "Floods of December 1964 and January 1965 in the Far Western States, Part 2: Streamflow and Sediment Data" and "Water Resources Data for Oregon, 1992" published by the U. S. Geological Survey, and "The Pacific Northwest Floods of February 6-11, 1996" published by the American Institute of Hydrology, all as cited by USGS Portland Office Information Specialist Suzanne Jo Miller to the author by letters dated Nov 29 and 30, 2000; Taylor & Hatton, 84, 86, 91, 97, 103.
[64] However, former mayor W. S. Ladd served as the first president of the Portland Board of Trade, predecessor organization to the Chamber of Commerce. MacColl, *Shaping*, 492.
[65] Dean Collins, in Aikman, 178.
[66] George P. Frank was no relation to Sigmund Frank of the Meier & Frank store. MacColl, *Shaping*, 194.
[67] MacColl, *Merchants*, 323.
[68] Inman was joint owner of the huge Inman-Poulson lumberyard which covered 37 1/2 acres along the east riverfront of the Willamette, a business which would become the largest lumber operation in Oregon by the turn of the century. Maddux, 135-36; MacColl, *Shaping*, 123. The lumberyard was located at the foot of S.E. Clinton Street, and had a wharf big enough for two ocean-going vessels. In 1891, Inman's partner, John Poulsen, built as his residence the historic castle with round tower and several spires still standing at the east end of the Ross Island bridge. Snyder, *Potpourri*, 151-57.
[69] Final election returns, which were unavailable until four days after the election because of the flood, were: Frank, 4,578; Inman, 4,095; independent republican W. B. Honeyman, 398; independent J. M. Caywood, 95. *Oreg.*, June 9, 1894, p 5, c 1.
[70] George Frank's term on the police board expired July 1891. *Proc. C. C.*, July 9, 1891. An 1889 charter amendment provided for voters to elect future police commissioners, but allowed commissioners to serve out their terms.
[71] *Oreg.*, June 16, 1891, p 1.
[72] MacColl, *Shaping*, 194.
[73] *Republican League Register*, 210; Lockley, *Columbia*, v 1, 457-58; Short, 135.
[74] *Oreg.*, Jan 1, 1895.
[75] MacColl, *Merchants*, 323.
[76] Ord #8881, approved July 23, 1894.
[77] Ord #8894, approved Aug 2, 1894, targeted steamboats operating between the north end of Ross Island and the south end of Swan Island.
[78] Vagrants were punishable by fines of up to $100 or imprisonment of five to ninety days. Ord #9036, approved Nov 22, 1894.
[79] Dozens of prostitutes were arrested under the vagrancy ordinance throughout the winter and early spring, but "most of them were immediately released." MacColl, *Shaping*, 199.
[80] Ord #9088, approved Jan 3, 1895.
[81] Potential trial evidence was excluded from property sales. Ord #9280, approved May 18, 1895
[82] Ord #9117, approved March 2, 1895.
[83] Ord #9186, approved March 21, 1895.
[84] Ibid.
[85] Ord #9329, approved June 20, 1895
[86] *Oreg.*, Jan 1, 1895.
[87] Hartwell, 20; Short, 33.
[88] Short, 35-36.
[89] *1895 Oregon Special Laws*, 522.
[90] *Oreg.*, Jan 1, 1895.
[91] Short, 32, 36.
[92] The bonded debt carried in the city's regular budget included $300,000 from the former City of East Portland; $150,000 from the former City of Albina; $56,500 of general city debt; and $675,000 worth of outstanding city hall bonds. The annual interest cost of these obligations was $64,000. Mayor Frank's annual message to council. *Proc. C. C.*, January 2, 1895.
[93] Patrolmen's salaries were cut from eighty to seventy-five dollars a month and detectives' salaries from one hundred dollars to ninety. In other police board business, Patrolman E. S. Nelson was suspended from duty for thirty days without pay for using "an opprobrious epithet" to a Vancouver streetcar conductor while riding on that line. *Oreg.*, Jan 1, 1895, p 40, c 3.
[94] MacColl, *Shaping*, 199-200; Maddux, 141.
[95] Edwards, G. Thomas, 172; MacColl, *Shaping*, 186-87.
[96] *Oreg.*, March 8, 1896, p 10, c 1.
[97] Ibid., c 2.
[98] *Oreg.*, Feb 14, 1896, p 8, c 1-3.
[99] MacColl, *Shaping*, 223; *Oreg.*, circa Nov 8, 1887; Gaston v 1, 214; Scott, *Oregon*, v 5, 131. An *Oreg.* article of March 28, 1887, p 4, c 4, details the steady disappearance of Couch Lake, once a "glorious skating field," before it was gradually filled in with earth dug from street excavations, etc.
[100] Edwards, G. Thomas, 173.
[101] The quote was attributed to realtor C. K. Henry. MacColl, *Shaping*, 187.
[102] Solis-Cohen was described as "the regular Republican nominee" in an *Oreg.* article dated May 31, 1902, p 13, c 2, and as the "protégé of Joe Simon" and "close friend of Joe Simon" in MacColl, *Shaping*, 194, 201, 213, 237, 253. However, Steven Lowenstein maintained otherwise in his 1987 *The Jews of Oregon*, p 63. "David Solis-Cohen and Joseph Teal, Jr., two Jewish Republican lawyers identified with liberal reform, strongly opposed the 'Simon machine,'" Lowenstein says. This conclusion by Lowenstein is puzzling, because the only other Republican umbrella under which Cohen could have been a major mayoral candidate or appointed twice to the board of police commissioners would have been as a Mitchell Republican—an unlikely possibility for a romantic idealist such as Lowenstein describes Solis-Cohen.
[103] Both Cohen and Beebe would later serve on the police board. MacColl, *Shaping*, 201, 213, 302-4, 401.
[104] *Oreg.*, May 31, 1902, p 13, c 2.

Chapter 16

[1] *Oreg.*, May 31, 1902, p 13, c 3.
[2] Geer, 332-33.
[3] A facsimile of Pennoyer's telegraphed reply, captioned "Pennoyer's Famous 'Mind-Your-Own-Business' Message," was printed in the *Oreg.* as part of Pennoyer's obituary on May 31, 1902, p 13. The text of both the original Washington D. C. letter and its reply are quoted in full in Turnbull, *Governors*, 49-50.
[4] At least two sources (Geer, 386 and Hays, 67) say Pennoyer's message related to Coxey's Army crusade. However, original documentation makes it clear that the Chinese exclusion act was Pennoyer's target. "[T)]hough audacious in the extreme," says Hays, Pennoyer's letter "was exactly like him.
[5] *Oreg.*, May 19, 1893, p 1; Scott, *Oregon*, v 1, p 279; MacColl, *Merchants*, 290.
[6] *Pennoyer v Neff* became a landmark case "in determining legal jurisdiction over citizens in differing states. ... The court ruled that ... Neff's property could be used only to satisfy the amount of the judgment, not more." Leeson, 47-48.
[7] Clark, *Pharisee*, v 2, 510. It was Deady who had bestowed upon Pennoyer the nickname "Silpester Annoyer." Clark, *Pharisee*, v 2, 550-51.
[8] Snyder, *We Claimed*, 198-99; Turnbull, *Governors*, 48-49; Corning, 194-95; Lockley, *Columbia*, v 1, 458; *Oreg.*, May 31, 1902, 13.
[9] Moynihan, 93.
[10] Turnbull, *Governors*, 49.
[11] *Oreg.*, May 19, 1890, as quoted in Scott, *Oregon*, v 5, 73-77.
[12] "This Was Portland: River View Cemetery," prepared by River View cemetery, circa 1998, p 5. Ladd's grave is in Sec 3, near the Failing and Corbett plots, close to the River View administration building and chapel.
[13] *Oreg.*, Nov 21, 1993, D3; *Oreg.* April 12, 1998, Sec F.
[14] *Oreg.*, May 31, 1902, p 13, c 2.
[15] *Ordinance Journal*, v 15, Ord #10120 through #10886.
[16] "Summary of Significant Dates and Events," prepared by the Portland Police Historical Society, circa 1990; MacColl, *Shaping*, 210-11.
[17] Corning, 6; Maddux, 143; MacColl, *Shaping*, 215-17; Bowman, 246-47.
[18] "Portland of Years Past," 1898 Section, *Oreg.*, April 23, 1998.
[19] Ibid., April 30, 1998.
[20] Scott, *Oregon*, v 3, 106; Corning, 24, 229; MacColl, *Shaping*, 303.
[21] Governor's Park is located at S.W. Thirteenth and Davenport. Snyder, *Portland Names*, 246; *Oreg.*, May 31, 1902, 13. E. Kimbark MacColl describes it as "a narrow six acre overgrown tract that runs up the hill from S.W. Broadway Drive." MacColl, *Shaping*, 211.
[22] MacColl, *Shaping*, 234-35; Maddux, 149-51.
[23] Edwards, G. Thomas, 176.
[24] "Portland of Years Past," 1900 Section, *Oreg.*, June 22, 2000, E3.
[25] Maddux, 149.
[26] The Portland-Vancouver route was also a popular streetcar ride. At least ten years before, a group of businessmen had built a narrow-gage track to connect the Stark Street ferry, via Albina, with a ferry landing on the Columbia. MacColl, *Shaping*, 120. Another popular bicycle path was built beside the road north from Portland to St. Johns. Pratt, 26.
[27] Pennoyer died in 1902. *Proc. C. C.*, v 20, p 445-46. His body was originally interred at Lone Fir Cemetery, but was later moved to River View. "This Was Portland: River View Cemetery," p 4.
[28] *OJ*, May 2, 1909, as quoted in MacColl, *Shaping*, 60.
[29] MacColl, *Shaping*, 212-13.
[30] Mason was the last Portland mayor to serve non-consecutive terms. Three other mayors had previously done so: William S. Ladd, Henry Failing, and James A. Chapman.
[31] All three new police commissioners appointed by Mason were Simon supporters: James E. Hunt; David Solis-Cohen, who had run against Pennoyer for mayor and had served a previous police commissioner term during Mason's first term; and George Bates, a well-to-do businessman who would later be a nominee to complete Mayor Mason's term. MacColl, *Shaping*, 213.
[32] Chief McLaughlin was the former mayor of Albina. He had served one year as a police commissioner under Mayor Frank.
[33] The wives of some saloon keepers in the suburbs handled bartending duties occasionally, and these men said the crackdown on women bartenders would force them to hire help or close down at times. "Portland of Years Past," 1898 Section, *Oreg.*, Aug 20, 1998.
[34] MacColl, *Shaping*, 213.
[35] Ibid., 214, 217.
[36] This new charter was filed with the Secretary of State's office on Oct 17, 1898, nine days after Simon was elected to the U.S. Senate. Gaston, v 3, 199.
[37] *1898 Oregon Special Laws*, 101-87; *Oreg.*, March 8, 1896, p 10, c 1.
[38] Mason's annual mayor's message, Administrative folder, 1899 Council documents file; MacColl, *Shaping*, 242.
[39] The mayor could also remove the municipal judge for cause, if recommended by the police board. The board and mayor were to decide together what constituted such cause and the mayor would appoint a replacement.
[40] The salary provisions were effective July 1, 1900. Council size remained at eleven—one representative from each of eleven specified wards. All terms of office remained at two years, with incumbents to serve until the end of their terms (except that the city surveyor's position expired immediately, to be replaced by a city engineer). The council was given authority to prevent and suppress bawdy houses or places where fornication was practiced; to prevent and suppress opium smoking and places kept therefor; to prohibit the sale of tobacco to minors; to protect the public from injury from runaways by punishing persons who left horses or carriages in the streets without fastenings; and to require prisoners to work on city projects during their confinement. *1898 Oregon Special Laws*, 101-87.
[41] Henry Failing's gravestone says: "He was a just man and loved mercy." The Failing family plot is located in Section 3, near the administrative building and chapel. The body of Henry's father, Josiah Failing, who died in 1877, was moved to River View after it opened.
[42] A survey form completed by the WPA Writers' Program says Henry Failing's will, signed in 1879, left a "large amount of property" to be used for a cemetery,

and that the cemetery "was later developed and is known as the Riverview Cemetery." *History of Portland, Oregon*, 1941.
[43] MacColl, *Shaping*, 242-43.
[44] MacKay was active politically as a Simon Republican. Ibid., 243.
[45] Letter from D. W. Hoelbing to Board of Public Works dated July 31, 1900. Administration folder, 1900 Council Documents file.
[46] Annual message from Mayor Mason to council, Administrative folder, 1899 Council Documents file.
[47] Mayor Mason died at his home following a bout with liver complications and grippe. Maddux, 142; MacColl, *Shaping*, 214-15.
[48] Previous mayors who died during their term of office were Thomas J. Holmes (1867) and John Gates (1888).
[49] Letter to the council dated April 1, 1899, from E. Scott, secretary of the Chamber of Commerce of San Francisco. Administration folder, Council Documents file, 1899.
[50] *Oreg.*, April 2, 1899, as quoted in Scott, *Oregon*, v 5, 275.
[51] Ord #11187, April , 1899. Documentation papers giving details of funeral expenses was found in Administration folder, Council Documents file, 1899.
[52] The impressive William Mason house was located on N.W. Irving between Twentieth and Twenty-first avenues. Hawkins, *Classic Houses*, 80.
[53] George Bates was a member of both the police board and Water Committee. He and his partner Lee Hoffman built the first Bull Run pipeline for $467,000. Supporting Bates as mayor were councilmen George J. Cameron, Fred W. Hansen, J. C. Luckel, John A. Martin, and William Showers. MacColl, *Shaping*, 140-42, 214-15, 217.
[54] Other Jameson supporters were councilmen Henry A. Belding, N. D. Beutgen, and J. D. Meyer.
[55] *OHQ*, Summer 1979, footnote 158, p 156-57.
[56] Council meetings of May 2 and 9, 1899. *Proc. C. C.*, v 18, 406, 408.
[57] MacColl, *Shaping*, 215.
[58] Maddux, 144; Lockley, *Columbia*, v 1, 458.
[59] "The Opinion of a Prominent Business Man and Heavy Taxpayer on Mayor Storey's Candidacy," *Oreg.*, June 3, 1900, p 24, c 2-3; MacColl, *Shaping*, 215.
[60] *Proc. C. C.*, July 6, 1891.
[61] "Portland of Years Past," 1900 Section, *Oreg.*, Jan 13, 2000, E11.
[62] Wemme had placed his automobile order eleven months before delivery. Wemme says in Lockley's *Oregon Folks*, 117-19, that the automobile cost him six hundred dollars (the equivalent of approximately twelve thousand dollars today) plus twelve dollars shipping, which was his net cost after three refunds of one hundred forty-seven dollars each from the three different railroads that had shipped various parts of his automobile. The *Oreg.* reported Wemme's cost at a little over a thousand dollars, perhaps not aware of the refunds that he would ultimately receive.
[63] Maddux, 151; Corning, 260; MacColl, *Shaping*, 215-17.
[64] "Portland of Years Past," 1899 Section, *Oreg.*, Nov 4, 1999, E4.
[65] Wemme sold his car to a Spokane man two years later for more than he had paid. Lockley, *Columbia*, v 1, 677.
[66] Scott, *Oregon*, v 3, 207; "Portland of Years Past," 1900 Section, *Oreg.*, Feb 24, 2000, E3.
[67] Ord #9117, approved March 2, 1895.
[68] "Portland of Years Past," 1900 Section, *Oreg.*, Feb 3, 2000.
[69] Explorations of these tunnels were conducted by historian Mike Jones and others in the 1970s and again in 1991. Jones became convinced that the rumors and folk tales were true; that these tunnels had been used for shanghaiing purposes by crimps, and also as escape routes for Chinese gambling houses and opium dens. *Oreg.* columnist Phil Stanford wrote of these excavation expeditions in 1991, during which he and Jones and two companions found bolted and cemented tunnel openings in several Old Portland locations (Stanford's *Oreg.* columns of April 5, 12, 19, and 26 1991; *OHQ*, Fall, 1992, 275). Author E. Kimbark MacColl was informed in 1976 that underground telephone wires had been discovered between a 1898 Chinese tong named "The Bishop's House" and an old 1898 police headquarters building site. MacColl, *Shaping*, 213.
[70] *OHQ*, Fall 1992, 263, 274-75; Phil Stanford column, *Oreg.*, April 5, 12, 19, and 26, 1991; Corning, 220; Dean Collins, in Aikman, 175-76; Holbrook (Booth), 182-90.
[71] Phil Stanford column, *Oreg.*, April 5, 1991.
[72] "According to one … tale, Kelly earned his nickname "Bunco" in 1885, when he stole a six-and-a-half-foot wooden Indian from the front of Wildman's Cigar Store …, wrapped it in a tarpaulin, and sold it as a drunk seaman to a ship for fifty dollars." *OHQ*, Fall, 1992, 275. Stewart Holbrook added this footnote to the story: "'I got your man,' [Kelly said to the skipper] with great satisfaction. 'He's pretty drunk, but he's a big son-of-a-bitch, and he'll make you a good man.' … Two days later, the Finn salmon fishermen of Astoria, a hundred-odd miles down the Columbia from Portland, were astonished to drag in their nets and find a cedar Indian amid the struggling fish." Booth, 183-84. Also see Bunco Kelly yarn in Worchester, 9, based on a radio series narrated by Nelson Olmsted.
[73] Holbrook (Booth), 185-89; *OHQ* Fall, 1992, 275.
[74] Holbrook (Booth), 185-89.
[75] *OHQ*, Fall 1992, 264-65.
[76] Ibid., 265-66.
[77] Clark, *Pharisee*, v 2, 609, footnotes.
[78] *OHQ*, Fall 1992, 280-81.
[79] Hartwell, 19-20.
[80] Moynihan, 207.
[81] *OHQ*, Summer 1997, 139.
[82] Monihan, 208; *OHQ*, Summer, 1997, 141.
[83] *OHQ*, June 1913, 191.
[84] *Oreg.*, June 4, 1900, p 1; June 5, 1900, p 1.
[85] Ibid., p 1; Lockley, *Columbia*, v 1, 473-74.
[86] *Oreg.*, June 7, 1900, p 7, c 3.
[87] *OJ*, Sept 2, 1912, p 2, c 1-2.
[88] Regarding the election of June 1904, MacColl quotes from a letter in the Jonathan Bourne Papers: "You cannot expect good faith in anything controlled by Matthews." Soon thereafter, MacColl says, "All the Matthews-Carey candidates won with a notable exception: honest Tom Ward defeated incumbent Sheriff William A. Storey." MacColl, *Shaping*, 280, 410.
[89] Ibid., 215.

Chapter 17

[1] Pratt, 1, 9-10, 27; MacColl, *Shaping*, 222, 226.
[2] Pratt, 28-29.
[3] "The first Italian colony in the city was set up on the edge of the Portland city dump, situated on the present site of Duniway Park, south of S.W. Sheridan and west of S.W. Fourth Street." Gould, Charles, "Portland Italians, 1880-1920," *OHQ*, v 77, 1976, p 242, 250. A 1920 photo in the same article shows a trolley car trestle spanning Marquam Gulch, "where city dump was located."
[4] Pratt, 10.
[5] Rosenkranz, 21; Peacock, 106-7; *OHQ*, Summer, 1985, 125.
[6] The city's next mayor, George Williams, also born in New York, was the eleventh and last mayor to claim such heritage.
[7] *Portrait and Biographical Record*, 59-60; Gaston, v 2, 314-16; MacColl, *Shaping*, 141, 176, 239; Short, 135.
[8] In addition to statistics given in Mayor Rowe's 1902 message to council, two biographers of his time credit Rowe with economical oversight over city expenses. *Portrait and Biographical Record*, 59-60; Gaston, v 2, 314-16. Rowe's obituary says his "policy of economy was one of the strong features of his administration." *Oreg.*, Mar 21, 1914.
[9] MacColl, *Shaping*, 238.
[10] Mayor's message to council, July 5, 1900, Administration file, 1900 Council Documents file.
[11] "An active movement for … creation and maintenance of a sufficient park system was set under way by well-known citizens (in 1898) … who realized that the first essential was to take control of the parks out of the hands of politicians." "Portland of Years Past," 1900 Section, *Oreg.*, April 27, 2000, E5.
[12] Draft *Portland Parks and Recreation, A Chronological History*, Dec 1998, 1900 section. The parks act that made the Portland vote possible applied to all cities over three thousand in population and specified a process for acquiring land for parks when agreement with the property owner could not be reached. *1899 Oregon General Laws*, 67-70.
[13] MacColl, *Shaping*, 268.
[14] Rufus Mallory served in Congress 1866-69 and as U.S. Attorney 1873-82. The first city engineer to serve on the commission was W. B. Chase. *History of the Bench & Bar*, 182-83; Gaston, v 1, 543, 573; Leeson, 57, 246.
[15] Gaston, v 1, 543; Minutes of Jan 3, 1901, Park Board Proceedings, No. 1, p 19, C.P. Arch..
[16] Snyder, *Potpourri*, 11.
[17] Undated letter and report form dated Apr 24, 1901. Administration folder, 1901 Council Documents file.
[18] "Portland of Years Past," *Oreg.*, Dec 7, 2000, Year 1900 Section, E7.
[19] Portland accounted for 88 percent of Multnomah County's population and nearly a fourth of Oregon's. Oregon's 1900 population was 413,536; Multnomah County's 103,167. Males totaled 59 percent of Portland's citizenry. Foreign-born women represented 28 percent of the female population. *1900 U.S. Census*, v 1, pt I, p 471 and 517; v 2, pt II, 141.
[20] Ward 9, the central eastside ward, had nearly twice the population of any of the other three eastside wards (from 12,240 to as low as 6,099). *1900 U.S. Census*, v 1, pt I, p 637.
[21] Pratt, 9-10.
[22] *Oreg.*, April 12, 1998, Sec F; "Portland of Years Past," E3; Board of public works letter, May 15, 1899, Finances folder, 1899 Council Documents file. Also see Corning, 109; Scott, *Oregon*, v 3, 158.
[23] Letter from George H. Himes to A. L. Mills, chairman of the board of public works, dated July 14, 1900. The OHS was incorporated on December 17, 1898. Finances folder, 1900 Council Documents file.
[24] Abbott, *Extravaganza*, 14; MacColl, *Shaping*, 265.
[25] Letter from W. H. Pope, Multnomah County auditor, to A. L. Mills, president of the board of public works, July 14, 1900. Finances folder, 1900 Council Documents file.
[26] The free Portland Public Library was organized in 1891, with its reading room located near First and Burnside prior to 1900. (Anderson, 13-14) An April 1901 letter to the council from George H. Williams, president of the PPL, said the free library had "more than 2000 volumes upon its shelves," and that more than 1,600 books had been in circulation since the first of January. Administration folder, 1901 Council Documents file. C.P. Arch. PPL records have been retained and are housed in the board room of the Multnomah County Library administrative offices, according to *OHQ* Fall 2002, 331, 337.
[27] Original officers of the Library Association of Portland were William S. Ladd, William Strong, Bernard Goldsmith, William Caldwell, and Henry Failing. Judge Matthew Deady, Leland Wakefield, and many others were also instrumental in founding the LAP. Anderson, 6.
[28] Ibid., 13; *General Laws of Oregon, 1901*, 19-22, approved Feb 13, 1901.
[29] Anderson, 15.
[30] While some businesses were still recovering from the depression, the *Financial Redbook of America*, as quoted in the *Oreg.*, Oct 14, 1903 (cited in MacColl, *Shaping*, App F, p 485) listed fifty-one Portland individuals and estates worth more than three hundred thousand dollars, including G. W. Bates, Jonathan Bourne, Jr., Helen Ladd Corbett, Sigmund Frank, William M. Ladd, A. L. Mills, P. F. Morey, Henry L. Pittock, H. W. Scott, Joseph Simon, Henry Weinhard, and the estates of H. W. Corbett, Frank Dekum, Henry Failing, William S. Ladd, and D. P. Thompson.
[31] General fund expenditures decreased from $173,000 in 1893 to $105,000 in 1901; fire department from $151,000 to $97,000; police department from $119,000 to $55,000; while interest increased from $48,000 to $122,000. Mayor Rowe's message to council, Jan 8, 1902. Administration folder, 1902 Council Documents file.
[32] Pratt, 24. See also MacColl, *Shaping*, 258.
[33] Unidentified newspaper account, Jan 17, 1902 (OHS Scrapbook #48, p 86), as quoted in MacColl, *Shaping*, 225.
[34] Unidentified 1902 newspaper account (OHS Scrapbook #48, p 111), as quoted in ibid., 225.
[35] *Oreg.*, Feb 23, 1936, p. 8, as quoted in ibid., 231.
[36] Ibid., 246.
[37] The vote was 62,024 for to 5,668 against. *1997-98 OBB*, 348-49.

[38] Eaton, Author's Preface, page v.
[39] More than thirty measures a year were on the ballot in 1910 and 1912, and more than twenty every election year in the 1990s. The June 1908 statewide ballot contained thirty-two measures; Nov 1910, thirty-two measures; Nov 1912, thirty-seven; Nov 1914, twenty-nine; Nov 1994, twenty-two; Nov 1996, twenty-three. *1999-2000 OBB*, 289-308.
[40] The members of the 1901-02 committee that drafted the 1903 charter were: mayor Henry S. Rowe, future mayor Harry Lane, city auditor Thomas C. Devlin, council president Rodney L. Glisan, council members Tyler Woodward, J. A. Strowbridge, and E. C. Bronaugh, future council president Louis Zimmerman, author and lawyer C. E. S. Wood, former legislator and police board member P. L. Willis, father of public docks Joseph N. Teal, *Oreg.* editor Harvey Scott, Dr. A. J. Giesy, lawyer and future state senate president Dan J. Malarkey, brewer Paul Wessinger, merchandisers Sigmund Frank and Solomon Hirsch, wealthy businessman Walter F. Burrell, eastside realtor William Killingsworth, lawyer Richard Montague, and William M. Ladd, John Montag, Ned E. Ayer, F. E. Beach, Harry Hogue, Fred V. Holman, T. D. Honeyman, J. T. Morgan, John F. O'Shea, Henry W. Fries, W. E. Robertson, Isam White, and Abbot Mills (chosen as committee chair by the other members). Proposed Charter of the City of Portland, 1902, Charter file, C.P. Arch.
[41] The vote was 10,810 for to 1,253 against. MacColl, *Shaping*, 250; *1903 Oregon Special Laws*, 3-172.
[42] Henry S. Rowe died in 1914 and was buried at Lone Fir Cemetery.
[43] The closest two in age were Sylvester Pennoyer at age sixty-five, and William Mason at age sixty-six.
[44] *Oreg.*, June 14, 1902, p 12, c 1, as quoted in Sidney Teiser, "Life of George H. Williams: Almost Chief Justice," *OHQ*, Dec 1946, 437.
[45] "Political History of Oregon, from 1853 to 1865," by George H. Williams, read before the legislature to commemorate Oregon's fortieth anniversary of statehood in 1899. Reprinted from *OHQ* in Carey, *Constitution*, as App C, p 502-3.
[46] George Williams was born in New York in 1823, and was elected as a judge in Iowa at age twenty-four. A friend of Abraham Lincoln from his Iowa days, Williams served as a pall-bearer at Lincoln's funeral. Scott, *Oregon*, v 5, 163-66; *1997-98 OBB*, 376, 387. See also Gaston, v 1, 552; Leeson, 12.
[47] Leeson, 35; MacColl, *Shaping*, 203. Williams's first wife, Kate Van Atwerp, died in July 1863. Williams married Mrs. Kate George in 1867 while he was serving in the U.S. Senate. Gaston, v 2, 13; Corning, 269.
[48] *Congressional Record*, April 25, 1874, p 3375, as quoted in a compiler's note, Scott, *Oregon*, v 5, 168.
[49] Harvey Scott vigorously defended Williams in his editorial pronouncements. *Oreg.*, July 16, 1907, as quoted in Scott, *Oregon*, v 5, 167-69.
[50] *Hamilton Fish Diary*, as cited in Nevins, Allan; *Hamilton Fish, The Inner History of the Grant Administration* (New York, 1936), as quoted in Sidney Teiser, "Life of George H. Williams: Almost Chief Justice," *OHQ*, Dec 1946, 428.
[51] President Grant had received "anonymous and scurrilous letters of a blackmailing nature written for the purpose of keeping Attorney General Williams in office. These letters had been traced to Mrs. Williams through peculiarities of phraseology and similarity of handwriting." Teiser, "Life of George H. Williams," 432.
[52] Ibid., 434-36.
[53] MacColl, *Shaping*, 245.
[54] Ibid., 253.
[55] Ibid., 235-36.
[56] The Lewis and Clark Exposition was held primarily to boost commerce and further trade with "the Orient." Little interest was shown in historical research about Meriwether Lewis, William Clark, or Sacajawea, but statues were erected of all three of these historic figures.
[57] Col. Dosch's words are taken from a lengthy interview with the *Evening Telegram* on April 22, 1899, as quoted in MacColl, *Shaping*, 265. An ironic reversal of perspective was to occur over the next seventy years, when the same natural resources and climate would prompt Governor Tom McCall to proclaim in 1971: "Come visit us again and again. This is a state of excitement. But for heaven's sake, don't come here to stay." Walth, 313-14.
[58] Abbott, *Extravaganza*, 13-14.
[59] "Indeed, a subcommittee of the Exposition Company voted for City Park in July, 1902, but reopened debate when the trolley companies refused to spend the $300,000 necessary to extend their lines." Abbott, *Extravaganza*, 20. Also see MacColl, *Shaping*, 269.
[60] Abbott, *Extravaganza*, 21.
[61] MacColl, *Shaping*, 254-56.
[62] The railroad companies accused of fraud were the City and Suburban Company and the old Portland Railway Company. *Oreg.*, June 20, 1906, and several *OJ* issues in Nov 1902, as related in MacColl, *Merchants*, 406.
[63] MacColl, *Merchants*, 345.
[64] Sec. 254 and 259 of the charter specify that "no member shall be ineligible as a member by reason of sex." The complete charter is contained in *1903 Oregon Special Laws*, 3-172.
[65] Proposed Charter of the City of Portland, 1902, C.P. Arch.. This pamphlet contains a list of charter board members, a summary of underlying principles followed in drafting the charter, and a comparison of the existing charter with the proposed charter.
[66] Sec 125, 1903 charter, *1903 Oregon Special Laws*, 62.
[67] Letter from Mayor Williams to auditor Thomas Devlin, dated January 23, 1903, notifying Devlin, in accordance with Section 160 of the charter, of his ten appointees to the executive board. Administration folder, 1903 Council Documents file. See also MacColl, *Shaping*, 257, 455.
[68] New civil service board appointees were A. A. Courteney, C. W. Hodson, and P. L. Willis. Mayor George Williams message to council dated January 6, 1904. Administration folder, 1903 Council Documents file.
[69] The new water board members were S. E. Josephi, C. H. Raffety, William M. Ladd, and L. A. Lewis. The latter two were also sons of original 1885 water committee members. Short, 41-47, 135—36.
[70] The Bull Run Trespass Act, Public Law #206, was signed by the president April 28, 1904. Ibid., 48-49.
[71] Article by Ray S. Baker, *Century* Magazine, March, 1903, 658-59, as quoted in MacColl, *Shaping*, 221-22.

[72] Abbott, *Extravaganza*, 21; MacColl, *Shaping*, 269-72.
[73] Letter from Louis Zimmerman to William D. Wheelwright, dated April 25, 1903. Administration folder, 1903 Council Documents file.
[74] Minutes of Sub-committee on Details, Visit of President Roosevelt, April 1903, Administration folder, 1903 Council Documents file.
[75] Pratt, front cover.
[76] Letter from Thomas Devlin to the executive board dated Aug 7, 1903. Administration folder, 1903 Council Documents file.
[77] Letter from Thomas Devlin to council dated July 9, 1903. Administration folder, 1903 Council Documents file.
[78] Scott, *Oregon*, v 4, 356; Scott, *Portland*, 525; Corning, 37.
[79] Report of Appraisement Committee, dated October 26, 1903. Administration folder, 1903 Council Documents file.
[80] The original Morrison Bridge was replaced soon after the report was made. Scott, *Oregon*, v 3, 206.
[81] Article by Burton J. Hendrick in *McClure's Magazine*, Sept, 1911, p 56, as quoted in Boag, Peter, "Sex & Politics in Progressive-Era Portland and Eugene: The 1912 Same-Sex Vice Scandal," *OHQ*, Summer 1999, 163; MacColl, *Shaping*, 228. See also *Oreg.*, March 18, 1904, p 10, c 1.
[82] *OJ*, May 23, 1905; MacColl, *Shaping*, 300.
[83] Report by a special council committee: H. R. Albee, chair, J. P. Sharkey, A. F. Flegel, C. E. Rumelin, and B. D. Sigler, dated April 6, 1904. Police chief at the time was Charles H. Hunt, who had served two years as chief under Mayor William Mason in 1892-94. Administration folder, 1904 Council Documents file.
[84] The group's first president was Walter J. Honeyman, a forty-six-year-old native of Scotland who had immigrated to Portland in 1881 at age twenty-four. He was to die June 3, 1904, less than a year after he spearheaded the founding of this activist organization. Gaston, v 3, 240-43.
[85] Ibid., v 1, 633-34.
[86] Ibid., v 1, 633-34.
[87] Lucy Ransom, "Country Schoolma'am," *OHQ*, Summer, 1985, 124, 130-32.
[88] Mayor George Williams message to council, Jan 6, 1904. Administration folder, 1904 Council Documents file.
[89] Letter to council from postmaster F. A. Bancroft dated April 2, 1904. Administration folder, 1904 Council Documents file.
[90] The St. Johns dry dock cost $377,342, according to MacColl, *Shaping*, 422. See also Purdy, 59.
[91] *Oreg.*, June 5, 1904, as quoted in MacColl, *Shaping*, 270-72.
[92] Mayor Katz announced in January 2001 that Ross Island, identified as part of the 1904 Olmstead Plan, would be gifted to the city by 2004. *Oreg.*, Jan 26, 2001, C1, 8; Houle, 9.
[93] Moynihan, 211-12.
[94] Dean Collins, in Aikman, 187-88.
[95] Ibid., 187-88.
[96] *Oreg.*, Jan 5, 1905, p 14, c 1 and Jan 8, 1905, p 1, c 3, as referenced by Teiser, "Life of George H. Williams," 439.
[97] Maddux, 157-58.
[98] MacColl, *Merchants*, 366.
[99] Pendleton newspaperman Charles S. "Sam" Jackson founded the *OJ* on July 23, 1902. Turnbull, *Newspapers*, 187-89; Maddux, 164; MacColl, *Shaping*, 251; Corning, 126.
[100] "Law Enforcement in Portland and Multnomah County," *Portland City Club Bulletin*, Feb 20, 1948, p 141.
[101] *OJ*, May 22, 1905, as quoted in MacColl, *Shaping*, 282-83; MacColl, *Merchants*, 366-67.
[102] The landfill ran nine blocks south from Sullivan's Gulch (where highway I-84 would one day run) to the Hawthorne Bridge, and four blocks eastward from the river with a dogleg to Ninth Street. MacColl, *Shaping*, 283-86; MacColl, *Merchants*, 367.
[103] A news story about the parade said: "The long line was made up of soldiers, cadets and blue-jackets ... and members of the official party in carriages. ... There were no stupid floats or long, tiresome arrays of civic organizations. These things had been wisely debarred as being out of harmony with the occasion." *Oreg.*, June 8, 1905, 1.
[104] Maddux, 165.
[105] The bonds for the new Morrison Bridge had been approved by the voters in June 1903. MacColl, *Shaping*, 286.
[106] O'Donnell and Vaughan, 49.
[107] Article by Jean Henninger, *Oreg.*, Aug 19, 1979, Northwest Mag, 10.
[108] This author visited the Forestry Building in 1962, and can personally attest to its grandeur.
[109] Culp, 11.
[110] *OJ*, May 23, 1905, p 1, c 1-2.
[111] MacColl, *Shaping*, 299, 301-2.
[112] Ibid., 299.
[113] "All the liquor associations of the city are officially back of the mayor," *OJ*, May 22, 1905, p 4, c 1; Sidney Teiser, "Life of George H. Williams: Almost Chief Justice," *OHQ*, Dec 1946, 439.
[114] Sidney Teiser, "Life of George H. Williams: Almost Chief Justice," *OHQ*, Dec 1946, 440.
[115] Mitchell was convicted on July 3, 1905, and died that December, while his conviction for receiving illegal fees was on appeal. Scott, *Oregon*, v 1, 347; Corning, 167-68; Leeson, 68-71. "Harry," he told his secretary, "you know they'd hadn't ought to prosecute me for that. All I ever got was some little checks." Lukas, 625. Mitchell had a scandalous personal life. He deserted his first wife (whom he had married because she was carrying his child at age fifteen), changed his name by reversing his middle and last names, fled Pennsylvania with a mistress and his three-year-old daughter, left that mistress, remarried without ever having been divorced, and subsequently took up a long-lasting relationship with his sister-in-law. These facts about his life "didn't surface in Oregon until Mitchell had established himself as a prominent lawyer and political powerhouse." Leeson, 30-31; Dodds, *Oregon*, 153.
[116] Lane defeated Williams by a plurality of 1,216 votes out of nearly fifteen thousand cast. *OJ*, June 6, 1905, 1.
[117] Scott, *Oregon*, v 5, 87-89. W. F. "Jack" Matthews had also served as city auditor in 1890-91, and on the police board in 1891-92. Lockley, *Columbia*, v 1, 471; MacColl, *Shaping*, 194.

[118] Dodds, Gordon, 154, 172.
[119] Hayes, 71.
[120] C. E. S. Wood's 1910 tribute to George Williams, "recalling his contributions in national, state, and Portland affairs" (Leeson, 74) is reprinted in *History of the Bench and Bar*, 286. Williams is buried at River View Cemetery.

Chapter 18

[1] MacColl, *Shaping*, 304.
[2] "Reminiscences of Oswald West," *OHQ*, September 1951, 152.
[3] The first was quirky Sylvester Pennoyer.
[4] Maddux, 159.
[5] MacColl, *Shaping*, 316; Corning, 142; Lockley, *Columbia*, v 1, 460-61.
[6] Lockley, *Columbia*, v 1, 460-61.
[7] DeMarco, 81; Lockley, *Columbia*, v 1, 461; MacColl, *Shaping*, 316.
[8] The state legislature chose Joseph Lane over George Williams for the U.S. Senate seat in 1861. "Reminiscences of Oswald West," 151; "Political History of Oregon, from 1853 to 1865," by George H. Williams, as reprinted from *OHQ* in Carey, *Constitution*, as App C (p 504-5.) Also see MacColl, *Shaping*, 302.
[9] www.ci.portland.or.us/auditor/Elecarchives2/GEN05.htm — [accessed May 31, 2000].
[10] *Oreg.*, June 8, 1905, 1.
[11] O'Donnell and Vaughan, 60-61.
[12] Ibid., 54.
[13] *OHQ*, Winter 1986, 407-8.
[14] Maddux, 189.
[15] Ibid., 189; Scott, *Oregon*, v 3, 113; MacColl, Shaping, 324.
[16] Maddux, 167; Davis and Weit, 32; Long, 134; Conversation with Mary Beth Coffee of Oaks Park by this author on July 17, 2000.
[17] Richard M. McCann, *Portland Chamber of Commerce Bulletin*, 4 March, 1906, p 8, as quoted in MacColl, *Shaping*, 309.
[18] Long, 27.
[19] Abbott, *Extravaganza*, 54.
[20] Ibid., 62, 65.
[21] Indians called the meteorite "Tamahnawus." The Willamette Meteorite was subsequently moved to the American Museum of Natural History in New York and placed in the Hayden Planetarium of that institution in 1936. Stone, 29, 38; Long, 27. In 2000, the museum and the Confederated Tribes of the Grand Ronde signed an agreement granting the tribe acccess to the meteorite for annual ceremonial and cultural purposes while maintaining its presence at the museum for scientific and educational purposes.
[22] Bowman, 260; *Oreg.*, Apr 19, 1906, 1.
[23] Five-year-old Dorothy McCullough lived with her family on Nob Hill, and remembered that her father, a military man, sent a mule-drawn wagon for her mother to save what household items she could and to evacuate their home. Pitzer, "Dorothy McCullough Lee," 8.
[24] Abbott, *Extravaganza*, 16. Abigail Scott Duniway persuaded the National American Woman Suffrage Association to hold its thirty-seventh annual convention in Portland in late June 1905. A group photo taken at the exposition grounds on June 30 shows suffrage leaders Susan B. Anthony, Anna Howard Shaw, Carrie Chapman Catt, and many others in attendance. Moynihan, 210; *OHQ*, Summer 1997, 138.
[25] Former Expo buildings which survive in private or semi private use are located in St. Johns, West Linn, and Aurora. *Oreg.*, June 4, 2000, A27. Also see Abbott, *Extravaganza*, 73; MacColl, *Shaping*, 269-70, 321-22; DeMarco, 80.
[26] MacColl, *Shaping*, 467-72; Article by Jean Henniger, *Oreg.*, Northwest Magazine, Aug 19, 1979, 9.
[27] If Portland did not act by October 1, 1905, the commission was authorized to offer the Forestry Building to the OHS, the Oregon Pioneers, the Oregon Grangers, or any other public Oregon society. HB 364 was approved Feb 21, 1905. Chapter 154, *1905 General Laws of Oregon*, 265-67.
[28] MacColl, *Shaping*, 321. The council's ways and means committee recommended purchase of the Forestry Building grounds for seven thousand dollars per acre on Sept. 20, 1905, according to author Carl Abbott in a May 30, 2000, letter to this author. Also see Abbott, *Extravaganza*, 73.
[29] Abbott, *Extravaganza*, 63; Joseph Gaston, v 1, 589; MacColl, *Shaping*, 321-22; letter to this author from Carl Abbott, dated May 30, 2000.
[30] "We can estimate that the Exposition drew approximately 800,000 customers for Portland hotels, when cheap rooms went for 50¢ and expensive for $5." Abbott, *Extravaganza*, 64.
[31] Ibid., 72.
[32] Maddux, 151-52.
[33] MacColl, *Shaping*, 345.
[34] Ibid., 315.
[35] From a memorial tribute by Richard Montague at Lane's death, Senate Proceedings of the sixty-fifth Congress, Sept 16, 1917, 18-20, as quoted in MacColl, *Shaping*, 318.
[36] The public benefit of hearing both sides of controversial issues from competing dailies would be part of Portland's heritage for the next eighty years—from the time of the *Journal*'s founding in 1902, through its sale to S. I. Newhouse in 1961, until its merger with the *Oreg.* newsroom in 1982. From 1982 until the present time, Portland has had no competing daily.
[37] The vote was 52,567 for to 19,852 against. *1997-98 OBB*, 349.
[38] The vote was 47,075 against to 36,902 for. Ibid., 349.
[39] Moynihan, 212; *OHQ*, Summer 1997, 152-53.
[40] "Starting in 1907, the city council passed an ordinance barring steam locomotives or freight trains from using Fourth Avenue, to become effective eighteen months later. When the city charged the railroad with violating that ordinance in November 1908, Southern Pacific … sought an injunction against the city in U.S. District Court. The litigation lasted five years, ending with a United States Supreme Court decision in 1913. … [The Court] held that the city had reserved the option of regulating use of the rail line. With that precedent established, city officials granted permission for steam engines to run on downtown streets for several more years." Leeson, 91-92. Also see MacColl, *Shaping*, 330-31.
[41] A Nov 1932 charter amendment approved the issuance of $195,000 in bonds for constructing a

"Fourth Street Extension" in cooperation with the state highway commission and Multnomah County, and authorized use of Reconstruction Finance Corporation Financing. www.ci.portland.or.us/auditor/elections/ELECARCHIVES/GEN32.htm — [accessed July 28, 2000].
[42] MacColl, *Shaping*, 330-33.
[43] *Proc. C. C.*, Oct 1, 1906, v 25, and July 3, 1907, v 26, as quoted in ibid., 331-34.
[44] John Terry, "Oregon Trails," *Oreg.*, April 18, 1999; Portland street map, 2000.
[45] MacColl, *Shaping*, 340-41.
[46] Lockley, *Columbia*, v 1, 461.
[47] MacColl, *Shaping*, 344-45; Maddux, 159.
[48] MacColl, *Shaping*, 344-45; Maddux, 159. Thomas Devlin would be elected to an at-large council position in 1909. Lockley, *Columbia*, v 1, p 476.
[49] www.ci.portland.or.us/auditor/Elecarchives2/GEN07.htm — [accessed May 31, 2000]; MacColl, *Shaping*, 345-46.
[50] Because the waterworks bonds were approved by a charter amendment referred to the voters by the council, a lawsuit challenged its constitutionality on the grounds that charter amendments had to be initiated by a citizen petition. A lower court barred issuing the bonds until the case of *McKenna v. Portland* was decided. The Oregon Supreme Court upheld the water board's authority to issue bonds in August 1908. Short, 52-53.
[51] Ibid., 11, 52-53.
[52] This veto record was not approached by any other mayor, although Mayor John Breck's two vetoes, both overridden in 1861-62, gave him a 100 percent override record.
[53] Maddux, 159.
[54] Eaton, 105-7, 173-74. The *Voters' Pamphlet*, although slightly modified over the years, remains an essential part of the Oregon elections process today, as does the Oregon Corrupt Practices Act.
[55] Prior to 1904, U.S. senators had been elected by state legislators with no regard to the popular vote. In 1904, a citizen-initiated measure in Oregon required legislative candidates to sign a pledge to vote for the people's choice. *Oreg.* editor Harvey Scott had scorned the idea as disruptive of party and as a trap to force Republican legislators to elect Democratic senators. Scott, *Oregon*, v 1, 98, 279-80; MacColl, *Shaping*, 374; Moynihan, 211-12. The 1908 measure *requiring* the state legislature to select the people's choice was considered the equivalent of direct election of U.S. senators, and Oregon was the first state to institute this reform. www.senate.gov/artandhistory/history/common/briefing/Direct_Election_Senators.htm.—[accessed Apr 14, 2003].
[56] *1997-8 OBB*, 349-50.
[57] In 1898, Portland had a population of 81,637 living in an area of 36.87 square miles; the density at that time was 2,214 people per square mile. Figures provided by John Acker, Urban Services, City of Portland Finance and Administration Division, Feb. 19, 1999.
[58] Gaston, v 1, 341, 346.
[59] Ibid., 340-41. Pintarich, Dick, "Guild's Lake." Portland: *The Neighbor* newspaper, April and May 1983.
[60] "Portland Police Historical Society history", p 4; *Oreg.*, Dec 4, 2000, B10; *A Municipal Mother: Portland's Lola Greene Baldwin, America's First Policewoman*, by Gloria E. Myers, Oregon State University Press, 1995.
[61] *Proc. C. C.*, April 28, 1909, v 30, p 379-81, as quoted in MacColl, *Shaping*, 370-71.
[62] MacColl, *Shaping*, 374.
[63] "Reminiscences of Oswald West," 152.
[64] Ibid., 153.
[65] O'Donnell and Vaughan, 62. Lane is buried at Lone Fir Cemetery, Lot 51, Block 9.
[66] Simon received 52 percent of the vote in incomplete returns. Munley had 35 percent and future mayor Albee had 16 percent. *Oreg.*, June 8, 1909, p 8, c 2; MacColl, *Shaping*, 375; www.ci.portland.or.us/auditor/Elecarchives2/GEN09.htm — [accessed May 31, 2000].
[67] Gaston, v 3, 199; MacColl, *Merchants*, 244.
[68] Gaston, v 3, 198-200; Leeson, 36; Hines, 269; Lowenstein, 61-63; MacColl, *Merchants*, 244.
[69] Stephen McCormick was born in Ireland; Thomas J. Holmes in England. Bernard Goldsmith and Philip Wasserman were both German-born Jews; future mayor Vera Katz was also born in Germany.
[70] *Oreg.*, June 8, 1909, p 14, c 2-3; www.ci.portland.or.us/auditor/Elecarchives2/GEN09.htm — [accessed May 31, 2000].
[71] Lowenstein, 62.
[72] Maddux, 167-68.
[73] Parks superintendent Emanuel T. Mische came to Portland in 1908 from Wisconsin, and would eventually be considered "one of the most influential leaders" in the history of Portland's parks, in part because of his "excellent abilities" as a landscape architect. He was to oversee the parks during a formative six-year period. Draft *Portland Parks and Recreation, A Chronological History*, Dec 1998, 1908 section.
[74] Women's suffrage lost by twenty-four thousand votes in 1910. *1997-98 OBB*, 350-51.
[75] Gaston, v 1, 633.
[76] MacColl, *Shaping*, 84.
[77] Terwilliger Boulevard was built on land donated by the family of blacksmith James Terwilliger. Gaston, v 1, 544; MacColl, *Shaping*, 382; Maddux, 196; Draft *Portland Parks and Recreation*, 1900 and 1909 sections; Abbott, *Portland*, 60-61.
[78] Two years before, the city had shut down the six-year-old "city baths" in the Willamette operated by a private company because the location was too close to a sewer outlet and the water was unsafe. Draft *Portland Parks and Recreation*, 1908 and 1910 sections.
[79] Draft *Portland Parks and Recreation*, 1909 section. Chapman Square runs between Main and Madison; Lownsdale Square between Salmon and Main. Snyder, *Portland Names*, 244, 249. See also Snyder, *Potpourri*, 107.
[80] A "Committee of 100" or a "Committee of One Hundred Taxpayers" had operated at various times in Portland's history, dating back to earliest days. The most recent Committee of One Hundred had been formed in 1906 by the Portland Board of Trade "in consultation with Mayor Harry Lane," and was composed of representatives from every city precinct. The committee's goals were "municipal construction of a belt-line railroad along Portland's waterfront, ... the building of public docks, the creation of a system of parks and boulevards throughout the city ... [and] municipal ownership of gas and light plants."

Blackford, Mansel G., "The Lost Dream: Businessmen and City Planning in Portland, Oregon, 1903-1914," *The Western Historical Quarterly*, Jan 1984, 45.
[81] MacColl, *Shaping*, 384-85; Blackford, "The Lost Dream," 47-48; Abbott, *Portland*, 61-62; Communication between Carl Abbott and the author, February 2001.
[82] Abbott, *Portland*, 61-62; Blackford, "The Lost Dream," 47-48; MacColl, *Shaping*, 384-85.
[83] *Oreg.* May 16, 1910, as quoted in MacColl, *Shaping*, 385-86.
[84] www.ci.portland.or.us/auditor/Elecarchives2/SPEC10.htm. [accessed May 31, 2000.]
[85] Gaston, v 1, 342; MacColl, *Shaping*, 386.
[86] MacColl, *Shaping*, 386.
[87] Harvey Scott made an unsuccessful bid for a U.S. Senate seat in 1903, when selection of Oregon's congressional delegation was still made by the state legislature. Scott was more responsible for the failure of Oregon's women's suffrage ballot measures than any other single individual. "Abigail versus Harvey," by Lee Nash, *OHQ*, Summer 1997, 142-43; 152-53.
[88] Scott, *Portland*, 5-6; Scott, *Oregon*, v 1, iii, 114.
[89] The sidewalks on N.E. Hancock were personally observed by this author in Aug 2000. Also see *Old Portland Today*, "The Foot and Its Place in Portland," circa May 1975. For sidewalk ordinance, see Ord #19680, approved July 14, 1909.
[90] *OS*, 44.
[91] O'Donnell and Vaughan, 62-63.
[92] Gaston, v 1, 337-38.
[93] Parks Inventory, July 1, 1999-June 30, 2000, obtained from Portland Parks & Rec, Dec 8, 2000.
[94] Gaston, v 1, 544.
[95] Portland had 653 acres in parks, Seattle 1,500 acres, and Tacoma 1,700. *OJ*, Aug 18, 1912; MacColl, *Shaping*, 424-25.
[96] *1993 Portland Fire Yearbook*, 16-20; "Fire Department history," ca 1946, 2; Maddux, 140, 155; Purdy, 25.
[97] Snyder, *Potpourri*, 37-43; Purdy, 49.
[98] Measures not approved included creation of "pension and relief" funds for police, fire, and street cleaning workers; 1.4 million dollars for a Willamette River bridge; one million dollars for a municipal paving plant; two hundred fifty thousand dollars for a Council Crest park; and increased salary for the city attorney. Narrowly defeated were measures to make it unlawful "to influence a person from entering any place of business," and a measure to increase the salary of the city engineer (which lost by only ninety-nine votes out of nearly twemty-four thousand cast.) www.ci.portland.or.us/auditor/Elecarchives2/GEN11.htm — [accessed May 31, 2000].
[99] MacColl, *Shaping*, 400-401.
[100] Ibid., 401. Simon is buried at Beth Israel Cemetery. Phone call by the author to the Beth Israel Cemetery caretaker, March 7, 2000.

Chapter 19

[1] Dean Collins, in Aikman, 191.
[2] Blankenship, 233, 244.
[3] Dodds, *Oregon*, 173.
[4] *Oreg.*, May 3, 1913, p 14, c 1.
[5] Ibid., Jan 7, 1930, 1, 4.
[6] Allen Rushlight died of a heart attack followed by pneumonia at age fifty-six. He served in the 1925, 1927, and 1929 legislatures. According to an *Oreg.* article, he also served in the 1909 legislature while he was a member of Portland city council, "but on account of important matters pending before the city council, he refused to go to the legislature and remained on guard at the city hall." Rushlight had long suffered from a throat affliction and was a poor public speaker who worked best in committees. *Oreg.*, Jan 7, 1930, p 1, 4. According to Edwards, Rushlight actually served in the 1911 legislature, not the 1909 session. Edwards, Cecil, 114.
[7] MacColl, *Shaping*, 402.
[8] *Oreg.*, Jan 7, 1930, 1. See also MacColl, *Shaping*, 362; Lockley, *Columbia*, v 1, 462.
[9] *Oreg.*, Nov 8, 1905, as quoted in MacColl, *Shaping*, 362.
[10] *Oreg.*, Jan 7, 1930, p 4, c 3, 4.
[11] The *Oreg.* article is quoted by Helen Barney in "Sporting Women," *Metropolis*, March 1973, p 4, according to MacColl, *Shaping*, 402, 512.
[12] Ord #23939, Aug 23, 1911.
[13] *Oreg.*, Jan 7, 1930, p 4, c 3.
[14] Gaston, v 1, 402-3; O'Donnell and Vaughn, 56-57; Corning, 209; Scott, *Oregon*, v 2, 269.
[15] MacColl, *Shaping*, 402.
[16] O'Donnell and Vaughan, 58.
[17] Dean Collins, in Aikman, 191; Boag, Peter, "Sex & Politics in Progressive-Era Portland & Eugene: The 1912 Same-Sex Vice Scandal," *OHQ*, Summer 1999, 163; De Marco, 85. See reconstructed map and prominent family names at MacColl, *Shaping*, 404-10. Included on the list of businessmen who owned vice properties are the names Failing, Corbett, Reed, Dolph, R.R. Thompson, D.P. Thompson, Weinhard, Ainsworth, Glisan, Hirsch, Wemme, Bates, Teal, T. Woodward, and Lansing Stout.
[18] Dean Collins, in Aikman, 192.
[19] MacColl, *Shaping*, 404; O'Donnell and Vaughan, 58.
[20] Marshall Dana, "The Greater Portland Plan of Edward Bennett" (Portland, 1912); Mansel G. Blackford, "The Lost Dream: Businessmen and City Planning in Portland, Oregon, 1903-14," *Western Historical Quarterly*, Jan 1984, 48; Abbott, *Portland*, 62-63.
[21] Foreword to "The Greater Portland Plan"; Blackford, "The Lost Dream," 51.
[22] A retail-focused promenade was proposed near this location in year 2000. *Oreg.*, Dec 12, 2000, C2; Dec 13, A1, 5; Dec 16, E8; Dec 17, E2, 3.
[23] Dana, "The Greater Portland Plan"; Abbott, *Portland*, 63-66; Blackford, "The Lost Dream," 48-49; MacColl, *Shaping*, 428.
[24] Blackford, "The Lost Dream," 49, 51.
[25] Simon Benson's daughter Alice quotes Benson in her book, *Simon Benson, Northwest Lumber King*. After the fountains were installed, she says her father sent an agent around to investigate, who reported back to Benson that many saloons had a sales decrease of up to 40 percent after the bronze fountains were turned on. Short, 55.
[26] In 1992, the water bureau started turning off fountains during summer months to conserve water.

"Let bubblers bubble," cried a summer 2000 *Oreg.* editorial urging the city to install timing mechanisms that would turn the four-armed fountains back on, at least during daylight hours. "Each summer since 1992, city water workers—flying the flag of conservation—have capped most of the 125 thirst-quenching and soul-refreshing Benson bubblers with ugly push-button faucets. … [A] one-time installation of battery-operated timers would return life to the fountains, at least during the daylight." *Oreg.* editorial, June 29, 2000, D8. Water for the downtown Benson fountains was subsequently restored with timers for daytime use.

[27] *OJ*, Sept 1, 1912, p 1-2.

[28] Ibid., p 1, 7.

[29] "Partners in Progress: Port of Portland, Celebrates 100 Years, 1891-1991," 12. The "pusher"-style aircraft had the engine and propeller mounted *behind* the pilot. A reproduction of this historic aircraft is at the Pearson Air Museum in Vancouver, Washington, along with a video documentary of a re-creation of the historic flight. Correspondence by the author with the webmaster, Port of Portland, April 14, 2003.

[30] Ibid., Sept 5, 1912, as quoted in MacColl, *Shaping*, 410-11.

[31] Ibid., Aug 26, 1912, as cited in MacColl, *Shaping*, 408.

[32] Ibid., Aug 29, 1912, as quoted in MacColl, *Shaping*, 408.

[33] Ibid., Sept 5, 1912, as cited in MacColl, *Shaping*, 410-11.

[34] MacColl, *Shaping*, 328.

[35] Ibid., 411, 459.

[36] Ord #26156, signed by Mayor Rushlight Oct 28, 1912; MacColl, *Shaping*, 411-12.

[37] Collins, in Aikman, 192-93.

[38] O'Donnell and Vaughan, 58-59.

[39] Collins, in Aikman, 192-93.

[40] *Civic Review* (Portland, Oregon, 1938-39), p 55, as cited in *History of Portland*, WPA Writers' Project, 11, 13; MacColl, *Shaping*, 492.

[41] Purdy, 59.

[42] MacColl, *Shaping*, 467-72; Jean Henniger, *Oreg.*, Northwest Magazine, Aug 19, 1979, 9.

[43] *OJ*, Sept 28, 1913, as quoted in MacColl, *Shaping*, 470-71.

[44] The Bull Moose Party got its nickname when Theodore Roosevelt was asked by a reporter how he felt. "I feel strong as a bull moose," he said.

[45] MacColl, *Shaping*, 411.

[46] The equal suffrage vote was 61,265 yes to 57,104 no, a margin of 4,161 votes. *1997-98 OBB*, 351.

[47] Stone, 99-100; Moynihan, 216; *OHQ*, Summer 1997, 153.

[48] *1997-98 OBB*, 351-52.

[49] The Nov 12, 1912, vote was 16,202 yes for adopting the Bennett plan to 7,996 no. www.ci.portland.or.us/auditor/Elecarchives2/SPEC12.htm — [accessed May 31, 2000]. See also Abbott, *Portland*, 66.

[50] The two million dollar "parks, boulevards and bridges over gulches" levy failed by a vote of 9,612 yes to 15,659 no. www.ci.portland.or.us/auditor/Elecarchives2/SPEC12.htm — [accessed May 31, 2000]; Blackford, "The Lost Dream," 52.

[51] Some of the volcanic rock from Mt. Tabor was placed in Laurelhurst Park Lake. Maddux, 193-94.

[52] *Oreg.*, Feb 3, 1913, p 14, c 1-4. Mayor Rushlight was the second mayor in the city's history to be married during his mayoral term (William S. Ladd was the first), but he would not be the last. Joe Carson would subsequently be married during his mayoral term.

[53] The Committee of Municipal Research was appointed "to inquire as to the feasibility of organizing a permanent Bureau of Municipal Research" in Portland. Members of the group that commissioned the study were C. S. Jackson, Kingman Brewster, W. B. Ayer, James B. Kerr, A. H. Devers, A. Feldenheimer, Richard Montague (added later), and Charles D. Mahaffie (added later). Introduction, "Organization and Business Methods of the City Government of Portland, Oregon," 1913.

[54] A similar study of Multnomah County government by the same New York group would be conducted in September.

[55] MacColl, *Shaping*, 438.

[56] "Organization and Business Methods of the City Government of Portland, Oregon," May 5, 1913. The original copy of this report is stored at the C.P. Arch.. See also ibid., 438-41.

[57] A few other states had previously passed women's suffrage laws, but a federal mandate would not be adopted until 1920.

[58] *Oreg.*, May 3, 1913, p 1.

[59] Besides Rushlight and Baker, other members of the 1913 charter committee were R. W. Montague, P. L. Willis, W. F. Woodward, T. M. Hurlburt, W. C. Benbow, W. B. Ayer, and Frank S. Grant. Charter Amendments File, 1913-42, Box 5 of 10, 3 May 1913 folder, C.P. Arch.. The committee had been appointed by council president George Baker (at Mayor Rushlight's direction) when the mayor was out of town. *Oreg.*, May 3, 1913, p 1.

[60] Officials currently elected who would thereafter be appointed by the council were the treasurer, municipal judge, and city attorney. 1913 Charter of the City of Portland.

[61] *Oreg.*, May 3, 1913, p 1; 1913 Charter of the City of Portland.

[62] *OS*, 44-45.

[63] *Oreg.*, Apr 22, 1913, as quoted in MacColl, *Shaping*, 443.

[64] *Oreg.*, Jan 7, 1930, p 4, c 4.

[65] Ibid., May 3, 1913, p 14; *OJ*, May 2, 1913, p 1, 2; MacColl, *Shaping*, 443; Blankenship, 237.

[66] *Oreg.*, May 3, 1913, p 1; MacColl, *Shaping*, 442.

[67] MacColl, *Shaping*, 442-43.

[68] *Oreg.*, April 20, 1913, as quoted in ibid., 442.

[69] *Oreg.*, May 3, 1913, p 1.

[70] Ibid., p 14, c 4.

[71] The vote was 17,317 for and 17,025 against. www.ci.portland.or.us/auditor/Elecarchives2/SPECMAY13.htm — [accessed May 31, 2000].*Oreg.*

[72] *Oreg.*, May 4, 1913, p 1, c 1.

[73] According to the *Oreg.* of May 4, 1913, p 1, the city had seventy-three thousand registered voters.

[74] Many sections of the 1903 charter, especially regarding the council's basic powers, were retained; the 1913 amendments made extensive changes to the 1903 charter, but did not repeal it entirely. By April 2001, citizens had approved many more amendments to the

1903 charter, but none that changed the commission form of government.

[75] *Oreg.*, May 4, 1913, p 4; May 5, 1913, p 1; May 6, 1913, p 1.

[76] Hampton was a doctor who had received a Progressive Party primary nomination for councilman-at-large over four male candidates. Mrs. Rosalie Goulding was a Democratic write-in candidate for councilman-at-large in the May election, but did not run again in June. Ibid., May 5, 1913, p 1, p 4, c 1; May 3, 1913, p 14, c 4.

[77] Snyder, *Portland Names*, 92.

[78] MacColl, *Shaping*, 445.

[79] This system, now known as "instant runoff" voting, was invented by Massachusetts Institute of Tchnology professor W. R. Ware in 1870, and was used in Portland mayoral elections until 1933. Ireland has for many years used the system to elect its president, and Australia its House of Representatives. In March 2002, San Francisco and the state of Vermont decided to introduce instant runoff voting. www.fairvote.org/irv/faq.htm [accessed Apr 14, 2003].

[80] C. L. McKenna received nearly ten thousand more second-place votes than did Rushlight, bringing McKenna within less than 1 percent (637 votes) of besting Mayor Rushlight as runner-up. *Oreg.*, June 17, 1913, p 1, c 2; Maddux, 162.

[81] George Baker's losing ballot slogan was: "A theatre manager who has had many years experience in municipal government." His winning slogan two years later was: "Faithful performance of my full duty to Portland, first, last, and always." Sample Ballots, 1905-1992, C.P. Arch..

[82] Lockley, *Columbia*, v 1, 478; www.ci.portland.or.us/auditor/Elecarchives2/GEN13.htm — [accessed May 31, 2000].

[83] www.ci.portland.or.us/auditor/Elecarchives2/GEN13.htm — [accessed May 31, 2000];Blackford, "The Lost Dream," 55.

[84] Blackford, "The Lost Dream," 54-55

[85] Lockley, *Columbia*, v 1, 462.

[86] MacColl, *Shaping*, 445.

[87] Lockley, *Columbia*, v 1, 462.

[88] Robert D. Johnston, "The Myth of the Harmonious City," *OHQ*, Fall 1998, 257.

[89] MacColl, *Shaping*, 445-46.

[90] *News* (Portland), July 1, 1913, 1, as quoted in "Police Response to Labor Radicalism in Portland and Seattle, 1913-19," by Dennis E. Hoffman and Vincent J. Webb, *OHQ*, Winter 1986, 343.

[91] Hoffman and Webb, "Police Response," 342-45.

[92] Neither site was in accord with the Bennett plan.

[93] The city bought property to relocate the displaced public market along both sides of S.W. Yamhill, from Third to Fifth streets, which proved to be a popular location. MacColl, *Shaping*, 450-55; www.ci.portland.or.us/auditor/Elecarchives2/GEN11.htm — [accessed May 31, 2000].

[94] "Only 17 percent of the original (1914-17) structure was salvaged when the facility was rebuilt from 1956-68 at a cost of nearly $4 million." MacColl, *Shaping*, 453.

[95] Ibid., 453-55.

[96] Johnston, "Harmonious City," 256-57; MacColl, *Shaping*, 455-56.

[97] Only fifteen thousand voters turned out for the election. www.ci.portland.or.us/auditor/Elecarchives2/SPECDEC13.htm — [accessed May 31, 2000].

[98] MacColl, *Shaping*, 432-33.

[99] *OJ*, March 17, 1914; *OHS Scrapbook 50*, p 84.

[100] The dock was dedicated March 28, 1914. Abbott, *Portland*, 68; MacColl, *Shaping*, 448; Leeson, 94-95.

[101] The vote tallies in the recalls were Albee 15,455 yes, 33,687 no; Brewster 17,896 yes, 28,976 no; Dieck 20,146 yes, 28,297 no. www.ci.portland.or.us/auditor/Elecarchives2/SPEC14.htm — [accessed May 31, 2000]; Maddux, 162; MacColl, *Shaping*, 459.

[102] Leeson, 76; MacColl, *Growth*, 21.

[103] The merger and prohibition measures passed by a comfortable margin. However, the measure to abolish the death penalty barely squeaked by with a one hundred fifty-seven-vote margin, after being rejected two years previously. In 1920, voters again reinstated the death penalty, and the measure continued to surface throughout the twentieth century. Stone, 58-69; *1997-98 OBB*, 351-52.

[104] Sample Ballots, 1905-1992, C.P. Arch..; *Oreg.*, April 3, 1915, p 1. St. Johns had been incorporated in 1903 and Linnton in 1910. *History of Portland*, WPA Writers' Project, 11-12. Linnton "was located on the west side of the Willamette about eight miles down the river from Portland. ... It had been laid out as early as 1844 by M. M. McCarver and Peter H. Burnett. ... In 1843 James Johns settled on the west side near the site of Linnton but soon removed across the river and opened a store. In 1852 he operated a ferry. ... He was something of a hermit, and because some religious characters of mediaeval days were hermits, he became known as St. John." Maddux, 169-70. See also MacColl, *Growth*, 30, 115.

[105] Snyder, *Portland Names*, 19; MacColl, *Shaping*, 341, 472-73, 492; MacColl, *Growth*, 30.

[106] Ibid., June 30, 1916; July 1, 1916, as quoted in MacColl, *Growth*, 21.

[107] Leeson, 97.

[108] *OJ*, July 7, 1916, as quoted in MacColl, *Growth*, 21; Leeson, 97.

[109] www.ci.portland.or.us/auditor/Elecarchives2/GEN15.htm [accessed May 31, 2000].

[110] Benson had bought Gordon Falls (renamed Wahkeena in 1915) in 1903 for twenty-one thousand dollars. *Oreg.*, June 3, 1915, p 13; McArthur, 766; MacCall, *Growth*, 24.

[111] Many sections of the historic Columbia River Highway were "demolished, abandoned or bypassed" during construction of highway I-84 that began in the 1950s. Today, ten miles of those original segments have been restored as bike paths and pedestrian hiking trails and were recently designated as a Millennium Legacy Trail by the White House Millenium Council and the highway itself listed in the National Register of Historic Places in 1983. Oregon Dept of Transportation web site, www.odot.state.or.us/hcrh/trail/trail.htm [accessed July 23, 2000].

[112] Benson purchased Multnomah Falls and surrounding 140 acres in summer 1915 for $5,250 after a complicated condemnation proceeding. Benson was an avid supporter of and activist regarding the Columbia River Highway. *Oreg.*, June 3, 1915, p 13; Sept

7, 1915, p 6; Sept 17, 1915, p 11; McArthur, 529; Corning, 27, 58, 113; Norman, 88; MacColl, *Growth*, 24-26; OHQ, Sept 1965, 263-65.
[113] At the beginning of the twenty-first century, Multnomah Falls was still the most-visited natural attraction in Oregon, with approximately 2.5 million visitors per year. Throughout most of the twentieth century, it was the overall number one state tourist attraction until overtaken by the Spirit Mountain Casino in the late 1990s. Letter from Julie Curtis, Assistant Director, Oregon Tourism Commission to the author, July 28, 2000.
[114] *Oreg.*, Aug 8, 1915, p 4.
[115] *OJ*, Oct 2, 1915, p 4.
[116] "75 Years," 1991 City Club of Portland Annual Report, 2; Lucia, 12-13.
[117] *1997-98 OBB*, 352; MacColl, *Growth*, 21.
[118] Maddux, 156.
[119] Abbott, *Portland*, 67.
[120] Abbott, *Portland*, 68.
[121] Houle, 10-11.
[122] The discharged officer "was said to have belittled the preparations for war, to have scoffed at the President, and otherwise to have manifested a spirit not in accord with the uniform." *Oreg.*, April 7, 1917, p 1, 9
[123] Ibid., April 7, 1917, p 1.
[124] Neuberger is quoted in DeMarco, 111.
[125] Harry Lane is buried in Lone Fir Cemetery.
[126] *Oreg.*, May 26, 1917, p 4, c 2.
[127] Widow Corbett kept the cow in a side yard by the Corbett home until the mansion was sold in 1936. "Portland the Spinster," by Wilbur Hall, *Collier's Weekly*, May 1917, 30-32, 34-36, 38; Culp, 56-57; MacColl, *Growth*, 19; *Oreg.*, June 17, 2002, B1, 4. The sixty thousand dollar value would be the equivalent of nearly one million of today's dollars.
[128] Hall, "Portland the Spinster," 30-31.
[129] Votes against getting rid of the commission form of government tallied 32,086, while yes votes totaled 14,196. www.ci.portland.or.us/auditor/Elecarchives2/GEN17.htm [accessed May 31, 2000].
[130] Ibid.
[131] O'Donnell and Vaughan, 60-61.

Chapter 20

[1] This one-time three and a half-year term shortened the waiting time between election and swearing-in to two months.
[2] "Until the very day before [the] election, Daly's election looked like a foregone conclusion." Silver, 49.
[3] Dodds, 181-82; Silver, 30, 46-47. Daly campaigned against an anti-conspiracy ordinance which would have made it difficult to "boycott, picket, or display a banner in any labor dispute"—a ballot measure which passed by only 283 votes out of some forty thousand cast. Dodds, 182; Silver, 50-51.
[4] Silver, 51; Robert D. Johnston, "The Myth of the Harmonious City," *OHQ*, Fall 1998, 265.
[5] Silver, 50; Johnston, "Harmonious City," 268-69.
[6] Baker won only 711 more first-choice ballots than Daly, but received a plurality of 1,575 votes out of more than forty-eight thousand first-, second-, and third-place votes tallied. Johnston, "Harmonious City," 269; www.ci.portland.or.us/auditor/Elecarchives2/GEN17.htm — [accessed July 28, 2000].
[7] Dean Collins, in Aikman, 195; Frank Sterrett, "Portland's Kissing Mayor," *Oreg.*, Northwest Mag, May 15, 1966, 24; Abbott, *Gateway*, 97.
[8] *Oregon Voter*, Oct 4, 1919, as quoted in MacColl, *Growth*, 167.
[9] Maddux, 145; Lockley, *Columbia*, v 1, 463; *OJ*, May 17, 1941, p 4, c 5.
[10] Baker did, however, enroll in night public speaking classes after he was elected mayor. *OJ*, May 17, 1941, p 1, c 1-2; Sterrett, "Portland's Kissing Mayor," 24
[11] Abbott, *Gateway*, 97.
[12] W. Kenneth Waters, Jr., "The Baker Stock Company and the Community," *OHQ*, Fall 1981, 229-31. Baker Stock Company actors included William Powell, Fay Bainter, and Jean Hersholt. DeMarco, 112-13. Also see Lockley, *Columbia*, v 1, 464; Maddux, 147.
[13] Sterrett, "Portland's Kissing Mayor," 24.
[14] *OHQ*, Fall 1981, 269.
[15] Dodds, Gordon, 182.
[16] Before Baker, the longest consecutive mayoral terms were the four years each of Harry Lane and H. Russell Albee. Both James Chapman and Henry Failing functioned as mayor more than four years, but their service was not consecutive. Chapman's nearly six years were in three different segments, while Failing's four and a half years were in two separate time periods. One mayor later matched Baker's sixteen-year record—Mayor Terry Schrunk, who served from 1957 to 1972.
[17] "Fifty Years of Commission Government, 1913-1963," unpublished paper written by E. Kimbark MacColl, 1985.
[18] Funk graduated from night law school in 1916, and was admitted to the Oregon bar the same year. "Northwestern College of Law Announcements," 1916-17, p 17; Lockley, *Columbia*, v 2, 545-46.
[19] When Bigelow's term was up, the *Oregon Voter* wrote that, at least in West Portland, "business men … are almost unanimous in dreading and opposing his [re]election." His constituency was eastside business owners and organized labor. *Oregon Voter*, May 19, 1917, as quoted in Johnston, "Harmonious City," 263, 292.
[20] Lockley, *Columbia*, v 2, 647-48; Snyder, *Portland Names*, 92.
[21] MacColl, *Growth*, 422-23.
[22] Kellaher served on the city council in 1905-08 and again in 1917-19. He was an "east-side grocer" who was the only Democrat on the fifteen-member council in 1905. MacColl, *Merchants*, 383.
[23] Kellaher ran for mayor in 1913 and 1920. The *Oreg.* once referred to reform-minded Kellaher as "an exploded bomb, a fired sky-rocket, a sagging balloon." *Oreg.*, June 1, 1913, as quoted in MacColl, *Growth*, 125; *Oreg.*, May 25, 1932, p 8, c 3.
[24] Sylvester Pier had previously served on Mayor Simon's executive committee and before his election was sales manager for Marshall Wells. *Oreg.*, Nov 7, 1918, p 1. Marshall Wells was a hardware wholesale business which occupied two city blocks at Fourteenth and Lovejoy. *1925 P.C. Dir.*, 118.
[25] "The people of St. Johns asked council to name the park in his honor." *Oreg.*, May 22, 1935, p 20, c 3.
[26] Stanhope Pier, like his father, worked for Marshall Wells. Ibid., June 30, 1923, p 6, c 2; Oct 12, 1930, sec 1, p 14, c 1; and Nov 26, 1952, p 13, c 4.

[27] Clyde had two years of prior council service (1911-13), and campaigned unsuccessfully for a council seat in 1915 and 1928. He was a commissioner of liberal bent.
[28] MacColl, *Growth*, 423.
[29] *Oreg.*, April 4, 1970, 1, 14, 15. Bennett served in the state legislature in 1925, 1929, 1931, 1947, 1963, 1965, 1967, and 1969. Edwards, Cecil, 8.
[30] MacColl, *Growth*, 140.
[31] Ibid., 147.
[32] Ibid., 149-50.
[33] Germantown Road in Linnton was in process of a name change at war's end. Snyder, *Portland Names*, 64.
[34] MacColl, *Growth*, 143-44.
[35] Ibid., 147.
[36] Ibid., 147.
[37] Ibid., 148.
[38] Diamond, 202. The influenza epidemic at the end of World War I killed twenty-one million people worldwide.
[39] For the two-year period that ended Sept 30, 1920, the flu epidemic took 3,786 Oregon lives. Ivan M. Wooley, "The 1918 'Spanish Influenza' Pandemic in Oregon," *OHQ*, v 77, 1976, 247-49, 252-53, 257; *Oreg.*, Oct 5, 1918; Nov 7, 1999, F1.
[40] In Portland, twenty thousand people caught influenza, and two thousand died. Deaths were mainly from secondary causes, such as pneumonia. McCormack and Pintarich, 121-24.
[41] Abbott, *Portland*, 70, 78-79; MacColl, *Growth*, 321-22.
[42] DeMarco, 113; *OHQ*, Winter 1986, 357-59. When the 1919 raids occurred, the IWW headquarters were located at S.W. Second near Burnside. MacColl, *Growth*, 158.
[43] Quotations are from an autobiographical sketch by IWW lawyer Burl A. Green as cited in MacColl, *Growth*, 158.
[44] National women's suffrage would be adopted the following year.
[45] MacColl, *Growth*, 21.
[46] Marsh, 182-87.
[47] Ibid., 187-89.
[48] MacColl, *Growth*, 276-77.
[49] Marsh, 183-86.
[50] City elections were moved to May and November because of a statewide referendum approved by the voters in 1917 that required all "city, town and state" elections to be held at the same time. *1997-98 OBB*, 353; Maddux, 162-63; www.ci.portland.or.us/auditor/Elecarchives2/GEN18.htm — [accessed May 31, 2000].
[51] Commissioners Mann and Barbur were also reelected handily. *Oreg.*, Nov 4, 1920, p 17, c 3-4.
[52] *Oreg.*, October 5, 1921, as quoted in MacColl, *Growth*, 273.
[53] Horowitz, 6.
[54] MacColl, *Growth*, 163-64.
[55] Dever, Lem, *The Confessions of an Imperial Klansman*, 40, as quoted in ibid., 167.
[56] Horowitz, 6; Silver, 78.
[57] *OJ*, Sept 9, 1923, Sec 1, p 1 and May 17, 1941, p 4, c 6; Clark, Malcolm, Jr., "The Bigot Disclosed: 90 Years of Nativism," *OHQ*, June 1974, 180; Silver, 78-85; *1997-98 OBB*, 387.
[58] Clark, "The Bigot Disclosed," 180.
[59] MacColl, *Growth*, 265.
[60] *Oregon Voter*, Oct 25, 1924, as quoted in MacColl, *Growth*, 280-81.
[61] MacColl, *Growth*, 264-79; Silver, 47, 85.
[62] Baker's opponents in 1924 were Rufus Holman, W. N. Gatens, Joseph Strowbridge, George Parrish, Charles DeLashmutt, and John Howard Rankin. Commissioners Mann and Barbur were also returned to office that year with no serious challenge. *Oreg.*, Nov 6, 1924, p 1, c 3; www.ci.portland.or.us/auditor/Elecarchives2/GEN24.htm [accessed July 28, 2000].
[63] *Oregon Voter*, Aug 30, 1924, as quoted in MacColl, *Growth*, 281.
[64] Draft *Portland Parks and Recreation, A Chronological History*, Dec 1998, 1924 section; MacColl, *Growth*, 550-51.
[65] *Oreg.* Dec 20, 1929, p 1, c 2.
[66] The council had adopted a zoning ordinance on March 17, 1920, with commissioners Mann and Pier dissenting, but later reversed itself to leave the decision to the voters. Abbott, *Portland*, 81, 84-85; www.ci.portland.or.us/auditor/Elecarchives2/GEN20.htm [accessed July 28, 2000].
[67] Abbott, *Portland*, 87.
[68] MacColl, *Growth*, 300-301. See also Abbott, *Portland*, 87.
[69] This 1929 rating was based on 1926-27 data. *The American City*, July 1929, as quoted in MacColl, *Growth*, 284.
[70] *The American City*, July 1929, as quoted in MacColl, *Growth*, 284.
[71] Maddux, 187. *Oreg.*
[72] *Oreg.*, Dec 4, 1950, C16; O'Donnell and Vaughan, 60.
[73] 1929 speech by Mayor Baker as quoted in ibid., 286.
[74] MacColl, *Growth*, 341.
[75] Paving of one and a half miles of Terwilliger Boulevard, for example, was completed for 62 cents per square yard, while private contractors were charging $1.25 to $1.45. MacColl, *Growth*, 284-86.
[76] Sterrett, "Portland's Kissing Mayor," 24. Also see *OJ*, May 18, 1941, p 11, c 7.
[77] *OJ*, March 5, 1925, p 1, c 7 and p 7, c 3.
[78] Dodds, Gordon, 182.
[79] *History of the Bench and Bar*, 188.
[80] *OJ*, June 19, 1927, Sec 1, p 1, 4, and June 26, 1927, Sec 1, p 1, 5. www.ci.portland.or.us/auditor/Elecarchives2/GEN26.htm & SPEC27.htm [accessed July 28, 2000].
[81] Paper dated June 20, 1927, by Richard W. Montague, Commission Chairman, titled "Arguments on Consolidation Amendment." An attached note page explained the Government Simplification Commission history.
[82] *1997-98 OBB*, 355.
[83] *Oreg.*, Sept 15, 1927, 1; MacColl, *Growth*, 249-51.
[84] Price, 49-50; MacColl, *Growth*, 232-34, 249-50; Maddux, 186.
[85] MacColl, *Growth*, 248-9.
[86] By a vote of 14,953 to 11,308, charter section 227, as amended, authorized the council to issue bonds for "carrying on the water system," provided that these bonds would be paid for out of the water fund. Official City Ballot for November 8, 1910, Sample Ballots, 1905-1992, C.P. Arch.. Also see Short, 61.

[87] Bull Run Dam Number 1, a two hundred-foot high gravity dam that was state of the art in the 1920s, was designed by D. C. Henny, who later designed Hoover Dam. Short, 65-67.
[88] John Mann and Asbury Barbur were again reelected to council, but by narrower margins than previously. *Oreg.*, Nov 8, 1928, p 1; Nov 10, 1928, p 6, c 6.
[89] Prof. James G. Ashbaugh, Department of Geography, Portland State University as stated in Price, 41.
[90] Price, 39; Abbott, *Portland*, 104; MacColl, *Growth*, 286, 501. Technically, the wall was over one hundred miles from the ocean, but it was usually called a seawall. The project was also called the Front Street Intercepting Sewer and Drainage Project.
[91] The council specified that the study should investigate "widening of Front Street to 100 feet, constructing an esplanade along the harbor wall, the acquisition of all the land between the widened Front Street and the harbor wall, and the cost of constructing a link railroad." *Oreg.*, Dec 21, 1929, p 1, c 3.
[92] MacColl, *Growth*, 361, 488-99.
[93] *Oreg.*, Feb 12, 1930, p 23, c 1.
[94] The three Oregon Supreme Court cases referred to are *Bethune v Funk*, July 1917; *State Ex Rel. Bayer v Funk*, July 30, 1921, and June 27, 1922; *Monahan et al. v Funk*, Oct 13, 1931. The Bethune case (166 Pac.931) concerned a three dollar claim for serving on a city elections board, which Funk refused because Bethune had already been compensated by Multnomah County. The Bayer case (105 Or. 134, *146, 209 P. 113, **114) concerned a $36,703 claim regarding construction of the city auditorium. The Monahan case (137 Or. 580, 3 P .2d 778) attempted to force Funk to place a measure on the ballot that Funk had refused on grounds that the council action questioned was an administrative matter, not a legislative one.
[95] MacColl, *Growth*, 390-95; *OS* 60-61.
[96] *Oreg.*, Jan 1, 1930, as quoted in MacColl, *Growth*, 390.
[97] Purdy, 34.
[98] Abbott, *Gateway*, 110; MacColl, *Growth*, 459; Pement and Keller, 34.
[99] Purdy, 34.
[100] *Oreg.*, Feb 13, 1930, p 1, 3.
[101] www.ci.portland.or.us/auditor/Elecarchives2/GEN30.htm [accessed July 28, 2000].
[102] Ord #61451, adopted Sept 23, 1931, was approved by a vote of 54,288 in favor and 52,479 against; and upheld by the Oregon Supreme Court on March 12, 1935. (*Safeway Stores, Inc. v. City of Portland, et al.*, Circuit Court of Multnomah County, Case #1099660.) Citations are from "The Crusade against Chain Stores: Portland's Independent Merchants, 1928-1935," by David A. Horowitz, *OHQ*, Winter 1988, 358-61.
[103] MacColl, *Growth*, 411-52, and 558-71. MacColl includes a full discussion of the private versus public power struggle in his *Growth of a City*, and concludes (p 571): "World War II saved PGE and its parent holding company, PEPCO."
[104] McKay, 67, 291.
[105] *Proc. C.C.*, Jan 9, 1931; v 93, 566, as quoted in MacColl, *Growth*, 421.
[106] MacColl, *Growth*, 421.
[107] Portland Chamber of Commerce papers, as quoted in MacColl, *Growth*, 421-22.
[108] Council papers, "Public Utility Box," as quoted in MacColl, *Growth*, 421.
[109] MacColl, *Growth*, 422-23.
[110] Ibid., 422.
[111] In 1999, city commissioner Erik Sten suggested that Portland look into creating its own public power utility, but "might as well have proposed an expedition to the planet Zargon," according to *WW*, Feb 28, 2001, p 10. The possibility of a renewed look at public power emerged during a critical energy shortage in winter 2000-01 and with subsequent scandals surrounding the bankruptcy of PGE's parent company, Enron, which had acquired PGE in 1997.
[112] *OJ*, May 18, 1941, p 11, c 6.
[113] *Oreg.*, April 20, 1932, p 5, c 3.
[114] *Sloan, for Use of City of Portland, v Baker et al.* (139 Or.370, 10 P .2d 362).
[115] Ord #60860, passed June 10, 1931.
[116] The court's decision was handed down on April 19, 1932. The decision further noted that municipal governments are a "mere creature of the law" which possess "only those properties which the charter confers upon it." *Sloan, for Use of City of Portland, v Baker et al.* (139 Or.370, 10 P .2d 362).
[117] *Oreg.*, April 20, 1932, p 5, c 3.
[118] Before he took the trip, friends had "raised a purse" for him "so that he wouldn't be cramped for money." *Oreg.*, April 20, 1932, p 5, c 3-4.
[119] The St. Johns Bridge, designed by David Steinman of New York, was dedicated June 13, 1931. Maddux, 183; MacColl, *Growth*, 350-53.
[120] MacColl, *Growth*, 623, 628-29. Fred Meyer stores are today part of "America's largest retail food company," the Kroger Co. www.fredmeyerstores.com [accessed Oct 23, 2000].
[121] Purdy, 34.
[122] Ralph Lloyd first purchased land in northeast Portland in 1923, launching "the most ambitious program of urban land acquisition by one person in Portland's history." Lloyd said he planned to spend upwards of twenty-five million dollars over the next twenty-five years to create "a little city within a city," a dream which would result in the building of Lloyd Center twenty-seven years later. However, property values in the Depression allowed Lloyd to acquire his properties for much less than he had anticipated—about three million dollars. MacColl, *Growth*, 325.
[123] *OJ*, October 30, 1931, p 1, c 6; p 4, c 1.
[124] *Oreg.*, Nov 8, 1931, p 9; Nov 13, p 1; Nov 14, p 1.
[125] Snyder, *Portland Names*, 65-67.
[126] Ord #61325, approved September 2, 1931; *OHQ*, Fall 1998, 322, footnote 1. House numbers were also specified in the ordinance. Maddux, 200.
[127] An exception to the Willamette River as the east–west divider was the north-only district (N) created for the eastside "peninsula" formed at the junction of the Willamette and Columbia rivers, a peninsula which included the community of St. Johns. Maddux, 200; Snyder, *Portland Names*, 65-67.
[128] Ibid., January 20, 1932, as quoted in MacColl, *Growth*, 499-500. See also Abbott, *Portland*, 103-8.
[129] Abbott, *Portland*, 108-9.
[130] MacColl, *Growth*, 499.

[131] Nearly eighteen thousand customers and two hundred forty-two farmers had protested the proposed move of the public market. Commissioner Ralph Clyde had vigorously opposed the new structure, calling it a "White Elephant" in the making. The council had approved the final building contract while Clyde, the commissioner of public utilities, was out of town. Clyde had understandably been furious, but had no recourse. *Oreg.*, April 30, 1932, p 1; MacColl, *Growth*, 282-83.
[132] *Oreg.*, April 28, 1932, p 1, c 3; April 29, 1932, p 1, c 8; MacColl, *Growth*, 494.
[133] MacColl, *Growth*, 494. The council approved building the new public market in April 1931. An extensive discussion of the public market "fiasco" is available in MacColl, *Growth*, 488-99.
[134] *Oreg.*, April 30, 1932, p 1, c 3.
[135] Sample ballot, Special Recall Election, Friday, May 20, 1932; Sample Ballots, 1905-1992, C.P. Arch..
[136] Ibid.
[137] The Baker vote was 38,585 for recall, 43,882 against—a difference of 5,279 votes out of 82,467 cast. www.ci.portland.or.us/auditor/Elecarchives2/RECALL32.htm [accessed July 28, 2000].
[138] Johnson was a former assistant to both Commissioner Barbur and Senator Jake Bennett. Bennett also lobbied for the appointment. *Oreg.*, May 22, 1932, p 1, c 8, and May 25, 1932, p 8, c 1-3; MacColl, *Growth*, 423. Former commissioner Stanhope Pier was also mentioned as a possible appointee, but Pier said he would not, "under any condition return to the commission unless elected by a vote of the people." No less than sixteen candidates sought to fill the eight months remaining in Commissioner Mann's term at the November 1932 election, including former commissioner Stanhope Pier. The winner was the man whom the council had declined to appoint, J. E. "Jake" Bennett. www.ci.portland.or.us/auditor/Elecarchives2/GEN32.htm [accessed July 28, 2000].
[139] Dirk DeJonge was arrested during the 1934 dock strike, charged with "criminally advocating the overthrow of the government," and sentenced to seven years. The U.S. Supreme Court found that DeJonge had not advocated such overthrow. *DeJonge v. Oregon*, 299 U. S. at 364-65. Long, 46; Leeson, 128-30; MacColl, *Growth*, 483-86; *OHQ*, Winter 1999, 390-91.
[140] *Oreg.*, Nov 10, 1932, p 1, c 6.
[141] Ibid. One woman, Laurie Palmer Weber, competed with 25 male candidates for these two commission seats. www.ci.portland.or.us/auditor/Elecarchives2/GEN32.htm — [accessed July 28, 2000].
[142] Under the November 1932 ballot measure, the mayor and two commissioners elected in 1932 (Carson, Bennett, and Bean) would take office July 1, 1933, and serve until January 1, 1937. The auditor and two commissioners elected in November 1934 would also serve only three and a half year terms from July 1, 1935, until January 1, 1939. Charter Amendments, 1913-42 file, C.P. Arch..
[143] *Oreg.*, Nov 10, 1932, p 1, c 6. However, commissioners continued to run at large. The two council candidates who received the highest number of votes were deemed elected. Charter Amendments, 1913-42 file, C.P. Arch..
[144] Draft *Portland Parks and Recreation, A Chronological History*, Dec 1998, 1932 section.
[145] Abbott, *Gateway*, 108. "Scrip" is a piece of paper containing a written promise that it can be redeemed for cash at some future date.
[146] E. Kimbark MacColl and others attribute Portland's good fortune in avoiding "what could have become a severe bank disaster" to the prompt and generous actions of Aaron Frank of the Meier and Frank department store. Frank loaned the American National Bank enough money to keep its doors open at the most critical time of the national banking crisis. MacColl, *Growth*, 404-5.
[147] Abbott, *Gateway*, 108.
[148] MacColl, *Growth*, 453.
[149] *OJ*, May 14, 1933, Mag sec p 5.
[150] That Mayor Baker was the city's "most colorful" mayor is arguable. Former mayor Sylvester Pennoyer and future mayor Bud Clark both come readily to mind.
[151] Sterrett, "Portland's Kissing Mayor," 24.
[152] *OJ*, May 18, 1941, p 11, c. 6-7.
[153] Ibid., May 17, 1941, p 4, c 6.
[154] Ibid., May 19, 1941, p 8, c 1-2.
[155] Joseph Kirtley Carson's name should not technically be termed "Jr." because he had a different middle name than his father, whose middle name was Kelly. Mayor Carson's mother disliked the name Kelly and insisted on a different name for her first-born son. But Joseph Jr. called himself Joe Jr. all his life. *OJ*, June 11, 1933, Mag sec, 3; *Oreg.*, May 3, 1933, p 1, 11.
[156] Purdy, 35.
[157] Abbott, *Gateway*, 110-11
[158] MacColl, *Growth*, 609.
[159] Purdy, 35.
[160] *Oreg.*, Dec 22, 1956, p 10, c 1-2.
[161] Thirty-seven-year-old Allen Rushlight (1911-13) and thirty-three-year-old Neil Goldschmidt (1973-9) were younger.
[162] *OJ*, June 11, 1933, Mag sec, 3.
[163] The bar held a special oral examination to speed up the process so these men could volunteer. Ibid.
[164] Ibid., June 18, 1933, Mag sec, 3. Fifteen years after his tenure as mayor, Carson served, by appointment, as a state senator for the 1955 session. Edwards, Cecil, 20.
[165] *OJ*, June 18, 1933, Mag sec, 3.
[166] Nov 1932 Sample Ballot, Sample Ballots 1905-1992, C.P. Arch..
[167] *OJ*, Nov 28, 1932, 6.
[168] Ibid., June 18, 1933, Mag sec, 3.
[169] Ibid., June 11, 1933, Mag sec, 3.
[170] Abbott, *Gateway*, 110-11.
[171] *Portland City Club Bulletin*, Oct 13, 1933.
[172] *Oreg.*, Aug 27, 1933, 1; Dec 5, 1950, A9.
[173] *Oregon Statesman*, Oct 18, 19, 20, 25, 27, 1933, as cited in McKay, 78.
[174] Voters approved the bonds by a two-to-one margin, but turned down measures regarding railway franchises, street lighting systems, and revision of the firemen's pension fund. www.ci.portland.or.us/auditor/Elecarchives2/SPEC33.htm [accessed July 28, 2000].
[175] The November 1934 sewer measure was defeated 46,886 to 33,013. *1955 Portland City Handbook*, 44.
[176] MacColl, *Growth*, 544-45.
[177] Ibid., 546-47.
[178] *1955 Portland City Handbook*, 43-45.
[179] *Oreg.*, Dec 6, 1933, p 1, c 7.

[180] Democrat Bert Haney had replaced long-time port chairman Frank M. Warren the previous fall in the Port's first public election of port commissioners.
[181] MacColl, *Growth*, 462-65.
[182] *Oreg.*, Nov 19, 1933, as cited in ibid., 465.
[183] MacColl, *Growth*, 465.
[184] *Oreg.*, Feb 16, 1934, p 1 and p 2, c 4.
[185] For a detailed description of the waterfront strike of 1934 and its underlying issues, see MacColl, *Growth*, 453-86, and "Portland's 'Silk Stocking Mob'" by Michael Munk, *Pacific Northwest Quarterly*, Summer 2000, 150-60.
[186] MacColl, *Growth*, 453-86; Munk, "Portland's 'Silk Stocking Mob'," 150-60; Dodds, Gordon, 217-18.
[187] Governor Charles Martin and Mayor Joe Carson were singled out for "special condemnation" by a group founded after Governor Martin "vetoed legislation designed to implement a public power scheme for Oregon in 1935." "Hunting Reds in Oregon, 1935-1939," by Gary Murrell, *OHQ* Winter 1999, 378-79.
[188] *Oreg.*, July 13, 1934, p 2, c 2.
[189] A member of the recall movement was charged with forging twenty petition signatures. Ibid., Oct 14, 1934, p 1, c 7, 8. Auditor Funk ruled out 34,732 names because "they were not registered voters" and because "the wording of the petition did not conform to that required by the 1933 law." Ibid., Feb 12, 1935, p 1, c 4.
[190] Quiett, 395.
[191] Draft *Portland Parks and Recreation, A Chronological History*, Dec 1998, 1934 section.
[192] *Oreg.*, Apr 12, 1998; "Historic City Hall Fact Sheet," April, 1998. Funds for the renovation came from both federal and city monies. Lawrence Howes, *OJ*, 1947, month and day unknown.
[193] "How It Was Then: The Pacific Northwest in the Twenties," by Frederick Bracher, *OHQ*, Summer 1984, 162.
[194] *Oreg.*, May 17, 1936, p 1, c 7. Other mayoral candidates were druggist John Witty and ex-boilermaker William Roberts. *Oreg.*, May 3, 1936, p 1, c 6.
[195] Ibid.
[196] Ibid.
[197] A charter amendment passed in 1934 assigned position numbers to commission seats, and provided that any candidate who received over 50 percent of the May primary vote would appear alone on the general election ballot. 1934 Sample Ballot, Sample Ballots book, 1905-1992, C.P. Arch..
[198] Bennett had a "little short of three to one" lead over the next highest vote-getter, Walter Snearly. *Oreg.*, May 17, 1936, p 1, c 7; www.ci.portland.or.us/auditor/Elecarchives2/GEN36.htm [accessed July 28, 2000].
[199] Prior to 1936, Honeyman served in the Oregon legislature for one term (1935) and was the third woman state representative ever elected from Multnomah County. The first, Mrs. C. B. Simmons, was elected to the Oregon House in 1923 and served one term. The second, Dorothy McCullough Lee, who later served as Portland's first woman council member and first woman mayor, was elected to the Oregon House twice (1929, 1931) and to the state senate five times, beginning in 1933. Dorothy Lee and Nan Wood Honeyman therefore both served in the state legislature during the 1935 session, in different branches. Edwards, Cecil, 145-46.
[200] Edith Green would later represent this district in Congress for twenty years, 1955-75. Chamberlin, 112-13; *1997-98 OBB*, 390.
[201] Nov 6, 1934 Sample Ballot, Sample Ballot Book, 1905-1992, C.P. Arch..
[202] Built by WPA craftsmen and artists, Timberline Lodge on the eastern slope of Mount Hood was to become a cherished National Historic Landmark. Bowman, 306; Roe, 149, 170.
[203] *Oreg.*, Sept 29, 1937, 1.
[204] MacColl, *Growth*, 570.
[205] Gunther, 129.
[206] Gunther, 129.
[207] Lucia, *Conscience*, 19.
[208] Carson married Myrtle Cradick of Portland on June 19, 1937. *Oreg.*, Dec 21, 1956.
[209] Ibid., June 16, 1937. Other mayors married while in office were William S. Ladd and Allen G. Rushlight. In May 1938, a daughter was born to Mayor Carson and his wife. *Oreg.*, May 31, 1938, 1.
[210] Abbott, *Portland*, 118.
[211] Ibid., 117-18.
[212] In 1974, a similar measure was proposed, but by that time the cost of a buyout had increased enormously. The measure went down on a three-to-one vote. www.ci.portland.or.us/auditor/Elecarchives2/GEN74.htm [accessed Sept 22, 2000]. A BPA administrator told a City Club study committee that all existing long-term power production had already been fully contracted for, and that no BPA power could be available to the city on a firm basis until 1987. *City Club Bulletin*, No 1, 1974, 142-43. In November 1976, petitioners would again place a measure on the ballot to purchase "certain Pacific Power" facilities, with costs to be financed by revenue bonds. The measure was soundly defeated. Sample General Election Ballot, Multnomah County, City Measure #54, Nov 2, 1976.
[213] This election took place in November 1938. MacColl, *Growth*, 530-34. Commissioner Jake Bennett called the proposal "communistic."
[214] *OJ*, Feb 3, 1939, as quoted in MacColl, *Growth*, 536.
[215] MacColl, *Growth*, 504-5.
[216] Mumford's City Club address was delivered July 15, 1938. Abbott, *Portland*, 123.
[217] *OJ*, July 15, 1938, as quoted in MacColl, *Growth*, 551.
[218] Abbott, *Portland*, 123; MacColl, *Growth*, 552-53.
[219] Lewis Mumford as quoted in McCormack and Pintarich, 156.
[220] Bean was appointed in May 1939 and "proved to be a champion of the consumer." McKay, 139. Bean would return to the council ten years later.
[221] MacColl, *Growth*, 514, 518. The 1.25 million-dollar bond measure passed by a vote of 65,121 in favor to 34,807 against on May 17, 1940. www.ci.portland.or.us/auditor/Elecarchives2/PRIM40.htm [accessed Sept 12, 2000].
[222] MacColl, *Growth*, 513-15, 518. No one would have believed, in his or her wildest dream, that Harbor Drive itself would be removed thirty-four years later, that the monstrous two-block concrete structure that flanked Harbor Drive on the west would be demolished, and that the entire area would be turned into a waterfront

park. The project was completed in November 1942.
[223] "A History of the Port of Portland," Jan 1998, p 8.
[224] MacColl, *Growth*, 571-73.
[225] *Oreg.*, Feb 15, 1947, 1; Feb 18, 1947, 1; Feb 22, 1947, 1.
[226] Purdy, 35; Leeson, 128.
[227] While Carson was living in Washington, D. C., his name was mentioned in a 1952 book titled *How to Get Rich in Washington*, which hinted "that the maritime commission of which he [Carson] was a member helped to make special favorites of the incumbent administration rich" by allowing special subsidies to a dozen ship lines. Carson said the accusation did not warrant or justify any comment. *Oreg.*, Apr 27, 1952, p 18 c 6.
[228] Carson was the Democratic nominee for governor against incumbent Paul Patterson. Carson passed away in Dec 1956. Turnbull, *Governors*, 96; *Oreg.*, Dec 21, 1956, p 1, c 7; *1997-98 OBB*, 372.

Chapter 21

[1] MacColl, *Growth*, 571.
[2] Abbott, *Portland*, 118. Earl Riley defeated Frank H. Hilton with 52 percent of the vote. During the campaign, charges were hurled back and forth about "allegedly libelous publications." *Oreg.*, Nov 7, 1940, p 6; Nov 8, 1940, p 6, c 7, 8.
[3] Abbott, *Portland*, 155. In another 1940 race, Commissioner Bill Bowes, the former linotype operator and printer who had been appointed to a council vacancy a year and a half before, had garnered enough votes in his primary race to be spared a November run-off. Purdy, 47; www.ci.portland.or.us/auditor/Elecarchives2/PRIM & GEN40.htm [accessed Sept 12, 2000].
[4] In an article written at the time of Bennett's death, *Oreg.* writer Harold Hughes said of him, "During his recent years in the Legislature, he was a kind of a time bomb, waiting to explode and upset the schedules of House leaders, be they Democrats or Republicans. But even when he couldn't command supporting votes, he commanded attention with his articulate and colorful language." *Oreg.*, Apr 4, 1970, p 15, c 3-4.
[5] *Pacific Northwest* Quarterly, Summer 2000, 155, 158; Oreg., Nov 7, 1940, p 6, c 6.
[6] Nowadays, a charter provision requires a runoff election if no candidate receives over 50 percent of the vote. Also, an elected official has to resign before an election can be scheduled for a replacement, which was not the case here. City Charter Sec. 2-206 (b), (c), and (d). In March 1942, the council passed Ord #76832, a charter reorganization and codification that required three indexing tables to track contents of the 1913 charter through a 1928 revision to the newest revision. Charter Amendments folder, 1913-42 file, Box 5 of 10, C.P. Arch..
[7] *Oreg.*, Aug 16, 1972, Sec 1, 40 and Sports Sec, 6; Purdy, 45.
[8] The council had appointed Edward W. Jones as interim city auditor in 1938. Gibson was designated America's Outstanding Municipal Finance Official "in recognition of public service and for establishing efficiency in accounting systems" by the National Association of Municipal Finance Officers in 1941. Purdy, 47-48.
[9] Mayor Riley's obituary says, "He was the son of a fire captain." *Oreg.* Aug 19, 1945, p 34, c 2. Lone Fir Cemetery records show that his father was Lester N. Riley, who died in 1928. An employee card at the Portland Fire Bureau says that L. N. Riley was appointed Aug 7, 1903; promoted to captain Dec 1, 1913; "suspended" Apr 25, 1921; and "pensioned" Apr 26, 1921.
[10] Earl Riley's grandfather, Robert R. Riley, came to Oregon via boat in 1851, walking across the Isthmus of Panama, according to Earl Riley's daughter, Dorislee Riley Hoffpauer of Richardson, Texas, in a telephone conversation with the author on Sept 26, 2000.
[11] *Who's Who for Oregon, 1942-1944*, 354; *Oreg.*, Jan 6, 1929, p 13, c 3 and Aug 19, 1965, p 34, c 2; *Oregon Journal*, Aug 20, 1965, p 10, c 1.
[12] Abbott, *Portland*, 119.
[13] MacColl, *Growth*, 609.
[14] Grand Coulee was a new dam being built further up the Columbia from Bonneville, ninety miles northwest of Spokane, in Washington State. It was built for both irrigation and hydroelectric power and was completed in 1942.
[15] Pitzer, 265; Hardin, 81-82; *Oreg.*, July 22, 2001, D1, D4.
[16] "Music, 1936," *The People's Chronology*, by James Trager, 1995, licensed from Henry Holt and Company, Inc.; Harden, 81-2.
[17] "Roll On, Columbia, Roll On" was adopted as the official Washington State folk song in 1987. www.leg.wa.gov/legis/symbols/symbols.htm [accessed Apr 9, 2003].
[18] Writer and later U.S. Senator Richard Neuberger was a foremost advocate of harnessing nature to serve humanity. Robbins, 295; Harden, 81-82.
[19] The *Star of Oregon* was christened Sept 27, 1942, by Blanche Sprague, wife of then-governor Charles Sprague. McKay, 130; Maben, 1; Long, 53.
[20] Abbott, *Portland*, 131.
[21] *History of Portland, Oregon*, WPA Writers' Project, Federal Works Agency, Work Projects Administration, 1941.
[22] For example, see *Oregon: End of the Trail*, WPA Writers' Project, Oregon, Binfords & Mort, 1940.
[23] For example, see *Inventory of the County Archives of Oregon, No 26, Multnomah County*, Oregon Historical Records Survey Project No. 65-1-94-25, Vol I, June 1940 and Vol II, May 1940.
[24] *Spec. Index*, 1846-1854, Vol I and II, WPA Newspaper Index Project, O. P. 665-94-3-66, May 1941.
[25] See *Guide to the Manuscript Collections of the Oregon Historical Society*, Portland: Federal Works Agency, WPA Official Historical Records Proj No. 65-1-94-25, August 1940.
[26] Abbott, *Portland*, 141.
[27] Ibid., 131-33; MacColl, *Growth*, 575. Columbia Villa had already been approved as a low-income housing project site in October 1941 because the city was eligible for defense-related housing money under a Supreme Court ruling. Ground breaking for Columbia Villa occurred in May 1942. Communications between Carl Abbott and this author March 1 and 2, 2001, and between former HAP Deputy Director Helen Barney and this author, March 2 and 3, 2001.

[28] Draft *Portland Parks and Recreation, A Chronological History*, Dec 1998, 1942 section.
[29] Ibid.
[30] Leeson, 137.
[31] *Oreg.*, Dec 5, 1950, A9.
[32] Long, 53. See also *Oreg.*, Dec 8, 1941, p 1, c 2.
[33] *History of Portland's African American Community*, Portland Bureau of Planning, Feb 1993, 64-65; Abbott, *Portland*, 133-34; Maben, 104; McKay, 130; *OHQ*, Spring 1990, 7.
[34] Maben, 1.
[35] Republican vice-presidential candidate Earl Warren said the same year, 1948, that "Grand Coulee had done nothing less than save America from atomic annihilation." Harden, 83.
[36] Even some toddlers contributed to the war effort. Long, blonde hair never touched by curling irons was needed for making bomb sights. The author's four-year-old sister, Sherry Beck, donated her hair (which had grown to three inches below her waist) to an airplane factory in 1943. A sample of her hair was first sent to a factory in Maryland to find out if it was usable.
[37] *Oreg.*, June 29, 1980, C3.
[38] Draft *Portland Parks and Recreation*, 1943 section.
[39] Henry Kaiser first experimented with a prepaid health plan for his Grand Coulee dam workers in 1938. "About Kaiser Permanente - Who We Are;" www.kp.org/about/whoweare.html and www.kp.org/newsroom/history.html [accessed Sept 20, 2000].
[40] MacColl, *Growth*, 583.
[41] *History of Portland's African American Community*, 62; McKay, 130.
[42] Discrimination was not unique to Portland. The U.S. Chinese Exclusion Act was not repealed until December 1943. *Seventy-Eighth Congress, Session I, 1943*; Chapter 344, 57 U.S. Statutes at Large, p 600-601.
[43] June 1945 memo from HAP staff member K. E. Eckert to executive director Harry D. Freeman, as quoted in MacColl, *Growth*, 580.
[44] *History of Portland's African American Community*, 67.
[45] Obituary of DeNorval Unthank, Jr., *Oreg.*, Nov 11, 2000, B3.
[46] Lucia, *Conscience*, 63.
[47] *Oreg.*, Feb 27, 1944, as quoted in MacColl, *Growth*, 583.
[48] McKay, 130.
[49] Pitzer, "Dorothy McCullough Lee," 11-12.
[50] Ibid.
[51] John O. Bredemeier was acting auditor from Dec 1943 until Dec 1945.
[52] MacColl, *Growth*, 584-85.
[53] Robert Moses started out as a reformer, but metamorphosed over the years into an abuser of power. *The Power Broker, Robert Moses and the Fall of New York*, Robert A. Caro, 1974.
[54] Edgar Kaiser had extended the invitation to Moses first, then convinced the PAPDC to follow through.
[55] Abbott, *Portland*, 138; MacColl, *Growth*, 587.
[56] Commissioner Bowes gave his radio address Nov 15, 1943. Abbott, *Portland*, 139; MacColl, *Growth*, 587-88.
[57] MacColl, *Growth*, 589.
[58] Communication with Carl Abbott by this author, Feb 12, 2001.
[59] Pitzer, "Dorothy McCullough Lee," 12-13; Maddux, 207.
[60] MacColl, *Growth*, 588-89; Abbott, Portland, 140; www.ci.portland.or.us/auditor/Elecarchives2/PRIM44 & GEN44.htm [accessed Sept 12, 2000].
[61] MacColl, *Growth*, 591-92; www.ci.portland.or.us/auditor/Elecarchives2/SPEC45.htm & GEN46.htm [accessed Sept 12, 2000].
[62] Houle, 11.
[63] Short, 48-49, 73.
[64] Harmon, Rick, "The Bull Run Watershed," *OHQ*, Summer-Fall 1995, 256-57.
[65] Lucia, 40-42; *Portland City Club Bulletin*, Jan 27, 1945.
[66] Victory in Europe Day was May 8, 1945.
[67] *Oreg.*, Aug 15, 1945, 1.
[68] *OS*, 77.
[69] Oregon Constitution, Article XI-A, *1997-98 Blue Book*, 457. By 2000, the Oregon Department of Veterans' Affairs had issued over 332,000 veterans' loans, with the program extended to subsequent military veterans. A successful 2000 ballot measure broadened eligibility for this program. *Oreg.*, Oct 22, 2000, C2.
[70] The survey was undertaken at the behest of the Portland committee for post-war planning, and conducted under the auspices of Dr. Chilton R. Bush, chair of the Stanford University journalism school. The Portland area included Gresham, Beaverton, Oregon City, Tigard, and points in between. When asked what aspect of living in the area had caused them most inconvenience, "none" and "transportation" were the two biggest categories. *Oreg.*, Feb 27, 1944, p 1, c 1; p 17, c 6-7.
[71] MacColl, *Growth*, 593-95.
[72] Robert Moses had noted during his visit two years before that many community leaders believed it was neither "possible nor desirable" for Portland "to keep all of the war workers attracted from other parts of the country," with the term "war workers" understood to mean blacks. "Portland Improvement," by Robert Moses, 1943, as quoted in O'Donnell and Vaughan, 66.
[73] Maben, 92-93.
[74] From this modest beginning, Portland State University would be established nine years later on the downtown South Park Blocks. The federal G. I. Bill of Rights would bring record enrollments at higher education facilities throughout the region. *Oreg.*, Feb 18, 2001, A23; *Oreg.*, Dec 4, 1950, B14.
[75] Maben, 74-80, 102-3.
[76] Those who deserve special credit for today's Forest Park include the Rev. Thomas Lamb Eliot, the Olmsted Brothers, and Portland businessman Garnett "Ding" Cannon, who persuaded the City Club to undertake a feasibility study in 1945, which Cannon chaired. Houle, 11, 13.
[77] Ibid., 12-13.
[78] Ibid., xi.
[79] Multnomah County commissioners in 1947-48 were Frank Shull, Tom H. West, and Alan Brown.
[80] O'Donnell and Vaughan, 184.
[81] Dorothy McCullough Lee ascribed her "reluctant" candidacy for mayor to this shocking incident. MacColl, *Growth*, 647-48; Pitzer, "Dorothy McCullough Lee," 13.

[82] MacColl, *Growth*, 613-14.
[83] *Oreg.*, Jan 15, 1948, as quoted in ibid., 614.
[84] *City Club Bulletin*, Feb 20, 1948, 132-48.
[85] Ibid., 133, 135; MacColl, *Growth*, 610-11.
[86] *City Club Bulletin*, Feb 20, 1948, 134-35.
[87] Uris, 60, 198.
[88] *City Club Bulletin*, Feb 20, 1948, 142-48.
[89] John Gunther, 1947, as cited in Uris, 61.
[90] Abbott, *Portland*, 156.
[91] Aug 8, 1979, interview with Dorothy McCullough Lee by E. Kimbark MacColl, as reported in *Growth*, 614. Also see *Growth*, 648.
[92] Prominent Portland businessmen who endorsed Riley's campaign for a third term included Portland Chamber of Commerce president Hillman Lueddemann and four former Chamber presidents, U.S. Bank president E. C. Sammons, Benjamin Franklin Savings and Loan president Ben Hazen, Iron Fireman executive T. Harry Banfield, architect Glenn Stanton, Meier and Frank department store executive Aaron Frank, and shopping center owner Fred G. Meyer. MacColl, *Growth*, 614.
[93] Ibid., 647.
[94] Abbott, *Portland*, 156. Commissioner Fred Peterson won resounding reelection at the same time. www.ci.portland.or.us/auditor/Elecarchives2/PRIM48.htm [accessed Sept 12, 2000].
[95] The 1948 flood was the largest flood on the Columbia River since 1894, and lasted for almost three weeks. The Columbia crested at thirty-one feet at Vancouver, Washington. It was the "most destructive flood in the Columbia River Basin in 180 years." Taylor and Hatton, 87, 98.
[96] *Oreg.*, May 31, 1948; Maben, 105-6, 121.
[97] Maben, 106-8.
[98] Maddox, 209.
[99] Maben, 116; Maddox, 209.
[100] Maben, 122.
[101] Ibid., 104.
[102] Abbott, *Portland*, 157.
[103] www.ci.portland.or.us/auditor/Elecarchives2/GEN48.htm [accessed Sept 12, 2000].
[104] MacColl, *Growth*, 614.
[105] The report also said, "A good twenty percent of the members of the active police are no longer fit to serve in the positions they are required to fill." *City Club Bulletin*, Feb 20, 1948, 135. Presumably, this conclusion referred to physical fitness.
[106] *1955 Portland City Handbook*, 21.
[107] The measure received 85,370 yes votes to 56,938 no. Effective July 1, 1990, members were no longer required to make contributions into the retirement plan. www.ci.portland.or.us/auditor/Elecarchives2/GEN48.htm [accessed Sept 12, 2000]; *City of Portland General Purpose Financial Statements for the Fiscal Year Ended June 30, 2000*, Note 17, Fire and Police Disability and Retirement Plan, p 55.
[108] Portland City Charter, Chapter 5, Sec 5-102 and 103, approved by the voters Nov 2, 1948, amended Nov 7, 1950.
[109] A 1980 City Club report called for requiring all "normal costs" to be paid on a current basis and sufficient money budgeted to amortize unfunded liabilities in already established plans. *City Club Bulletin*, July 4, 1980, 33.
[110] Correspondence from Richard Tracy, Portland Director of Audits, to the author, Oct 29-31, 2000.
[111] Pitzer, "Dorothy McCullough Lee," 9.
[112] Ibid., 5, 8, 34; *Oreg.*, Feb 20, 1981, C1.
[113] Pitzer, "Dorothy McCullough Lee," 9.
[114] Ibid., 10. At the time of her election to the House in 1929, Lee was the sixth woman to serve in the Oregon legislature and the third woman in the state Senate. Edwards, Cecil, 145.
[115] Pitzer, "Dorothy McCullough Lee," 11.
[116] *1997-98 OBB*, 152.
[117] Pitzer, "Dorothy McCullough Lee," 11.
[118] Ibid.
[119] Lee received 85,567 votes to 22,078 for Riley and 20,298 for Frank M. Learned. www.ci.portland.or.us/auditor/Elecarchives2/PRIM48.htm [accessed Sept 12, 2000].
[120] Pitzer, "Dorothy McCullough Lee," 14.
[121] Maddux, 205. See also MacColl, *Growth*, 649.
[122] Pitzer, "Dorothy McCullough Lee," 16-17. Sometime during the Lee administration, the Press Club's six illegal slot machines were dumped in the Willamette River. The club closed in the mid-50s. "Press club blended ink, alcohol in an era of different ethics," by R. Gregory Nokes, *Oreg.* Anniversary Special, Dec 4, 2000, 44.
[123] Pitzer, "Dorothy McCullough Lee," 16. Pitzer based his conclusion about Lee's motivations on Dorothy Lee biographical notes written by W. Scott Lee, a copy of which is available at the Oregon Historical Society.
[124] Contemporary readers may wonder at Lee's conclusion that slot machines are the root of all evil, when such devices were readily available to the public at the beginning of the twenty-first century at Indian casinos all over the United States.
[125] Punchboards were thick cardboard rectangles with rows of small covered holes that had messages secreted inside. When the holes were punched out, some of the messages awarded prizes. This author observed merchandise-prize punchboards in restaurants, bars, and grocery stores in Montana in the 1940s.
[126] Pitzer, "Dorothy McCullough Lee," 23-24.
[127] *OJ*, Sept 1 and 2, 1949, as cited in ibid., 24.
[128] Pitzer, "Dorothy McCullough Lee," 17.
[129] Ibid., 23.
[130] The recall against Elliott passed by a 12,700 margin out of 105,000 votes cast. MacColl, *Growth*, 652-53; Maddux, 204; Pitzer, "Dorothy McCullough Lee," 25.
[131] *OJ*, Nov 24, 1949, as quoted in Pitzer, "Dorothy McCullough Lee," 25.
[132] "Portland of Years Past," 1950 segment, *Oreg.*, March 16, 2000, E3.
[133] MacColl, *Growth*, 655.
[134] www.ci.portland.or.us/auditor/Elecarchives2/PRIM50.htm & SPEC50.htm [accessed Sept 12, 2000].
[135] MacColl, *Growth*, 555.
[136] By comparison, the city had 1,927 inhabitants in 1851, and encompassed only 2.1 square miles.
[137] 1900 U. S. Census; "Population of the City of Portland, 1850-1975," prepared by the City Finance Office.
[138] *OS*, 89. By 2000, the percentage of white Oregon residents had decreased 12 percent, to 86.6 percent, while Portland's percentage had decreased to 79.2

percent. http://quickfacts.census.gov/qfd/states/41/41051.html [accessed June 15, 2002].

[139] Lee and the rest of the council "stayed remarkebly distant" from the "emotional issue" involved when Dr. Ruth Barnett was raided, arrested, and put on trial for performing abortions in summer 1951. *OJ*, May 1, 1951, as cited in Pitzer, "Dorothy McCullough Lee," 29.

[140] Abbott, *Portland*, 159; Pitzer, "Dorothy McCullough Lee," 26.

[141] "Portland of Years Past," 1950 segment, *Oreg.*, Jan 6, 2000, E7.

[142] *Oreg.*, Feb 20, 1981, C1.

[143] Abbott, *Portland*, 158.

[144] "Portland of Years Past," 1950 segment, *Oreg.*, June 8, 2000, E3; *OJ*, Apr 11, 1958.

[145] The official city flag, adopted by council ordinance in 1971, hung in council chambers and on a flagstaff by the Fourth Avenue entrance to city hall in April 2001. The flag has undergone several updates over the years. *OJ*, Dec 18, 1969; City Code section 1.06.010, adopted as Ord #132219, Feb 18, 1971; correspondence between the author and researcher Ted Kaye dated Sept 4, 2002.

[146] At the state capital in Salem, Bennett had "rushed across the hearing room, and [begun] a fistfight with Carl W. Hogg, a state liquor control commissioner." Pitzer, "Dorothy McCullough Lee," 27.

[147] *OJ*, April 5, 1951, as cited in ibid. 27-28.

[148] Maddux, 200-201; MacColl, *Growth*, 653; *Oreg.*, Feb 20, 1981, C1.

[149] Abbott, *Portland*, 157; Pitzer, "Dorothy McCullough Lee," 26.

[150] *OS*, 91.

[151] Pitzer, "Dorothy McCullough Lee," 27; "Portland of Years Past," 1950 segment, *Oreg.*, Sept 21, 2000.

[152] The vote on the equal rights measure was 60,969 yes to 77,084 no. www.ci.portland.or.us/auditor/Elecarchives2/GEN50.htm [accessed Sept 12, 2000].

[153] Autobiographical sketch by Dorothy McCullough Lee obtained from E. Kimbark MacColl; Pitzer, "Dorothy McCullough Lee," 22-23.

[154] Mayor Frank Ivancie is quoted in the *Oreg.*, Feb 20, 1981, C1: "Dottie—we all used to call her that—will always be a fascinating figure in Portland's history." Ivancie credited Lee with "changing the city's image to a 'more rightful mode.'"

[155] Lee subsequently helped the company gain a needed fare increase, and they "grudgingly" provided new motorized busses to replace all old rail lines. At one time Portland had "one of the most enviable electric trolley systems in the United States," but got rid of it to make way for automobiles. Leeson, 185. "The last cars on the Council Crest, Willamette Heights, and Twenty-third Avenue lines ran earlyy in the morning of Sunday, February 26, 1950, and thereafter service was provided by motor busses." Maddux, 112. Abandonment of rail right-of-ways was, in retrospect, unfortunate, because by the end of the twentieth century, light rail was generally viewed as a more efficient and pollution-free method of travel than gasoline-powered vehicles. "However, the rail system in Portland was antiquated and would have been impossible to operate" under today's circumstances, said Bob Baldwin, former Multnomah County Planning Director. Letter to the author, Nov 26, 2000.

[156] Pitzer, "Dorothy McCullough Lee," 11, 13, 16-17.

[157] MacColl, *Growth*, 185-87, 626.

[158] Notson, 48.

[159] Scott Lee was said to have a "corny" sense of humor. He was employed by Standard Oil, and once jested that when there were problems "he simply put oil on the troubled waters." Ibid. 11.

[160] Ibid., 25, 34.

[161] Ibid., 10, 15.

[162] *Oreg.*, June 16, 1949, 18; MacColl, *Growth*, 652.

[163] *OJ*, Mar 31, July 6, and Aug 23, 1951, as cited in Pitzer, "Dorothy McCullough Lee," 16.

[164] Donald McNamara would later serve another nine years as police chief (1964-73) under Mayor Terry Schrunk, then a year under Mayor Neil Goldschmidt until replaced by outsider Bruce Baker.

[165] "The Rise and Fall of the Portland Hotel," by G. Douglas Nicoll, *OHQ*, Fall 1998, 298, 325, 328; O'Donnell and Vaughan, 67.

[166] O'Donnell and Vaughan, 69; Pitzer, "Dorothy McCullough Lee," 29.

[167] *OS*, 91.

[168] Sample ballot, May 16, 1952 Special Recall Election, Sample Ballots, 1905-1992, C.P. Arch.

[169] Pitzer, "Dorothy McCullough Lee," 28. See also *Oreg.*, April 4, 1970, 14-15.

[170] Sample ballot, May 16, 1952 Special Recall Election, Sample Ballots, 1905-92, C.P. Arch.

[171] Pitzer, "Dorothy McCullough Lee," 5.

[172] Peterson won 38 percent, Lee 36 percent, a candidate named Lew Wallace 19 percent of the May vote for mayor, with the remaining three candidates together receiving the other 2 percent. Dorothy Lee received twenty-eight thousand fewer votes than she had in her victorious primary four years before. On the same May 1952 ballot, Bill Bowes easily won reelection. www.ci.portland.or.us/auditor/Elecarchives2/PRIM52.htm [accessed Sept 12, 2000]. A measure Lee had pushed to prohibit punchboards was not on the ballot because the state supreme court ruled that an emergency clause Lee had attached to the referendum ordinance did not constitute a valid emergency. www.ci.portland.or.us/auditor/elections/Meas1942.htm [accessed Aug 9, 2000].

[173] www.ci.portland.or.us/auditor/Elecarchives2/GEN52.htm [accessed Sept 12, 2000]. Stanley Earl was the union official who had been the main author of the City Club report on vice four years before.

[174] "Portland of Years Past," 1950 segment, *Oreg.*, Jan 13, 2000, E11.

[175] www.ci.portland.or.us/auditor/elections/Meas1942.htm [accessed Aug 9, 2000].

[176] Autobiographical sketch by Dorothy McCullough Lee; Pitzer, "Dorothy McCullough Lee," 32-33.

[177] As the Democratic nominee for state treasurer in 1976, this author was the speaker at a Business and Professional Women's meeting that Lee attended. Lee was polite, but aloof. She looked frail and disengaged. Her husband had died earlier that year and Lee herself underwent extensive surgery for cancer shortly after the meeting.

[178] Dorothy Lee taught classes at Portland State University, Warner Pacific College, and the University of Portland. Pitzer, "Dorothy McCullough Lee," 33.

[179] *Oreg.*, Feb 20, 1981, C1. Lee was buried in River View Cemetery.
[180] Pitzer, "Dorothy McCullough Lee," 30.
[181] *Oreg.*, Feb 20, 1981, C1.

Chapter 22

[1] Pitzer, "Dorothy McCullough Lee," 31.
[2] Republican Connie McCready subsequently served as the appointed mayor in 1979-80, but lost her election bid.
[3] *Oreg.*, Oct 18, 1985, C7; *Who's Who in the West*, 1956 edition, 500.
[4] Elsewhere in the same issue, a letter to the editor championed Mayor Lee's hats. *Oreg.*, June 16, 1949, 18 and June 22, 1949, 1; *Oreg.*, Nov 13, 1984, PM2, c 1; MacColl, *Growth*, 652.
[5] Bean had had "youthful allegiance to housing reform" and continued to favor "structural changes to city government." Abbott, *Portland*, 158-59. Also see *OJ*, Aug 27, 1958, p 5, c 1 and Dec 31, 1958, p 43.
[6] Correspondence from *Oreg.* columnist John Terry to the author, Nov 3, 2000.
[7] *OS*, 89.
[8] *Oreg.*, Apr 21, 1999.
[9] Ibid., Oct 18, 1985, C7.
[10] MacColl, *Growth*, 355, 550-51; Draft *Portland Parks and Recreation, A Chronological History*, Dec 1998, 1954 section.
[11] www.ci.portland.or.us/auditor/elections/Meas1942.htm [accessed Aug 9, 2000].
[12] De Marco, 142.
[13] Abbott, *Portland*, 162-63.
[14] MacColl, *Growth*, 589. In 1987-89, the council considered two major alignment changes to I-5: moving the freeway away from the east bank, and building a southbound ramp onto I-5 near the east side of the Marquam Bridge. The council decided against both projects after contentious hearings, mainly because of enormous after-the-fact costs and other needs for transportation funds. The Central Eastside Industrial Council was pushing for access to I-5 southbound from the east side, a proposed ramp that would have jutted out into the river. City land-use planner Michael Harrison estimated the cost to relocate the freeway further east with an alignment along Eighth and Ninth avenues at up to 335 million dollars. "Crowd packs forum on proposed I-5 relocation," by Carla Thompson, *Oreg.*, Nov 3, 1987, B4, c 2; Letter from former city planning director Ernie Bonner to the author, Dec 15, 2000.
In May 1993, the council reaffirmed a goal of reclaiming and redeveloping the Willamette River Eastbank. A citizens' committee recommended that the I-5 freeway be removed from the Eastbank "over the long term" of 15 to 25 years." Council Resolution #35141 dated May 1993. "Willamette River Eastbank Review Report and Recommendations," Nov 29, 1993, p 11. Mayor Vera Katz again breathed life into the issue in her January 2001 State-of-the-City speech to the Portland City Club.
[15] Price, 45.
[16] The Portland Arts Commission told Governor Hatfield that the Marquam Bridge was "so gross, so lacking in grace, so utterly inconsistent with any concept of esthetics that the Art Commission feels called upon to offer a formal protest." However, others noted that the bridge was "unduly criticized for its uncomplicated practicality." Wood, 43; "Art Commission Opposes Marquam Bridge Design," by Carl Gohs, *Portland Reporter*, Aug 12, 1963, 10, as cited in Price, 52-53.
[17] At the June 18, 1954, meeting, the new E-R commissioners met with the mayor, three council members, the city attorney, a city photographer, and representatives of KOIN-TV, KPTV-TV, the *Oreg.*, and the *Journal* in city hall chambers. E-R Commission minutes, June 18, 1954, 1. Metropolitan Exposition-Recreation Commission office. KGW-TV broadcast its first color network program in 1954, but did not cover this local event. *OS*, 91.
[18] E-R Commission minutes, June 18, 1954, 1-2. Metropolitan Exposition-Recreation Commission office.
[19] MacColl, *Growth*, 253-55, 462-67.
[20] The other three E-R commissioners were John T. Carson, James J. Richardson, and Carvel Linden. E-R Commission minutes, 1-4, MERC, 777 N.E. MLK Jr. Blvd, Portland, OR 97232.
[21] When the water bureau's new chief engineer, H. Kenneth Anderson, warned Peterson that the city needed another dam at Bull Run, and cautioned that such projects required time for careful planning and design, Peterson said, "Put the dam in this summer, and then you can plan and design it next winter during the slow time!" Bull Run dam #2 was begun in 1958 and completed in 1962. Harmon, Rick, "The Bull Run Watershed," *OHQ*, Summer-Fall 1995, 260-61.
[22] Uris, 202.
[23] *Oreg.*, Apr 19, 1956, 1.
[24] Uris, 171.
[25] Leeson, 150-52.
[26] Baker would run for council, unsuccessfully, against Connie McCready in 1970. Uris, 172.
[27] Ibid., 86, 93, 171, 193, 212.
[28] Ibid., 68-71.
[29] Ibid., 5.
[30] Ibid., 5, 78, 197, 213.
[31] Seventy hours of tape recordings were ultimately involved. Notson, 47.
[32] Uris, 206.
[33] Morgan testified at the U.S. Senate hearings that this is what he had told the press. Ibid., 121.
[34] Notson, 47; *Oreg.*, Apr 19, 1956, 1.
[35] Uris, 79, 203, 219.
[36] Nine candidates were on the ballot in the May 1956 mayoral contest. www.ci.portland.or.us/auditor/Elecarchives2/PRIM56.htm [accessed Sept 12, 2000].
[37] The pinball measure was placed on the ballot by a Teamster signature drive challenging a council-passed ordinance outlawing pinball machines. Uris, 114; www.ci.portland.or.us/auditor/Elecarchives2/PRIM56.htm [accessed Sept 12, 2000].
[38] Telephone conversation with Don Clark by the author on November 1, 2000.
[39] Uris, 220-21, 224.
[40] Voters also rejected fluoridation of the city water supply. www.ci.portland.or.us/auditor/elections/Elecarchives2/PRIM56.htm & GEN56.htm [accessed Sept 12, 2000].

[41] Uris, 91.
[42] Ibid., 92.
[43] Ibid., 138-41; 186-92.
[44] Leeson, 150-53; "Portland Vice Quiz Proves Fizzle," by Drew Pearson, *OJ*, Apr 23, 1958, Sec 4, p 4.
[45] *Oreg.*, Sept 16, 1956, p 1, c 7.
[46] Ibid..
[47] Schrunk polled 61 percent to Peterson's 39 percent. www.ci.portland.or.us/auditor/Elecarchives2/GEN56.htm [accessed Sept 12, 2000].
[48] The pinball ban was upheld 62 percent to 38 percent in November 1956. www.ci.portland.or.us/auditor/Elecarchives2/GEN56.htm [accessed Sept 12, 2000].
[49] Uris, 232.
[50] *Oreg.*, Nov 13, 1984, PM2, c 1, and Oct 22, 1985, D16, c 1.
[51] Ibid., Nov 13, 1984, PM2, c 1. A year after the *Oreg.* interview, Fred Peterson died of lingering cancer at age eighty-nine. *Oreg.*, Oct 18, 1985, C7, and Oct 22, 1985, D16, c 1. Peterson is buried at Willamette National Cemetery, Sec L 562. Letter to the author dated March 31, 2000, from James Brewster of Willamette National Cemetery.
[52] City offices were nonpartisan, but political affiliations of candidates were well known. The only Democrats elected mayor after Philip Wasserman in 1871 were Sylvester Pennoyer (1896-98), Harry Lane (1905-09), and Joe Carson (1933-40).
[53] *1999-2000 OBB*, 311, 347.
[54] *OJ*, March 4, 1975.
[55] *Who's Who for Oregon*. Portland: R. O. Norman, Book Publisher, 1961, 245.
[56] Uris, 171.
[57] Twenty-five years later, there was "remarkable consensus" in Portland that the Senate Committee was unjust and that "the treatment afforded witnesses was unfair." Ibid., 222-23.
[58] Pearson, "Portland Vice Quiz," p 4.
[59] Allegations against Schrunk were presented to a grand jury three times, after Attorney General Thornton was pressured by the *Oreg.* to do so, before an indictment of Schrunk was issued. *OJ*, March 15 and 30, 1957, 1; Uris, 78, 92, 204.
[60] *OJ*, Apr 1 and 2, 1957, 1.
[61] "Schrunk's Record: He Should Resign," *Oreg.*, March 30, 1957, p 10, c 1.
[62] Leeson, 153-54.
[63] Ibid., 154; *Oreg.*, June 28, 1957.
[64] The trial ended June 29, 1957. Leeson, 153-55; Uris, 92, 191-92, 203-4, 219.
[65] This author knows District Attorney Michael D. Schrunk personally and holds him in high regard. However, she never met Mayor Schrunk, although she saw him on television numerous times. The author moved to Salem, Oregon, from out of state in fall 1957, and to Portland in late summer 1961.
[66] Telephone conversation with Don Clark by the author on November 1, 2000.
[67] Leeson, 150.
[68] *Oreg.*, Sept 25, 1957, p 1, c 3; Leeson, 150-53; Uris, 5, 94, 221, 277; Pearson, "Portland Vice Quiz," p 4.
[69] *Elkins v United States*, June 28, 1960, as cited in Uris, 183.
[70] Uris, 177.
[71] Ibid., 88, 124.
[72] *OJ*, Apr 8 and Apr 14, 1957, as quoted in ibid., 173, 186-87.
[73] Uris, 211.
[74] Ibid., 60, 198; *City Club Bulletin*, Feb 20, 1948, 1.
[75] *Oreg.* editorial at the time of Earl's death, Mar 6, 1970, 38.
[76] Taped interview with former city commissioner Lloyd Anderson by Ernie Bonner on Feb 27, 1995, p 7, copy furnished to the author with Anderson's permission on Oct 11, 2000.
[77] Uris, 79, 114-15, 146, 198-99.
[78] Pearson, "Portland Vice Quiz," p 4.
[79] Uris, 198-99.
[80] Ibid., 146-47.
[81] Ibid., 144.
[82] Pearson, "Portland Vice Quiz," p 4.
[83] Notson, 47-48; Leeson, 150; Pearson, "Portland Vice Quiz," p 4.
[84] Notson, 48. Racketeers were said to have made a handsome profit from the sale of land (close-in, eastside) on which the E-R center was built. Uris, 58, 71-74, 194.
[85] Uris, 156-57.
[86] Ibid., 54, 223, 232.
[87] Kell-Uris interview of 1981, as cited in ibid., 204.
[88] Uris, 193.
[89] *Oreg.*, Feb 14, 1937, as cited in MacColl, *Growth*, 536-37.
[90] Elkins suffered a heart attack and died at age sixty-seven when his car "crashed into a utility pole" in August 1972. Uris, 193.
[91] The Fair Housing Act made it illegal to refuse to rent or sell because of a person's race. *Oreg.*, Apr 21, 1999; *OS*, 90-91.
[92] Credit for conceiving the Willamette Greenway concept belongs to Dean Karl W. Onthank of the University of Oregon, who got the idea from the American River Greenway near Sacramento. Onthank sent materials about his proposal to both McCall and Bob Straub, and Straub first proposed the Willamette Greenway publicly. McCall, with Neal, 68.
[93] Walth, 402-3; McCall with Neal, 68, 183, 186-87.
[94] www.ci.portland.or.us/auditor/Elecarchives2/PRIM58.htm [accessed Sept 12, 2000].
[95] *OJ*, Sept 9, 1959, p 3B, c 4-6.
[96] John Kenward, head of the Urban Renewal Section of the city Planning Bureau, as quoted in Abbott, *Portland*, 171.
[97] Guest editorial by Miss Elsie R. Perry, "Why Owners Fight Urban Renewal Job," *OJ*, Sept 8, 1959, p 22, c 7.
[98] MacColl, *Growth*, 47, 54-60.
[99] DeMarco, 143.
[100] One of these parks was named for Portland founder Asa Lovejoy, and nearby Pettygrove Park for founder Francis Pettygrove. O'Donnell and Vaughan, 143-47; Price, 58-59; Abbott, *Portland*, 212-14.
[101] Interview with Donald Sterling, former *OJ* editor, by Ernie Bonner in March 2000, p 5. www.pdxplan.org/DonSterlingweb.html [accessed Oct 1, 2000].
[102] Interview with Richard Brainard, principal staff member of the CH2M Hill team working with Dick Ivey on the Portland Downtown Plan, by Ernie Bonner on Jan 16, 1995, Part II, p 3. Brainard says, "Keller was probably the richest man in Oregon at the time. He was like a little Napoleon or little Caesar." Richard Ivey says

that meetings regarding the Downtown Plan were sometimes held in Keller's boardroom at Willamette Industries. www.pdxplan.org/Ivy2.html, p 5 [accessed Dec 1, 2000].

[103] Abbott, *Portland*, 170.

[104] Interview with Donald Sterling, by Ernie Bonner, p 5; www.pdxplan.org/DonSterlingweb.html [accessed Oct 1, 2000]; Abbott, Portland, 171.

[105] "Fifty Years of Commission Government, 1913-1963," unpublished manuscript by E. Kimbark MacColl, 1985, p 16.

[106] Ira Keller Fountain was designed by Angela Danadjieva of Lawrence Halprin's San Francisco firm. Gleason and Orloff, 26, 33, 41; Abbott, *Portland*, 214; De Marco, 149.

[107] "The Resurrection of Portland's Streetcars," by Randall B. Kester, *Oregon Benchmarks*, U.S. Dist. Ct of Oregon Historical Society newsletter, Spring 1999.

[108] "Key Events leading to Tri-Met's Formation," www.tri-met.org/keyevents.htm [accessed Sept 28, 2000].

[109] Ord #115674. "Key Events leading to Tri-Met's Formation," www.tri-met.org/keyevents.htm [accessed Sept 28, 2000].

[110] Communication with Carl Abbott by the author, Feb 12, 2001. The commission was appointed in January 1969.

[111] Schrunk was a charter member of the Town Affiliation Association (the "sister city" organization). *OJ*, Mar 4, 1975. Also see Long, 153.

[112] The formal name of Tri-Met was the Tri-County Metropolitan Transportation District, and its boundaries included urban areas in Multnomah, Washington, and Clackamas counties.

[113] Abbott, *Portland*, 216-17; "Key Events leading to Tri-Met's Formation," www.tri-met.org/keyevents.htm [accessed Sept 28, 2000].

[114] Abbott, *Portland*, 253.

[115] Price, 139.

[116] DeMarco, 142.

[117] Sale of the *OJ* to the Newhouse chain was completed in August 1961, after which the *Journal* offices were moved to the *Oreg.* building. Notson, 51-52. When the *Journal* building was torn down in 1969, the process took three or four weeks. Huge fragments of reinforced concrete were used for fill at the south end of Willamette Park, big hunks of which are still visible today on the west bank of the river. Interview with Donald Sterling, by Ernie Bonner, p 2. www.pdxplan.org/DonSterlingweb.html [accessed Oct 1, 2000].

[118] Bean was considered a champion of the consumer during his tenure as Gov. Charles Sprague's Public Utilities Commissioner in 1939-41. McKay, 139.

[119] www.ci.portland.or.us/auditor/Elecarchives2/PRIM60.htm [accessed Sept 22, 2000].

[120] *OJ*, Mar 4, 1975.

[121] Interview with Lloyd Anderson by Carl Abbott, as cited in Abbott, *Portland*, 159. See also *Oreg.*, Dec 20, 1966, p 23, c 2; *OJ*, Feb 15, 1975, p A4, c 1.

[122] Lloyd Center, which opened Aug 1, 1960, included motels, a hotel, office buildings and 1.3 million square feet of shops. Its sales were almost equal to those of downtown merchants. Abbott, *Portland*, 274-75; *OS*, 93.

[123] Draft *Portland Parks and Recreation*, 1960-61 Section. Memorial Coliseum opened November 3, 1960. *OS*, 103.

[124] Maurine Neuberger was elected in Nov 1960 to complete the rest of the term of her late husband, Richard L. Neuberger, as well as to a full senate term. *1997-98 OBB*, 387.

[125] Abbott, *Portland*, 159.

[126] Taped interview with Lloyd Anderson by Ernie Bonner, p 5-6.

[127] At the same time, voters turned down a two-year one-twentieth mill levy that would have raised seventy thousand dollars for a charter revision study to modernize city government. Primary 1958 sample ballot, Sample Ballots, 1905-92, C.P. Arch..

[128] Letter dated March 11, 1966, from Harold S. Hirsch, general chairman, addressed to 623 petition carriers and 189 sponsors of the Citizens League for Effective Government, an umbrella group that included the League of Women Voters, Junior Chamber of Commerce, Council of Churches, and both the young Democrats and young Republicans. Documents obtained from files of the City Club of Portland.

[129] *Oreg.* editorial of March 3, 1965, as quoted in a 1965 brochure published by the Citizens League for Effective Government; *Oreg.* May 1, 1966, 4F.

[130] 1965 brochure published by the Citizens League for Effective Government, Mrs. Dale W. Barker, Executive Secretary.

[131] *OJ* editorial of August 21, 1965, as quoted in a 1965 brochure published by the Citizens League for Effective Government.

[132] *Portland City Club Bulletin*, May 13, 1966, 178.

[133] A 1959 Survey Report by the Public Administration Service of Chicago had concluded that Portland was enjoying a "reasonably high level of municipal service at a rather modest cost" and that it was "at least as well governed as the average large American city." Source: MacColl, "Fifty Years of Commission Government," p 17-18. Also see *Oreg.*, May 1, 1966, F4.

[134] 1966 campaign brochure of Citizens For Good Government, p 1, c 4.

[135] Each of the thirty-eight legislators in the four counties had appointed one member. Letter from McKay Rich to the author, Dec 12, 2000,

[136] April 13 and 14, 1966, minutes of the Portland City Government Committee of the Portland City Club.

[137] The proposal was rejected by 68,158 votes to 41,848. www.ci.portland.or.us/auditor/Elecarchives2/PRIM66.htm [accessed Sept 12, 2000].

[138] ORS 199.730(6), transmittal letter by Chairman George Joseph, Proposed Charter, City-County of Portland - Multnomah, Oregon. City - County Charter Commission, November 1, 1973.

[139] CRAG included Columbia County, Oregon, and Clark County, Washington, as well as Multnomah, Washington, and Clackamas counties. Abbott, *Portland*, 242, 262.

[140] After a five-year zoo levy passed in 1976, Portland transferred operation and ownership of the Washington Park Zoo to MSD. Conversation by the author with McKay Rich, former seventeen-year assistant zoo director, Nov 30, 2000.

[141] *Oreg.*, May 25, 1978, C1; Conversation by the author with McKay Rich.

[142] For example, a City Club report urging support of the strong-mayor form of government measure had noted that, because of the council's failure "to designate a location inside the city" for the I-205 freeway, the State Highway Commission had located that new freeway east of the city limits. It was a "well-known State Highway Commission policy" that no freeway would be located in a city "without that city's consent." *City Club Bulletin*, May 13, 1966, 178.

[143] Former commissioner Lloyd Anderson told the following story about Commissioner Buck Grayson. "Stanley [Earl] would say, now listen to this ... And Buck would say, you've got the horse before the cart. And of course all of us laughed because Buck didn't even realize that that was the way it ought to be!" Taped interview with former city commissioner Lloyd Anderson by Ernie Bonner.

[144] www.ci.portland.or.us/auditor/Elecarchives2/PRIM56.htm [accessed Sept 12, 2000].

[145] "Ivancie the Terrible," by Steve Forrester, *WW*, Nov 10, 2000.

[146] *OS*, 104.

[147] Abbott, *Portland*, 212.

[148] "The Stadium Freeway ... razed and paved-over 282 houses and 131 apartment houses, and displaced 1,700 persons along with many small shops, cafes and hotels." McCormack and Pintarich, 156; *OS*, 102. Mayor Vera Katz was to float a proposal in the late 1990s to cap two and a half blocks of I-405 near the downtown core, between S.W. Taylor and Alder streets, to regain valuable real estate. Response ranged from enthusiastic support to ridicule. Katz convened a group of experts to study the proposal, who pronounced the idea "eminently feasible." *Oreg.*, Jan 29, 2000, A11; "Committee says I-405 cap possible in five years," by Scott Learn, *Oreg.*, Sept 28, 2000, A1, 7. As of April 2001, capping I-405 was a future possibility but no specific plan had been designed.

[149] Price, 52.

[150] Soon after McCall took office in 1967, he started exploring how to close Harbor Drive. He put his state planning director, Arnold Cogan, to work on the proposal. "I was assigned the job of going up to the city [around late 1967]," Cogan said, "and announcing to mayor Terry Schrunk and his assistant, Frank Ivancie, and my old boss, Lloyd Keefe, that we're going to remove Harbor Drive. Their mouths just absolutely dropped. I mean, they were totally stunned. And the compromise [was] ... a special ramp off I-405 ... into the Northwest Industrial area." Interview with Arnold Cogan by Ernie Bonner, March 10, 1999, p 2 and 3, www.pdxplan.org/ArnoldCoganweb.html [accessed Nov 30, 2000].

[151] Harbor Drive was begun 1940, completed November 1942. MacColl, *Growth*, 513-18; Abbott, *Portland*, 216; Price 43.

[152] *City Club Bulletin*, Aug 8, 1969, p 21.

[153] Minutes of July 7, 1969, joint meeting of the City Club Board of Governors and representatives of a special City Club committee concerning *Journal* building site use.

[154] Undated *Oreg.* and *OJ* articles, circa July 8, 1969, from City Club Journal Site file; City Club Board of Governors minutes of July 14, 1969.

[155] *City Club Bulletin*, Oct 1969, p 74.

[156] Also in 1969, a group of two hundred fifty adults and one hundred children calling themselves Riverfront for People held a picnic between Front Avenue and Harbor Drive, with four lanes of traffic running on both sides, to demonstrate public support for a waterfront park . Abbott, *Greater Portland*, 136-38.

[157] Abbott, *Portland*, 216; Taped interview with Lloyd Anderson by Ernie Bonner, p 4.

[158] Historical background presented by David Bragdon at Clinton Street Theater, June 14, 1994, as transcribed by Ernie Bonner.

[159] Abbott, *Portland*, 197, 239, 255; "Highway to Hell," by Bob Young, *WW*, Nov 10, 1999, 9.

[160] "A Summary History of I-205," Oregon Department of Transportation, 1973, p 4 and 5. Obtained from the ODOT archives, Nov 17, 2000.

[161] Draft *Portland Parks and Recreation,* 1962 Section. Big Belle had been "elephanticipating" for 635 days. *Oreg.*, Apr 15, 1962, 1.

[162] *Oreg.*, Nov 22, 1970, A31.

[163] Draft *Portland Parks and Recreation,* 1964 Sec.

[164] Ibid.; Price, 121.

[165] MacColl, *Shaping*, 453.

[166] Voters approved a 2.5 million-dollar ballot measure to purchase a civic stadium in 1966. www.ci.portland.or.us/auditor/elections/Meas1942.htm [accessed Aug 9, 2000].

[167] West Delta Park golf course (name later changed to Blue Heron) opened May 1, 1971, and the Delta Raceway hosted the National Hot Rod Association meet and the National Go-Carts Race in 1971. Draft *Portland Parks and Recreation*, 1971 page.

[168] Tryon Creek State Park opened in 1970. *Oreg.*, Oct 30, 2000, E1 and E7.

[169] *OJ*, July 5, 1973, Sec 7, p 7, as cited in Price, 48; "Riverside Project Unveiled," by Paul Pintarich, *Oreg.* Dec 30, 1971, 1, as cited in Price, 45, 46, 47.

[170] Lucia, *Blow*, 43, 63; *OS*, 96; Draft *Portland Parks and Recreation,* 1962 Section.

[171] *OS*, 96.

[172] *OJ*, Dec 23, 25, and 26, 1964, 1.

[173] Interview with Richard Brainard by Ernie Bonner on Jan 16, 1995, Part I, p 2, www.pdxplan.org/BrainrdWeb1.htm [accessed Dec 1, 2000].

[174] *Oreg.*, Aug 2, 1992, A20.

[175] Price, 39.

[176] "Floods of December 1964 and January 1965 in the Far Western States, Part 2: Streamflow and Sediment Data," and "Water Resources Data for Oregon, 1992," published by the U.S. Geological Survey; and "The Pacific Northwest Floods of February 6-11, 1996," published by the American Institute of Hydrology; all as cited by USGS Portland Office Information Specialist Suzanne Jo Miller to the author in letters dated Nov 29 and 30, 2000.

[177] Draft *Portland Parks and Recreation,* 1968 page. This curfew would be a bone of contention in Ivancie's reelection bid two years later. Abbott, *Portland*, 174.

[178] Walth, 284-85.

[179] Ibid., 286.

[180] Ibid., 289.

[181] Ibid., 290-91.

[182] Ibid., 291.

[183] Ibid., 294.

[184] Ibid., 296.

[185] Ibid., 299.
[186] Ibid., 301-5.
[187] Queen's Bench Fiftieth Anniversary Commemorative Calendar, 1998; Leeson, 160, 247.
[188] Anderson did have solid credentials: he was a former Multnomah County planning director, and was director of planning for the CH2M Hill engineering firm as well as its Portland regional manager. Taped interview with Lloyd Anderson by Ernie Bonner, p 2.
[189] *Oreg.*, March 6, 1970, 18; *Voters Pamphlet*, May 25, 1976, 161; Notson, 65.
[190] "Highway to Hell," by Bob Young, *WW*, Nov 10, 1999, 9.
[191] Abbott, Portland, 174-75; www.ci.portland.or.us/auditor/Elecarchives2/PRIM70.htm [accessed Sept 22, 2000].
[192] www.ci.portland.or.us/auditor/Elecarchives2/GEN70.htm [accessed Sept 22, 2000]. Tom Walsh would later head the region's Tri-Met Transit Authority as General Manager from 1991 to 1998.
[193] "Legends in Their Spare Time," *WW*, Oct 11 - 17, 1990, 13.
[194] www.ci.portland.or.us/auditor/Elecarchives2/GEN70.htm [accessed Sept 22, 2000].
[195] "The Goldschmidt Era," by Ron Buel, *WW*, Nov 10, 1999.
[196] Remarks by Vera Katz's 1970 neighbor, Sally Landauer, at a Clinton St. Theater gathering on June 14, 1969, to celebrate the early years of the Goldschmidt era. www.pdxplan.org/LandauerWeb.html. [accessed Oct 1, 2000].
[197] www.ci.portland.or.us/auditor/Elecarchives2/GEN68.htm & GEN70.htm [accessed Sept 22, 2000]. Also see Leeson, 193-94.
[198] *Oreg.*, Dec 19, 1982. Also see *Daily Journal of Commerce*, Nov 26, 1982, p 2.
[199] "Doubts Raised About Auditor Office," by Robert Landauer, Financial Editor, *Oreg.*, Oct 16, 1970 Sunrise Edition, 1.
[200] *Oreg.*, Oct 13, 1970; *OJ*, Oct 29, 1970; Landauer, "Doubts Raised About Auditor Office," 1.
[201] Yerkovich had previously challenged Auditor Will Gibson for the auditor's title in 1954, and garnered only 15 percent of the vote at that time. www.ci.portland.or.us/auditor/Elecarchives2/PRIM54.htm & GEN70.htm [accessed Sept 12 & Sept 22, 2000].
[202] *Oreg.*, Nov 22, 1970, 1 and 31.
[203] Ibid., Nov 23, 1970, 1.
[204] No measures are listed for 1972 in the C.P. Arch..; www.ci.portland.or.us/auditor/elections/Meas1942.htm [accessed Aug 9, 2000].
[205] Cover page of web page, "Planning in Portland in the '70s," www.pdxplan.org [accessed Oct 1, 2000].
[206] Interview with Donald Sterling, by Ernie Bonner, p 3-4. www.pdxplan.org/DonSterlingweb.html [accessed Oct 1, 2000].
[207] Abbott, *Portland*, 192-94.
[208] Price, 81-82.
[209] Abbott, *Portland*, 196-97.
[210] Ibid., 197-98.
[211] Ibid., 215.
[212] Interview with Richard Ivey by Ernie Bonner, Jan 13, 1995, p 1. www.pdxplan.org/Ivy1.html [accessed Dec 1, 2000].
[213] Abbott, *Portland*, 215; Price, 59-61; *Oreg.*, June 21, 2000, C7.
[214] Funding for staff work by private consultants on the plan (excluding government employees on loan to the project) was paid for by contributions from downtown businessmen. In the words of project director Richard Ivey: "[W]e held a meeting at the old First National board room and I went through my presentation again and Julian Cheatham … went around the table and extracted $10,000 (each) from 10 people—a remarkable performance." Interview with Richard Ivey by Ernie Bonner, Jan 13, 1995, Part I, p 2, www.pdxplan.org/Ivy1.html [accessed Dec 1, 2000]
[215] Dick Ivey of the engineering firm CH2M Hill was project director and primary force of the plan, assisted by Bob Baldwin, Multnomah County Planning Director, on loan from the county part time; Richard Brainard of CH2M Hill, full time; City Planner Rod O'Hiser, full time; and Judy Galantha, Bill Blosser, and John McCormick, all of CH2M Hill, varying amounts of time. City Planning Director Lloyd Keefe was also involved. Stan Goodell represented the Building Owners and Managers Association as advisor to this staff. Lawyer Dean Gisvold chaired the Citizens' Advisory Committee. The DeLeuw-Cather firm did traffic and transportation studies, paid for by Glenn Jackson's state highway commission. Influential Portlanders involved besides Glenn Jackson included Ira Keller, Bill Roberts, Melvin "Pete" Mark, Jr., Frank Warren, Hib Johnson, Ed Steidle, Paul Murphy, Ralph Voss, Ed Finn, Al Aus, and many others (see Bob Baldwin interview for names of other city staffers and individuals involved from other organizations). Interview with Bob Baldwin by Ernie Bonner, Dec 30, 1994, p 2 - 3, www.pdxplan.org/BaldwinWeb.html [accessed Oct 1, 2000]. Letter from Bob Baldwin to the author dated Nov 28, 2000; Interview with Richard Ivey by Ernie Bonner, Jan 13, 1995, Part I, p 3-5; Part II, p 2, www.pdxplan.org/Ivy1.html and Ivy2.html [accessed Dec 1, 2000]; Interview with Richard Brainard by Ernie Bonner, Part II, p 4, www.pdxplan.org/BrainrdWeb2.html [accessed Dec 1, 2000]; Conversation with Lloyd Keefe by the author, Dec 19, 2000.
[216] Interview with Richard Brainard by Ernie Bonner, Part II, p 3. www.pdxplan.org/BrainrdWeb2.html - [accessed Dec 1, 2000].
[217] Abbott, *Portland*, 215-28.
[218] Ibid., 222.
[219] These oral histories were compiled by 1970s city planning director Ernie Bonner. See www.pdxplan.org.
[220] Interview with Richard Brainard by Ernie Bonner, Part III, p 1, www.pdxplan.org/BrainrdWeb3.html [accessed Dec 1, 2000];
[221] Abbott, *Portland*, 220; Interview with Richard Brainard by Ernie Bonner, Part III, p 3, www.pdxplan.org/BrainrdWeb3.html [accessed Dec 1, 2000].
[222] Interview with Richard Brainard by Ernie Bonner, Part III, p 2, www.pdxplan.org/BrainrdWeb3.html [accessed Dec 1, 2000]; Interview with Lloyd Anderson by Ernie Bonner, p 10.
[223] Interview with Richard Brainard by Ernie Bonner, Part II, p 2, www.pdxplan.org/BrainrdWeb2.html

[accessed Dec 1, 2000]; Questionnaire response from former *Oreg.* editorial writer Larry Hilderbrand, Oct 10, 2000.

[224] Letter from Ron Buel to the author dated November 7, 2000; www.ci.portland.or.us/auditor/elections/ELECARCHIVES/PRIM72.htm — [accessed Sept 22, 2000].

[225] Schrunk died two years after he left office and was buried in Willamette National Cemetery, Sec H 3537. Willamette National Cemetery was founded in February 1951. Letter to the author dated March 31, 2000, from James Brewster of Willamette National Cemetery.

[226] *OJ*, Mar 4, 1975.

[227] The move to name the plaza for Schrunk after his death in March 1975 was begun by his former secretary, Jean Briedwell. *Oreg.*, Sept 30, 1976, C1, c 5; Aug 26, 1977, C10, c1; Conversation with the Portland office of the General Services Administration by the author on Dec 11, 2000.

[228] The federal government bought the two blocks between Madison and Jefferson , one block of which was adjacent to city hall.At one time, they proposed a two-block-long building with a tunnel for Avenue traffic to pass through, but later decided to put up a tower on one block and a park on the other, with parking underneath the park plaza. The 1972 Downtown Plan called for a plaza on the western block to be coordinated with the Chapman and Lownsdale squares adjoining it on the north. Conversations with former city planner Rod O'Hiser by the author, Dec 15, 2000, and Jan 3, 2001; Interview with Richard Brainard by Ernie Bonner, Part III, p 4, www.pdxplan.org/BrainrdWeb3.htm [Dec 1, 2000]; Letter from Ernie Bonner to the author, Dec 14, 2000; Letter from Bob Baldwin to the author, Dec 17, 2000.

[229] Former mayor Connie McCready (1979-80) died at age 79 on December 22, 2000, after suffering a series of strokes. *Oreg.*, Dec 23, A1 & 11.

Chapter 23

[1] Five mayors in the first fourteen years of the city's history were younger than Neil Goldschmidt (Simon Marye, William Ladd, James O'Neill, Stephen McCormick, and Henry Failing), all in the days when being Portland mayor was a one-year volunteer job. John M. Breck was only five months older than Goldschmidt when he served as mayor.

[2] Long, 58.

[3] Abbott, *Portland*, 223.

[4] Goldschmidt's campaign manager for this University of Oregon election was Ron Buel, who would later run Goldschmidt's first city council race, along with Neil's brother, Steve Goldschmidt.

[5] Neil Goldschmidt biography received by the author from his office Dec 29, 1999; *1982-83 Who's Who in America*, 1242; "The Goldschmidt Era," by Ron Buel, *WW*, Nov 10, 1999; Abbott, *Portland*, 173-74; *Voters' Pamphlet*, 1976 May primary, 157.

[6] Letters from Ron Buel to the author dated Nov 26 & Dec 3, 2000; Abbott, *Portland*, 173-74.

[7] Taped interview with Lloyd Anderson by Ernie Bonner, p 4.

[8] Leeson, 185-86.

[9] "Mildred Schwab dies at home in Portland," by Spencer Heinz, *Oreg.*, Jan 16, 2000, A1, 18; *Oreg.*, Jan 14, 1999, A1; *Oreg.*, Feb 2, 1999, B1, 18.

[10] Correspondence to the author from Don Barney, Nov 2000.

[11] Correspondence from *Oreg.* columnist John Terry to the author, Nov 3, 2000.

[12] Former commissioner Mike Lindberg, Apr 23, 2002, speech at Classroom Law Project dinner.

[13] Walth, 356-61, 403; Dept of Land Conservation and Development, www.lcd.state.or.us/history.html [accessed Nov 22, 2000].

[14] *Public Records and Meetings Manual*, Oregon Attorney General, rev. June 1984, p v, II-3.

[15] The required three-fourths of states necessary to ratify the federal ERA fell short by three, so the amendment was never adopted. However, the Oregon legislature reaffirmed its support for ERA in 1977 after a bill introduced to rescind Oregon's ratification had the word "reaffirm" substituted for the word "rescind." HJR 62, 1977 Oregon Legislature.

[16] Edwards, Cecil, 148-49.

[17] *City Club Bulletin*, Oct 21, 1988, 108.

[18] *OS*, 114.

[19] Ibid., 101.

[20] For example, PDC Chair Elaine Cogan and Fred Rosenbaum of HAP consulted with each other and both decided not to resign. Conversation between the author and Arnold Cogan, Elaine Cogan's husband, on Sept 27, 2000; Abbott, *Portland*, 169.

[21] Abbott, *Portland*, 178-79. Other Goldschmidt staff members included executive assistants Ron Buel (who would leave later that year to found the *WW* newspaper), Bill Scott, and Doug Capps; David Kottkamp, Betsy Welch, Jayne Carroll, Alan Webber, Susan Kerr, Don Barney, Pam Dunham, Angus Duncan, George Russill, Phil McLaurin, Len Bergstein. Letter from Ron Buel to the author dated Nov 26, 2000; letter to the author from Doug Capps dated Dec 5, 2000.

[22] Abbott, *Portland*, 223.

[23] O'Bryant Square, located between S.W. Washington and Stark streets on land originally platted as part of the Park Blocks, was named for Portland's first mayor, Hugh O'Bryant. The park was built on land donated to the city in 1971 as a bequest by Donald C. Sloan, a former prime minister of the Royal Rosarians, and converted into a public square with financial assistance from a federal Housing and Urban Development grant. Snyder, *Potpourri*, 132; www.parks.ci.portland.or.us/Parks/OBryantSq.htm [accessed Nov 29, 2000].

[24] Questionnaire response from Ron Buel to the author dated Nov 25, 2000; letter from Bob Baldwin to the author dated Nov 28, 2000.

[25] Portland's Yamhill District was added to the National Register of Historic Places in 1976. *OS*, 116. Lair Hill and Ladd's Addition were designated as a historic conservation district by the city in 1977. Abbott, *Portland*, 185, 202, 225; DeMarco, 146. The Portland Saturday Market, a popular crafts-oriented bazaar located in Old Town began in 1974. *OS*, 114.

[26] Price, 61.

[27] Individual building owners who wanted to develop connections between buildings could still do so under the plan. Letter to the author from Bob Baldwin dated Nov 28, 2000.

[28] Questionnaire response from former *Oreg.* editorial writer Larry Hilderbrand, Oct 10, 2000.
[29] A list of all city police chiefs and dates of tenure, based on photograph captions in the Portland Police Museum, was compiled by retired police officer Larry Grant in Oct 2000 at the request of this author.
[30] Sylvester was "a 20-year-old divorced mother of four." *WW*, Nov 10, 2000, 1974 section.
[31] *Voters' Pamphlet*, Nov 5, 1974, 145; Interview with Mary Catherine Pedersen-Blackett by Ernie Bonner, Dec 15, 1999, p 12, www.pdxplan.org/ BlackettWeb1.html [accessed Oct 1, 2000].
[32] The City-County Charter Commission was established under authority of ORS 199.730(6) passed by the 1971 Oregon legislature. Members of the City-County Charter Commission were lawyer George Joseph, chair; Gresham newspaperman Lee Irwin, vice-chair; citizen activist Ruth Hagenstein, secretary; William E. Bradley, Polly Casterline, Joseph M. Edgar, Joseph A. Labadie, Loyal Lang, Glen Otto, Frank Roberts, and Morton A. Winkel. Members who resigned early in the process were Richard Bogle, Sylvia Davidson, R. W. deWeese, and Earl Klapstein. "Proposed Charter, City-County of Portland-Multnomah, Oregon, 1973."
[33] The commission completed a final charter draft by November 1, 1973. Transmittal letter, "Proposed Charter, City-County of Portland-Multnomah, Oregon, 1973."
[34] *OJ*, May 28, 1974, 1; Abbott, *Portland*, 260-61.
[35] Tabloid published by "Vote No on 7 Committee," John H. Wilson, chairman, printed May 11, 1974; *OJ*, May 28, 1974, 1.
[36] *OJ*, May 29, 1971, 1.
[37] www.ci.portland.or.us/auditor/elections/ ELECARCHIVES/PRIM74.htm & GEN74.htm [accessed Sept 22, 2000].
[38] In May 1974, Alice Corbett won the Democratic primary for county commissioner and future city auditor Jewel Lansing won the Democratic primary for county auditor. At that time, winning the Democratic primary was tantamount to election in Multnomah County. *OJ*, May 29, 1974, 2, 16.
[39] *OJ*, May 29, 1974, 2.
[40] Conversation by the author with George Joseph, Chair of the 1974 City-County Charter Commission, on Nov 27, 2000; *Consolidation Study Task Force, Final Report*, Sept, 1998, 7.
[41] The consultant firms were Booze-Allen and Hamilton and the Arthur Young CPA firm. Multnomah County Audit #5-77, "Payroll Function: Internal Control and Reporting Systems," Nov 1977.
[42] Letter from former city accounting manager Marino Bual to the author, Dec 15, 2000; Letter from PDC controller and former city accountant Bill Blauvelt to the author, Dec 12, 2000; "Portland of Years Past," 1975 Section, *Oreg.*, March 16, 2000, E3.
[43] "Portland of Years Past," 1975 Section, *Oreg.*, Jan 6, 2000, E7.
[44] *Oreg.*, Aug 22, 1975, B5; *OJ*, Aug 22, 1975.
[45] Schwab's assertion was an oversimplification; inability to correctly assign costs to individual budgeted line items was the quandary. Letter from former city accounting manager Marino Bual to the author, Dec 15, 2000.
[46] Abbott, *Portland*, 177, 191-99, 204-5; DeMarco, 146.
[47] The Rajneeshees were in Oregon from 1981 to 1985. *OS*, 124-25, 128; McCormack and Pintarich, 199-212; Interview with Mary Catherine Pedersen-Blackett by Ernie Bonner, p 1, 12-19. www.pdxplan.org/ BlackettWeb1.html [accessed Oct 1, 2000]. Mary Pederson-Blackett, who had a doctorate from Yale University in political science, credits Lloyd Anderson with being "the father" of the process that included neighborhood associations in council decisions (p 15).
[48] Portland's S.E. Ninety-sixth Avenue - West Linn was the approved I-205 route. "A Summary History of I-205," Oregon Dept of Transportation, 1973, p 1-2, 4-5, 26.
[49] Leeson, 185; Abbott, *Portland*, 197; Price, 83, 139.
[50] "Highway to Hell," by Bob Young, *WW*, Nov 10, 1999, 9-10.
[51] Ibid., 10.
[52] Abbott, *Portland*, 256-57.
[53] "A Summary History of I-205," p 4 and 5. Members of the Multnomah County Board of County Commissioners who requested the Mt. Hood Freeway moratorium on construction and condemnation were M. James Gleason, chair; Larry Aylsworth, Donald E. Clark, Mel Gordon, and Ben Padrow.
[54] Abbott, *Portland*, 256; "A Summary History of I-205," p 1-2, 4-5, 26. Suburban Lake Oswego had set a precedent for rejecting freeways in 1963 when ODOT proposed running I-205 through that city, at which time its city council passed a resolution banning such construction. "A Summary History of I-205," p 1.
[55] *OS*, 114.
[56] Lui, Ben-Chieh, 1975, Quality of Life Indicators in U. S. Metropolitan Areas, 1970: A Comprehensive Assessment. Washington D. C., U.S. Environmental Protection Agency. Lui was a geographer with the Midwest Research Institute, per Price, 191, 206.
[57] Another scenario that could have made Waterfront Park possible would have been a lack of private development in the former Harbor Drive area as downtown continued to move westward, leaving a low-intensity-use area for future urban renewal and redevelopment. Communication with Carl Abbott by the author, Feb 15, 2001.
[58] The 1860 warehouse was built in defiance of a council order. *Oreg.*, March 24, 1860.
[59] Price, 49; *Oreg.*, Oct 17, 1999, E-1; Parks Inventory, July 1, 1999-June 30, 2000, obtained from Jean Hamilton, Portland Parks and Rec, Dec 8, 2000.
[60] "Portland of Years Past," 1975 Section, *Oreg.*, Sept 28, 2000, F5.
[61] The application for Transit Mall funding was put together by Bill Roberts, head of the Tri-Met Board, Lloyd Anderson, and Neil Goldschmidt, and submitted in September 1973. At the time, the U.S. Department of Transportation was "looking for a viable, innovative transit project with more political glamour than additions to city bus fleets." Credit for shepherding the Transit Mall project through all its phases belongs in large part to Bill Roberts. Abbott, *Portland*, 223.
[62] *WW*, Nov 10, 1999, 1976 section.
[63] O'Donnell and Vaughan, 90-91.
[64] Abbott, *Portland*, 253.
[65] Tri Met Ord #27, dated Nov 4, 1974.
[66] *WW*, Nov 10, 1999, 10.

[67] Questionnaire response by *Oreg.* reporter Fred Leeson, Sept 22, 2000.
[68] Commissioner Mildred Schwab got ninety-two write-in votes for mayor. www.ci.portland.or.us/auditor/elections/ELECARCHIVES/PRIM76.htm [accessed Sept 22, 2000].
[69] *Oreg.*, June 7, 1977, p A1, c 5. "Blazers win!" *Oreg.*, June 6, 1977, A1 banner headline.
[70] *OS*, 112. Columnist Bill McDonald, writing in the *P. Trib.*, Feb 9, 2001, A8, says: "Let's face it. There are really only two major events in our short history: the Lewis and Clark Expedition and the Trail Blazers' championship of 1977."
[71] *Oreg.*, May 25, 1978, C1; Price, 138; Abbott, *Portland*, 242, 249, 256-57, 262; Communication to the author from McKay Rich, Dec 22, 2000. The margin of voter approval was 110,600 yes and 91,090 no. *1997-98 OBB*, 333, 364.
[72] Interview with Downtown Plan leader Richard Ivey by Ernie Bonner, Jan 13, 1995, www.pdxplan.org/Ivy1.htm [accessed Dec 1, 2000].
[73] Price, 176; *OS* 116.
[74] Draft *Portland Parks and Recreation, A Chronological History*, Dec 1998, 1978 section.
[75] President Carter announced Goldschmidt's appointment July 27, 1979, and Goldschmidt resigned Aug 15, 1979. *Oreg.*, Sept 8, C6, c1. After Goldschmidt's return to Portland, he would be elected Oregon governor in 1987.
[76] Abbott, *Portland*, 180; "Hatfield to Harding, many could've been bigger contenders," Gerry Frank, *Oreg.*, Aug 18, 2000, A19; "Big plan raises large issues about future of Portland," Randy Gragg, *Oreg.*, June 4, 2000, E2.
[77] *Oreg.*, June 7, 1978, D1, c 4, and Sept 1, 1979, A8, c 4.
[78] Questionnaire response from *Oreg.* reporter Fred Leeson, Sept 22, 2000.
[79] Ivancie had previously offered Jordan his vote, which Jordan refused. Jordan said he turned down the offer because he believed Ivancie would try to ambush his every move as mayor, and was not sincere. *Oreg.*, Sept 5, 1979, A1, c 1; Sept 6, 1979, A1, c 1; Sept 8, 1979, C1, c 1; Conversations with Charles Jordan by the author, Dec 6 and 8, 2000; Conversation with Jim Kuffner, former exec to Mayor Ivancie by the author, Dec 6, 2000; Letters from Ron Buel to the author, Nov 7 and Dec 7, 2000; Letter from Lloyd Anderson to the author, Dec 7, 2000; Interview with Charles Jordan by Ernie Bonner, Nov 3, 1999, p 8. Jordan gave the author permission to use the interview on Dec 15, 2000. 7-8.
[80] *OHQ*, Summer 1979, footnote 158, p 156-57.
[81] *Oreg.*, Sept 5, 1979, A1, c 1.
[82] The Federal Reserve Board action took place Oct 6, 1979. *OS*, 117.
[83] Candidates for Lindberg's seat included labor official and state representative Jim Chrest, former state labor commissioner Bill Stevenson, and Goldschmidt's former exec, Doug Capps. The final vote was three to one for Lindberg, with Ivancie voting for Chrest. *Oreg.*, Sept 19, 1979, B1, c 1, and Sept 20, 1979, A1, c3; Letter from Ron Buel to the author dated Dec 7, 2000.
[84] *Voters' Pamphlet*, Nov 1988, 110; *Oreg.*, Metro Section, Dec 3, 1987; *WW*, Nov 10, 1999.
[85] *Voters' Pamphlet*, May 1976, 161, and May 1980, 122; *Oreg.*, Dec 23, 2000, A1 and 11.
[86] *Oreg.*, Sept 7, 1979, B6, c 4; *Oreg.* Anniversary Special, Dec 4, 2000, p 43.
[87] "Mayor's ties to paper bring no favoritism," by J. Richard Nokes, *Oreg.*, Sept 7, 1979, B6, c 4. Editor J. Richard Nokes also said, "But isn't it amazing that that good looking gal reporter who sat across the desk from me back at Sixth and Alder should wind up mayor?"
[88] *Oreg.*, Feb 15, 1978, B1, c 5, and Nov 13, 1980, B1.
[89] *The I Hate to Cook Book*, by Peg Bracken, 1960. By 1985, three millions copies of the book had been sold. This author treasures a well-worn copy, and occasionally refers to such old favorites as "Stayabed Stew" and "Sweep Steak."
[90] *Oreg.*, Nov 3, 1979, p 1, c 1-4.
[91] "Reaching for the Sky," by Steffen Silvis, *WW*, Nov 10, 1999, 1982 section; *Oreg.*, July 25, 2000, A1, c1.
[92] www.parks.ci.portland.or.us/Parks/PioneerCourthouseSq.htm [accessed Dec 10, 2000].
[93] Others on the local design team included J. Douglas Macy, landscape architect; Terrence O'Donnell, author and historian; Spencer Gill, writer; Robert Reynolds, artist and photographer; and Lee Kelly, sculptor. Script prepared by Gregg Kantor and former Portland planning director Ernie Bonner for airing on Portland Cable Access TV, Summer 1986, p 5; "The Rise and Fall of the Portland Hotel," by G. Douglas Nicoll, *OHQ*, Fall 1998, 325, 328; O'Donnell and Vaughan, 67.
[94] "Editor's Note, Conflict ahead over Pioneer Square," *Oreg.*, June 29, 1980, C3.
[95] *Volcano, First Seventy Days, Mount St. Helens, 1980*, (Beautiful America Publishing Company, Beaverton, Oregon), p 4-6.
[96] "Fire and Ice," by Patti Wentz, *WW*, Nov 10, 1999, 1980 section.
[97] www.ci.portland.or.us/auditor/elections/ELECARCHIVES/PRIM80.htm [accessed Sept 22, 2000].
[98] The charter section amended was Sec 2-206. www.ci.portland.or.us/auditor/elections/ELECARCHIVES/PRIM80.htm [accessed Sept 22, 2000]. Another part of this charter amendment established the following order of succession to council membership if three members of council were unable to perform their duties: city auditor, city attorney, city engineer, city treasurer, police chief, fire chief, then council assistants in order of seniority. Charter Sec 2-206(g).
[99] www.ci.portland.or.us/auditor/elections/ELECARCHIVES/GEN80.htm [accessed Sept 22, 2000]; *1997-98 OBB*, 333. Civic Stadium, today known as PGE Park, reopened on April 30, 2001, after a major facelift and construction to bring it into conformance with seismic standards. The renovation was financed with thirty-three million dollars from increased hotel/motel taxes and car rental taxes, along with five and a half million dollars from Portland Family Entertainment. *Oreg.*, Feb 9, 2001, A1 and 15.
[100] Ord #150580 was adopted Oct 16, 1980.
[101] Abbott, *Portland*, 203.
[102] Interview with former Planning Commissioner Joan Smith taped Sept 27, 2000, by Ernie Bonner, www.pdxplan.org/JoanSmith.htm [accessed Jan 28, 2001]; Abbott, *Portland*, 204, 258, 265, 274; "A Line in the Sand," by Nick Budnick, *WW*, Nov 10, 1999, 1978

Section; Letter from Bob Baldwin to the author, Nov 26, 2000.

[103] *Oreg.*, Nov 13, 1980, B1, c 2-5.

[104] "A tribute to Connie McCready at her memorial service held at the Old Church, January 7, 2001," by Steve Jolin, www.pdxplan.org/commentary.html [accessed Jan 11, 2001]. McCready died Dec 22, 2000, as the result of a stroke. Her ashes were scattered on family-owned acreage in the Columbia Gorge. Telephone conversation with McCready's granddaughter, Laura Gunderson, by the author, Jan 30, 2001.

[105] Conversation by the author with Helen Barney, aide to Multnomah County Executive Don Clark during this period; *Oreg.*, Dec 23, 2000, A11; *Oreg.*, Dec 24, 2000, D4; *Oreg.*, Jan 8, 2001, B6.

Chapter 24

[1] *Voters' Pamphlet*, May 1976, 158.

[2] For example, Richard Ivey states in his interview by Ernie Bonner, Jan 13, 1995, that he thought Ivancie was a Republican. www.pdxplan.org/Ivy1.html, p 5 [accessed Dec 1, 2000].

[3] Conversation with Margaret Strachan by the author, Dec 4, 2000.

[4] www.ci.portland.or.us/auditor/elections/ELECARCHIVES/SPECFEB81.htm [accessed Sept 22, 2000].

[5] According to Strachan, Blumenauer spent about a hundred twenty thousand dollars and she spent sixty-three thousand. Conversations with Margaret Strachan by the author, Sept 25, 1999 and Dec 4, 2000. The city archives does not retain old contribution and expenditure reports.

[6] Conversations with Margaret Strachan by the author, Sept 25, 1999 and Dec 4, 2000; Abbott, *Portland*, 199, 201.

[7] www.ci.portland.or.us/auditor/elections/ELECARCHIVES/SPECMAR81.htm [accessed Sept 22, 2000].

[8] Dorothy Lee, Connie McCready, and Mildred Schwab—all Republicans—had gained their council seats by appointment, although all three were subsequently elected.

[9] Women staffers who worked for Strachan included Julia Pomeroy, Austin Chown (Raglione), Beverly Stein, Ruth Roth, Elise Anfield (Marshall,) Rachel Jacky, and Loretta Young. Conversations with Strachan by the author, Sept 25, 1999 and Dec 4, 2000. Pomeroy, Chown, and Young stayed on in city hall to work with Commissioner Earl Blumenauer, who hired more women in management positions than had any of his predecessors. Blumenauer managers included Felicia Trader, Mary Nolan, Sue Keil, Elsa Coleman, Anne Larkin, Grace Crunican, and Joan English.

[10] "Ivancie the Terrible," by Steve Forrester, *WW*, Nov 10, 1999.

[11] "Playing Possum," by Philip Dawdy, *WW*, Nov 10, 1999, 1981 section.

[12] www.ci.portland.or.us/auditor/elections/Meas1942.htm [accessed Aug 9, 2000].

[13] The official name of the committee created in 1982 was the Police Internal Investigative Auditing Committee (PIIAC). *LWV Voter*, Newsletter of the League of Women Voters of Portland, Dec 2000/ Jan 2001 issue, 1, 3; Interview with Charles Jordan by Ernie Bonner, Nov 3, 1999, p 8.

[14] *OJ*, Aug 27, 1980, p 2, c 5, and May 30, 1981, p 1, c 2, and p 5, c. 3; *Oreg.*, Dec 24, 1980, B2, c 1, and May 30, 1981, A1, c 5.

[15] Chief Still was later to reminisce about his first luncheon meeting with Schwab as his boss. She said, "Honey, let's go to lunch every Wednesday if we're both in town. I'll pay one week and you pay the next." During the next two and a half years, Still said, she bought lunch three times while he paid for the rest. It was always, "Honey, I forgot my pocketbook." "City pays homage to a civic work of art," by Steve Duin, *Oreg.*, Feb 2, 1999, B1.

[16] *Oreg.*, Jan 1981, 1. Pioneer Courthouse Square application for Bruner Award completed by Barbara Walker on Feb 2, 1987. The city would later receive the prestigious Rudy Bruner Foundation award for "excellence in urban design" in 1989. MacColl, "Portland: First Class on a Steerage Ticket," *The New Pacific*, Summer 1990, 47.

[17] List of PDC board members and chairpersons obtained from PDC; Interview with Richard Ivey by Ernie Bonner, January 13. 1995, p 4. www.pdxplan.org/Ivy1.html - [accessed Dec 1, 2000].

[18] Information taken from a script prepared by Gregg Kantor and former Portland planning director by Ernie Bonner for airing on Portland Cable Access TV, Summer 1986, p 5-6.

[19] Three hundred thirty-five people had contributed one hundred thousand dollars between Dec 1870 and Feb 1871, as demanded by Ben Holladay, for this purpose. Scott, *Oregon*, v 4, 352-54.

[20] The Friends of Pioneer Square campaign was led by Karen Whitman, Michael Powell, Barbara Walker, Pete Mark, and Commissioners Charles Jordan and Mike Lindberg. Dozens of organizations, businesses, and individuals were involved. Application for Bruner Award completed by Barbara Walker Feb 2, 1987; Letter from Ernie Bonner to the author dated Dec 10, 2000; "Reaching for the Sky," by Steffen Silvis, *WW*, Nov 10, 1999, 1982 section; Interview with Charles Jordan by Ernie Bonner, Nov 3, 1999, p 9-10.

[21] Letter from Stephanie Leeper of Pioneer Courthouse Square to the author dated Jan 12, 2001.

[22] Script for airing on Portland Cable Access TV, Summer 1986, p 5-6.

[23] www.parks.ci.portland.or.us/Parks/PioneerCourthouseSq.htm [accessed Dec 10, 2000].

[24] The bronze sculpture "Allow Me" was by artist J. Seward Johnson, a gift from Harry H. Schwatz to the city. The bronze sculpture "Running Horses" was by artist Tom Hardy, a gift from Bill Roberts to the city. Public Art Walking Tour brochure produced by the Regional Arts and Culture Council, circa 1992.

[25] "The Rise and Fall of the Portland Hotel," by G. Douglas Nicoll, *OHQ*, Fall 1998, 299-304, 331; O'Donnell and Vaughan, 67.

[26] "Reaching for the Sky," by Steffen Silvis, *WW*, Nov 10, 1999, 1982 section.

[27] www.parks.ci.portland.or.us/Parks/PioneerCourthouseSq.htm [accessed Dec 10, 2000].

[28] Ibid.

[29] Houle, 9; *Oreg.*, June 5, 1904, as quoted in MacColl, *Shaping*, 270-72. As of November 2000, the city owned over ten thousand acres of park land. (Parks Inventory, July 1, 1999-June 30, 2000, obtained from Jean Hamilton, Portland Parks and Rec, Dec 8, 2000.)

[30] Much of the Springwater Corridor walking/biking/ riding trail was completed in the late 1990s. A Metro open spaces bond measure approved in May 1995 provided much of the funding, along with the aid of many different groups. A three-mile segment from OMSI to Sellwood opened in Nov 2002. *Oreg.*, Jan 17, 2001, C2; www.portlandparks.org/Planning/ SpringwaterOMSI.htm - [accessed Jan 20, 2001 and Apr 11, 2003].

[31] "Money needed to fill gap in trail," by Wade Nkrumah, *Oreg.*, Jan 17, 2001, C2; communication with Mel Huie, Regional Trails Coordinator for Metro, by the author, Jan 19, 2001.

[32] Conversation with Barbara Walker, a founding and current member of the 40-Mile Loop Land Trust, by the author, Dec 16, 2000; www.parks.ci.portland.or.us [accessed Apr 11, 2003].

[33] The plant at Bull Run Dam #1 was to generate twenty-four megawatts; Dam #2, twelve megawatts. The total output was projected at one hundred million kilowatt-hours per year. The Federal Energy Regulatory Commission (FERC) which "encouraged construction of small hydro plants at existing dams," approved licensing for the dams. Short, 109-13.

[34] Financial Statement titled: "Hydroelectric Power Project Profits Made Available to the General Fund, 1984 through November 2000," plus letter dated Dec 12, 2000, from Frank Galida, Portland Hydro Project Manager, and conversation with the author on Dec 11, 2000.

[35] The four aquifers (underground, water-bearing geological formations) chosen were part of a "vast aquifer 'network' that extends from Clark County, Washington, to Clackamas County, and from the Willamette River to the Sandy River." Short, 124-25.

[36] "Ivancie muscled the project through despite critics doubts," says reporter Eric Goranson. "City's backup water wells fail to fulfill promise," *Oreg.*, Aug 2, 1992, A20.

[37] Ibid.; Short, 125-27; www.water.ci.portland.or.us/ groundwater.htm [accessed Dec 14, 2000].

[38] Between 1992 and 2000, the city used the wells seventy-three days in Aug 1994 as a seasonal supplement, twenty-seven days in Nov 1995 because of the landslide and conduit failure in the Bull Run watershed, eight days during the Feb 1996 flood, twenty-seven days in Sept 1996 as a seasonal supplement, five days in Dec 1998 due to a rain-on-snow event, and nineteen days in Nov 1999 because of turbidity in the Bull Run supply. www.water.ci.portland.or.us/groundwater.htm #gwuse [accessed Dec 14, 2000].

[39] www.water.ci.portland.or.us/groundwater.htm [accessed Dec 14, 2000].

[40] Goranson, "City's backup water wells," A20; "Bull Run water system passes crucial tests," by R. Gregory Nokes, *Oreg.*, Dec 14, 1995.

[41] O'Donnell and Vaughan, 101.

[42] DeMarco, 150.

[43] *Time* and other magazines ran color photos of the building soon after its completion. Ibid., 150; *Oreg.*, July 25, 2000, A1, 7.

[44] "Reaching for the Sky," by Steffen Silvis, *Willamette Week*, Nov 10, 1999, 1982 section.

[45] *Oreg.*, July 25, 2000, A1,7.

[46] Michael Graves received many commissions based on his Portland work. He received the American Institute of Architects' gold medal, its highest honor, in February 2001. Ibid., Dec 4, 2000, D12.

[47] "Train in Vain?" by Bob Young, *WW*, Nov 10, 1999, 1986 section.

[48] *OJ*, Sept 4, 1982, 1, as quoted in the *Oreg.* Anniversary Special, Dec 4, 2000, 44.

[49] City hall television coverage utilized a new government channel operated by Rogers Cable. Conversation with Diane Linn, former programming director for Rogers Cable, by the author, Aug 10, 2000.

[50] *OS* 128.

[51] With the 1997 completion of the Mark O. Hatfield Federal Courthouse next door to the Justice Center, the federal component of the government center envisioned by the Downtown Plan was complete. This included the Wendall Wyatt/Edith Green Federal Building south of the Justice Center Building and Terry Schrunk Plaza.

[52] The Schnitz (named for Harold and Arlene Schnitzer) was originally built as the Portland Publix (sic) Theatre in 1928, and later changed its name and venue to the Paramount movie theater. www.pcpa.com/ halls.html [accessed Dec 18, 2000]; Letter from Margie Humphreys of PCPA to the author dated Jan 5, 2001.

[53] The civic auditorium is now known as the Keller Auditorium.

[54] The other two theaters, located across Main Street from the Schnitz, were the Intermediate Theater (now the Newmark Theater), seating capacity 880, and the Delores Winningstad Theater, seating capacity 292. These two theaters opened in 1986 on three-fourths of a block shared with the First Congregational Church. O'Donnell and Vaughan, 86-87; www.pcpa.com/ halls.html [accessed Dec 18, 2000].

[55] The Performing Arts Center committee had pledged that six million dollars in private funds would be raised before the nineteen million dollars in public bonds were sold. The project was in jeopardy, one million dollars short of that goal, when Arlene and Harold Schnitzer stepped forward to complete the required funding. Information obtained from Margie Humphreys of the Performing Arts Center by the author, Dec 27, 2000.

[56] *1997-98 OBB*, 333; www.multnomah.lib.or.us/metro/ merc/facil.html [accessed Dec 18, 2000].

[57] Conversation with Margaret Strachan by the author, Sept 23, 2000; Conversation with Dave Aschenbrenner, former production technician for Rogers Cable, by the author on Sept 22, 2000; Conversation with Diane Linn by the author, Aug 10, 2000.

[58] "Personalities pivotal in commission system," by Elaine Cogan, *OJ*, Feb 22, 1983.

[59] *Voters' Pamphlet*, May 1984, 127.

[60] Ivancie dedicated the book to the "420 loyal employees of the Portland Water Bureau." In fall 1982, 40 percent of the city's water supply was being sold to neighboring communities. Short, Foreword and 122.

[61] The author of this book, Jewel Lansing, served as the elected auditor of Portland for four years, from January 1983 through December 1986.

[62] Auditor's Citizens' Task Force members were Steve Schell, chair; Richard Botteri, Cliff Carlsen, Jr., Tanya Collier, Ross Hall, Joe Kershner, Wanda Mays, Kathleen Peasley, Nancy Rangila, and Robert Scanlan. "Citizens' Advisory Task Force Report to Jewel Lansing," Portland City Auditor, October 1983. Based on the recommendation of this task force, the council referred a successful charter amendment to the voters in 1984 requiring all future auditors to be certified public accountants. This charter section (2-501) was expanded in 1986 to include certified internal auditors, and again in 1994 to include certified management accountants. A second 1984 amendment referred to the voters at Lansing's urging required elimination of masculine and feminine terms from the charter (unless context dictated otherwise). Charter section 2-513. Previous proposals for change in city government had replaced the elected auditor with appointed personnel. Early drafts of the Multnomah County Home Rule Charter passed in 1966 had eliminated the elected county auditor until incumbent Jack O'Donnell warned that he would publicly and vigorously oppose the charter if his position were axed.

[63] "Lansing a Blow at City Hall," by Linda Keene, *WW*, June 14-20, 1983, 8; "Pursuit of performance audit creates unease in City Hall," by Linda Williams, *Oreg.*, June 22, 1983.

[64] Two months before the council vote, Lansing had refused to authorize funds for the mayor's office to buy wine for an official city function. She invoked her seldom-used, but charter-mandated "pre-audit of claims" power in Section 2-506, meaning that no city money could be dispersed unless and until the auditor "was satisfied" that the money was for an appropriate city expenditure. Lansing notified council members that if they wanted to buy alcohol with public funds, they would have to do so out of the council's emergency fund (five thousand dollars) or the mayor's emergency fund (two thousand dollars), both provided for in the charter, neither of which required vouchers or explanation of usage. Memo from auditor Jewel Lansing to council members dated May 19, 1983, "Intent to Disallow Any Expenditure of City Funds for Alcoholic Beverages."

[65] Keene, "Lansing a Blow," 8

[66] "Lansing wins OK for city audits," by Linda Williams, *Oreg.* Street Edition, July 28, 1983, p 1. Lansing hired Richard Tracy from the California Auditor General's office to establish the performance auditing function.

[67] Voters subsequently approved a 1986 charter amendment which specified that the auditor should conduct both financial and performance audits of city government in accordance with generally accepted governmental auditing standards, and "appoint, coordinate and monitor" the annual certified audit of the city's finances required by state law. Bureaus and managers were required to respond to the auditor's recommendations in writing. All audit reports were to be made public. Charter Sec. 2-505 (a)-(e). See also "Alter charter for audits," *Oreg.* editorial, Dec 24, 1983.

[68] Oregon Department of Transportation newsletter, Vol 7, No. 12, December 1982; "The Glenn L. Jackson Memorial Bridge," publication of the Oregon Department of Transportation, received from the ODOT Archives by the author on Nov 17, 2000.

[69] City Council Resolution #33327, adopted Feb 23, 1983, as cited in "Urban Services Report IAR #3-86," City Auditor's Office, Sept 1986, p 1, 111, 113; Yeates, 23.

[70] "City at a Crossroad, Creating a Framework for Change," a paper prepared by Mark Gardiner, former City of Portland fiscal administrator, June 9, 1989.

[71] Yeates, 23.

[72] Communications with former city commissioners Earl Blumenauer and Mike Lindberg by the author, Jan 9, 2001.

[73] Members of both boards deserve credit for this historic agreement. City council members were Mayor Frank Ivancie, Charles Jordan, Mike Lindberg, Mildred Schwab, and Margaret Strachan. County Executive Dennis Buchanan, and his staff member, Steve Telfer, were key players. County commissioners were Arnold Biskar, Earl Blumenauer, Gladys McCoy, Caroline Miller, and Gordon Shadburne. Others involved in either the early negotiations or later implementation included previous county executive Don Clark, county commissioners Pauline Anderson and Gretchen Kafoury, subsequent mayor Bud Clark, and city commissioner Dick Bogle. City financial administrator Mark Gardiner worked out details of the plan on behalf of mayors Ivancie and Clark.

[74] *Consolidation Threshold Study, Final Report,* Sept 1998, 8.

[75] Multnomah County cut funding for its parks in 1982, planning to phase them out, and transferred four county parks—Sacajawea Park, Floyd Light Park, John Luby Park, and Cherry Park—to the city on October 15, 1985. The following year, the county transferred two acres on top of Rocky Butte, Brentwood Park, and Park 51. Draft *Portland Parks and Recreation, A Chronological History,* Dec 1998, 1985 and 1986 sections.

[76] For the effects of early 1920s prohibition on other "vice" activities, see Marsh, 182-89.

[77] Draft *Portland Parks and Recreation,* 1984 section.

[78] "City Club of Portland Annual Report, 1991," p 3.

[79] The Oregon Lottery was approved by voters in November 1984. *1997-98 OBB*, 365. There was no connection between this new state law and the opening of a popular Indian casino, Spirit Mountain, sixty miles southwest of Portland eleven years later. Indian casinos operate under federal jurisdiction. In a switch from prohibited vice activity to legitimate business, gaming devices formerly prohibited, such as slot machines, roulette, and video poker, had now become legally and socially acceptable. *OS*, 140.

[80] Among those considering an Ivancie challenge were Commissioner Charles Jordan; future county commissioner Pauline Anderson (the first woman president of the Portland City Club and spouse of former city commissioner Lloyd Anderson;) and State Representative Rick Bauman. *Oreg.*, Feb 19, C1, c 2, and May 6, 1983, C1, c 2; *WW*, June 28 - July 4, 1983.

[81] "This Bud's for You," by John Schrag, *WW*, Nov 10, 2000.

[82] Letter to the author from Bud Clark dated Nov 20, 2000.
[83] Excerpt from a May 1984 campaign brochure with the following inscription at the bottom: "Paid for by the Mayor Ivancie Committee."
[84] Over four hundred thirty thousand copies of the poster had been sold in the sixteen years after its 1978 publication. The caption "expose yourself to art" was chosen from contest entries submitted to *The Neighbor* newspaper, which Clark founded. The poster photo was taken in 1977 by Bud Clark's friend, Mike Ryerson. Proceeds from autographed copies of the poster helped pay off Clark's campaign debt. The poster had been seen in Europe and South America. Long, 80. In 2002, the poster copyright was owned by Mike Beard of ErrolGraphics studio; www.errolgraphics.com.
[85] Questionnaire response from *Oreg.* reporter Fred Leeson dated Nov 22, 2000.
[86] www.ci.portland.or.us/auditor/elections/ELECARCHIVES/PRIM84.htm [accessed Sept 22, 2000].
[87] Forrester, "Ivancie the Terrible."
[88] *Oreg.*, May 9, 1984, B12.
[89] www.ci.portland.or.us/auditor/elections/ELECARCHIVES/PRIM84.htm [accessed Sept 22, 2000].
[90] In November, Ivancie supporters conducted a write-in campaign, in which Ivancie took no part, that resulted in an impressive forty-two thousand write-in votes for Ivancie.
[91] Government critic Bill Sizemore placed fifth in the balloting.
[92] Bogle received 34,865 votes to 27,870 for Cawthorne. www.ci.portland.or.us/auditor/elections/ELECARCHIVES/EMERG84.htm — [accessed Sept 22, 2000].
[93] Dick Bogle's mother, Kathryn Bogle, wrote an article for the February 14, 1937, *Oreg.* describing the difficulty she experienced, because of the color of her skin, in finding a job in downtown Portland when she graduated from high school. Employment as a domestic was the only option open to her. MacColl, *Growth*, 536; *Voters' Pamphlet*, Nov 1988, 111.
[94] Petition for divorce and decree of dissolution of marriage, Multnomah County Circuit Court, January 11, 1985 and April 16, 1986.
[95] *Oreg.*, Aug 30, 1985, D1, c 6, and Oct 18, 1985, D2, c 2; *Business Journal*, Jan 13, 1986, p 15, c 1.
[96] Questionnaire response from Sue Keil, former Ivancie staff member, to the author, Dec 6, 2000, and email from Keil dated Apr 16, 2003.
[97] Questionnaire response from Sue Keil, former Ivancie staff member, to the author, Dec 6, 2000.
[98] Forrester, "Ivancie the Terrible."
[99] *Voters' Pamphlet*, May 1984, 126.
[100] Clark listed himself as owner of Mother Goose Antiques and northwest neighborhood rental properties; co-owner and operator of Forsstrom & Clark Waterfowl Specialties and Duck Stuff; and former owner of the Spatenhause and Aardvark Pest Control. Ibid., 126.
[101] The old community of Goose Hollow, west of downtown in the vicinity of Jefferson Street, was so named for the geese maintained by the Thomas Carter family. *OHQ*, Fall 1993, 337. Purdy, at page 16, says that most of the women who lived nearby "raised geese while their husbands farmed or hunted gold."
[102] *1985-1986 Who's Who in the West*; *Voters' Pamphlet*, May 1984, 126.
[103] *Oreg.* editorial, Dec 29, 1983, as quoted in the *Voters' Pamphlet*, May 1984, 126.
[104] Billy Hults and Phil Thompson organized the first Bud's Ball, which raised seventy thousand dollars. Letter from Bud Clark to the author, Dec 17, 2000; Letter from Billy Hultz to the author, Dec 19, 2000.
[105] Letter from Billy Hultz to the author, Dec 19, 2000; Letter from Bud Clark to the author, Dec 17, 2000.
[106] Letter to the Editor from Philip Thompson, *Oreg.*, Sept 16, 1999, D10.
[107] The Mayor's Ball was to become an annual charity event during Bud Clark's eight-year tenure. At times there was controversy among organizers and musicians, and at some point musicians decided they needed to get paid. *WW*, Nov 10, 1999, 1984 Section; Letter from Bud Clark to the author, Dec 17, 2000; Letter from Billy Hultz to the author, Dec 19, 2000; "Bring Back Bud's Ball," *Oreg.* editorial, Sept 8, 1999, B12.
[108] Conversation with E. Kimbark MacColl by the author at MacColl's office, April 6, 2000.
[109] "Badge of Honor," by Philip Dawdy, *WW*, Nov 10, 1999, 1986 section.
[110] "Don't Choke 'Em, Smoke 'Em," by Philip Dawdy, *WW*, Nov 10, 1999, 1985 section.
[111] Ibid.
[112] *Portlandia* is a modern-day version of Lady Commerce, the female figure on the city seal. www.ci.portland.or.us/inside/seal.htm [accessed Sept 30, 2000].
[113] *Portlandia* arrived at her permanent perch on October 6, 1985. She was created by East Coast artist Raymond Kaskey using the same *espousee* technique (hammering copper into a negative mold) as that used for the Statue of Liberty, which is three times *Portlandia*'s size. Kaskey spent three years creating *Portlandia* after his design won a national competition. www.webports.com/dmt/article.htm [accessed Sept 26, 2000]; Abbott, *Gateway*, 193; OS 121; Price, 62-64.
[114] *OJ*, Sept 5, 1912, as quoted in MacColl, *Shaping*, 410-11.
[115] "Don't pillory innocent," *Oreg.*, Nov 20, 1985.
[116] "Prostitution Continues to Erode Livability of Northeast," *Portland Observer*, Mar 5, 1986, 2.
[117] The homeless plan was written by former Multnomah County Commission chair Don Clark at the behest of Mayor Bud Clark. The two Clarks were not related.
[118] "Embattled Portland mayor puts heart into soul of city he loves," by Susan Gilmore, *Seattle Times, Seattle Post-Intelligencer*, May 24, 1987, B2.
[119] *WW*, Feb 27 - Mar 5, 1986.
[120] "Ruffled furrier to treat vagrants to drinks at mayor's place," by John Snell, *Oreg.*, Apr 9, 1986.
[121] "Mayor must exert firm control to guide commission," by E. Kimbark MacColl, *Oreg.*, Mar 20, 1986, E9.
[122] Clark had known about the investigation for five months. "Clark aide suspected of drug tie," by Leslie L. Zaitz, James Long, and Tom Hallman Jr, *Oreg.* Apr 4, 1986, A1 and C5.

[123] "Clark rips critics, defends record," by Richard Read, *Oreg.*, April 9, 1986.
[124] In addition to Lezak, commission members were John C. Beatty, Jr., and H. Doyle Watson. "Harrington misled probe, witness says," by Richard Read, *Oreg.*, April 29, 1986, A1.
[125] Ibid.
[126] "Clark ends briefings, limits interviews," by Richard Read, *Oreg.*, May 13, 1986.
[127] "Sigrid Clark: Adjusting to a new lifestyle," by Rick Rubin, *This Week* newspaper, May 28, 1986.
[128] The city charter now required all candidates for the city auditor's position to hold professional auditor or accountant certification. www.ci.portland.or.us/auditor/elections/ELECARCHIVES/GEN86.htm [accessed Sept 22, 2000]. Barbara Clark and Mayor Bud Clark were not related.
[129] www.ci.portland.or.us/auditor/elections/ELECARCHIVES/GEN86.htm [accessed Sept 22, 2000].
[130] "Badge of Honor," by Philip Dawdy, *WW*, Nov 10, 1999, 1986 section.
[131] "Clark undercut chief," *Oreg.*, June 4, 1986.
[132] "Harrington judged in Wonderland," by David Sarasohn, *Oreg.* editorial page, June 4, 1986.
[133] "Schwab considering 1988 run for mayor," by Kathie Durbin, *Oreg.*, June 25, 1986, B1.
[134] The poll was taken by Bardsley and Haslacher. "Mayor Clark's approval rating drops, poll says," by Kathie Durbin, *Oreg.*, Aug 24, 1986, B1-2.
[135] "Clark joke a gaffe, brings apology to Schwab," by Kathie Durbin, *Oreg.*, Sept 19, 1986. This author wrote down the wording of the remark when she heard it rebroadcast on the radio.
[136] Clark's staff sent the card to Brokaw, who sent back a thank you and a picture of himself. Letter from Bud Clark to the author dated Dec 17, 2000.
[137] Durbin, "Clark joke a gaffe."
[138] However, some later questioned whether MAX ever fulfilled the potential its backers had envisioned. "[I]n retrospect, it seems clear that the MAX tracks were laid in the wrong place. They weren't close enough to the Lloyd Center, didn't go to downtown Gresham and, worse yet, ran in a ditch along the Banfield Freeway, which kept MAX from spurring denser development. … [Now, on other rail lines] developers build housing that's geared to transit users." "Train in vain?" by Bob Young, *WW*, Nov 10, 1999, 1986 section.
[139] "Clark says administration 'over the hump,'" by Kathie Durbin, *Oreg.*, Oct 13, 1986, C1-2.
[140] "Controversy tests mayor's rookie staff," by Kathie Durbin, *Oreg.*, Oct 13, 1986, C2.
[141] The poll was conducted by Bardsley and Haslacher for the *Oreg.*. "Poll gives Strachan strong lead in race," Gordon Oliver, *Oreg.*, Aug 25, 1986, B1.
[142] "The Central City Plan (1988) called for the historic downtown to grow outward rather than upward, spreading north and south along the river and across the river to the east side." Abbott, *Gateway*, 195.
[143] "East-Side Story," by Jim Redden, *WW*, Nov 13-19, 1986, 11; *Voters' Pamphlet*, Nov 1982, 64, and May 1986, 100; www.ci.portland.or.us/auditor/elections/ELECARCHIVES/GEN86.htm [accessed Sept 22, 2000]..
[144] "Urban Services Report, IAR #3-86," City Auditor's Office, Sept 1986.
[145] According to Bud Clark, County Executive Dennis Buchanan never got the credit he deserved for helping to persuade the governing bodies of all three counties and the city to pass convention center resolutions so that the funding measure could be placed on the ballot. Letter to the author from Clark, dated Nov 20, 2000.
[146] Newsletter of the Committee on Regional Convention, Trade, and Spectator Facilities, November 1986; www.oregoncc.org/faq.html [accessed Dec 18, 2000].
[147] Other city employees were covered by the state Public Employees Retirement System, PERS. "Review of the Fire and Police Disability and Retirement Plan, IAR 4-86," City Auditor's Office, Dec 29, 1986; *Oreg.*, Dec 30, 1986, B1; *Portland Business Today*, Dec 30, 1986; *Statesman-Journal*, Dec 30, 1986.
[148] *Oreg.*, Dec 30, 1986, C1. Lansing's auditor colleagues nicknamed her "Mother of Performance Auditing in Oregon Government."
[149] "Mayor fires Police Chief Davis," by Dee Lane and Tom Hallman, *Oreg.*, Apr 8, 1987, A1; "Chief's firing proper," *Oreg.* editorial, Apr 8, 1987; "Firing Line," *WW*, Apr 16-22, 1987; "The skinny on Fat City," by Jonathan Nicholas, *Oreg.*, Apr 9, 1987.
[150] "The Transition to Community Policing in Portland, Oregon, 1984 through 1992," paper prepared by J. E. "Bud" Clark, Nov 18, 1996, p 4.
[151] Lane and Hallman, "Mayor fires Police Chief Davis," A1.
[152] "Portland mayor puts heart into city's soul, Critics call him walking disaster," by Susan Gilmore, *Seattle Times, Seattle Post-Intelliger*, May 24, 1987, B1.
[153] "Embattled Portland mayor puts heart into soul of city he loves," by Susan Gilmore, Ibid., B2.
[154] Clark received 63,531 votes in the primary; Ron Still, 43,321; Lloyd Anderson, 13,954; Jim Davis, 5,271. The other seven candidates received less than seven hundred each. www.ci.portland.or.us/auditor/elections/ELECARCHIVES/PRIM88.htm [accessed Sept 22, 2000]. Both Mike Lindberg and Dick Bogle were reelected with no serious opposition.
[155] Part of the credit for Clark's strong showing at the ballot box belongs to a strong campaign organization, which included pollster Tim Hibbitts, benefactor Robert McCracken, and campaign manager Julie Williamson. "Portland's mayor tough candidate to manage," *Oreg.*, April 18, 1988, B1 and 4; Telephone conversation with Tim Hibbitts by the author, Dec 20, 2000; www.ci.portland.or.us/auditor/elections/ELECARCHIVES/GEN88.htm [accessed Sept 22, 2000].
[156] The City Club board said the committee's recommendations were not adequately documented for publication. "No fire this time from City Club study," by Donald J. Sterling Jr., *Oreg.*, May 16, 1989.
[157] Abbott, *Gateway*, 193-94.
[158] *OS*, 128.
[159] County Measure 17 regarding salaries was adopted Nov. 4, 1986. Multnomah County Charter, Sec 4.30. The 1987-88 county commissioners were Gladys McCoy, chair; Pauline Anderson, Gretchen Kafoury, Caroline Miller, and Polly Casterline. www.multnomah.lib.or.us/cc/pastboar.html [accessed Dec 28, 2000].
[160] *Oreg.*, April 23, 1998, M1 and 3.

[161] Ord #161573, proposed by Commissioner Earl Blumenauer, passed Jan 25, 1989; *WW*, Feb 21, 1991, p 6, c 1. Portland was the first city in the Northwest to enact a polystyrene ban for food containers, and one of the first in the nation. Long, 153.
[162] July 12, 1989. *OS* 127.
[163] "Willamette River Eastbank Review," Report by Citizens' Advisory Committee, Nov 29, 1993, 11; Letter from Ernie Bonner to the author dated Dec 15, 2000.
[164] *WW*, Nov 10, 1999, 1989 section.
[165] Draft *Portland Parks and Recreation,* 1989 section; www.ci.portland.or.us/auditor/elections/ELECARCHIVES/SPECJUNE89.htm [accessed Sept 22, 2000].
[166] Draft *Portland Parks and Recreation,* 1989 section.
[167] "Clark's leadership spurs controversy," by Gordon Oliver and Sarah Carlin Ames, *Oreg.*, Oct 29, 1989.
[168] "Crime catches City Hall off guard," by Larry Cowen and James Long, *Oreg.*, Oct 1, 1989.
[169] "Meanwhile, back in Bozo land," by Phil Stanford, *Oreg.*, Oct 16, 1989.
[170] Salmon Street Springs is maintained by the Portland Water Bureau. "At full capacity the fountain recycles 4,924 gallons of water per minute." Letter from water bureau webmaster@water.ci.portland.or.us to the author dated Dec 8, 2000.
[171] "Clark's leadership spurs controversy," by Gordon Oliver and Sarah Carlin Ames, *Oreg.*, Oct 29, 1989.
[172] "I will do my best to become a more sensitive human being and expunge any racism that I might discover in myself, now and in the future," Clark said. "Mayor tells blacks he's sorry," by Gordon Oliver, *Oreg.*, Nov 14, 1989, A1.
[173] "Political sparks ignited at City Hall," by Gordon Oliver, *Oreg.*, Oct 15, 1989.
[174] *Oreg.*, Oct 29 and 30, 1989. See also "Clark taking his message directly to the public," *Oreg.*, Nov 1, 1989, B1 and 8.
[175] "Poll shows mayor at lowest ebb," by Gordon Oliver, *Oreg.*, Feb 11, 1990, B5 and 8.
[176] "Witness says Clark under pressure to remove Chief Harrington," by John Painter Jr., *Oreg.*, Mar 14, 1990, E1.
[177] "Mayor's aide testifies negative publicity led her to suggest panel," by John Painter Jr., *Oreg.*, Mar 10, 1990.
[178] "Duffy says Harrington wasn't fired," by John Snell, *Oreg.*, Mar 8, 1990.
[179] Clark's attorney had advised him not to comment about his alleged remark when it became public. "Quote of the Week," *WW*, June 22-28, 1989.
[180] Conversation by the author on Jan 30, 2001, with John Russell, an Arlington Club member instrumental in getting the club policy changed. The U.S. Supreme Court ruled in late 1988 that local governments could prohibit male-only social clubs. *WW*, Dec 12-18, 1988. "Council asks 2 clubs to admit women," by Sarah Carlin Ames, *Oreg.*, Oct 5, 1989, A1 and&15.
[181] "Clark says he's sorry for remark," *Oreg.*, Mar 23, 1990.
[182] "Harrington suit costs Portland taxpayers $304,688 in legal fees," Mar 23, 1990, F4.
[183] Harrington's pension benefits would be paid from the city's Fire and Police Disability and Retirement Fund.
[184] "Harrington to drop appeal of bias case," by John Painter Jr., *Oreg.*, Aug 1, 1990.
[185] "Clark and the press: Bloom off the roses," by Gordon Oliver, *Oreg.*, Apr 10, 1990, B7.
[186] Ibid.; "Clark shows little interest in hiring press secretary," by Barnes C. Ellis and Sarah Carlin Ames, *Oreg.*, Apr 16, 1990.
[187] "Civic leaders get mandate to map city's future," by Sarah Carlin Ames, *Oreg.*, Apr 10, 1990, B8.
[188] "Burch cites tension, files for stress disability," by Sarah Carlin Ames, *Oreg.*, May 11, 1990.
[189] "Dick Bogle to pay settlement," by Barnes C. Ellis, *Oreg.*, July 26, 1990, A1 and 18.
[190] *Oreg.*, Aug 25 and 28, 1990.
[191] City Commissioner Earl Blumenauer won reelection with no serious challenge. *Voters Pamphlet*, Nov 1990, 170-11; www.ci.portland.or.us/auditor/elections/ELECARCHIVES/PRIM90.htm [accessed Sept 22, 2000].
[192] Yeates, 23, 33.
[193] The Oregon Convention Center cost eighty-five million dollars to build. www.oregoncc.org/faq.html [accessed Dec 21, 1990]. Eleven years later, a one hundred sixteen million-dollar addition to the Convention Center got underway in February 2001, to be paid for with revenues from an increase in hotel/motel taxes and car rental taxes, new revenue sources which went into effect in April 2000. (Voters had turned down a twenty-five-year property tax measure for this purpose in November 1998.) *P. Trib.*, Feb 9, 2001, B4; *Oreg.*, Feb 9, 2001, D2.
[194] "[D]esigned by Bob Murase, and completed in 1990, the Plaza is a miniature landscape of bronze sculpture and granite boulders engraved with haiku." Abbott, *Gateway*, 203. The plaza was initiated and brought to fruition by civic leader Bill Naito, who was himself a living demonstration of that assimilation.
[195] Pioneer Place cost one hundred thirty-five million dollars to build. *WW*, Nov 10, 1999, 1990 section; *OS*, 140.
[196] Chief Walker and Clark's police liaison, Steve Moskowitz, who joined the mayor's staff in late 1986, had kept police relations with Clark and the rest of the city on an even keel. *Oreg.*, Oct 13, 1986, C2.
[197] Ibid., Nov 18, 1990, A29.
[198] *Oreg.*, Nov 16, 1990, A1 and 27.
[199] Ibid., Nov 15, 1990.
[200] Steve Duin column, *Oreg.*, Jan 13, 1991; *Oreg.*, Apr 14, 1992; telephone conversation with Tim Hibbitts by the author, Dec 20, 2000. Eight years after Clark left office, columnist Duin put it this way, "As nostalgic as many Portlanders may be for Bud's openness and accessibility, they aren't ready to cast another vote for his manner of unpredictability." *Oreg.*, May 1, 2000.
[201] "City's backup water wells fail to fulfill promise," by Eric Goranson, *Oreg.*, Aug 2, 1992, A20; Letter from Ross Walker of the Portland Water Bureau to the author, Dec 18, 2000; www.water.ci.portland.or.us/groundwater.htm [accessed Dec 14, 2000].
[202] Communication with Mike Lindberg by the author, Dec 24 and 30, 2000.
[203] *Oreg.*, Apr 14, 1992.
[204] Measure 50 (approved by voters in 1997) changed the value used to test Measure 5 limits to real market

value only. Insert to November 1997 Multnomah County property tax statements; *OS* 133-34; "The Ballot Measure That Ate Oregon," by Patty Wentz, *WW*, Nov 10, 1999, 1990 section.
[205] Vera Katz was speaker of the Oregon House of Representatives for the 1985, 1987, and 1989 regular sessions and the 1990 special legislative session. She lost that position when Republicans gained control of the House in 1991. Edwards, Cecil, 149 and 158.
[206] *WW*, Nov 10, 1999, 1992 section.
[207] Hales won by six thousand votes out of one hundred eighty-six thousand cast. www.ci.portland.or.us/auditor/elections/gen92.htm [accessed Sept 22, 2000].
[208] *Voters' Pamphlet*, May 1992, 113.
[209] Hales resigned in mid-2000 to take a job with a national engineering firm. He had proved his independence from the Homebuilders Association when the organization contributed to his opponent in the 2000 election, which Hales won easily. He had referred to houses with big garages in front as "snout houses" that were "ugly" and "stupid"—a description which had enraged the Homebuilders. *Oreg.*, Apr 24, 2000, E5; *Oreg.* Aug 20, 1999, C8.
[210] Abbott, *Gateway*, 195. In 1999, OMSI placed seventh in popularity among Oregon's tourist attractions, while the Washington Park Zoo rated fourth. Indian casinos ranked first, third and sixth; Multnomah Falls, second; the D River Wayside on the coast was fifth. "Oregon Attractions," Oregon Tourism Commission, obtained July 28, 2000.
[211] Abbott, *Gateway*, 203; *Oreg.*, Jan 10, 1991, A18; Long, 122.
[212] Portland was an informal, laid-back town, *WW* noted, and "people here don't respond well to stern father figures." "How Good a Mayor?" *WW*, Oct 13-19, 1988, 8.

Chapter 25

[1] Only one of the seven members of the first council, Loren Hastings, was married.
[2] One could argue that legislative approval of Portland's charter (Jan 23, 1851) properly marks the city's birthday, or the date the governor signed that bill (Feb 8, 1851,) or the first city election (April 7, 1851.) This author used April 14, 1851, the date the first city council met. A 1949 city attorney letter to Mayor Lee cites three possible dates as the city's birthday: Feb 8, April 7, and April 14. Historian E. Kimbark MacColl says at *Merchants*, 469, published in 1988, that April 6 (sic) had become "the generally accepted date for Portland's birthday." In 2001, Mayor Katz hosted a public one hundred fiftieth Portland birthday party at City Hall on Feb 8.
[3] Among the one hundred largest cities in the U.S. governed by women mayors, Portland ranked second behind San Diego in order of city population. "Women in Elective Office 2000," Center for American Women and Politics (CAWP), Eagleton Institute of Politics, Rutgers University. www.cawp.rutgers.edu/pdf/elective.pdf - [accesssed Jan 2, 2001].
[4] The six foreign-born mayors were Stephen McCormick, Thomas J. Holmes, Bernard Goldsmith, Philip Wasserman, Joseph Simon, and Vera Katz.
[5] One mayor (J. A. Chapman) served three different times and three mayors (William Ladd, Henry Failing, and William Mason) served at two different times.
[6] "Just Like a Woman," by Foster Church, *Governing* magazine, Sept 1990, 26-28; "She never had the desire to travel," by Steve Duin, *Oreg.*, June 21, 1990; "The Politics of Vera Katz," by Susan Hereford, *This Week* magazine, Sept 11, 1991; *Who's Who of American Women*, 2000-2001 Edition, 662.
[7] Church, "Just Like a Woman," 29.
[8] Ibid., 26-28.
[9] In 1998, pollster Tim Hibbitts said Vera Katz was "more popular than predecessors Neil Goldschmidt and Bud Clark, with approval ratings in the 65-70 percent range." *WW*, Dec 12-16, 1998, 23. However, Katz won only 55 percent of the vote in May 2000, which engendered a *Oreg.* editorial suggesting several reasons why her percentage was down 26 percent from four years before: an aggressive opponent (nineteen-year-old Jake Oken-Berg), police payroll scandals, May Day riot control where there was no rioting, sloppy handling of a PDC computer contract, and a behind-the-scenes Civic Stadium deal cut by the mayor. "Voters to mayor: Open up!" *Oreg.* editorial, May 20, 2000.
[10] George Baker and Terry Schrunk each served sixteen years.
[11] Edwards, Cecil, 149; Yeates, 39, 41.
[12] Blumenauer replaced the incumbent congressman, Ron Wyden, who in turn had been elected to replace Bob Packwood after he resigned his U.S. senate seat.
[13] "Oregon Democrat pushes livability in Congress," by Dave Hogan, *Oreg.*, Feb 7, 1999.
[14] www.ci.portland.or.us/auditor/elections/prim96, spec96, and gen96.htm [accessed Sept 22, 2000].
[15] *Voters' Pamphlet*, May 1996, M-12.
[16] Ibid., M-11.
[17] Yeates, 17, 23, 25, 33-37, 49, 56.
[18] *Voters' Pamphlet*, Nov 1998, 71.
[19] www.ci.portland.or.us/auditor/elections/prim98 and gen98.htm [accessed Sept 22, 2000].
[20] *Voters' Pamphlet*, Nov 1998, 69.
[21] Sten was thirty-three; Hales, forty-six; Saltzman, forty-eight; Francesconi, forty-nine; Blackmer, fifty-one; and Katz, sixty-eight; for an average age of forty-nine.
[22] In fall 2002, State Representative Randy Leonard, president of the Portland firefighters' union, bested Multnomah County Commissioner Serena Cruz in a runoff election to fill Charlie Hales' open council seat. *Oreg.*, Nov 6, 2002, E1. For the third time out of the four most recent campaigns, a male candidate had won a spirited runoff against a female challenger. So in spite of laying claim to three women mayors in its history, the city of Portland had been served by only eight women in city elective office as of year 2003.
[23] "About Sam Adams," *Oreg.*, Apr 7, 1996.
[24] The twentieth annual Gay Pride Day parade on June 17, 1995, was attended by Mayor Katz, Chief Charles Moose, former chief Tom Potter and his daughter Katie. *Oreg.*, June 18, 1995, D1.
[25] *Oreg.*, Aug 3, 1999, B6; *P. Trib.*, Nov 1, 2002, C3.
[26] *Oreg.*, Dec 10, 1999, A1.
[27] Ibid., Feb 6, 2001, B3. At least two previous chiefs from outside the bureau had experienced difficulties

assimilating. Mayor Lee's chief, Charles Pray (1949-51), complained that nobody would tell him things "that were common knowledge." *OJ*, Mar 31, July 6, and Aug 23, 1951, as cited in Pitzer, Paul C., *OHQ* Spring 1990, 16. Mayor Goldschmidt's Chief Baker (1974-81) once recommended that he "be the last or one of the last" chiefs to be chosen from outside the bureau." "'Outsider' tag makes new chief's job tougher," Fred Leeson, *Oreg.*, Feb 11, 1994.

[28] Calls came for Kroeker's firing a year after he arrived in Portland over a police crackdown at a May Day rally and because of remarks Kroeker had made eleven years before to a Christian group in California, which became publicly known at this time. Kroeker's 1989 remarks disparaged gays, said wives should be "submissive" to their husbands, and spoke of "disciplining disobedient children with a boat oar." *Oreg.*, Nov 10, 2000, D1; *Oreg.*, Nov 5, 2000, B1; *Oreg.*, Nov 4, 2000, B1; *WW*, Nov 1, 2000, 16.

[29] *OS* 141.

[30] Fact sheet of the Center for American Women and Politics (CAWP), Eagleton Institute of Politics, Rutgers University. www.cawp.rutgers.edu/facts/Summary2000.html [accesssed Jan 3, 2001]; Letter from CAWP Program Coordinator, Information Services, dated Jan 2, 2001, to the author.

[31] Synopsis prepared by the author based on information from Multnomah and Washington county property tax statements, the 1997-98 Summary of Assessments and Taxes prepared by the Multnomah County Tax Supervising and Conservation Commission, and through correspondence between the author and Linda Burglehaus, TSCC Director, May 22, 2002.

[32] *1999-2000 OBB*, 307-8.

[33] A Marion County judge ruled Measure 7 unconstitutional in February 2001, and the decision was upheld by the Oregon Supreme Court in October 2002. *Oreg.*, Feb 23, 2001, A1 and 11; Oct 5, 2002, E1.

[34] Fact sheet of the Center for American Women and Politics (CAWP), Eagleton Institute of Politics, Rutgers University. www.cawp.rutgers.edu/facts/Summary2000.html [accesssed Jan 3, 2001].

[35] In *City of Portland v Jim Atwood*, July 21, 1994, the Oregon Tax Court ruled that City Ord #167514, adopted March 30, 1994, which assessed fees based on use of property rather than ownership of property (City Code Sec 6.06), was not subject to Measure 5 property tax limitations. This business property-management license fee was based on the size of the building footprint and the carrying capacity of non-freight elevators, and exempted owner-occupied and low-income housing. Communications with Terri Williams, audit manager of the City License Bureau, and Dan Vizzini, former manager of the Assessment and Liens Division, by the author on Feb 21, 24, 26, and March 2, 5, 2001; "Stewards for Downtown: APP Marks 20 Years," 1999; *Oreg.*, June 21, 2000, C7.

[36] *OS* 126.

[37] Abbott, *Gateway*, 195-97.

[38] "Floods of December 1964 and January 1965 in the Far Western States, Part 2: Streamflow and Sediment Data," and "Water Resources Data for Oregon, 1992," published by the U. S. Geological Survey, and "The Pacific Northwest Floods of February 6-11, 1996," published by the American Institute of Hydrology, all as cited by USGS Portland Office Information Specialist Suzanne Jo Miller to the author by letters dated Nov 29 and 30, 2000; Taylor and Hatton, 84, 103.

[39] The plaque, dated February 14, 1996, was located on the river at the Salmon Street Plaza. "I hope you will always remember for as long as you live," President Clinton said, "what the people of Portland did in one remarkable day."

[40] "Beyond Bull Run," by R. Gregory Nokes, *Oreg.*, Feb 25, 1996.

[41] "Council gets too far out Front," *Oreg.*, June 22, 1996; "Front's new name alters city's history," by Bill Stewart, *Oreg.*, June 23, 1996.

[42] Martin Luther King, Jr., was assassinated April 4, 1968.

[43] "City Council begins Front Ave. Renaming," by Bill Stewart, *Oreg.*, July 4, 1996.

[44] "John and Lucy Buchanan," by Foster Church, *Oreg.*, June 8, 1997, L4; "Money for art's sake," by John Foyston, *Oreg.*, Nov 19, 1995, E1; www.orsymphony.org/orchestra/conductors/jdepreist.html [accesssed June 13, 2002].

[45] The tally for the May 21, 1996, city term-limits measure was 40,572 yes: 57,305 no. www.ci.portland.or.us/auditor/elections/Meas1942.htm [accesssed Aug 9, 2000].

[46] "Portland term limits fail to make ballot," by Scott Learn, *Oreg.*, Aug 3, 2000, D3.

[47] Draft, *Portland Parks and Recreation, A Chronological History*, Dec 1998; 1995, 1996, and 1997 sections. In 2000, an eighteen-member Citywide Off-Leash Task Force unanimously recommended increasing dog license fees (to be collected by Multnomah County Animal Control) to cover enforcement and other costs of fencing off-leash areas. *Oreg.*, Feb 7, 2000, B1, 5. The license fees were not adopted.

[48] City hall first opened to the public on January 2, 1895. *Oreg.*, Jan 1, 1895.

[49] Of the 29.3 million-dollar cost to renovate city hall, construction costs consumed twenty million dollars, 85 percent of which was for bringing the structure into compliance with code; 2.8 million dollars was for architectural and engineering services; three million dollars for temporary employee offices; 1.3 million dollars for art, equipment, and other systems; 1.2 million dollars for furnishings; one million dollars for project administration, permits and miscellaneous. "City Hall reopens, flaunting face-lift," by Michele Parente, *Oreg.*, Mar 30, 1998, A1 and 6.

[50] Moyer actually donated five million dollars to the Oregon Community Foundation for purchase of the block, and the foundation was to turn the block over to the city for public use. Conversations between the author and Parks Block Foundation president, Jim Westwood, on June 10 and 11, 2002; *Oreg.*, Dec 13, 2000, A1 and 5.

[51] The proposed retail-focused promenade was patterned after the famous Las Ramblas in Barcelona, Spain, to feature an underground European-style robotic parking garage with thirty-five hundred stalls. Opponents argued that the underground parking would act as a magnet that would draw traffic tie-ups and cause loss of housing and existing businesses. *Oreg.*, June 4, 2000, E1 and 2; Dec 14, 2000, C2, c 2; Jan

28, 2001, B1 and 5; *WW*, Dec 20, 2000, 23; Conversations between the author and Parks Block Foundation president Jim Westwood on June 10 and 11, 2002.

[52] The northernmost of the original "missing" south park blocks, now O'Bryant Square, was donated to the city in 1973. In 1865, a court decree awarded six park blocks to the heirs of Nancy Lownsdale in the absence of a written will bequeathing them to the city. Benjamin Stark refused to donate two blocks of his property in between the south and north park blocks. Snyder, *Potpourri*, 123-33; Maddux, 195-96; MacColl, *Merchants*, 17.

[53] *WW*, Nov 10, 1999, 1998 section.

[54] *Consolidation Study Task Force, Final Report*, Sept 1998, xv-xvii. This author was a member of that task force, but voted with the minority, recommending that further discussion of consolidation cease unless east Multnomah County showed interest in such consolidation in the future.

[55] "Bills provide Gresham option to quit county," *Oreg.*, May 15, 1999.

[56] *Oreg.*, Sept 29, 1998, B1 and 5; Oct 2, 1998, Portland page.

[57] "A tug of war of two cities," *Oreg.*, Oct 20, 1990; Conversation with George Joseph, Chair of the 1974 City-County Charter Commission, on Nov 27, 2000, by the author. Joseph said he would not vote for Portland-Multnomah County consolidation if it were on the ballot today.

[58] According to the PDC Web page, tax increment financing worked this way: "When the city defines an urban renewal boundary, the county assessor 'freezes' the assessed value of real property within the urban renewal district. As the city and others invest in the urban renewal area, property values go up. The property taxes above those that were collected when the values were 'frozen' are used to pay for the improvements in the urban renewal area." www.portlanddev.org/faq01.html, p 5 [accesssed Mar 4, 2001]. www.portlanddev.org/about/pdfs/intro.pdf [accesssed Mar 7, 2001].

[59] "Steering a course with new power," by Scott Learn and David Austin, *Oreg.*, Oct 8, 2000, D1 and 3.

[60] Other city urban renewal districts existing in October 1998 were the downtown/waterfront, Oregon Convention Center, South Park Blocks, Central Eastside industrial area, and Airport Way. After that time, Lents, North Macadam, and Interstate renewal districts were added to PDC's list, and a Gateway district was approved in June 2001. *Oreg.*, Jan 30, 2001, B3; Oct 15, 1998, C2; and Dec 15, 1998, A10; www.portland.dev.org [accessed Apr 11, 2003].

[61] The Portland Development Commission was authorized to issue up to two hundred thirty-four million dollars in bonds through 2018 for the River District project. Opinion piece, "Examine renewal districts: Do benefits outweigh losses?" by Debbie Aiona and Shelley Lorenzen, *Oreg.*, Oct 29, 1998; "PDC Five Year Business Plan," www.portlanddev.org [accesssed Mar 7, 2001].

[62] "Urban renewal heads into the Corridor," by Fred Leeson, *Oreg.*, Aug 13, 2000, B1 & 2; "Divided by the tracks," by Spencer Heinz, *Oreg.*, Aug 6, 2000, D1 & 12.

[63] The mayor of Seattle cancelled plans for a citywide celebration on December 31, 1999, for fear of terrorists. "While they were sleeping in Seattle, we partied in Portland," said Commissioner Charlie Hales. "I think that's a nice contrast." "Y2K afterglow warming up City Hall," by Scott Learn, *Oreg.*, Jan 4, 2000, B1.

[64] Unfortunately, a New Year's Eve celebration at Pioneer Square the following year turned out badly. Would-be-celebrants-turned-vandals "broke windows, stole property, threatened officers and pelted them with bottles." *Oreg.*, Jan 3, 2001, B10. An *Oreg.* editorial supported the mayor's call for institutionalized New Year's Eve celebrations in the square for the future.

[65] *WW*, Apr 12, 2000, 17; "Katz, being treated for cancer, urges women to get breast exams," by Scott Learn and Oz Hopkins Koglin, *Oreg.*, Apr 4, 2000, A1.

[66] Portland will build fiber-optic network," by Scott Learn, *Oreg.*, May 25, 2000, B1 and 7.

[67] www.surfpac.navy.mil/pressrelease/June99/00-150.htm [accesssed Jan 3, 2001].

[68] Portland had nine sister cities as of April 2001. In addition to Sapporo, Japan, and Suzhou, China, the other cities were in Israel, Mexico, Nicaragua, Russia, South Korea, Taiwan, and Zimbabwe. The city also had a friendship city association with Tallinn, Estonia. www.ci.portland.or.us/mayor/international/ [accesssed Jan 8, 2001].

[69] *Oreg.*, Sept 15, 2000, C1 and 8; Sept 14, 2000, D1.

[70] "A waterfront view will be as close as a walk in the park," by Bill Stewart, *Oreg.*, Nov 14, 2000, B3; "Eastbank Riverfront Park moves closer to reality with agreement," by Bill Stewart, *Oreg.*, Sept 4, 1999, D1, 5. The new esplanade extends from the Hawthorne Bridge to the Steel bridge, with access steps at the Morrison and Burnside bridges.

[71] *Oreg.*, July 10, 2000, E6; April 30, 2002, A1 and 7. Computer vendor Severn Trent subsequently agreed to pay the city seven million dollars of the city's estimated loss. *Oreg.*, Jan 3, 2003, A1, A4.

[72] *Oreg.*, Mar 4, 2001, A1 and 8; *P. Trib.*, Mar 3, 2001, A3; *Oreg.*, Mar 2, 2001, A1.

[73] "U. S. grows 13% in decade," *Oreg.*, Dec 29, 2000, A1 and 19. The story was based on U.S. Census data collected in 2000. The entire Portland metropolitan area had a population of nearly two million people by 2000.

[74] *Oreg.*, Dec 19, 2000, A14.

[75] In 1960, there were no Nguyens in Portland; in 1992 there were 338, and by 2000 there were 903. In 1960, there were six families named either Gonzales or Gonzalez; in 1992 there were 172, and by 2000 there were 422. The 1960 and 1992 figures are from Abbott, *Gateway*, 201; the 2000 figures are based on a count by the author of names in *The White Pages, 2001 Qwest Portland Telephone Directory*.

[76] Statistical Section, 1, 5, 9, 18, 20, 22-23, *Portland Comprehensive Annual Financial Report*, FYE June 30, 2001. Actual water main mileage—1,935; actual lane miles of streets—3,843; general fund outlays—366 million dollars.

[77] *P. Trib.*, Feb 9, 2001, A9.

[78] *Oreg.*, Feb 8, 2001, B2; "Portland's Missing Children," by Todd Murphy, *P. Trib.*, Feb 16, 2001, A1 and 2. "Some of the luster has worn off our neighborhood

system," said Dan Saltzman, commissioner in charge of the Office of Neighborhood Involvement and Associations. *The Multnomah Village Post*, Sept 1999. A 1990 Portland history says, "At present the neighborhood movement has apparently peaked as a political power." DeMarco, 146.

[79] Abbott, *Gateway*, 199.

[80] The council created the powerful position of chief administrative officer in early 2000 and told appointee Tim Grewe to reduce city administrative costs by 10 percent. "Bureau budget cuts won't come easy," by Scott Learn, *Oreg.*, Dec 26, 2000, B2.

[81] *Oreg.*, Mar 20, 2000, A1 and 4; "The Willamette's poisoned heritage," *Oreg.*, Dec 17, 2000, A1, 14-15; *Oreg.*, Dec 21, 2000, C8; *Oreg.*, Jan 27, 2001, A1 and 11; "Portland Harbor Joins Superfund," *River Monitor*, a publication of American Rivers in Washington D. C., Dec 2000, p12, c 2.

[82] *Oreg.*, Dec 17, 2000, A1 and 14.

[83] *Consolidation Study Task Force, Final Report*, Sept 1998, 151; *WW*, Nov 20, 2000, 27.

[84] "Managing the Costs of Environmental Responsibility, Fact Sheet 4," www.enviro.ci.portland.or.us/CPR.htm [accesssed Aug 20, 2000].

[85] *Oreg.*, June 13, 1867, p 2, c 1; Dec 4, 1950, B2, c 7.

[86] "Partners in Progress: Port of Portland Celebrates 100 Years, 1891-1991," 1-2; MacColl, *Merchants*, 292.

[87] "Request to dredge river denied," by Jonathan Brinckman, *Oreg.*, Sept 30, 2000, A1 and 9.

[88] "Pro & Con: Should Columbia channel be deepened?" *Oreg.*, July 6, 2000, D9; Brinckman, "Request to dredge river denied," A1 and 9.

[89] Two of the biggest citizen complaints reported in the auditor's tenth annual survey released January 2, 2001, were traffic congestion on main thoroughfares and fast drivers on neighborhood streets. *Oreg.*, Jan 3, 2001, B2.

[90] The 1996 Telecommunications Act "opened the door to frantic competition." "Trapped in the slow motion of slush hour," by Steve Duin, *Oreg.*, June 29, 1999. "The number of companies licensed to lay fiber in Portland is expected to swell from 19 to 32 during the next few months." "Fiber-optics installation snarls traffic downtown," by Jim Lynch, *Oreg.*, May 15, 2000.

[91] Mayor Katz and Commissioner Francesconi spoke of plans for "when the freeway is moved away from the river" in Nov 2000. Bill Stewart, *Oreg.*, Nov 14, 2000, B3. In May 1993, the council passed resolution #35141, reaffirming "the goal of reclaiming and redeveloping the Willamette River Eastbank." A 1993 citizens' committee appointed by Commissioner Hales recommended that the I-5 freeway be removed from the Eastbank "over the long term" of fifteen to twenty-five years. "Willamette River Eastbank Review Report and Recommendations," Nov 29, 1993. Aesthetic blight, air pollution, noise pollution, and loss of valuable land for parks, housing, commercial, and industrial use were east-bank issues. Conversations and communications with Ron Paul (exec asst to Comm. Hales), Ernie Bonner, Jane Cease, Ron Buel, Mike Lindberg, and others in fall 2000. In 1987, the estimated cost of relocating the freeway with an alignment along Eighth and Ninth avenues was 335 million dollars. *Oreg.*, Nov 3, 1987, B4 and C2.

[92] "A crucible for creativity," by David Sarasohn, *Oreg.*, May 30, 1999, F1.

[93] Voters turned down statewide gas tax increases in 1994 and 2000 that would have funneled needed dollars for roads to Portland.

[94] *Tenth Annual Performance Report and Citizen Survey*, Office of the City Auditor; *Oreg.*, Jan 3, 2001, B2.

[95] A 5.4-mile light-rail line was part of the Interstate Corridor Urban Renewal Area approved by the council in August 2000. "Urban renewal heads into the Corridor," by Fred Leeson, *Oreg.*, Aug 13, 2000, B1 and 2; "Streetcar promises to start up in July," by Bill Stewart, *Oreg.*, Jan 11, 2001, C2; "Train in Vain," by Bob Young, *WW*, Nov 10, 1999, 1986 section.

[96] *Oreg.*, Jan 12, 2001, C3; "Portland 2001: The city at 150," *Oreg.*, Jan 1, 2001, F8; *P. Trib.*, Feb 20, 2001, B4.

[97] *Oreg.*, Jan 29, 2000, A11; Sept 28, 2000, A1 and 7.

[98] "Telco hotels" are bunker-like buildings filled with phone switching devices and computer servers. "'Telco hotels' divide City Council," by Randy Gragg, *Oreg.*, Nov 22, 2000, D2; "High-tech bunkers pit tax revenue, livability," by Randy Gragg, *Oreg.*, Nov 6, 2000, E1.

[99] Between 1993 and 1999, the City of Portland contributed thirty-seven million dollars to Portland-area schools. *Oreg.*, Jan 29, 2000, A11 and D6.

[100] Robert Reich, former secretary of labor for Bill Clinton, as quoted in "Reich displays designer hips and a deft mind," by Steve Duin, *Oreg.*, Dec 3, 2000, B1.

[101] The Portland - Vancouver area scored second nationally in gains in the high-technology area from 1995 to 1999, growing from 5.3 billion dollars billed in 1995 to 12.7 billion dollars billed in 1999, an increase of 137 percent. "Oregon cities rate high on tech list," by Elisa Williams, *Oreg.*, June 19, 2000, B1. Also see "'Cybercities' list ranks Portland 19th for technology employment," *Oreg.*, Dec 11, 2000, D1.

[102] Short, 11, 33; *Oreg.*, Jan 1, 1895.

[103] "Beyond Bull Run," by R. Gregory Nokes, *Oreg.*, Feb 25, 1996, A1.

[104] There were three winter emergency uses between 1996 and 1999: eight days during the February 1996 flood; five days starting December 28, 1998, because of a rain-on-snow event, and nineteen days starting November 25, 1999, due to turbidity in the Bull Run supply. www.water.ci.portland.or.us/groundwater.htm#gwuse [accesssed Dec 14, 2000].

[105] "Portland sweats as 'burbs shop for water," by Scott Learn, *Oreg.*, Dec 31, 2000, C1 and 12; "Sewer/water rate won't end fee," by Scott Learn, *Oreg.*, Apr 5, 2000, D2; "Water providers look at backup systems rather than costly, big regional supply," by R. Gregory Nokes, *Oreg.*, Mar 29, 2000, C4; "The Muddied truth about Bull Run water," In My Opinion, by Douglas W. Larson, *Oreg.*, Dec 12, 1999, F5.

[106] "Customers must use less water to meet conservation goal," by Scott Learn, *Oreg.*, Dec 31, 2000, C12.

[107] The city's police and firefighters' pension fund "threatens its bond rating and funding for basic services like parks and public safety. 'It's a crucial issue that could one day break the budget,' said historian Kimbark MacColl.'" *WW*, Dec 12, 1998, 29. "Rethink city pension funding," *Oreg.* editorial, Feb 10, 1999.

[108] *LWV Voter*, Newsletter of the League of Women

Voters of Portland, Dec 2000/ Jan 2001 issue, 1, 3; *Willamette Week*, May 31, 2000, 29-31. Among issues discussed by the council and Police Chief Kroeker in December 2000 were "lessons from May Day's police clashes with protesters, the best ways to handle demonstrations, ways to strengthen police oversight and the role of the Portland-FBI joint task force on terrorism." "Police issues prompt council workshops," by Maxine Bernstein, *Oreg.*, Dec 27, 2000, B3.

[109] *City of Portland General Purpose Financial Statements for the Fiscal Year Ended June 30, 2000*, Note 17, Fire and Police Disability and Retirement Plan, 52-56. In addition, because of compression of tax levies caused by Oregon Measure 5 in 1990, the pension and disability fund could cause the city's general fund to lose revenue it would otherwise receive if growth of real property market values slowed significantly or declined. Correspondence between the author and Ken Rust, Acting Manager, Bureau of Financial Management, Feb 3 and 7, 2001; Correspondence between the author and Linda Burglehaus, Director of the Multnomah County Tax Supervising and Conservation Commission, Feb 3, 6, and 7, 2001; May 22, 2002.

[110] Council members were reluctant to propose or support changes in the Fire and Police Pension and Disability Fund because of intense pressure from powerful police and fire unions. For example, Commissioner Jim Francesconi was not endorsed by the Portland Fire Fighters Association in 2000, because, the president said, "Francesconi's recent support of reforming the city's pension board didn't win the commissioner many union friends." *Oreg.*, Apr 3, 2000, E3. Also see "The Pension Fund that Ate Portland, and why city officials are afraid to take on the cops and firefighters who run it," by Bob Young, *WW*, Mar 25, 1998; "Too timid by far," by Robert Landauer, *Oreg.*, Aug 19, 1998; "Tension Fund," by Nick Budnick, *WW*, Nov 10, 1999.

[111] In 1946, Portland was among the ten largest cities governed by commissions. After that time, the other nine cities—New Orleans, Newark, Jersey City, Memphis, St. Paul, Birmingham, San Antonio, Omaha, and Des Moines—changed their form of government. Questionnaire response, City Auditor Gary Blackmer to the author, Nov 6, 2000; Kneier, 292.

[112] This author had formerly advocated changing the city's form of government, but no longer does.

[113] "Increasing Density in Portland," City Club Report dated November 1999. "The ... City Club ... came out swinging with a scathing report on Portland's long-range planning. Lost in the fracas is an equally blistering attack on what club members see as the underlying problem: the city's commission form of government." The fragmented nature of city government is cited, and the lack of cooperation between individual commissioners. "City Clubbed," *WW*, Nov 10, 1999.

[114] *OJ*, May 29, 1974, 1.

[115] In May 2002, for the seventh time since the commission form of government was adopted in 1913, Portland voters firmly rejected a proposal—76 percent to 24 percent—to change their form of government. Signatures to place the initiative measure on the ballot were secured by paid signature gatherers in a well-financed campaign that outspent opponents, led by former mayor Bud Clark, by ten to one. The measure proposed a strong mayor and a legislative council of nine, seven of whom would be elected by district instead of citywide. *Oreg.*, May 10, 2002, C3; May 22, 2002, E1; June 24, 2002, B2; www.ci.portland.or.us/auditor/elections/elecarch/pastformvotes.htm—[accessed Apr 21, 2003].

[116] In addition to preparing the council meeting agenda, overseeing the conduct of outside audits, and performing ongoing internal audits of city functions, bureaus, and financial affairs, Auditor Gary Blackmer had recently added a city ombudsman to his staff and agreed to oversee operation of the Independent Police Review Division (IPR), successor organization to the Police Internal Investigative Auditing Committee (PIIAC).

[117] The League study was conducted in 1991 and reaffirmed as a current position in May 1999. Member Handbook, League of Women Voters of Portland, 2001-02.

[118] *Tenth Annual Performance Report and Citizen Survey*, Report #270, Office of the City Auditor, ii, iv, 18, A-1 and A-17. Thirty-two percent of residents responding rated their neighborhood's livability very good; 52 percent rated it good. The random sample had a plus or minus 1-1/2 percent margin of error; the return rate was 41 percent; a total of 3,758 city residents returned their surveys. Also see *Oreg.*, Jan 3, 2001, B2.

[119] *Financial World*, March 19, 1995, 52.

[120] *Forbes* quotations as cited in Abbott, *Gateway*, 199; *Time* magazine Jan 20, 1997, 55-57.

[121] As quoted in *Oreg.*, May 4, 1999, A1 and 8.

[122] *Money* magazine, Dec 2000, 150.

[123] Mrs. C. M. Cartwright, "Early Days in Oregon," *OHQ* v 4 (1903), 58.

[124] Wortman, v. The ten bridges are, from north to south, St. Johns, Burlington Northern Santa Fe Railroad, Fremont, Broadway, Steel, Burnside, Morrison, Hawthorne, Marquam, and Sellwood.

[125] Abbott, *Gateway*, 27.

[126] The captain protested his fine in court, and won his case. *Proc. C.C.*, June 16, 1855, 287-88; O'Donnell and Vaughan, 18;

[127] "Downtown Open Today for Skaters," Spencer Heinz, *Oreg.*, Jan 26, 2001, C3; "Rebel with a clause," *WW*, Nov 29, 2000, p 9.

[128] www.census.gov/population/cen2000/phc/-t5/tab02.pdf [accesssed April 5, 2001].

Appendix A

[1] Belknap, 13, 47.

[2] The charter broadside printed by the *Oregonian* was a single sheet of paper in five columns. Although Territorial Governor John P. Gaines signed the law on February 8, 1851, his name was not included on the broadside.

[3] *Oregon Special Laws, 1850-51*, 16-22. The eleven-page handwritten version of the bill is available on microfilm at the Oregon State Archives. The *1850-51 Laws of the Territorial Legislature*, a rare volume, was available for public viewing at the Oregon Supreme Court Library.

[4] April 1969 auction catalog of Parke-Bernet Galleries,

Inc., New York (Affiliated with Sotheby & Co., London), Streeter Collection, v 6, p 2330.

[5] The auction price paid by the Library Association of Portland (LAP) is handwritten in the margin of the auction catalog for Item 3368, the broadside copy of the Portland City Charter, in the index (v 8, p 348), Multnomah County Library Rare Book Room. The same price is penciled in the margin of v 6, p. 2330, next to item #3368, Portland charter. The notation says, "LAP 350." Correspondence to the author from Cindy Gibbon, Central Multnomah County Library, Aug 7, 1999.

[6] Bancroft, at v 2, 717, says, "There is no copy of the incorporation act of 1851 in my library, but the act is mentioned by its title in the *Oregon Statesman* for March 28, 1851" Examples of inaccurate information about the first charter include Scott, *Portland*, 176, 188, 319; Gaston, v 1, 5-10, 336, and 549; *History of Portland*, WPA Writers, 9.

[7] A list of city charters, amendments, and dates compiled by the UO Bureau of Municipal Research and Service in Nov 1941 was attached to City Ord #76832, a major charter recodification ordinance adopted March 11, 1942. This author obtained her copies of 1851 through 1903 charters and amendments from the Oregon Supreme Court Library.

[8] *19979-8O BB*, 349.

Appendix B

[1] The two-story residence where O'Bryant lived, according to the 1850 territorial census, was at the same location, Alder and Front, the home of Job and Hannah McNamee and their seven small children. Lacy, 63. It is possible that if O'Bryant donated a "library room" it was his own winter sleeping quarters, since he might also have had a cabin on his Swan Island claim. Space was critically short in early Portland.

[2] Corning, 178; Lockley, *The Fact Is*, 13; *History of Portland*, 18; *OHQ* (Dec 1955), 354; Maddux, 51-52. Also see Lockley, *Columbia*, v 1, 516, and Fred Lockley column, *OJ*, Nov 28, 1932.

[3] "A Narrative of the Life of William P. Abrams," compiled by his descendant, Seth L. Pope from the diaries of William Abrams. OHS Mss #701, Folder 25, Pope Family papers, 16-19.

[4] A history of the Library Association of Portland published in 1964 omits reference to this earlier organization, and gives only the one-hundred-year history of the Library Association of Portland, which remained in business and was the nucleus for the present-day Multnomah County Library. Anderson, 5, 34-36. A recently published history of Portland's Central Library erroneously states that "Portland's first library was in its infancy in 1865" in a photo caption at the front of the book. Ritz, 1.

[5] *Oreg.*, Nov 8, 1903, p 40.

[6] Portland Library Association papers, OHS Mss #429.

[7] Ibid., 1-5.

[8] *Oreg.*, Nov 8, 1903, p 40; Anderson, 13-15. For a history of the 1891-1902 free Portland Public Library that was housed for a time in city hall, see Cheryl Gunselman's "Pioneering Free Library Service for the City," *OHQ* Fall 2002, 327-37.

Appendix F

Sources: City invoices and minutes of council meetings, and "History Shows Council Changes Meeting Sites Often," by Don Holm, *Oreg.*, Mar 1, 1964, p 36.

Bibliography

Abbott, Carl. *Greater Portland, Urban Life and Landscape in the Pacific Northwest.* Philadelphia: University of Pennsylvania Press, 2001.

———. *Portland—Gateway to the Northwest.* Northridge, CA: Windsor Publications, 1997.

———. *The Great Extravaganza.* Portland: Oregon Historical Society, Rev. edition 1996.

———. *Portland: Planning, Politics, and Growth in a Twentieth-Century City.* Lincoln, NE: University of Nebraska Press, 1983.

Adams, William Lysander. *A Melodrame Entitled "Treason, Stratagems, and Spoils."* Edited by George N. Belknap. Hamden, CT: Archon Books, 1968.

Aikman, Duncan, ed. *The Taming of the Frontier.* Freeport, NY: Books for Libraries Press, Inc., 1967. First printed 1925.

Anderson, Katherine E. *Historical Sketch of the Library Association of Portland.* Portland: Library Association of Portland, 1964.

Arlington Club and The Men Who Built It: Centennial Anniversary. Portland: The Arlington Club, 1968.

Balcomb, Raymond E. *Portland's First Church / The Sesquicentennial History.* Portland: First United Methodist Church, 1996.

Bancroft, Hubert Howe. *History of Oregon, Vol. 2, 1848-1888.* San Francisco: The History Company, 1888.

Belknap, George N. *Oregon Imprints, 1845-1870.* Eugene, OR: University of Oregon Books, 1968.

Bennett, Robert A., *Walla Walla, Portrait of a Western Town, 1804-1899.* Walla Walla, WN: Pioneer Press Books, 1980.

Blankenship, Warren Marion. *Progressives and the Progressive Party in Oregon, 1906-1916.* Ph.D. dissertation, University of Oregon, 1966.

Booth, Brian, ed. *Wildmen, Wobblies & Whistle Punks: Stewart Holbrook's Lowbrow Northwest.* Corvallis, OR: Oregon State University Press, 1992.

Bourke, Paul, and Donald DeBats. *Washington County, Politics and Community in Antebellum America.* Baltimore and London: The Johns Hopkins University Press, 1995.

Bowman, John S., ed. *The World Almanac of the American West.* New York: Pharos Books, 1986.

Brandt, Patricia, and Nancy Guilford, ed. *Oregon Biography Index, Bibliographic Series Number 11.* Corvallis, OR: Oregon State University Press, 1976.

Buan, Carolyn M., ed. *The First Duty, A History of the U.S. District Court for Oregon.* Portland: U.S. District Court of Oregon Historical Society, 1993.

Carey, Charles Henry. *A General History of Oregon Prior to 1861, v 2.* Portland: Metropolitan Press, 1936.

———. *History of Oregon, v 1.* Chicago-Portland: The Pioneer Historical Publishing Co., 1922.

———, ed. *The Oregon Constitution and Proceedings and Debates of the Constitutional Convention of 1857.* Salem, OR: State Printing Department, 1926.

Cartwright, Mrs. C. M., "Earlyy Days in Oregon," *Oregon Historical Quarterly,* v.4 (1903).

Castor, Henry. *Fifty-Four Forty or Fight!* New York: Franklin Watts, Inc., 1970.

Chamberlin, Hope. *A Minority of Members: Women in the U S. Congress.* New York: Praeger Publishers, 1973.

The Charter and Ordinances of the City of Portland, Oregon, 1895. Portland: Multnomah Printing Company, 1895.

Charter of the City of Portland and General Ordinances in Force, September 1886. Portland: R. H. Schwab & Bro., 1886.

City of Portland, Proceedings of the Common Council, v 1-20. Portland: City of Portland, 1851-1902.

City of Portland, Ordinances, v 1-9. Portland: City of Portland, 1851-1890.

Clark, Hugh. *Portland's Chinese: The Early Years, Ethni-City Series.* Portland: Center for Urban Education, 1975; rev. 1978.

Clark, Malcolm H., Jr. *Eden Seekers, The Settlement of Oregon, 1818-1862* Boston, MA: Houghton Mifflin Company, 1981.

———. ed., *Pharisee among the Philistines, The Diary of Judge Matthew P. Deady, 1871-1892, 2 vol.* Portland: Oregon Historical Society, 1975.

———. "The War on the Webfoot Saloon," *Oregon Historical Quarterly,* March 1957.

Clarke, Samuel A. *Pioneer Days of Oregon History.* 2 vols. Portland: J. K. Gill Company, 1905.

Cole, George E. *Early Oregon, 1850 to 1860; Jottings of Personal Recollections of a Pioneer of 1850.* Spokane, WA: Shaw & Borden Co., 1905.

Collins, Dean. *Stars of Oregon.* Portland: Binfords & Mort, 1943.

Corning, Howard McKinley, ed. *Dictionary of Oregon History.* Portland: Binfords & Mort, 1956.

Culp, Edwin. *Oregon The Way It Was.* Caldwell, ID: The Caxton Printers, Ltd., 1981.

Davis, Judi Siewert, and Kathryn Weit. *Around Portland with Kids.* Portland: Discovery Press, 1993.

De Marco, Gordon. *A Short History of Portland.* San Francisco: Lexikos, 1990.

Diamond, Jared. *Guns, Germs and Steel, The Fates of Human Societies.* New York: W. W. Norton & Company, 1998.

Dicken, Samuel E., and Emily F. Dicken. *The Making of Oregon: A Study in Historical Geography.* Portland: Oregon Historical Society, 1979.

Dimon, Elizabeth F. *'Twas Many Years Since; 100 Years in the Waverley Area, 1847-1947.* Milwaukie, OR: Elizabeth F. Dimon, 1981.

Dobbs, Caroline C. *Men of Champoeg.* Portland: Metropolitan Press, 1932.

Dodds, Gordon B. *Oregon, A Bicentennial History.* New York: W. W. Norton & Company, 1977.

Donald, David Herbert. *Lincoln.* New York: Simon & Schuster, 1995.

Duniway, Abigail Scott. *Path Breaking.* Reprinted from the James, Kerns, & Abbott edition of 1914. New York: Schocken Books, 1971.

Eaton, Allen H. *The Oregon System: The Story of Direct Legislation in Oregon.* Chicago, IL: A. C. McClurg & Co., 1912.

Eberhart, Edith Whitcraft, and Adaline Marye Robertson. *The Maryes of Virginia, 1730-1985.* Baltimore, MD: Gateway Press, Inc., 1985.

Edwards, Cecil L., comp. *Alphabetical List of Oregon's Legislators.* Salem, OR: State of Oregon Legislative Administration Committee, 1993.

Edwards, G. Thomas. *Sowing Good Seeds, The Northwest Suffrage Campaigns of Susan B. Anthony.* Portland: Oregon Historical Society Press, 1990.

Ermenc, Christine. *Voices of Portland.* Portland: Neighborhood History Project, 1976.

Fogdall, Alberta. *Royal Family of the Columbia, Dr. John McLoughlin and His Family.* Fairfield, WA: Ye Galleon Press, 1978.

Gaston, Joseph. *Portland Oregon: Its History and Builders.* Vol. 1, 2 & 3. Chicago, IL: The S. J. Clarke Publishing Co, 1911.

Geer, T. T. *Fifty Years in Oregon.* New York: The Neale Publishing Company, 1912.

Genealogical Material in Oregon Donation Land Claims, Volume 1. Portland: Genealogical Forum of Portland, Oregon, 1957.

Genealogical Material in Oregon Provisional Land Claims, 1845-1849. Portland: Genealogical Forum of Portland, Oregon, Inc., 1982.

Gilbert, Frank T. *Historic Sketches of Walla Walla, Whitman, Columbia and Garfield Counties, Washington Territory, and Umatilla County, Oregon.* Portland: A. G. Walling Printing and Lithographic House, 1882.

Gleeson, Norma Catherine, and Chet Orloff. *Portland's Public Art.* Portland: Western Imprints, the Press of the Oregon Historical Society, 1983.

Grover, LaFayette. *Oregon Archives: Including the Journals, Governors' Messages and Public Papers of Oregon (1843-49).* Salem, OR: A. Bush, Public Printer, 1853.

Guide to the Manuscript Collections of the Oregon Historical Society. Portland: Federal Works Agency, Work Projects Administration Official Historical Records Project No. 65-1-94-25, August 1940.

Gunther, John. *Inside U.S.A.*, revised edition. New York: Harper & Brothers, 1951.

Harden, Blaine. *A River Lost, The Life and Death of the Columbia.* New York: W. W. Norton & Company, 1996.

Hartwell, Barbara Bartlett. *Sprigs of Rosemary.* Portland: National Society of the Colonial Dames of America in Oregon, 1975.

Hawkins, William John III. *The Grand Era of Cast Iron Architecture in Portland.* Portland: Binford & Mort, 1976.

———. *Classic Houses of Portland, Oregon, 1850-1950.* Portland: Timber Press, 1999.

Hawthorne, Julian. *The Story of Oregon, v 1-2.* New York: American Historical Publishing Company, 1892.

Hays, Jeff W. *Looking Backward at Portland.* Portland: Kilham Stationery & Printing Co., 1911.

Heider, Douglas, and David Dietz. *Legislative Perspectives, A 150-Year History of the Oregon Legislatures From 1843 to 1993.* Portland: Oregon Historical Society Press, 1995.

Hines, H. K. *An Illustrated History of the State of Oregon.* Chicago,IL: The Lewis Publishing Company, 1893.

History of the Bench and Bar of Oregon. Portland: Historical Publishing Co., 1910.

"History of Portland, Oregon," Oregon Writers' Project. Federal Works Agency, Work Projects Administration, 1941.

History of Portland's African American Community (1805 to the Present). Portland: City of Portland Bureau of Planning, 1993.

Holbrook, Stewart H. *The Portland Story; Written in Observance of Lipman's One Hundredth Anniversary.* Portland: Lipman Wolfe & Co., 1950.

Horn, Huston. *The Old West: The Pioneers.* New York: Time-Life Books, 1974.

Horowitz, David A. *Inside the Klavern, The Secret History of a Ku Klux Klan of the 1920s.* Carbondale, IL: Southern Illinois University Press, 1999.

Houle, Marcy Cottrell. *One City's Wilderness, Portland's Forest Park.* Portland: Oregon Historical Society Press, 1988.

Huffman, Doris. *Oregon's Flamboyant Fourth: 1876.* Portland: Doris A. Huffman, 1976.

Hussey, John A. *Champoeg: Place of Transition.* Portland: Oregon Historical Society, 1967.

Jackson, Ronald Vern, ed. *Washington 1860 Territorial Census Index.* Bountiful, UT: Accelerated Indexing Systems, Inc., 1978.

———. *Washington 1870 Territorial Census Index.* Bountiful, UT: Accelerated Indexing Systems, Inc., 1979.

———. *Washington 1880 Territorial Census Index.* Bountiful, UT: Accelerated Indexing Systems, Inc., 1980.

———, and Gary Ronald Teeples, ed. *Oregon 1850 Territorial Census Index.* Bountiful, UT: Accelerated Indexing Systems, Inc., 1978.

Judson, Katharine Berry. *Early Days in Old Oregon.* Portland: Metropolitan Press, 1935.

Kelso, Linda. *Volcano, First Seventy Days, Mount St. Helens, 1980.* Beaverton, OR: Beautiful America Publishing Company, 1980.

Kneier, Charles M. *City Government in the United States.* New York: Harper & Brothers, 1947

Labbe, John T. *Fares, Please! Those Portland Trolley Years.* Caldwell, ID: The Caxton Printers, Ltd., 1980.

Lacy, Ruby. *Oregon Territory 1850 Census.* Ashland, OR: Ruby Lacy, 1984.

Lang, Herbert O. *History of the Willamette Valley.* Portland: Himes & Lang, 1885.

Lansing, Ronald B. *Juggernaut: The Whitman Massacre Trial: 1850.* Pasadena, CA: Ninth Judicial Historical Society, 1993.

"Law Enforcement in Portland and Multnomah County," *Portland City Club Bulletin*, Feb 20, 1948, p 132-48.

Laws of the City of Portland, 1886. R. H. Schwab & Bro., *Morning Oregonian* edition, 1886.

The Laws of Oregon and the Resolutions and Memorials of the Thirteenth Regular Session of the Legislative Assembly Thereof, 1885. Salem, OR: W. H. Byars, State Printer, 1885.

Leeson, Fred. *Rose City Justice, A Legal History of Portland, Oregon.* Portland: Oregon Historical Society Press, 1998.

Lockley, Fred. *History of the Columbia River Valley, From The Dalles to the Sea, Vol. 1, 2, & 3.* Chicago, IL: The S. J. Clarke Publishing Co., 1928.

———. *Oregon Folks.* New York: The Knickerbocker Press, 1927.

———. *Oregon's Yesterdays.* New York: The Knickerbocker Press, 1928.

———. *The Fact Is.* unpublished typewritten sheets, date unknown.

Long, James Andrew. *Oregon Firsts, Past and Present.* North Plains, OR: Pumpkin Ridge Productions, 1994.

Lowenstein, Steven. *The Jews of Oregon, 1850-1950.* Portland: Jewish Historical Society of Oregon, 1987.

Lucia, Ellis. *The Big Blow: The Story of the Pacific Northwest's Columbus Day Storm.* Portland: Storm Book, 1963.

———. *The Conscience of a City, Fifty Years of City Club Service in Portland.* Portland: The City Club of Portland, 1966.

Lukas, J. Anthony. *Big Trouble.* New York: Simon and Schuster, 1997.

Lyman, Horace S. *History of Oregon, The Growth of an American State, Vol. 1-4.* New York: The North Pacific Publishing Company, 1903.

Lyman, William Denison. *The Columbia River, Its History, its Myths, Its Scenery, its Commerce.* New York: G. P. Putnam's Sons, 1909.

Lynch, Vera Martin. *Free Land for Free Men, A Story of Clackamas County.* Portland: Artline Printing Co., 1973.

Maben, Manly. *Vanport.* Portland: Oregon Historical Society Press, 1987.

MacColl, E. Kimbark. *The Shaping of a City; Business and Politics in Portland, Oregon 1885 to 1915.* Portland: The Georgian Press, 1976.

———. *The Growth of a City; Power and Politics in Portland, Oregon 1915 to 1950.* Portland: The Georgian Press, 1979.

——— with Harry H. Stein. *Merchants, Money and Power, The Portland Establishment, 1843 - 1913.* Portland: The Georgian Press, 1988.

Maddux, Percy. *City of the Willamette, The Story of Portland, Oregon.* Portland: Binfords & Mort, 1952.

Magazine Miscellany, v. 6. Unknown national publisher and place, circa 1910.

Marsh, Floyd R. *20 Years A Soldier of Fortune.* Portland: Binford & Mort, 1976.

Mayor's Message and Annual Reports. Portland: City of Portland, 1923.

Mayor's Message and Annual Reports, 1923. Portland: City of Portland, Oregon, 1924.

McArthur, Lewis A. *Oregon Geographic Names.* Portland: Western Imprints, Fifth Edition, 1982.

McCall, Tom, with Steve Neal. *Tom McCall: Maverick.* Portland: Binford & Mort, 1977.

McCarthy, Linda. *A History of the Oregon Sheriffs, 1841-1991.* No city specified: Oregon State Sheriffs' Association, Taylor Publishing Company, 1992.

McCormack, Win, and Dick Pintarich. *Great Moments in Oregon History.* Portland: New Oregon Publishers, Inc., 1987.

McCurdy, James. *By Juan de Fuca's Strait.* Portland: Binfords & Mort, 1937.

McKay, Floyd J. *An Editor for Oregon; Charles A. Sprague and the Politics of Change.* Corvallis, OR: Oregon State University Press, 1998.

Miller, Emma Gene. *Clatsop County, Oregon.* Portland: Binfords & Mort, 1958.

Mills, Randall V. *Stern-Wheelers Up Columbia.* Palo Alto, CA: Pacific Books, 1947.

Milner, Clyde A., Carol A. O'Connor, and Martha A. Sandweiss, ed. *The Oxford History of the American West.* New York: Oxford University Press, 1994.

Mirengoff, William, and Lester Rindler. *The Comprehensive Employment and Training Act, An Interim Report.* Washington, D. C.: National Academy of Sciences, 1976.

Mooney, Ralph James. "Formalism and Fairness: Matthew Deady and Early Portland Land Title Disputes," *Oregon Benchmarks,* Bulletin of the U.S. District Court of Oregon Historical Society, Summer 1989.

Moynihan, Ruth Barnes. *Rebel for Rights: Abigail Scott Duniway.* New Haven, CT: Yale University Press, 1983.

Morrison, Dorothy Nafus. *Outpost, John McLoughlin and the Far Northwest.* Portland: Oregon Historical Society Press, 1999.

Munk, Michael, "Portland's 'Silk Stocking Mob.'" *Pacific Northwest Quarterly,* Summer 2000.

Nelson, Herbert B. *The Literary Impulse in Pioneer Oregon.* Corvallis, OR: Oregon State College, 1948.

Norman, James B., Jr. *Portland's Architectural Heritage, National Register Properties of the Portland Metropolitan Area,* 2d. ed. Portland: Oregon Historical Society Press, 1991.

Notson, Robert C. *Making the Day Begin, A Story of the Oregonian.* Portland: Oregonian Publishing Company, 1976.

O'Donnell, Terence. "Oregon History," in *1997-98 Oregon Blue Book.* Salem, OR: Oregon Secretary of State, 1997.

———, and Thomas Vaughan. *Portland: An Informal History and Guide.* Portland: Western Imprints, 1984.

Oregon Digest, Annotated, Vol. 7, Covering Cases from State and Federal Courts. San Francisco, CA, and St. Paul, MN: Bancroft-Whitney Company and West Publishing Co., 1957.

Oregon: End of the Trail. American Guide Series. Federal Writers' Project, Oregon. Work Projects Administration. Portland: Binfords & Mort, 1940.

The Oregon Law Index: An Index to Oregon Territorial and State Laws up to 1886. Portland: Stevens-Ness Law Publishing Co., 1937.

Oregon Native Son, v 1-2. Portland: Native Son Publishing Company, February 1900 and December 1900.

Oregon Spectator Index, 1846-1854, Vol. 1 & 2. W. P. A. Newspaper Index Project. Portland: Sponsored by City of Portland and Oregon Historical Society, May 1941.

The Oregonian Souvenir Book. Portland: The Lewis & Dryden Printing Company, 1892.

The *Oregonian*, staff of. *The Oregon Story, 1850 - 2000.* Portland: Graphic Arts Center Publishing, 2000.

Organization and Business Methods of the City Government of Portland, Oregon. Portland: Bureau of Municipal Research, New York City, May 5, 1913.

Papas, Bill, and Tessa Papas. *Papas' Portland.* Portland: Chetwynd Stapylton, Inc., 1994.

Partners in Progress: Port of Portland, Celebrates 100 Years, 1891-1991 Portland: Port of Portland, 1991.

Peacock, John. *Costume 1066-1966.* London: Thames and Hudson Ltd., 1986.

Pement, Jack, and Paul Keller. *Oregon Historical Vignettes.* Portland: Binford & Mort, 1974.

Pietsch, Margaret. *Riverwood, Yesterday and Today.* Lake Oswego, OR: Lake Grove Printing Co., 1980.

Pitzer, Paul C. *Grand Coulee, Harnessing a Dream.* Pullman, WA: Washington State University Press, 1994.

———. "Dorothy McCullough Lee: The Successes and Failures of 'Dottie-Do-Good.'" *Oregon Historical Quarterly*, Spring 1990, 4-42.

Population of Oregon Cities, Counties, and Metropolitan Areas, 1850 to 1957. Eugene, OR: Bureau of Municipal Research and Service, University of Oregon Information Bulletin No. 106, 1958.

Portland City Directory. Portland: S. J. McCormick, 1863-75, 1878-81; A. G. Walling, 1876-77; J. K. Gill, 1882, 1884; R. L Polk, 1889-90.

Portland Fire Department Year Book. Portland: City of Portland, 1905, 1976, and 1993.

The Portland Handbook. Portland: City of Portland, 1953, 1955, 1964, and 1982.

Portland, Our Community, Children's Readings, Grade 3 Social Studies. Portland: Portland Public Schools, 1992.

Portrait and Biographical Record of Portland and Vicinity, Oregon. Chicago, IL: Chapman Publishing Co., 1903.

Portrait and Biographical Record of the Willamette Valley, Oregon. Chicago, IL: Chapman Publishing Co., 1903.

Potential Historic Conservation Districts, An Inventory of Historic Resources. Portland: Portland Historical Landmarks Commission and Portland Bureau of Planning, 1978.

Pratt, Laurence. *I Remember Portland, 1899-1915, A Vivid Look at Sturdy Days.* Portland: Metropolitan Printing Company, 1965.

Price, Larry W., ed. *Portland's Changing Landscape.* Portland: Geography Department, Portland State University and Association of American Geographers, 1987.

Prosch, Thomas W. *McCarver and Tacoma.* Seattle, WA: Lowman & Hanford Stationery and Printing Company, 1906.

Purdy, Ruby Fay. *The Rose City of the World.* Portland: Binfords & Mort, 1947.

Quiett, Glenn Chesney. *They Built the West, An Epic of Rails and Cities.* New York: D. Appleton-Century Co., Inc., 1934.

Republican League Register, A Record of the Republican Party in the State of Oregon. Portland: The Register Publishing Company, 1896.

Ritz, Richard E. *An Architect Looks at Downtown Portland.* Portland: The Greenhills Press, 1991.

———. *Central Library, Portland's Crown Jewel.* Portland: The Library Foundation, Inc., 2000.

Robbins, William G. *Landscapes of Promise: The Oregon Story, 1800-1940.* Seattle, WA: University of Washington Press, 1997.

Roe, JoAnn. *The Columbia River, A Historical Travel Guide.* Golden, CO: Fulcrum Publishing, 1992.

Scott, Harvey W. *History of the Oregon Country.* 6 vols. Compiled by Leslie M. Scott. Cambridge, MA: The Riverside Press, 1924.

———, ed. *History of Portland Oregon.* Syracuse, NY: D. Mason & Co., 1890.

Scott, Leslie M. *Masonic Papers, v 2.* Portland: Research Lodge of Oregon No. 198, A. F. and A. M., 1938.

Short, Casey. *Water: Portland's Precious Heritage.* Portland: City of Portland, 1983.

Silver, Philip. *George Luis Baker, An Inquiry into the Methods and Psychology of Municipal Leadership.* B. A. thesis, Department of Political Science, Reed College, 1926.

Snyder, Eugene E. *Early Portland; Stump-Town Triumphant.* Portland: Binfords & Mort, 1970.

———. *Portland Names and Neighborhoods.* Portland: Binford & Mort, 1979.

———. *Portland Potpourri: Art, Fountains & Old Friends.* Portland: Binford & Mort, 1991.

———. *Skidmore's Portland: His Fountain and Its Sculptor; From Buckboards to Bustles.* Portland: Binfords & Mort, 1973.

———. *We Claimed This Land: Portland's Pioneer Settlers.* Portland: Binford & Mort, 1989.

Somerset Fry, Plantagenet. *The Dorling Kindersley History of the World.* New York: Dorling Kindersley Publishing, Inc., 1994.

Statutes of a General Nature Passed by the Legislative Assembly of the Territory of Oregon. Oregon City, OR: Asahel Bush, Territorial Printer, 1851.

Stein, Harry, Kathleen Ryan, and Mark Beac. *Portland: A Pictorial History.* Virginia Beach, VA: The Donning Company, 1980.

Stone, Stephen A. *Oregon Memorabilia; Stories from the Files of an Oregon Newsman.* Eugene, OR: Parkstone Company, 1967.

Taylor, C. W., Jr. *Eminent Judges and Lawyers of the Northwest, 1843-1955.* Palo Alto, CA: C. W. Taylor, Jr., 1954.

Taylor, George H., and Raymond R. Hatton. *The Oregon Weather Book.* Corvallis, OR: Oregon State University Press, 1999.

Teaford, Jon C. *City and Suburb, The Political Fragmentation of Metropolitan America, 1850-1970.* Baltimore: The Johns Hopkins University Press, 1979.

Throckmorton, Arthur L. *Oregon Argonauts: Merchant Adventurers on the Western Frontier.* Portland: Oregon Historical Society, 1961.

Tobie, Harvey Elmer. *No Man Like Joe, The Life and Times of Joseph L. Meek.* Portland: Binfords & Mort for the Oregon Historical Society, 1949.

Turnbull, George S. *Governors of Oregon.* Portland: Binfords & Mort, 1959.

———. *History of Oregon Newspapers.* Portland: Binfords & Mort, 1939.

Thwaites, Reuben Gold. *Original Journals of the Lewis and Clark Expedition, Vol. 4.* New York: Arno Press, 1969.

Uris, Joseph Samuel. *Trouble in River City: An Analysis of An Urban Vice Probe.* Portland: PhD thesis, Urban Studies Department, Portland State University, 1981.

Van Arsdol, Ted, ed. *Frontier Soldier, The Letters of Maj. John S. Hatheway, 1833-1853.* Vancouver, WA: Vancouver National Historic Reserve Trust, 1999.

Walth, Brent. *Fire at Eden's Gate, Tom McCall and the Oregon Story.* Portland: Oregon Historical Society Press, 1994.

Who's Who for Oregon, 1942-1944. Portland: Capitol Publishing Company, 1942.

Who's Who in America, 42nd Edition, 1982-1983, v 1. Chicago, IL: Marquis Who's Who, 1982.

Who's Who in the West, 1956 Edition, Chicago, IL: Marquis Who's Who, 1956.

Who's Who in the West, 20th Edition, 1985-1986. Chicago, IL: Marquis Who's Who, 1985.

Who's Who of American Women, Millenium (22nd) Edition, 2000-2001. New Providence, NJ: Marquis Who's Who, 2000.

Wilkinson, John C. *History of the Grand Lodge of A. F. & A. M. of Oregon, From 1846 to 1951.* Portland: Grand Lodge of Oregon, 1954.

Willamette Lodge No. 2, A. F. & A. M., 1850-1950, Portland, Oregon. Portland: Bede-Hibbitt Inc., 1950.

Wills, Charles A. *A Historical Album of Oregon.* Brookfield, CT: The Millbrook Press, 1995.

Winther, Oscar Osburn. *The Old Oregon Country.* Lincoln, NE: University of Nebraska Press, 1969.

Women in Congress 1917 - 1990. Washington, D. C.: U.S. Government Printing Office, 1991.

Wood, Erskine. *Life of Charles Erskine Wood.* Vancouver, WA: Rose Wind Press, 1991.

Woodward, Walter Carleton. *The Rise and Early History of Political Parties in Oregon.* Portland: The J. K. Gill Company, 1913.

Worcester, Thomas K. *Bunco Kelly and Other Yarns of Portland and Northwest Oregon.* Beaverton, OR: TMS Book Service, 1983.

Wortman, Sharon Wood. *The Portland Bridge Book.* Portland: Oregon Historical Society Press, 2001.

Yeates, Marian. *The Story of Gretchen Miller Kafoury.* Salt Lake City, UT: Marian Yeates, Publisher, 1998.

Index

Note: The names listed in Appendices C-F are not included in this index, nor are the names of many other people and places that played a passing role in city history. Page numbers in italics refer to photographs or illustrations.

C

E

F

G

H

R